W9-CAX-338

Cognition

Drawing on a modern neurocognitive framework, this full-color textbook introduces the entire field of cognition through an engaging narrative. Emphasizing the common neural mechanisms that underlie all aspects of perception, learning, and reasoning, the text encourages students to recognize the interconnectivity between cognitive processes. Elements of social psychology and developmental psychology are integrated into the discussion, leading students to understand and appreciate the connection between cognitive processing and social behavior. Numerous learning features provide extensive student support: chapter summaries encourage students to reflect on the main points of each chapter; end-of-chapter questions allow students to review their understanding of key topics; approximately 200 figures, photos, and charts clarify complex topics; and suggestions for further reading point students to resources for deeper self-study. The textbook is also accompanied by 800 multiple-choice questions, for use before, during, and after class, which have been proved to dramatically improve student understanding and exam performance.

Arnold Lewis Glass is a professor in the Department of Psychology at Rutgers University.

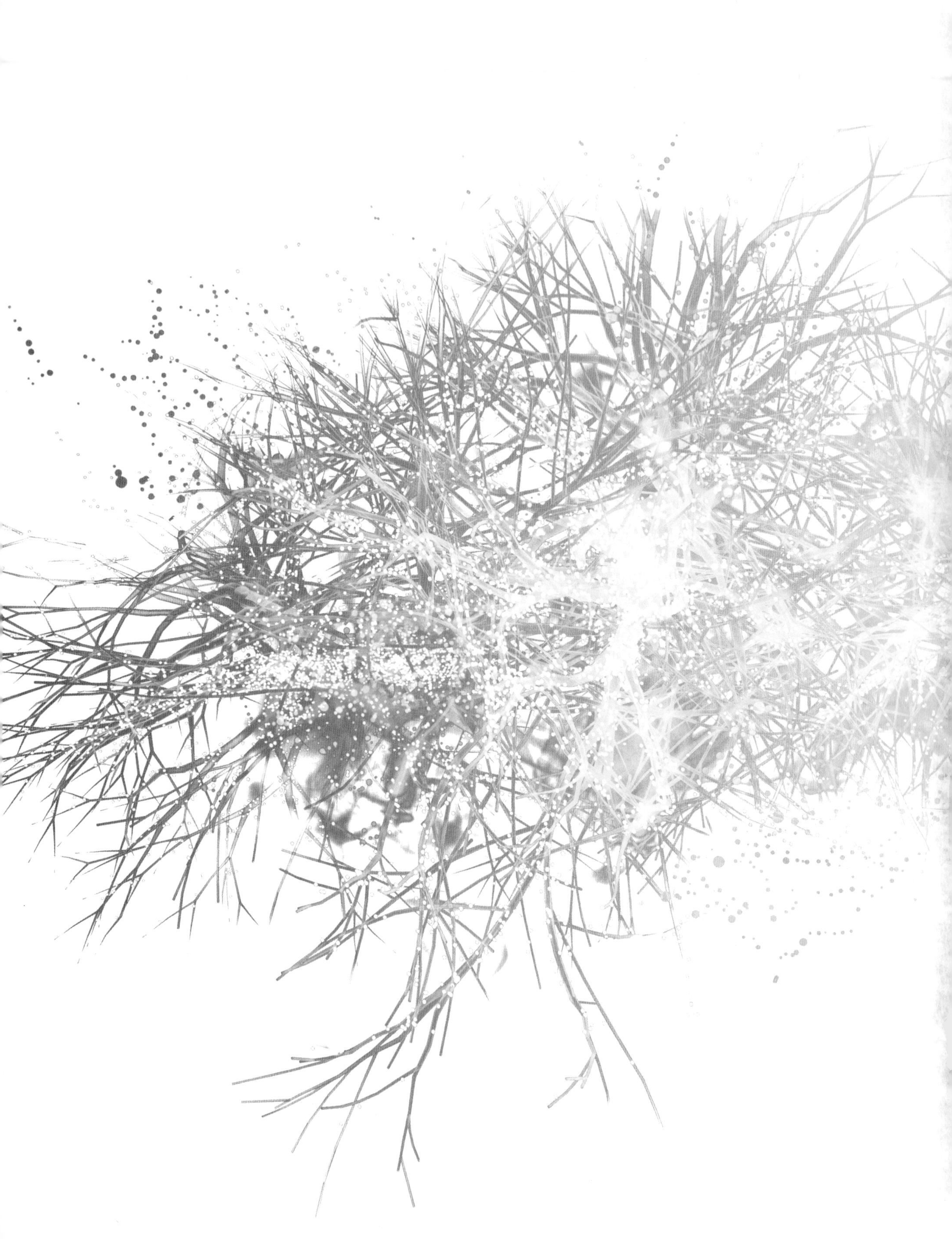

COGNITION

Arnold Lewis Glass

CAMBRIDGE
UNIVERSITY PRESS

University Printing House, Cambridge CB2 8BS, United Kingdom

Cambridge University Press is part of the University of Cambridge.

It furthers the University's mission by disseminating knowledge in the pursuit of education, learning and research at the highest international levels of excellence.

www.cambridge.org
Information on this title: www.cambridge.org/glass

First published 2016

Printed in United States of America by Sheridan Books, Inc.

A catalogue record for this publication is available from the British Library

Library of Congress Cataloguing in Publication data
Glass, Arnold Lewis, 1951–
Cognition / Arnold Lewis Glass.
pages cm
Includes bibliographical references.
ISBN 978-1-107-08831-3 (hardback) – ISBN 978-1-107-57273-7 (paperback) 1. Cognition. I. Title.
BF311.G5423 2016
153–dc23
2015020973

ISBN 978-1-107-08831-3 Hardback
ISBN 978-1-107-57273-7 Paperback

Additional resources for this publication at www.cambridge.org/glass

To my wife, Lynne, and my son, Brian, because the writing of this book was a family project that benefited from their enthusiasm, insights, and general good judgment.

CONTENTS

PREFACE

The modern study of cognition began with the associative theory in the eighteenth century. According to this theory, spatial contiguity and temporal contiguity cause more simple visual and auditory features to be combined into more complicated representations, and the manipulation of these representations corresponds to thoughts. Associative theory motivated the experimental studies that began the science of cognitive psychology in the nineteenth century. In the early twentieth century behaviorism provided an alternative theoretical framework for psychology, whose content was observable behavior instead of mental states. The focus on behavior led to important advances in the experimental methodologies for observing behavior coupled with a complete lack of progress in explaining the mental processes causing the behaviors. This non-mental psychology came to an abrupt end with the publication of Ulric Neisser's (1967) *Cognitive Psychology*. Although the theories that followed its publication were much more sophisticated, they were within the associative tradition. Thought was represented as the manipulation of sensory features. My contribution at that time was a textbook that was a best-seller and certainly influenced those that came after it. Even the most recent textbooks published today still follow the same basic organization and cover the same basic topics.

Because of their theoretical orientation, all current cognitive textbooks are now out of date. The theoretical framework is not wrong but it is incomplete. The conceptualization of cognition in terms of the combination of sensory features suggests that a good place to begin is with perception – i.e. with the construction of a representation of the world from sensory features. Unfortunately, this means that we begin with a passive description of cognition. An observer is not doing anything other than constructing a representation of the surrounding environment. This leads to analogies with passive mechanical recording devices such as cameras. The passive, perception-first, approach to the study of cognition has dominated introductory psychology textbooks, as well as much research, ever since Neisser's (1967) seminal work. This was not Neisser's fault. The theory he presented, called analysis-by-synthesis, was an active approach to all of cognition, including perception. However, it was difficult to understand and not as influential as the classical organization of the material around perception. In this century it has become increasingly difficult to describe cognition within the framework of the traditional organization beginning with simple visual features because of new findings demonstrating that basic units of memory represent purposeful actions to meaningful targets and that novelty rather than contiguity drives learning. The central purpose of this textbook is to present cognition as purposeful action. This approach provides a more accurate description of what cognition is.

This new textbook is a rethink of the entire field, reflecting what is known and what is under active research today. Both neuroscience and social psychology are much more important, and influence this text. Instructors and students alike will benefit by being introduced to relevant topic areas that they may not be well versed in and that will give them a new way of looking at the discipline.

The text includes more and better neuroscience, social, and developmental perspectives, which are absent from other texts. This is evident from the first two chapters, which provide a foundation not available in other texts. In terms of neuroscience, the emphasis is always on functional systems. In Chapter 1 we see how reflexes emerged in the spinal cord and brain stem and how conditioning emerged in the brain stem, midbrain and cerebellum. Not every instructor will have time to include the pre-cognitive evolution of the nervous system in a human cognition course. It is available for those instructors who are interested. In Chapter 2 we see how voluntary action emerged through the functioning of the frontal cortex, striatum, and hippocampus. The advantage of this approach is that, rather than have an introductory chapter on the brain, right from the beginning the emphasis is on behavior, how neural computation makes behavior possible, and how inter-species behavioral competition has led to the increasing complexity and sophistication of behavior and the neural computational systems that make behavior possible. There is complete integration from the social level down to the neural, and each evolutionary advance emerges inevitably from the challenges provided by the increasing sophistication of competitors. By explaining to students the "Why?" of "cognition" they acquire a framework for understanding the "What?" as well.

In Chapter 2 the habit system and instrumental system are both introduced. The seminal animal work on these systems is widely influential in the behavioral cognitive neuroscience literature. Here it is introduced into a cognitive psychology text for the first time. Once this foundation is laid, we can see in Chapters 3, 4, and 5 how both systems cooperate to control motor and mental action, respectively. In Chapters 5 and 6 we see how the ability to rapidly encode task-relevant perceptual targets makes possible the accumulation of knowledge of the world. We see that both systems are necessary components of the meaningful encoding of events in semantic memory and are necessary components of the neural systems for language production and comprehension. Throughout the later chapters of the text we see how both systems influence our abilities to learn, remember, and reason. Hence, Chapter 2 provides an organizing framework for the entire textbook.

It is argued in Chapter 2 that higher cognitive functions evolved to support social behavior. Evidence for this claim is presented throughout the second half of the book. Chapter 8 is about how infants learn, and especially how infants are able to learn language. We see that caretaker–infant social interaction is the driver of the development of cognitive abilities, especially language development. In Chapter 9 categorization, causal learning, and reasoning are shown to be largely social in nature. Throughout the later chapters of the text we continue to see how the higher cognitive functions have been shaped for social ends.

In addition, beginning with the discussion of the amygdala in Chapters 1 and 2, the role of emotion in cognition is discussed with respect to attention, learning, and reasoning.

The effect of this organization is that the cognitive psychology course is no longer a collection of research areas – perception, attention, language, learning, memory, reasoning, and problem solving – that are treated as a set of independent topics without reference to a common neural mechanism or overarching function. Instead, it is the single story of how cognition makes action more effective by solving two great problems: how to respond to novel events and how to respond to familiar events. It is the story of how the control of mental action evolved from the control of physical action, and so reasoning and problem solving ultimately evolved from motor control.

The brilliant research of the past twenty years has illuminated both the common frontal-temporal neural system that underlies all these abilities and the common social function they all share. Beginning in Chapter 2, the common neural system and the common social function will be used to integrate all human cognitive abilities, and consequently all the research topics, within a single narrative. It is much easier for students to understand a single story, whereby one chapter follows naturally from its predecessor, than to understand a loose connection of topics. Consequently, my students have found the material not only accessible but also intriguing and even exciting.

To facilitate the presentation, some new terminology is introduced in the hope that it will be widely adopted. Despite wide agreement within the cognitive and behavioral neuroscience research communities on the basic brain systems for cognition, there has been no agreement on what to call them. This has had the unfortunate effect of masking the underlying consensus. In their classic foundational review describing the two systems in detail, Yin and Knowlton (2006) call one system the action–outcome (A–O) system and the other system the stimulus–response (S–R) system. However, virtually no subsequent report has adopted this nomenclature. Yin and Knowlton refer to the function of the S–R system as habit learning, so it is simply called the habit system here. The complementary A–O system is called the instrumental system, which implies an action and its outcome.

The central audience is anyone taking cognitive psychology at any college or university. However, anyone with an interest in the topic will find the book accessible. It will therefore be of benefit to students and instructors in other areas who are interested in this exciting area of study.

In addition to presenting the astounding new findings of this century, it is worthwhile to present the new and old methodologies that produced these findings. However, I have not done this by providing an introductory historical chapter. Physics and chemistry texts do not begin with such a chapter. I have always felt that such a chapter was unnecessary and betrayed a defensive attitude about what was actually known. It seemed to say, "We don't know much yet about mental life but here is how we have been trying to find out about it." Such a chapter often introduced a text that appeared to be a collection of experimental results rather than a description of how the mind works. Instead, I have integrated the methods and conclusions through the use of elaborate figures that illustrate both the experimental method and its result. Each chapter contains visual descriptions of one or two iconic experiments.

When I began teaching forty years ago, I felt that I had a special obligation to my students to teach effectively. After all, the course I was teaching was called cognitive psychology. One of the main topics was learning and memory. If I was presenting myself as an expert on learning and memory, how could I not fail to use what I claimed to know to help my students learn the material?

For many years it was not possible for me to carry out my intention to apply cognitive psychology to instruction. I could not collect enough information about student knowledge throughout class to assess the effectiveness of what I was doing. Finally, advances in technology in this twenty-first century have made my original plan possible. The introduction of personal response systems (clickers) made it possible to continuously monitor student knowledge in class and the use of an online course platform made it possible to measure what they knew from studying at home.

The use of these technologies has greatly benefited my instruction, and through this book I hope to confer those benefits on you. Because I teach multiple large sections with hundreds of students at the same time, I was able to perform counterbalanced within-student, within-item experimental studies of the comprehensibility of the study materials and of the effects of different instructional strategies.

One benefit was the development of highly effective question sets, which are integrated with the text and provide an effective means of learning the material through the instructional methodology known as distributed questioning. About 150 question sets cover the principles and facts that comprise the discipline of cognitive psychology. Each set contains four or more questions such that all questions query the same principle or fact statement. The correct answers to all the questions in the set may be inferred from this single principle or fact statement. Three questions from the set are integrated with instruction, including a pre-lesson, post-lesson, and review question. The remaining question from the set becomes the exam question. Many studies (including my own) have now been published demonstrating the effectiveness of this instructional methodology in peer-reviewed journals. Distributed questioning has proved to be effective whether the questions are presented online or in the classroom, but appears to be most effective when the questions are presented as clicker questions in class. An extensive set of PowerPoint slides coordinated with the printed text is available that can be used in a lecture or integrated in an online presentation. These include the clicker question from the question sets.

A second benefit was that the student responses to specific questions provided the feedback necessary to repeatedly revise the content of this text, page by page and paragraph by paragraph, to make it clearer and more accessible.

A third benefit is that the technology, along with my varied teaching schedule, has made it possible to adapt the text and supporting materials to a variety of contexts. The book has been used in large lectures and small seminars. It has been used by undergraduate psychology students and by graduate students from a variety of disciplines who wanted to learn about human cognition. It has been used in hybrid courses in which much of the material was presented online. The result is a robust presentation in which the individual chapters can be presented as written, in a new order, or as stand-alone introductions to their topics. I am vividly aware that the first thing instructors (including me) do with a text they like is to tear it apart and reorganize it to conform to their own priorities for their students. I welcome this, and I am eager to hear from you all about what you used, what you did not use, and what you missed; what you liked and what needs to be improved.

Arnold Lewis Glass aglass@rutgers.edu

ACKNOWLEDGEMENTS

I thank my editor, Matthew Bennett, the development editors, Valerie Appleby and Claire Eudall, the editor, Carrie Parkinson, the art director, Charles Howell, and the copy-editor, Mike Richardson, for making this book a reality. I would also like to thank the anonymous reviewers, who invariably made helpful suggestions, including several suggested studies that have been incorporated into the text. I thank Nicole Owens for the original drawings on which Figures 1.6, 3.2, and 4.1 are based. I thank Karen Ternosky, Daniel Wilmott, and James Wilmott for the research and original drawing on which Figure 14.1 is based. I thank Peter Balsam for introducing me to studies of conditioning mentioned in Chapter 1.

1 The evolution of the pre-cognitive control of action

If you dropped a newborn infant into a swimming pool, do you think that it would swim? Remarkably, it would. A newborn infant cannot roll over and can barely manipulate its fingers. Yet, when placed in a pool, the infant swims both vigorously and happily. I can still remember the first time I saw this, in a grainy movie shown in an undergraduate developmental psychology class. It seemed almost too amazing to believe. I had to wait many years to confirm it, and then my son was born, and as soon as we got him home I took him to a pool, placed him in it, and let go. He swam from one end to the other. So, I can assure you from my own experience. Infants can swim!

Why infants can swim illuminates one of the important milestones in the evolution of cognition. The evolution of cognition begins with the control of action. Almost all animals, except for the very simplest, are born with a set of automatic responses to things they will encounter in the world. Though not of importance to human survival, the infant swim reflex is a reminder that we evolved from creatures for which automatic action was a larger portion of their behavior than it is of ours. Initially, the nervous system evolved to automatically control action. Little learning was possible and reasoning was unnecessary.

1.1 The control of action

Cognition evolved from the control of action. An **action** is the movement of a body part in response to some **target** perceived by an animal. So, falling off a cliff and being blown in the wind do not count as actions. Rather, action implies **sensation**, because the animal must be able to detect the stimulus that the action is in response to. If you cannot move about and have an effect on your place in the world then there is no value to you in perceiving and thinking about the world. That is why there is a psychology of animals but there is not a psychology of plants. There is no survival value in being able to perceive the world around you if you cannot respond to what you perceive. The sole purpose of cognition is to make action more effective (Barsalou, 2008).

Every action has two components: a stimulus from the world detected by an organism, and its response to it. So, action begins with the ability to respond to the world. The ability to respond to the world begins with the evolution of the nervous system, which made it possible to detect changes in the world and respond to them. The simplest responses are called reflexes.

Reflexes by themselves are not cognitive. They do not require thought. However, they were the important first step in the evolution of cognition. The neural mechanisms of reflexes formed the basis of the enhanced neural mechanisms that made cognition possible.

1.2 Reflexes

It is the nervous system that makes action possible. The simplest actions that an animal can produce regulate activities within the animal's own body. Life functions in all except the simplest animals are performed by several distinct systems. The digestive system breaks food down into nutrients, the respiratory system provides oxygen to burn them for energy, and the circulatory system delivers oxygen to all the cells of the body. These various systems do not function independently but are under the control of the **nervous system**, which regulates their activities to make them more effective. For example, the nervous system regulates heartbeat, stomach movements, contractions of the bladder and rectum, and secretions of glands.

The simplest form of action is the reflex, in which a stimulus elicits a response. All reflexes are performed by a sequence of neurons called the **reflex arc**, which begins with a sensory neuron and ends with a response neuron. A **sensory neuron** detects a change in the environment or in the animal itself, and a **response neuron** activates a muscle (or gland) in response to it. The other neurons in the arc, whose function is to transmit a signal from the sensory neuron to the response neuron, are called interneurons (Figure 1.1). Interneurons connect stimulus neurons to response neurons in complex patterns that combine many simpler reflexes into sophisticated responses to the world.

Each neuron is separated from the next neuron in the circuit by a small gap called a **synapse**. Because they are impossible to draw correctly in detail, illustrations such as Figure 1.1 and schematic diagrams of the neural mechanisms of reflexes are always misleading. Reflex arcs do not consist of one sensory neuron and one response neuron. Rather, they consist of hundreds of sensory and response neurons. Thousands of sensory–response neuron pairings are included in the arc; that is, each of the hundreds of sensory neurons forms synapses with each of the hundreds of response neurons, and vice versa.

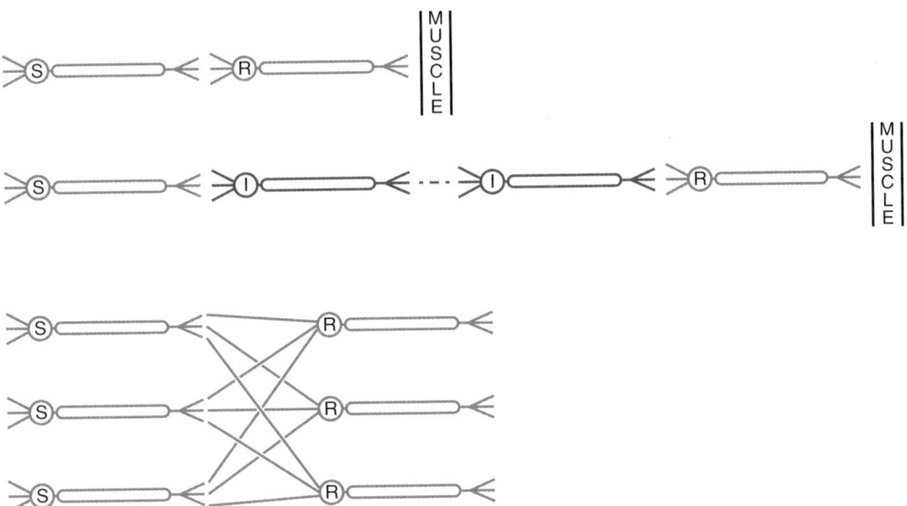

Figure 1.1 The reflex arc from a sensory neuron (S) to a response neuron (R) may consist of only those two neurons or the pathway may also contain one or more interneurons (top). Even the simplest reflex arc contains hundreds of sensory and response neurons and thousands of synapses between different pairs of neurons (bottom).

Most neurons communicate with the adjacent neuron by releasing a chemical signal called a **neurotransmitter**, which floats across the synapse and is taken up by the next neuron and stimulates it. (Some interneurons communicate by generating an electrical charge in the gap between them, but their function is not well understood: (Apostolides and Trussell, 2013.)

Many reflexes respond to stimulation from the environment. For example (as the great physiologist Ivan Pavlov discovered), placing a small amount of meat in a dog's mouth causes it to salivate, which begins the process of digesting the meat. The **pupillary light reflex** varies the size of the pupil so that the right amount of light for vision enters the eye. The **accommodation reflex** varies the shape of the eyeball so that the image projected on the retina is not blurred. In addition to regulating purely life functions through simple actions, reflexes evolved to perform increasingly complex actions in response to stimuli in the animal's environment.

Reflexes are also called **unconditioned responses**, because of a mistranslation from Russian. Pavlov described reflexes as unconditional because the same stimulus always caused the same response regardless of other conditions; "unconditional" was mistranslated as "unconditioned." The same mistranslation has been extended to the stimulus of the reflex, which is called the **unconditioned stimulus**. In many texts, stimulus and response are simply referred to by the initials US and UR.

Motor neurons are response neurons that initiate muscle contraction or relaxation, producing body movement. For example, blowing a puff of air in someone's eye causes it to blink, thus protecting the eye from harm.

The sea snail

In the simplest creatures that have reflexes, the reflexes are the only kinds of actions that the creature performs. One such creature is the sea snail, *Aplysia*, shown in Figure 1.2. In the

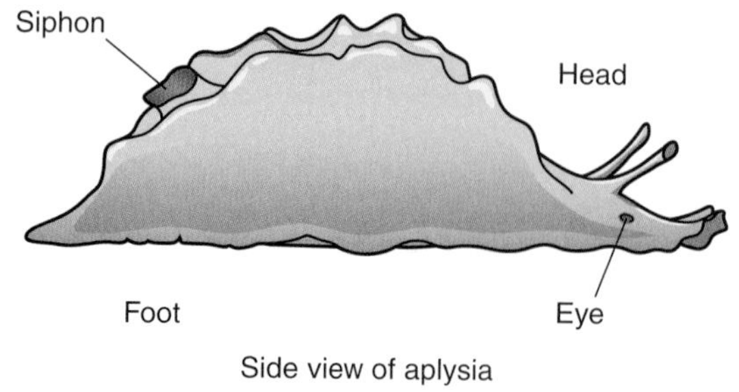

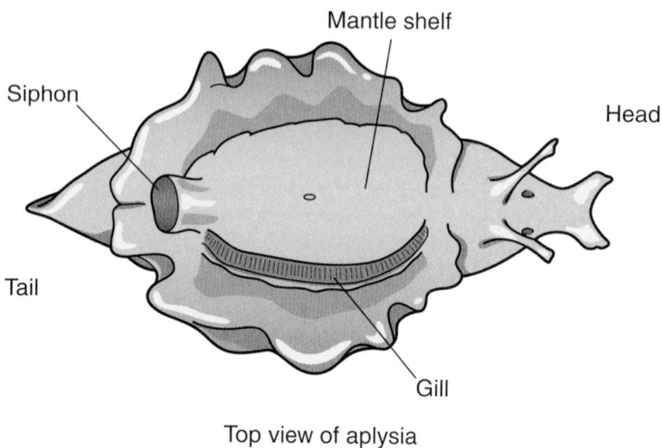

Figure 1.2 The siphon and gill are within the mantle cavity. When the siphon is touched, the entire gill withdraws into the mantle cavity for protection (Kandel, 2006).

Aplysia, six different reflexes, including the gill withdrawal reflex, are controlled by a group of 2,000 neurons (Kandel, 2006). As shown in the figure, in the top center of its body, called the mantle, there is an opening that contains its gill, which it breathes through, and its spout, through which it expels seawater and waste. Touching its siphon lightly produces a brisk defensive withdrawal of both the siphon and the gill.

The gill withdrawal reflex of the sea snail was studied intensively by Kandel (2006) because it had a nervous system that was simple enough that it appeared to be possible to figure out the neural mechanism that produced the reflexive movements in response to stimuli. It was expected that what was true of the neural mechanism producing reflexes in *Aplysia* would generally be true for the neural mechanisms of all animals with reflexes. This did turn out to be true, so the study of the neural mechanism of the reflexes of *Aplysia* was an extremely useful enterprise.

Neural mechanisms

The sensory neuron is separated from the response neuron by a small gap called a **synapse**. At the tips of the sensory neurons there are many tiny **terminal nodes**, which are containers filled with chemicals called **neurotransmitters**. When the sensory neuron is activated by a stimulus, its terminal nodes open and spill the neurotransmitter into the synapse, from which it is absorbed by receptors at the end of the response neuron. If the response neuron absorbs enough neurotransmitter, it becomes active and initiates the response. Kandel and his colleagues studied the neurons that were part of the neural pathway for the gill withdrawal reflex of *Aplysia*. They found that a single sensory neuron had about 1,300 terminal nodes, of which about 40 percent were active, contacting about twenty-five motor neurons; that is, about 40 percent spilled neurotransmitter into the synapse when the neuron was stimulated.

1.3 Habituation and sensitization

Despite Pavlov's characterization of reflexes as unconditional, the response to a repeated stimulus changes. Over successive repetitions, the strength of the response to a weak stimulus decreases and the strength of the response to a strong stimulus increases. These changes in response strength are called habituation and sensitization.

Functional characteristics

Habituation is when the response to a weak stimulus becomes weaker with each repetition of the weak stimulus. In this situation there may be complete habituation, so that eventually the response is not made at all. **Sensitization** is when the response to subsequent stimuli becomes stronger after a very strong stimulus is presented. Recall that touching an *Aplysia*'s siphon produces withdrawal of both the siphon and the gill. The force of the touch required varies with the experience of the individual snail. Repeated light touch produces **habituation** – that is, after each touch the withdrawal of the siphon is slower, until it doesn't withdraw at all. In contrast, a strong shock to either head or tail produces **sensitization** – that is, after the strong shock, a weak touch that previously did not cause the withdrawal of the siphon now does.

Habituation and sensitization adjust the strength and probability of a reflex to the current level of stimulation in the world around it. If the snail is pulling its way through some vegetation, it is counter-productive for it to withdraw into its shell every time it brushes against a leaf. Habituation decreases the sensitivity of the reflex to prevent this. On the other hand, the stronger the stimulus, the more potentially damaging it is. Sensitization increases the sensitivity of the reflex so that there is a fast and certain response to a potentially damaging stimulus.

How long the change in the sensitivity of the reflex persisted depended on the training routine to which the *Aplysia* was subjected. Carew and Kandel (1973), and their colleagues, found that forty weak electrical stimuli administered consecutively resulted in short-term habituation of the gill withdrawal that lasted only one day, but ten stimuli every day for four days produced long-term habituation that lasted for weeks. Similarly, Pinsker *et al.* (1973) found that four strong shocks on each of four successive days produced long-term sensitization that lasted for three weeks. The presentation of stimuli over a brief interval is called **massed** presentation. The presentation of stimuli over a long interval is called **distributed** or **spaced** presentation.

The short-term effect of massed training allows the creature to respond immediately to a current change in conditions. The long-term effect of distributed training allows the creature to adjust to a **routine** change in conditions. Thus, the neural mechanism makes sophisticated adjustments to changing conditions. Massed training is treated as the conditions of a single event, implying nothing about the future. Adjustments are short-term, hence temporary. Distributed training is treated as a repeated event, and the repeated event is treated as a routine event that may continue into the future. Hence, the adjustments are long-term and, given the continued routine, permanent.

The short-term versus long-term changes in siphon withdrawal are caused by different changes in the snail's nervous system. Short-term changes included the amount of neurotransmitter released into a synapse by the sensory neuron. Short-term habituation of the reflex occurred because, after each weak stimulus, the sensory neuron released less neurotransmitter into each synapse. Short-term sensitization of the reflex occurred because, after the strong stimulus, more neurotransmitter was released into each synapse. Such a short–term change had long been predicted by earlier investigators of the nervous system. However, it was the previously unknown, long-term changes in the neuron that were of particular interest. These demonstrated that, for even the simplest modification of action, the neural mechanisms were far more complicated than had been imagined.

Neural mechanisms of long-term changes in sensitivity

Recall that, in the gill withdrawal reflex, Kandel (2006) found that a single sensory neuron had approximately 1,300 pre-synaptic terminals, 40 percent of which were active, with which it contacted about 25 different motor neurons (Figure 1.3). This changed with both habituation and sensitization. In long-term habituation, the number of terminal nodes dropped to 850, of which 12 percent were active. In long-term sensitization, the number of terminal nodes increased to 2,700, of which 60 percent were active. In addition, there was outgrowth from the motor neuron to receive the output of the new terminals. Kandel suggested that, because building new terminals or removing old ones requires the availability of limited resources in the neurons, there could be only a limited decrease or increase in

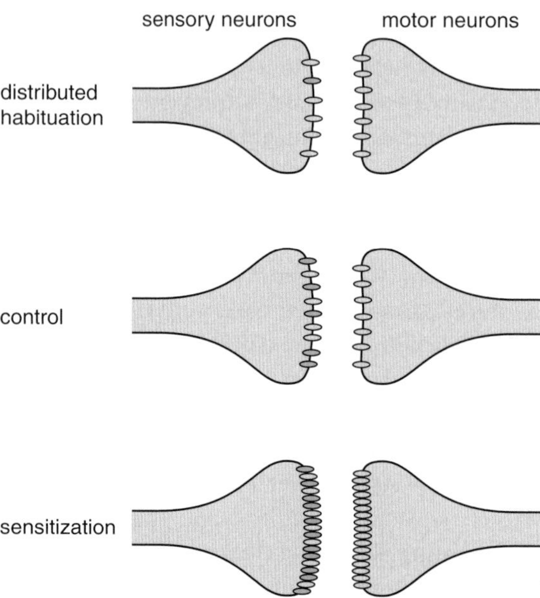

Figure 1.3 The number of terminal nodes on the presynaptic sensory neuron change as the result of distributed habituation (top) and distributed sensitization (bottom). Active nodes are shown darker. In sensitization, there is also a change in the number of post-synaptic receptor terminals (Kandel, 2006).

the number of terminals over a given training period regardless of the number of stimuli. Specifically, proteins used to make long-term changes in the cell take time to synthesize. Distributing the stimuli over a longer period of training results in more protein being available (Abbott and Kandel, 2012).

1.4 Complex reflexes and the organization of behavior

Animals do not perform individual voluntary actions independently of one another. Rather, as the result of evolution, they engage in behaviors such as foraging, stalking, chasing, feeding, and courting. A **behavior** consists of a sequence of complimentary actions towards a common purpose. Such behaviors may be complex, extended, reflexive responses in which earlier reflexes in the sequence generate stimuli that elicit later ones (Lorenz, 1958).

The aggregation of reflex arcs increased the sophistication of reflexive actions

To create more specific, precise, and effective responses, simpler reflex arcs were combined to generate more complex responses to more specific stimuli. For example, when a painful stimulus is applied to the foot of many animals, from amphibians such as frogs to mammals such as humans, there is a defensive withdrawal response (Tresilian, 2012). Precisely where the foot is touched determines the exact trajectory of its withdrawal movement in order to ensure that it no longer is in contact with the painful stimulus (Schouenborg, 2008). A stimulus may direct an action towards a target, as well as away from it. The wiping reflex of the frog will cause the leg to move into position and then wipe away an irritating particle. Again, the action is directed by an integrated set of reflexes that direct it to the irritating particle (Berkinblit, Feldman, and Fukson, 1986).

Furthermore, a pattern of stimuli may elicit a sequence of responses through feed-forward stimulation, in which each response becomes the stimulus for the next response in the sequence. Hence, reflexes may include complex behaviors such as locomotion and feeding. When the response has several components extended over time, it is called a **modal action pattern**. In a modal action pattern, the initiation of some reflexes results in feed-forward stimulation that initiates other reflexes that form part of the action pattern. For example, a bird that sees an egg (or egg-like object) just outside its nest will push it into the nest.

Reflexes in complex animals

In the life of an animal, stimuli do not randomly activate its reflexes independently of events in its world. If this were the case then the reflexes would have limited functional value. Rather, the stimuli are parts of larger events that are relevant to the life of a creature. For example, a stimulus activating the gill withdrawal reflex of a sea snail may be part of a larger event in which other parts of the creature are pelted, perhaps by rain, or by gravel, or by another creature. For another example, the stimulus activating salivation is almost always part of a larger event in which the animal eats and digests a meal.

In complex animals, reflexes do not operate independently of each other but either as components of complicated, sophisticated systems of voluntary action or as withdrawal responses that prevent inadvertent injury from voluntary action. Reflexes consist of **cranial**

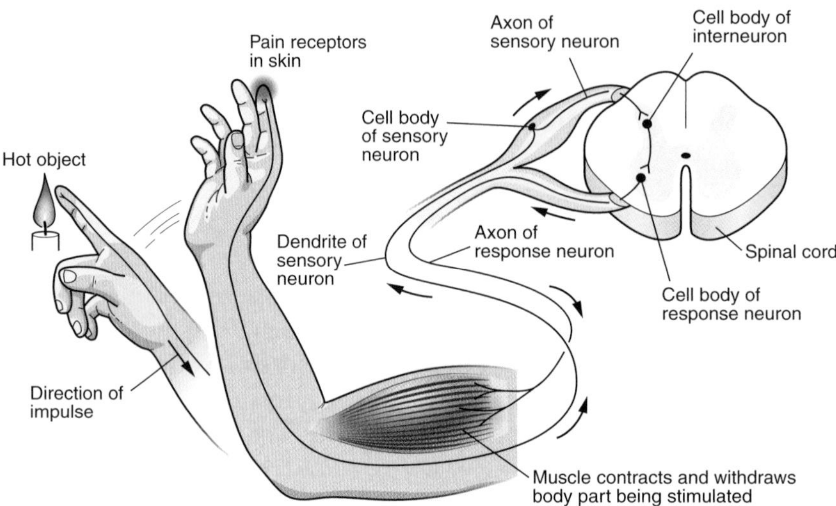

Figure 1.4 A simple spinal motor reflex.

reflexes in the head and **spinal reflexes** in the body. Spinal reflexes consist of both **segmental reflexes**, whose junctions between the stimulus and response neurons are in the spinal cord, and **intersegmental reflexes**, whose junctions are in the brain stem. Throughout the body, reflexes prevent muscles from being stretched too far to cause injury. Reflexes rapidly move body parts out of harm's way, so that touching a hot surface does not result in a severe burn (Figure 1.4), and adjust the tension of muscles in response to changes in the body's center of gravity caused by voluntary movement. This prevents someone from inadvertently toppling over every time one reaches across a counter.

Cranial reflexes in the brainstem again either have protective functions or are components of complex systems. The gag and cough reflexes help clear the throat of noxious substances. A variety of blink reflexes lower the eyelid to protect the eye from harm. As the result of distinct reflexes, people blink in response to a tap on the forehead, a mild shock to the wrist, an intense sound, a flash of light and pressure on the cornea by a touch or puff of air (Aramideh and Ongerboer de Visser, 2002). Three brainstem reflexes, the pupillary reflex, the accommodation reflex, and the vestibulo-ocular reflex, make vision possible. When you go from a dark room to a light one or from a light room to a dark one, the small holes in the surface of each eye called **pupils** reflexively respond to the change in light and close or open just enough to maintain the same amount of light falling on the retina. When you focus on something, muscles contract and relax to change the shape of the eyeball so that a clear image continues to fall on the retina. When you turn your head while you are looking at something, muscles contract and relax so that your eyes roll in the exact opposite direction to maintain a clear image at your fixation point (Figure 1.5).

Collections of segmental reflexes in the brainstem are organized by the superior colliculus and inferior colliculus in the midbrain as **supersegmental** functional systems that orient the body towards visual and auditory stimuli, so you automatically turn towards a bright flash or loud noise. In addition, the eyes automatically fixate on a moving target (Gnadt *et al.*, 1997). These automatic responses are part of an **orientation reaction** that directs perceptual

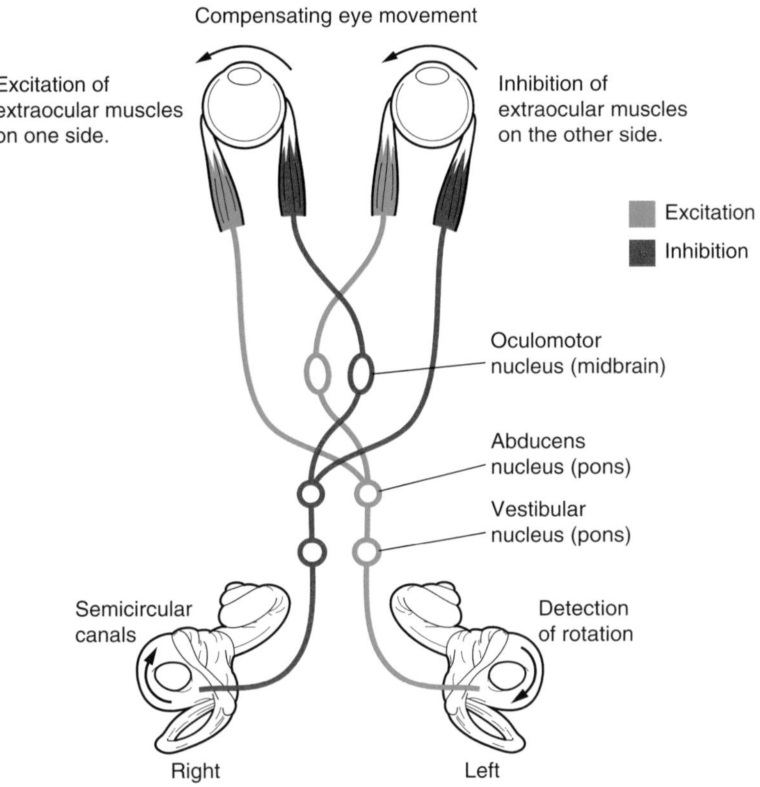

Figure 1.5 The vestibular-ocular reflex is initiated by the vestibular nucleus in the pons of the brain stem. The eyes move in response to changes in the fluid levels of the semicircular canals of the ear, which change as the result of head movement.

processing to a novel input. As shown in Figure 1.6, above the midbrain are three structures that further organize reflexes into functional systems. First, the hypothalamus regulates **cranial** and **spinal** reflexes related to eating. The hypothalamus sensitizes salivation and stomach contraction reflexes when a hungry animal is about to eat. Second, the cerebellum modulates cranial withdrawal reflexes, such as the blink reflex and spinal reflexes that stabilize the body in different postures and during locomotion. To coordinate body movements, the **vestibular** system keeps track of the orientation of the body, and this information is used by the cerebellum in making both reflexive and voluntary movements. As you move about you agitate the fluid in the semicircular canals in your ears. The movement of the fluid signals the tilt of your body and activates compensatory vestibular reflexes in the brainstem that keep you from falling (Figure 1.5).

Third, the amygdala aggregates and modulates responses of the superior colliculus and inferior colliculus into a comprehensive orienting or startle response that categorizes the stimuli as good or bad and orients the body towards or away from it and prepares the body for action in response to it. Finally, as shown in Figure 1.6, the amygdala, cerebellum, hypothalamus, superior colliculus, and inferior colliculus receive inputs from the areas in the frontal, parietal, and occipital cortex that modulate their supersegmental responses so that they support rather than conflict with voluntary movements that are part of the same

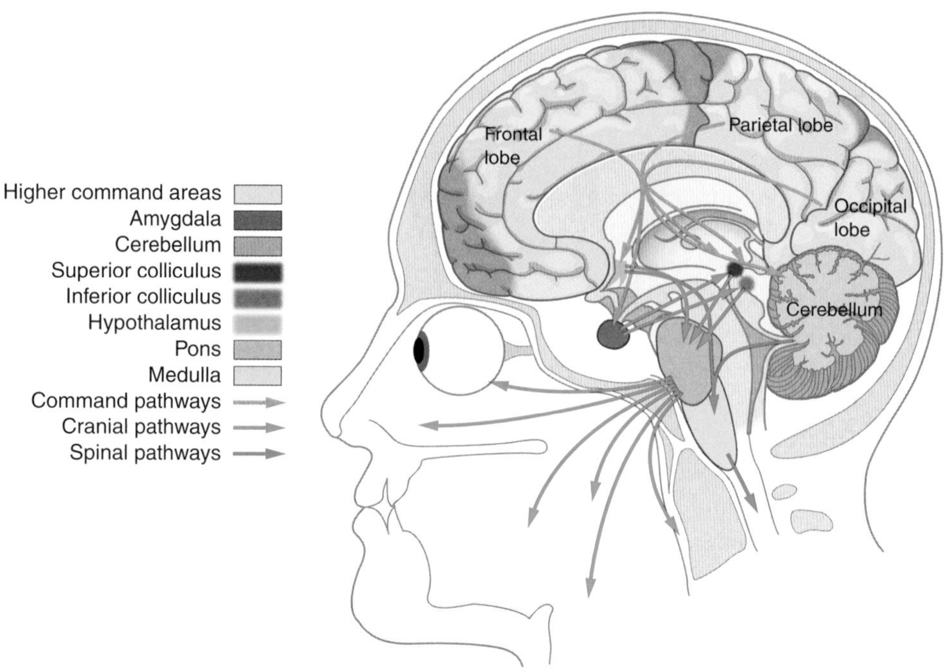

Figure 1.6 Functional systems of reflexes include: the hypothalamus regulates reflexes related to eating; the cerebellum modulates reflexes that stabilize the body; and the amygdala aggregates responses by the superior and inferior colliculus into the orienting response (after an original) figure by Nicole Owen).

functional response. For example, the reflexes controlled by the superior colliculus are part of the visual scanning system that makes visual perception possible (Chapter 3).

The automatic reflexes play important, though secondary, roles in the regulation of voluntary action. A reflex provides an innate fast response to a single, simple, stimulus. A reflex can be fast because it involves only a few sensory neurons and interneurons, so very little processing takes place and there is only a short time before the response is activated. The reflex always occurs without any conscious decision to perform the action. Speed is an advantage. A hand pulls away from a burning stimulus before the person even feels the pain. But simplicity is a limitation. There are no reflexes to things that must be recognized. Recognition requires many computations, so is not simple. Some reflexes have no purpose at all in humans but are vestiges of reflexes that were useful to an ancestor. When a hairy animal is cold, neurons sensitive to the cold activate motor neurons that cause the skin to pucker up, which causes little air pockets close to the skin that are surrounded by hair. This has exactly the same effect as putting on a sweater. The pockets of air are warmed by the animal's body heat and, in turn, help keep the animal warm. In humans, the puckering in the skin is called goose bumps. Goose bumps have no function but remind us that we evolved from creatures whose bodies were covered by hair. In addition, touching the cornea elicits a slight movement of the skin over the jaw. It is not known why this response evolved.

Reflexes are encoded into the nervous system at birth. They are innate. However, innate does not mean permanent. Some reflexes that are present at birth disappear as the infant matures as part of normal development. They are suppressed by signals from the brain as it takes control of the motor system. These early, temporary reflexes present a conundrum. Do they perform useful functions until the motor system matures or are they, like goose bumps, vestiges that serve no purpose? In the case of the sucking and grasp reflexes, the purpose seems obvious. For other reflexes, it is not. The most elaborate automatic response that humans perform is the amazing, temporary **infant swim reflex**. When a newborn infant is placed in the water, such as in a swimming pool, the infant swims for a few meters. Water that enters the infant's mouth is diverted to its stomach, so the infant does not drown. The infant swim reflex disappears a few weeks after birth, to make way for a much more complex method for controlling action.

1.5 Conditioning

The next step in the evolution of the nervous system was the expansion of the kinds of stimuli that automatically elicited responses. When the nervous system became sufficiently complex, it was capable of encoding not just a variety of stimuli but the temporal relationship of one stimulus to another. Within this more complex system it became possible for a stimulus that was predictive of an unconditioned stimulus to come to elicit its response. This becomes a possibility when two stimuli, such as an air puff and a tone, have pathways to a response, such as an eye blink, but only the unconditioned stimulus – the air puff – causes a strong enough signal to cause the response. When both stimuli are presented together, the response neuron becomes more sensitive to signals from the second sensory neuron, for the tone, so now the second stimulus also initiates the response by itself. When this occurs, the second stimulus is called the **conditioned stimulus** (CS).

Kandel and his colleagues (Carew, Walters, and Kandel, 1981) demonstrated conditioning in the sea snail. Conditioning makes it possible to extend the set of stimuli that elicit a reflex by presenting one that doesn't innately elicit the reflex just before one that does. In the gill withdrawal reflex, presenting a mild electric shock to the tail of the sea snail causes it to withdraw its gill. The electric shock to the tail is the unconditioned stimulus and the gill withdrawal is the unconditioned response. When the mantle shelf skin of the snail was lightly brushed, by itself this degree of stimulation produced no response. However, when an electric shock was given to the tail while brushing the mantle, after several brushing–shock pairings the gill withdrew as soon as the mantle skin was brushed, without the shock being applied. At this point, the brushing of the mantle skin had become a conditioned stimulus or CS, because through conditioning (that is, pairing with a US) it had come to elicit a response.

In order for the potential conditioned stimulus in the environment to ultimately elicit the unconditioned response, there must be (a) an innate CS–UR pathway and (b) an interneuron that connects the US with the CS–UR pathway. In *Aplysia*, an interneuron connects the sensory neuron in the tail with the synapse between the sensory neuron in the mantle and the motor neuron contracting the siphon (Figure 1.7).

There are two critical stages in conditioning. First, the stimulus that will become the conditioned stimulus generates a large response in a sensory neuron because it is novel. When a neuron generates a response, it becomes briefly vulnerable to alteration through another signal to it. This occurred when the mantle was lightly brushed. Second, the unconditioned

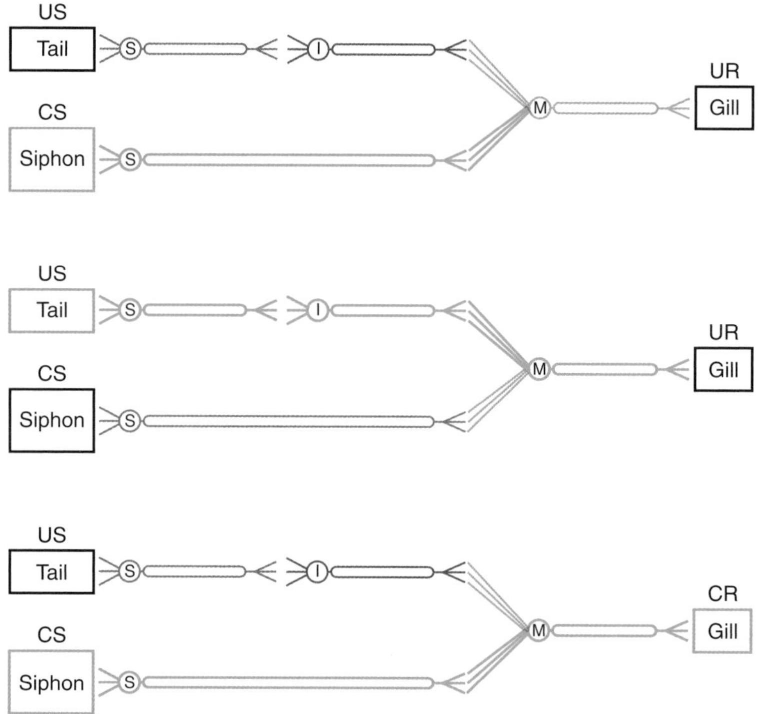

Figure 1.7 Conditioning of gill withdrawal in aplysia. Unhabituated novel stimulus (CS) generates strong signal (top). Unconditioned stimulus (US) modifies pathway between CS and response (UR) to strengthen the signal from the sensory neuron and the response from the response neuron (middle). Conditioned stimulus elicits response (bottom) (Kandel, 2006).

stimulus, which elicits the unconditioned response, sends a signal through an interneuron that alters the strength of the pathway from the novel stimulus to the response. This occurred when an electric shock was applied to the tail.

The consequence of this sequence of events is that the strength of the signal from the novel stimulus is increased and the excitability of the response neuron to the signal is also increased. The result is the conditioning of the UR to the CS. When the CS elicits a response, the response is called the **conditioned response (CR)** in other texts. Using this terminology, exactly the same response would be called the UR when it was elicited by the US and the CR when it was elicited by the CS. Calling the same response by two different names is misleading and confusing, so here the same response will continue to be called the UR even when it is elicited by a CS.

The functional value of conditioning is that it tends to elicit a reflex sooner in a context in which it is useful. When other stimuli besides the unconditioned stimulus have their own sensory pathways to the same response, they are likely to occur in the presence of other stimuli that are part of the same event containing the unconditioned stimulus that initiates the reflex. When these other stimuli precede the unconditioned stimuli they may be reliable signals that the unconditioned stimulus is about to occur. For example, when you eat, the smell and sight of the food that you are about to place in your mouth is a reliable signal that you will soon be eating it. Salivating just before the food enters your mouth prepares your mouth so that digestion and the enjoyment of its flavor begins a few moments sooner.

Conditioning requires contingent relationship between novel stimulus and unconditioned stimulus

In mammals, the eye blink reflex has proved convenient for the studying of conditioning for several reasons. First, it can be easily and harmlessly initiated by a puff of air in the eye. Second, it can be conditioned easily. Third, it has been possible to trace the neural pathway controlling the eye blink. Specifically, the neural pathway for eye blink conditioning is in the cerebellum for rabbits (Christian and Thompson, 2003) and humans (Woodruff-Pak, Papka, and Ivry, 1996), which probably means that the cerebellum serves this function and related functions for all mammals. In other words, even though the junction between the sensory and response pathways for the eye blink reflex is in the brainstem, conditioning of the reflex is the result of a pathway descending from the cerebellum. For example, when a tone sounds, the output of the ear follows a pathway first to the brainstem, then on to the cerebellum, where it intersects with a pathway extending down to the junction of the eye blink reflex in the brainstem. A **novel stimulus** is one that has not been recently presented. When a contingent relationship exists between an appropriate novel stimulus, such as a sound, and the unconditioned stimulus, such as an air puff or food particle, and the necessary neural pathways exist, the novel stimulus comes to elicit the unconditioned response (Ward, Gallistel, and Balsam, 2013).

A potential CS–US pair must be contingent so that both are unhabituated

Why must the CS–US pair be contingent, and how does the brain identify a contingent pair in the first place? The answer is that sensory neurons produce a much larger response to a first-time stimulus than to a repeated stimulus. Every time a mild stimulus is repeated over a short period of time, the response from the sensory neurons that detect it is reduced. This is the same change in neuronal response that causes habituation. When a novel stimulus is presented, it stimulates a set of previously resting neurons that have not recently been stimulated to make a response. Hence, their response is strong. It is the strong responses of sensory neurons of the CS–US pair to novel stimuli that initiate conditioning (Groves and Thompson, 1970).

This effect of short-term habituation partly explains why a contingent relationship must exist between the novel stimulus and the unconditioned stimulus. When the conditioned stimulus or the unconditioned stimulus has occurred shortly beforehand, it is not novel, has become habituated and has occurred **non-contingently** in relation to the pair (Randich and Lolordo, 1979). Consequently, it does not cause a signal sufficiently strong to initiate conditioning. The restriction to contingent stimuli prevents conditioning from extending reflexive responses to ubiquitous but functionally meaningless stimuli in the animal's environment. Only stimuli that are contingently related to the unconditioned stimulus, and so are predictive of it, will come to elicit the reflex precisely in those contexts in which it is appropriate. Furthermore, during conditioning the interval between the conditioned stimulus and unconditioned stimulus is encoded by neurons in the cerebellum (Johansson *et al.*, 2014). Consequently, the conditioned response occurs at the interval after the conditioned stimulus when the unconditioned stimulus is most likely to have also occurred. So, conditioning is not a epiphenomenon resulting in a meaningless response, such as biting at air or salivating in response to a tone. Rather, its purpose is to sensitize what is likely to be a meaningful response by signaling a context in which the corresponding unconditioned stimulus is likely to imminently occur.

Extinction, recovery, and context

Once a CS is established through conditioning, subsequent presentations of the CS that are not paired with the US do not elicit the unconditioned response forever. Instead, if the CS is consistently presented alone, it elicits the unconditioned response less and less, until it does not elicit it at all. This process is called **extinction**. However, after extinction occurs and a subsequent rest period when the CS is not presented, if it is again presented alone it may again elicit the unconditioned response. This is called **spontaneous recovery** (Todd, Vurbic, and Bouton, 2013).

Recall that a variety of different sensory neurons may have **overlapping** pathways to the same response neuron that transmit signals to the neuron that are not strong enough to elicit a response. Nevertheless, the signals from these sensory neurons influence the probability of a response, and the variety of stimuli to which the sensory neurons respond constitute the context of the response. When the CS is presented, but is not followed by the US, the signals of the various other sensory neurons encoding features of the context alter the pathway from the CS to the UR to weaken the response to the CS. The result is that subsequently, when the CS is presented in the extinction context, the signal from the CS to the response neuron is weakened so that it no longer elicits the response. Hence, extinction is a **context-specific** effect. When the CS is presented later in a different context in which the same set of contextual stimuli are not present, its signal is no longer as weakened and again sometimes elicits the response, thus exhibiting spontaneous recovery. A variety of internal or external stimuli may have pathways that intersect the US–UR pathway and be part of the context for a response. External stimuli may include sights, sounds, and smells from the environment. Internal stimuli may include the hunger, thirst, and degree of tiredness of the animal and may be experimentally manipulated through the administration of drugs (Todd, Vurbic, and Bouton, 2013). Spontaneous recovery may occur because the internal stimuli partly defining the context of the extinguished CS have changed.

In addition to spontaneous recovery, there are a variety of other situations in which a change of context causes a CS that has undergone extinction to again elicit a response (Todd, Vurbic, and Bouton, 2013). In **renewal**, extinguished responding returns when the CS is tested in a different environmental context from the extinction context (for example, Bouton and Bolles, 1979). In **reinstatement**, the response to the CS recovers even if the unconditioned stimulus is presented by itself again after extinction (for example, Rescorla and Heth, 1975), because the US was part of the original training context but was not part of the extinction context. In **rapid reacquisition**, responding can return to the CS quickly if CS–US pairings are resumed after extinction (for example, Napier, Mcrae, and Kehoe, 1992).

Extinction and recovery mark an important advance in the control of action. An action may not be appropriate in all contexts. Servers may not salivate to the smell of the food they bring because the context for them is different from what it is for the customers. They are not about to eat it. The additional neural complexity of pathways from multiple sensory neurons to a response neuron makes it possible to control an action so that it is made only in an appropriate context. This is accomplished through an increased sophistication of the nervous system, which operates not only through activation but **inhibition** as well. The appropriate contexts for a response are selected by inhibiting it in contexts for which it is inappropriate.

Three characteristics of conditioning

To summarize, conditioning has three characteristics that make it useful for controlling action. First, the sensory systems do not impartially respond to all inputs from the environment but preferentially detect what is new in the immediate environment. Second, it is not sufficient for a stimulus to be novel to be encoded; it must predict some stimulus eliciting action, namely the US–UR pair (Lubow, 1965). Third, in addition to the unconditioned stimulus, there may be additional circuits between other stimuli and the unconditioned response that define contexts in which the response is appropriate and contexts in which it is inappropriate. Extinction and spontaneous recovery demonstrate that the conditions for eliciting a reflex may be fine-tuned so that it occurs only in a variety of specific contexts in which it is appropriate.

Delay versus trace conditioning

For conditioning to occur, the novel stimulus must begin prior to the unconditioned stimulus. When the novel stimulus ends in relation to when the unconditioned stimulus begins determines two different situations in which conditioning may occur. The more common and robust form of conditioning is called delay conditioning. **Delay conditioning** occurs when the US **overlaps** the CS. For example, a tone is sounded, and while the tone is still being sounded a puff of air is sent to the eye, so that the termination of the tone and the application of the air to the eye coincide (Thompson, 1986). The name "delay conditioning" could not be more misleading for this procedure, because, by definition, there is **no delay** between the CS and US. Rather, the CS is initiated first, and during the interval over which it is presented the US is also presented, so that they terminate together. Hence, **delayed conditioning** describes the situation in which there is **no delay** between the end of the novel stimulus and the beginning of the unconditioned stimulus.

In humans the neural pathways for delay conditioning for avoidance reflexes are clustered in two structures of the brain (Figure 1.6), the cerebellum and the amygdala. As mentioned above, pathways extending through the cerebellum cause the conditioning of the eye blink. Avoidance reflexes to painful and unpleasant stimuli are conditioned to warning stimuli by a pathway from the thalamus that sends sensory input directly to the amygdala. The conditioning of responses to simple tones and light flashes paired with foot shocks require an intact thalamus-to-amygdala pathway. The conditioning of such reflexes is called fear conditioning, because the avoidance response involves several coordinated reflexes that are associated with the emotion of fear in humans and appear to have the same effect on other mammals. "Fear" can be measured in terms of any one of the several different responses associated with it, including the skin conductance response as the result of sweating, increased heart rate, freezing or moving behavior, or some combination of these measures (Eichenbaum, 2008).

On the top of the midbrain in mammals is the **forebrain**, which contains numerous structures, including an anatomical area called the **hippocampus** (Figure 1.6). The hippocampus makes an additional form of conditioning, called **trace conditioning**, possible. **Trace conditioning** describes the situation in which the novel stimulus ends before the unconditioned stimulus begins. Hence, there is a delay between the end of the novel stimulus and the onset of the unconditioned stimulus, which may be as brief as half a second. In order for conditioning to occur, therefore, some representation of the novel stimulus, called a trace, must remain in the brain after it has ended; hence the name: trace conditioning.

As shown in Figure 1.8, for eye blink conditioning of rats, delay conditioning produced a 75 percent response rate but trace conditioning produced only a 50 percent response rate (Beylin *et al.*, 2001). However, trace conditioning was an enormous evolutionary advance over delay conditioning. In delay conditioning, the nervous system need only associate two stimuli that occur at the same time. In trace conditioning, the nervous system must associate a later stimulus with an earlier stimulus that is no longer

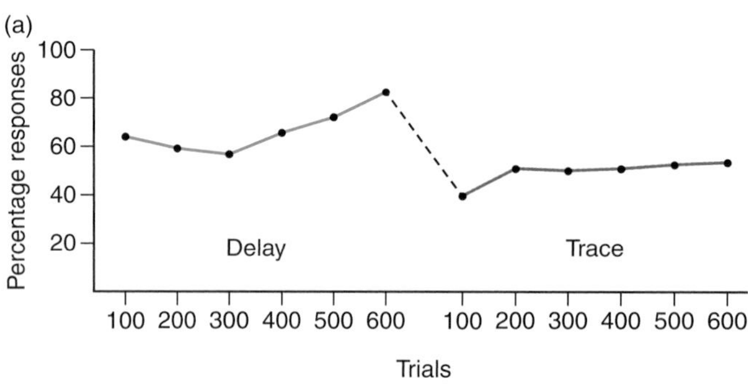

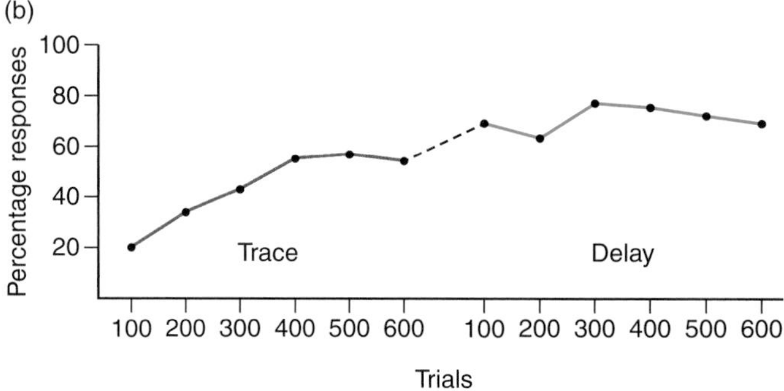

Figure 1.8 In the trace condition, rats heard 250 milliseconds of noise, 500 milliseconds of silence, and then received a mild 100 millisecond shock that caused an eyeblink. In the delay condition, the rats heard 850 milliseconds of noise. During the last 100 seconds of the noise, they received a 100 millisecond shock that caused an eyeblink. Regardless of whether the delay condition was first (a) or second (b), the response rate was 75 percent in the delay condition and 25 percent in the trace condition (Beylin *et al.*, 2001).

present. Accordingly, it must contain some mechanism for preserving the trace of the earlier stimulus (hence the name of the condition). The interval between the end of the novel stimulus and beginning of the unconditioned stimulus is rarely longer than a second in trace conditioning experiments. Nevertheless, the preservation of the trace over this brief interval is associated with an important elaboration of the animal brain. In addition to whatever structure is necessary for delay conditioning, trace conditioning requires a functioning **hippocampus** (Figure 1.8). Both the cerebellum and the hippocampus are active during trace conditioning of the eye blink reflex (Tseng *et al.*, 2004) and both the amygdala and the hippocampus are active during trace fear conditioning (Desmedt *et al.*, 2003). Damage to the hippocampus eliminates trace conditioning but leaves delay conditioning intact. Furthermore, if the hippocampus is damaged after trace conditioning, the reflex continues to respond to the conditioned stimulus. So, the role of the hippocampus in trace conditioning is specifically to associate the unconditioned stimulus with the trace of the novel stimulus during training. Once that association has been formed, a functioning hippocampus is not required to preserve it. However, its role in trace conditioning is only one of many functions the hippocampus has. We shall see that there is no more important structure among the neural mechanisms for cognition than the hippocampus.

In conditioning, the environment controls an animal's actions by activating a reflex. For example, when you salivate, you do not choose to salivate. This occurs as the result of an external stimulus.

SUMMARY

The evolution of cognition begins with the control of action. Almost all animals, except for the very simplest, are born with a set of automatic responses to things they will encounter in the world. Such automatic responses are called reflexes. They include effective responses to threats (a turtle withdrawing into its shell) and opportunities (a bird turning to the song of a potential mate) alike. Automatic responses can be as simple as an eye blink or as complicated as swimming in a pool. To make such automatic responses possible, an elaborate nervous system evolved that responded to stimuli in the environment with effective actions. Today, many creatures, such as birds, live their entire lives being guided by primarily automatic, albeit elaborate, courting, mating, foraging, feeding, and child-rearing responses, which are collectively called instinctive behavior. In fact, automatic responses play important roles influencing the behaviors of all animals. Insects', reptiles', and birds' behaviors such as foraging, stalking, chasing, feeding, and courting are generated by complex unconditioned responses (Lorenz, 1958). In humans, the sexual response – and so sexual orientation – is largely automatic, hence uninfluenced by upbringing.

Automatic responses play only a limited, albeit important, role in our behavior because life is not perfectly predictable. If a lifetime of events was perfectly predictable then every animal could be born able to automatically make every response it would ever need to make and cognition would be unnecessary. However, life is not perfectly predictable.

Let me recapitulate the evolution of these basic abilities.

- Initially, the nervous system evolved to automatically control action. Little learning was possible and reasoning was unnecessary.
  - Automatic responses, called reflexes, involve muscle movements and hormone secretions in response to stimuli from the environment. A specific response, such as salivation, is elicited by a specific stimulus – in this case the presence of food on the tongue. Each stimulus activates specific sensory neurons and each response is initiated by specific response neurons. Which stimuli elicit which responses is determined by the transmission of a signal from a specific sensory neuron to specific response neurons.
  - The intensity of the stimulus necessary to elicit a response is modulated by the strength of previous stimuli. A sequence of low-intensity stimuli insufficient to elicit a response causes the habituation of the response, so that even a stimulus strong enough to previously elicit the response no longer does so. A single high-intensity stimulus far above the threshold necessary to elicit a response causes the sensitization of the response, so that even a stimulus previously too weak to elicit the response now does so.
    - A variety of sub-cellular processes cause habituation and sensitization.
    - Massed presentation of stimuli produces short-term habituation or sensitization. Distributed (or spaced) presentation of stimuli produces long-term habituation or sensitization.
  - A stimulus that elicits a response without prior training is called an unconditioned stimulus (US). The response this elicits is called an unconditioned response (UR). The nervous system contains pathways from sensory neurons to the response neurons over which the signal that is transmitted is too weak to activate the UR. However, when the stimulus, called the conditioned stimulus (CS), is contingently paired with the US for that response, so that when the CS occurs the US always follows it, the signal between the CS neuron and UR neuron strengthens such that the CS comes to elicit the UR. Conditioning widens the stimuli in an environment that may come to elicit a response; for example, the smell of food comes to elicit salivation.
    - There are two forms of conditioning. The more common form is delay conditioning. In delay conditioning there is *no delay* between the termination of the CS and the onset of the US. They overlap so that the US begins before the CS ends. Delay conditioning results from intersections of stimulus and response pathways at various locations in the brain. Moving up from the spinal cord, on which the brain rests, these include the brain stem, cerebellum, midbrain, and amygdala.
    - The other form of conditioning is trace conditioning. In trace conditioning there is a delay between the termination of the CS and the onset of the US. Trace conditioning requires a functioning hippocampus. Trace conditioning was an important advance that made it possible for something that had occurred in the past to come to elicit a response. An animal was no longer restricted to responding to what was present in its immediate environment.

QUESTIONS

1 In a reflex, is the response controlled by the organism or an external stimulus?
2 What is the behavioral effect of repeating a weak stimulus on an unconditioned response? What are the neural mechanisms causing the behavioral effect?
3 What is the behavioral effect of a strong stimulus on an unconditioned response? What are the neural mechanisms causing the behavioral effect?
4 What is the difference between an unconditioned stimulus and a conditioned stimulus? What is the difference between an unconditioned response and a conditioned response?
5 In delayed conditioning, how long is the interval between the offset of the unconditioned stimulus and onset of the conditioned response?

FURTHER READING

Kandel, E. R. (2006). *In Search of Memory: The Emergence of a New Science of Mind*. New York: W. W. Norton.

Lorenz, K. Z. (1958). The evolution of behavior. *Scientific American*, 199, 67–83.

Tresilian, J. (2012). *Sensorimotor Control and Learning: An Introduction to the Behavioral Neuroscience of Action*. Basingstoke, UK: Palgrave Macmillan.

2 The evolution of cognition

Automatic responses play only a limited role in our behavior because life is not perfectly predictable. If a lifetime of events was perfectly predictable then every animal could be born able to automatically make every response it would ever need to make, and cognition would be unnecessary. However, life is not perfectly predictable. To make it possible to respond to unpredicted challenges in the world, an elaborated nervous system evolved that made voluntary action possible. The advantage of voluntary over automatic, involuntary action is that it can be ad hoc. Faced with something unexpected, an animal can craft a response it has never made before. Social creatures face a lifetime of new social experiences that require ad hoc responses. For example, dogs that are allowed on furniture often sit where other family members sit. This is how I came to share a chair with my golden retriever. The dog would have to move whenever I wanted to sit down. Across the room was the sliding door to the backyard. The retriever learned that, to go out, he should touch the door. One day, when I was sitting in the chair, the dog touched the door. I got up and walked over to the door. Before I could open it, the dog ran back and sat in the chair!

Cognition begins with the control of voluntary action. In this chapter we will see that cognition evolved to make it possible for an animal to perform novel actions in response to novel, hence unexpected, events.

- To make voluntary action possible, at the top of the spinal cord, layer upon layer of representational, computational, and control structure was added, forming brains of increasing complexity, which provided increasingly sophisticated control of voluntary action. The great advantage of a voluntary ad hoc system of action is that it can craft new responses to novel situations, and so respond to change. The great advantage of learning is that successful new actions can be incorporated into future behaviors.
- Voluntary action is synonymous with consciousness. The control of voluntary action is synonymous with cognition.
- Social groups are so effective at dominating their environments that a member's success at raising a family depends more on his or her social standing than any other factor. This is truer of the most social of animals, humans, than of any others. The rapid increase in human cognitive abilities in the past million years occurred to support the social skills that are essential for success. In the last million years humans became smarter and smarter not to outwit plants and other animals but to ingratiate themselves with, and sometimes outwit, each other.

2.1 Voluntary action and learning

The system of unconditioned and conditioned responses is a complex neural system that supports a sophisticated set of behaviors. Nevertheless, it has two significant limitations. First, reflexes respond to stimuli only as they occur. They cannot react to things in the past or prepare for the future. Second, the domain of stimuli that reflexes may ever respond to is fixed at birth. They do not respond at all to novel conditions outside this domain. To deal with these two limitations, the nervous system evolved three new capabilities: voluntary action, short-term memory, and learning.

Voluntary action

If every situation an animal may encounter can be predicted at birth then there is no need for it to have the ability to construct new actions. Rather, it may be born with the ability to perform the actions appropriate for the situations it will face. All responses would be automatic. There would be no need for the ability to construct a novel response to an unanticipated situation. There are many creatures whose environments have remained stable over very long periods of time and that have little ability to construct new actions. For example, although insects engage in some complex behaviors, their behaviors are determined at birth.

However, for many creatures life was not perfectly predictable. One cause of unpredictability has always been climate change. Another cause of unpredictability has been the increasing sophistication of inter-species predator–prey relations. As predators became better at tracking prey, the ability to construct novel escape strategies and find novel hiding places to thwart them would be of great advantage to the prey. As prey became better at avoiding predation, the ability to adopt novel hunting strategies and search new locations would be of great advantage to the predators.

Voluntary action evolved to respond to novel situations. The evolution of voluntary action required a large enhancement of the capabilities of the nervous system. The first step towards voluntary action is the ability to construct a representation of the target of the action. This means that the sensory input is used by the brain to construct a mental three-dimensional representation of the world and to describe specific objects in the world. Consequently, animals do not merely detect shapes but see both the animate and inanimate objects in their surroundings. Furthermore, they can hear sounds and identify the sounds with the objects making them. The process of using sensory input to construct a representation of the surroundings is called **perception**.

The cortex. A basic function of cognition is to compute from the sensory input the relationships necessary to represent the animal's world. The mental representation of the world, along with the actions themselves, is the product of cognition. In mammals, and especially in humans, the mental representation of the world is accomplished by the forebrain, and especially by the thick outer layer of the forebrain, called the cerebral cortex, which is shown in Figure 2.1. As shown in the figure, the **cortex** has a large surface area, much too large to fit smoothly within the skull, which is why it is crumpled together. The deep folds that result are called **sulci**, and appear in about the same positions for all humans. Therefore, they are conventionally used to partition the cortex into four different functional areas, called **lobes**, as shown in Figure 2.1. The function of the occipital and temporal lobes is to construct the mental representation of the world from the sensory information available. They are responsible for perception and recognition.

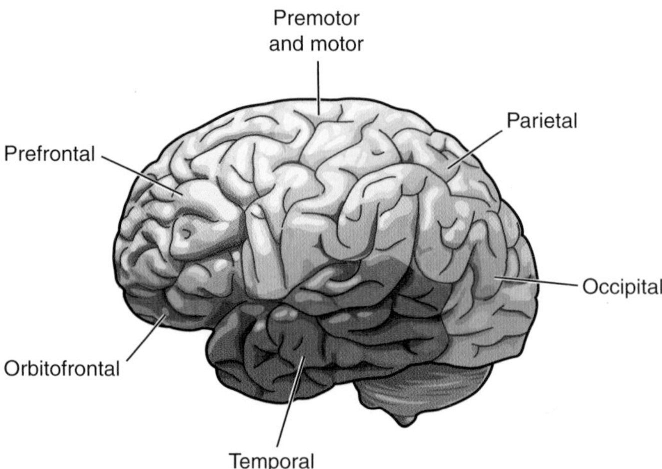

Figure 2.1 The cerebral cortex is conventionally divided into four lobes. The occipital and temporal lobes construct a mental representation of the world. They perform the computations necessary for perception and recognition. The premotor and motor areas of the frontal lobe and parietal lobe plan and direct voluntary actions. The prefrontal area is involved in reasoning and the orbitofrontal area is involved in emotion.

The second step towards voluntary action is the coordination of a variety of motor movements to direct an action towards a perceived target. A voluntary action is entirely different from a reflex. An animal is born with a fixed set of reflexes that perform an unchanging set of actions. In contrast, an animal is not born with the ability to perform any particular voluntary action but, rather, the ability to construct ad hoc voluntary actions to perceptual targets as the need for them arises. The task of planning some purposeful action, directed to a perceptual target, then determining all the muscles in the body that must be contracted and relaxed to perform it, as well as the precise temporal sequence of the muscle movements, and then finally to execute and direct them, is computationally intense. Virtually all the rest of the cortex that is not involved in perception – the frontal and parietal lobes – is involved in planning and executing voluntary actions.

In the mammal brain, the forebrain exploded in size to increase the number and sophistication of the possible computations, hence the detail of the representation of the world and the sophistication of the actions that may be performed in response to it. If we slice the mammalian forebrain in half, the entire back half of the forebrain is involved in processing sensory input, the top part (parietal lobe) for directing action and the bottom part (occipital and temporal lobes) for constructing a representation of the immediate surroundings. Much of the front half of the forebrain, as well as the midbrain, cerebellum, and spinal cord, is involved in planning and executing such an action.

Voluntary action is completely different from conditioning. In conditioning, the environment controls an animal's actions by activating a reflex. For example, when you salivate, you do not choose to salivate; it occurs as the result of an external stimulus. However, when you pour yourself a glass of water and put it to your lips, you choose to perform these voluntary actions. In Pavlov's classic experiment, a bell came to elicit salivation. In contrast, in Skinner's classic experimental paradigm, an animal is given the opportunity to press a bar to obtain bits of food or water. Given this opportunity, an animal will press the bar repeatedly to obtain the reward of food or water. The ability to remember a reward is an example of **learning**. So, learning is entirely different from conditioning. In conditioning, a stimulus *precedes* and elicits an automatic response. In learning, a reward *follows* the voluntary action and increases the probability that it will be performed again. Learning has been called **operant conditioning**. When this is done, conditioning is called **classical conditioning** or **Pavlovian conditioning**. Since these terms are not descriptive and imply a false similarity between conditioning and learning, here conditioning will continue to be called conditioning and learning will be called learning.

Consciousness. Another name for voluntary action is **consciousness**. To see why this is so, consider if you regard an action you performed while unconscious as voluntary. Of course, you would not. In order for the action to be voluntary, it would have to be accompanied by an intention to act, and without consciousness there could not be such an intention. At a minimum, therefore, voluntary action implies consciousness. However, does consciousness imply voluntary action? What about when a person is lying still, awake, and so perceives the surrounding environment? In fact, as described in Chapter 3, seeing and hearing require the mental actions of looking and listening, which involve exactly the same neural mechanisms of voluntary motor actions except that fewer (or no) muscles are ultimately moved. Consciousness implies (sometimes mental) voluntary action, and consciousness and voluntary action are two names for the same thing.

Behavior. Animals do not perform individual voluntary actions independently of one another but sequences of related actions towards a common purpose such as foraging, hunting, or feeding. Such a sequence of actions constitute a **behavior**. One behavior that may be a sequence of voluntary actions is when an animal builds its home. Rats build a complex maze of tunnels and burrows underground. Of course, they have no trouble navigating the tunnels they live in, which raises the issue of how rats – and, indeed, all animals, including humans – find their way around. Studying how rats learn their way through mazes has been a productive area of research in the study of how animals learn to navigate through their environments for over 100 years. It has provided a deep insight into the more general question of how animals learn.

Place versus response learning

For more than a century psychologists have been providing rats with the opportunity to run through mazes to obtain rewards. This is a task that the rat is well suited for, and if the reward is consistently hidden in the same place then the rat soon learns where to find it. The question is: what does the rat learn when it learns the maze? One possibility is that the rat learns a sequence of actions that result in reaching the goal, such as left turn, right turn, etc. This is called **response learning**. Another possibility is that the rat forms a mental map of the maze that guides its journey through it. This is called **place learning**. These two alternatives have been salient since the work of Edward Tolman (1932), the great promoter of place learning. Tolman collected considerable evidence of place learning during his career, but there was also always evidence of response learning over the many decades that maze learning was studied. The response versus place learning controversy was finally resolved by Packard and McGaugh (1996), more than sixty years after Tolman's great work. Their experiment resoundingly demonstrated that place and response learning both occur. It led to the determination that the mammalian cognitive system includes two distinct, interrelated, and complementary systems of learning and memory. The **instrumental system** is responsible for place learning, and controls the animal's response early in the training. The

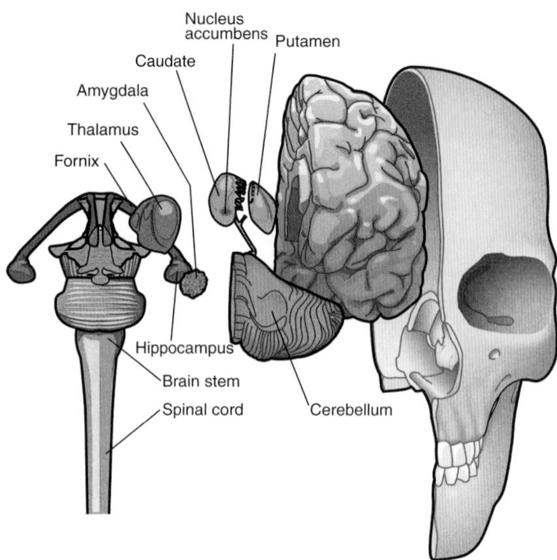

Figure 2.2 The hippocampus is a key structure of the instrumental system and the caudate is a key structure of the habit system. The amygdala and nucleus accumbens influence learning by influencing the robustness of a representation (after an original drawing by Nicole Owen).

hippocampus is a key structure. As shown in Figure 2.2, the hippocampus lies deep within the temporal lobe near the center of the brain. The **habit system** is responsible for response learning and controls the animal's response after extensive practice. The caudate nucleus of the striatum is a key structure (Figure 2.2). Not shown in the figure, the caudate lies close to the hippocampus and is literally wrapped around it.

The experiment. Packard and McGaugh (1996) employed the simplest of mazes: the T-maze. As shown at the top left of Figure 2.3, the rat was trained to go down the runway and turn right at the crossbar to obtain the reward. After the rat had been trained to do this, the runway was flipped, as shown at the bottom left of Figure 2.3. If the rat had learned the location of the reward, then when it reached the crossbar it would now turn left rather than right. If the rat had learned to turn right to obtain the reward then it would continue to turn right.

As shown in the top right of Figure 2.3, the result was that, after one week of practice, the rats turned left, providing clear evidence for place learning. Packard and McGaugh investigated this finding further. They had inserted two tiny pipettes into the brains of their rats, one into the caudate nucleus of the striatum and one into the hippocampus. By squirting a small drop of anesthetic down a pipette, they could render either the caudate or hippocampus inactive in an otherwise awake and functioning animal. When the caudate was put to sleep, it had no effect on the rat's performance, indicating that the caudate played no role in the animal's left turn. However, when the hippocampus was put to the sleep, instead of always turning to the left, the rats turned left or right equally often, indicating that they had no idea where to go. A functioning hippocampus therefore appeared necessary to remember the place of the reward.

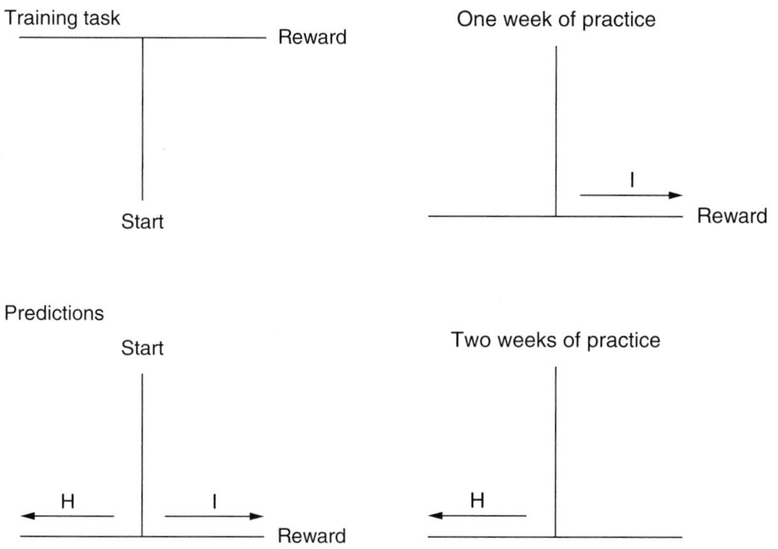

Figure 2.3 Rat is trained to find reward at end of right branch of T – maze (top left). Then the runway is flipped (bottom left). If instrumental system controls response, so rat goes to the same place, then rat will now turn left to go to same place, as indicated by the arrow labeled I. If habit system controls response, so rat makes same response, rat will turn right, as indicated by the arrow labeled H. After one week of training, performance indicates place learning, hence response is controlled by instrumental system (top right). After two weeks of training (bottom right), performance indicates response learning, hence response is controlled by habit system (Packard and McGaugh, **1996**).

This was only the first half of Packard and McGaugh's experiment. For other rats, the runway was flipped after two weeks of practice. As shown at the bottom right of Figure 2.3, in this case the rats turned right, providing clear evidence of response learning. This time putting the hippocampus to sleep had no effect on performance, indicating that it was not in control of an intact rat's response after two weeks. However, putting the caudate nucleus of the striatum to sleep did affect performance. The rats now turned left instead of right. So, when the caudate was no longer inhibiting it, the hippocampus again took control of the animal's response.

Packard and McGaugh's (1996) results indicate that during the first week of training the rat made a sequence of ad hoc actions to move towards the place of reward that it had marked on the mental map guiding those actions. These actions were controlled by the instrumental system. After two weeks of practice the rat automatically executed a sequence of actions that in the past had brought it to the place of reward. These actions were controlled by the habit system.

Learning. To summarize, once voluntary action is possible, learning is useful. Voluntary action makes new kinds of actions possible. Learning preserves a record of successful actions so that they may be employed again when a similar situation arises. Together, the instrumental and habit systems address two issues in learning: how to learn something new and how to remember something. Through the use of a mental map the instrumental system makes it possible for you to learn your way to class on the first day of school. Through the encoding of a repeated sequence of actions the habit system makes it possible to effortlessly retrace the route to class for the rest of the school year.

The instrumental system in the brain and initial learning

The functions and characteristics of the instrumental and habit systems are summarized in Table 2.1. The instrumental system encodes both visual and temporal representations of the world. These include maps of the environment but also descriptions of objects, faces, tunes – everything that can be recognized. Notice that this is because all spatial representations, whether of the environment or of a face, are of the same form: the relationship to each other of a set of points in space. Similarly, a tune is a temporal representation of a set of notes in relationship to each other in time.

Mental maps. Experiments with rats have shown that the hippocampus is part of the neural system for encoding spatial maps of the environment. **Place cells** in the hippocampus are activated every time an animal returns to the same location (O'Keefe and Dostrovsky, 1971). **Grid cells** in the entorhinal cortex, adjacent to the hippocampus within the temporal cortex, encode the location and position of a rat as it moves from place to place (Stensola *et al.*, 2012). Place and grid cells combine to identify the location of the rat in a mental map (Azizi, Schieferstein, and Cheng, 2014).

The use of a mental map by a rat to find a location is demonstrated by the water maze task. The water maze task is simply a platform just below the surface of the water. A swimming rat can use the platform as a place to rest. We can put a little milk in the water and make it cloudy so that the rat cannot see the platform beneath the water. But, once the rat has found the platform and uses it as a rest stop, the rat can use its mental map to find it again.

Mental maps are part of the cognitive systems of all mammals, including humans. When you stand at your front door, can you point where your bedroom is? Can you point correctly even with your eyes closed? To perform this task, you are using your mental map. One advantage of a mental map is that you don't have to be able to see something to know where it is. You need only to know where it is on your mental map. Stimulating the entorhinal cortex with a mild electric current while humans played a virtual taxi game, in which the goal was to drop off passengers as quickly as possible in an unfamiliar city, improved performance on the task. Entorhinal stimulation applied while the subjects learned the locations of landmarks enhanced their subsequent memory of these locations: the subjects reached

TABLE 2.1 Dual system of memory

Instrumental system	Habit system
Does not require a visible target	Requires a visible target
Encodes mental map	Encodes a sequence of actions
Influenced by reward magnitude	Influenced by reward consistency
Controls responses during initial learning	Controls responses after extended practice
Requires functional hippocampus	Requires functional striatum

Source: Yin and Knowlton (2006).

these landmarks more quickly and by shorter routes, as compared with locations learned without stimulation (Suthana *et al.*, 2012).

The instrumental system is not restricted to the medial region of the temporal cortex. The instrumental system extends forward from the hippocampus, through the dorsomedial striatum (putamen and caudate), to the anterior cingulate gyrus and associated areas in the dorsomedial prefrontal cortex. The prefrontal cortex uses place and location information to plan actions, as will be described in Chapter 3.

Reward. Instrumental learning is influenced by both pleasure and pain, which are possible emotional reactions to the consequence of an action. Positive emotional responses, which are collectively called **rewards**, include various degrees of joy and pleasure, including sexual attraction. At the tip of the caudate is the **nucleus accumbens**, which is the pleasure center of the brain (Feltenstein and See, 2008). When the nucleus accumbens responds to an input, that input is perceived as pleasurable. The nucleus accumbens is strongly activated by food, water, and sex. Unfortunately, it is also strongly activated by amphetamines, cocaine, opiates, and alcohol, thus leading to self-destructive addictive behavior.

Rewards cause instrumental learning, consequently increasing the probability of the action being performed again to the same target (Yin and Knowlton, 2006). Having once enjoyed a car ride, a dog may subsequently leap in when its door is opened. Animals are responsive to changes in reward over time. Animals initially trained on large food rewards work less hard for less food (Justel, Pautassi, and Mustaca, 2014). Animals initially trained on small food rewards work harder for more food (Dwyer, Lydall, and Hayward, 2011). Hence, two groups of animals will respond differently for the same reward if their training rewards have been different.

Pain, also called punishment, also causes instrumental learning. However, pain reduces the probability of an action being performed again in the same context. Any mammal, including a human, is much less likely to again touch a surface that has given it a painful electric shock. As shown in Figure 2.2, the tip of the hippocampus is adjacent to the **amygdala**, which controls a reflexive avoidance response (Chapter 1). When a painful target is encountered, the avoidance response becomes the initial component of a more general emotional response that causes the encoding of the action, target, and context causing it.

Short-term memory

As mentioned in Chapter 1, animals do not perform individual actions independently of one another. The advantage of voluntary action is that completely novel behaviors may be constructed for different environments. For example, different actions are required to catch birds, mice, and fish. Rather than having a single, automatic, hunting behavior, cats can combine different sequences of voluntary actions to prey on almost anything.

For an animal to engage in a behavior that is a sequence of voluntary actions, at each point in the sequence the animal must know what it has done and what it must do next. Awareness of what was done and what must be done both require memory. Without memory, a cat stalking a mouse or bird would forget what it was doing when the prey was out of sight. The next step in the evolution of cognition, the ability to plan a sequence of voluntary actions, makes this possible. The ability to plan an ad hoc sequence of actions and remember which action in the sequence has just been performed is often called **short-term memory**. For most behaviors this name is descriptive, because the actions constituting the behavior are performed consecutively over an interval measuring minutes or at most hours. An ad hoc sequence of actions necessary to perform a novel task is under the control of the instrumental system.

The habit system, distributed retention, and long-term retention

Through practice the habit system encodes the sequence of actions for performing a task, and so controls the long-term performance of routine tasks. Because the habit system does not encode mental maps, it does not learn the location of an invisible target. When the hippocampus has been rendered inactive, a rat will never learn the location of a hidden platform in the water maze no matter how many times it finds it accidentally while swimming around.

The robustness of the representation formed is determined by the consistency of the reward rather than its magnitude. If every time the same sequence of actions is performed the animal retrieves some small benefit, the robustness of its representation will be strengthened. Furthermore, as was the case for habituation and sensitization, the robustness of the representation is much more influenced by the distribution than by the number of times a task is performed. Again, distributed trials result in longer retention than massed trials, so that the actions necessary to perform routine tasks are not forgotten. This is a basic feature of the nervous system. Through a variety of neural mechanisms, distributed practice, training, or study always causes a more permanent change than massed experience.

The complementary functions of the instrumental and habit systems

In the normal functioning of learning and memory the instrumental and habit systems work seamlessly together as part of a single system. The first time you are in a new supermarket, you must remember where you have already been while searching for items on your list. A mental map makes it possible for you to keep track of locations you have already visited. When you return to a familiar store, you retrieve and retrace the steps you made on previous trips to find the items you need.

Win-shift; win-stay. These complementary roles of the instrumental and habit systems are revealed by the responses of rats to two different reward schemes when they search a radial arm maze (eight arms radiating from a central platform) for food. These schemes are called, respectively, the win-shift and win-stay tasks, shown in Figure 2.4. The win-shift task rewards exploratory behavior. On each trial the animal must shift to a new pathway not previously investigated to obtain all the food. The win-stay task rewards routine behavior. The animal must repeatedly visit the same pathway to obtain all the food. Packard, Hirsh, and White (1989) trained different rats on the win-shift and win-stay tasks in a radial maze. In the win-shift task, all maze arms contained one reward each day, and the rat had to visit each arm just once and then shift to a new arm to obtain all the food. This task requires that the rat remember where he has just been, which is what the hippocampus does. Rats with caudate damage performed normally on this task but rats with hippocampus damage were impaired. In the win-stay task, four of the eight maze arms were illuminated each day, and a rat could repeatedly search any one to find a reward. This task requires that the same action be repeated, which is what the caudate does. Rats with caudate damage were impaired on the task but rats with fornix

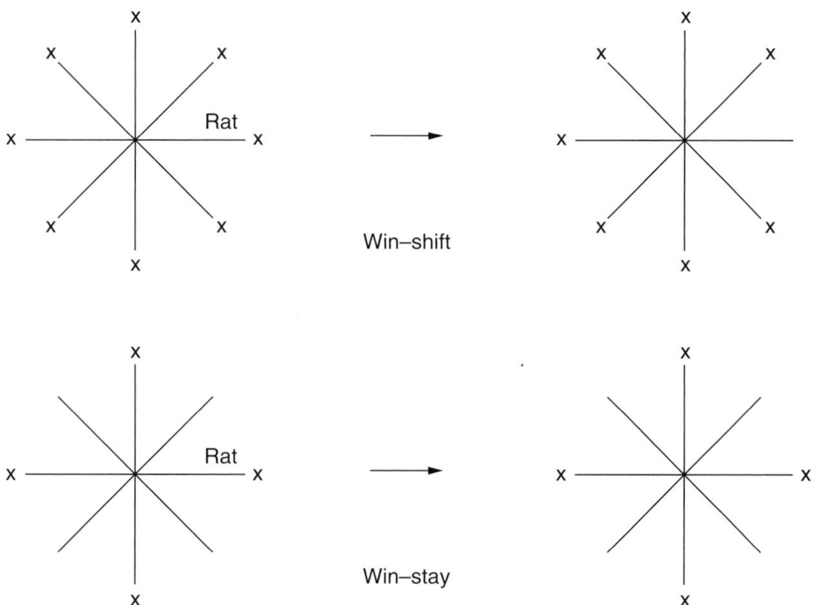

Figure 2.4 The x's are food pellets at the end of the arms of a radial maze. On the left, word mouse indicates a mouse at the end of that arm of the maze eating a pellet. As shown at the top right, in the win-shift task, the arms of the radial maze containing food are not rebaited, so the rat must visit all the arms to find all the food. As shown at the bottom right, in the win–stay task, the arms with food are rebaited, so the rat must revisit those arms where it has found food (Packard, Hirsh, and White, **1989**).

damage performed better than normal rats. As shown in Figure 2.2, the fornix is adjacent to the hippocampus and is also part of the instrumental system.

Episodes. There are not separate representations of an experience in memory, one in the instrumental and another in the habit system. Rather, there is a single representation of an experience, though different features of it are encoded in different areas of the brain. The single representation of an experience in the animal brain, whose construction is initiated by the hippocampus (Iordanova, Good, and Honey, 2011), is called an **episode.** An episode consists of voluntary action, the target of the action, the context of the target, and the result of the action. When an episode is retrieved and the action specified is used to achieve the result specified, the action is **intentional** – that is, it has an intended result. When an action is planned and executed under the control of an episode, the intended result is the **goal** of the action.

Episodes make it possible to act effectively in routine situations. Most of life is routine. In the case of a routine event, the most effective response is to anticipate the event, prepare whatever action was effective last time in advance, and then execute it as the soon as the event is recognized. Predictable events do not require novel voluntary action. Instead, automatic, hence rapid and unconscious, action is more effective. Episodes guide our behavior from the moment we wake up. When you first open your eyes, you do not look around and think to yourself, "Oh, I see that I am home. I guess that a good plan would be to get out of bed and look for the bathroom." Rather, before you open your eyes you have a strong expectation about where you are and have prepared an action to begin your day. When you open your eyes, you process the visual field around you just enough to confirm your expectation and then execute the prepared action. The expectation and action are both determined by the "waking episode" that both describes and determines the first event in your daily routine. Since most of life is routine, most of cognition involves retrieving from memory each successive episode in one's daily routine and repeatedly automatically executing a prepared action to an expected target.

Fear. Although most of life is routine, unexpected challenges do occur, intermittently. Therefore, the key to effective action is to anticipate life events and then rapidly determine whether each experience has any unexpected elements. If not, then the prepared action is automatically executed by the habit system. Otherwise, the instrumental system performs an ad hoc modification of the action that takes account of the unexpected elements of the situation. In a familiar store, you walk straight to the item you want. In an unfamiliar store, you begin to explore.

Although the instrumental and habit systems cooperate in the encoding of episodes, the emotional state of the creature influences what is encoded. Recall that a large reward drives instrumental learning (Yin and Knowlton, 2006). It might seem consistent that a terrifying experience would also drive instrumental learning, because pleasure and fear are both emotional experiences. However, the opposite is the case; when fear is generated, instrumental learning is inhibited, thereby increasing habit learning in the situation (Packard, 2009). Perhaps the reason for this is that, if the animal escapes the situation, encoding by the habit system ensures the long-term retention of the action resulting in the escape.

Learning is thus influenced by both the magnitude and the valence of the emotional response. Fear produces robust traces in the habit system. Presumably, the most important things are lethal, hence terror-inducing. So, if an animal escapes a terrifying situation there will be one-trial learning, and the animal will not forget that situation nor the action effecting the escape. For example, if you ever fall out of an airplane and manage to survive, you will not forget it. If you survive by pulling the ripcord on your parachute, you will never, ever forget to pull your ripcord in the future.

Recall that the hippocampus merges into the amygdala (Figure 2.2). Recall that the amygdala controls avoidance responses, which are composed of avoidance reflexes to threatening, painful, or noxious stimuli. In fact, the amygdala generates fear, anger, and disgust responses to appropriate stimuli in the environment that include the appropriate avoidance responses. A neural center within the amygdala called the **basolateral complex** is the neural mechanism by which the amygdala influences the type of memory formed. The basolateral complex responds to adrenalin, which prepares the body for action and is produced in quantity as part of the response to a terrifying situation. The basolateral complex inhibits instrumental learning as part of the fear response, thus increasing the contribution of habit learning to the episode.

2.2 Neural bases of learning

Kandel's finding of more than one sub-cellular mechanism contributing to habituation/sensitization in the *Aplysia* was the beginning of the accumulation of evidence of numerous sub-cellular, cellular, and super-cellular mechanisms that contribute to learning. The work mentioned here is a hint of the many layers of a complex system that is just beginning to be discovered.

Sub-cellular mechanisms of learning

Kandel and his colleagues showed in *Aplysia* that long-term habituation and sensitization were the result of a variety of sub-cellular changes, primarily to the terminals of the pre-synaptic neuron, which changed the amount of neurotransmitter sent across the synapse. Changes in the strength of the signal from the pre-synaptic to the post-synaptic neuron are collectively referred to as **synaptic plasticity**. Figure 2.5 shows a variety of sub-cellular changes that influence learning.

Long-term potentiation (LTP). Neurons are like tiny living batteries. The electrical charge on the inside of the neuron is different from the charge on its surface. Neurons transmit information across their bodies by depolarizing – that is, equalizing or reversing the charge difference between the inside and the outside, so that an electrical charge rolls from one end of the neuron to the other. The larger the change in charge is, the greater the response strength of the neuron. When a series of high-frequency stimuli is applied to neurons in the major pathways of the hippocampus, there is a long-term increase in the amplitude of the electrical potential produced by theses neurons in response to subsequent stimuli (Kandel, Schwartz, and Jessell, 2000: 1259). For some tasks, learning is also associated with a decrease in the electrical potential for some neurons, which is called **long-term depression (LTD)**, perhaps because it contributes to the specificity of the response (Caporale and Dan, 2008).

Change in number of synapses. There may also be a change in the number of synapses between a pair of neurons, including an increase, called **synaptogenesis**, and a decrease, called **synaptic extinction** (Hongpaisan and Alkon, 2007). Conditions similar to those producing LTP and LTD may also change the number of synapses (Rosenkranz, Kacar, and Rothwell, 2007).

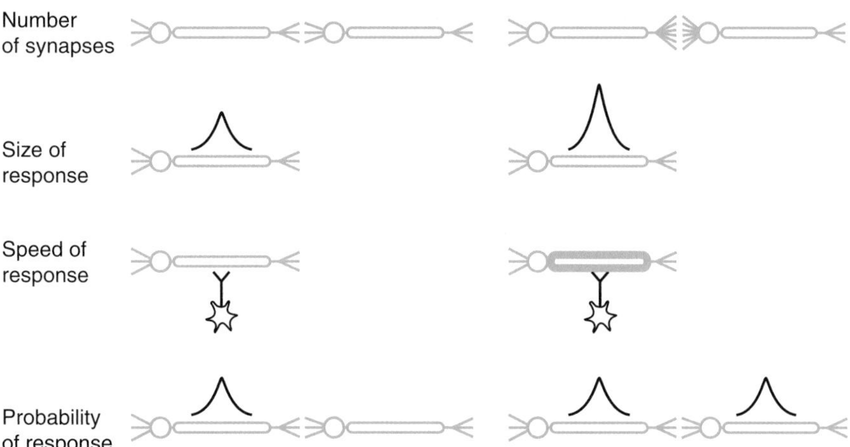

Figure 2.5 A variety of neuronal changes are associated with learning. The number of synapses between neurons may change (top). The size of a neuron's response, called long-term potentiation (LTP) (Kandel, Schwartz, and Jessell, **2000**) or long-term depression (LTD) (Caporale and Dan, **2008**), may change (second). Glial cells may influence the neuronal response; for example, they may increase the speed of response by increasing myelination of the neuron's axon (third) (Fields, **2008**). The probability of a neuron's response, called intrinsic excitability, may increase (bottom) (Daoudal and Debanne, **2003**).

Intrinsic excitability. The excitability of a neuron is its probability to respond to an input signal. Changes in excitability have been found in the nervous systems of a variety of animals (Daoudal and Debanne, 2003).

Neuronal–glial interaction. The majority of the cells in mammal brains are non-neuronal cells called glial cells. These cells both interact with neurons to influence synaptic plasticity and even generate signals themselves. For example, glial cells myelinate a neuron's axon, which increases the speed of the neuron's response (Bains and Oliet, 2007; Fields, 2008). In addition, glial cells called astrocytes provide neurons with a chemical necessary for a long-term change in response (Suzuki *et al.*, 2011).

Neurogenesis

A key mechanism that supports trace conditioning and learning in mammalian, including human, memory is **neurogenesis**, which includes two processes: proliferation and survival (Shors, 2009). **Proliferation** refers to the fact that new neurons are born every day in various parts of the brain, especially the hippocampus (Eriksson *et al.*, 1998). Diet, exercise, and rest all influence the number of neurons born in the brain each day. Most of these new neurons die within two weeks, but learning a spatial or temporal task causes some of the new neurons to **survive** (Gould *et al.*, 1999). Those new neurons that are incorporated into the neural representation of what has been learned become a permanent part of the nervous system. Unsurprisingly, neurogenesis is particularly prominent in the hippocampus, which is so important for learning. In other words, our brains are of our own making. If you want a bigger brain then you must adopt a healthy lifestyle but also learn something new every day. Ultimately, neurogenesis and synaptogenesis contribute to an increased area of the cortex being devoted to supporting a highly practiced task. We each have a designer brain, and we are the designers. Areas that are associated with knowledge and skill grow in size with expertise. Furthermore, these processes, along with synaptic extinction, may lead to a reorganization of the area controlling the skill.

Just as habituation and sensitization effects last longer with distributed training than with massed training, distributed training results in longer retention of the learned response than does massed training. For example, when rats were trained to find the hidden platform in the water maze task, performance was better two weeks later after distributed training than after massed training. Performance was correlated with the number of new neurons incorporated into the hippocampus (Sisti, Glass, and Shors, 2007).

2.3 Social organization

Through the cooperation of the instrumental and habit systems, animals get better at what they do. Two kinds of advantages accrue with experience and practice. The first kind of advantage that accrues with experience is the performance advantage that results from practice. The **performance advantage** is the improvement in performance on a motor or perceptual task as the result of practice. For example, the more an infant practices, the more skillful it becomes at walking. The more a student reads, the more quickly he or she reads. Such an advantage occurs through the encoding of sequences of action by the habit system that are performed automatically. Notice that improvement in performance on a task does not necessarily imply any memory of having performed the task previously. You can walk but do not remember learning to walk.

The second kind of advantage is the **associative advantage**: the animal learns what is good and what is bad. For example, after a larger dog attacks a smaller one, the smaller one subsequently expresses fear and runs from the bark or sight of the larger one. Notice that an animal (or person) may have an emotional response to something without having a memory of ever encountering it before. When a larger dog has attacked a smaller dog, for the smaller dog's safety it is necessary only that it runs from the larger dog. In order for this to occur, it is necessary only for the smaller dog to fear the sound and sight of the larger dog at subsequent encounters. It is not necessary for it to remember their first encounter. Therefore, because the smaller dog exhibits fear of the one that attacked it, we cannot assume that it is aware that it has encountered the larger dog before. In general, associative advantages that result from the modification of behavior on the basis of good and bad experiences could occur without any memory of those experiences. You could develop preferences for good things over bad, and for routes that lead to useful locations and avoided dangerous ones, without encoding any memory of the experiences producing those preferences. Why, then, do we have memories of past experiences at all? The cause of event memory is an extremely useful behavior shared by many animals: the desire to live in groups.

Collective action. Many kinds of animals are social, and there are great advantages to living in groups over living alone. A group of animals can collectively perceive more of the environment than any one animal, and collective action can be more effective than individual action for attack and defense. Several members of a group can scout a wider area for food and water than a single individual. Furthermore, the perceptual abilities of all group members are available for detecting foe. A group can arrange themselves in a defensive formation with the strongest members facing outward all the way around and the weaker members in the middle. Finally, a minor and temporary injury to a solitary individual can result in a downward spiral, inability to forage, hunger, weakness, and death. A group member may be sustained by other members of the group until it recovers.

The effectiveness of collective action is limited by the ability of the group members to communicate with each other. Once communication begins, a group of animals is no longer just a group but a social organization. Consequently, social animals have signal systems of varying degrees of complexity. More complex signal systems make more sophisticated social structures possible. The larger and more sophisticated the social structure, the more elaborate the coordination of action among group members, and the more control the social organization exerts over its environment. The more control it collectively exerts over its environment, the less likely any member of the society in good standing is ever going to starve to death or be killed by a predator. Success in life no longer depends on the animal's ability to act effectively in the natural environment on its own but, instead, on its ability to rise to a protected level in its society. Members of a successful social group are both comrades and rivals. They are comrades in achieving the success of their group but rivals in the distribution of the benefits of that success. In simple social organizations, brute individual strength is sufficient to obtain the largest share of the rewards. However, in advanced social organizations it is possible to form alliances so that personal physical strength is no longer determinative. Success in obtaining rewards depends not only on the ability to intimidate other members of the group but also on the ability to ingratiate oneself to raise your status among them.

To raise your status, one must have effective responses to the social behavior of family and friends. This requires recognizing them as individuals and remembering everything they have ever done to you and for you and everything you have ever done to them and for them. The ability to recognize someone (or anything) and remember what he (or she, or it) has done is called **declarative memory**. This detailed knowledge makes a sophisticated social organization possible. Declarative learning and memory are central to social skill. Declarative memory evolved because it supported advanced social skills that were beneficial to the member of an advanced social group because they made it possible for an individual to rise to a leadership position. Effective leaders benefited from their advanced social skills in two ways. First, through their leadership, group action became more effective, so there were more benefits of collective action to distribute. Second, the leader was able to claim the single largest share of the benefits.

Humans are the most social of all animals, as measured by the size and sophistication of their groups, and by far the smartest creatures, as measured by the sizes of the cortex and hippocampus and the sophistication of their cognitive abilities (Shultz and Dunbar, 2010). As human society became more complex, positive feedback between cognitive ability and social organization produced an astounding increase in the cognitive capabilities of humans (Dunbar and Sutcliffe, 2012).

As inter-species competition became less important to the survival of the social group member, evolutionary pressure did not slow; it accelerated. The likelihood of group members having progeny became determined by their standing in the social order, which depended on their social skills, which depended on their cognitive abilities. Thus, an accelerating positive feedback loop developed between social skills and cognitive abilities. As social skills became more important, the cognitive abilities on which they depended improved, which led to increased social skills, which further increased their importance. Furthermore, as social skills improved, the group was ever more effective at dominating its environment. Hence, increased cognitive abilities and social skills did not merely benefit the individual but the group as a whole (Dunbar, 2013).

The extreme cognitive abilities that humans have developed, therefore, including self-awareness, personal identity, and the ability to infer the intentions of others, have not been acquired to outwit dogs and cats but to make it possible to either ingratiate oneself or outwit members of one's own species. Indeed, they are for interactions with the most intimate members, including family members, of one's own group. This is why the anthropologist Robin Dunbar (2013) calls this collection of cognitive abilities "the Machiavellian mind."

Declarative memory. So, when you meet someone for the first time, they appear novel and you know that you have not seen them before. However, when you see this person again, they appear familiar and you know that you have seen them before. **Recognition**, the awareness that something has been perceived or done before, is called **declarative learning** or **declarative memory**. Within philosophy, declarative memory is called "**knowing what**," as in knowing what something is. **Recognition** is another word for declarative knowledge.

Declarative knowledge is not only the experience of familiarity but the knowledge of what something is. When you see a chair, it not only looks familiar, you know what to use it for. This created another form of the performance advantage: the knowledge advantage. Knowledge is used to direct action. For example, the more people explore their environment, the more complete their mental map and the easier it is to find their way around. The more words that a student can recognize, the more sentences containing them he or she can comprehend. Declarative knowledge is possible through the integration of the instrumental and habit systems to construct a single representation: the episode. An episode containing a chair as a target includes a mental map of its appearance constructed by the instrumental system and identifies its function, something to sit on, through the sequence of actions necessary for sitting that is constructed by the habit system.

Declarative memory is often contrasted with changes in behavior as the result of experiences that do not involve awareness of the past. A kitten may become better and better at swatting a moving object without remembering the hours of practice to do so, just as none of us remembers the practice required in learning how to walk. Such changes in behavior as the result of experience without any accompanying memories of the experience are sometimes called **implicit learning**. When the change is an improvement in the performance of some task, it is called **procedural learning** or **procedural memory**. Procedural memory has a variety of other names. It may be called motor, perceptual, or perceptual-motor skill learning depending on the context. Within philosophy, it is called "**knowing how**," as in knowing how to do something.

2.4 The invention of human language

Over the past million years the verbal communication abilities of humans rapidly improved. This led to the second striking difference between the brains of humans and of most other animals. As shown in Figure 2.6, the human brain, like all animal brains, is partitioned into two hemispheres. The left hemisphere controls the right side of the body, and the right hemisphere controls the left side of the body. In describing hemispheric

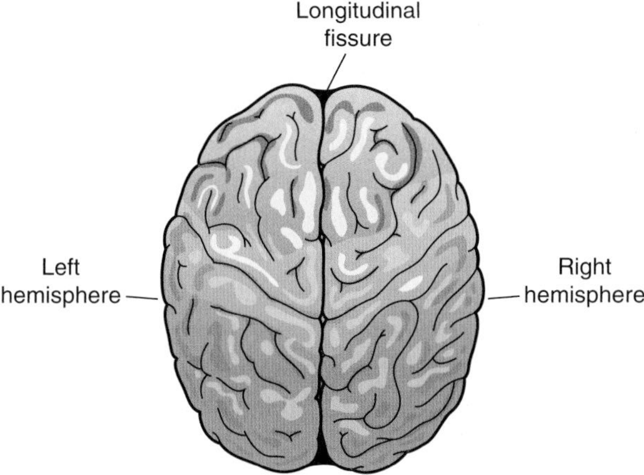

Figure 2.6 The cerebral cortex is divided by the central sulcus into a left and right hemisphere.

control, the term for opposite is **contralateral**. The left is contralateral to the right. In nearly all animal species, the functional organization of the two hemispheres is perfectly symmetrical. Whatever function a particular area in the right hemisphere performs for the left side of the body, the corresponding area in the exact same location of the left hemisphere performs for the right side of the body. However, the pressure to rapidly generate many precise speech sounds breaks that symmetry. Shared left and right control of the tongue, lips, and throat would result in slower, coarser movements that would reduce the speed with which distinct speech sounds were produced. So, for nearly all individuals, the left hemisphere contains specialized areas for the production and comprehension of speech that do not exist in the right hemisphere. The ability to rapidly generate and comprehend individual speech sounds, and so individual words, made possible the final leap in the development of human cognition.

About 60,000 years ago there was a human family just like us, with one important exception. They did not yet speak the equivalent of a modern human language. Then they invented modern human language and became just like us, our immediate ancestors. Human language was invented once and carried all over the world by the people who spoke it. All languages spoken today are variants of that original language (Fitch, 2010).

The invention of human language led to a profound reorganization of human memory, resulting in an enormous expansion of human abilities. With the invention of language, narrative became possible. With the invention of narrative, planning, storytelling, vicarious learning, and the cultural transmission of knowledge all became possible. Once storytelling had been established, autobiographical memory and the details of personal identity became possible. Self-awareness and autobiographical recollection emerged in their modern form.

2.5 What is cognitive science?

Every science has two components: its subject matter and the descriptive theory that explains it. Beginning with the control of action, the content of the study of human cognition has been explored. I conclude by considering what is necessary to explain it.

Cognition requires the processing of information, and the human cognitive system may also be called the human information-processing system. Information requires a code, content, one or more operations that change the content, and a medium to represent the code. For example, the code for representing binary numbers is ones and zeros, the content is the particular number being represented, the operations include addition, subtraction, multiplication, and division, and the medium may be ink on paper, chalk on blackboard, electric charges in a computer memory, etc. Notice that the content within an information-processing system represents entities outside the system. For example, numbers represent quantities of objects. In the human cognitive system, the medium is the neurons and pathways of the brain, and the content is the representation of the world and an individual's actions in it. Cognitive psychology describes the code used to represent the world, the operations that encode a representation of the world from sensory input, and the operations that direct a person's actions.

SUMMARY

Automatic responses play only a limited, albeit important, role in our behavior because life is not perfectly predictable. If a lifetime of events was perfectly predictable then every animal could be born able to automatically make every response it would ever need to make, and cognition would be unnecessary. However, life is not perfectly predictable, and there are two challenges to a purely automatic behavioral response. First, environments change, such as through climate change. Old behaviors may not be effective in a new environment. For example, if potential food sources change, unchanging foraging behaviors may no longer be effective and so the creature starves. Second, natural selection guarantees that there will always be new competitors in the inter-species competition for survival. When dealing with a changing, hence inherently unpredictable, field of competitors, an instinctive, therefore predictable, pattern of behavior is not an asset. For example, if a herbivore always automatically moves to its best food source then a carnivore that eats it can evolve that automatically moves to the same locations. However, the food source of the carnivore is the herbivore. Being a predictable meal for someone else is not a recipe for survival.

To make it possible to respond to unpredicted challenges in the world, an elaborate nervous system evolved that made voluntary action possible. The advantage of voluntary over automatic, involuntary action is that it can be ad hoc. Faced with something unexpected, an animal can craft a response it has never made before. To be likely to craft an *effective* new response, the animal must be able to perceive its current situation accurately, remember a similar past situation and what action was effective then, and modify the previous action for the current circumstances. Cognition begins with the control of voluntary action. **Cognition** refers to an animal's representation of itself in the world and the computations on that representation that are required for an animal to construct a novel action appropriate to its situation.

Chapters 3 to 5 begin the description of cognition with the description of the control of action. This is the natural place to begin, because the neural mechanisms that originally evolved for the control of muscle movements (Chapter 3) were subsequently repurposed for the control of other cognitive tasks. As discussed in Chapter 3, the ability to perform ad hoc actions requires two stages: first, the planning of the action occurs in the frontal cortex and parietal cortex; then the performance of the action is directed by the sub-cortical structures – the basal ganglia and the cerebellum. Skilled action is the result of repeated practice on a task. Practice results in the encoding of sequences of actions in a plan in the habit system. Subsequently, the plan is retrieved by the habit system and the sequence of actions is performed automatically. Chapters 4 and 5 describe how the control of neural processing by the prefrontal cortex, parietal cortex, and basal ganglia was extended from motor actions that move body parts to mental actions that direct perceptual processing by closing gates in the thalamus, through which all perceptual pathways pass. Sophisticated perceptual skills such as face recognition and reading are learned from repeated practice on those tasks. Practice results in the encoding of representations of the perceptual targets and a plan by the habit system in the habit system for a sequence of actions directing processing to locations in the environment containing predicted target features. As long as predicted and observed features match, perception and recognition occur automatically.

Chapters 6 and 7 describe the declarative knowledge that is encoded by the perceptual skills described in Chapters 4 and 5. Chapter 6 describes visual perception and recognition and Chapter

6 describes semantic memory. Semantic, including visual, representations reside in the temporal cortex and adjacent areas of the parietal cortex. As described in Chapter 7, semantic memory is the basis of language. Language involves the production and perception of novel sequences to encode new information, so language processing requires the instrumental system. However, for language processing to be fast it must be predictive, and so it requires the habit system as well. Finally, language processing makes use of specialized control centers in the left hemisphere that make it possible for people to intentionally encode and reproduce the complex sequences of speech sounds they hear through verbal rehearsal.

Chapters 8 to 10 describe how human experience is transformed into the declarative knowledge that is the basis of identity and that directs human life. As described in Chapter 8, learning is initially a social experience between infant and caregiver. It begins with the infant's innate ability to make and understand emotional responses, which makes meaningful social interactions with a caregiver possible. This provides the basis for referential communication and for language learning. Chapter 9 describes how language provides a useful tool for labeling experiences and organizing them in semantic memory. Chapter 10 describes the roles of the instrumental and habit systems in the sophisticated, mature learning system. The purpose of the system is to encode the targets, contexts, and results of successful actions in semantic memory. Memory may thus be viewed as the incidental product of action. To this end, events are characterized as novel or familiar, and only novel experiences are encoded as unique experiences by unique episodes in semantic memory. The robustness of the episode is determined by the emotional response associated with it. A strong emotional response indicates an important event, which results in a robust representation. Familiar experiences influence semantic memory by increasing the robustness of the episodes in semantic memory describing them.

The evolution of prefrontal and parietal control of processing through the instrumental system also makes intentional learning possible. A person can attempt to learn any perceptual sequence or pattern through verbal or visual rehearsal, though for completely novel sequences this is a difficult task that results in a fragile representation of a short sequence. The set of skills includes mnemonic skills, which direct sequences of actions that rapidly associate familiar visual and auditory targets with representations in semantic memory, making possible the elaboration of information in semantic memory.

Chapters 11 to 13 describe the retrieval of declarative knowledge from semantic memory and its use in the construction of autobiographical memory, which provides each person with an identity. The world that people inhabit is a complicated social world in which many social situations are somewhat novel and several different novel actions are possible. The past is an incomplete guide to the future, and a person cannot rely on the automatic execution of a previously effective action. Chapters 14 and 15 describe visual reasoning, verbal reasoning, problem solving, and intelligence, which all describe the construction of novel actions in novel situations. This required the final evolution of the neural system for generating ad hoc actions, which first evolved for motor action (Chapter 3) and then was extended to perception (Chapter 4), intentional learning (Chapter 10), and intentional recollection (Chapter 12). These tasks, like motor action (Chapter 3), involve two stages: planning and performance. Mental actions initiated by the prefrontal cortex and parietal cortex through the basal ganglia construct semantic representations of the task and a possible solution to the task before a motor action is taken. The application of the ability to solve novel problems, called fluid intelligence, to daily life requires making decisions under uncertainty; one cannot be certain of the course of future events or what the full effects of one's actions will be. The emotional system plays an important role in the choice among possible actions by making people risk-averse.

To recapitulate the evolution of these basic abilities.

- An innate, automatic response system may come to be ineffective in a changing world. The great advantage of a voluntary ad hoc system of action is that it can craft new responses to novel situations, and so respond to change.
- The ability to perform ad hoc voluntary actions makes learning useful. When an ad hoc voluntary action is successful it is encoded so that when the same situation again arises it may be retrieved and executed again. The basic unit of mammalian memory is the episode, which has four components:
  - the target of a voluntary action;
  - the context of the target;
  - the action; and
  - the consequence (which is called the reward when positive).
- Learning in mammals, including humans, is controlled by two distinct but integrated systems: the instrumental system and the habit system.
  - The instrumental system includes the hippocampus and controls the response during the initial stage of learning. The instrumental system encodes a mental map of the target and context. Instrumental learning is sensitive to the size of the reward.
  - The habit system includes the caudate nucleus of the striatum and encodes a sequence of actions. It controls a practiced response in a familiar situation – that is, it determines long-term memory for an episode. Habit learning is sensitive to the consistency of the reward.
- Voluntary action is synonymous with consciousness. The control of voluntary action is synonymous with cognition.
- Social groups are so effective at dominating their environments that a member's success at raising a family depends more on his or her social standing than any other factor. This is most true for the most social of animals, humans, than for any others. The rapid increase in human cognitive abilities in the past million years occurred to support the social skills that are essential for success.

QUESTIONS

1. Is a voluntary action controlled by the organism or an external stimulus?
2. What role does the instrumental system play in learning?
3. What role does the habit system play in learning?
4. What influences the probability that a voluntary action will be made to a target?
5. What is the definition of consciousness?

FURTHER READING

Carruthers, P., and Chamberlain, A. (2000). *Evolution and the Human Mind: Modularity, Language and Meta-Cognition*. Cambridge University Press.

Dunbar, R. I. M. (2005). *The Human Story: A New History of Mankind's Evolution*. London: Faber & Faber.

Packard, M. G., and McGaugh, J. L. (1996). Inactivation of hippocampus or caudate nucleus with lidocaine differentially affects expression of place versus response learning. *Neurobiology of Learning and Memory*, 65, 65–72.

Whiten, A., and Byrne, R. W. (1997). *Machiavellian Intelligence II: Extensions and Evaluations*. Cambridge University Press.

Yin, H. H., and Knowlton, B. J. (2006). The role of the basal ganglia in habit formation. *Nature Reviews Neuroscience*, 7, 464–76.

3 Motor action and motor skills

There is a sense in which the entire modern age is a fortuitous consequence of the human ability to make an ad hoc voluntary response. People did not specifically evolve to be able to drive a car or to be able to type a text message into a smartphone. However, we did evolve to be able to do whatever we were able to imagine. There once was a one-legged high school athlete who played football without an artificial leg but who nevertheless could hop so quickly and forcefully that he could catch and tackle a runner. Such a skill demonstrates the flexibility, hence the robustness, of the motor system.

In this chapter, we shall see that voluntary action involves two distinct stages: planning and performance.

- During the planning stage, involving the parietal and the premotor or supplementary motor cortex, various final postures from previous successful acts are retrieved, and one is selected and modified for the current situation.
- During the performance stage the plan is encoded for specific body parts in the motor cortex, initiated by the basal ganglia, and translated into a motor program for making the necessary muscle movements by the cerebellum. The neural system includes multiple top-down pathways that exert multiple levels of control of the action towards its target under the guidance of feedback. Furthermore, unrelated perceptual and motor activity is inhibited.
- A successful action results in the encoding of the final posture of the action. Over time, when a familiar action is repeated in a similar context, it is necessary only to retrieve and execute a posture plan for rapid, errorless performance. Skill learning is the result of the accumulation of posture plans.
- The ability to learn skills makes a wide range of actions possible. A boy does not even need two legs to be able to play football.

Consider all that is involved in the simple act of pointing at a target. In order to perform the action, the motor system must be able to encode the location of the target and the hand, initiate the movement of the hand, encode the changing location of the hand in real time, and use this information to adjust its motion to the target and initiate the movement of the fingers into a pointing posture. Action requires perception of the target, awareness of the location of a movable body part, the ability to move the body part, the ability to detect sensory feedback from the motion of the body part, and the ability to use the feedback to detect errors and to readjust the movement accordingly (Figure 3.1). This requires a large number of computations, hence a sufficiently complex nervous system to perform them.

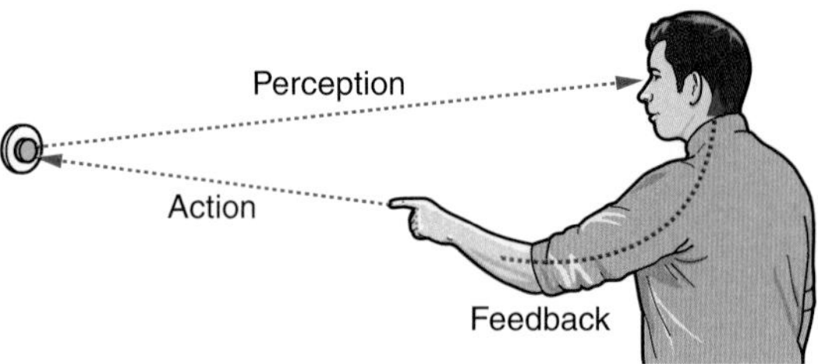

Figure 3.1 Action requires perception of the target, awareness of the location of a body part, the ability to move the body part, and the ability to modify the movement on the basis of feedback from the body part.

As described in Chapter 2, the neural mechanisms for unconditioned responses were elaborated in three ways to make voluntary action possible. First, the sensory system was elaborated into a perceptual system so that the animal could construct a representation of its environment. Second, the response was decoupled from a specific, innate stimulus and placed under the control of the actor. Any object in the representation of the environment is a possible target for an action. Thus, a chicken will reflexively peck at only small bits that look like grain. A person can bite at anything. Third, the target, context, and result of a successful action were encoded along with the action, so the performance of routine actions improved with practice. In short, the episode is the basic unit of memory because it is the basic unit of action. Action is not just motor movement. It is a movement towards a target in a specific context intended to have a specific result.

It is only through the coordination of the instrumental and habit systems that daily activities are possible. The instrumental system can plan and perform only one ad hoc voluntary action at a time, and during that time other perceptual and motor processing is inhibited. This creates a response bottleneck. If all actions were planned and performed by the instrumental system, you could not walk and chew gum at the same time. However, not all actions are planned and performed by the instrumental system. Successful actions are encoded by the habit system, and so routine actions are retrieved and performed without much planning at all. As long as they are coordinated so that they do not interfere with each other, more than one routine action can be performed at a time, along with a single action under instrumental control. Thus you can unwrap and eat a candy bar while walking, a musician can play an instrument while marching, and a quarterback can throw a football while running. Furthermore, when an unexpected obstacle occurs, the instrumental system immediately assumes control. You do not choke on an unexpected bit of nut in a candy bar, marchers rarely stumble and fall regardless of the terrain, and some quarterbacks are exceedingly difficult to tackle.

There are two reasons why action is the subject of Chapter 2. First, because the entire reason for cognition is to make action more efficient, an understanding of action is useful in understanding cognition. Second, the motor system for performing voluntary physical action evolved to perform mental actions as well. So, the neural systems for performing action are the neural systems for cognition as well. In Chapters 4 and 5 we will see that the same neural system that makes ad hoc and automatic action possible makes it possible to converse while dining, take notes during a lecture, and shop for a list of items in a new store. In short, it makes multitasking possible, if not always advisable. Therefore, it is wrong to think of the motor system as merely a system for twitching muscles; it is the core of a more general neural system that is essential to the creative skills that define what it means to be human (Chapter 5).

3.1 The four human motor systems

The human brain includes four distinct motor systems, which have different functions and which control different parts of the body. The **locomotion system** moves the torso and limbs to make it possible for us to crawl, walk, skip, run, jump, climb, swim, etc. The **manipulation system** (top panel of Figure 3.2) moves the fingers and hands for grasping, catching, writing, pointing, gesturing, etc. The **vocalization/ingestion system** moves the vocal cords, tongue, throat, and mouth for talking, singing, eating, etc. The **visual search system** directs, moves, and focuses the eyes for searching, scanning, tracking, reading, etc. This chapter draws most of its examples from the locomotion and manipulation systems. The visual search system will be described in Chapters 4 to 6 and the vocalization system will be described in conjunction with language in Chapter 7.

When we act, the intention and the act are perceived as simultaneous. When you pick something up, you do not perceive an interval between your intention to grasp it and the motion of your hand; you just grasp it. However, this simultaneity between thought and deed is an illusion. Voluntary action consists of two distinct stages: planning and performance. During the planning stage the target body posture of the action is retrieved or constructed. During the performance stage the plan is executed and the muscle contractions are initiated to move the body into this posture.

3.2 Planning an action

The motor system is shown schematically in Figure 3.3. Voluntary action begins with a goal generated in the prefrontal cortex. This area of the cortex is outside the motor system proper but is the focal point for purposeful behavior in general. We will take it as the starting point for the idea to do something – for example, to throw a Frisbee. The prefrontal cortex communicates this intent to the premotor area of the cortex, which plans a sequence of actions designed to accomplish the intended purpose. In order to throw a Frisbee you must grasp it, pick it up, pull it back, and fling it forward while releasing it. These are four separate actions but we refer to them as if they were one. Treating a sequence of actions with a single purpose as a single action is not just a figure of speech. The **motor plan** specifies the sequence of actions to be taken – that is, the movement of the hand into a grasping position, the movement of the arm to place it in contact with the projectile, the lifting of the arm to place it in the initial throwing position, and the force and direction of the toss. To effectively fling a Frisbee to hit a target, the motor plan must be constructed on the basis of perceptual information describing both the Frisbee and the location of the target. The premotor cortex constructs such a motor plan on the basis of visual and tactual information provided by the parietal cortex, as shown schematically in Figure 3.3. The motor plan describes a sequence of actions to be carried out by one or more body parts. It is important to keep in mind here that the motor plan is specified in terms of body parts, at a higher level of abstraction than individual muscle contractions.

Cortical areas for action planning

Three areas of the cortex are responsible for the planning of actions (top panel of Figure 3.2). The parietal cortex contains neurons that respond to both visual and tactual inputs. It

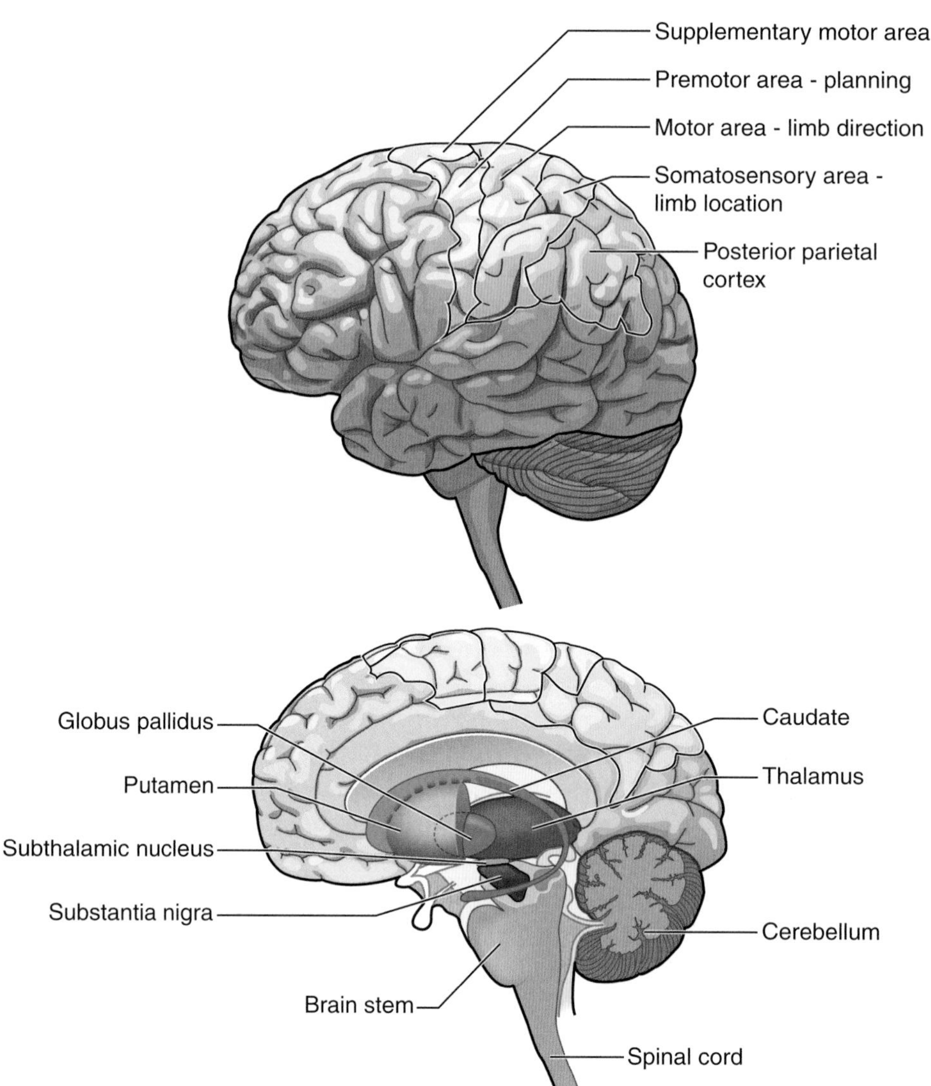

Figure 3.2 The motor system for locomotion and manipulation. The top panel shows the cortical areas involved in planning and directing the movement. The bottom panel shows the sub-cortical areas involved in executing the movement and transmitting feedback from it to the cortex.

integrates these two sources of information, so that you can see the things you feel (Andersen *et al.*, 1997). The premotor cortex in the frontal lobe receives an intention to do something, such as grasp an object, activates descriptions of appropriate body postures to accomplish this task, and selects the best one among them on the basis of the visual information it receives from an area of the parietal cortex called – appropriately – the parietal reach region (Yttri *et al.*, 2014). The same intention is also sent to the supplementary cortex, which is just above the premotor cortex. The supplementary cortex activates descriptions of appropriate body postures to accomplish this task and selects the best one among them without using

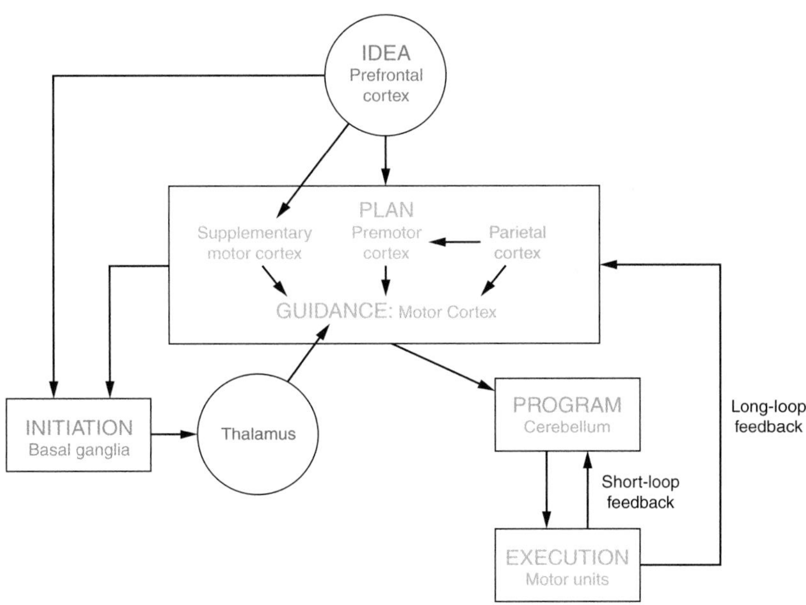

Figure 3.3 The action system is organized into several levels of control: planning, programming, guidance, initiation, and execution. The basal ganglia initiate movement and inhibit irrelevant processing.

visual information. Hence, exactly the same action, such as writing your name, may be planned and executed by two different parts of the brain depending on whether your eyes are open or closed.

Mirror neurons, imitation, and stimulus–response compatibility

The premotor cortex contains neurons called mirror neurons. These neurons respond when the individual performs a specific action or sees that action performed by another individual (Cook and Bird, 2013). Mirror neurons provide a neurological basis for social animals learning to perform actions by observing and imitating one another. Observed actions are initially encoded as a movement of a body part towards a target. When the action is attempted, the mirror neurons guide the selection of the limb and its posture to imitate the action, rather than the exact muscle movements. Mirror neurons therefore provide evidence that the premotor cortex plans goal-oriented actions rather than specific movements. The same mirror neurons respond to different actions with the same goal as long as they have the same stimulus–response compatibility between the target location and the action.

Suppose you come to a detour and see a large arrow pointing to your right. To stay on the road you must turn the car to the right by turning the steering wheel to the right. Moving to the right by turning the steering wheel to the right is an example of **stimulus–response compatibility** (Fitts and Seegar, 1953). The target and action are embedded within the same spatial representation. Turning the wheel in the direction of the target is an example of stimulus–response compatibility. Turning the wheel in the opposite direction from the target is an example of stimulus–response incompatibility. As you might intuit, responding is more difficult when there is incompatibility between the target and response representations. This is why parallel parking requires some effort to learn, and why it is first easier to comb your hair without looking in the mirror.

Responses are faster and most accurate when the response is made towards the location of its target, responses are next fastest and accurate when there is a simple relationship between the direction or location of the response and its target, and responses are slowest when there is no relationship between the location or direction of the response and its target (Fitts and Deininger, 1954). It is not the position of a body part that determines the degree of stimulus–response compatibility but, instead, the spatial location at which the response is made. When a participant crosses his or her hands so that he or she controls the right response switch with the left hand, and vice versa, it does not decrease stimulus–response compatibility (Anzola *et al.*, 1977; Brebner, Shephard, and Cairney, 1972). The same motor neurons respond whether the action is performed with crossed or uncrossed hands (Cook and Bird, 2013). Furthermore, the spatial representation determining stimulus–response compatibility may be activated through verbal labels. Responses are faster when made to compatible verbal labels such as *left* and *right* as well as to compatible visual labels, such as arrows (Weeks and Proctor, 1990).

The effect of planning on performance

Povel and Collard (1982) cleverly demonstrated the role of planning in action by instructing people to repeat exactly the same tapping sequence according to two different plans and showing that the pauses came in different places. They had subjects learn the same sequence of finger movements as two different pairs of sub-sequences. One pattern was index (i), middle (m), ring (r), ring, middle, index. The other pattern was middle, ring, ring, middle, index, index. Participants repeatedly tapped out the sequence, and the average latency between taps was computed over all the repetitions.

The left panel of Figure 3.4 shows the initiation latencies for the finger movements coded in order of sequence position for both patterns. In each case, the latency is largest for the first and fourth positions, indicating that each pattern is composed of two three-movement sub-sequences. When people were told to repeat imrrmi they first planned and executed imr and then rmi. For this set of sub-sequences, the first pause came before the first index finger stroke and the second pause came before the second ring finger stroke. When people were told to repeat mrrmii they first planned and executed mrr and then mii. With this different set of sub-sequences, the first pause came before the first middle finger stroke and the second pause came before the second middle finger stroke.

In fact, the two sequences were cleverly defined so that, when a participant was repeating either sequence over and over, the movements of the two differently defined sequences were identical except for the very first finger movement. Thus, when the sequences are repeated, both contain the sub-sequence imrrmi. The right panel of Figure 3.4 shows the data from the left panel replotted for the sequence imrrmi. The latency profile is different for exactly the same sequence of movements when produced according to two different plans.

Posture planning

One challenge to motor planning is selecting the most efficient plan of action. There is often more than one way to move your body towards a particular target. Suppose that you want to pick up a pencil just out of reach. There are several ways it might be gripped, but you were born with a motor program for the **pincer grip** between the thumb and index finger for yourself (Vingerhoets, 2014). There are also several ways to reach for the pencil, and

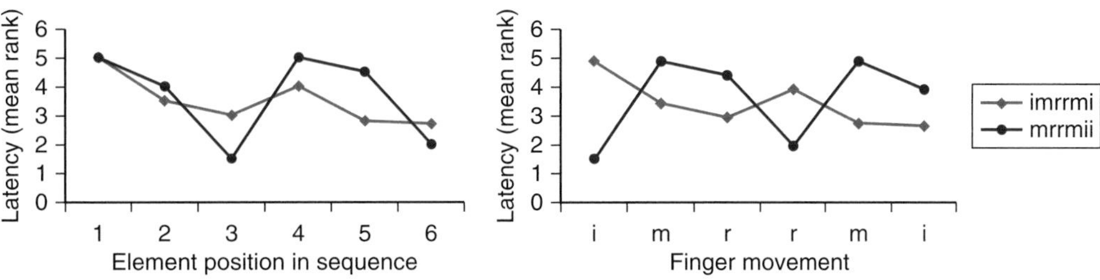

Figure 3.4 When the same repetitive motor sequence is learned from two different start points, the time to initiate a movement is determined by its position in the learned sequence (Povel and Collard, 1982).

in this case there is no innately specified response. You may lean your entire body towards it, or stretch out your arm, or perform some combination of these two actions. In addition, you may reach with your right hand or your left hand. The premotor planning area first selects a particular constellation of body parts for performing the action, such as the right hand, right arm, and torso, and then selects the final postures that the body parts will take when each movement is complete. To determine the final posture, first, representations of final postures when the action was performed in the past are retrieved from memory, and then the posture that brings the body part closest to the target is selected. If necessary, the selected posture is modified to bring it into perfect alignment with the target (Rosenbaum *et al.*, 2001).

The steps in planning the simple action of reaching out and grasping a pencil are shown in Figure 3.5. To begin, as shown schematically at the top, representations of postures that were used to grasp pencils in the past are retrieved from memory. Next the grasping posture that best satisfies the task constraints is selected, as shown in the next panel down. The one that involves the least twisting and turning of the rest of the body is selected. After the hand posture has been selected, representations of arm postures consistent with it are retrieved from memory, as shown in the third panel of Figure 3.5. Finally, as shown in the bottom panel, the best arm posture is selected.

3.3 Performing an action: overview

As shown in Figure 3.3, once the motor plan is complete the frontal cortex sends commands to the motor cortex, the basal ganglia, the cerebellum, the brain stem, and the spinal cord to initiate and control the performance of the planned action. The motor system provides redundant sources of control through a **heterarchy** of parallel top-down pathways that exert multiple levels of control, ultimately making fine, smooth, precise movements, and thus accurate actions, possible.

Directional guidance by the motor cortex and somatosensory cortex

The **motor cortex** in the posterior frontal lobe guides the direction of a body part's movement. Located conveniently adjacent to the motor area, the **somatosensory cortex** in the anterior parietal lobe receives feedback indicating their locations (top panel of Figure 3.3).

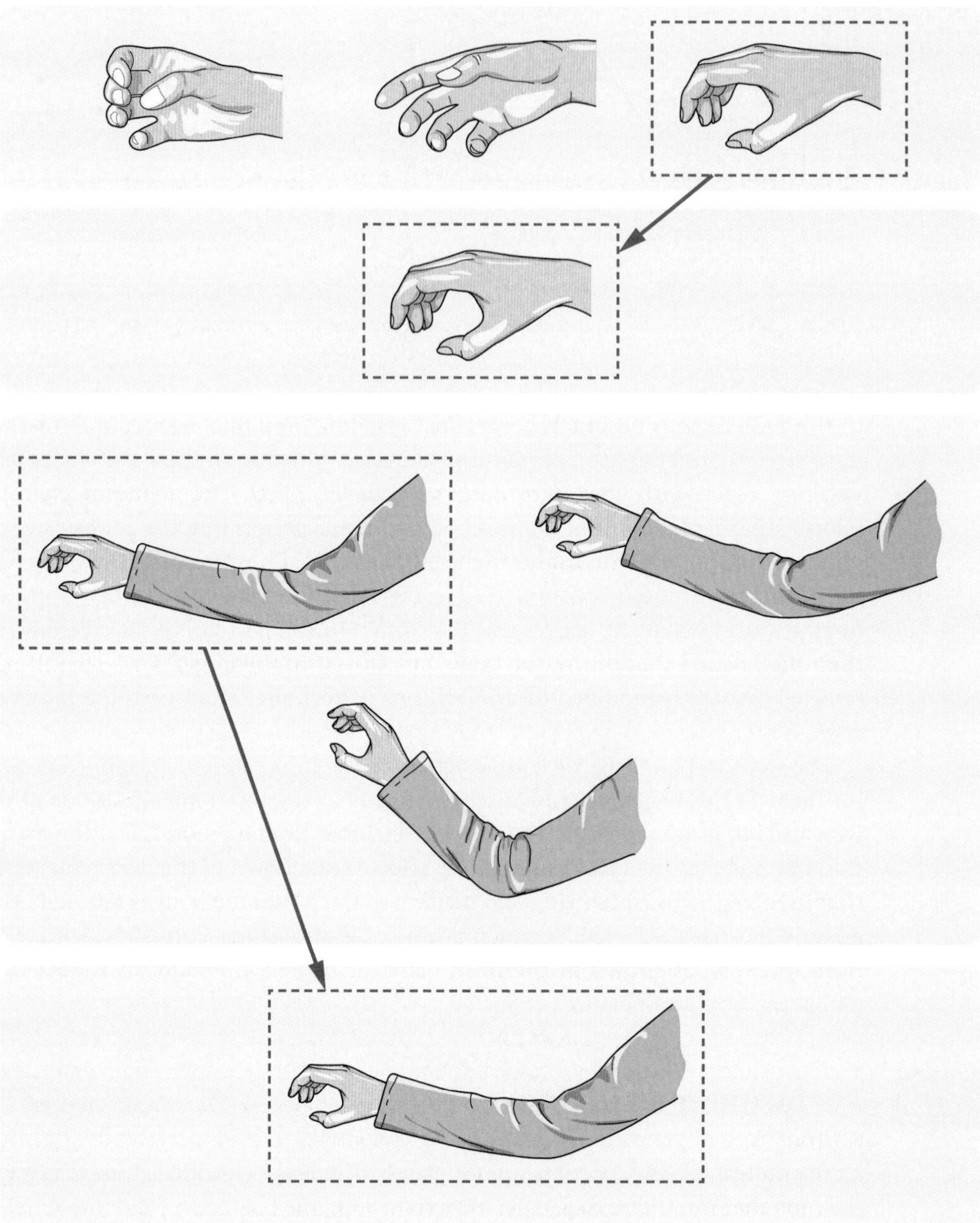

Figure 3.5 Four steps in planning a grasping action. Representations of grasping hand postures are retrieved from memory (top panel). The hand posture providing the closest fit to the target is selected (second panel). Representations of arm extensions are retrieved from memory (third panel). The arm extension providing the best fit with the grasp posture and its location is selected (bottom panel) (Rosenbaum *et al* 2001).

As shown in Figure 3.6 (Penfield and Rasmussen, 1950), both the motor area (left panel) and the somatosensory area (right panel) contain detailed representations of movable body parts. The map appears distorted because body parts such as the tongue and hands, which require fine control, have large areas devoted to them and areas that require only gross

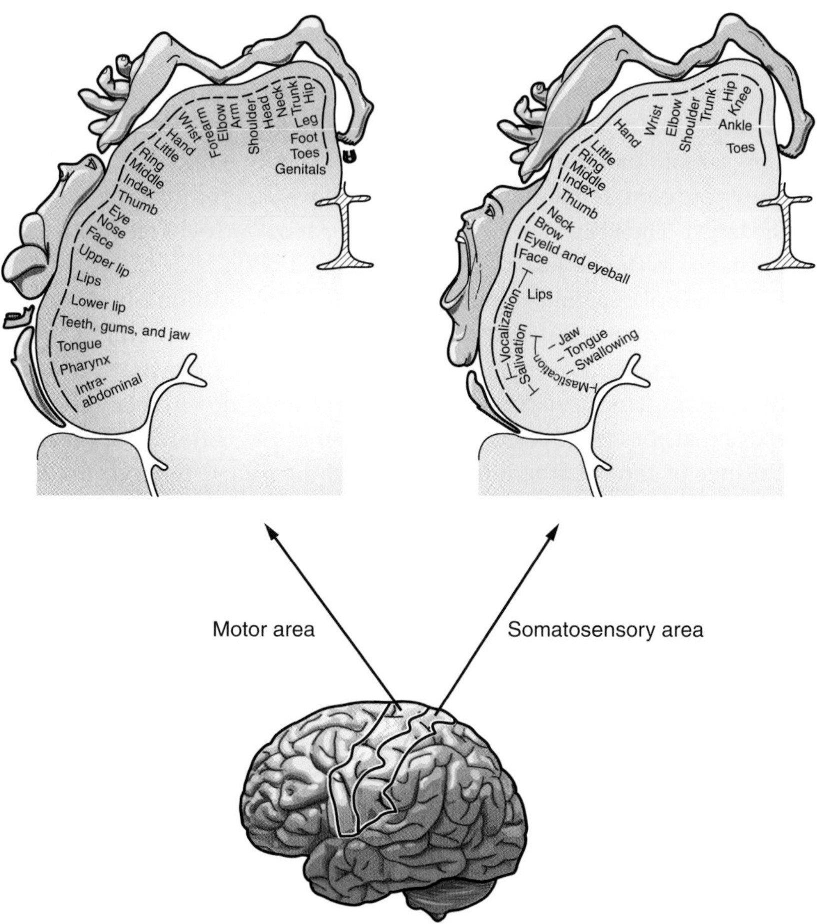

Figure 3.6 Body map in motor area of frontal cortex (left) and somatosensory area of parietal cortex (right) (Penfield and Rasmussen, 1950).

control, such as the trunk, have small areas devoted to them. The somatosensory area is where you experience the sensation of your own body. When you shake hands, the sensory neurons in the hand send signals that ultimately arrive at the part of the somatosensory cortex corresponding to your hand in your body map. It is the activation of these cortical neurons that produces the feeling of having a hand.

Feedback. Motor movements generate kinesthetic, vestibular (Chapter 1), and visual feedback (Gaveau *et al.*, 2014) that is used to guide an action during execution. The **kinesthetic** system detects body movements. Neurons in your joints keep track of where your arms, legs, and fingers are as you move them. Information about the location of body parts is called **proprioceptive** feedback. There are two kinds of feedback: gross short-loop proprioceptive feedback from the spinal cord and brain stem and fine long-loop proprioceptive and vestibular feedback from the cerebellum (Figure 3.3). The short-loop feedback allows rapid, approximate corrections to the motion of the limb. Proprioceptive feedback can reach the brain from a variety of muscles in less than 25 milliseconds (msec) and from tongue and eye muscles in only 4 to 6 milliseconds (Adams, 1976: 215). The long-loop feedback allows slower, fine corrections to the motion of the limb. When a grasping action is filmed and examined in detail it is found to have two components. Most of the distance to the target is covered by a rapid **ballistic phase**. The hand is simply pointed at the target, and a series of motor units are contracted that cause a rapid movement of the limb that places the hand close to the target. Then the hand is guided, under the control of feedback, over the remaining short distance to the target.

Hence, the control of a guided movement during its execution is not continuous. Rather, the maximum control is exerted at the beginning of the action and at the end. Thus the speed profile of a guided movement is not much different from the speed profile of an airplane. Just as an airplane speeds up at take-off and slows down at landing, a guided movement speeds up at the beginning and slows down at the end. Just as the airplane is under the finest degree of control at landing (the rest of the time it is necessary only to point the plane in the correct direction and leave it on autopilot), a guided movement is under the finest degree of control just before it reaches the target. As was the case for the airplane, the rest of the time it is necessary only to point the body part in the correct direction and move it as rapidly as possible without feedback. It is the time it takes to process the long-loop feedback at the end of a guided movement and to make any necessary motor adjustment that slows the movement at the end. Since most of the distance traveled by a guided movement consumes only a small portion of its travel time, the total movement time increases only modestly as a function of distance.

Fitts' law. The relationship between movement time and the distance and size of the target,

$$T = a + B \log_2 (2D/W)$$

where T = movement time, a,B = constants, D = distance of movement from start to target center, and W = width of the target, is called **Fitts' law** after the psychologist who formulated it, Paul Fitts (Fitts, 1954). Movement time changes as the log of the distance, reflecting the fact that movements to targets further away do not take much longer than movements to close targets. The constants a and B in the equation are determined by the body part that is being moved. As we move from finger to wrist to arm the effect of distance on movement time increases. Notice that the more cortical area is devoted to a body part, hence the finer control of it, the less effect that distance has. Fitts' law has practical significance for the design of tools and work spaces, because it allows us to predict in advance how rapidly someone will be able to perform a task requiring guided movements (Proctor and Van Zandt, 1994; Sanders and McCormick, 1993).

To determine whether sensorimotor cortical activity was consistent with Fitts' law, Ifft, Lebedev, and Nicolelis (2011) implanted two monkeys with multielectrode arrays in the motor and somatosensory cortices. The monkeys performed reaches with a joystick-controlled cursor towards targets of different size. Consistent with Fitts' law, the reaction time (RT), movement time, and movement velocity changed with target size, and motor and somatosensory activity reflected these changes.

Error detection. When a correction based on feedback comes too late, an error is detected. West (1967) found that experienced typists detected 50 percent of their errors even when they could not see what they were typing. Rabbitt (1967; 1968) reported even higher error detection rates for a simpler key-pressing task.

Internal control. Some well-learned tasks that are normally performed under the guidance of feedback can be performed accurately without any feedback at all. Evidence that manipulation movements may be made without feedback comes from a rare disability called a **neuropathy** in which a patient loses the sensory neurons in a limb so there is no proprioceptive feedback to guide movement (Rothwell *et al.*, 1982); however, the motor neurons are preserved. Such a patient was still able to make a complex hand movement, such as tracing a circle in the air in the dark, even though no visual or proprioceptive feedback was available.

Phantom limbs. Suppose that a person is unfortunate enough to lose a body part, such as a finger, hand, arm, or leg. After the limb has been amputated, the person often still feels its presence as a phantom limb. This is because the somatosensory cortex still contains a representation of it, and immediately after the amputation begins to receive input from another part of the body that it interprets as coming from the missing limb (Ramachandran, Rogers-Ramachandran, and Stewart, 1992). If you look again at Figure 3.6 you will see that the area in the body map for the hand is next to the area for the face. When Ramachandran reached out and touched the cheek of a man whose arm had been amputated, the patient reported that Ramachandran had not only touched his cheek, but also his phantom hand (Ramachandran, Rogers-Ramachandran, and Stewart, 1992).

Ramachandran and his colleagues (Ramachandran, Rogers-Ramachandran, and Cobb, 1995) made use of the fact that limb movements can be guided by purely visual feedback to diagnose and treat an unusual kind of pain. Some amputees are able to move the phantom limb as easily as a fleshly one. Other amputees are unable to move their phantom limb. For this latter group, it feels as if the limb is curled into an uncomfortable position, and the individual feels excruciating pain in the phantom limb. Ramachandran reasoned that if he could make the phantom limb visible then the amputee would be able to move it under visual control, thus relieving the pain. To accomplish this, Ramachandran cut two holes in a box and had such an individual insert his remaining hand through one hole and his phantom hand through the other. On the other side of the box was a mirror that reflected an image of the remaining hand, so that when he looked over the top of the box he saw two hands: the remaining physical hand and its reflection in the position of the phantom hand. Ramachandran told the patient to try to move his two hands in some cooperative pattern, such as clapping, twirling, etc. Under visual control, the patient discovered that he could move his phantom hand perfectly well, and when he could move it the pain went away.

Artificial limbs. Ramachandran, Rogers-Ramachandran, and Cobb's (1995) results with the mirror box suggested that amputees might one day be visually trained to feel their artificial limbs. To test whether this was possible, Shokur *et al.* (2013) had two monkeys watch a video in which a ball brushed a hand. At the same time, the monkey's actual hand was brushed. During the brushing, activity was recorded from the areas in the motor and somatosensory areas for the hand. Afterwards, when the brushing occurred in the video but not for real, at least 40 percent of the time the activity in the motor and somatosensory areas indicated that the monkeys perceived the video hand as part of their body and felt it being brushed (Figure 3.7).

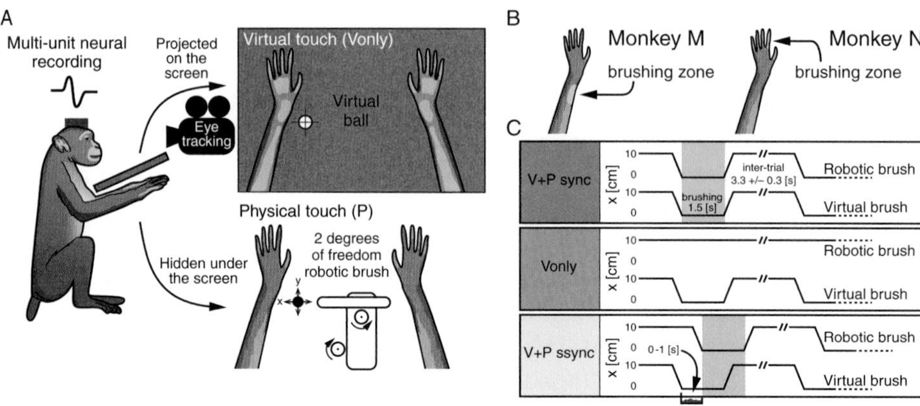

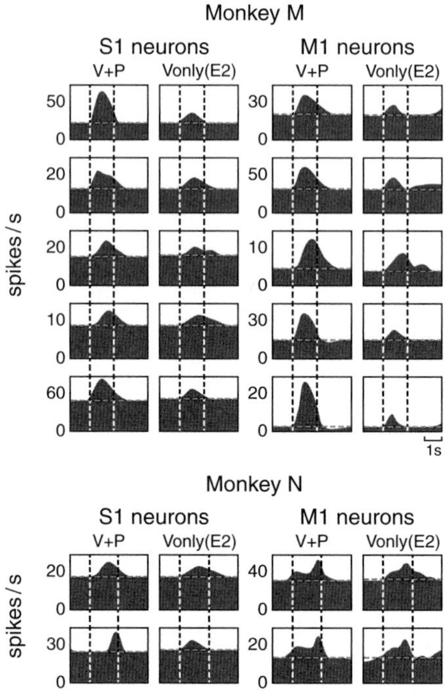

Figure 3.7 The top shows the task. Two monkeys with their hands and arms hidden saw a video of a ball brushing an arm (A).The arm was not brushed on a virtual only (Vonly) trial but was brushed at the same time as the video image on a virtual plus physical (V + P) trial (B, C). The bottom shows the results. Both the motor area and the somatosensory area for the brushed are responded on both V + P and V only trials. The pink line shows baseline (Shokur *et al*., 2013).

Encoding direction in the motor cortex. By recording the responses of individual neurons within the sub-area for a body part, Georgopoulos (1995) determined how movement is directed at the neuronal level. Within each body part sub-area, there are neurons that direct that body part to move in various directions. Each neuron in the sub-area for a body part directs the body part in a particular direction. However, these neurons are broadly tuned, as shown in the top panel of Figure 3.8. Each neuron will be somewhat active if a movement is made within 90 degrees of the one causing its strongest response. In other words, a neuron that is most active when the hand is moving straight away from the body will only be a little less active when it is moving forward to the right or left. Each possible direction is represented by many neurons in the area. When direction is represented in the motor area, many of the direction neurons for the body part are active so that the direction actually specified is the average of the directions indicated by all the individually active neurons, as shown in the bottom panel of Figure 3.8.

Damage to any part of the body map in the motor area causes the loss of voluntary control over whatever body part is represented in that portion of the map. Effectively, the part of the body represented by the map becomes paralyzed. This paralysis is called **hemiplegia**.

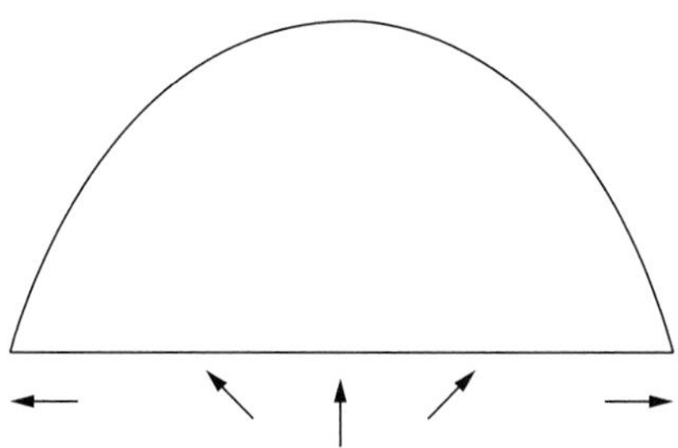

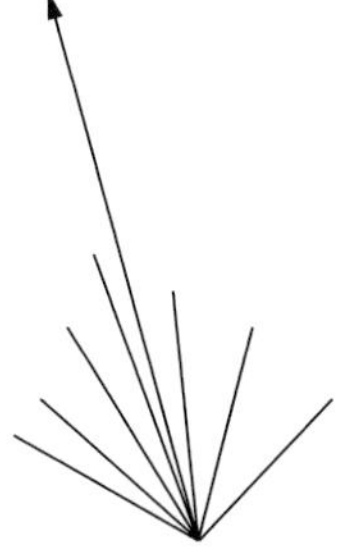

Figure 3.8 Representing limb direction in the motor cortex. Each motor neuron responds to a wide range of directions but has a greatest response for a particular direction of movement away from the body (top panel). A direction is represented on an area of the cortex by the activation of many neurons, represented by the straight lines. The length of each line represents the strength of the neuron's activation and the orientation of the line is the direction the neuron encodes. The average of the activation of all the neurons is the direction that the body part moves, shown by the arrow (bottom panel) (Georgopoulos, 1995).

The motor cortex encodes the direction of a planned action but it does not initiate the action. When monkeys were first cued as to the direction of a response and then given a 'Go' signal after a fixed interval, the activation of the direction neurons in the motor cortex began following the cue and was maintained throughout the interval (Georgopoulos, 1995). Actions are initiated by the basal ganglia.

Initiation and the basal ganglia

The basal ganglia comprise a collection of structures within the frontal cortex that play an important role in the fine control of voluntary action by inhibiting all irrelevant movement and perceptual processing when a voluntary action is initiated. The basal ganglia receive input from the prefrontal, frontal, and parietal areas of the cortex and influence cortical processing by inhibiting the flow of perceptual information through the thalamus to the cortex (Figure 3.9 (a)). All perceptual information passes through the thalamus, so perceptual feedback from the motor action passes through the thalamus to the parietal cortex, where it is used to direct the action. Furthermore, the processing of all sensory input that is not relevant to the target is terminated by closing the gates through which it passes in the thalamus.

A variety of disorders result from damage to the basal ganglia, producing either decreased or increased inhibition of the thalamus. In either case, the normal flow of only action-relevant feedback is disrupted, so voluntary movement is impaired. Deterioration of the nuclei in the **striatum** ultimately results in decreased inhibition to the thalamus, which results in the jerky, involuntary movements that are a defining characteristic of **Huntington's disease** (Figure 3.9 (b)). As the deterioration proceeds, the person's ability to make voluntary movements becomes more impaired, until the person is unable to make deliberate actions at all. The rare disorder called **hemiballismus** results from damage to the part of the basal ganglia between the midbrain and thalamus called the **subthalamic nucleus**. Damage here disrupts the usual inhibition sent to the thalamus. So, instead of a precise voluntary action, a violent flinging motion occurs. Yet another basal ganglia disorder is **Tourette's syndrome**. Voluntary action may be unaffected, but, as the result of a decrease in inhibition from the basal ganglia, involuntary movements occur in the form of twitches and tics. One rare but particularly unpleasant symptom is involuntary vocalization, including barks and curse words.

Parkinson's disease results from damage to the part of the basal ganglia extending into the midbrain, called the **substantia nigra**, that ultimately increases inhibition to the thalamus, which reduces the activation from the thalamus to the cortex (Figure 3.9 (c)). When the damage is severe the behavioral effect is **endo-akinesia**, the inability to make a voluntary movement without an external stimulus. Without a perceptible target, people with Parkinson's disease will sit or lie still indefinitely. However, if you put a bar of soap in their hand, they will wash themselves. If you put a toothbrush in their hand, they will brush their teeth. As the disorder becomes more severe, more extreme stimulation is required to elicit a response.

Programming

The cerebellum is comprised of three parts. The **vestibulocerebellum** contains the reflexes for maintaining balance and coordinating eye movements, such as the vestibulo-ocular reflex, which facilitates voluntary movement and perception (Chapter 1). The **neocerebellum**

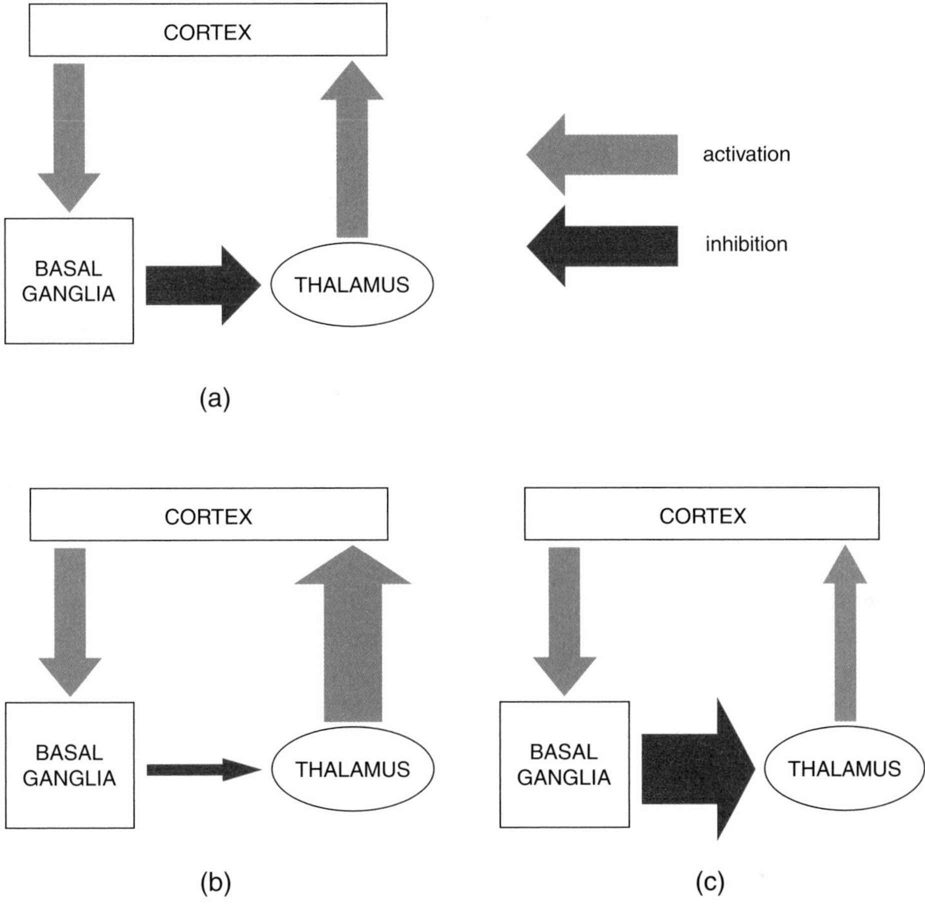

Figure 3.9 The circuit between the cortex, basal ganglia, and thalamus. The basal ganglia regulate the flow of activation from the thalamus to the cortex by inhibiting the thalamus (a). In Huntington's disease the ability of the basal ganglia to inhibit the thalamus is impaired (b). In Parkinson's disease the basal ganglia over-inhibit the thalamus (c).

and **spinocerebellum** turn motor plans into motor programs transmitted to the brain stem and to the spinal cord, which contains the motor neurons that execute the motor unit contractions necessary to produce smooth movements (Braitenberg, 1967).

When the cerebellum is damaged, and so the timing of the muscle movements is coarsened, voluntary movements become less precise and the ability to rapidly alternate movements that require antagonistic muscles is lost (Holmes, 1939). Ivry and Keele (1989) directly tested the role of the cerebellum in timing by having patients with cerebellar damage perform both a motor and a perceptual timing task. The patients' performance was more variable than normal when they tried to tap to a beat of 550 milliseconds. They were also less accurate than normal at discriminating two short (less than half a second), slightly different temporal intervals defined by pairs of tones, suggesting that the ability to perceive a rhythm evolved from and depends on the ability to produce a rhythm. When the timing of muscle movements is impaired, the individual suffers from a motor coordination problem called **ataxia**. Walking becomes wobbly, reaching attempts lead to overshoots, and it becomes difficult to touch your finger to your nose. Alcohol causes these symptoms because it disrupts cerebellar activity.

The control of action is complicated by the bifurcated nature of the brain and the need to control movements on both sides of the body. The left cortex is connected with the right cerebellum, which is connected with the right side of the body. The right cortex is connected with the left cerebellum, which is connected with the left side of the body. Each cortex therefore plans the movements of the opposite side of the body. But, during the actual execution of the plans, movements on both sides of the body must be coordinated. During execution one cortex is ultimately responsible for cross-body coordination. Cross-body coordination keeps you from getting in your own way and makes it possible to coordinate different movements on each side of the body (for example, in playing an instrument or swinging a bat or racket). Since one hemisphere or the other normally takes control of coordinating cross-body coordination, it is normally difficult to move opposite body parts independently. For example, point your index fingers towards each other and then try to twirl one finger towards you and one away from you. You will find them both going in the same direction.

Cross-body coordination is normally assisted by the **corpus callosum**, which transmits information between the left and right cortex, and the **massa intermedia**, which transmits information between the left and right thalamus. Nonetheless, the cognitive functioning of individuals born without a massa intermedia is indistinguishable from everyone else. Similarly, when the corpus callosum was severed in a few individuals as a treatment for intractable epilepsy, the operation did not impair their motor coordination. However, it did make it possible for them to make more independent hand movements than are seen in normal individuals, such as copying two different pictures at the same time. Since cross-body coordination is rarely a problem, there must be redundant pathways for maintaining it when the corpus callosum is damaged and the massa intermedia is absent.

3.4 Skill learning

With practice, a routine action becomes faster and more accurate, and so is called a **skill**. Although there is continuous improvement in the performance of a task with practice, skill learning can be conventionally divided into three stages as control of the action passes from the instrumental system to the habit system (Fitts and Posner, 1967). The first stage is the **declarative stage**. When a novel action is required, the individual knows what must be done but does not yet know how to do it. So the instrumental system must construct the posture plan, perhaps from the plans from simpler or similar actions. This process is slow and does not necessarily produce an accurate response. Because the response is under the complete control of the instrumental system, it is under conscious control, and attempting to perform another ad hoc voluntary action at the same time will interfere with its execution.

The second stage is the **associative stage**. From the very first attempt, a fragile representation of the sequence of actions that comprise the response is encoded by the habit system. With practice, the representations in the habit system of those components of the response that are consistent across successful responses become more robust. During the associative stage the instrumental and habit systems cooperate. Those sequences of actions encoded by the habit system execute the plan constructed by the instrumental system. Performance is faster and more accurate but still subject to interference from another ad hoc voluntary task.

The third stage is the **autonomous stage**. A single plan describing the final body posture for the entire action is retrieved and executed by a sequence of actions encoded in the habit system. Because there is no construction involved in this now routine task, a different, ad hoc, action may be planned and executed by the instrumental system at the same time without interfering with it. This is how you can carry on a conversation while walking, reaching for something, feeding yourself at dinner, etc., since none of these well-practiced actions require conscious planning.

Some people may be better at skill learning because they have slightly larger habit systems. A group of investigators (Erickson *et al.*, 2010) examined whether individual differences in improvement in performance on a demanding video game, the Space Fortress game, could be predicted by the pre-training volume of either the striatum (of the habit system) or the hippocampus (of the instrumental system). Hippocampal volumes did not predict learning improvement. However, the volumes of three different parts of the striatum, the caudate nucleus, the putamen, and the nucleus accumbens (Figure 3.10), did.

Routine tasks are often performed in similar but slightly different contexts. We may need to grasp a wide variety of different objects, sometimes closer to us, sometimes a little further away, sometimes when we are sitting, and sometimes when we are standing. These different contexts require slightly different final body postures for perfect performance. When a task is practiced, not one but many different body postures for it are encoded. Subsequently, when the task must be performed in a particular context, all the body postures for it are retrieved and then the one best suited for that context is selected on the basis of visual and/or tactual information provided by the parietal cortex (Figure 3.5). It is the accumulation of ever more specific body postures that causes task performance to become more accurate. The accumulation of body posture plans also causes the execution to become faster, because the occasions on which either the plan or its execution must be modified on the basis of feedback become rarer. Hence skill learning occurs through the accumulation of posture (or action) plans.

If skill performance improves as the result of the accumulation of plans then most of the improvement will occur at the very beginning of learning, when many of the posture plans encoded will be for contexts being encountered for the first time, and so encoding successful posture plans for them will lead to immediate, large improvements in the speed and accuracy of performance. As the number of encoded postures increases, the contexts being encountered will be only slightly different from one practiced earlier, and so result in only slight improvements in performance. This model predicts that the improvement in performance will be a power function of the amount of practice, as it approaches, but never quite reaches, an asymptote.

To test this prediction, Crossman (1959) visited a cigar factory to observe the effect of years of practice on cigar rolling. Crossman measured the performance of the operators of cigar-making machines of different years of experience. Figure 3.11 (top) shows an initial large decrease in cigar-rolling time for novice workers and after that an apparently negligible decrease for experienced workers. However, it is not really possible to tell from Figure 3.11 (top) whether experienced workers continue to improve, because their speeds are compressed into a narrow range when compared with those for novice workers.

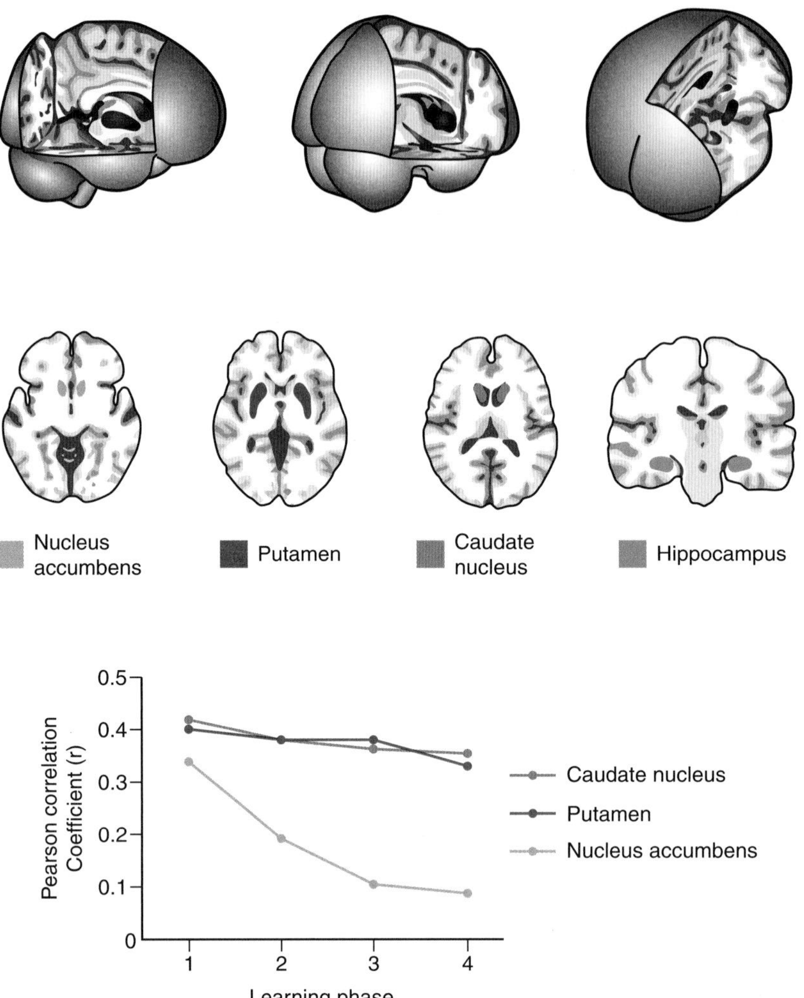

Figure 3.10 The top panel shows the four areas of the brain for which cortical volume was measured for participants learning a video game. The cortical volume of the hippocampus was uncorrelated with performance. As shown at the bottom, the cortical volume of the nucleus accumbens was correlated with performance at the beginning of training and the cortical volume of the caudate nucleus and putamen are correlated with performance throughout training (Erickson *et al.*, 2010).

Figure 3.11 (bottom) shows exactly the same data replotted on a graph in which the production and time scales are logarithmic scales rather than linear ones. From Figure 3.11 (bottom), it is clear that, even during the autonomous phase, practice on a skill continues to improve performance for years. Crossman found that the time to operate a cigar-rolling machine decreased for at least two years and 3 million cycles, at which time the operator approached the mechanical operating limit of the machine. Figure 3.11 (bottom) illustrates the **exponential law of practice** (Heathcote, Brown, and Mewhort, 2000). This is described by the function

$$T = A + Be^{-aN}$$

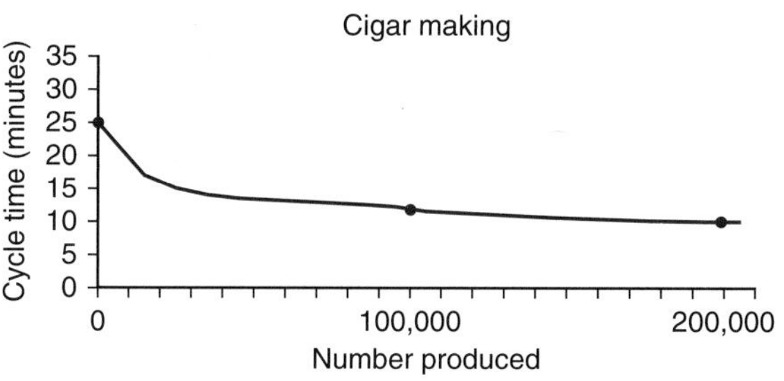

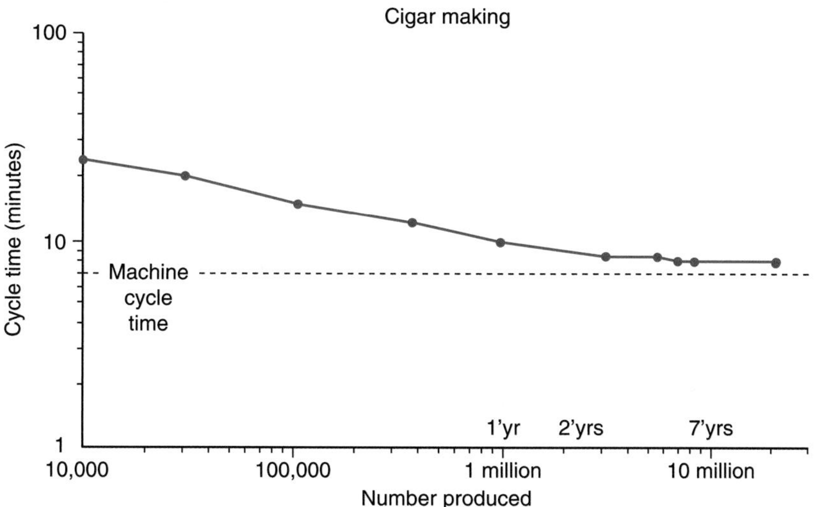

Figure 3.11 The effect of practice on the time to roll cigars plotted on a linear time scale (top panel). The function is the average cycle time for making a cigar over one week's production for one operator. The x-axis is the total production by the operator since beginning work. The bottom panel shows the effect of practice on the speed of cigar making plotted on logarithmic time and production scales (Crossman, 1959).

where T = time to perform task, N = number of times task has been performed, A = asymptotic time to perform action, and B = change in time as function of learning.

As can be seen in the figure, the improvement in performance between successive repetitions of a task decreases as the number of repetitions increase. Exponential functions are always plotted on a logarithmic time scale axis, as in Figure 3.11 (bottom), rather than on a linear time scale, as in Figure 3.11 (top), so that the small differences that continue with extended practice can be seen on the graph. However, even though the function approximates a straight line when plotted on a log scale, do not lose sight of the fact that the actual relationship between speed of performance and practice is as shown in Figure 3.11 (top). Although the improvement in the performance of a motor skill with practice eventually becomes tiny, as far we know there is no point at which improvement in task performance, however slight, ceases altogether. The asymptote (A) is never quite reached in motor skill learning. There is always improvement with practice.

Feedback in skilled performance

Skilled performance requires, first, that possible posture plans be retrieved, and then that the most appropriate plan for the situation be selected on the basis of tactual and visual information. The tactual and visual information used for selection is determined by the feedback available when the skill was learned. Adams, Goetz, and Marshall (1972) showed that reducing perceptual information was even more disruptive to skilled performers than to unskilled performers. What is available during training determines the kind of feedback needed during skilled performance. For example, Notterman and Tufano (1980) showed that a repetitive motion learned under visual control required less proprioceptive feedback. Conversely, when Proteau, Marteniuk, and Levesque (1992) had people practice hitting a target without visual feedback, they found that later letting them see what they were doing hurt performance. Depending on how it was learned, a skilled movement may make use of both or either of visual and proprioceptive feedback for guidance, or it may be performed without the use of feedback at all.

Relationship between declarative and autonomous control of skilled performance

One important role of feedback is to signal that a routine action under the autonomous control of the habit system has failed to achieve its goal, so it is necessary for the instrumental system to take control of the response. Hence, control shifts from autonomous habit control to declarative instrumental control (Jeannerod, 1994). Even though the instrumental system is in control in a novel situation, it has access to the posture plan in the habit system and need only modify this plan, rather than construct a new plan from scratch, in order to accommodate the novel context. For example, Slachevsky *et al.* (2003) devised a computer game in which participants copied a slanted line on a screen without being able to see their hand or their copy while drawing it (Figure 3.12). Nevertheless, this is still an easy task. To make it more difficult, the computer displaced the angle of motion produced by the participant to the right when plotting it on the computer screen. Therefore, in order to trace the line shown on the screen, participants would have to displace their angle of motion to the left (see Figure 3.12). Normal participants explicitly reported the correct strategy to correct for the added right-angle displacement (move the hand at an angle to the left of the target) and were able to implement the strategy and trace over the target line by displacing the hand motion to the left. However, participants with frontal damage that impaired the functioning of the instrumental system were unable to report the correction strategy (though they noticed that their lines deviated from the target line). Their performance was significantly worse than for the individuals who were able to state the correction strategy. These results demonstrate the importance of declarative representation in learning. It is first necessary to understand what has to be done and to repeatedly make conscious efforts to do it in order to be able to encode an accurate autonomous habit representation of how the motion should be made.

As this computer game demonstrates, the cooperation of the instrumental and habit systems makes it possible for humans to extend their motor skills not only to novel and unusual environments but even to bizarre ones. When the normal visual–proprioceptive correlations do not apply, so your hand feels as though it is in one place and looks as if it is in another, the visual–proprioceptive correlations are recalibrated so that accurate movements can be made. Perhaps you remember how difficult it was the first time you

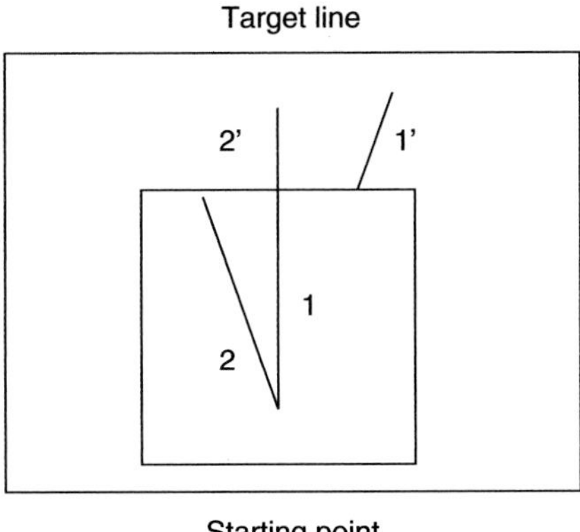

Figure 3.12 The target is a vertical line. When a participant attempts to trace the target by drawing a vertical line as shown in 1, the line drawn emerges from under the mask as shown in 1′. When the participant compensates by drawing a line with a 22 degree angular displacement to the left as shown in 2, the line drawn emerges from under the mask as shown in 2′ (Slachevsky *et al*., 2003).

tried to comb your hair while looking in the mirror. Nonetheless, after a few attempts it became less disturbing to see your hand move away from you in the mirror as you moved it towards you. Stratton (1897) demonstrated just how far the motor system could accommodate to the visual system when he wore an inverting lens over one eye (the other eye was patched). When looking through the lens, down appeared up and right appeared left. Over a period of days his motor system recalibrated so that he could reach for objects and move about normally.

Generalization across limbs and tools

The high level of complexity of joint instrumental/habit control confers one enormous advantage on the performance of skills. Even though the skill has been learned through the repeated action of the same body part, in appropriate context the posture plan may be used to direct an entirely different body part. For example, after thousands of trials performing a task by pressing a lever with his foot while hanging from rings by his hands, a monkey used its hand to press the lever the first time it had the opportunity to perform the task while sitting on a perch (Rumbaugh, 2003).

The ultimate example of abstraction and generalization is tool use, when an object is used to substitute for a body part. In this case, the posture plan describes the manipulation of a tool, which is not an end in itself but the means to an end. A screwdriver is not turned for its own sake but to insert or remove a screw. Posture plans permit both tool and body part substitution when performing a skill. Children learn to write with pencils on paper by moving their wrists. However, this skill generalizes to writing with chalk on blackboard, in which the wrist is held rigid and the entire arm is moved. On the other hand, the encoding of the posture plan in the left hemisphere places an important constraint on generalization. Most people can manipulate a tool much more effectively with one hand than the other, and most individuals are right-handed. This corresponds to the left parietal posture plan. The posture plans for tool use are overwhelmingly encoded in the left parietal cortex. There is increased activation in the left somatosensory cortex when a tool is manipulated (Vingerhoets, 2014). To accommodate the posture plans, the amount of cortex devoted to a skill increases with practice. The sub-area in the right motor cortex for the left hand's fingers, which do the fingering, is enlarged in expert violinists (Schwenkreis *et al.*, 2007).

Apraxia

Damage to the parietal, premotor, or supplementary motor areas of the cortex, to subcortical pathways connecting them, and to the basal ganglia impairs the ability to carry out routine actions. Even though the person can still move his or her hands, arms, and legs, he or she has difficulty combining movements to perform a purposeful action. For example, a person may no longer be able to get dressed. Somehow, everything gets all tangled up, with the arm in the wrong sleeve and the vest inside out. Using a knife and fork, piling up a pile of blocks, writing a brief note may all now be insurmountably complex. Sometimes an injury results in an action being performed in a less efficient way. For example, a person who has lost the fine control for grasping objects now overshoots them and must search the area with a cupped hand before the target is obtained. The normal cutting of meat may be replaced with a rapid sawing motion. Although the symptoms vary with the location of the damage, all these disorders are sometimes collectively referred to as **apraxia**. However, all apraxic disorders are not the same, and milder forms reveal the different levels of organization of posture plans (Cubelli *et al.*, 2000; Rothi, Ochipa, and Heilman, 1997).

Frontal injuries that affect planning. Frontal injuries appear to affect access to a plan rather than the representation of the plan (in the parietal cortex) itself. Access can be impaired in a variety of ways, resulting in a variety of remarkably specific impairments. Normally, action begins with intention. However, sometimes as a result of frontal damage, an intention is not enough. Some patients are apraxic for actions that do not require tools but can still perform actions requiring tools such as a toothbrush when the tool is placed in their hand. In this case, the tool apparently acts as a strong cue for the action. On the hand, skills involving tools tend to involve more complex plans than simple actions that do not require tools. Other patients are apraxic for skills requiring tools but not for simple actions that do not require tools (Cubelli *et al.*, 2000).

If we consider only actions that use tools, some patients are able to perform a familiar action when given the appropriate tool but are unable to pantomime it. For example, a patient who cannot pantomime how to use a knife and fork may perform adequately when the actual utensils are placed in his or her hand. The patient can still turn a screwdriver correctly, but when he or she attempts to pantomime it he or she fails to put the hand in a grasping posture before turning. This deficit suggests that the habit posture plan of the action is intact in the left parietal cortex but the patient has difficulty retrieving it through the instrumental system. Some patients are able to both perform and pantomime familiar actions, such as using a knife and fork, correctly, but are unable to imitate novel actions. This deficit suggests that posture plans are intact but the instrumental system's ability to construct a novel action is impaired, which makes the imitation of novel actions impossible (Bartolo *et al.*, 2001). Conversely, a woman became unable to perform familiar actions, though she could imitate novel actions perfectly. In this case, it seems that the habit system's control of familiar actions was impaired, but instrumental control of novel actions was intact (Bartolo *et al.*, 2001).

Visuospatial disorders. As will be described in Chapter 6, a visuomotor pathway extends from the retina of the eye, where light is encoded, to the thalamus and then to the parietal cortex, where the visual information is used to plan and direct motor movements. Damage to the visuomotor pathway causes a deficit in the visual control of actions that is called a **visuospatial** or **visuoconstructive disorder**, or **visual ataxia.** Visual guidance of reaching, the manipulation of objects, and even of moving about are poor. In mild cases, people may get only the left and right confused. For example, they might make an error when asked to point with their right hand to the examiner's right eye. In more severe cases people may have difficulty putting on their clothes and be unable to find their way about (Benton and Tranel, 1993; Kolb and Whishaw, 1980). Patients with visual ataxia may have difficulty reaching in the correct direction and/or adjusting the orientation of their hand to the object (Karnath and Perenin, 2005), and/or adjusting their grasp to the shape and size of the object (Goodale *et al.*, 1991) and/or fixating on the object (Milner and Goodale, 1995). Different patients have different difficulties, so it appears that different regions of the parietal cortex control different actions.

Visuospatial deficits may also be detected by having a person do some simple drawings, such as a daisy, the face of a clock (Rouleau, Salman, and Butters, 1996), a house, or a cube (Moore and Wyke, 1984). Patients produce badly distorted drawings, such as those in Figure 3.13. Notice that the drawings in the figure are distorted on the left. When the shape representation is constructed, the separate representations of right and left visual space must be integrated within a single hemisphere. For visuospatial representation, integration takes place in the right hemisphere. The right hemisphere therefore contains many neurons that respond to visual and tactual inputs from both sides of space. Hence, when the left hemisphere is injured, the right hemisphere can take over much of its processing. However, the left hemisphere contains neurons that respond to visuospatial inputs only from the right side of space. So when the right hemisphere is damaged the left hemisphere cannot take over the processing of these neurons, and distortions in the left sides of drawings, as shown in Figure 3.13, are one result.

Figure 3.13 Drawings indicate parietal injury: the verbal instructions were to draw a clock with the hands set at 10 past 11 (left) and to draw a daisy (right) (Goodglass and Kaplan, 1972).

The effect of distributed practice on skill learning and long-term retention

Today, cellphones and text messaging have made typing on a keyboard an important skill for everyone to have. This raises the issue of when and where children should be taught this skill and how much practice they should have, daily. It was not long ago that typing on a keyboard was a specialized skill performed by secretaries, reporters, some authors, and almost no one else. Then technology increased the contexts in which it was necessary, which provided an opportunity to study the best training schedule for learning it.

In the 1970s mechanical letter-sorting machines were introduced, which required postal workers to type postal codes on their keyboards. Postal workers had to learn how to type for the first time. The (British) Royal Mail service was faced with the prospect of teaching large numbers of postal workers to type so that they could operate keyboard-driven sorting machines. They turned to the Applied Psychology Unit of the Medical Research Council, whose director, Alan Baddeley, conducted a study of different practice schemes (Baddeley and Longman, 1978). Psychologists already knew that the training schedule had an effect on learning, so the effects of four training schedules were compared by Baddeley and Longman (1978) to determine the best one. Trainees were each given one of four different practice schedules: a single one-hour practice session a day, two one-hour practice sessions a day, a single two-hour practice session a day, and two two-hour practice sessions a day. Figure 3.14 (top) shows performance as a function of the number of days over which training was received. The number of days to learn the keyboard were thirty-five, twenty-two, twenty-two, and thirteen for the respective groups. The more time per day that was spent practicing, therefore, the fewer the number of days in which the skill was learned. Performance improved most rapidly when the task was practiced four hours a day. So, if you have to learn do something right away, it is best to spend a lot of the short time available practicing it.

However, Figure 3.14 (bottom) shows exactly the same results, but this time performance is shown as a function of the number of hours of practice. When the same data are examined as a function of the number of hours to learn the keyboard, the results are thirty-five, forty-three, forty-three, and fifty, for the respective groups. When examined this way, it can be seen that the skill was learned with fewer hours of practice when the practice was distributed over more days. Performance improved most rapidly when the task was practiced only one hour a day. In fact, with one hour of practice a day, eighty keystrokes per minute was achieved after only fifty-five hours of practice – a level of performance not achieved when practicing four hours a day after eighty hours of practice. So, if you have plenty of time to learn a task, you can minimize the time you spend learning it by distributing your effort into as many short practice sessions over as long a training period as possible. Distributed practice is more efficient than massed practice for skill learning.

The advantage of distributed practice is caused by the sophisticated interaction of the instrumental and habit systems during skill learning. During a single practice session a posture plan may be retrieved once by the habit system, and then used for repeated actions with ad hoc adjustments to its execution by the instrumental system. These ad hoc adjustments are not completely ephemeral. A representation survives long enough to be available if the action is immediately repeated in the same context.

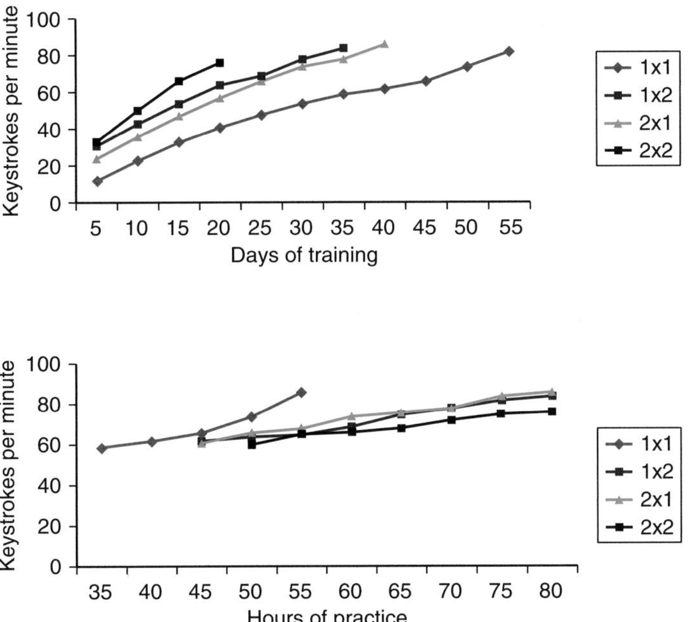

Figure 3.14 Typing speed as a function of number of days of training (top) and number of hours of practice (bottom) (Baddely and Longman, 1978).

However, the plan itself in the parietal cortex is not revised. If the plan itself is not revised and re-encoded by the habit system then there is not a long-term improvement in skill performance. Only at the start of a practice session, when the posture plan is first retrieved by the habit system, is it re-encoded in a more robust form. So, the number of practice sessions has more effect than the duration of each practice session on the improvement in skilled performance. Hence, distributed practice is more efficient than massed practice.

Baddeley and Longman (1978) also studied the effect of the different training schedules on the retention of the typing skill. Recall that Kandel and his colleagues found that distributed training produced longer habituation and sensitization than massed training. Similarly, Baddeley and Longman found that there was longer retention of the typing skill following distributed practice than following massed practice. In fact, superior retention following distributed practice is a ubiquitous aspect of animal behavior, supported by a variety of neural mechanisms. Consider an animal constructing ad hoc novel action in a novel situation. If this situation is unique and will not occur again, there is no value in having a record of the action. So, only a fragile representation of it is encoded, which will soon disappear from memory. However, suppose that, before the representation disappears, the situation occurs again and the action is again performed. This second occurrence classifies the situation as routine, and the representation of the response to it is made sufficiently robust to survive an interval longer than between the first and second occurrences of the situation requiring it.

Figure 3.15 shows the final level of performance after sixty hours of practice for the single-hour-a-day group and eighty hours of practice for the other three groups, and

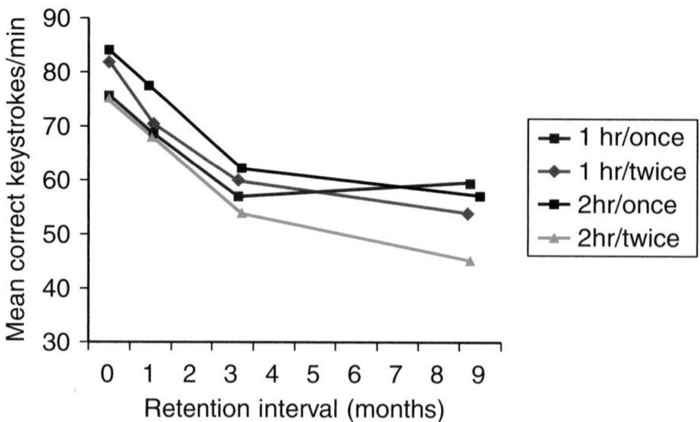

Figure 3.15 The retention of typing learned under four different practice schedules (Baddeley and Longman, 1978).

the level of performance after **retention intervals** of one, three, and nine months. (The retention interval is the period of time between training and test; no typing was done during this interval.) The figure illustrates the two ubiquitous aspects of the forgetting function. There is an initial, relatively short, period when performance declines and a much longer period of asymptotic performance, often lasting the entire life of the animal, when there is no further decline in performance. The effect of distributed practice is not on the duration of the initial decline but on the asymptote of performance. Distributed practice causes a higher asymptote; that is, it causes a higher permanent level of performance. Figure 3.15 shows that, for one or two hours of practice a day, the decline in performance occurs within the first three months and then asymptotes. However, performance continued to decline over the nine-month period for the postal workers who trained four hours a day, hence for the fewest number of days. At nine months they had the poorest retention of all.

Thus, if there is sufficient distributed practice of a skill, it is never forgotten. The familiar example is that no one ever forgets how to ride a bicycle. A variety of other motor skills have been tested over retention intervals of up to several years, and no forgetting has been found (Fleishman and Parker, 1962; Hammerton, 1963).

SUMMARY

The emergence of the instrumental system made voluntary action possible. The emergence of the habit system made the learning of routine actions possible. Together, the two systems make skill learning possible. The paradox of the joint instrumental/habit (hence, both conscious and automatic) control of action is that it seems so easy not because it is simple but because nearly all the levels of computation necessary to make it possible are occult. The irony of the study of motor control is that no matter how complicated the neural mechanisms for even a simple action appear, further research reveals them to be even more complicated.

- Voluntary action involves two distinct stages: planning and performance. During the planning stage, involving the parietal cortex and the premotor or supplementary motor cortex, various final postures from previous successful acts are retrieved, and one is selected and modified for the current situation.
- During the performance stage the plan is encoded for specific body parts in the motor cortex, initiated by the basal ganglia, and translated into a motor program for making the necessary muscle movements by the cerebellum. The program for the movements is transmitted to the brain stem and spinal cord, and ultimately to the muscles that perform them. The neural system consists of parallel top-down pathways so that multiple levels of control are exerted on the antagonistic muscles whose movements perform the action. The performance of the action produces feedback that is used to guide it. Furthermore, at the same time as the target and feedback from the action are being used to direct it, all other perceptual processing and all other movement is inhibited. The resulting smooth movements produce fine, precise, accurate actions.
- A successful action results in the encoding of the final posture of the action. Over time, when a familiar action is repeated in a similar context, it is necessary only to retrieve and execute a posture plan for rapid, errorless performance. Skill learning is the result of the accumulation of posture plans.
  - The fewer the number of plans that have been encoded, the larger the effect that the addition of a single plan has. Consequently, the greatest improvement in performance occurs at the beginning of training, for a novice.
  - When performance is plotted as a function of the amount of practice, it is found that distributed practice results in a faster rate of improvement than massed practice.
  - Long-term retention has two components: an initial period, over which performance declines; and an asymptote, which may extend for the rest of the person's life, over which performance is stable and does not decline. Distributed practice results in a higher asymptote than massed practice.
- The joint instrumental/habit control of skilled action makes generalization to new situations possible. Anyone who has learned to write on paper with a pencil can write on a blackboard with chalk.

QUESTIONS

1. Name three everyday tasks that are performed autonomously and three everyday tasks that cannot be performed autonomously.
2. How long are motor skills remembered without practice? Why are they remembered so long?
3. When does forgetting of a motor skill occur?

FURTHER READING

Andersen, R. A., Snyder, L. H., Bradley, D. C., and Xing, J. (1997). Multimodal representation of space in the posterior parietal cortex and its use in planning movements. *Annual Review of Neuroscience*, 20, 303–30.

Cook, R., and Bird, G. (2013). Do mirror neurons really mirror and do they really code for action goals? *Cortex*, 49, 2944–5.

Keller, C. M., and Keller, J. D. (2008). *Cognition and Tool Use: The Blacksmith at Work*. New York: Cambridge University Press.

Latash, M. L. (2012). *Fundamentals of Motor Control*. New York: Academic Press.

Rosenbaum, D. A. (2009). *Human Motor Control*, 2nd edn. New York: Academic Press.

Vingerhoets, G. (2014). Contribution of the posterior parietal cortex in reaching, grasping, and using objects and tools. *Frontiers in Psychology*, 5, article 151.

4 Mental action: attention and consciousness

People like to look for things. From *Where's Waldo?* to countless video games, searching for visual targets is considered by many people to be fun. Paleontologists hunt for dinosaur bones, anthropologists hunt for human bones, and archeologists hunt for the debris of ancient civilizations. Quarterbacks search for the open receiver and point guards search for the open shooter. Merchants stock miles of shelves in giant stores with confidence that customers will be able to find what they look for. People can routinely detect and respond to task relevant targets so quickly that they can drive vehicles through crowded streets safely much more quickly than any person can walk or run. The general name for this ability to control perception so that what is important is seen or heard is attention.

Attention refers to voluntary actions that are used to control perception. Seeing and hearing are the consequence of looking and listening. The control of perception involves either of two tasks. One task is to select a single target for processing, such as when you listen to a single conversation during a party. The other task is to divide attention among several targets, such as when you drive a car down a crowded street. In this chapter we will see the following.

- Selective attention involves three stages: target specification, search, and target identification. The frontal cortex, where the target is specified, selects for the target by the inhibition of all perceptual input that is not target-related.
- Because the human information-processing system can plan and perform only one ad hoc voluntary response at a time, the bottleneck imposed by serial responding limits the number of targets that can be identified and responded to. Tasks that require independent ad hoc responses to multiple targets are called divided attention tasks. Divided attention inevitably results in missed targets and lower responses. Multitasking results in poorer performance than performing the tasks separately.
- Target selection is not entirely determined by top-down control from the prefrontal cortex and parietal cortex. Emotional arousal may also play a role. Emotional arousal increases the inhibition of distracters, narrowing perceptual processing to just the emotionally significant target. In other words, one cannot ignore something sufficiently threatening.

4.1 About attention

People do not passively see and hear but actively look and listen. The same neural systems that evolved to control motor movements control perception as well.

Definitions

Attention begins with action. As mentioned in Chapter 2, the fundamental unit of action is the same as the fundamental unit of memory: a voluntary action is made to a target in a context, producing a result. Similarly, the fundamental unit of attention is the same as the fundamental unit of action: a voluntary action is made to a target in a context, producing a result. The only difference between *action* and *attention* is that *action* implies movement but *attention* includes both the initiation of movements and mental actions that do not involve movement. Listening for the sound of a starting gun, refusing to move until "Simon says," and trying to remember the answer to a question are all voluntary mental actions that do not require motor movement.

The ability to make a voluntary response is the central subject matter of psychology, and there are many names for the experience of performing a voluntary action. When a target enters awareness, just as this sentence is in your awareness, you can do something in response to it. Saying that you are **aware** of something, that you are **conscious** of something, that you **experience** something, that you **perceive** something, and that you can make a **voluntary response** to something are all ways of describing the target of an action (Table 4.1).

While these various words tend to be used in different contexts and emphasize different aspects of experience, they do not name different related things; they are all names for the same thing. This can be proved by a test in which any two of the words are selected and we try to imagine whether one can be true of something without the other. For example, you cannot be aware of something without being conscious of it, so awareness and consciousness must be the same thing. We must therefore avoid the trap of "explaining" consciousness as your awareness of something. We cannot describe or explain something by simply giving it different names. Rather, we can begin to explain voluntary action by describing its consequences.

Consciousness: the consequence of a voluntary action to a target

There are important consequences of directing a voluntary response to a target (Table 4.2). First, you perceive the target, its context, your action, your intention, and the result of the action. These elements comprise your experience of that moment in time. Second, a representation of the episode may be encoded in your brain. The action is recorded by the habit system, which is procedural learning. A perceptual representation of the target is encoded in the brain by the instrumental system, which activates a familiar representation so that the target is perceived as familiar (Somers and Sheremata, 2013). One functional consequence is that you are aware of the entire representation, so that, when you hear the notes of a tune, you hear the tune rather than just single notes. Moreover, you see an entire face, rather than just a nose, an eye, or an ear (Chapter 5).

TABLE 4.1 Different ways of describing the target of voluntary action

Target is in...
Awareness
Consciousness
Experience
Perception

TABLE 4.2 Differences between targets and distracters

	Targets	Distracters
Part of present	Yes	No
Procedural learning	Yes	No
Declarative learning	Maybe	No

4.2 Selective attention: target specification, search, and identification

Voluntary action consists of two stages: planning and performance (Chapter 3). One advantage of having voluntary movements controlled by a two-stage process is that a planned action can be withheld until just the right moment for execution. For example, a projectionist plans the motion to turn on the second projector and then waits until the second splotch appears. When the plan and execution of an action are separated in time because the execution is deliberately delayed, we are aware of the plan and call it an **intention**. When the plan is immediately executed, as when you reach for your toothbrush, the planning stage is too brief to be noticed. However, it is always present.

Planning often begins with the retrieval of an episode. Even when movies were sent to movie theaters in boxes of fifteen-minute reels, the audience saw a movie lasting more than an hour without interruption. A projectionist used two projectors focused on the screen and switched reels and projectors as needed. The projectionist's behavior was directed by an episode in memory describing the end of every reel. The episode described two successive target splotches in the upper left-hand corner of a movie screen, the second one coinciding with the end of the reel, as well as the action of turning on the other projector when the second splotch appeared. The episode **specified** the target of the action – that is, the second splotch. So, the projectionist knew what the splotch looked like and when it would appear, which is why he or she was able to rapidly detect it and was prepared to initiate the action of turning on the other projector upon its appearance. The first stage of selective attention will therefore be called **target specification**.

Second, the location of a potential target is identified through the comparison of perceptual input with the target representation. This will be called **search**. The search process often involves eye movements under the control of the habit system. The search stage ends when the comparison produces a match **identifying** the target, which causes a response indicating that the target has been found within the instrumental system. As a result of the match, input from non-target locations is inhibited.

The gate model of the visual search system

Figure 4.1 shows the parts of the brain involved in controlling the identification of a target. These include some of the same parts of the brain that control motor action (compare Figure 4.1 with Figure 3.2, in Chapter 3), as well as the visual system (Chapter 6). When you choose to look here or there, the prefrontal cortex selects a target by inhibiting the processing of the visual field around it and moving your eyes towards it. The selection versus inhibition of visual information from different locations in the visual field may be conceptualized as the opening versus closing of gates along the visual pathway for sensory input from different locations in the visual field.

The visual scanning system uses a two-stage process of target identification. In the first stage, sensory information from multiple locations in the visual display is subjected to feature analysis to determine whether it contains a feature that identifies the target. For example, suppose that the task is to find a red "O" in a field of green "X"s and "O"s (Figure 4.2, top). The visual system organizes the sensory input into several distinct maps. One map contains all the locations where the input is red and one contains all the locations where a circle has been detected. In the second stage, the eyes move among the locations of one of these feature maps. At each location a more complete description of the input at that location is constructed, until the target is found. When a feature map contains many fewer locations than the entire field, selecting possible target locations on the basis of that feature correspondingly decreases the number of locations that must be

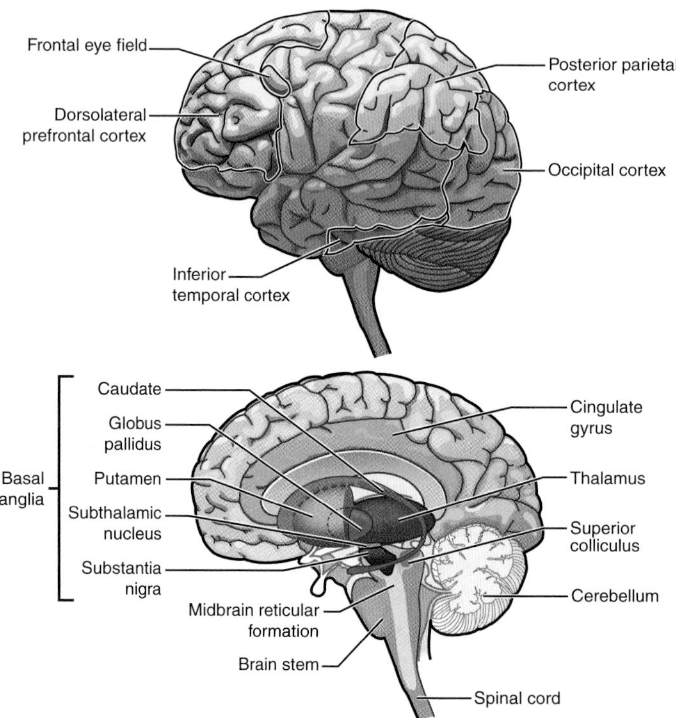

Figure 4.1 The top panel shows the cortical areas that direct visual target selection. The bottom panel shows the medial areas that carry out the selection and the reticular formation, which influences target selection by modulating arousal.

```
X O X O X O X O X O X O X O X
O X O X O X O X O X O X O X O
X O X O X O X O X O X O X O X
O X O X O X O X O X O X O X O
X O X O X O X O X O X O X O X
O X O X O X O X O X O X O X O
X O X O X O X O X O X O X O X
```

```
O X O X O X O X O X O X O X O
O X O X O X O X O X O X O X O
O X O X O X O X O X O X O X O
O X O X O X O X O X O X O X O
O X O X O X O X O O O X O X O
O X O X O X O X O X O X O X O
O X O X O X O X O X O X O X O
```

Figure 4.2 Selective attention to feature conjunction. Red circle can be effortlessly selected on the basis of color (top); but red circle requires effort to select on the basis of color and shape (bottom).

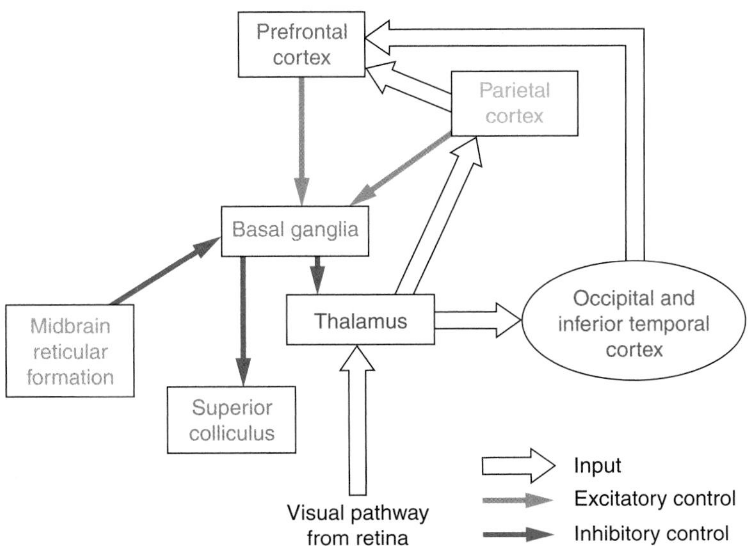

Figure 4.3 The basal ganglia control the thalamic gate and hence regulate the flow of information to the cortex.

examined to find the target. For example, in the display at the top of Figure 4.2 there is only a single location with a red feature, so this location will be searched and the red "O" will be found immediately.

The brain system for target selection is shown schematically in Figure 4.3. By opening one gate and closing the others, a particular input may be selected for further processing. At the top of the figure we have the prefrontal cortex, parietal cortex, and basal ganglia, components of the motor system (Chapter 3). Together, the prefrontal cortex and the posterior parietal cortex specify both the target and the target-selection feature that determines the locations that must be searched. They activate the basal ganglia, which, among their many functions involving the control of action, control

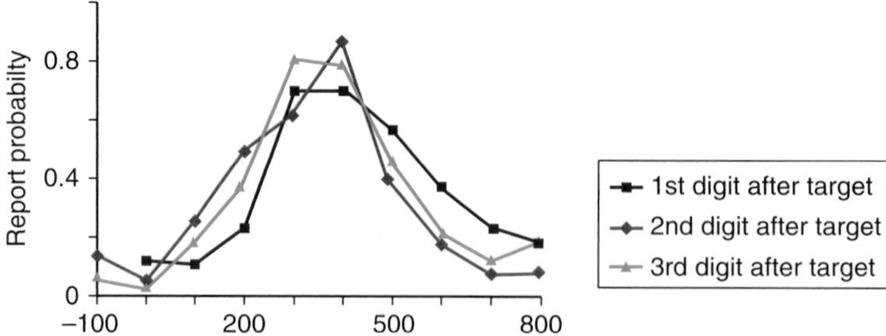

Figure 4.4 The probability of a report peaks at 400 milliseconds after the cue to switch attention (Weichselgartner & Sperling, 1987).

eye movements and the processing of visual information from specific locations. In turn, the basal ganglia signal the superior colliculus to compute the trajectory of the eye movement to each location. The basal ganglia also inhibit thalamic processing of input from all non-target locations and disinhibit thalamic processing of input from the target location.

To the center and right of Figure 4.3 we have the thalamus controlling the flow of sensory input from the retina to the visual processing areas in the cortex (Desimone and Duncan, 1995; Heilman, Watson, and Valenstein, 1993; Posner and Petersen, 1990). In the thalamus is a system of gates that distributes visual sensory input to the occipital cortex and inferior temporal cortex, and to the parietal cortex. The visual cortex is where the analysis of the visual input into simple features and patterns occurs and the inferior temporal cortex is where these patterns are compared with a representation of the visual target (Chapter 6). The posterior parietal cortex marks the spatial location of the visual target and passes this information to the prefrontal cortex.

At the bottom of Figure 4.3 are the superior colliculus and the reticular formation. The superior colliculus moves the eyes to fixate on a visual target (Fischer and Breitmeyer, 1987; Posner and Cohen, 1984). The basal ganglia direct the eyes to particular locations by inhibiting their movement to other locations. The reticular formation is part of the general arousal system, which exerts a general level of control over action through inhibition of the basal ganglia.

Notice that the processing of the input from a location leads rather than follows the eye movement to it. Complete information about the target is not obtained until after an eye movement has been made to fixate on it. Remington (1980) found that the thalamic shift to the new target occurs within 150 milliseconds of its initiation by the basal ganglia. Weichselgartner and Sperling (1987) confirmed this estimate in a behavioral study. They presented continuous streams of characters at the rate of 10 or 12.5 characters per second at two locations. Observers watched for the presence of the letter "C" in one location and then reported the first four digits seen in the adjacent location. In fact, the probability of reporting a digit depended on how long after the "C" it appeared. The first digits detected appeared 100 msec after the "C" (Figure 4.4). Processing of the target is not complete until about 300 msec after the initial processing of the location began. Weichselgartner and Sperling (1987) found that the probability of reporting a digit peaked at 300 to 400 msec after the "C" was shown (Figure 4.4).

4.3 Visual target detection

When a target is selected through the closing and opening of thalamic gates to sensory input, the process is called **early selection**. How the visual system organizes visual information will be described in Chapter 6. How that organization is used for target selection is described here.

Early selection during target search

The speed of target selection is determined by the perceptual organization of the visual field containing the target. When the target is distinctively different from its surroundings, it is found rapidly. Either a distinctive shape or a distinctive color may mark a target as distinct. For even three-month-old infants, a single plus sign will pop out from among six "L"s and a single "L" will pop out from among six plus signs, as shown in Figure 4.5 (Rovee-Collier, Hankins, and Bhatt, 1992). When the target has a unique shape or color, it **pops out** of the visual field. This is because the visual system organizes the sensory input so that a visual pathway transmits only the sensory input that contains the distinctive feature. Hence, when the target pops out, it reduces the number of locations that are searched to find the target to only the one (or few) containing its distinctive feature.

How quickly the pop-out occurs depends on how different the target is from the surrounding distracters and how far it is from the initial fixation point of the target search (Theeuwes, Kramer, and Atchley, 1999) and how many adjacent targets contain the target feature. Marking a target with a distinctive feature initiates its processing in less than 100 milliseconds (Bay and Wyble, 2014). For example, in Figure 4.6, the column of "O"s pops out. Figure 4.6 illustrates that adjacent locations that all contain the same feature result in rapid pop-out for the target they collectively form. Pop-out can also occur for separated locations with the same distinctive feature. When two of four briefly presented letters were cued by red bars, two simultaneous letters were recognized as accurately as one (Bay and Wyble, 2014).

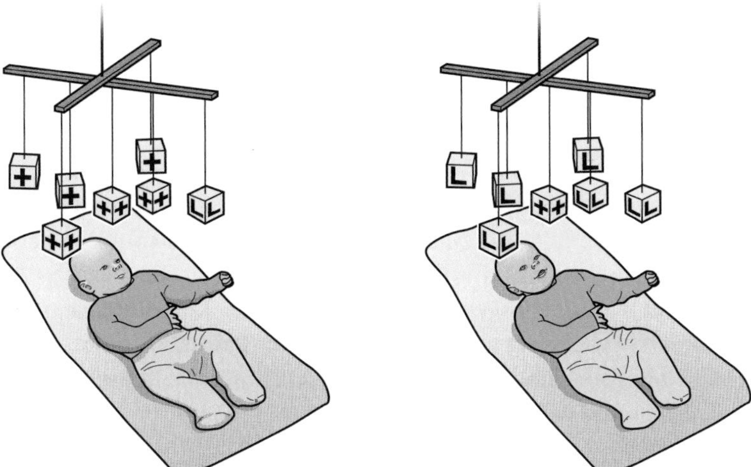

Figure 4.5 For even three-month old infants, a single plus sign will pop out from among six "L"s and a single "L" will pop out from among 6 plus signs (Rovee-Collier, Hankins, and Bhatt, 1992).

ZPORF
AQOSG
BROTH
CSOUI
DTOVI

Figure 4.6 Attention can be directed by perception to the vertical pattern by the "o"s. Attention can also be directed by memory to the horizontal letter string that forms the word "broth."

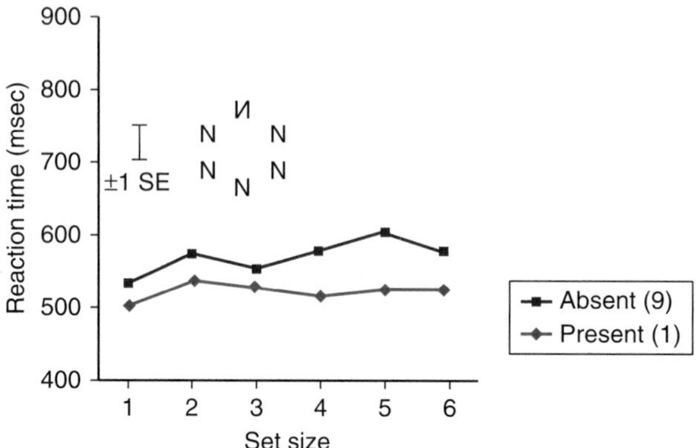

Figure 4.7 Reaction time does not vary as a function of number of display elements (set size) when searching for a novel target (mirror-image N) among familiar distracters (N). Observers responded whether 1- to 6-element displays contained only identical elements (target absent condition) or contained one different element (target present condition). The slopes for correct target-present and -absent regressions are shown in parentheses (Wang *et al*., 1994).

Memory also plays a role in early selection. The features used to restrict the locations searched for a target not only include innate features, such as color and orientation, but familiar patterns, such as the shapes of letters. Wang, Cavanaugh, and Green (1994) found that a mirror image "Z" pops out from a field of "Z"s and a mirror image "N" pops out from a field of "N"s, even though the only difference between the novel target and familiar texture is the orientation of a single diagonal line (Figure 4.7).

Rather than marking a target with a distinctive feature such as a color or shape that causes it to pop out from the background, its location can be indicated by an external visual (such as an arrow) or a verbal cue that is not part of the target itself. Of course, a person can move his or her eyes where directed, but this top-down selection is slower than the automatic bottom-up selection that is an effect of perceptual organization. Marking a target with a distinctive feature initiates its processing in less than 100 msec (Bay and Wyble, 2014). In contrast, marking the location of a target with an external cue does not initiate its processing in less than 300 msec (Müller and Rabbitt, 1989).

Late visual target selection

When a target does not have a unique feature and is not marked by an external cue, locations throughout the visual field must be fixated and the sensory input from each location compared with the target representation one at a time until it is found. This is a much slower process, dependent on the number of locations in the visual field containing targets (Duncan and Humphreys, 1992; Northdurft, 1993; Treisman and Gormican, 1988). This is called **late selection**. For example, in Figure 4.6, the word "BROTH" in the figure is an example of late selection. It can be found only by serially reading each letter until it is found.

Generally, late selection is required whenever the target is not distinguished by a unique visual feature such as its color or shape. A target with a unique conjunction of shape and color does not pop out from a display containing distracters that have either the same color or the same shape. It can be selected only by either serially examining each display item of the target color to determine its shape or by serially examining each display item of the target shape to determine its color. It therefore takes longer to find a conjunction of a letter and a color among colored letters (Duncan and Humphreys, 1992; Treisman, 1991; 1992) than to pick out a unique color or a unique letter that pops out. In the top panel of Figure 4.2, the visual system organizes all the green "X"s and circles into a single pattern called a **texture**, and the red circle into another pattern. The red circle thus pops out, and the time it takes to detect it is independent of the number of green "X"s and circles in the display. In the bottom panel of Figure 4.2, the visual system organizes the visual field into an "X" map, a circle map, a red map, and a green map. The single red circle is not the sole member of any of the maps, so it does not pop out from among either the circles or the red shapes. The red circle can be found only by comparing the representation of each element in either the circle or red map, one at a time, with a representation of a red circle in memory. As a result, the time to find the red circle is proportional to the number of display elements.

Attentional blink for simultaneous targets. Recall that, during the identification of a target, the processing of information at all non-target locations is inhibited. When an observer has to make independent responses simultaneously or near-simultaneously to targets, the voluntary response to one target inhibits the perception of other targets, so one target may be missed. The period during which the ability to detect a target is momentarily reduced by a voluntary response to another target is called a **refractory period**. Duncan (1980) devised a pair of tasks for measuring the refractory period. The failure to detect one target as the result of detecting another target is called an **attentional blink**.

One task for studying the attentional blink is the simultaneous, brief, presentation of two targets in two different locations. Duncan (1980) presented a cross consisting of four characters. An observer had to look for a digit target among letter distracters. In one experiment there were independent probabilities that a digit could appear in either the vertical or horizontal bar of the cross. Thus, a cross could contain zero-, one-, or two-digit targets. In the single response condition the observer had a single key and was told to press it whenever a cross contained at least one digit. In this condition, even though the observer had to press a key when he or she saw even a single digit, he or she was more likely to press it when the vertical and horizontal bars both contained a digit. Thus, the probability of pressing the key indicated that, when both the vertical bar and the horizontal bar contained a digit, both targets were seen. Furthermore, it did not matter whether the two bars of the cross were presented simultaneously or successively, half a second apart.

In the dual-response condition the observer had one key for the horizontal bar and another key for the vertical bar and had to press the key for the bar where the digit target appeared. Hence, zero, one, or two independent responses might be made to a display. In this condition the probability of detecting a digit target in one bar was negatively correlated with the probability of detecting a digit target in the other bar. Furthermore, performance was better when the bars were presented successively than when they were presented simultaneously. Since the results of the single-response condition demonstrated that the observer saw both targets when only one response was required, it must be that in the dual-response condition making a response to one target interfered with detecting the other.

Detection versus counting. Because counting requires an independent response to each target counted, Duncan (1980) found that reporting the number of targets increased the likelihood that one would be missed. Four characters were presented in a square display. In one condition either no or one target appeared and the observer had to press one of two keys to indicate which. In the other condition either one or two targets appeared and the observer had to press one of two keys to indicate which. Detection was more accurate in the zero or one condition, presumably because the detection of one target requires one response, but the detection of two targets requires two responses, because the observer must count to two. Moreover, in the one- or two-target condition, accuracy was much better when each side of the square was presented successively than when the entire square was presented simultaneously, presumably because successive presentation made it possible to make successive responses to each side of the square. Similarly, Duncan and Nimmo-Smith (1996) found a decrement for simultaneously presented targets when the target was selected early on the basis of a variety of features, including color, brightness, texture, length, location, and motion, generalizing the finding that more than one response cannot be made at a time regardless of how the target is defined.

Attentional blink for successive targets. Another task for studying the attentional blink is the simultaneous, brief, presentation of two targets in two different locations. Converging evidence that during the response to one target another target may be missed comes from target detection in the RSVP task. Broadbent and Broadbent (1987) used the RSVP method to present words at the rate of eighty milliseconds per word (about twelve words per second). The target was either a word in capital letters or an animal name. When two targets were presented within half a second of each other, the probability of reporting the second target was significantly reduced. Furthermore, the likelihood of missing the second target was greater when the first target was detected than when it was missed, so the probability of detecting both targets was very low.

Illusory conjunctions. Another consequence of late selection for a briefly presented target is an illusory conjunction between a target feature and a non-target feature. Recall that target detection is a two-stage process: first a single target feature is detected, and then a complete representation of the target is identified by comparison with memory representations. When a sequence of visual patterns occurs one after the other in the same location at a rate of twenty per second, there is sufficient time to detect a single target feature but not enough time to assemble the other features appearing with it into a complete target representation.

Lawrence (1971) flashed successive words at observers at rates of twenty words a second so that each word was available for processing for fifty milliseconds before it was replaced by its successor. All the words but one were in lower case, and the observer had to report the upper-case word. However, after case detection, when the processing of information from the target location was disinhibited, there were representations of several words presented in the temporal window just before and after the target upper-case word that were available for identification. Furthermore, these representations did not include case information (Adams, 1979). Consequently, **illusory conjunctions** between the case of one word and the identity of another word frequently resulted. The error rate was 42 percent for a presentation rate of twenty words per second, and 72 percent of the errors were the reporting of lower-case words that were also presented. Of these errors, 69 percent of the time a word following the upper-case word was reported and 31 percent of the time a word preceding the upper-case word was reported. Lawrence's task is called a **rapid serial visual presentation (RSVP)** task.

Using the RSVP technique, Broadbent and his colleagues (Gathercole and Broadbent, 1984; McLean, Broadbent, and Broadbent, 1982) demonstrated illusory conjunctions between digits and their colors, and Intraub (1985) demonstrated illusory conjunctions between pictures and the kinds of frames around them. In each case a feature was sometimes perceived as part of a distracter either preceding or following the target. Using a similar technique, Treisman and Schmidt (1982) presented colored letters and created illusory conjunctions between a letter's shape and color for spatially adjacent colored letters that were presented simultaneously. For example, if a display contained a red "B" next to a black "R," an observer might see a black "B."

Botella *et al.* (2011) used the RSVP method to show that an attentional blink and an illusory conjunction can both occur in the same refractory period. Participants had to identify two letters in target colors in a multicolored letter sequence (Figure 4.8, top). Figure 4.8 (middle) shows the probability of detecting the second target as a function of the number of intervening letters between the first and second target. The second target is most often missed when there is one intervening letter between it and the first target. Botella *et al.* reasoned that towards the end of the refractory period an observer would have time to detect and report some features, and so illusory conjunctions would result. Figure 4.8 (bottom) shows that illusory conjunctions between the target color and a non-target letter were most often reported towards the end of the refractory period, when there were four intervening letters between the first and second target.

Practice and visual target search

Recall that a reverse "N" or a reverse "Z" pops out from among the familiar orientations of the letters. As the result of practice with familiar shapes such as letters and numbers, maps of familiar shapes are constructed when the visual field is organized. This potential organization is realized when an observer repeatedly searches for one kind of target, such as letters, among another kind of target, such as numbers (Schneider and Shiffrin, 1977; Shiffrin and Schneider, 1977). When unpracticed observers searched for a letter among numbers, the results were as shown in Figure 4.9. The time to find a letter among digits was proportional to the number of distracters in the display, because each display element was compared with memory one at a time until the target was found. However, as the result of practice, searching for a letter was associated with the inhibition of numbers, hence the inhibition of the number texture. After fourteen days of practicing searching for a letter among digits (during

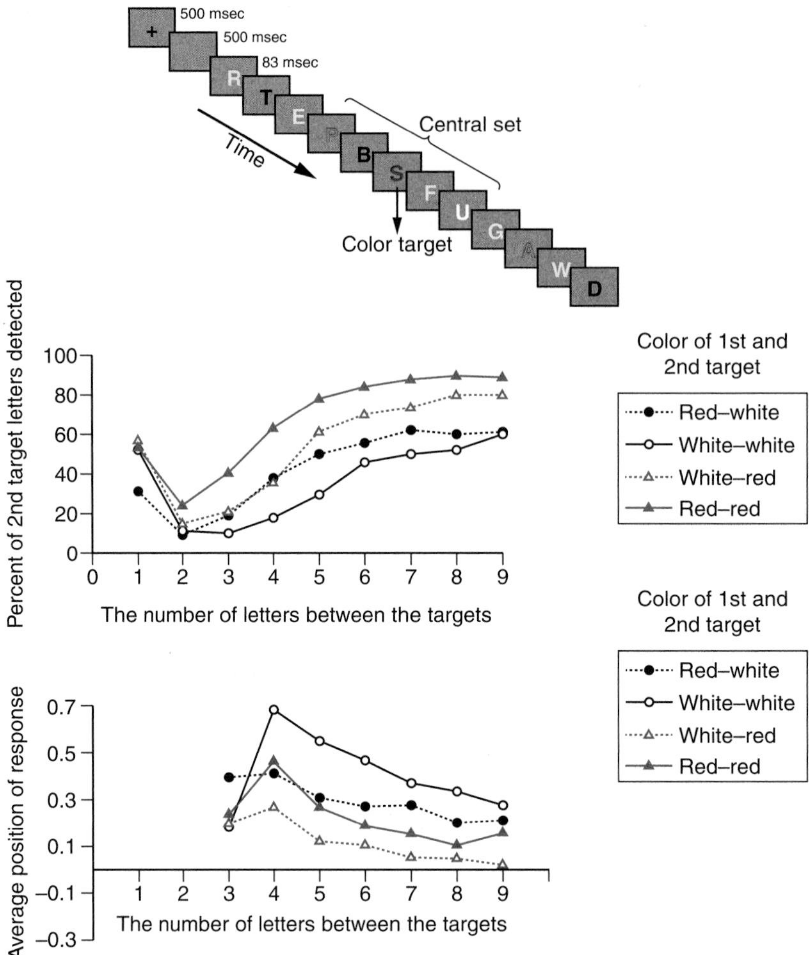

Figure 4.8 The task is to detect the letter in the target color in an RSVP of letters (top). The probability of detecting a second target letter is a function of the number of letters between the targets (middle). The average position response is the position of the letter reported as the second target. If the second target were always reported correctly then this value would be zero. The probability of an illusory correlation between a target color and letter peaks at a lag of 4 (bottom) (Botella *et al.*, 2011).

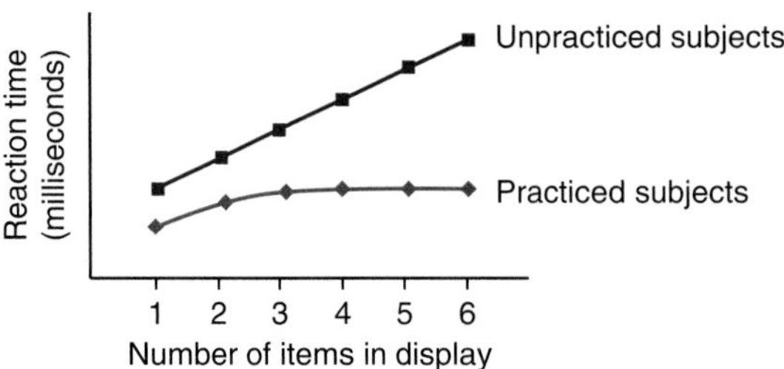

Figure 4.9 Performance on an item recognition task for one or more items from a fixed set as a function of display size (Schneider and Shiffrin, 1977; Shiffrin and Schneider, 1977).

which over 4,000 searches were conducted), the detection of a combination of distinctive features at a location rapidly resulted in inhibition if they indicated a number and further processing if they indicated a letter. Furthermore, multiple locations in the visual field were checked simultaneously for distinctive features. The time to detect a letter target was therefore no longer linearly related to the number of display items when the distracters were letters (Figure 4.9). So, combinations of orientation features that defined particular characters as letters or numbers, such as a horizontal line meeting a top-right to bottom-left diagonal for a "7," and a circle intersecting top-right to bottom-left diagonal for a "Q," were used by the visual system to sort them into numbers or letters for inhibition or further processing.

Furthermore, as the result of practice, a set of features rather than a single feature was compared with each of several locations in the visual field at the same time. When an unpracticed observer searched for a "Q" or a "T," because more than one distinctive feature had to be checked at each location, it took longer to search for any one of a set of two or more targets than for only a single one, indicating that each location had to be serially checked first for one feature and then for the other. However, after an observer practiced finding any one of a small set of targets, it took no longer to search for any one of the set than for a single member. In other words, a practiced observer can find either a "Q" or "T" as quickly as when looking for just a "Q" or just a "T" (Neisser, 1963; Schneider and Shiffrin, 1977; Shiffrin and Schneider, 1977).

There was a downside to practice in visual search. When Shiffrin and Schneider (1977) reversed the task, practicing searching for letters among digits made it difficult for the students to search for digits among letters. The now automatic inhibition of digit features and disinhibition of letter features could not be immediately reversed. The students found that they could not ignore the familiar letters; the former letter targets kept intruding on their awareness when they tried to search for the digits.

Long-term improvement in visual target search. During the first months of life, features such as color and shape determine pop out (Bahrick and Lickliter, 2014), making early selection possible. Subsequently, as the infant practices visual search as it looks for things in familiar environments as part of daily life, late selection in familiar environments improves. Performance on visual search tasks improves all through childhood and peaks somewhere between the ages of twenty and thirty. Lane (1980) measured the amount of task-relevant and task-irrelevant information remembered after the completion of a selective-attention task to measure what was attended to during the task. For children, the memory of targets and distracters was positively correlated. This result implies that the children were not selectively identifying targets and inhibiting distracters but, rather, were indiscriminately identifying every input they fixed on. In contrast, for college students, the memory for targets versus distracters was negatively correlated, implying that target identification inhibited the processing of distracters. High school and college students remembered fewer distracters than elementary school children (Druker and Hagen, 1969; Hagen, Meacham, and Mesibov, 1970; Wagner, 1974).

Inattention blindness. As mentioned above, when searching for a target, children still see some distracters. However, by college age, when a target is detected, observers see only a single target, not the details of the background. Consequently, what observers see is a consequence of what they are looking for. Experiments using realistic materials confirmed the narrowness of perception. People counting the number of passes during a basketball game failed to notice either a woman with an umbrella or a gorilla strolling across the court in the middle of play. Simons and Chabris (1999) found that more than a third of the observers keeping track of the number of bounce versus aerial passes failed to notice the intruder in plain view. Inattention blindness does not only afflict naive observers engaged in an unfamiliar task. It also occurs for expert searchers who have spent years honing their ability to detect small abnormalities in specific types of images. Twenty-four radiologists performed a familiar lung nodule detection task. A gorilla, forty-eight times the size of the average nodule, was inserted in the last X-ray that was presented. The gorilla was not seen by 83 percent of the radiologists. Eye tracking revealed that the majority of those who missed the gorilla looked directly at its location (Drew, Võ, and Wolfe, 2013).

Vigilance

When targets requiring late selection are infrequent, another difficulty arises. Life includes a variety of late-selection tasks in which the environment must be monitored for an extended period of time. Such a task, called a **vigilance task**, is the assignment of a sentry, lookout, or watchman. During World War II the vigilance task required of sonar operators stimulated interest in the problem. A small blip on a sonar screen could indicate a school of fish, while a larger blip could be a ship. The operator's task is to alert the rest of the crew if a larger blip is seen. When distracters are sufficiently similar to the target, so that they are rejected only after comparison with the target representation, the target representation is disrupted after a few minutes and the probability of detecting the target is reduced. Therefore, when the similarity among targets and distracters is high, performance deteriorates over time. The seminal study was reported by Mackworth (1948). How long a time passes before the decrement in performance becomes noticeable depends on a host of task variables, environmental variables, and subject variables (Mackie, 1977; Stroh, 1971) that influence the degree of processing of a target. When targets are rare and similar distracters are common, a decrement occurs within ten minutes of the task's onset (Jerison, 1977; Mackworth, 1964). Vigilance is important in a variety of services, including security, quality control, and traffic control. So, eliminating the vigilance decrement has practical value. One obvious way is to provide breaks in the task. However, each successive break beyond the first has a smaller effect on the decline in performance. Ross, Russell, and Helton (2014) found that, when one-minute breaks were inserted twenty and thirty minutes into a forty-minute task, only the first break improved performance.

4.4 Auditory target detection

A parallel auditory system for target specification, search, and identification operates along with the visual system. During auditory target identification, the prefrontal cortex and parietal cortex jointly regulate the processing of auditory input in the superior temporal cortex through the basal ganglia–thalamic pathway by inhibiting the processing of auditory distracters while an auditory target is being processed. Knight and his colleagues (Knight, Scabini, and Woods, 1989) found evidence of the inhibition by making a recording of the electrical activity (an electroencephalogram: **EEG**) of the **auditory** (area of the superior temporal) **cortex** in both healthy individuals and individuals with damage to the prefrontal cortex. When clicks were presented, the electrical activity in the *auditory cortex* to the clicking sounds was *greater* in individuals with *prefrontal cortical* damage than in healthy individuals. The increase in electrical activity in the auditory cortex when the prefrontal cortex was damaged suggested that, in healthy individuals, the prefrontal cortex normally inhibits its activity. Thus, when the prefrontal cortex was damaged, activity in the auditory cortex increased.

To examine the effect of prefrontal activity on target selection, electrical activity from both the left and right auditory cortex was recorded in a study in which listeners heard a sequence of clicks in both ears at the same time. The listener was told either to attend to the clicks in the right ear or to attend to the clicks in the left ear. As was mentioned in Chapter 2, and will be considered in more detail in Chapter 7, the right auditory cortex processes sounds located on the left, and the left auditory cortex processes sounds located on the right. Consequently, the right auditory cortex *initially* processed the clicks in the left ear, and vice versa. For healthy listeners, the electrical activity was greater in the auditory cortex that initially received input from the attended ear than in the auditory cortex receiving input from the ignored ear. When input to the right ear was the target, the processing of input to the left ear was inhibited, and vice versa.

For individuals with damage to the right or left prefrontal cortex, the different levels of EEG activity indicated that, while the right hemisphere processes auditory input only from the left side of space, the left hemisphere ultimately controlled auditory input from both the right and left sides of space. Damage to the right prefrontal cortex eliminated the difference in EEG activity between the right and left ear for left ear targets but did not affect the difference from right ear targets. This result indicates that the right prefrontal cortex controls the processing of auditory input only from the left side of space. In contrast, damage to the left prefrontal cortex reduced but did not eliminate the difference in EEG activity for right ear and left ear targets alike. This result indicates that the right prefrontal cortex responds to auditory input from both the left and right sides of space (Knight *et al.*, 1981; Knight, Scabini, and Woods, 1989). As mentioned above, the prefrontal cortex does not control auditory selection alone. Similar results were obtained when the inferior parietal cortex was damaged (Woods, Knight, and Scabini, 1983).

Early selection for pitch

The auditory system can search for a single target in a specific location or a single target with a distinctive pitch, so that it pops out, producing early selection. In a famous experiment, Treisman and Riley (1969) demonstrated that target detection based on pitch was independent of its location. They presented one spoken message to each ear of the listener. In this case, both messages were lists of digits that also included an occasional letter spoken in a different voice from the digits. The listeners had to shadow one of the messages, ensuring attention to that location. In addition, the listeners were told that, when they heard a letter in either ear, they should stop shadowing at once and tap their desk with a ruler. The listeners, then, had to selectively attend both to the digits presented in one ear and, at the same time, to all the letters presented to either ear, which they could do by attending to the distinctive pitch of the voice the letters were spoken in. In fact, Triesman and Riley's results showed that nearly all the letters presented to both ears were detected. Therefore, a listener can selectively attend to sounds distinguished by their pitch even when he or she is also attending to sounds distinguished by their location. So, there is **early selection** for pitch.

Besides pitch, there is not much auditory processing beyond the target location. The identification of a target or targets at one location is accompanied by inhibition of the sensory input, other than pitch, at other locations. In a famous experiment, Cherry had listeners wear earphones while one spoken message was presented to the right ear and another spoken message was presented to the left ear (Cherry, 1953; Wood and Cowan, 1995). Listeners had to repeat everything they heard in the right ear. This is called **shadowing**. Its purpose was to make certain listeners were selectively attending to the target message in the right ear and to provide a measure of when listening shifted to the left, which produced a shadowing error. The input in the left ear always began and ended with normal English spoken in a male voice. However, the middle portion of the left ear's input either remained the same or changed to English spoken in a higher-pitched female voice, to reversed male speech (that is, a segment of tape-recorded speech played backwards), or to a single tone. People rarely remembered any word or phrase heard in the left ear, and only a shadowing error for the speech in the right ear indicated that they had briefly switched to listening to the left ear message. Furthermore, although all listeners knew that the ignored input was speech, some listeners were unable to definitely identify it as English. Listeners who briefly listened to the left ear remembered the reversed speech as having something queer about it, but it was thought to have been normal speech by others. Only the change of voice from male to female or the introduction of a tone was almost always noticed. Moreover, after four minutes of practice shadowing the right ear, switches to the left ear decreased. Selection on the basis of location was highly effective, therefore. Everything in the target message was perceived but very little of the distracter input was perceived.

Late selection in audition

When an auditory target is not distinguished by its pitch or location, and so does not pop out from the background sounds, each sound at a different location in the environment must be serially compared with the target representation. This is a slower process, dependent on the number of distinct sounds at different locations and the similarity among them. Selective listening becomes difficult when the inputs are similar in pitch and location (Treisman, 1964). Recall that Treisman and Riley (1969) presented lists of digits that also included an occasional letter to each ear of a listener. The listener had to shadow the list in one ear and detect all the letters. When the letters were spoken in a different voice from the digits, they popped out and were detected. However, when the letters were spoken in the same voice as the digits, they no longer popped out, so each spoken character had to be categorized as a digit or letter by matching it with its representation in memory. When every character presented in either ear had to be compared with memory and identified, the comparison process was overwhelmed, and some targets were missed. Thus, late selection was not perfect in Treisman and Riley's (1969) task, as about 75 percent of the letters presented in the attended ear and only 33 percent presented in the unattended ear were detected.

Moray *et al.* (1976) found an attentional blink for briefly presented tones. A listener had to detect a target tone of a particular pitch or loudness. The target tone always occurred in one of two locations. The listener had to press one key if the target was heard in one location and the other key when the target was heard in the other location. In addition, when target tones were presented simultaneously in both locations the listener was required to press both keys. When both tones occurred simultaneously the probability of detecting a tone in one location was reduced.

Auditory target identification has the same two stages as visual target identification: first, a feature unique to the target is detected, and, second, the entire target is identified. When the identification system is overwhelmed by too many briefly present items, so there is more than one target representation following feature detection, auditory illusory conjunctions are observed for pitch and location (Cutting, 1976; Efron and Yund, 1974) just as visual illusory conjunctions are observed for shape and color. Furthermore, when a click was used as an external cue for a visual target, an illusory conjunction was found between auditory and visual features. When a visual target digit was signaled by an auditory click, distracters that both preceded and followed the target were erroneously reported, indicating an illusory conjunction between the click and the visual presentation of the digit (Weichselgartner and Sperling, 1987).

As was the case for visual late selection, the ability to selectively listen to an auditory target increases as its familiarity increases (Poltrock, Lansman, and Hunt, 1982). However, again, the same practice that makes a specific message, such as a familiar song, easier to hear in the presence of other sounds also makes it more difficult to ignore (Johnston, 1978).

4.5 Hypnosis

The basic function of selective attention is to make looking and listening possible – that is, to interact with the world. However, some individuals are extremely adept at inhibiting all other processing when responding to a target. The ability to concentrate on a target can have other purposes besides following a conversation. A hypnotic trance is not something that one person, the hypnotist, induces in the other but, instead, a selectivity of attention that some people are able to voluntarily attain. People develop no special abilities under hypnosis that they do not have when they are not hypnotized (Barber, 1969; Orne, 1959). Rather, hypnotizable individuals are highly susceptible to suggestion (Kirsch and Braffman, 2001). A hypnotizable individual will be compliant with a hypnotist's requests whether or not the individual is told he or she is undergoing hypnosis (Orne, 1966).

In a test of hypnotic susceptibility, a person is given a set of suggestions (external cues), such as that his or her arm is growing heavy, his or her eyelids are glued shut, or there is a fly buzzing about. Notice that these targets may be the perception of an internal state or a memory. The more suggestions the person translates into a perceptual experience, the more hypnotically susceptible the person is said to be. There are three standardized tests of hypnotic susceptibility. The Stanford Hypnotic Susceptibility Scale (Weitzenhoffer and Hilgard, 1959; 1962) and the Barber Suggestibility Scale (Barber and Glass, 1962) must be administered to individuals. The Harvard Group Scale of Hypnotic Susceptibility (Shor and Orne, 1962) may be administered to groups. Perhaps 15 percent of all people respond to nearly all the test items and hence are highly susceptible to hypnosis.

What distinguishes the hypnotic state is the kind of perceptual and cognitive experiences the hypnotized individual is capable of avoiding (Orne, 1977). A hypnotized individual may not feel pain from an input that would cause an unhypnotized individual to feel pain (Hilgard and Hilgard, 1975). In addition, as described in the next chapter, readers cannot avoid reading words when identifying the color of the ink they are printed in. However, hypnotized individuals can inhibit reading in this task (Raz *et al.*, 2002).

4.6 Distributing voluntary actions among tasks

Multiple target detection is a part of everyday life. When someone drives a car, traffic signals, traffic signs, pedestrians, and other vehicles are all potential targets. Furthermore, different targets may require different responses, including speeding up, slowing down, or stopping. When targets requiring different responses may appear at more than one location, and more than one target may appear at the same time, the task presents the challenges of monitoring more than one possible target location and preparing more than one voluntary response. Divided attention tasks are challenging for two reasons. First, only one voluntary action may be made at a time (Chapter 3). Second, as implied by the description of selective attention above, ad hoc voluntary action inhibits all task-irrelevant perceptual processing.

Visual dominance: cross-modal inhibition

The inhibition associated with a voluntary response does not occur across modalities. A response to a visual target does not disrupt an auditory target, and vice versa. Eijkman and Vendrik (1965) and Moore and Massaro (1973) found little or no decrement in people's accuracy in detecting a simultaneous tone and light pair in comparison with their accuracy in detecting only a single target. Gescheider, Sager, and Ruffolo (1975) found a similar result when using tones and brief vibrations as inputs.

However, even though the simultaneous auditory and visual targets are both detected, they may not be perceived as having occurred simultaneously. For example, when a light and a tone are presented simultaneously, the light is likely to be detected first (Colavita, 1974; Egeth and Sager, 1977). This phenomenon is called **visual dominance** (Posner, Nissen, and Klein, 1976). Tactual targets dominate over auditory targets in the same way that visual targets do (Gescheider, Sager, and Ruffolo, 1975). When required to make two separate voluntary responses to two separate inputs in different modalities, most people give priority to the visual input. When people are given instructions stressing that they should attend to the auditory input, the difference in the time it takes them to detect the visual and auditory targets is virtually eliminated (Egeth and Sager, 1977). The misperception of simultaneous visual and auditory targets has actually been known for centuries. Eighteenth-century astronomers used the ticks of a metronome to time the transits of stars they were observing. It was they who first noticed and recorded the fact that simultaneously occurring visual and auditory targets (a star crossing and a tick) were not perceived as having occurred simultaneously. This observation was confirmed by Wilhelm Wundt, one of the first experimental psychologists, and in 1908 it appeared in a textbook (Titchener, 1908) as the "law of prior entry."

Target specification and working memory

Voluntary action can specify and maintain a complicated target representation. For example, you can follow the direction to make a left at the third traffic signal. You typically maintain the representation of the direction through **verbal rehearsal** – that is, you silently tell yourself three lights, now two lights, etc. Verbal rehearsal is commonly used to retain information briefly. Conrad (1964) found that even printed letters were remembered verbally. However, this was a choice, not a constraint. Kroll *et al.* (1970) found that, when verbalization of the letters was impossible, they were remembered visually. The rehearsal of a complicated target representation is inaccurately called **working memory**. Working memory refers to target specification through the voluntary action of rehearsal. It is not the name of a special kind of memory.

Just as the effect of verbal rehearsal on target specification is inaccurately called **verbal working memory**, the effect of a repeated sequence of responses to visual targets is called **visual working memory**. Since you can perform only one ad hoc voluntary action at a time, the voluntary actions of working memory necessarily reduce the kinds of ad hoc voluntary actions that may be made during target search and identification. Recall that a response to a target inhibits the perception of other targets in the same perceptual modality but not the perception of targets in another perceptual modality. This implies that, when a target must be specified and maintained through voluntary action, maintaining the target description will interfere with its detection but an external cue for the target in a different perceptual modality will not interfere with its detection. Brooks (1968) confirmed this prediction.

Brooks asked students to form either a visual image (for example, a block letter H) or an auditory image of a simple sentence. For the H, the students had to determine which corners were convex as they navigated around a mental image of the H. For the sentence, they had to report whether or not each word was a noun. The students responded either manually, by pointing to either a "Y" or an "N" (for "Yes" or "No") on a page for each corner or word, or vocally by saying "Yes" or "No" for each corner or word. The students responded more rapidly vocally than manually for the visual imagery task but more rapidly manually than vocally for the linguistic task. Presumably, forming the visual image of the H interfered with visual control of the manual response, and forming the auditory image of the sentence interfered with the construction of the vocal response. This pattern of results is called **selective interference**, because forming an image selectively interferes with perception or production in the same modality. For example, as just mentioned, forming a visual image interferes with the scanning of a visual display.

Cross-modal multitasking

Because a response to a target in one perceptual modality does not prevent the detection of a target in another modality when two tasks involving different modalities do not require two independent but simultaneous responses, after sufficient practice, some or all of the participants can perform both tasks together as quickly and accurately as either one alone. Schumacher *et al.* (2001) performed an experiment to investigate the conditions under which dual-task performance was equivalent to single-task performance. They combined an auditory-verbal task with a visual-manual task. In their first experiment the auditory-verbal task was to say "One," "Two," or "Three" in response to a low, medium, or high tone, respectively. The visual-manual task was to respond with the index, middle, or ring finger to the visual targets "O–," "–O–," and "–O," respectively. Half a second after a warning signal, an auditory, a visual, or both kinds of targets were presented. Hence, the instant when at least one target would appear was perfectly predicted by the warning signal.

The results of the experiment are shown in Table 4.3. As can be seen, when the participants were novices their responses were slower and less accurate when two targets appeared (a dual task) than when only one appeared (a single task). However, after practice, the responses were equally fast whether one or two targets appeared, though still slightly more accurate for a single target. How were the practiced participants able to make two responses

TABLE 4.3 The effect of practice on reaction time (and percentage error) for tasks that have different completion times

Task	Trial type	Novice	Practiced
Auditory-visual	Dual-task	725 (6.5)	456 (5.4)
	Single-task	655 (5.3)	447 (3.3)
Visual-manual	Dual-task	352 (2.4)	283 (5.6)
	Single-task	338 (1.3)	282 (2.7)

Source: Schumacher *et al.* (2001).

TABLE 4.4 The effect of practice on reaction time (and percentage error) for tasks that have similar completion times

Task	Trial type	Novice	Practiced
Auditory-visual	Dual-task	1178 (6.8)	565 (4.8)
	Single-task	821 (2.9)	466 (4.1)
Visual-manual	Dual-task	965 (10.2)	522 (5.3)
	Single-task	778 (6.9)	466 (6.9)

Source: Schumacher *et al.* (2001).

as rapidly as one? Notice from the table that the auditory-verbal task took longer to perform than the visual-manual task. Suppose we assume that the decision processes for the auditory and visual targets could occur in parallel, but the planning and performance of the verbal and manual responses could be performed only sequentially. Practiced participants made use of the fact that the visual-manual task required a much shorter decision process than the auditory-verbal task, as indicated by the shorter response times for it. The practiced participants created a plan to execute the fast manual response first, and then the slower verbal response. By the time that the slower decision process for the verbal response was completed, the manual action (button press) had already been initiated. The first response therefore did not interfere with the second.

To test this explanation of the equally fast dual- and single-task responses, another experiment was performed in which the preparation times for the two responses were equalized by making the visual-manual decision more difficult. Again the auditory-verbal task was to say "One," "Two," or "Three" in response to a low, medium, or high tone, respectively. This time the visual-manual task was to respond with the ring, index, little, or middle finger to "O–––," "–O––," "––O–," and "–––O," respectively. Again, a warning signal occurred half a second before one or both targets were presented.

The results of the experiment are shown in Table 4.4. Notice that making the visual-manual task more difficult had the effect of slowing responses in both tasks. This time, practiced responses to two targets remained slower than responses to one target. These results are consistent with the results of other studies (Ruthruff, Pashler, and Klaassen, 2001) indicating that there is an absolute limit to performing one voluntary action at a time. When a task requires that two voluntary actions be performed at exactly the same time, one or the other must give way.

Task switching when responses conflict

It is possible for you to try to perform more than one task with conflicting responses at the same time by distributing your actions among all the tasks. However, attempting to do more than one task at a time and succeeding at doing them all well are two different things.

In a seminal study, Jersild (1927) presented observers with two-digit numbers to which they had to either add or subtract a number to determine how quickly a person could switch from addition to subtraction and back again. Jersild presented his participants with columns of two-digit numbers. In one condition a participant had to add six to each number in the column. In a second condition the participant had to subtract three from each number in the column. In the third condition the participant had to alternately add six to the first number, subtract three from the second number, and so on. In order to determine the time to switch from addition to subtraction and back again, the average time to complete the first two homogeneous (all addition and all subtraction) conditions was subtracted from the time for the alternating condition. The difference was the time it took to repeatedly switch from addition to subtraction and back again. Jersild also performed an otherwise identical experiment in which a participant had to add seventeen or subtract thirteen from each digit. The more difficult computations produced a longer switching time.

Spector and Biederman (1976) proposed that switching time reflected the time required to retrieve from memory the plan for performing the next task. They reasoned that if switching time were the time to retrieve a representation from memory then a cue for that representation would reduce retrieval, hence switching, time. They repeated Jersild's experiment with an easier addition task. This time participants had to add three or subtract three from each digit. Again, performance was slower in the alternating condition. In another alternating condition, "+3" or "–3" was printed next to each number in the column, indicating which operation had to be performed. These redundant visual cues reduced switching time, confirming the retrieval hypothesis. Subsequently, other studies found evidence consistent with the retrieval hypothesis. Rogers and Monsell (1995) alternated runs of two or more trials before switching tasks. If switching time represents the time to retrieve the task representation on a "switch" trial, then response time should increase only for the first trial in a run of same-task trials. This is what Rogers and Monsell found.

The study of multitasking in this modern world has taken on new urgency because electronic devices entice many users to multitask in situations in which it is unproductive or even dangerous. Carrying on a conversation on an interesting topic demands enough attention to interfere with braking to a light that has changed from green to red while driving (Strayer and Johnston, 2001).

The cellphone is a serious threat to life because of the inattention blindness it induces for everything other than the conversation on the cellphone. Conversation impairs not just target detection but target memory as well. As a consequence, it impairs performance on any task in which you must keep track of what you are doing or in which you must remember what has occurred (such as listening in class). Strayer and Drews (2007) examined the effects of hands-free cellphone conversations on simulated driving. Even when participants looked directly at objects in the driving environment, they were less likely to create a durable memory of those objects if they were conversing on a cellphone. This pattern was obtained for objects of both high and low relevance, suggesting that very little semantic analysis of the objects occurred. In-vehicle conversations did not interfere with driving as much as cellphone conversations did, because drivers were better able to synchronize the demands of driving with in-vehicle conversations than with cellphone conversations.

Even when cellphone use is not life-threatening there remains the possibility of severe disruption of daily life. People now routinely multitask between a cellphone activity and some other activity while in class, at a business meeting, or a social situation. The results of the cross-modal multitasking and task-switching studies described above provide evidence that multitasking between a cellphone and anything else causes slower, poorer performance on both tasks compared with performing the tasks one at a time. On the other hand, perhaps the human brain is sufficiently flexible that infants born with a cellphone in hand will learn to multitask efficiently. So far, the results are not encouraging. Ophir, Nass, and Wagner (2009) compared the multitask performance of those Stanford University students who reported both extensive multitasking experience and that they were good at it with the performance of Stanford students who reported being less adept at multitasking and doing it less often. The experienced multitaskers who reported being good at it actually did more poorly than the students who multitasked less. Thus, there is no evidence that practice improves performance on multitasking, though it may make multitaskers less aware of how poorly they do it.

4.7 Alerting and arousal

When you are reading this book you are not aware of extraneous auditory, tactual, temperature, and visual inputs. It is normally quite satisfactory not to be aware of such inputs, since they are usually not very important. In fact, these extraneous signals receive so little attention that we are tempted to believe that they are not processed at all. However, the complete failure to process such inputs could have disastrous consequences. For example, if you were not processing the temperature, and the room suddenly became very hot, you might be trapped in a fire. If sounds were being totally ignored, then an explosion would bring no response. It would also be inconvenient if you did not hear your name when addressed unexpectedly. In order to survive, you must be able to detect and respond rapidly to unexpected changes in the environment. Fortunately, a variety of unconditioned responses to unconditioned stimuli (Chapter 1) serve the function of alerting humans to important distracters. Reflexes that rapidly withdraw the body from harmful inputs also provide alerts that direct the perceptual system so that the input may be perceived and the reflexive response followed by a voluntary response if necessary. If you unexpectedly prick your finger, a flexor reflex not only pulls your hand back but also sends an alerting signal to the brain, so that you will perceive your hand's location and the injury.

Startle reflexes to intense stimuli such as loud noises and sharp changes in brightness generate responses, such as turning the head and eyes towards the stimulus, that make it a perceptual target, hence the target of a voluntary response. The various startle reflexes in the (superior and inferior) colliculus generally do not occur independently of each other but are modulated by control pathways extending downward from the amygdala to the colliculus. These top-down pathways control the likelihood that a stimulus will evoke a response by inhibiting (or disinhibiting) the response. As the result of this top-down control, the various reflexes tend to occur together and form an **orienting response** to the intense stimulus or stimuli eliciting them. Orienting responses have several components, including pupil dilation, contraction of the blood vessels in the limbs, dilation of the blood vessels in the head, and changes in the galvanic skin response and the electrical activity of the brain. As mentioned, some of these responses make the stimulus the target of further perceptual processing. The remaining responses prepare the body for whatever action may be directed towards that target. Recall that a response may be either a motor response or the release of a hormone. Collectively, the variety of responses are said to **arouse** the individual or to increase the individual's arousal level. Differential stimuli result in orienting responses composed of different reflexes. Different orienting responses are perceived as fear, anger, disgust, hunger, sexual arousal, or surprise.

Emotional arousal

The emotional arousal system provides a more primitive alternative to the cognitive system of voluntary action for directing actions to targets and performing responses to them. Unlike the motor system, which provides a general system for performing any action in response to any target, the emotional system generates specific behaviors to specific targets. The four "F"s of emotion-determined behaviors are fear, fighting, feeding, and sexual activity. Voluntary action and emotional arousal sometimes compete and sometimes cooperate in the production of responses.

The amygdala is the structure in the brain that modulates the orienting responses elicited by alerting stimuli for fear, anger, and disgust (LeDoux, 1993). The amygdala is a key structure in the conditioning of fear to novel stimuli. More generally, the amygdala modulates the likelihood that a stimulus will elicit an avoidance response on the basis of the context in which the stimulus occurs. So, the same scream or grotesque image that may frighten you when alone in a strange place may only mildly excite you in an amusement park funhouse or on television. Figure 4.10 shows schematically the principal brain circuits containing the amygdala. The amygdala is at the center of a network comprised of six principal pathways. Two pathways, from the thalamus and perceptual processing areas of the cortex, direct input to the amygdala. Through its anatomical connections, the amygdala is influenced by simple features, whole objects, the context in which the objects occur, the semantic properties of objects, images and memories of objects, and the like. It may be influenced by a present, imagined, or remembered target. Four pathways from the amygdala, to the hypothalamus and colliculus, to the basal ganglia, and to the hippocampus, make it possible for the amygdala to regulate reflexes, voluntary responses, and memory, respectively. The input and output pathways may be partitioned into two input-output circuits: a low road, providing a rapid, reflexive response to a simple stimulus; and a high road, providing a slower, voluntary response to a perceptual target.

Low road. A pathway from the thalamus directly to the amygdala sends visual input to the amygdala without being first transmitted to the cortex. In contemporary mammals this

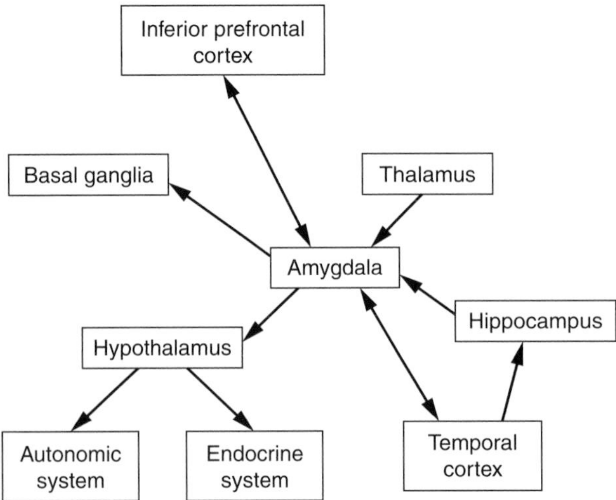

Figure 4.10 The amygdala is at the center of several circuits that generate fear, anger, and disgust.

pathway functions as an early warning system, allowing the amygdala to be activated by simple stimulus features. In response, through the pathway to the hypothalamus, the amygdala initiates a response appropriate to the stimulus. The hypothalamus initiates endocrine and autonomic responses associated with emotional arousal. Pathways to the forebrain and hypothalamic areas are also involved in the control of hormones released by the pituitary gland.

High road. In humans the emotional and cognitive memory systems operate together. Pathways for representations of visual and auditory targets proceed forwards to the prefrontal cortex and then downwards to the amygdala. Through the combined effects of the low road and high road, the emotional arousal influences the voluntary action directed towards the target. The influence of emotion on action is first demonstrated by the Kluver–Bucy syndrome. This is a complex set of behavioral changes brought about by damage to the amygdala in primates (Kluver and Bucy, 1937; Weiskrantz, 1956). Following such lesions, animals lose their fear of previously threatening stimuli, attempt to copulate with members of another species, and attempt to eat a variety of things that normal primates find unattractive (such as feces and rocks).

Easterbrook's hypothesis. A high level of emotional arousal prepares an individual to do one thing: flee, fight, feed, etc. Easterbrook (1959) proposed that, as arousal increases, the inhibition of non-target processing associated with voluntary action increases. Consequently, as arousal increases from low to moderate levels, the inhibition of distracters increases. Consequently, performance is less likely to be disrupted by the processing of distracters. However, as arousal further increases from moderate to high levels, further increases in inhibition increase the refractory period between voluntary actions. Consequently, the number of voluntary responses to task-relevant targets is reduced. Consequently, performance is disrupted because of an inability to process all the targets.

The distribution of attention is usually tested with an experimental paradigm in which a primary task and secondary task are performed concurrently. If increasing arousal restricts the distribution of attention, then as arousal increases there should be more processing of the primary task and less processing of the secondary task, resulting in better performance on the primary task and poorer performance on the secondary task. Most of the experiments that have examined the effect of arousal have used either electric shock or noise to increase it. Easterbrook (1959) reviewed a large number of studies that found that an increase in arousal either improved performance on the primary task or impaired performance on the secondary task. An updated review by Eysenck (1982) found that, in seven out of ten further studies using electric shock and eight out of fourteen studies using noise, performance on the secondary task deteriorated. Moreover, in five of the fourteen studies in which noise was used to increase arousal, performance on the primary task improved.

Although the entire point of a fear response is to facilitate escape behavior by narrowing processing to escape-relevant targets, fear can sometimes result in a paralyzing narrowing of processing to the fear-producing target. Consequently, fear can make a dangerous situation even more dangerous by causing paralysis rather than escape. Baddeley (1972) found that this explained the difference between diver performance in the open sea and pressure chamber simulations. The degree of danger was a crucial variable affecting performance. Baddeley was stimulated to review findings on people's performance in dangerous environments, including deep-sea divers, soldiers in combat, army parachutists, and soldiers subjected to extremely realistic, simulated, life-threatening emergencies (see also Weltman, Smith, and Egstrom, 1971). He found that a dangerous situation tends to produce a high level of arousal – that is, fear – thus reducing target detection and decreasing task performance. Just at the moment that correct performance becomes essential, it is impaired. This leads to the tragedy of an individual in a car stalled on railroad tracks unable to figure out how to open the door while the train approaches.

Another task relevant to Easterbrook's (1959) hypothesis is the vigilance task. Recall that, in a vigilance task, interference from the distracters degrades the target's representation. Any factor that increases arousal delays the onset of the performance decrement by reducing the number of distracters processed. Arousing factors include noise, paying monetary rewards (Bergum and Lehr, 1964), and telling participants that the task is a selection task for a high-paying job (Nachreiner, 1977).

Social behavior. The amygdala responds to complex, socially relevant stimuli (LeDoux, 1993). For social creatures, the emotional system plays an important role in regulating their social behavior. Camras (1977) observed that the display of distress cues (a sad facial expression) resulted in the termination of aggression in four- to seven-year-olds. Blair (1995) suggested that, for humans, the perception of distress (that is, a sad facial expression, the sight and sound of tears) makes it hard to stay angry with someone who is upset.

Task difficulty and distraction

The probability of an orienting response depends on more than the intensity of the distracter. Whether a distracter causes an alert depends in part on the working memory demands of the task. If an individual is maintaining the target through verbal rehearsal then other perceptual processing is inhibited, so there is little chance for a distracter to stimulate a response and alert him. As a result, a very difficult task, requiring immediate, serial, voluntary action to specify the target, is also more difficult to interrupt than an easier one. Kahneman (1973: 14, emphasis in original) put it this way:

> First try to mentally multiply 83 x 27. Having completed this task, imagine that you are going to be given four numbers, and that your life depends on your ability to retain them for ten seconds. The numbers are seven, two, five, nine. Having completed the second task, it may appear believable that, even to save one's life, one *cannot* work as hard in retaining four digits as one must work to complete a mental multiplication of two-digit numbers.

Mental multiplication requires repeated voluntary rehearsals to maintain the intermediate products as targets of subsequent action during the computation. This continuous voluntary activity reduces the likelihood that a distracter will stimulate a response and cause an alert.

An experiment by Zelniker (1971) demonstrated this principle. Zelniker used a very distracting input called **delayed auditory feedback** (DAF). People spoke into microphones while their own speech was played back to them through earphones two-thirds of a second later. DAF is so distracting that people usually stutter and stop when they try to speak under these conditions. Zelniker subjected people to DAF both while they were performing an easy task and while they were performing a difficult task. The easy task was to shadow a string of three numbers as they heard them; thus, no more than three numbers ever had to be rehearsed. The difficult task was to repeat one string of three numbers while at the same time listening for and remembering the next string of three numbers; six numbers therefore had to be rehearsed in two three-number sequences. The speech of the participants was much more filled with stutters and stops when they were performing the easy task than when they were performing the difficult one.

Sometimes the entire point of performing a sequence of voluntary actions is to block painful distracters. In the Lamaze method of natural childbirth, controlled breathing techniques are used to divert attention from the pain of labor. The breathing techniques serve other purposes as well, but pain reduction is the most important one. In using this method the woman takes over conscious control of what is usually unconscious activity: breathing. Because awareness is directed to the task of breathing in a carefully controlled way, attention is less likely to be diverted to the strong pain signals being generated by the contractions of labor.

4.8 Neglect

Neglect is a disorder in which an individual does not respond to sensory input from some locations in space, or even from some parts of his or her own body. An individual with severe neglect will be completely unaware of everything on one side of space, including his or her own body. Look at Figure 4.11. It shows six self-portraits of the artist Anton Raderscheidt. Portrait (a) was done before he had a stroke in his right hemisphere. Portrait (b) was the first one done after the stroke. Notice that in the first portrait after the stroke he completely neglected to draw the left side of his face. Yet when asked about it he saw nothing odd about it. As he recovered, the neglect lessened in subsequent portraits (b) through (e), and had disappeared by the time he painted portrait (f).

Figure 4.11 Self-portraits of the painter Anton Raderscheidt before and after he suffered a right-hemisphere stroke in October 1967: in 1965 (a); December 1967 (b); January 1968 (c); March 1968 (d); April 1968 (e); June 1968 (f) (Jung, 1980).

Since many different brain structures contribute to the voluntary control of action, damage to many different brain structures can cause some form of neglect, including damage to the parietal cortex, prefrontal cortex, basal ganglia, or thalamus. Depending on the location of the cortical damage, two major behavioral manifestations of the neglect syndrome are **sensory neglect** and **motor neglect** (Heilman, Watson, and Valenstein, 1993). **Sensory neglect** is the failure to respond to sensory inputs from a particular location. For example, a patient may be unaware of his wife standing to his left but be able to see and hear her when she steps to his right. **Motor neglect** is the failure to make responses with a particular portion of the body. For example, when asked to clap hands, a patient may uselessly lift only his or her right hand in the air.

Neglect to various portions of space has been observed (Rapcsak, Cimino, and Heilman, 1988; Shelton, Bowers, and Heilman, 1990), but usually neglect is observed for the left side of space. Recall that the different effects of damage to the left versus right prefrontal cortex indicate that areas in the right hemisphere integrate the representations of sounds from the left and right sides of space. Similarly, the different effects of damage to the left versus right hemisphere, especially the posterior parietal cortex, indicate that the integration of the visuospatial representations of the left and right sides of space usually takes place in the right parietal cortex, where there are many neurons that respond to inputs from both the left and right. The right parietal cortex contains maps encoding the locations of visual targets across the entire visual field (Somers and Sheremata, 2013). When only the left hemisphere is damaged the right parietal cortex is often able to immediately compensate, because its visual map includes the right side of the visual field, and so no neglect is observed. However, the left hemisphere responds only to inputs from the right and the visual map of the left parietal cortex includes only the right side of space. Hence, when only the right hemisphere is damaged, the left hemisphere cannot compensate and neglect is observed.

The neglect syndrome may be subcategorized into three different levels of severity. In its mildest form, a patient responds to a single input in any location but when inputs are presented simultaneously to more than one location the patient is unaware of the input in the neglected location. This phenomenon is an exaggeration of the normal non-response. The interval over which a normal individual may miss a second target is about half a second, and there is not an irreversible bias to miss targets in a particular location (Chapter 4). In the patient with neglect, briefly presented targets in the neglected location are always missed when another, competing target appears in another location.

In the moderate form of sensory or motor neglect, a patient will neglect inputs in a particular location even when there is no limitation on the time available to detect it. For example, if a person with left sensory neglect is asked to put a line through all the letter "A"s on a page placed in front of him or her, he or she may cross out only the "A"s on the right side. However, if the patient's attention is called to the "A"s on the left by someone pointing them out, he or she can momentarily respond appropriately to the neglected side.

The neglect extends to visual imagery. Bisiach *et al.* (1981) asked patients with right hemisphere lesions to describe a location familiar to them: the cathedral square in Milan. The patients first described the features of the square from the vantage point facing the cathedral from the opposite side of the square. Then the patients were asked to describe the square again, this time imagining their vantage point to be the central entrance to the cathedral looking out onto the square. The patients were able to correctly report more details on their right for both perspectives.

The severest form of the neglect disorder is coupled with **anosognosia.** The patient not only completely ignores some area of space but also denies having a deficit. Not only is the patient aware only of sights and sounds from one side of the environment, but the patient will wash, shave, and comb one side of his or her face and head, eat the food off one side of the plate, etc. For example, Raderscheidt thought the self-portrait shown in Figure 4.11 (b) looked perfectly normal. Patients with anosognosia cannot be talked out of it. If you point out to them that they cannot move their left arm, they will respond that there is nothing wrong with their left arm. If you challenge them to move it you get an evasive reply, such as "I am not going to do it just because you told me to." To provide a powerful alerting stimulus that would arouse the damaged hemisphere, Bisiach, Rusconi, and Vallar (1992) poured ice water in the left ear of a neglect patient. Cold water in the left ear causes the eyes to move to the left. Sure enough, for about a half-hour the patient became aware that half her body was paralyzed and that she perceived only part of visual space. Ramachandran repeated the experiment and wrote a vivid account of it (Ramachandran and Blakeslee, 1998: 145).

Before he administered the ice water, Ramachandran asked:

Mrs. M. how are you doing?
Fine.
Can you walk?
Sure.
Can you use your left hand?
Yes
Are they equally strong?
Yes.

After administering the ice water he again asked:

Can you use your arms?
No, my left arm is paralyzed.
Mrs. M., how long have you been paralyzed?
Oh, continuously, all these days.

This was an extraordinary remark, for it implies that even though she had been denying her paralysis each time I had seen her over these last few weeks, the memories of her failed attempts had been registering somewhere in her brain, yet access to them had been blocked.

Twelve hours later a student of mine visited her and asked,
Do you remember Dr. Ramachandran?
Oh, yes, he was that Indian doctor.
What did he ask you?
He asked me if I could use both my arms.
And what did you tell him?
I told him I was fine.

The effect of the cold water was therefore temporary. When the shock wore off the denial returned. Fortunately, as is dramatically apparent in the self-portraits shown in Figure 4.11, over a period of weeks spontaneous recovery from severe neglect is common.

SUMMARY

Mental action to control perceptual processing is the same as motor action except that it does not involve the movement of muscles. Any ad hoc voluntary action, whether involving a motor or non-motor response, is associated with the inhibition of all other processing not associated with the action. During the control of perceptual processing, the inhibition of processing not associated with the action is the entire point of the action. A perceptual target is selected by inhibiting the processing of distracters.

- The control of perception makes use of the same neural system that controls physical action, the prefrontal cortex, the parietal cortex, the basal ganglia, and the thalamus. Looking and listening

are the voluntary actions that determine perception. Perceptual control involves two kinds of tasks:
  - selective attention, in which a response must be directed to a single target in the presence of distracters; and
  - divided attention, in which responses must be directed to multiple targets that may be present at the same time.
- Selective attention involves three stages: target specification, search, and target identification. The prefrontal cortex, where the target is specified, selects for the target by inhibiting all perceptual input that is not target-related.
  - Early selection of the target occurs when the target is encoded as a distinct part of the perceptual representation, and so pops out without a search for it.
  - Late selection of the target occurs when it must be identified by comparing the perceptual representation to a specification of the target in memory.
- Because the human information-processing system can plan and perform only one ad hoc voluntary response at a time, the bottleneck imposed by serial responding limits the number of targets that can be identified and responded to in a divided attention task.
  - Tasks requiring divided attention inevitably involve missed targets when more than one occurs simultaneously within the same perceptual modality.
  - Cross-model divided attention is possible as long as only a single response at a time is required.
  - Multitasking inevitably results in poorer performance than if the tasks were performed separately.
- Target selection is not entirely determined by top-down control from the prefrontal cortex and parietal cortex. Bottom-up alerting and emotional arousal also play a role. Emotional arousal increases the inhibition of distracters, narrowing perceptual processing to just the target. In other words, one cannot ignore something sufficiently threatening.
- When both the intentional control of perception and the alerting system are damaged for a specific part of the perceptual field, the result is neglect of that area, so nothing in that location is perceived. Left field neglect is the most common form, because the left hemisphere processes information only from the right field and cannot compensate when the right hemisphere is damaged.

QUESTIONS

1 Describe a product package that would be easily found on a supermarket shelf.
2 Should people get better with practice playing a visual search game such as *I Spy* and *Where's Waldo?*?
3 Would talking on a cellphone while driving be safe if conducted through a hands-free Bluetooth device?
4 What is the effect of practice on multitasking? Why does it have this effect?
5 What mental task might you perform to block the pain of an injury?

FURTHER READING

Bahrick, L. E., and Lickliter, R. (2014). Learning to attend selectively: the dual role of intersensory redundancy. *Current Directions in Psychological Science*, 23, 414–20.

Roda, C. (ed.) (2014). *Human Attention in Digital Environments*. Cambridge University Press.

Simons, D. J., and Chabris, C. F. (1999). Gorillas in our midst: sustained inattentional blindness for dynamic events. *Perception*, 38, 1059–74.

Somers, D. C., and Sheremata, S. L. (2013). Attention maps in the brain. *WIREs Cognitive Science*, 4, 327–40.

Strayer, D. L., and Drews, F. A. (2007). Cell-phone-induced driver distraction. *Current Directions in Psychological Science*, 16, 128–31.

5 Serial learning, perceptual skills, and talent

Once upon a time I was a projectionist for a college film club. Each movie reel was a half-hour long and each projection booth had two projectors. About five seconds before the end of a reel a large colored splotch appeared in the upper right-hand corner of the screen, as a signal to the projectionist to be ready to turn on the second projector. This is easy to do, so the audience never notices that the reel has changed. Nor does the audience notice the splotch in the corner of the screen. However, for some years afterwards, whenever I sat in the audience, as a former projectionist I always noticed the splotch in the corner. There are two morals to this story. The first is that no one sees everything. The second is that sometimes it is a disadvantage to see too much, and an advantage to see only what is necessary.

The tendency to notice the splotch in the upper right-hand corner was the result of a visual scanning strategy encoded by the habit system. The habit system does not just encode actions. The habit system encodes *sequences* of actions, such as the sequence of actions to traverse a maze (Chapter 2). Performing a sequence of actions in the correct order is essential for performing the routine tasks that are part of daily life. The encoding of sequences of actions by the habit system makes possible such mundane skills as washing, dressing, and cooking. These are not merely motor skills, as described in Chapter 3, but perceptual–motor skills, requiring the identification of a sequence of targets. The age of the cellphone has increased the importance of order, as this is what defines phone numbers, passwords, etc. Therefore, the ability of the habit system to encode target sequences is an essential twenty-first-century cognitive ability.

The ability to encode a sequence of actions is called **serial learning**. In this chapter we will see the following.

- Serial learning is performed by the habit system, yet involves the encoding of the spatial location of responses.
- Serial learning is the basis of the encoding of the predictable spatial locations of the targets that make possible the rapid encoding of targets in familiar visual tasks such as reading. It is essential for the skillful navigation of daily life.
- Serial learning is also the basis of musical and artistic talent. These wonderful abilities should not be overlooked, because they make human life about more than mere survival. Because the habit system makes it possible to encode and effortlessly perform sequences of actions in endless variation, it makes possible sublime skills such as playing an instrument.

5.1 Serial learning

Serial learning is studied by having participants perform a serial reaction time task. A **serial reaction time (SRT) task** is a task in which a person repeatedly responds as rapidly as possible to one of a small set of targets. For example, suppose that your cellphone is your test device and each key may light up. Every time a key lights up you must press it. Each response triggers the presentation of the next target. For the first ten trials there is no way to know which target will appear next, but then, unbeknownst to you, the same ten-target sequence repeats itself over and over. In this situation, people generally do not notice that the same sequence is repeating itself. Nevertheless, each time the sequence repeats, the reaction time to respond to each target decreases. To prove that the decrease in reaction time is the result of the encoding of the repeated sequence, a novel sequence of targets is presented. Reaction times increase with this shift, indicating that the repeated sequence had been learned (procedurally), thereby speeding responses for that sequence. However, the procedural learning of the sequence does not have to be accompanied by declarative learning. As just mentioned, when the repeated sequence is longer than nine members and/or a participant is distracted by performing another task at the same time, there is little or no recognition or recall of the sequence. The participant has no awareness that he or she has been responding to a repeated sequence nor any ability to recognize the sequence (Nissen and Bullemer, 1987).

What sort of representation causes the faster response times to the sequence? One possibility is a representation of the target sequence. Another possibility is a representation of the response sequence. To compare these possibilities, Willingham, Nissen, and Bullemer (1989) recorded response times for three different kinds of repeated sequences. For one sequence, a sequence of targets was repeated in different locations, which determined the responses, meaning that there was a repeated sequence of targets, not a repeated sequence of responses. For another sequence, different targets were presented in a repeating sequence of locations determining the responses, which meant that there was not a repeated sequence of targets but, instead, a repeated sequence of responses. Performance was not faster in either sequence than for a third sequence, in which repetition of neither the target nor the response occurred, demonstrating that serial learning did not occur for either of these sequences. Serial learning cannot therefore be the result of learning the target sequence nor of learning the response sequence.

What, then, is learned in the serial reaction time task? The answer is supplied by the basic unit of mammalian memory, the episode. As described in Chapter 2, an episode consists of an action and its effect, along with the target and context of the action. Applying the episode representation to the serial learning task, the action would be the response that a participant made, and its effect would be the target that appeared next. Ziessler and Nattkemper (2001) performed an experiment whose results demonstrate that this was indeed the case. To demonstrate the causal role of response–target associations in serial learning, they performed an experiment to determine whether serial learning depended on target–target (TT), response–response (RR), or response–target (RT) (that is, response–effect) contingencies. If reaction time decreases every time a target sequence is repeated, the decrease in reaction time implies that the participant has encoded the contingencies between successive targets in the sequence. For example, in the first sequence shown in Figure 5.1 (top), a "W" is always followed by a "G," a "G" is always followed by an "N," etc. Because each target is always followed by only one other target, the sequence is designated as TT1. In contrast, in the second

W/S left middle (1)
F/X left index (2)
N/P right middle (3)
G/H right index (4)

RR1/TT1/RT2: W G N F S X P H W G N F S X P H W G N F S X P H W G N F S X P H ...
1 4 3 2 1 2 3 4 1 4 3 2 1 2 3 4 1 4 3 2 1 2 3 4 1 4 3 2 1 2 3 4

RR1/TT2/RT4: W G N F S X P H S H P X W F N G W G N F S X P H S H P X W F N G ...
1 4 3 2 1 2 3 4 1 4 3 2 1 2 3 4 1 4 3 2 1 2 3 4 1 4 3 2 1 2 3 4

RR1/TT4/ RT4: W G N F S X P H S H P H W F N G W H N X S F P G S G P F W X N H ...
1 4 3 2 1 2 3 4 1 4 3 2 1 2 3 4 1 4 3 2 1 2 3 4 1 4 3 2 1 2 3 4

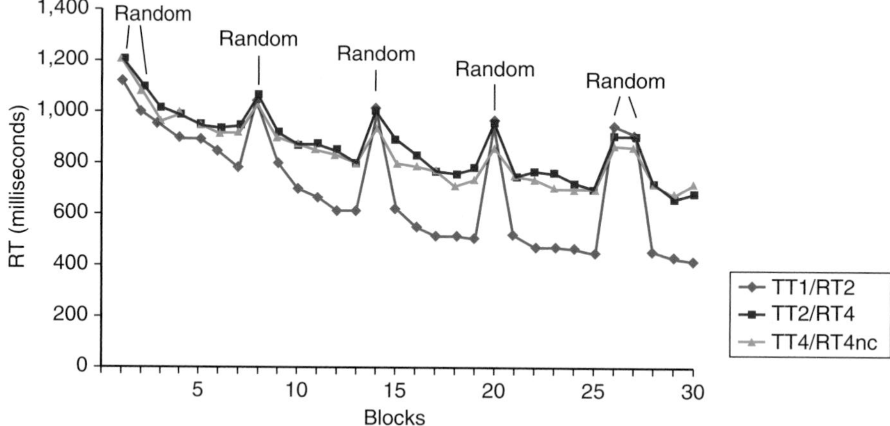

Figure 5.1 Three different sequences were used by Ziessler and Nattkemper (2001) to test what is learned in serial learning (top). The eight consonant targets and two finger responses (by key press) to each of them are shown at top. Below, the three target sequences and the sequences of responses to them are shown. For all three sequences each response is always followed by the same response (RR1). For the first, second, and third sequences, a target may be followed by one (TT1), two (TT2), or four different targets (TT4), respectively. For the first sequence, a response may be followed by one of two different targets (RT2) but for the second and third sequences a response may be followed by one of four different targets (RT4). Mean response time (RT) as a function of sequence type (bottom).

sequence shown in Figure 5.1 (top), each target is followed by one of two other targets, and so is designated as TT2. For example, "W" is followed by either a "G" or an "F." Since the second sequence is less predictive than the first of the target–target contingencies, learning the second sequence should result in a smaller reduction in reaction time than learning the first sequence.

Ziessler and Nattkemper (2001) constructed three different sequences that had different TT, RR, and RT contingencies. When they measured serial learning for all three sequences, they found that only the response–target contingencies predicted the relative reaction times for the three sequences. As shown in Figure 5.1 (top), for all three sequences, each response was followed by only one other response. Consequently, if response–response contingencies are learned, then the reaction time should be the same for all three sequences.

For the first sequence, each target was followed by only one other target in the sequence. For the second sequence, each target was followed by one of two other targets. For the third sequence, each target was followed by one of four other targets. Consequently, if target–target contingencies are what are learned, then the reaction time should be fastest for the first sequence, second fastest for the second sequence, and slowest for the third sequence.

For the first sequence, each response was followed by one of two different targets. For the second and third sequences, each response was followed by one of four different targets. Consequently, if response–target contingencies are what is learned, as predicted by the response–effect hypothesis, reaction time should be faster for the first sequence, with no difference between the second and third sequences. Figure 5.1 (bottom) shows that the results were consistent with the response–effect hypothesis. As shown in the figure, each repeated sequence was occasionally interrupted by a novel sequence, and the difference in reaction time between the repeated sequence and the novel sequence was the measure of learning. As shown in the figure, the first sequence was faster than the second and third sequences, between which there was no difference.

Spatial location plays a critical role in response–effect serial learning. Either the targets must be at different locations or the response keys must be at different locations. When this condition is satisfied, more than just the location of the target and/or response is encoded. Any perceptual information correlated with the location information is encoded as well. Any task-relevant perceptual information (including feedback from the response itself) on the one trial that predicts what will happen on the next trial will be encoded so that it comes to prime its consequent (Ziessler and Nattkemper, 2001). Hence, spatial memory appears to be the engine that organizes events into sequences and drives other kinds of learning (Deroost and Soetens, 2006). These include auditory stimuli (Hartman, Knopman, and Nissen, 1989; Hoffmann, Sebald, and Stöcker, 2001).

The fact that spatial location is important for serial learning suggests that the instrumental system plays a role. However, the fact that the learning occurs without conscious awareness or recognition of the sequence indicates that the response–effect representation is part of the habit system. This is confirmed by the effects of brain damage. Sequence learning is not impaired in patients with amnesia (Nissen and Bullemer, 1987; Nissen, Willingham, and Hartman, 1989; Reber and Squire, 1998). It is impaired in patients with moderate Parkinson's disease (Deroost *et al.*, 2006; Vandenbossche *et al.*, 2013), and in patients with Huntington's disease (Knopman and Nissen, 1991), which are both the result of damage to the basal ganglia. Hence, sequence learning is the result of a representation in the habit system.

To summarize, serial learning occurs because someone learns to perform a sequence of actions to distinct locations. The evidence that serial learning is the result of response–effect learning confirms the results of animal studies that the episode, which is a representation of an action, its target, its effect, and its context, is the fundamental unit of mammalian – including human – memory. That spatial location is necessary for serial learning confirms that the episode representation contains both habit (action) and instrumental (mental map) components. However, the autonomous non-declarative quality of the representation demonstrates that the component of the episode that causes serial learning is within the habit system.

5.2 Visual scanning as a skill

The search for a meaningless target in an unknown location has been a useful task for determining the limits of human visual search ability, as described in Chapter 4. However, with the possible exception of a child who hates chocolate on an Easter egg hunt, this task is not part of human experience. The visual targets that are part of everyday experience have predictable locations and a purpose. Consequently, serial learning improves target search in everyday life. Early in life, visual scanning becomes controlled by a collection of task-specific skills. Each visual scanning plan is adapted for its particular task or target, such as a face, a page of text, or moving traffic.

Perceptual skills make possible the rapid encoding of complicated visual patterns such as scenes and faces. They make possible the rapid encoding of information-rich narratives by listening and reading. They also make possible the reproduction of complicated visual patterns and temporal sequences through drawing and the playing of instruments. The area of highest visual acuity in the retina, the fovea, is too small to encode more than a small component in a single fixation. When fixated on the nose, sufficiently detailed information about the eyes, mouth, etc. encoded by the area of the retina outside the fovea, called the **parafovea**, is not encoded to distinguish one face from another in a single glance. However, in each case, the overall perceptual representation is comprised of predictable component targets in predictable locations, such as eyes, nose, mouth, etc. for faces. Hence, the repeated encoding of patterns and sequences results in the encoding of the response–effect sequences that result in efficient search for the components.

The visual search system

For you to obtain detailed information about the visual world it is necessary for your eyes to move to fixation points of high information in the visual field. Eye movements are controlled by the visual search system, which is a hierarchical system extending from the midbrain to the cortex.

At the lowest level of the system, it is important that an extraneous head movement does not blur the retinal image, in the way that moving a camera blurs the image in a photograph. Therefore, the vestibulo-ocular reflex (Chapter 1) keeps the eyes focused on a point during a fixation even when the head is turning (Brown and Deffenbacher, 1979). At the next level, the superior colliculus moves the eyes to areas of contrast, since these are usually areas of high information that are likely to mark the boundaries of objects and parts of objects. The superior colliculus contains the entire visual system for reptiles and birds but was reduced to only controlling eye movements in mammals when the ability to process patterns evolved in the cortex for mammals (Levinthal, 1983: 58).

Each eye movement is directed by information in the periphery of the visual field, so that, for example, when you read, your eyes are directed to fixate at the beginnings of words, rather than in between them. About three or four times a second your eyes move in unison, and fixate on the same new location in space (Yarbus, 1967; Henderson, 2003). These jumps are called **saccades**. A saccade takes anything from twenty milliseconds to 300 milliseconds. The duration of the saccade is directly proportional to the distance traveled (Becker, 1991). Both eyes fixate on a common point in space.

Figure 5.2 shows visual scanning of a face. The visual search tends to move to new rather than old locations. Theeuwes, Kramer, and Atchley (1998) found that, when observers

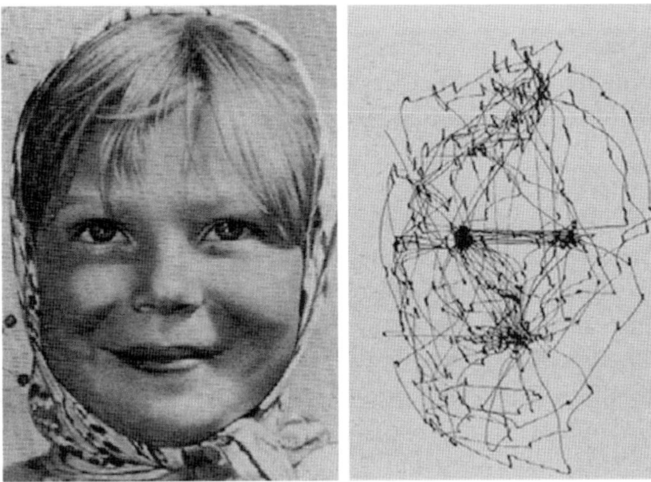

Figure 5.2 Eye movements: (a) picture observed; (b) record of eye movements made in continuous observation of picture (Yarbus, 1967).

search the visual field, they preferentially fixate on objects they have not seen beforehand, which means that the visual system is marking objects that it has already seen. On the other hand, fixations follow a coarse-to-fine pattern, so that the distance of successive saccades become shorter and the duration of successive fixations become longer so that informative areas are processed in more detail (Godwin, Reichle, and Menneer, 2014). In Figure 5.2 you can see that, when a face is examined, the eyes return repeatedly to specific, high-information parts, such as the eyes.

Control of eye movements is shared between the superior colliculus, responding to the visual input, with areas of the cortex, responding to the intentions of the observer. The superior colliculus is directed by signals from the basal ganglia, which in turn translate directions from the **frontal eye fields** and the **posterior parietal cortex** so that eye movements are made only to novel, task-relevant locations (Figure 4.1). At the highest level, the frontal eye fields may make use of nonvisual information, such as the expectations of the viewer, to direct the eyes to particular points. It is at this level that serial learning has its effect. For familiar targets, a representation of likely target locations directs eye movements. Although the expectations of the observer influence eye movements, they do not completely determine them. A startle reflex controlled by the superior colliculus (Chapter 1) can override the intentions of an observer. Even when an observer directed his or her eyes to a distinctly colored target, the eyes were likely to move in the direction of a new input suddenly appearing in the visual field (Godijn and Theeuwes, 2002; Theeuwes *et al.*, 1999).

Blind sight. The visual information used by the posterior parietal cortex to direct saccades is also used by the manipulation system (Chapter 3) to direct reaching, pointing, etc. This implies that healthy observers may exhibit the bizarre behavior called **blind sight**, in which they can physically indicate the locations of flashes that they have not seen. To test this possibility, Skavenski and Hansen (1978) asked observers to strike with a hammer in the dark at very briefly illuminated points presented during the observer's saccades. The observers claimed to be unable to see the targets, yet their hammer strikes were quite accurate. Furthermore, individuals rendered blind by lesions to the visual cortex that spare the posterior parietal cortex should have blind sight. Consistent with this prediction, Weiskrantz *et al.* (1974) described patients with lesions in the visual cortex who could accurately reach in space for targets that they said they could not see.

Initial development of visual scanning skill. In order for visual scanning to be effective, the entire visual field must be scanned. This skill develops early in life. At two months of age visual attention is focused on a narrow segment of the visual field. But by three months the infant begins to explore his or her world. This early development was demonstrated in a cleverly designed experiment by Rovee-Collier, Earley, and Stafford (1989), who trained two- and three-month-old infants to kick mobiles (this task will be described in detail in Chapter 8). Half the infants were shown a mobile composed of five identical blocks that each contained a different pattern on each of five sides. The other infants were shown a mobile composed of five different blocks that each contained one pattern on five sides. Both mobiles therefore contained five patterns, but in the same-side mobile each pattern could be seen on only one block, whereas in the different-side mobile each pattern could be seen on all the blocks. Infants were trained for two days and tested twenty-four hours later with either the same-side or the different-side mobile. If the infant recognized the mobile then he or she kicked to move it. Otherwise, the infant did not kick. The results confirmed that two-month-old infants scanned less of the visual field during each training session. The two-month-old infants failed to recognize the same-side mobile but did recognize the different-side mobile. Apparently, the two-month-old infants fixated on a single block each session, and if the fixation block differed from session to session they treated the mobile as novel. On the other hand, the three-month-old infants recognized both mobiles, indicating that they scanned the visual field containing all the different blocks during the training sessions.

Reading

One particular visual scanning skill that you are using now is reading. Reading involves the two distinct stages of visual target search described in Chapter 4. The first stage occurs when the word is to the right of the central fixation area, and so falls on the parafovea. During this stage some of the features of the initial letter cluster of the word are identified, and possible candidate words are retrieved from memory. The second stage occurs when the eyes fixate on the beginning of the word so that it is in the fixation area. During this stage a specific word is identified and integrated with the text. Unlike target search for targets in unknown locations, the location of each successive word is predictable. Moreover, through serial learning, the spelling patterns of words are encoded. So, for experienced readers, this memory-guided process is under the control of the habit system, hence autonomous with respect to the instrumental system (Chapter 3). Consequently, the inhibition of non-target locations plays an important role in reading. During a fixation you can see about three letters to the left and up to fourteen letters to the right of the fixation point. Letters further to the left are inhibited. No more than the three letters to the left and three letters to the right fall on the rod-dense fovea and are seen clearly. The remaining letters to the right fall on the parafovea, which encodes word length information as well as some feature information (McConkie and Rayner, 1975).

Saccades during reading take about thirty milliseconds (Kliegl, Nuthmann, and Engbert, 2006). The information encoded in the parafovea to program an eye movement to its next fixation point were revealed by synchronizing changes in the visual display with the movement of the eyes. In the altered-preview paradigm, a preview letter string appears on the screen in place of the target word (Rayner, 1975) that will ultimately be fixated. A sequence of three fixations is shown in Figure 5.3. The preview letter string is replaced with the correct target word only when its position is fixated. In the experimental conditions, some of the target word features are in the preview letter string to determine which features are encoded during the preview. For example, in Figure 5.3, to examine whether a reader is sensitive to word shape in the parafovea, letters in the preview have visually similar letters to the target. Reduced reading times demonstrate that, during the preview, skilled adult readers process information regarding the length, shape, orthography, and phonology of the target word prior to fixation (Rayner, 2009).

In the disappearing-text paradigm, each word literally disappears once it is fixated, but then reappears once the eyes move to another word within the sentence (Figure 5.4). This makes it possible to determine how long it takes to activate a fixated word's meaning. When each word disappeared sixty milliseconds after the onset of fixation on that word, there was very little disruption to the participants' eye movement behavior or reading comprehension (Rayner *et al.*, 2003).

During a fixation, the meaning of a familiar word is activated by the visual input of the word – that is, you do not have to sound a word out, or identify individual letters, in order for its meaning to be automatically activated. The meaning of the word is integrated with the meaning of the previous text, and the grammatical structure and meaning of the part of the sentence that has already been read predict what is likely to come next. As each word of a sentence is identified, possible completions of the sentence are generated. As each word is matched to a possible completion, it winnows the number of possible completions that remain in the comparison set. Consequently, although a fixated word's meaning is activated in about sixty milliseconds, the eyes linger on the fixation location until the meaning of the

```
This is an example of the| dansheug paradigm.
              *
This is an example of the| dansheug paradigm.
                         *
This is an example of the| boundary paradigm.
                               *
```

Figure 5.3 In the preview paradigm, a preview letter string appears on the screen in place of a target word that will ultimately be fixated. A sequence of three fixations is represented here, with the position of each fixation denoted by an asterisk. An invisible boundary (represented here by the vertical line) is placed in front of the target location, and the preview letter string is replaced with the correct target word during the first saccade that crosses the boundary. Reading times are fastest in a target-preview control condition, in which the preview and the target are identical, and reading times are slowest in a no-preview control condition, in which the preview (e.g. "xxxxxxxx") contains none of the features of the target word (Rayner, 1975).

This an example of the disappearing text paradigm.
*
This is example of the disappearing text paradigm.
*
This is an of the disappearing text paradigm.
*
This is an example of disappearing text paradigm.
*
This is an example of the text paradigm.
*

Figure 5.4 In the disappearing-text paradigm, each word literally disappears once it is fixated but then reappears once the eyes move to another word within the sentence. Here, the position of each fixation is denoted by an asterisk under the text (Rayner *et al.*, 2003).

word is integrated with the preceding part of the sentence and its completion is predicted. First, the frequency of a word has an effect on fixation durations even after the word has disappeared. Second, the more predictable a word is from the preceding passage, the less time is spent fixating on it (Ehrlich and Raynor, 1981). On average, you fixate on each word for about a quarter of a second, though this average is misleading because there is great variability in the length of each fixation. Figure 5.5 shows the record of the eyes of a person moving across a line of text. As the figure shows, most eye fixations last between 200 and 400 milliseconds, but a fixation can last from less than 100 milliseconds to more than a second (Just and Carpenter, 1980). Furthermore, because two words are being processed at the same time, the one at the fixation point and the next word to its right, the fixation time on a word is influenced by the word fixated before it and the word fixated after it (Kliegel, Nuthmann, and Engbert, 2006). Sometimes a mismatch between a predicted sequence and a fixated word results in a comprehension error. In this case, the left-to-right fixation pattern is briefly aborted. During reading, a small number of regressions also occur: the eyes move to the left and fixate on a word for a second time when the wrong representation was selected the first time. A college student makes about seventy-five forward fixations and fifteen regressions to read 100 words of text (Crowder, 1982: 9). A reading speed of about 300 words a minute is the upper bound on the speed of comprehension. (In comparison, you speak at no more than 120 words a minute.)

Masked priming. Converging evidence that as yet unseen visual targets to the right of the fixation point influence which word representations in memory are activated and which are inhibited comes from experiments on masked priming. These experiments do not involve eye movements. Rather, the observer fixates on a point at which two strings appear in rapid succession, a word and a meaningless sequence, such as a string of "X"s, which is called a **mask**. If the mask is presented for a quarter to a half of a second and the word is presented for about a twentieth of a second, only the mask is seen, and the word is said to be masked. If the mask occurs before the word it is called forward masking and if the mask occurs after

1 2 3 4 5 6 7 8 9 1 2 3
1566 267 400 83 267 617 767 450 450 400 616 517
Flywheels are one of the oldest mechanical devices known to man. Every internal combustion

5 4 6 7 8 9 10 11 12 13 14
684 250 317 617 1116 367 467 483 450 383 284
engine contains a small flywheel that converts the jerky motion of the pistons into the smooth

15 16 17 18 19 20 21
383 317 283 533 50 366 566
flow of energy that powers the drive shaft.

Figure 5.5 Eye fixations of college students reading scientific passages vary in duration. Gazes within each sentence are sequentially numbered above the fixated words, with the durations (in milliseconds) indicated below the sequence number (Carpenter and Just, 1980).

the word it is called backward masking. Even a masked word can still reduce the time to perceive a word that immediately follows it. When it does, it is called a **masked prime**. Just as in the dictionary, human lexical memory is organized by word **onset** (the initial vowel or consonant cluster of a word). A masked word primes the following word when it has the same initial consonant cluster (Forster and Davis, 1991; Grainger and Ferrand, 1996).

Other evidence for letter sequence representations comes from the effect of neighborhood. The neighborhood of a word is the set of words that differ from it by one letter; for example, *dig, dug, don,* and *dot* are the neighborhood of *dog*. When a word is part of a large neighborhood its neighbors are also primed and compete with it for recognition. Priming effects are therefore larger for hermit words without neighborhoods (Forster and Taft, 1994). In addition, there are priming effects on nonword targets such as *dag* (Perea and Rosa, 2000), so letter sequences can be primed as well as words.

Inverted text. If motor skill learning is the result of the accumulation of motor plans (Chapter 3) and reading is the result of the accumulation of letter, word, and sentence representations, then the relationship between practice and performance should be the same for both skills. That the relationship of practice to improvement in performance is the same for reading as for motor skill learning was established by a clever study by Kolers (1976). Over a semester, college students read 200 pages of text in which the typescript was inverted (Figure 5.6 (top)). The speed of performance for the perceptual skill of reading inverted text was a power function of the amount of practice, as shown in Figure 5.6 (bottom). Notice that the function is a straight line because the axes are log scales. At first the readers were extremely slow, as you might expect. The subjects took more than sixteen minutes to read their first page of inverted text, as compared with only 1.5 minutes for normal text. But, by the time they had finished 200 pages distributed over a semester, they were reading inverted text almost as quickly (1.6 minutes per page) as normal text. The students were retested a year later. Figure 5.6 (bottom) shows almost no decline, and the students continued to improve.

READING A YEAR LATER 555

Recognition seems so simple, direct, immediate. The skillful processing of information that must be involved is not itself apparent, forthe object seems familiar as soon as eye encounters it. in part, recognition seems so immediate because we spend most of our time in familiar surroundings, we work in the same rooms, see the same people, walk the same streets, live in the same houses for long periods of time. the perceptual information we receive each ordinary day isusually repetitious and redundant. we come to know the things we will encounter even before we encounter them. Put us on unfamiliar ground and we are much slower to realize what an object is, We hesitate, look several times, and make mistakes.

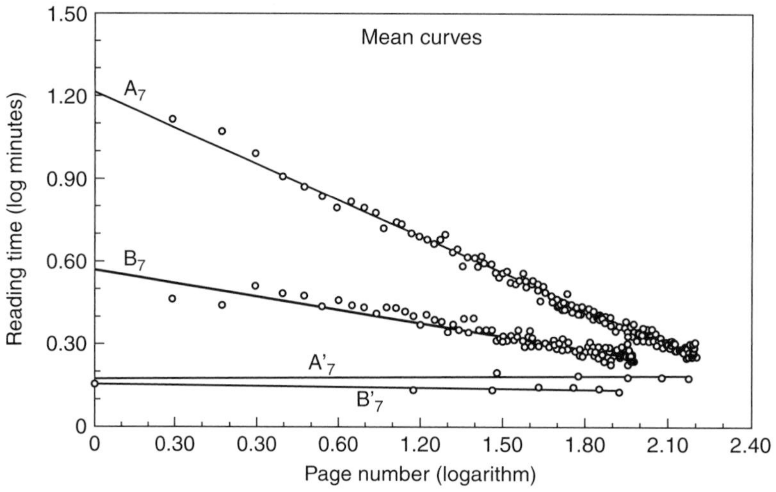

Figure 5.6 Over a semester, college students read 200 pages of text in which the typescript was inverted (top) (Kolers, 1976). The speed of performance for the perceptual skill of reading inverted text was a power function of amount of practice (bottom).

Furthermore, Figure 5.6 (bottom) shows that neither the normal nor the upside-down reading speed reached an asymptote. When the college students' reading speed for normal text was tested at times that were one year apart (A' versus B' in Figure 5.6 (bottom)), their reading speed was faster a year later. After all the pages they had read in their lives, they were still reading a little more quickly each year.

The Stroop effect. There is a small downside to an autonomous skill such as reading in which a verbal response is automatically generated to a printed word. If another task requires a different response to the word that conflicts with the automatic verbal response, the conflicting automatic response must be inhibited before the task-relevant voluntary action is made. The most famous example of such a situation is the Stroop task. Stroop (1935) showed people a list of color names that were printed in colored ink. Each color name was printed in a color different from the color it named. For example, the word *red* might be printed in blue ink and the word *blue* in green ink. Seventy college students had to read a second list printed in black ink. Stroop found little difference in the reading times for the two lists. Apparently, the students could largely ignore ink color while reading. However, students required an average of sixty-three seconds to identify colors on the color patch list but an average of 110 seconds to identify the ink colors on the list of color names. The students could not avoid reading the words when they tried to name their ink colors, and the conflict between the word and the ink color slowed down their responses. The conflict arises because there are two color names generated when the person tries to say aloud the name of the ink color of a printed word naming another color. One is the ink color, which is the correct response. The other is the word that is automatically read. Hence, if the person does not have to make a verbal response but, rather, indicate in some other way what color the ink is, the interference is greatly reduced (Flowers, Warner, and Polansky, 1979; McClain, 1983a; 1983b; Zakay and Glicksohn, 1985).

The interfering effect of reading words on another response to the words first appears when children learn to read, and peaks around the second or third year of primary school (Comalli, Wapner, and Werner, 1962; Schiller, 1966). It then slowly declines (Comalli, Wapner, and Werner, 1962; Wise, Sutton, and Gibbons, 1975) as the ability to selectively attend improves until at about sixty years of age, when it begins to rise again as the frontal lobes shrink and the ability to inhibit responses degrades (Comalli, Wapner, and Wener, 1962; Cohn, Dustman, and Bradford, 1984).

Response interference occurs in a wide variety of other tasks more or less similar to the original Stroop task. For example, interference occurs when a printed word is superimposed on a picture that a person is trying to name (Lupker, 1979; Smith and Magee, 1980). The magnitude of the interference increases with the relatedness of the word's meaning to the color (Klein, 1964) or picture (Lupker and Katz, 1981). Providing an incongruent name for an auditory input, such as calling a low tone "high," produces interference (Hamers and Lambert, 1972; Zakay and Glicksohn, 1985). In addition, naming the number of digits in a row of digits when the digit and row length are incongruent, as shown in Figure 5.7, produces interference (Windes, 1968). As an experiment, try to read aloud, as quickly as you can, the number of digits in each row of Figure 5.7. You will find it difficult to ignore the digits as you count them.

Since automatic word reading is itself the effect of practice, with practice a reader should be able to increase his or her speed on the Stroop task. In fact, Reisberg, Baron, and Kemler (1980) found that, with practice on the counting task shown in Figure 5.7, the digits counted interfered less and less with the report of the number of characters on each row. The effect was highly specific. Practice in ignoring the numbers "2" and "4" did not improve performance on rows containing the numbers "1" and "3" or the words "to" and "for." However, consistent with a **semantic** (that is, word meaning) locus, there was good transfer when the words "two" and "four" had to be ignored.

Negative priming. Dalrymple-Alford and Budayr (1966) identified a second reason color naming is slow in the Stroop effect besides the conflicting response from the word.

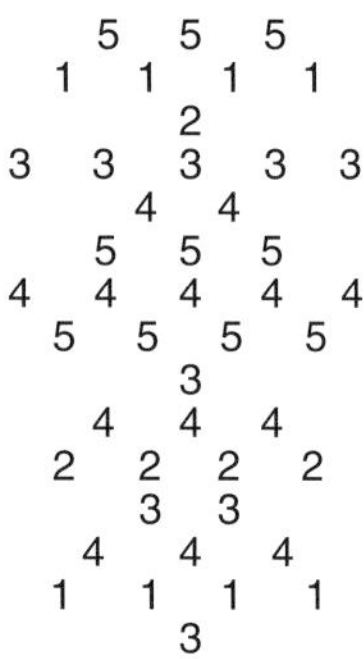

Figure 5.7 Stroop effect. Say aloud the number of characters in each row as fast as you can.

They compared the total color-naming time for a list of unrelated color words with that for a list in which each word named the ink color of the next word on the list; for example, "blue" written in red ink was followed by "yellow" in blue ink. Color naming was slower in the latter condition. Thus, there is a delay in executing a correct response that has previously been activated in a context in which it was incorrect. To state this effect more generally, ignoring an item, such as the word "blue," slowed a subsequent response – that is, saying the word "blue." In terms of the neural mechanism, inhibiting an action on one trial slowed its activation on the very next trial. This effect is called **negative priming**, which indicates that it is a short-term effect of the response to one target on the next (Grison and Strayer, 2001; Malley and Strayer, 1995; Strayer and Grison, 1999). Negative priming occurs during a task in which a response is sometimes correct and sometimes incorrect, so not only is it delayed by inhibition from the previous trial on which it was correct but it undergoes a verification check on the next trial on which it is correct (Neill and Joordens, 2002; Strayer, Drews, and Albert, 2002; Tipper, 2001).

Target identification in a changing world

Recognition of a complex target, whether a face, a scene, or a page of text, requires the integration of the images encoded at successive fixations into a single target representation. The visual search system aligns successive images within a common set of spatial coordinates to make their integration into a single representation possible. Eriksen and Collins (1967) demonstrated the existence of the temporal integration of distinct images. They prepared two random dot patterns, like those shown in the top panels of Figure 5.8, which formed a nonsense syllable when superimposed, as shown in the bottom panel of Figure 5.8. When each dot pattern was shown for six milliseconds with a 25 msec interval between them, observers saw the nonsense syllable 85 percent of the time (see also Brockmole, Wang, and Irwin, 2002). Hence, the visual system combined the information from two images that were encoded 25 msec apart.

The alignment and integration of successive images is not a particularly challenging task for static images, such as words on a page. However, when navigating the world, the changes in the successive images induced by the motion of the observer and by objects in the image make the task considerably more challenging. Not all successive visual images can or should be integrated. The visual attention system must sort between changes in successive images as the result of the motion of the observer and the successive fixation points of the eyes, changes that result from movement by an object in the object, and a change in a fixed

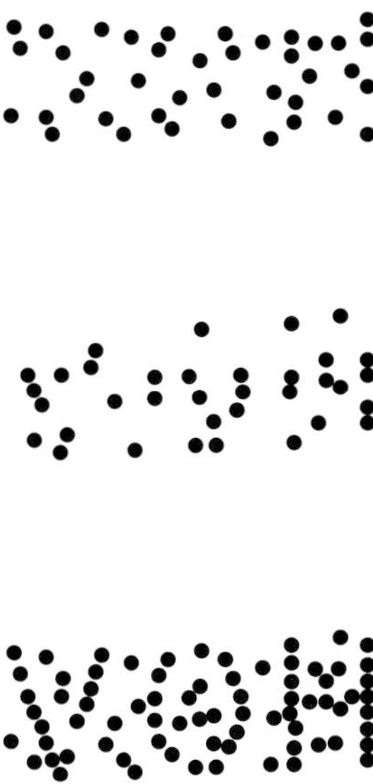

Figure 5.8 When superimposed, the upper two dot patterns result in the bottom pattern in which the syllable VOH can be read. When each dot pattern was shown for 6 milliseconds with a 25 millisecond interval between them, observers saw the nonsense syllable 85 percent of the time (Eriksen and Collins, 1967).

location, such as a blinking light. To reduce the computational load, the visual system concentrates on whether there is continuity or difference between successive images of the target. The comparison of the two target images can have one of two outcomes, therefore: either a disparity is detected and the images are encoded as separate target representations, or a disparity is not detected and the images are encoded as the same target.

Disparity detection. During the normal comparison of successive images at successive fixations, there is a brief blurring of the image during the saccade. A change that occurs in the visual field during the saccade may not be noticed when the two images are integrated into a single representation. To investigate the integration process, Currie *et al.* (2000) introduced changes in a scene that an observer was scanning. During an observer's saccade to a target object, one of three kinds of changes occurred in the scene: the location of just the background was displaced (that is, moved slightly up or down), the location of just the target object was displaced, or the entire picture was displaced. The results provided evidence of a multilevel integration process that directs eye movements.

The displacement that was detected least often was the displacement of just the background. Observers detected the displacement of the background about 40 percent of the time. Since visual acuity is good only at the fixation point, the visual system did not have sufficiently detailed information about the background to detect a change more than half the time. The displacement that was detected next most often was the displacement of the entire picture. Observers detected the displacement of the entire picture over 70 percent of the time. Notice that, when the entire picture is displaced, the target's location is displaced. The sensitivity to the change in the target's location suggests that this is the key element in the integration of the successive images. Presumably, when the target was displaced, the detection of the change in its location occurred at the feature analysis stage. The posterior parietal cortex detected features indicating an object in the periphery, moved the eyes there, and found no such features when it got there. However, notice that the detection of the displacement of the target was still only 70 percent. In fact, even under normal viewing the eyes occasionally undershoot the fixation of a target, so a failure to find the target does not signal an image disparity *unless* its displacement is beyond a critical distance.

The displacement that was detected the most often was the displacement of just the target. When only the target's location was displaced, detection of the displacement increased to over 80 percent of the time. In this case, it was possible for detection of the displacement to occur at either the feature analysis or object construction stage. Even if the displacement of the target was not detected at the feature analysis stage on the basis of the distance between the fixation point and the target, it could still be detected at the object construction stage, because the location of the target object in relation to all the objects in the scene had shifted. The new location of the target object did not correspond to the representation of the scene based on previous saccadic movements.

Change blindness. The failure to detect a change in successive images is called **change blindness**. Change blindness occurs at disruptions and interruptions that vary from small and brief, such as twenty milliseconds, to large and quite long, such as several seconds. The longer the interruption of the comparison process is, the larger are the disparities that go undetected (Simons and Ambinder, 2005). Observers fail to notice changes introduced during an eye movement, a blank screen, a blink, or a motion-picture cut or pan. Similarly, they fail to notice a change that is accompanied by other visual signals that distract attention from the change location, or a change that occurs gradually over a period of several seconds so that the change signal is not sufficiently strong to draw attention. The extent of change blindness is particularly striking, with remarkably large changes going unnoticed when the change is unexpected and incidental to the observer's task. One-third of the observers frequently failed to detect the substitution of a different actor in a motion picture. Moreover, in a real-life situation, some observers failed to notice when a person conversing with them who was briefly obscured was replaced with a different person (Levin and Simons, 1997; Simons and Levin, 1998).

Change blindness has proved to be a useful tool for the investigation of the neural areas performing target integration. Recall that the right posterior parietal cortex plays an important role in updating spatial representations, directing visuospatial attention (Chapter 4), and planning actions (Chapter 3). Consequently, the posterior parietal cortex is involved in the integration of successive images in the perceptual pathway. Its activation level positively correlates with successful conscious change detection (Beck *et al.*, 2001). Furthermore, Figure 5.9 shows that disruption of its activity increases the occurrence of change blindness, thus suggesting a causal role for the right posterior parietal cortex in change detection (Beck *et al.*, 2006).

Tseng *et al.* (2010) briefly disrupted cortical function by applying transcranial magnetic stimulation in a change detection task. While subjects attempted to detect changes between two image sets separated by a brief time interval, transcranial magnetic stimulation was applied either during the presentation of the first picture or during the second picture. Change blindness occurred more often when transcranial magnetic stimulation was applied during the viewing of the first picture, indicating that posterior parietal cortex plays a crucial role in the processes of encoding and/or maintaining feature information. In addition, the picture

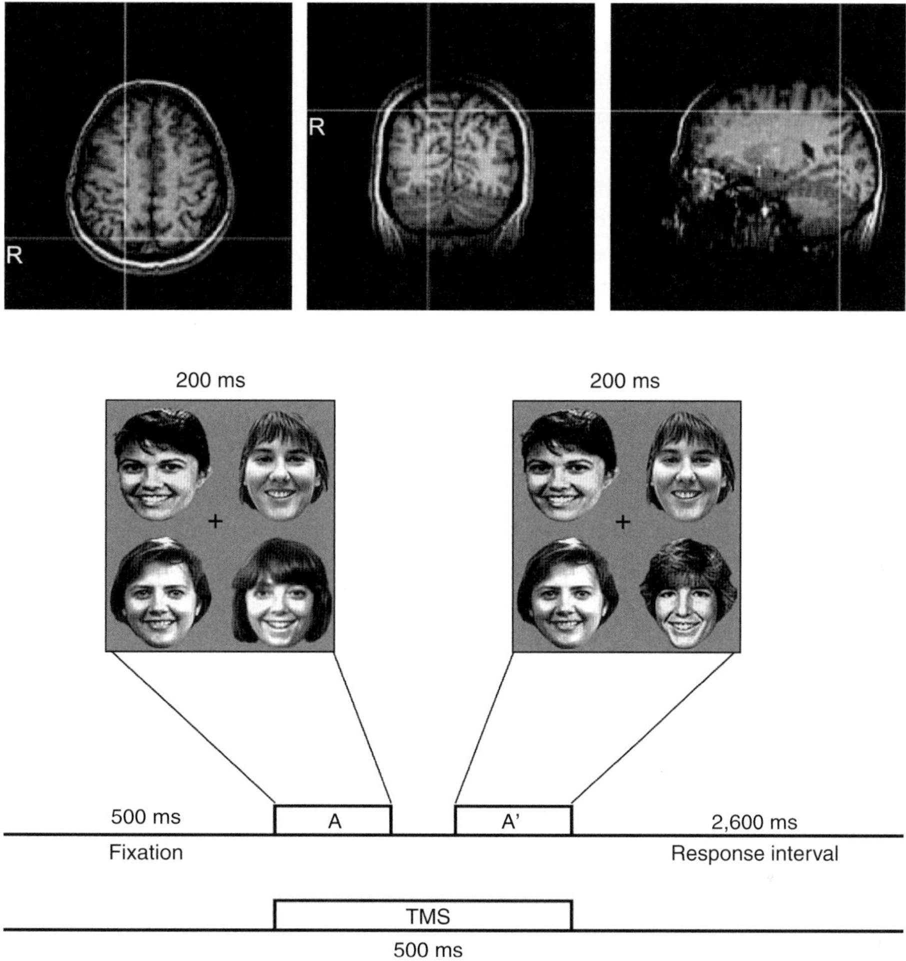

Figure 5.9 The task was to determine whether all the faces were the same in the first and second displays. Applying transcranial magnetic stimulation to the left parietal cortex at the point indicated by the cross hairs in the top three brain Images induced change blindness (Beck *et al.*, 2006).

changes did not involve changes in spatial locations, suggesting that the posterior parietal cortex may be involved in the encoding of figural as well as spatial information.

To summarize, when viewing the world, a task-relevant change in the target is noticed but any other change not intense enough to cause a reflexive alert is missed. Change blindness is related to inattention blindness (Chapter 4). In both cases, something is not seen because task-irrelevant information is not encoded. In the service of effective action, the visual system prioritizes the encoding of task-relevant information, while task-irrelevant information may not be encoded at all. Because we see whatever we are looking for, we mistakenly believe that we see all there is to see.

Response to novelty. When a target image disparity is detected and an unexpected target is encoded, this is a new challenge to the visual attention system. As long as daily life is predictable, voluntary action consists of the execution of prepared actions in response to confirmed expectations. However, sometimes an unexpected target is detected: a new word while reading, a new item on the menu, a red light on the way home. When this occurs, and the prepared action is no longer the appropriate response, control of the response seamlessly transfers from the habit system to the instrumental system without the awareness of the participant. The key neural structure in the construction of the unprepared response is the anterior portion of the cingulate gyrus (Posner, 1994), the oldest part of the cortex, deep beneath its surface, surrounding the central area containing the basal ganglia (Figure 4.1). The anterior cingulate gyrus is active when generating novel responses, such as generating semantic associates to words (Snyder *et al.*, 1995). It also becomes active when an incorrect response is made to a target (Dahaene, Posner, and Tucker, 1994; Gehring *et al.*, 1993). Sometimes you must make an ad hoc voluntary response to a target that automatically activates a conflicting response. This is another situation in which the anterior cingulate gyrus is active (Pardo *et al.*, 1990).

Yerkes–Dodson law

Skilled performance is influenced by the emotional arousal of the performer. The relationship between arousal and task performance is known as the Yerkes–Dodson law (Yerkes and Dodson, 1908). As shown in Figure 5.10, each task has an optimal level of arousal: the level at which performance is best. The optimal level of arousal is not the lowest level of arousal, nor the highest level of arousal, but some level in between. If a person's performance on a task is measured at various levels of arousal, performance first increases and then decreases as the level of arousal increases. Furthermore, as shown in Figure 5.10, the more difficult the task, the lower the level of arousal at which performance is optimal.

Why should an increase in arousal be associated with first an increase and then a decrease in task performance? One possibility is that the change in the performance is the result of the reduction of the number of targets receiving processing as arousal increases (Easterbrook's hypothesis, discussed in Chapter 4). As arousal increases from low to moderate, the number of task-irrelevant distracters that are processed is reduced, increasing task performance. The optimal level of performance is at the arousal level at which no task-irrelevant distracters but all task-relevant targets are processed. As arousal increases above the optimal level, the number of task-relevant targets that are processed is reduced, degrading task performance.

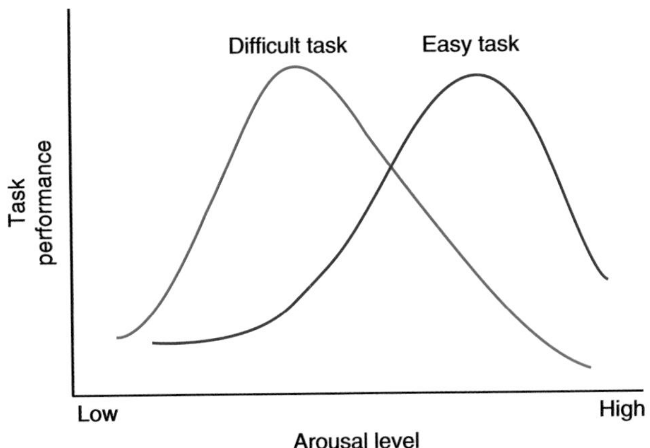

Figure 5.10 Yerkes–Dodson law. Performance on easy tasks peaks at a higher arousal level than performance on difficult tasks (Yerkes and Dodson, 1908).

A second possibility is that the change in performance is the result of a shift in control from the instrumental system to the habit system. Fear increases control of the response by the habit system at the expense of the instrumental system (Packard, 2009). Because the habit system generates fast, accurate responses, it may be that, as arousal increases from low to moderate, increasing control by the habit system results in better task performance. However, situations often differ from each other in some details, and so habitual responses require instrumental modification. As arousal increases above the optimal level, it may be that total control by the habit system causes inflexible, hence inaccurate, responses in a somewhat novel situation, degrading task performance. Because fear increases control by the habit system, armies throughout the world subject recruits to repetitive drill. The terror of combat causes habit system control, so the soldiers perform as trained. However, training on one task may result in poor transfer to a similar task that requires somewhat different responses. The probability of a correct response by a pilot to a flight emergency is predicted by the number of hours the pilot has flown that model of aircraft, not by the total number of hours flown by the pilot on all aircraft. Safety is therefore increased by having a pilot fly only one model of aircraft, though efficiency is increased by having each pilot fly more than one model of aircraft in the fleet.

The effects of target selection and habit are not mutually exclusive. Arousal may influence task performance through multiple pathways, including one or more that have not been identified.

5.3 Savant learning

When a novel task is performed, representations are encoded in both the habit and instrumental systems. For most individuals, responses are initially under the control of the instrumental system but with practice come under the control of the habit system, as response–effect sequences are encoded within the habit system as the result of serial learning. However, some individuals, for some tasks, are born with the ability to immediately encode response–effect sequences the first time they are encountered. Consequently, the habit system is in control of the responses from the very beginning, and these individuals demonstrate unusual expertise. This kind of extraordinary ability is called talent. The existence of talent is especially apparent in child prodigies, who may have extraordinary skill at a task despite a pervasive deficit in declarative learning.

Precocious art

Nadia was a three-year-old autistic child with little language who suddenly evinced an unprecedented drawing ability (Figure 5.11). Nadia drew rapidly and creatively. She had perfect control, so she never had to correct (Selfe, 1977). When she became older and more social, Nadia drew less often, and eventually she stopped drawing altogether (Selfe, 2011). This abandonment of an ability by a savant is unusual (Treffert, 2014).

Although some autistic individuals may have extraordinary artistic abilities, extraordinary artistic ability is not specifically associated with autism. A prodigy may have impaired intelligence, normal intelligence, or superior intelligence. Extraordinary artistic ability is often associated with an extraordinary visual memory, so that an individual can draw precisely in detail everything that he or she has seen. After a single forty-five-minute helicopter ride over London, Stephen Wiltshire drew a five-foot-wide panorama, including all the buildings he had seen, in their correct location, and sufficient detail to determine that he had gotten the number of windows in each building correct (Figure 5.12). He repeated the feat after helicopter rides over Rome and New York (Dwyer, 2009). Stephen has a gallery in London where he displays his work.

Figure 5.13 shows portraits a young French boy painted of his parents nearly 200 years ago. The boy did not grow up to become an artist. The portraits were painted by Louis Pasteur, one of the greatest scientists of all time. So, while some individuals have both

Figure 5.11 Drawing by Nadia when three years old (Selfe, 1977).

Figure 5.12 Aerial view of London by Stephen Wiltshire.

Figure 5.13 Portraits drawn by Louis Pasteur when he was a boy.

great talents and severe deficits, other individuals appear to be true polymaths; they are talented at everything. You may know that the engineering genius Leonardo da Vinci was a great artist but you probably did not know that Galileo Galilei, the founder of modern physics, had great artistic ability as well. Furthermore, you probability did not know that both were skilled musicians and that Leonardo composed music. The existence of polymaths means that talent cannot be explained as the overdevelopment of one ability in compensation for a deficit in another. Polymaths do not have deficits to compensate for.

Precocious music

The same pattern is observed with musical ability. Some autistic individuals demonstrate musical ability as young as three years old. Many of these individuals are blind. They not only learn to play an instrument well but have perfect pitch and an extraordinary musical memory, so they can play anything they heard once, or at most a few times (Ockelford, 2007; Pring, Woolf, and Tadic, 2008; Sloboda, Hermelin, and O'Conner, 1985; Treffert, 2014).

As if savant abilities are not mysterious enough, some individuals acquire abilities after brain injury, including as a result of being hit by lightning (Neal, 2012; Treffert, 2014). Furthermore, frontotemporal dementia, which otherwise causes a general decline in cognitive abilities, is sometimes associated with a preserved creative musical or visual ability. To investigate this association systematically, Miller *et al.* (2000) examined the records of every one of the sixty-nine patients diagnosed with frontotemporal dementia at the University of California, Los Angeles, Medical Center and found twelve who had creative musical (such as piano playing) or artistic (such as painting, photography, crafts) abilities that emerged sometime between the teens and age sixty-eight. In some cases the abilities emerged before and in other cases the abilities emerged after the onset of the frontotemporal dementia. They compared the performance of these individuals on a broad spectrum of cognitive and neurological tests with the performance of forty-six individuals with frontotemporal dementia who did not have creative abilities. The comparison revealed that nine of the individuals with creative abilities had abnormalities in the left anterior temporal cortex. This area is associated with verbal processing but not at all with the habit system. Miller *et al.* (2000) suggest that, as verbal abilities deteriorate, not only is the inhibition of nonverbal processing reduced but individuals may come to rely on a specific preserved ability, which causes its development. For the rare individual who has a latent extraordinary ability, the shift in processing reveals this ability.

SUMMARY

- When a sequence of voluntary actions is repeatedly made to a repeated sequence of targets, the actions are faster each time the sequence is repeated. This is called serial learning.
  - Serial learning is performed by the habit system, yet involves the encoding of the spatial location of responses.
  - Serial learning occurs below the level of awareness, and a person may be able to respond rapidly to a repeated sequence without having any ability to recognize it.
  - Serial learning is response–effect learning. An action and its consequence are encoded as an episode, which is the basic unit of memory.
- Serial learning is the basis of the encoding of the predictable spatial locations of the targets that make possible the encoding of familiar visual displays, such as faces and written text.
- Serial learning is also the basis of musical and artistic talent. Exceptional musical or artistic talent is unrelated to other abilities.

Perceptual skills are habit learning in the service of declarative knowledge. As the result of serial learning, perceptual skills are encoded in the habit system. Perceptual skills are sequences of actions that efficiently encode the representations, from scenes to faces (Chapter 6) to narratives (Chapter 7), that comprise declarative knowledge. Most of life is routine, and routine life is under the control of automatic response–effect sequences. When you awake in the morning, you do not open your eyes to discover where you are. You already have retrieved from memory a detailed episode describing your location. Furthermore, this episode also describes whatever action you take when you wake up. Hence, before you even open your eyes, you have both a target and response specified. When you open your eyes, only enough visual feature information is analyzed to confirm the target, and then the response is executed.

Similarly, throughout the day, actions are prepared in advance and then executed when the appropriate target is detected. When a familiar context is scanned, only enough information is encoded to confirm the target. This is why change blindness and inattention blindness (Chapter 4) occur. Whether driving, shopping, or ignoring the teacher in class, most of life is routine and is encoded as familiar episodes. The episodes in turn direct perceptual skills that process only enough of the world to confirm your expectations of it and execute actions prepared in advance. Only when a novel or unexpected target is encountered is ad hoc voluntary action required.

QUESTIONS

1 Is the improvement in typing speed as the result of practice the result, at least in part, of serial learning?
2 What evidence indicates that serial learning is habit learning?
3 During reading, are eye fixations most often between, at the beginning, or in the middle of words?
4 During reading, what processes occur during a word fixation?
5 How old must a child be to have enough understanding to begin to learn to play the piano?

FURTHER READING

Godwin, H. J., Reichle, E. D., and Menneer, T. (2014). Coarse-to-fine eye movement behavior during visual search. *Psychonomic Bulletin and Review*, 21, 1244–9.

Henderson, J. M. (2003). Human gaze control during real-world scene perception. *Trends in Cognitive Science*, 7, 498–504.

Hoffmann, J., Sebald, A., and Stöcker, C. (2001). Irrelevant response effects improve serial learning in serial reaction time tasks. *Journal of Experimental Psychology: Learning, Memory, and Cognition*, 27, 470–82.

Simons, D. J., and Ambinder, M. S. (2005). Change blindness. *Current Directions in Psychological Science*, 14, 44–8.

Treffert, D. A. (2014). Savant syndrome: realities, myths, and misconceptions. *Journal of Autism and Developmental Disorders*, 44, 564–71.

6 Vision

In November 1966 a twenty-five-year-old soldier who was home on leave accidentally suffered carbon monoxide poisoning from leaking gas fumes. This accident was a serious one, since exposure to carbon monoxide can cause brain damage and death. Following resuscitation, the soldier was able at first to converse with relatives. But the next day he lapsed into a coma, from which he recovered only slowly. In a month he was alert and talkative again. However, he experienced severe visual problems.

Seven months after the accident the soldier was admitted to Boston Veterans Administration Hospital for extensive tests. Most of his cognitive abilities, such as language use and memory, appeared normal. Most of his perceptual system was also intact. He could readily identify and name things through their feel, smell, or sound. In addition, his most elementary visual abilities were also preserved. He was able to identify colors, discriminate between lights of different intensities, and tell in what direction an object was moving. Nevertheless, the soldier's visual perception was severely impaired. He was unable to recognize objects, letters, or people when he saw them. His impairment was so severe that on one occasion he identified his own reflection in a mirror as the face of his doctor!

A common factor in these recognition failures appeared to be the inability to identify any visual shape or form. To test this hypothesis, two neurologists, Benson and Greenberg (1969), gave the soldier a variety of tests in which he had to verbally identify a pattern, copy a pattern, select which two of several patterns were the same, or simply say whether two patterns were the same or different. The results of a typical task are shown in Figure 6.1. In this task the soldier had to mark which one of four comparison patterns was the same as a standard pattern on the left. He was unable to match any of them correctly. All the results from this and similar tests were equally dismal. The soldier was simply unable to distinguish visual shapes from one another. He could not even tell a circle from a square.

The soldier's disorder dramatically demonstrates that pattern perception requires much more than the eye's ability to detect a beam of light. A great number of computations are required to determine whether a light beam falling on the retina has been reflected off a square object or a round one.

In this chapter we will see that the visual pathway that results in visual perception has three distinct stages.

Figure 6.1 Matching task: a soldier who suffered from carbon monoxide poisoning was unable to mark the appropriate matching figure in any of these examples (Benson and Greenberg, 1969).

- During the sensory registration stage, light stimulates rods and cones on the retina of the eye. The sensory information is encoded within the retina and transmitted along the visual pathway, first to the thalamus and then to the occipital cortex.
- During the feature analysis stage, the visual pathway divides into many sub-pathways that extend through the occipital cortex and down into the temporal cortex. Each sub-pathway initially encodes a different feature of the visual display. Then the representations of different sub-pathways are combined to construct increasingly complex features of the visual display.
- During the shape construction stage, the visual pathway extends down through the inferior temporal cortex. Complex features are combined into representations of three-dimensional objects. Ultimately, the visual display is organized into a three-dimensional scene containing three-dimensional objects, which are compared with representations in memory and recognized.

6.1 The perception of reality

You have good reason to believe that you usually perceive the world accurately. If you look out your window and see a tree, quite likely a tree is really there. This fact is so unremarkable that you hardly ever stop to think about it. Yet the task is quite a formidable one. How are the shapes and locations of objects determined through vision? For example, when you see a square, the image of it that falls on your retina is not square-shaped. How, then, do you know that it is a square and not a rectangle, a parallelogram, or a trapezoid?

Retinal image theory

The first step towards answering this question is to realize that the answer is not obvious – that is, you don't simply see the square as a square because that's its shape. The case study of the soldier demonstrates that perceiving light is not equivalent to perceiving the shapes of objects. Figure 6.2 shows the image of an object on the retina. When you look at an object, the light reflecting from the object passes through the lens of the eye, which focuses an upside-down image on the retina at the back of the eyeball. The retina is a curved surface containing light-sensitive cells that transmit signals along the optic nerve to the brain. According to the retinal image theory of pattern recognition, when you look at an object like a square the retinal image is transmitted to the brain, where it is turned right side up and recognized immediately. The problem with this simple theory is that, unless you are looking at the square head-on in absolutely even illumination (which almost never occurs in ordinary life), the image of a square does not fall on your retina. Instead, the image will most likely be some trapezoidal shape, because the side of the square closest to you will produce a longer edge in its retinal image (Figure 6.3). Often the shape will be even less square-like, since the square will be broken into light and dark areas by glare and shadow.

When we turn from this artificial example of viewing a single simple shape to the everyday perception of the environment, the problems of a retinal image theory of perception increase a thousand-fold. Consider what you see when you look around a room. Perhaps you see walls, tables, chairs (all with rectangular surfaces), a round clock on the wall, a picture, and a tree through a window. But, if you stop to analyze what the retinal image must be like, you realize that no shape in the retinal image is actually as you perceive it. The right angles you see everywhere as parts of walls, tables, etc. are almost all acute or oblique angles when they fall on your retinas. Similarly, the round clock is likely to be an ellipse in the retinal image.

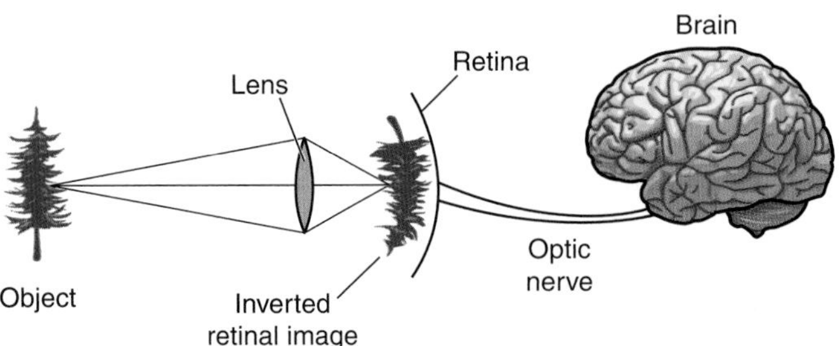

Figure 6.2 Visual processing begins with an inverted image of an object on the retina.

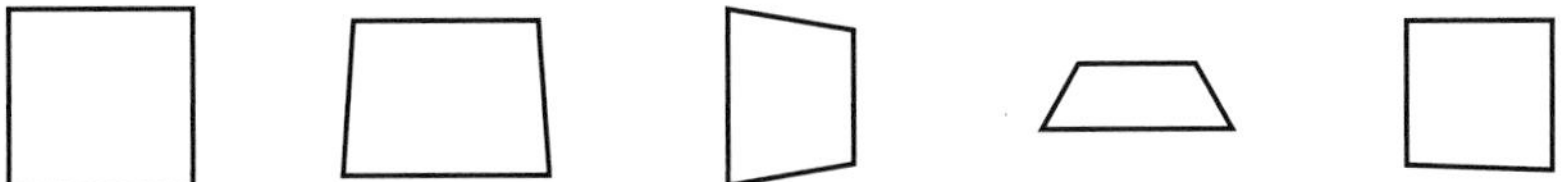

Figure 6.3 How a square may appear when viewed from different perspectives.

Colors and sizes also differ between the retinal image and your perception. A shadow falls across an orange couch, yet the entire couch appears to be the same color. One chair of two is closer to you, yet both appear to be the same size. You can easily tell the difference between the picture and the window, though the images they present to your retinas are very similar. The most remarkable aspect of the discrepancies between the retinal image and perception is that usually it is perception, not your retinal sensation, that is veridical. Your eyes lie, but your mind tells you the truth!

Overview of visual processing

Much of what the visual system does is below awareness, which makes it seem effortless. However, the effortlessness of visual perception is misleading. The way you actually see is much more complicated than the effortless process revealed by introspection. It is the result of an enormous number of computations being performed below the level of awareness. Hundreds of millions of years of evolution have endowed you with a supercomputer that performs millions of computations on the visual input before you are aware that you have seen anything at all.

Figure 6.3 shows that a square can cast many different images on the retina. The image that the square casts is determined by its position in relation to the observer. For example, images (b) and (d) occur when the bottom edge of the square is closer to the observer than the top edge, so the square is either above or below the observer. Furthermore, as the relative position of the square in relation to the observer changes, its image changes in a predictable way. For example, if the eyes fixate first to the left, then on the center, then to the right of a square, its image on the retina will successively be as shown in (c), (a), and (e). An accurate three-dimensional representation of a three-dimensional shape can be constructed from two or more two-dimensional images of it when seen from different locations. This is exactly what the visual system does. It constructs a three-dimensional representation from a sequence of pairs of two-dimensional retinal images.

The anatomical locations of the main components of the visual processing system are shown in Figure 6.4. The system is also shown schematically in Figure 6.5. Visual processing begins when light passes through the lens embedded in the front of the eyeball and is focused on the back of the eyeball, called the **retina**. After light falls on the retina, the visual input passes through three stages of processing before perception occurs.

The first stage is the **sensory registration** stage. The retinal images are encoded and sent up the optic pathway to the thalamus. The retinal images are sharpened, and the different kinds of information they contain are sorted out and sent on to specific cortical locations for further processing.

The second stage is **feature analysis**. The most detailed description of the input is sent from the thalamus to the **primary visual cortex** of the occipital cortex. Two retinal images are combined to form a three-dimensional representation of the **visual field**. Neurons there extract simple features, such as edges and angles, from the retinal image. The **visual field**

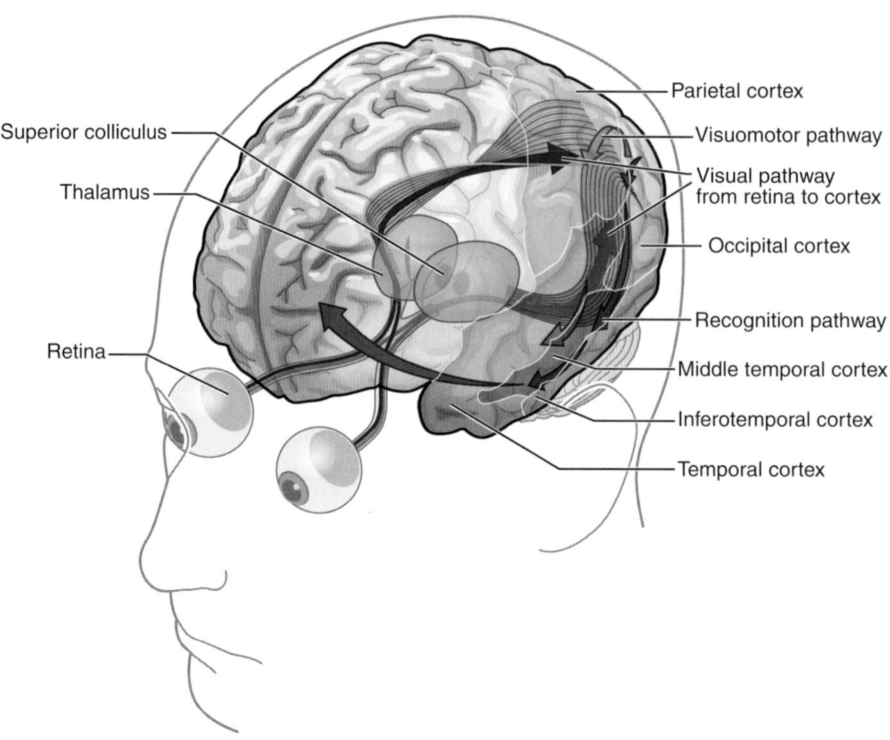

Figure 6.4 Visual information is transmitted from the retina by the visual pathway to the superior colliculus and thalamus and from the thalamus to the occipital cortex and parietal cortex.

is everything you can see. The processing of the input is continued in adjacent occipital, temporal, and parietal regions. The features in adjacent areas of the image are combined to form patterns that correspond to surfaces in the visual field.

From the visual cortex, the visual processing pathway splits into two processing pathways. The *how* pathway extends upwards into the parietal lobe, where visual and tactual information are integrated within a single representation that is used to direct limb movements in such tasks as reaching and grasping, as described in Chapter 3. The *what* pathway extends downwards into the temporal lobe. Here the third stage is the **object construction stage**. Pattern representations corresponding to surfaces are combined and compared with memory to construct shape representations. Ultimately, all the shape representations are combined into a single representation of a three-dimensional world filled with three-dimensional objects, which corresponds to your perception of the world.

6.2 Sensory registration

When light falls on the **retina** of the eye it stimulates the **photoreceptors** embedded in it. The photoreceptors signal the **bipolar** cells, which in turn signal the **ganglion** cells. Already at the retina there is some sorting out of the signal, because different areas of the

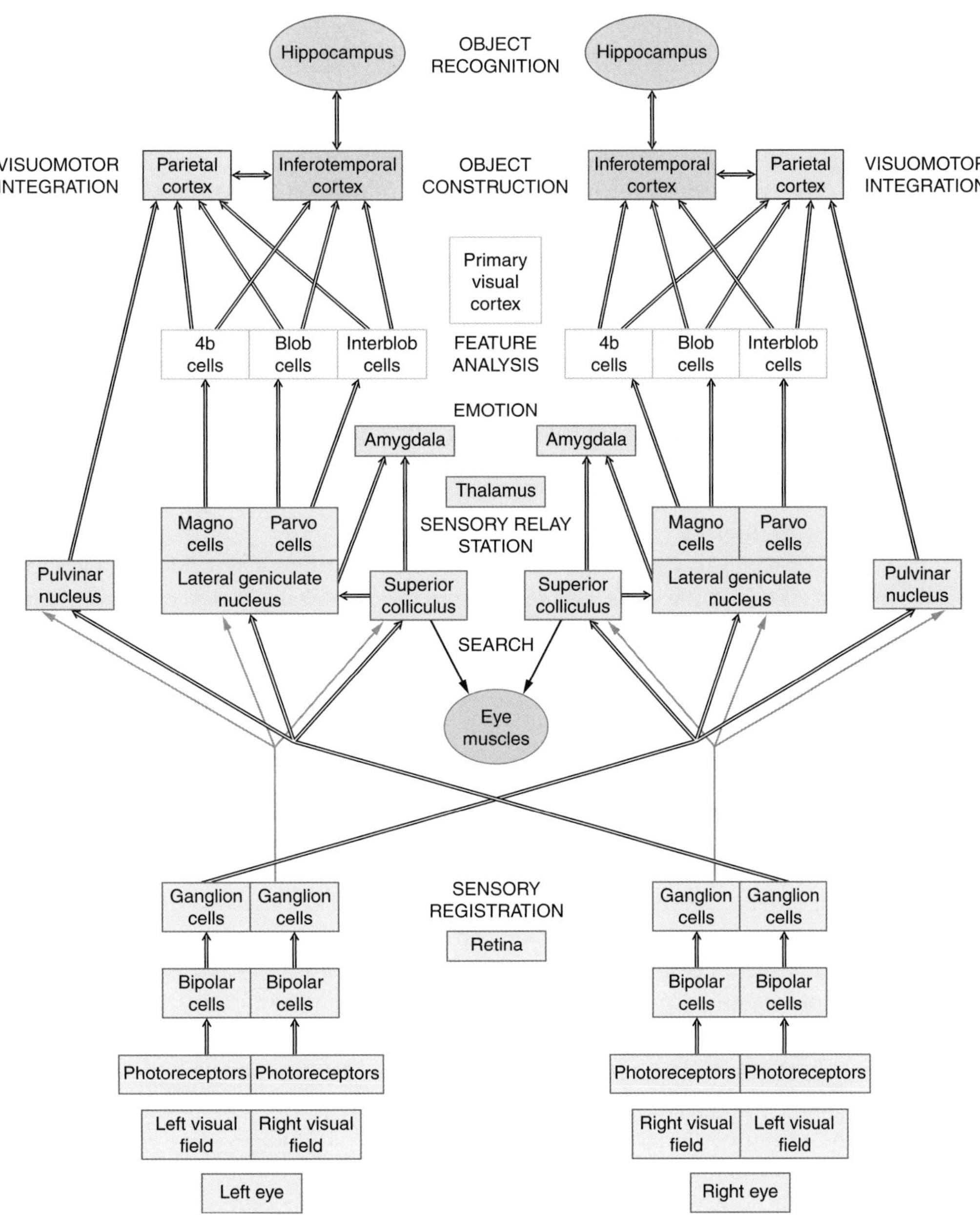

Figure 6.5 Visual information is distributed by the visual pathway to four different systems: the emotional system, the visual search system, the visuomotor system, and the perceptual system.

retina are sensitive to different information. The photoreceptors consist of **rod** neurons and **cone** neurons, and only the cone neurons are frequency-sensitive and hence transmit color information. There are three different types of cone cells, and each type is maximally sensitive to one of three different frequencies that produce the perception of red, green, or blue, respectively. However, people perceive four, rather than three, primary colors. When observers are presented with a large number of color samples and asked to pick out those that do not appear to be mixtures of other colors, they tend to pick out four colors: red, green, blue, and yellow (Bornstein, 1973). Furthermore, it is only in particular ways that the four primary colors can be mixed. You cannot see a reddish green or a bluish yellow. This is because input from the three kinds of cones is combined to form red-green, blue-yellow, and lightness pathways within the color lane of the optic pathway.

The cones exist only in the central area of the eye, called the fovea. If you move a crayon across your visual field while keeping your eyes fixated on a point, you will find a point at which you can no longer see its color. The visual field for color is smaller than the visual field for form. Moreover, the rods are most numerous immediately outside the fovea and thin out towards the periphery of the retina. If you continue to move the crayon away from the center of your visual field, you will find a point at which you cannot see it at all. However, while the rods are too sparse for form detection, motion detection is still possible. If you wiggle your finger at the location where you can no longer see the crayon, you will see something out there.

Visual acuity

As discussed in Chapter 5, about three or four times a second your eyes move in unison, and fixate on the same new location in space (Yarbus, 1967). Eye movements are essential in order to see more than a tiny portion of the world in detail. Visual acuity is the amount of detail that can be seen. The number of rods and cones packed together in a given area is the primary determinant of visual acuity, so it is much higher for the area near the center of the retina, called the **fovea**, than for the rest of the retina. Estes, Allmeyer, and Reder (1976) showed just how important eye movements are for good visual acuity by training observers to hold their eyes still while staring at a fixation point. A string of four letters was shown to the right or left of the fixation points. The observers had either 150 milliseconds or 2.4 seconds to see the string without making an eye movement. They were asked to report all four letters. The results are shown in Figure 6.6. The observers did not always report all four letters accurately. Without making an eye movement, visual acuity is not sufficient to always clearly see a novel letter string of four random letters extending to the right or left of the fixation point.

You perceive the visual field as having uniform clarity. However, this cannot be the case, because, as Estes, Allmeyer, and Reder (1976) demonstrated, only the area immediately around the fixation point is seen clearly. The constant motion of the eyes keeps the center of clarity always changing, and what you perceive is actually the integration

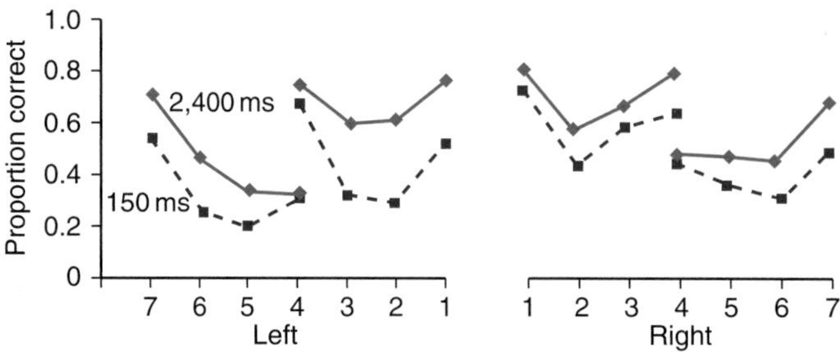

Figure 6.6 Serial position curves for identification of four-letter strings extending to the left or right of the fixation point. The most central was at position 1 (the fixation point) or position 4. The strings were observed for 2,400 or 150 milliseconds without an eye movement (Estes *et al.*, 1976).

of several images. The representation you perceive at any given instant is put together from retinal images collected over the past few seconds as your eyes jumped from fixation point to fixation point in the visual field directed by the visual search system (Chapter 5). When all the images at different fixation points are stitched together, an apparently equally clear perception of the entire visual field is constructed and constantly updated.

One effect of integrating successive representations is the filling in of the blind spot. Each retina contains a **blind spot**, where the optic pathway exits from it. You do not notice the blind spot for two reasons. First, when the eyes fixate on a location, the blind spot on one retina rarely covers the same area of the visual field as the blind spot on the other retina, so at least monocular information is received from all parts of the visual field. Second, when the blind spots do line up, the visual scanning system fills in the spot with part of an image from an earlier fixation.

Optic pathway

As mentioned above, rods and cones transmit their output to bipolar cells, which in turn transmit their output to ganglion cells. Some ganglion cells also respond to light (Lok, 2011). However, the primary function of the ganglion cells is to further the analysis begun by the bipolar cells and to transmit the information they encode to the superior colliculus and the thalamus.

When you fixate on a point in space, light from one side of the point falls on the right side of each retina, and light from the other side of the point falls on the left side of each retina. So the right sides of both retinas have images of one half of the visual field and the left sides of both retinas have images of the other half of the visual field. The axons from the ganglion cells that receive the input from the right sides of each retina form the **optic pathway**, which proceeds first to the thalamus and ultimately to the left hemisphere of the cerebral cortex. Similarly, the images from the left sides of the retinas are ultimately transmitted to the right hemisphere (Figure 6.5). Otherwise, there would not be the efficient visual control of motor movement that was described in the last chapter. The right optic pathway transmits visual input to the left hemisphere, and vice versa.

In each hemisphere, the optic pathway divides and terminates in several locations. One small sub-pathway terminates in the superior colliculus. The superior colliculus is part of the visual scanning system (Chapter 5) and uses the output from this pathway in the control of eye movements. The next largest sub-pathway goes to the **pulvinar nucleus** of the thalamus. By far the largest portion arrives at the **geniculate nucleus.**

From the superior colliculus a sub-pathway carries visual input by this second route to the pulvinar nucleus and from there to the amygdala. In addition, a small pathway from the suprageniculate nucleus also carries visual information to the amygdala, which generates a fear response to a frightening visual stimulus (Morris *et al.*, 2001), as described in Chapter 4.

The second largest visual sub-pathway, going to the **pulvinar nucleus** of the thalamus and from there to the parietal cortex, becomes part of the procedural or *how* pathway, which constructs a representation that is used to control motor movements involved in reaching and grasping for things you can see (Chapter 3).

The largest portion of the visual input is transmitted by a sub-pathway that goes to the **lateral geniculate nucleus** of the thalamus and from there to the primary visual area in the occipital cortex. From there, most of the pathway extends downwards into the temporal cortex, where it is called the ***what* pathway** and is used for visual recognition. However, some of this pathway extends upwards into the parietal cortex as the ***how* pathway**, and its visual information is added to that from the pulvinar nucleus and is used to direct voluntary action.

6.3 Feature analysis

The key problem that the visual system has to solve to make three-dimensional visual perception of the world possible is that there is a many-to-one mapping between three-dimensional and two-dimensional representations. In other words, any two-dimensional representation may be the image of many different three-dimensional objects. Nevertheless, your three-dimensional perception of the world is not ambiguous. You do not see an object as an approximate size or one of several sizes but unambiguously as a specific shape and size at a specific distance from you. This is because the visual system constructs the most likely three-dimensional representation of all those consistent with the two-dimensional retinal images. This is the one you perceive unambiguously.

To do this, the visual system consists of a heterarchy of feature detection neurons that encode features of the retinal image that can be combined to reveal possible three-dimensional scenes that could have produced the images. Parallel columns of neurons initially encode simple features and then combine them into successively more complex features. Visual processing is partly hierarchical, therefore, as the input moves from registration to feature analysis to construction, and partly parallel, as many separate analyses are carried out simultaneously at the analysis stage. The partly hierarchical, partly parallel, system is called a **heterarchy**.

To begin, Figure 6.5 shows schematically the main parallel pathways involved in feature analysis. The lateral geniculate nucleus (**LGN**) contains two kinds of neurons, **magnocellular** (large) and **parvocellular** (small), which are named for their size, and which project to different layers of the **primary visual cortex** of the occipital cortex (also called the **striate cortex**). In the primary visual cortex, neurons that receive information from both eyes combine the two-dimensional retinal images from each eye to form a three-dimensional representation of the visual field encoded on the retina. From the striate cortex the input is sent to the **secondary visual cortex** (also called the **prestriate** or **extrastriate** cortex) in adjacent occipital, temporal, and parietal regions, where the results of the basic analyses on adjacent areas of the image are combined to form patterns that correspond to surfaces in the visual field.

The cells in the primary visual cortex that receive their input from magnocellular neurons are called **4b** cells. The parvocellular neurons project to two kinds of neurons of the visual cortex. One kind of neuron forms clumps that appear as blobs when a small area is stained with a dye; these are called **blob** cells. The remaining cells, which fall between the blobs, are called **interblob** cells.

As summarized in Table 6.1, 4b cells, blob cells, and interblob cells are sensitive to three different kinds of information that is available in the visual input. The 4b cells are most sensitive to motion and contrast, and so are responsible for the representation of motion. Blob

TABLE 6.1 Functions of parallel visual pathways

System	4b	P-blob	P-interblob
Contrast	High	High	Low
Location	Low	Low	High
Motion	High	Low	Middle
Color	Low	High	Middle
Orientation	Middle	Low	High

TABLE 6.2 Constructing a three-dimensional visual image from a two-dimensional retinal image

Color encoding
Contrasts, including color contrasts, are encoded (Figure 6.7)
Feature detection
Orientation is encoded (Figure 6.8, Figure 6.9, Figure 6.10)
Orientation activates basic convex and corner features (Figure 6.11)
Textures are defined by adjacent features in the same average orientation (Figure 6.13)
Adjacent symmetry also defines textures (Figure 6:14)
Textures and edges are the features that define surfaces (Figure 6.15)
Depth construction
Binocular disparities (Figure 6.17)
Monocular cues make use of surfaces to select three-dimensional representations
Size and orientation create perspective (Figure 6.18, Figure 6.19)
Convex shapes create occlusion, which selects for depth (Figure 6.21)
The most likely depth representation is selected (Figure 6.26)

Note: For each feature, the figure illustrating the effect of each feature on perception is also mentioned.

cells are most sensitive to color and contrast, and so are responsible for the representation of color. Interblob cells are sensitive to location and orientation, and so are responsible for the representation of form.

Because of the inherent ambiguity of the two-dimensional retinal image with respect to possible three-dimensional scenes it might represent, as activation spreads through the heterarchy from the **bottom up**, multiple possible three-dimensional representations are activated. At each level, there is **top-down** selection of the most likely representations based on object representations encoded in the temporal cortex.

The interblob pathway (Table 6.2) encodes orientation features that activate convex and corner features that activate textures and edges. Textures and edges are used to construct possible surfaces.

First, binocular disparities between the left and right retinal images of the same area of space are used to construct possible three-dimensional representations. Then, these representations are combined with the monocular features of the interblob pathway. Using monocular features such as oriented lines and convex features, the most likely surfaces are selected, and then the convex feature activates the monocular depth cue occlusion and combines it with the representations activated by binocular disparities to restrict the possible three dimensional representations of the surfaces. On the basis of experience, the single most likely depth representation is perceived.

Color/contrast as an elementary feature

In the primary visual area of the cortex there are many feature detector neurons that each receives input from a few cells in the LGN of the thalamus, which in turn have received input from small adjacent areas on one or both retinas. The retinal area is called the LGN neuron's receptive field. Each receptive field consists of a center and a surround. The response of the feature detector neuron is determined by the *difference* between the input to the center and the surround. The encoding of relative differences in light frequency, hence color, by the blob color/contrast sub-pathway is shown in Figure 6.7. The perception of the shade of pink is determined by whether it is surrounded by green or white.

Orientation as an elementary feature

Within the interblob pathway there are more specialized sub-pathways for the detection of brightness contrast, hence edge detection and orientation, as shown in Figures 6.8 and 6.9. The LGN neuron responds when the brightness of the center of the receptive field is different from the brightness of the surround. Figure 6.8 shows the center and surround sending input to a single LGN cell. When the center and surround are both illuminated, as in Figure 6.8 (a), or both unilluminated, as in Figure 6.8 (b), the LGN cell does not respond. However, when the center is illuminated and the surround is not, as in Figure 6.8 (c), then the LGN neuron responds and sends input to the visual cortex.

A feature detector neuron responds when it receives input from a sufficient number of LGN neurons with overlapping receptive fields; thus, the response of the feature detector neuron depends on the retinal receptive fields of the LGN neurons that provide its input, as shown in Figure 6.9. These fields are organized into several simple shapes, called **features**. Among the most common are the **orientation features**, such as the vertical line shown in Figure 6.9 (a). The receptive fields of these cortical neurons contain a center that is in the shape of a line in a specific orientation. So, ultimately, a single cortical neuron

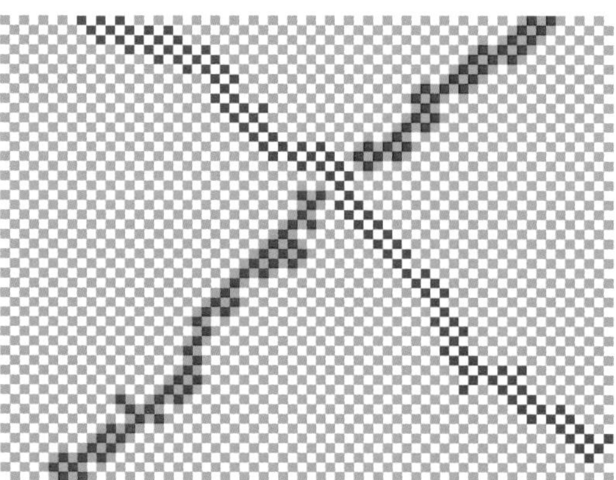

Figure 6.7 There are only three colors: white, green, and pink.

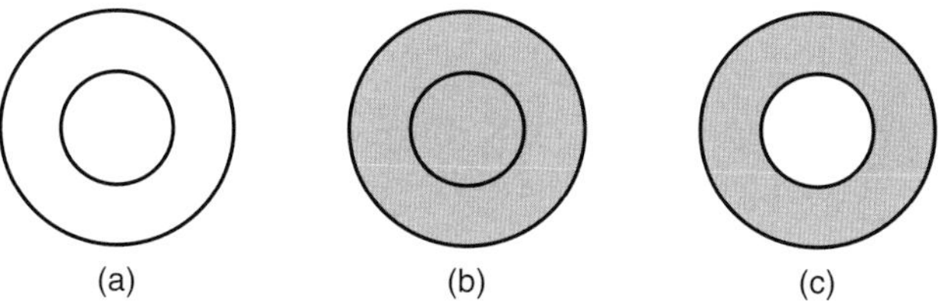

Figure 6.8 The receptive field of an LGN neuron contains a center and surround. When the center and surround are the same brightness (a, b) the LGN neuron does not respond. Only when there is a difference in brightness is there a response (c).

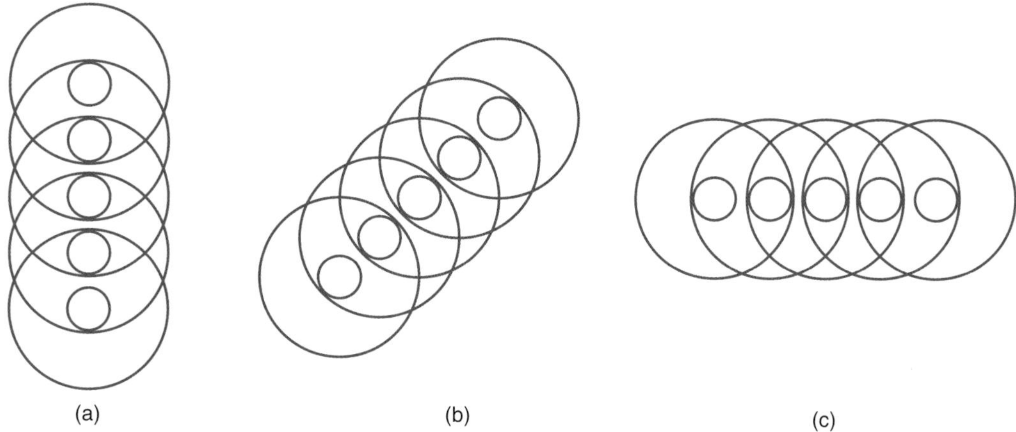

Figure 6.9 Receptive fields of orientation neurons that respond to vertical (a), diagonal (b), and horizontal lines (c).

responds to a line in a single orientation. There are many different cortical feature detector neurons that are sensitive to many different orientations (Knierim and Van Essen, 1992). For example, cortical receptive fields for a vertical, a diagonal, and a horizontal line are shown in Figures 6.9 (a), (b), and (c), respectively. The representation is a kind of feature map, therefore, in which the visual input has been segmented into a large number of highly localized features, each recording the orientation of a line at that location.

An edge is any sharp change in brightness. Notice that, if the edge of a bright field moves across the receptive field of an orientation detector that is oriented parallel to the edge, it will activate the feature detector when it passes through its center, as shown in Figure 6.10. Edges in specific orientations activate simple orientation features, and orientation detectors are also called edge detectors. Orientation is thus one of the basic features out of which both the edges and surfaces of objects are ultimately constructed. As soon as the orientation features are encoded they are combined into more complex features, called convex features and corners (Pomerantz, 1981), as shown in Figure 6.11. A convex feature is an angle or curve. Corners are three-line features that can be the images of the corners of three-dimensional objects. Convex features and corner features are **local features**.

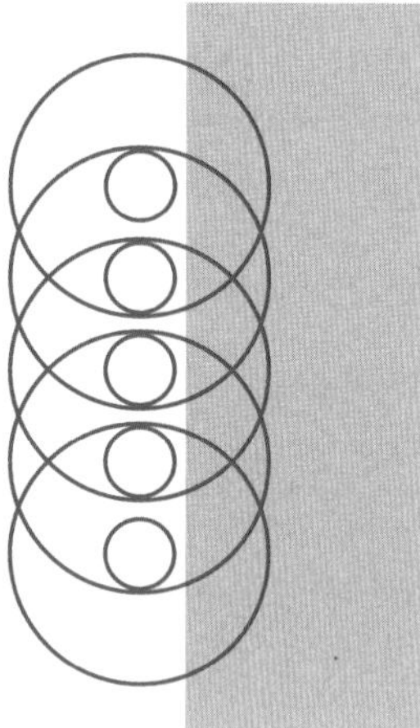

Figure 6.10 Edge detection by an orientation neuron results from a difference in brightness across its receptive fields.

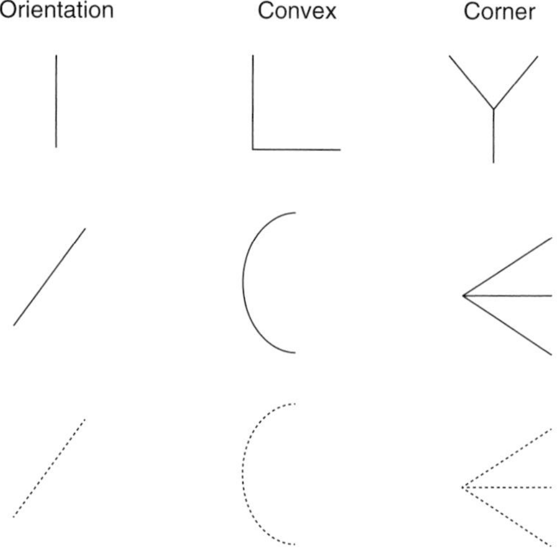

Figure 6.11 Orientation, convex, and corner features are detected early in a visual pathway (Pomerantz, 1981).

Visual organization

A **texture** is a pattern made up of adjacent repetitions of the same local feature. When the orientation of the feature varies unsystematically over the texture then the texture is defined by that local feature. Texture encoding by the visual system is apparent through the phenomenon of **pop-out** (Chapter 4). Just as LGN neurons with overlapping visual fields input to a common feature detector neuron in the visual cortex, feature detector neurons with overlapping fields for a common orientation input to a common texture detector neuron, which is thus activated by a texture consisting of adjacent identical features. If a visual display contains two textures, then the visual system organizes the display into the two areas corresponding to the two textures, so that one texture pops out from the other. For example, in Figure 6.12 (a) the one line in a different orientation pops out because the seven lines in the same orientation are combined into a single texture. The visual system puts not only lines in the same orientation together into textures but also features of the same type. In Figure 6.12 (b) a convex feature pops out from among lines. The strength of the pop-out effect increases with the size of the texture. When all the repetitions of the feature have the same orientation, that orientation is a global feature that also defines the texture. Figure 6.13 shows pop-out for four adjacent vertical lines among diagonal lines but not for one vertical line among diagonal lines.

Figure 6.14 provides a striking illustration that symmetrical adjacent areas are also organized into successively larger areas. First, look at the right pattern, which is perceived as symmetrical. In contrast, the left pattern appears to be just random noise. In fact, a central cross of random noise makes the otherwise symmetrical left pattern appear entirely random and a central cross containing a symmetrical pattern makes an otherwise random right pattern appear entirely symmetrical. On the left there are no adjacent areas with identical features to be detected and combined by a texture detection neuron. The figure is not organized into a pattern, therefore, and remains random noise. On the right, the symmetrical pattern within the central cross incorporates the symmetrical pixels on each side of the course and so extends the contiguous geons where symmetry is perceived. The operation of feature detection and texture detection neurons was impaired in the visual system of the unfortunate soldier

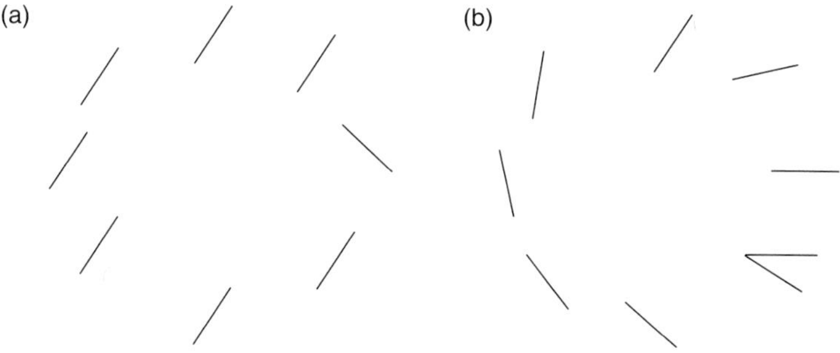

Figure 6.12 Pop-out is the result of texture segmentation, such as a distinct orientation (a) or a convex feature among lines (b).

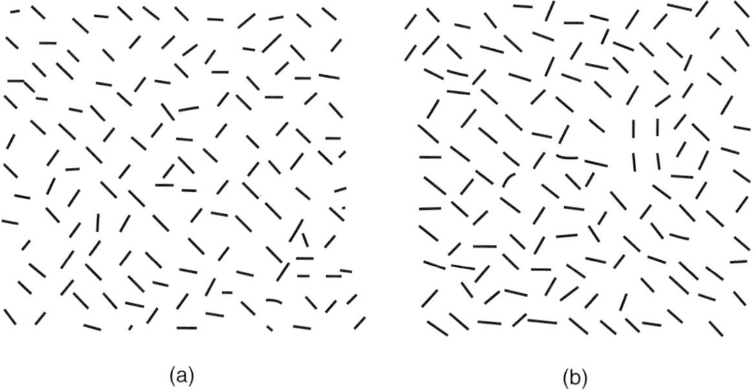

Figure 6.13 Finding the single vertical line is more difficult in (a) than finding the four vertical lines together in (b).

Figure 6.14 A central cross of random noise makes an otherwise symmetrical pattern appear entirely random (left) and a central cross containing a symmetrical pattern makes an otherwise random pattern appear entirely symmetrical (right). (Julesz, 1975).

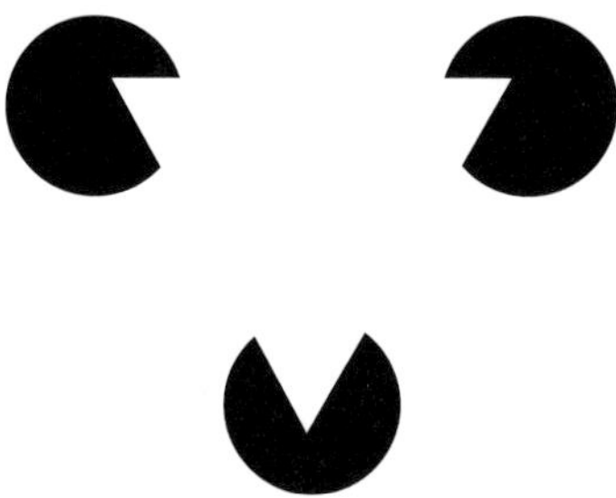

Figure 6.15 The representation of a triangle may be constructed from illusory contours resulting from closure.

described at the beginning of the chapter. So, to him, the patterns in Figure 6.14 would look the same. For the rest of us, what is easy versus what is difficult to see is determined by the organization of the visual input.

Textures and edges activate the representations of surfaces, which will ultimately be the surfaces of three dimensional objects, as described below. In Figure 6.15, corner and shape features are grouped together by the visual system and are experienced as illusory contours of a white triangle.

Visual stress

Each feature detection neuron in the visual cortex ultimately responds to the pattern of light and dark falling on its receptive field in the retina. Each receptive field consists of a central area that excites the neuron and a surround that inhibits it. Light/dark patterns, such as stripes, that activate the central areas of some neurons but not their surrounds cause the greatest levels of excitation in the visual cortex. Furthermore, the greatest level of excitation in the visual cortex occurs when the thickness of the stripes (technically called their spatial frequency) most closely matches the thickness of the central receptive fields of the maximum number of neurons in the visual cortex. The maximum response is to a pattern such as that in Figure 6.16. For some individuals, the visual cortex has such a large response to such

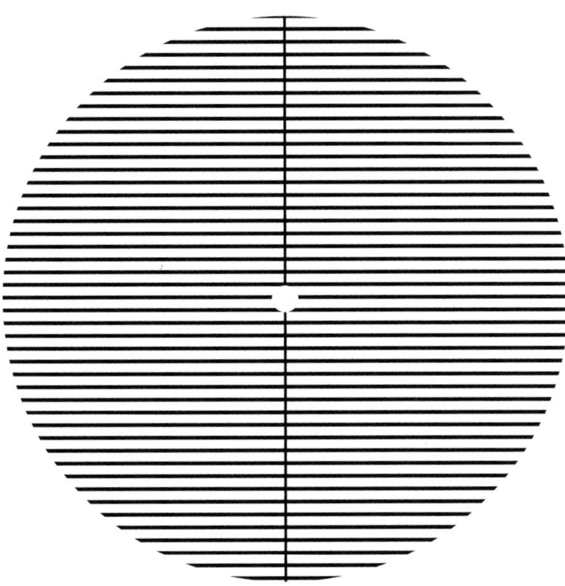

Figure 6.16 This spatial frequency pattern causes maximum firing in the visual cortex and maximum discomfort (Wilkins, Binnie, and Darby, 1981).

a pattern that they have a seizure when they look at it – that is, the neurons start firing out of control (Wilkins, Binnie, and Darby, 1981).

Fewer than 1 percent of people have such an extreme response. However, many more people find looking at such a pattern uncomfortable. Unfortunately, most books are typeset so that the letters form a similarly annoying spatial frequency pattern (Wilkins and Nimmo-Smith, 1987). This is why many people find reading tiring and suffer migraine headaches because of it. They are much poorer readers than they would be if the type were spaced differently. Fortunately, there is a remedy. Neurons that respond to different frequencies of light are not all equally sensitive to the same spatial frequency patterns. By wearing colored glasses while reading, people can reduce the frequencies to which they are most sensitive and read much more comfortably. The same result can be achieved by reading through covered overlays (Wilkins and Lewis, 1999). This is called the Mears–Irlen effect, after its discoverer (Mears) and popularizer (Irlen). The key is to get a proper diagnosis of the frequencies that need to be filtered out.

6.4 Depth construction

Some cells process only **monocular** responses from cells in a single retina while others compute **binocular** differences between the output of corresponding cells in the right and left retinas stimulated by light from the same location in space. Both kinds of responses contribute to the construction of the three-dimensional representation of the visual field. On the one hand, binocular responses are essential for precise representation, because a single two-dimensional representation is consistent with many possible three-dimensional representations. Only by comparing the differences between two images of the same visual field from difference perspectives (the left eye and the right eye) can a three-dimensional representation that represents the relative depth of objects be constructed with certainty. On the other hand, monocular cues provide converging evidence of the absolute distance of objects from the observer.

Binocular cues

Many neurons receive input from both the left and right eyes and detect binocular cues that require both eyes. They detect differences between the right and left retinal images. These differences, called **disparities**, are an important source of depth information. As shown in Figure 6.17, when you fixate on a point from two different locations, such as your left and right eyes, the images cast on each eye are slightly different. The closer an object is to you the closer together its retinal images are to the center of the visual field in each retinal image. For example, as shown in the figure, if you slightly cross your eyes so that the images in the figure merge, you see them in three dimensions, with the distance depending on the sizes of the disparities between the merged images. The combination of these separate images to form a single representation is called **stereopsis**.

Figure 6.17 When you fixate on two objects such that one is behind the other the images of the closer object are displaced more on each retina than the images of the farther objects. When you cross your eyes to merge the images, the visual system treats them as displaced images of a single object and so the three-dimensional effect of the figure is increased.

Another way to attempt to fuse the images is to attempt to look through the page to a point beyond it. Image fusing is not always easy. However, there are several ways of making the task easier that you may have experienced. For example, if one picture was printed in red and the other in green, and you looked at them through glasses with one red and one green lens, then each eye would see only one picture and it would be much easier to fuse them. Alternatively, the two pictures could be printed on top of each other. The pattern produced is called an **autostereogram**. If you fixate intently on an autostereogram for a while your eye muscles become tired, your eyes diverge a little from the fixation point, so the two retinal images diverge a little and the disparities between them produce the perception of depth – that is, the yellow and red flowers in front of the blue ones (Figure 6.17). However, for a small percentage of the population small difficulties in fixation early in life prevented the normal development of binocular vision, and for these people the form in the stereogram remains flat (Von Noorden, 1995).

Depth construction does not only make use of the comparison of simultaneous images in the right and left eyes. It also makes use of successive retinal images from the same eye (Hadani *et al.*, 1994). Moreover, **occlusion** aids in binocular depth perception. When seen from two different angles, slightly more of the occluded object appears in one image than in the other (Anderson and Nakayama, 1994).

Monocular cues

The local features detected by the interblob neurons are combined with the possible three-dimensional representations activated by binocular disparities to narrow the range of possible distances in a three-dimensional representation.

Size and perspective. When you look at something, the further away something is, the smaller the retinal image that it has; in other words, the points that comprise the retinal image are closer together. As a result, lines receding from you into the distance that are actually parallel seem to come together in the distance at a vanishing point, as shown in Figure 6.18. This cue for depth is called perspective, and it is used by the visual system to assign distances and relative sizes to other objects in the visual field. For example, notice that the horizontal line in the foreground looks smaller than the horizontal line in the background even though they are exactly the same size. The effect of perspective is to make the line in the background appear further away. But, since they both are objectively the same size on the paper, and hence have the same retinal images, the line further away must actually be larger, and so is assigned a greater size by the visual system to the line below it. This effect is called the Ponzo illusion, after its discoverer. To see the horizontal lines as the same size, it is necessary only to cover the diagonal lines creating the perspective. Another depth cue is size, which is often combined with perspective. Notice that in Figure 6.18 the smaller square appears to be further away.

Another perspective illusion is shown in Figure 6.19. Notice that line AB looks shorter than line BC, even though they are both the same size. This is because the line between them creates a corner feature that may be the apex of a pyramid such that BC is receding into the background, hence further away, and AB is projecting into the foreground, hence closer. But, if BC is both further away than AB and has the same retinal image, then it must actually be

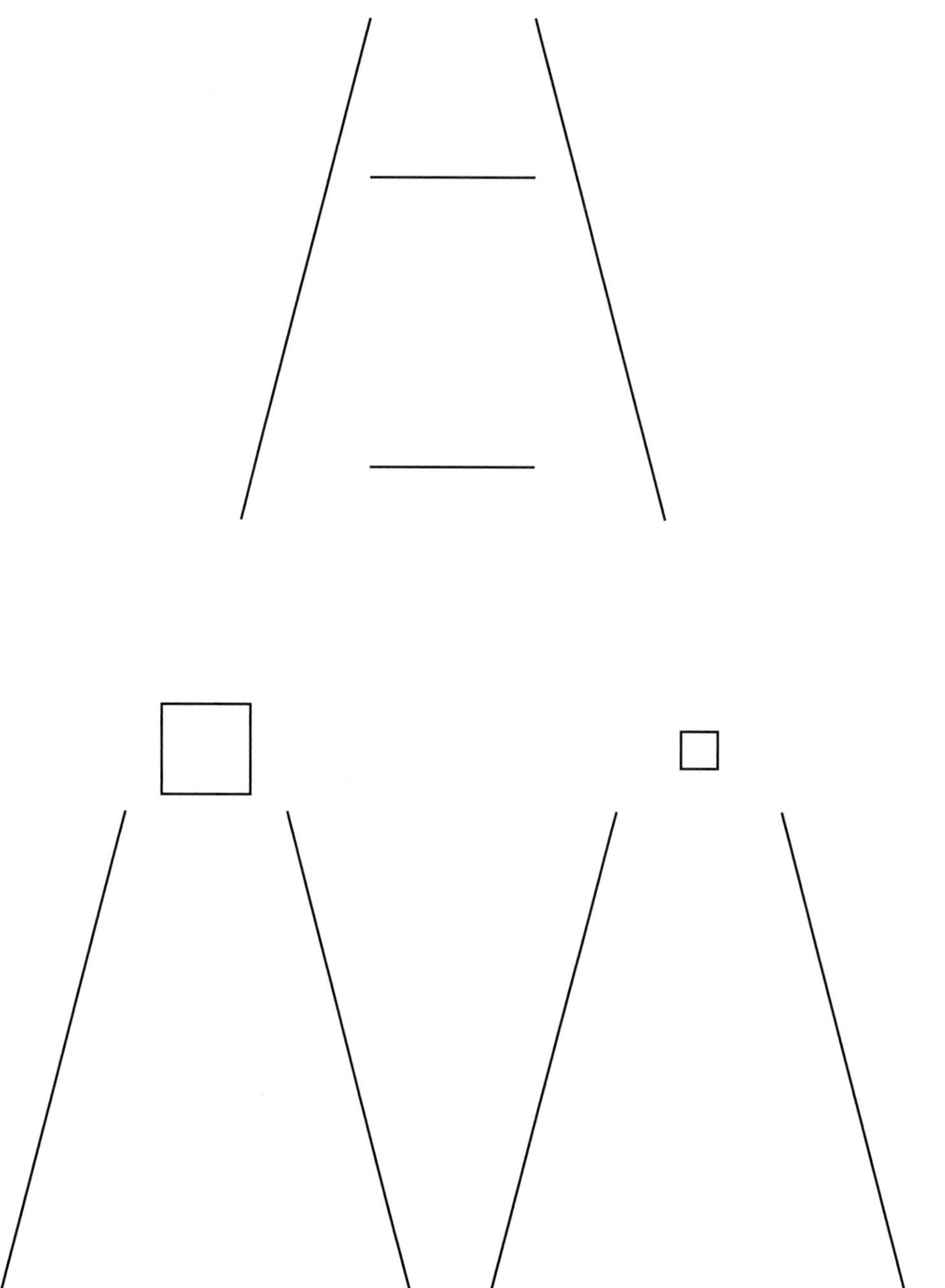

Figure 6.18 Perspective is a depth cue. Top: The Ponzo illusion. Upper horizontal line looks larger. Bottom: Size and perspective combine to make smaller square look further away.

larger, and so it is assigned a larger size in the representation of the visual field. To see that AB and BC are actually equal-size sides of a triangle it is necessary only to cover the line dividing angle B (Gregory, 1998).

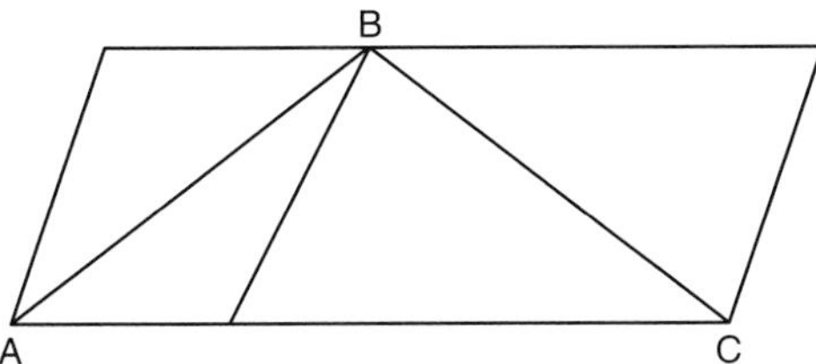

Figure 6.19 Line AB appears shorter than BC because they are the same length but BC appears farther away; hence it must be longer. Cover the middle line to break the three-dimensional representation and they look their correct sizes (Gregory, 1978).

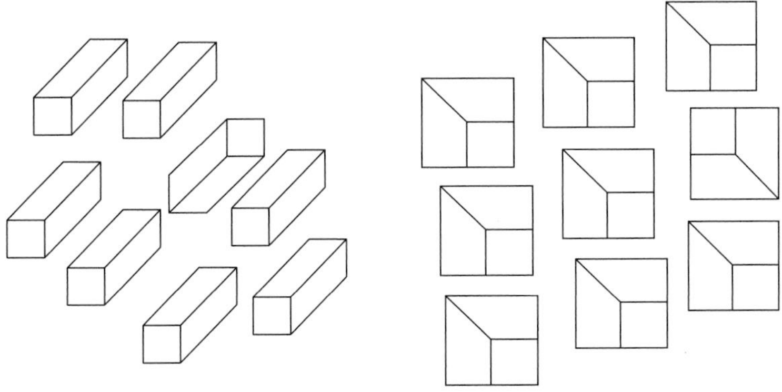

Figure 6.20 No form on the right is distinguished by a unique feature so "pop-out" does not occur. One form on the left is distinguished by a unique feature so "pop-out" does occur.

Perspective and size are therefore cues for the relative sizes and distances of objects seen in the visual field. A texture can be formed by combining patterns that have a common orientation in depth, as shown in Figure 6.20. In fact, the figure shows that three-dimensional depth is a more powerful organizing feature than two-dimensional orientation. On both the right and left of Figure 6.20 one pattern is distinguished from the others by the same visual feature. On the left side the patterns are organized into three-dimensional box representations, and the distinctive feature encodes a different orientation in three dimensions for one of the three-dimensional objects in the array. Hence, it pops out. But on the right side of Figure 6.20 the same distinctive feature is part of one of the two-dimensional shapes in the array, and its distinctive orientation does not cause the shape to pop out.

Occlusion. If you put a plate down on a table, the tabletop does not seem to disappear under the plate, making the plate look as if it floats unsupported in space. Rather, you see the plate on the table. The representation of the tabletop includes the unseen area under the plate. An important property of three-dimensional shape representation is that it includes both the parts of the object that can be seen and the parts that are occluded and hence can't be seen.

In constructing a representation of the occluded part of an object, the visual system makes use of convex features to determine that something is occluded. Figure 6.21 (a) illustrates how an occlusion is interpreted. You see this display as one circle partially occluded by

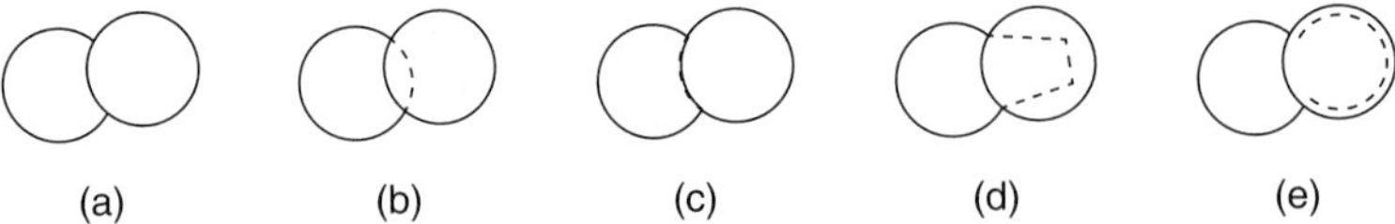

Figure 6.21 Overlapping circles? Potential completions are shown.

Figure 6.22 The fragments on the left do not form recognizable patterns because there is no appearance of occlusion to suggest they are connected. The fragments on the right form recognizable patterns because the overlaying pattern creating apparent occlusion suggests they are connected (Bregman, 1981).

another. The striking thing is that this representation seems like the only natural one, even though there are many other possibilities. A few of the alternative completions are depicted in Figures 6.21 (b), (c), (d), and (e). In each case the occluded portion of the left figure is represented by a dotted line. Figure 6.21 (b) represents the natural interpretation of 6.21 (a) as overlapping circles. In this case, the occluded edge is represented as continuing its path. However, as Figure 6.21 (c) shows, 6.21 (a) might simply be perceived as a chipped circle adjacent to a complete one. In this case, the convex feature would be interpreted as a *concave* feature. Furthermore, as 6.21 (d) and 6.21 (e) indicate, the occluded portion of the left figure might have a noncircular completion.

The filling in of missing parts makes it possible to see separated areas as part of the same surface. For a striking example of how the visual system completes occluded objects, examine Figure 6.22. There is no occlusion in the left panel of Figure 6.22, just some odd shapes that form no obvious pattern. Now look at the right panel of the figure. Here a new shape has been added that appears to occlude the fragments. The visual system connects them even though they are not adjacent. When the fragments are connected, the pattern of hidden letters is obvious.

Ambiguity and camouflage. The individual features of a two-dimensional representation can always be organized in more than one way to create a pattern. This is illustrated in Figure 6.23. Notice that the "X" on the left can be perceived as two vertical lines crossing or as two arrows whose points are touching. Most observers tend to see it as two vertical lines crossing. In addition, the hourglass-like figure on the right can be perceived as an "X" whose top and bottom endpoints are connected by horizontal lines or as two triangles whose points are touching. Most observers tend to see it as two triangles whose points are touching. When a pattern has more than one representation it is called **ambiguous**. In the pattern on the left the center crossing is represented as two diagonal lines intersecting, but in the pattern on the right exactly the same center crossing is represented as the tips of two triangular shapes touching. When more than two lines meet at a point there is always more than one possible representation. In each representation different pairs of lines are connected. Only one of the possible representations is selected and incorporated into the perceptual experience.

The way the visual system tends to perform this selection process is illustrated by the two patterns in Figure 6.24. The hexagon on the right is in fact contained in the striped parallelogram on the left. However, this is not apparent, because the visual system organizes the line segments of the figure on the left into a representation of a parallelogram whose

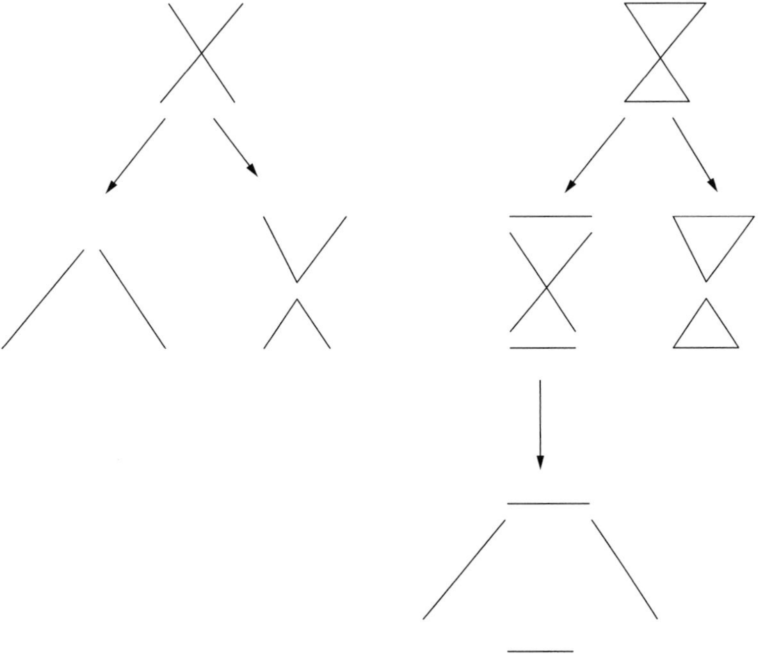

Figure 6.23 Crossing is usually perceived as crossing diagonal lines on left but as touching triangle points on right.

Figure 6.24 Hexagon is camouflaged in striped parallelogram.

Figure 6.25 Camouflage can make the familiar invisible. Cover the left side of the figure to find familiar patterns.

surface is covered with a striped texture. Neither of these representations (the parallelogram or the striped texture) contains the hexagon. Another way of saying this is that the hexagon is not a **good part** or **gestalt** of the striped parallelogram. When one pattern is contained in but not a good part of another, the hidden pattern is said to be **camouflaged**. Camouflage is the opposite of pop-out. A pattern pops out from a visual field when it is assigned a distinct representation. A pattern is camouflaged in the visual field when it is not assigned a distinct representation but, instead, its elements are partitioned among different features or embedded in a texture.

Predator versus prey

The inadequacy of the information about depth provided by monocular cues has influenced the evolution of the facial features and surface coverings of many animals. If an animal is a herbivore – that is, the prey of a carnivore – then it is useful to have the eyes far apart to provide a wide field of vision. In fact, some animals have their eyes on the sides of their head, giving them a view all the way around, making it impossible to sneak up on them in daylight when they are alert. Of course, an animal with eyes wide apart, giving it a wide field of vision, gives up the ability to construct an accurate three-dimensional representation of the world, because its left and right retinal images overlap little or not at all. However, for most purposes a precise three-dimensional representation of the world is unnecessary, and this is a small price to pay for survival. It is also useful to be invisible to whatever would prey on you. Some animals have camouflage that makes them invisible in their natural surroundings. For example, their stripes cause zebras to blend into the tall grass that is their home. If the claim that camouflage makes something invisible may seem exaggerated, try to find the familiar pattern in Figure 6.25.

On the other hand, if you are a predator, then you need to be able to find your prey. Camouflage exists only in an ambiguous two-dimensional representation. When the single possible three-dimensional representation consistent with them is constructed from the disparities of a pair of overlapping two-dimensional representations of the same visual field seen from two slightly different locations, there is no such thing as camouflage. So predators often have close-set eyes, creating overlapping fields of vision that provide many opportunities to detect disparities. Hence they construct an accurate three-dimensional representation of the field for a certain distance in front of them. Any prey within that distance is seen in

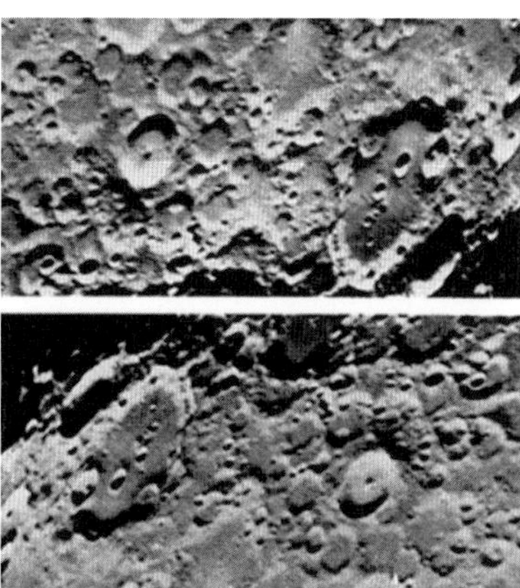

Figure 6.26 Images of faraway objects are ambiguous: upright and inverted moonscape.

three dimensions regardless of its camouflage. Cats, the premier predators of the mammal world, have the closest-set eyes.

Humans also have close-set eyes, indicating that we are more predator than prey. Binocular cues make it possible to compute the precise distance from you of an object close by. However, binocular cues are useful only for objects a few feet away from you. For distant objects there are no detectable disparities between the retinal images, and the differences in vergence are also undetectable. Only monocular cues are available. When objects are viewed in the distance, or in limited light, or in photographs, depth cues are reduced, so that more than one three-dimensional representation is consistent with the sensory input. In this case, the visual system relies on memory to select a single probable three-dimensional representation. What you actually perceive is the three-dimensional representation selected from memory, which you do not experience as ambiguous or indeterminate. For example, under normal illumination you have no difficulty discriminating the different sizes of a real chair and of a much smaller toy chair. But, if the visual information is reduced, then the size of a visual object may be determined by the typical size of the object whose memory representation it matches. Size judgments become more difficult, and a toy chair may appear to be the size of a real one (Franklin and Erickson, 1969; Schiffman, 1967; Slack, 1956).

Pictures have less information than three-dimensional objects, so they are useful for demonstrating ambiguity and the effect of memory on visual perception. For example, the shaded circles in the photograph of the surface of the Moon in Figure 6.26 are ambiguous. They may be images of holes or bumps. In one orientation they look like holes and in the other orientation they look like bumps. The reason is that, most of the time in the real world, the light source is from above. The reversal is the consequence of your perceptual experience with the shadows of real holes and real bumps. In each case the ambiguous representation is perceived as the most common representation that it matches in memory. The three-dimensional representation that is selected is the one that would produce the image if illuminated from above – which, of course, it almost always is. Memory therefore informs perception.

When humans engaged in modern warfare, the inadequacy of visual depth information for faraway objects became important. When the British and Americans sent bombers flying over Nazi-occupied Europe during World War II, the limits of monocular cues for visual perception became apparent. High-altitude reconnaissance photographs had no more information than the photograph in Figure 6.26. When human intelligence officers examined the photographs, all they saw were indecipherable dark smudges. The solution was to use twin cameras separated by a fixed distance when taking aerial reconnaissance photographs. Afterwards, the pair of photographs was placed in a stereoscope (what most of the world knows as the Viewmaster toy) for viewing three-dimensional pictures. When the aerial photographs were viewed stereoscopically, the objects on the ground popped out in three dimensions and became identifiable.

During World War II, although people knew how to create three-dimensional images with a stereoscope, no one knew how three-dimensional representations were constructed by the brain. However, the wartime intelligence work led directly to this discovery. In addition to aerial intelligence, the British and Americans received information from spies inside Nazi-occupied Europe. One of these was a Hungarian electrical engineer, and later a scientist, named Bela Julesz. Through his work in intelligence, Julesz became aware that camouflage was not possible in a three-dimensional representation. Many years after the war, when he had the opportunity to work on visual perception, this was the clue that inspired him to do the studies showing that binocular information was available near the beginning of the visual pathway and that a three-dimensional representation of the visual field was one of the first representations constructed (Julesz, 1995).

6.5 Recognition of three-dimensional objects

The perceptual system must do more than construct an accurate representation. It must construct a representation that may be compared with representations in memory to identify it. Recognition may be either in the short term or the long term. If you momentarily cover this page with your hand, you want to be able to see it as the same page, and not an entirely new page, when you remove your hand. On the other hand, you want to recognize people you know for the rest of your life, no matter how long it has been since the last time you have seen them.

Orientation and comparison

The great enemy of recognition is orientation. For example, unless an object has horizontal symmetry, it literally has an entirely different representation when turned upside down. This is easy to overlook for a familiar object whose identity you already know. However, it is obvious when a comparison of unfamiliar objects is attempted.

Figure 6.27 shows pairs of unfamiliar objects. The perception of the unfamiliar objects is immediate and automatic. However, the identification of an unfamiliar object as the same object when seen in two different orientations is slow, effortful, and prone to error. This is demonstrated by the three pairs of objects shown in Figure 6.27. The two members of each pair are shown in different orientations, and the task is to determine whether they are the same object in two different orientations or two different objects. This determination is obviously difficult. Presenting one member of each pair on a study list and then presenting the other member of each pair on a test list, thus turning the task into a recognition task for a study object in a new orientation, would make the task even more difficult.

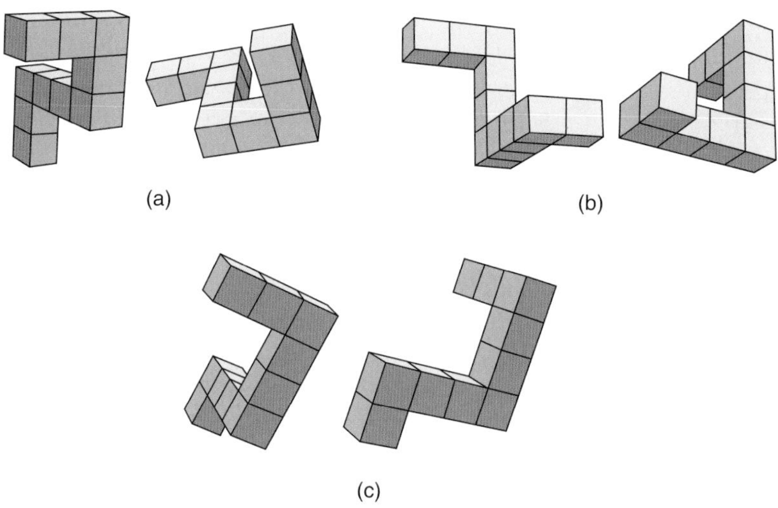

Figure 6.27 Pairs of patterns used for shape comparisons. (a) A "same" pair that differs by an 80 degree rotation in the picture plane. (b) A "same" pair that differs by an 80 degree rotation in depth. (c) A "different" pair that cannot be matched by any rotation (Shepard and Metzler, 1971).

Recognition is almost never as difficult as the same/different task in Figure 6.27 implies. How, then, do people usually recognize unfamiliar objects in unfamiliar orientations? The answer is that you perceive the unfamiliar object as composed of parts that are familiar **geons** (Biederman, 1985). Geons are the representations of convex shapes that are assembled in the construction of the representation of a three-dimensional object by the visual system. Geons are simple enough shapes to be only modestly altered by a change in orientation. In the limit, a round bulge remains a bulge regardless of orientation. A square block turned part-way becomes a diamond, but when completely inverted it becomes a square again.

The visual system matches the simple, *familiar* geons in the representation of a rotated, *unfamiliar* object and puts them together to identify the object. Biederman calls this **recognition by components**. Once a spatial representation of the familiar geons of a novel object has been encoded it will be matched with its representation in memory in any orientation that preserves the representations of its individual geons. Biederman and Bar (1999) called the parts of a figure that have similar representations in different orientations **non-accidental properties**.

To demonstrate that people used non-accidental properties to recognize objects, Biederman and Bar (1999) performed an experiment in which the objects in two different pictures were either the same or different. First, they predicted that observers were more likely to detect differences between the study and test images when they were in the same orientation, because when they were in the same orientation a difference between a part of the study image and a part of the test image in the same location of the respective images would be immediately apparent. Second, they predicted that, when the study and test images were in different orientations, when objects in different orientations had different geons it would still be possible to notice they were different, because the detection of a geon unique to one of the objects did not require a fixed orientation.

Biederman and Bar (1999) had observers determine whether two briefly presented pictures were of the same novel object or different novel objects, as shown in Figure 6.28 (b). First, the fixation point was shown for 500 milliseconds, then the study picture for 400 mil-

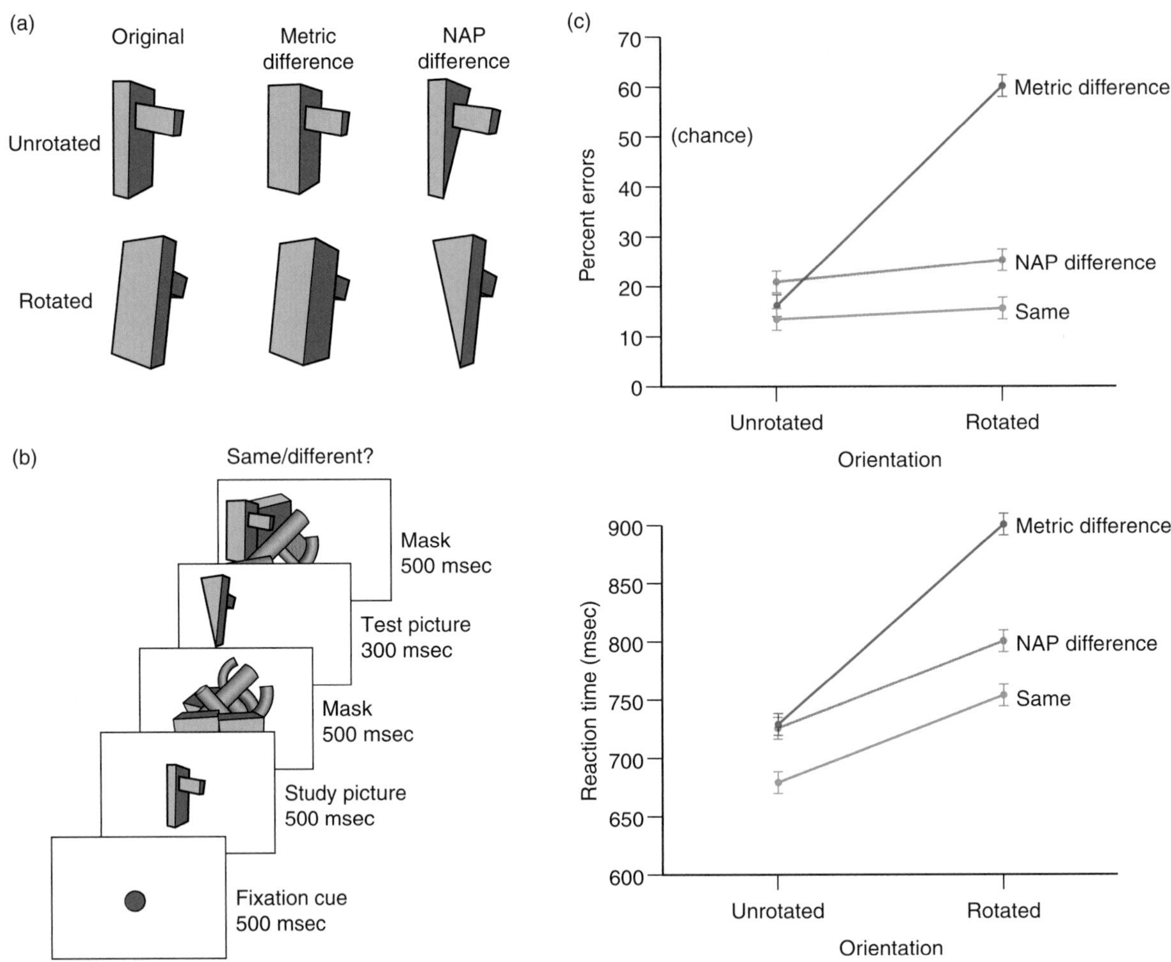

Figure 6.28 Comparison of unrotated and rotated forms. Examples of original form and transformations that preserve (metric) and alter (NAP) geons that remain visible under rotation (a). Sequence of events on an experimental trial (b). Mean error rates (upper panel) and mean correct RTs (c) as a function of orientation and type of change (same versus NAP difference versus metric (MP) difference). Vertical bars through points show standard errors of the means (Biederman and Barr, 1999).

liseconds, then a mask for 500 milliseconds, then the test picture for 300 milliseconds, and finally another mask for 500 milliseconds. As shown in Figure 6.28 (a), when the objects were different, they either had slightly different dimensions but the same geons, called a metric difference, or they had a different geon, which was called a non-accidental property (NAP) difference. Half the time the test picture was rotated with respect to the study picture and half the time it was not. As shown in Figure 6.28 (c), when study and test pictures showed the objects in the same orientation, error rates were about 20 percent for different judgments and did not differ for metric and NAP differences. In contrast, when the test picture showed a rotated object, the error rate did not change for forms that differed on non-accidental properties but rose to about 60 percent for those with only metric differences. Kim and

Biederman (2012) found that the performance of this task was associated with activation of the lateral occipital cortex. Textures are therefore combined into shapes relatively early in the perceptual pathway.

As is also shown in Figure 6.28 (c), even though the error rate was not greater for different judgments to rotated objects than for unrotated objects that differed in non-accidental properties from the object in the study picture, the response time to make the judgment did increase. An object that has been seen only once beforehand has only one representation in memory. When seen again in a novel orientation, it may be necessary for the visual system to first perform computations on the input representation that mentally rotate it to the orientation in which it was just seen in order to match the representation in memory. This mental rotation process adds time to the process of identification (Hayward and Tarr, 1997).

Geons and familiar objects

If geons are used to identify unfamiliar objects in new orientations then they must also be available to identify familiar objects in typical orientations. So, when a three-dimensional object representation is constructed, it is guided by the identification of familiar geons. As we have seen, geons are constructed from corner features, so these should be critical for recognizing objects. Figure 6.29 (a) shows line drawings of some familiar objects, and Figure 6.29 (c) shows the same drawings with the corner features erased to obscure the geons that comprised them. In Figure 6.29 (b) the same amount of erasure, leaving the corner features intact, does not obscure the geons. When shown to students, over 80 percent of the pictures like those in Figure 6.29 (c) were unrecognizable, but fewer than 5 per cent of the pictures like those in Figure 6.29 (b) were unrecognizable.

To provide evidence that geons actually exist, Biederman and Cooper (1991) performed a priming task (Chapter 5). In this task, two pictures were presented in succession to determine whether the first picture, the prime, influenced the processing of the second picture,

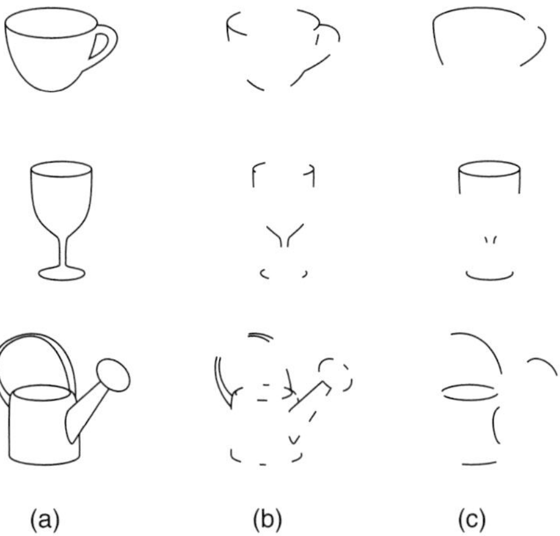

Figure 6.29 The effects of different deletions on the perception of pictured objects. Column (a) shows intact pictures. Column (b) shows deletions that preserve convex parts. Column (c) shows deletions that destroy the convex parts (Biederman, 1985).

the **target**. In order to test the geon theory, Biederman and Cooper created prime–geon target pairs from line drawings of familiar objects by deleting every other edge and vertex from the drawing to create the prime and using these deleted segments to create the target. In the top row of the panel the picture of a grand piano is divided into two images (left and center) such that each image contains exactly the same set of geons. Notice that the left and center images do not overlap but, combined, form the complete original picture of the piano. Biederman and Cooper used one of these images as the prime and the other image as the geon target. In addition, they used 50 percent of a picture of an upright piano as a semantic target (which will be defined below). Biederman and Cooper also created prime/part target pairs from line drawings of familiar objects by deleting every other object part from the drawing to create the prime and using these deleted parts to create the target.

The two complementary images therefore had different geons, as shown in the bottom row of Figure 6.30 (a). Biederman and Cooper used one of these images as the prime and the other as a part target. Again, 50 percent of a different picture was used as the semantic target. In Biederman and Cooper's experiment college students in an introductory psychology course had to identify the briefly presented picture fragments. The procedure is shown in Figure 6.30 (b). Each observer first saw a prime block of trials and then a target block of trials. In the prime block, for each object, the observer first saw a fixation point for 500 milliseconds, then the prime for 500 msec, and then a mask for 500 msec that was a random line drawing. Since it was presented for half a second, the prime was visible, unlike the priming task described in Chapter 5. A voice key recorded the onset of the observer's voice when he or she named the pictured object. The prime block took about seven minutes and was followed by the target block. In a target block the sequence of events was the same except that each target was presented for only 200 msec. There were four kinds of target blocks. The targets were identical to the primes, geon targets, part targets, or semantic targets. Each observer saw one of the four kinds of target block.

When the same picture of an object is shown more than once you can name it a little more quickly the second time. This is called **repetition priming**. Moreover, when two different pictures of objects with the same name, such as two pianos, are shown, the second picture is named a little more quickly. This is called **semantic priming**. In other words, repetition priming occurs for the repeated picture and semantic priming occurs for the second picture that has the same common name as the first picture. In general, there is a larger reduction in naming time for repetition priming than for semantic priming. Figure 6.30 (c) shows that Biederman and Cooper (1991) found this (usual) pattern of naming times: the students named the targets more quickly than the primes. In addition, as is typically found in experiments that involve priming, they named the identical targets (repetition priming) more quickly than the semantic targets (semantic priming). The purpose of Biederman and Cooper's experiment was the comparison between the geon targets and the part targets. They reasoned that, if geons existed, then the prime and geon targets would have exactly the same geons. Therefore, the prime and its geon target would activate the same visual representation – that is, repetition priming would occur. In contrast, since the prime and its part target had different geons, they would activate different visual representations of the same object. The part target would function as a different picture with the same name that is, semantic priming would occur. As shown in the bottom panel, identical and geon targets had the same naming times and part and semantic targets

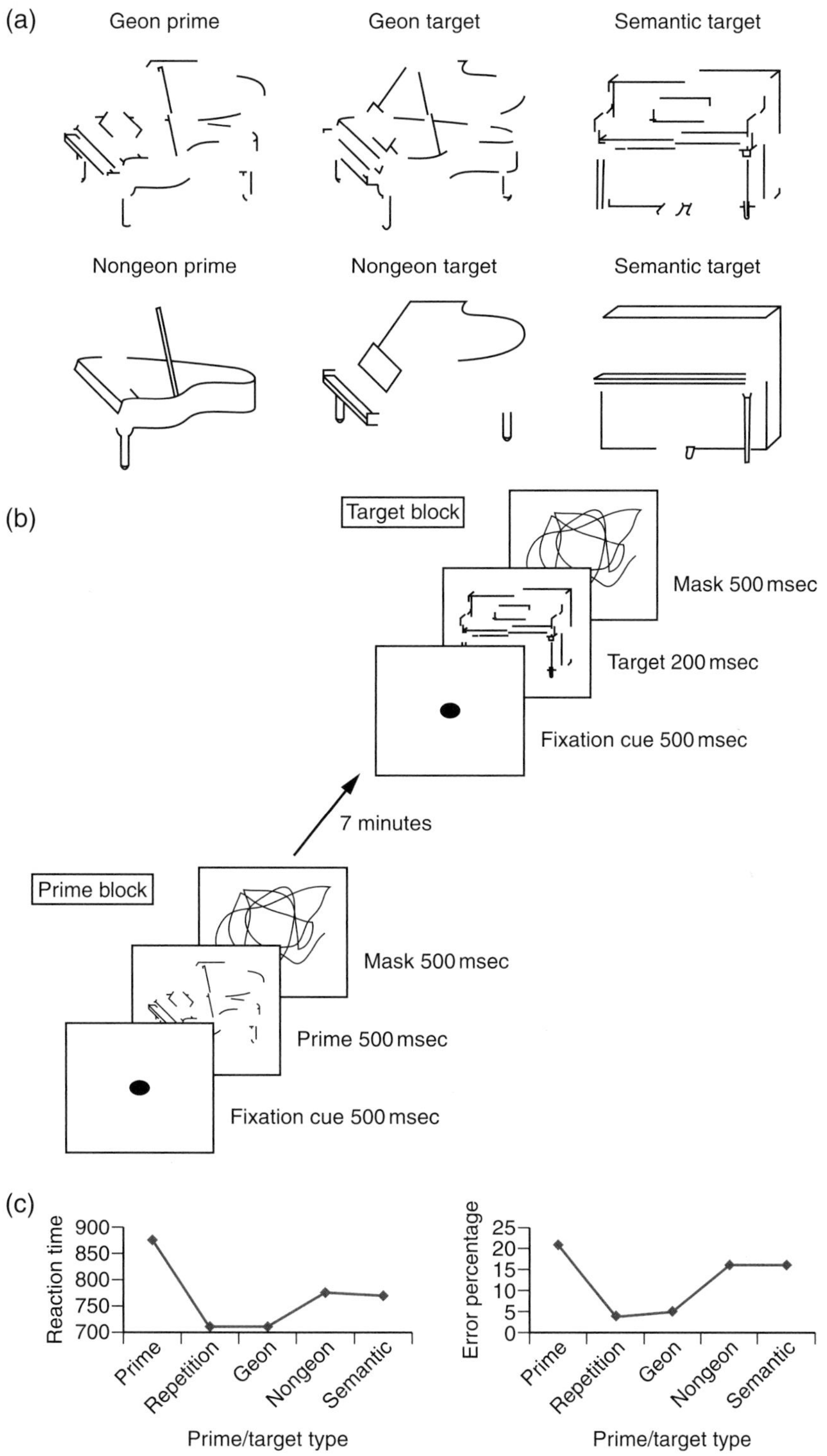

Figure 6.30 Prime/target pair at top of panel (a) have same geons but prime/target pair at bottom have different geon. Experimental procedure (b). Geon primes produce same results as repetition primes and nongeon primes produce same results as semantic primes (c) (Biederman and Cooper, 1991).

had the same naming times. As also shown in the figure, the same pattern was found for error rates.

Recall from Chapter 5 that priming plays a role in visual skills such as reading. Just as geons are features of the representations of three-dimensional objects, letters are features of the representations of words. Recall from Chapter 5 that the initial letters of a word may be used to retrieve a representation of the entire word during reading. Recall that you cannot always see four random letters to the right or left of a fixation point (Estes, Allmeyer, and Reder, 1976). In contrast, when reading familiar words, you can see up to fourteen letters to the right of a fixation point (McConkie and Rayner, 1975). Memory therefore guides perception. The role of whole-word representations in perception becomes apparent when perception is made more difficult. Suppose that a word or letter is presented under conditions that make it very difficult to identify. When a letter is presented in very small type (Prinzmetal and Silvers, 1994) or for a very short time (Reicher, 1969; Wheeler, 1970), it may be identified less often when it is presented by itself than when it is presented as part of a word. The advantage for the letter when it is part of a word is called the **word superiority effect**. The word superiority effect shows that visual memory contains word representations that are independent of the letter representations, so that the entire word can be perceived without first perceiving the individual letters.

Further evidence for word representations that are independent of letter representations is the fact that the individual letters are not seen when reading very familiar words. Healy (1980) demonstrated this effect of the whole-word pathway by instructing college students to read a prose passage at their normal reading speed and to encircle all the "t"s they came across. The students missed more "t"s in common words such as *fact* than in rare words such as *pact*. Similarly, function words are more frequent than content words, and Schindler (1978) found more letter detection errors on function words than content words. The most common word of all in the English language is *the*. In one passage Healy (1980) found that students missed "t"s in 38 percent of the *the*s but only in 20 percent of the other words containing "t" (see also Corcoran, 1966; Healy, 1976). Similarly, Haber and Schindler (1981) found that misspellings that changed the overall shape of a word were more likely to be detected than ones that did not (see also Holbrook, 1978). Because whole-word recognition makes letter detection more difficult, it makes the detection of spelling errors that preserve the overall shape of the word more difficult. Healy (1981) also asked college students to read passages at their normal reading speed but to mark any spelling errors they noticed while reading. She created the spelling errors by substituting one letter for another in the passage. For example, "c" was substituted for "e," creating *studcnts*, and "s" was substituted for "o," creating *absut*. According to the feature analysis hypothesis, "c" and "e" differ by only a single feature: the horizontal line that is present in the "e" but not in the "c." However, "s" and "o" differ by more than one feature. The students failed to notice 60 percent of the "c"-for-"e" substitutions but failed to notice only 5 percent of the "s"-for-"o" substitutions. More generally, Healy found that if the substitution maintained the outer configuration of the original, as in "c" for "e" or "C" for "G," the student was more likely to fail to detect the substitution than if the outer configuration was changed.

Spatial relations

Although geons aid in object identification, including face recognition, and letters aid in word recognition, the representation of a three-dimensional object is more than the sum

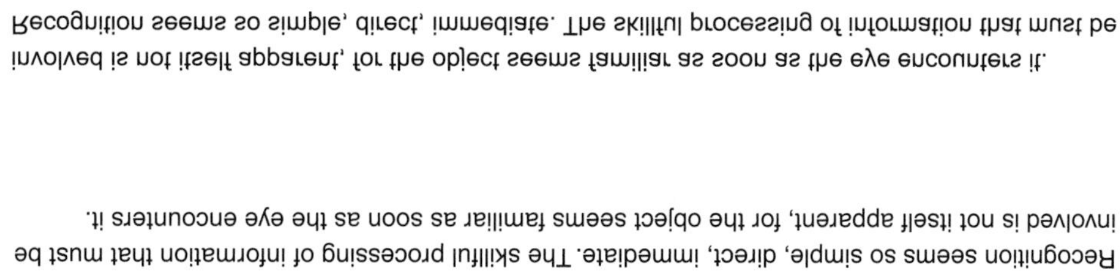

Recognition seems so simple, direct, immediate. The skillful processing of information that must be involved is not itself apparent, for the object seems familiar as soon as the eye encounters it.

Recognition seems so simple, direct, immediate. The skillful processing of information that must be involved is not itself apparent, for the object seems familiar as soon as the eye encounters it.

Figure 6.31 When an entire line of text is turned upside down the spatial relationships among letters are preserved (bottom). When the each letter in a line of text is inverted, the spatial relationships among the letters are changed (top).

of its geons, and the representation of a word is more than its individual letters. Compare the difficulty of reading two lines of inverted text in Figure 6.31. The bottom two lines are what you see when you turn a page of text upside down. Even though you are forced to read from right to left instead of from left to right, this can be done with only moderate difficulty. The top two lines were created by inverting each individual letter but otherwise leaving the text intact. As discussed in Chapter 5, Kolers (1976) found that initially reading inverted-letter text is very slow, despite the preservation of normal left-to-right scanning. The reason that the bottom lines are easier to read than the top lines is that, in the bottom, the spatial relationship of one letter to the next is preserved, even though the orientation is altered with respect to the reader. However, in the top two rows the spatial relationship of each letter with respect to its neighbors is altered. The greater difficulty of reading the top rows is caused by the elimination of the spatial relations among letters that are encoded in whole-word representations. Spatial relations are sometimes called **global features**, and geons, corners, etc. are called **local features**.

Thatcher illusion. A similar effect occurs when faces are rotated, though it is not so obvious. The representation of an inverted face contains a sufficient number of facial features (such as eyes, nose, and mouth) that it can still be matched with representations in memory, so the elimination of the whole-face pathway, which represents spatial relationships among the facial features, is not noticed. The effect of inversion on face perception was first demonstrated by the Thatcher illusion (Thompson, 1980), so called because it was first demonstrated with two inverted pictures of Margaret Thatcher, who was the UK prime minister at the time (Figure 6.32). Both faces are recognizable through feature matching even though they are inverted. The importance of spatial relations encoded in the whole-face pathway in upright face perception becomes apparent when you turn the book around and look at the faces right side up. Murray, Yong, and Rhodes (2000) confirmed that spatial relations among geons are represented only during the perception of upright faces, but geons are represented during the perception of both upright and inverted faces. They found that when individual geons, rather than spatial relations, were distorted the resulting face looked equally bizarre whether upright or inverted.

Face blindness. Face recognition is one of the major challenges of human cognitive development. It is imperative for normal social interaction to be able to recognize the faces of relatives, friends, and acquaintances, but detailed representations encoding the

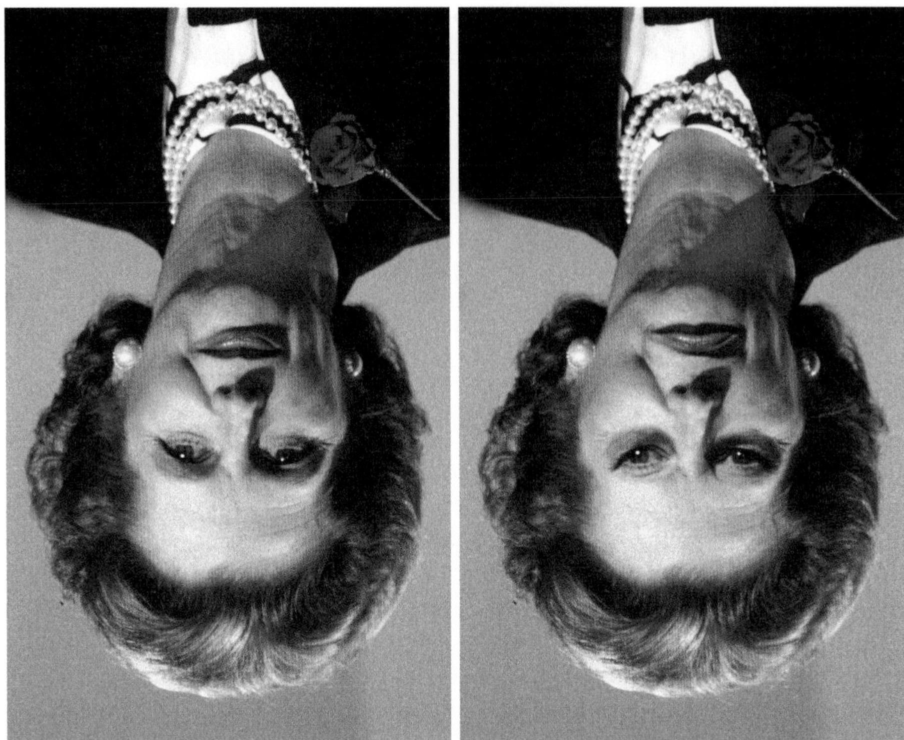

Figure 6.32 Thatcher illusion: invert and compare faces (Thompson, 1980).

precise spatial relationships among the geons of the face, eyes, nose, mouth, etc. are necessary to discriminate among faces. Consequently, practice in the skill of encoding faces begins in infancy and extends into adulthood (Susilo, Germine, and Duchaine, 2013). Consequently, improvements in face recognition emerge early in life. Six-month-old infants are equally adept at recognizing monkey and human faces but by nine months the lifelong advantage for human faces emerges (Pascalis, de Haan, and Nelson, 2002). There is remarkable variability among humans in how well they learn this important skill. Some individuals are much better, and others much worse, than most other people at recognizing faces. The skill depends on the ability to precisely encode the spatial relations among geons. Those who are born impaired in this ability are unable to discriminate among even familiar faces (Yovel and Duchaine, 2006). They are said to have **developmental prosopagnosia** or **face blindness**. Consistent with an inability to encode spatial relations, face-blind individuals do not show the normal recognition advantage for upright over inverted faces (Behrmann *et al.*, 2005; Carbon *et al.*, 2007; Susilo *et al.*, 2013; Yovel and Duchaine, 2006).

The effect of face blindness on social relations illustrates how cognitive abilities and social skills are intertwined. It is difficult to maintain close friendships if you cannot recognize your close friends; apparently ignoring them at school or play (because you don't recognize them) unwittingly creates hurt feelings. In addition, you cannot understand movies and television shows if you cannot tell one character from another. Face blindness runs in families

(Duchaine, Germine, and Nakayama, 2007), and even family life is strained when you and your mother do not recognize each other, and you do not even recognize yourself in home movies and pictures (Sellers, 2010).

At the other end of the ability continuum from face blindness, some individuals are super-recognizers who rarely forget a face (Russell, Duchaine, and Nakayama, 2009). These individuals are superior at encoding the spatial relations among facial features; they show even a greater advantage for normal over inverted faces than normal individuals. Although face blindness impairs social relations, super-recognition does not necessarily enhance them. As one super-recognizer put it, telling someone they once stood in line in front of you while shopping a year ago is not a good ice-breaker. Someone with a normal memory for (and hence forgetting of) faces could mistake this for obsession and stalking.

Scene perception. Ultimately, all visual representation consists of spatial representations. As mentioned above, among the first kinds of information encoded are the orientations of edges. Whether reading a sentence, recognizing a face, or navigating the environment, the visual representation encodes the spatial relations among features. Furthermore, because the construction of perceptual representation is guided by memory, the spatial relationships among the elements of a display influence how rapidly the representation of each element is constructed. Elements in typical, hence expected, locations are seen more rapidly than those in atypical locations. Biederman, Mezzanotte, and Rabinowitz (1982) told an observer the name of the target, such as a hydrant, that might appear in a briefly presented display. A fixation point, presented for 500 milliseconds, was followed by a 150-msec presentation of a scene, which, in turn, was followed by a cue marking some position in the scene that had just been presented. The observer had to report whether the target had appeared in the location marked by the cue.

Figure 6.33 (a) shows a normal scene in which the target is the fire hydrant. In Figure 6.33 (b) the fire hydrant is out of position. Observers failed to detect the target in an appropriate context, such as in Figure 6.33 (a), only 28 percent of the time. They missed it 40 percent of the time in Figure 6.33 (b).

(a)

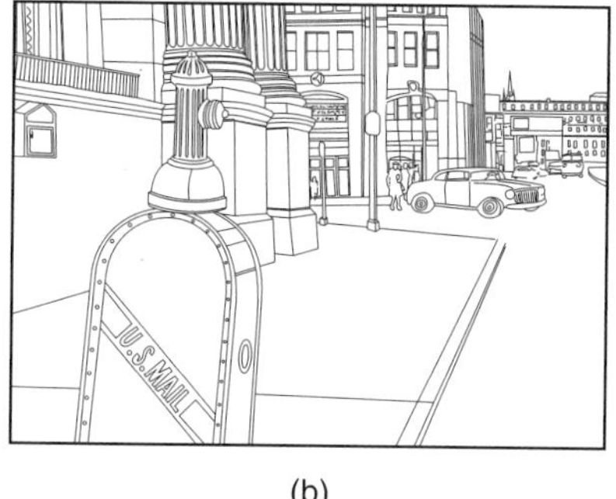

(b)

Figure 6.33 Scene recognition. (a) The target (hydrant) appropriately positioned in a probable context; (b) the target in a position violation (Biederman *et al*., 1982).

6.6 Vision and touch

Recall that the *what*-pathway constructs the perceptual experience while the *how*-pathway controls actions to perceptual targets. While the pathways are anatomically distinct, they are functionally integrated. In the normal course of events you reach for things that you see. In the parietal lobe, visual and tactual input is compared with the same spatial representation of an object, so cross-modal recognition is possible. If you visually examined an object, such as a toy block, before it was thrown into a bag with several blocks of other shapes, you would not have difficulty in reaching into the bag and selecting the one that you had seen. Neurons in the parietal cortex respond to both visual and tactual inputs. When you look at the things that you handle, the task of the perceptual system is sensory integration: combining tactual and visual inputs to construct a single representation. But how does information from the different senses come to be integrated? Do things look the way they feel or do they feel the way they look?

A classic experiment answered this question by placing information from the visual and tactual modalities in conflict. Rock and Victor (1964) asked students to grasp a square while simultaneously examining it through a lens that contracted its visual width to half its original size. The hands of the observers were covered with a cloth so that they could not see their fingers. Following the examination period the students were asked to pick a match, visually or tactually, from an array of undistorted similar items or else to draw the standard. The students selected or drew a square that was the size that it had appeared visually, rather than its actual size. Thus, vision dominates completely over touch: the square felt the way it looked.

Very strong or complete visual dominance over touch has been demonstrated many times in a variety of perceptual tasks, including judgments of size (Kinney and Luria, 1970; Miller, 1972), curvature (Easton and Moran, 1978), length (Teghtsoonian and Teghtsoonian, 1970), and spatial location (Hay, Pick, and Ikeda, 1965; Warren and Cleaves, 1971). The results of these studies indicate that vision completely predominates over touch in the perception of form. In contrast, when there is a conflict between vision and touch with regard to texture, the perceived roughness of the surface is an even compromise between vision and touch (Lederman and Abbott, 1981). Thus, the degree of visual dominance depends on the nature of the task. If the conflicting information is a kind that is usually obtained visually, such as shape information, vision dominates completely. But, if the conflicting information is of a kind usually obtained tactually, such as texture information, then tactual information also strongly influences the perception.

6.7 Visual agnosia

Damage to some part of the primary visual area destroys the feature analysis of some part of the visual input. It therefore generally results in a deficit in form and/or color perception, which is revealed by discrimination and matching tasks. The deficit may vary from mild to severe depending on the extent of the injury. A mild deficit might be loss of color vision or a blind spot in the visual field. A severe deficit would be total blindness (Morris *et al.*, 2001). A bilateral injury to the secondary visual area leaves perception sufficiently intact for the navigation of space. However, visual recognition is impaired.

The purpose of visual perception is not merely to accurately encode the locations of three-dimensional objects but to recognize the targets of possible actions. The soldier mentioned at the beginning of this chapter could no longer do this. Damage to the part of the perceptual pathway extending from the lateral occipital cortex down into the inferior temporal cortex causes a deficit in visual recognition called **visual agnosia**. An individual with visual agnosia will not trip over things, will not have trouble reaching for them, will move clumsily about, and may be able to copy a picture quite well (Behrmann, Moscovitch, and Winocur, 1994). However, the person will be unable to recognize what he or she is copying. The recognition deficit in visual agnosia is limited to the visual modality. A male agnosic patient who does not recognize his wife standing beside him will recognize her voice as soon as she speaks. Likewise, if he does not recognize a key lying before him he will recognize it tactually as soon as he picks it up and manipulates it, and will use it appropriately to open a lock.

Apperceptive and associative visual agnosia

There are two distinct forms of visual agnosia. One form results from a defect in feature analysis or the integration of visual features into perceptual representations in the occipital cortex. This is sometimes called **apperceptive visual agnosia**. The other form results from a disconnection in the temporal cortex that disrupts the comparison of perceptual representations with object representations in memory. This is sometimes called **associative visual agnosia**.

Apperceptive agnosia results from bilateral damage to the same part of the perceptual pathway in each hemisphere, which can produce a very specific deficit in feature integration or pattern organization that is nonetheless severe enough to disrupt object construction, hence recognition. When the agnosia results from a defect in the integration of features into patterns it is called **simultanagnosia** (Cooper and Humphreys, 2000; Humphreys and Price, 1994). The effect is that only a very small portion of the visual input may be represented at one time. So, when looking at a face, an observer can see each eye, the nose, the mouth, etc. perfectly well. He or she just cannot see any more than one eye, a nose, etc. at any one time. It is like going through life looking at the world through a narrow tube. Only it is worse. If you look at the world through a tube you can put the pieces together in your memory and eventually recognize what you are looking at. But someone who has lost the ability to integrate the features can never put the pieces together. The patterns in Figure 6.14 look identical: two squares of noise. In severe cases, such as the soldier at the beginning of the chapter, familiar objects become unrecognizable. In a mild case the individual retains enough visual features to recognize things at a general level and so can recognize an object as a face, car, building, or dog. But the person does not retain sufficient features to recognize his or her own home, car, pet, or face (Benton and Tranel, 1993).

Visual agnosia varies in severity depending on the extent and location of the damage to the perceptual pathway. In even the mildest forms there is some impairment of face recognition, indicating that faces require especially detailed and precise representations to discriminate among them in memory. In one case, existing patterns were left in place and only the learning process was disrupted. Farah and her colleagues (Tippett, Miller, and Farah, 2000) described a thirty-five-year-old male who could recognize people he knew before his injury but could not learn to recognize any new faces. When only face recognition is impaired the disorder is called **prosopagnosia**, as mentioned above. On occasion, recognition for something familiar other than faces is selectively impaired. Humphreys and Rumiata (1998) reported on a seventy-two-year-old female who could not visually recognize familiar objects but was in the normal range for visual recognition of faces and words. Prosopagnosia can result from damage anywhere along the visual perceptual pathway, hence from damage to either the occipital cortex or to the temporal cortex (Farah, 1990). Farah (1990) found that in 29 percent of the cases of prosopagnosia there was damage to only the right hemisphere and in only 6 percent of the cases there was damage to only the left hemisphere. (In 65 percent of the cases there was bilateral damage.) The preponderance of cases resulting from right hemisphere damage alone versus left hemisphere damage alone indicates that the right hemisphere is usually responsible for integrating the images of the right and left visual fields and generating a recognition response, as mentioned in Chapter 4 (Somers and Sheremata, 2013). Hence, when there is only damage to the visual pathway in the left hemisphere, face recognition is usually preserved.

SUMMARY

The construction of a three-dimensional visual representation of the world from the light stimulating the retina is a computationally intense process.

- During the sensory registration stage, light stimulates rods and cones on the retina of the eye. The sensory information is encoded within the retina and transmitted along the visual pathway, first to the thalamus and then to the occipital cortex.
- During the feature analysis stage, the visual pathway divides into many sub-pathways that extend through the occipital cortex and down into the temporal cortex. Each sub-pathway initially encodes a different feature of the visual display. Then the representations of different sub-pathways are combined to construct increasingly complex features of the visual display.
  - The images from the two eyes are combined to construct a three-dimension representation from the disparities between the two two-dimensional representations.
  - Successive images, occlusion, and other cues are also used to construct the three-dimensional representation
- During the shape construction stage, the visual pathway extends down through the inferior temporal cortex. Complex features are combined into representations of three-dimensional objects. Ultimately, the visual display is organized into a three-dimensional scene containing three-dimensional objects, which are recognized.

QUESTIONS

1 Is the movement of eyes from fixation point to fixation point automatic or are they ad hoc actions? When the eyes rest on a fixation point for a few seconds, is that an automatic resting state or an ad hoc action?

2 Why do people see a three-dimensional world? Is it because the world is three-dimensional or because the brain constructs a three-dimensional representation?

3 Should deer have eyes that are wide apart or close together? Should wolves have eyes that are wide apart or close together?

4 How are people able to perceive the size of something far away?
5 What does someone with face blindness see in the mirror?

FURTHER READING

Hoffman, R. R., Hancock, P. A., Scerbo, M. W., Parasuraman, R., and Szalma, J. L. (2014). *The Cambridge Handbook of Applied Perception Research*. Cambridge University Press.

Julesz, B. (1995). *Dialogues on Perception*. Cambridge, MA: MIT Press.

Rock, I. (1984). *Perception*. New York: Scientific American Books.

Van der Helm, P. A. (2014). *Simplicity in Vision: A Multidisciplinary Account of Perceptual Organization*. Cambridge University Press.

Walsh, V., and Kulikowski, J. (2010). *Perceptual Constancy: Why Things Look as They Do*. Cambridge University Press.

7 Semantic memory and language

Some 60,000 years ago, at the end of an ice age, there were humans over much of the world. They all encoded their world into episodes and used tools to act upon it. After the ice age ended, the descendants of one family who lived in east central Africa began to migrate north, and then west into Europe and east into Asia. Wherever they went, the people who already lived there went extinct (there was a small amount of interbreeding in Europe). Everyone in the world today is therefore descended from this one family. Clearly, this family had some enormous advantage that allowed them to conquer the world. One likely possibility is the invention of human language.

The fundamental unit of memory is the episode, in which a voluntary action to a target in a specific context, and its result, are encoded. This is a polymodal representation involving more than one sensory modality and more than one representation. So, when a visual target is matched to a representation in memory, the response is the activation of an entire episode that includes a previous action to the target in a specific context and its consequence. This knowledge of the previous encounter with the target may be used to guide behavior during the current event. As mentioned in Chapter 2, this kind of knowledge is called declarative knowledge. Declarative knowledge is of two kinds: semantic knowledge and episodic knowledge. **Semantic knowledge** is knowledge of what something is, and **episodic knowledge** is knowledge of when it has been encountered previously. Episodic knowledge will be discussed in Chapter 12. We begin the discussion of semantic knowledge here. The representation of semantic knowledge is commonly called **semantic memory**.

The components of an episode – the target, the action, etc. – are associated with verbal and written labels called **words**. When a visual target is matched to a representation in memory, the response to it includes the word naming it as well as the episode. Conversely, when a word is heard, the episode whose component it names is activated. Consequently, when people encounter or hear about a target, everything they know about it immediately becomes available to guide their action.

Essential as they are, individual words are limited in how much information they communicate. To let someone know what you wish to do or what you have done, entire sentences are necessary. Sentences make it possible to communicate complete episodes in detail rather than merely hinting at them by naming their components. Human language enormously increases the amount of knowledge that people can communicate to each other and collectively encode in the first place. The second half of this chapter reviews the evolution of human language and how it is produced and understood.

This entire chapter is about cognitive processes that take only a few hundredths of a second. That is how long it takes for a perceptual target to activate an episode in memory. A perception does not begin as a mystery; all the information you need to make sense of what you see is available as part of the perceptual experience. So, when you sit in class, you do not merely see a room full of objects; you see a familiar classroom, fellow students, and a teacher. Hence, you are oriented to place because all your declarative knowledge is immediately available in semantic memory.

- Semantic memory consists of:
  - interrelated response nodes that designate components of episodes and the associated perceptual and motor representations of the targets and actions of the episodes; and
  - response nodes for words, called logogens, which designate targets and actions.

Furthermore, it is the rapidity and sophistication of recognition within the semantic system that made naming possible, so people could communicate by naming things in addition to pointing to them. Then, about 60,000 years ago, modern human language was invented by this one family in east central Africa. For the first time people could communicate in sentences (Chapter 2). As mentioned above, this gave them the power to conquer the world. Speech understanding and production involves almost every system in the brain.

- The sensory registration and feature analysis stages of auditory processing:
  - are anatomically parallel and functionally similar to the corresponding stages of visual processing; and
  - make a distinction between speech (left hemisphere) and non-speech (right hemisphere) sounds for which there is no analogy in vision.
- The system that processes speech and language includes:
  - the primary auditory cortex in the superior left temporal cortex, for feature analysis;
  - the middle temporal cortex, for feature analysis and comparison at the word level; and
  - syntactic processing areas in the temporal cortex and prefrontal cortex, for the construction of clauses and episodes.
- The purpose of speech perception is to represent the sounds the speaker actually produces rather than the sounds that have been encoded.
  - A speaker produces only an approximation of the speech sounds that he or she intends to produce because of the sluggishness of the speech production system. As a result, speech input tends to be ambiguous – that is, small segments of the input approximately match the representations of several different speech sounds and can be put together to match representations of more than one word.
  - The speech-processing system makes use of syntactic representations of meaningful word sequences to reduce the possible representations of the speech input to those that are meaningful. As the length of the input sequence increases, the number of meaningful representations is reduced until only one remains.

- Speech recognition is thus performed through a repeated process of comparison (temporal cortex) and response selection (prefrontal cortex), sometimes called analysis by synthesis.

About 5,000 year ago writing and reading were invented, providing a permanent record of human language.

- The process of word recognition during reading includes three redundant pathways:
  - a visual whole-word pathway;
  - an auditory whole-word pathway; and
  - a letter sequence pronunciation pathway.
- An impairment of specific recognition and production pathways produces distinctive impairments.
  - Alexia – the inability to recognize printed words.
  - Agraphia – the inability to write.
- An impairment of logogens or syntactic processing produces a general impairment of language comprehension and production called aphasia.

7.1 Semantic memory

As mentioned in Chapter 2, everything you know about the world is collectively called declarative knowledge. The representation of declarative knowledge in memory is called **semantic memory**. Recall that the fundamental unit of semantic memory, the episode, involves both perceptual and motor representations. For example, an episode representing knowledge of a chair includes its appearance, its context, and its use (the motor actions required to sit down). Semantic memory is therefore composed of representations distributed throughout the cortex, including visual and verbal representations in the temporal cortex and motor representations in the parietal cortex and frontal cortex.

Neurons have electric charges, which play a role in intra-neuronal communication. Hence, neurons generate small magnetic fields, and these fields become stronger when the neurons are using oxygen while, presumably, actively processing information. In functional magnetic resonance imaging (fMRI), the magnetic activity of different areas of the brain is measured and used to construct a map of brain activity during a task. Figure 7.1 is a map of the temporal, parietal, and frontal areas that together comprise semantic areas. The coloured areas contain the perceptual, motor, and emotion representations involved in semantic

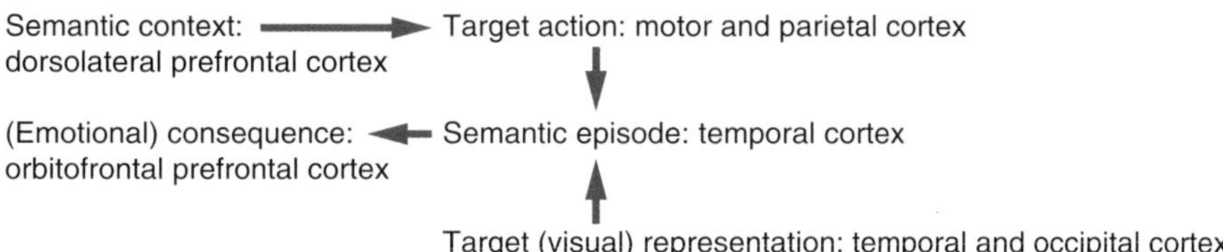

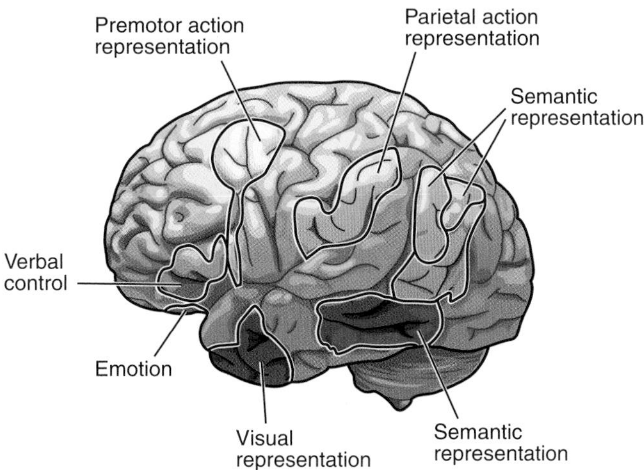

Figure 7.1 At the bottom, the temporal, parietal, orbitofrontal areas containing components of the episodes comprising semantic memory are shown in purple, green, and red. The frontal areas involved in the activation of semantic memory are shown in yellow (action towards a target) and orange (verbal control through naming). At the top, the schematic shows that the top-down initiation of an action to a target activities the bottom-up activation of its entire episode.

memory revealed by fMRI during semantic tasks (Binder and Desai, 2011). The visual representation area (purple) encodes the target, and context. The action representation (green) encodes the action. The semantic areas (green and purple) encode complete episodes along with the words naming their compenents. The emotion area encodes the emotional component of the outcome of the action (whether it was good or bad).

Organization

Figure 7.2 is a schematic showing the basic organization of semantic memory. In the schematic, the pictures represent the episodes containing the target. In the upper half, the schematic shows episode representations for *dog* and *cat* and four different response nodes, for *dog*, *cat*, *animal*, and *living thing*. The response nodes are interconnected and provide the organizational structure of semantic memory. So, everything you know about dogs is associated with its **response node**, which is indicated by the circle, the dotted line (the activation level), and the solid line (the criterion) through it. The response nodes are associated in various relationships that may be called associative or semantic. A relationship is often called **associative** if one item is the cue for the other, so that, when someone is asked what comes to mind, one word is sometimes given as a response to the other; for example, *cat* is a response to, hence an associate of, *dog*. A relationship is called **semantic** if there is some obvious connection in the meaning of the items; for example, *lad* is a synonym of *boy*, though rarely given as a response to *boy*. Obviously, by these criteria, many relationships are both associative and semantic. In Figure 7.2, the category–instance semantic relationships among *living*

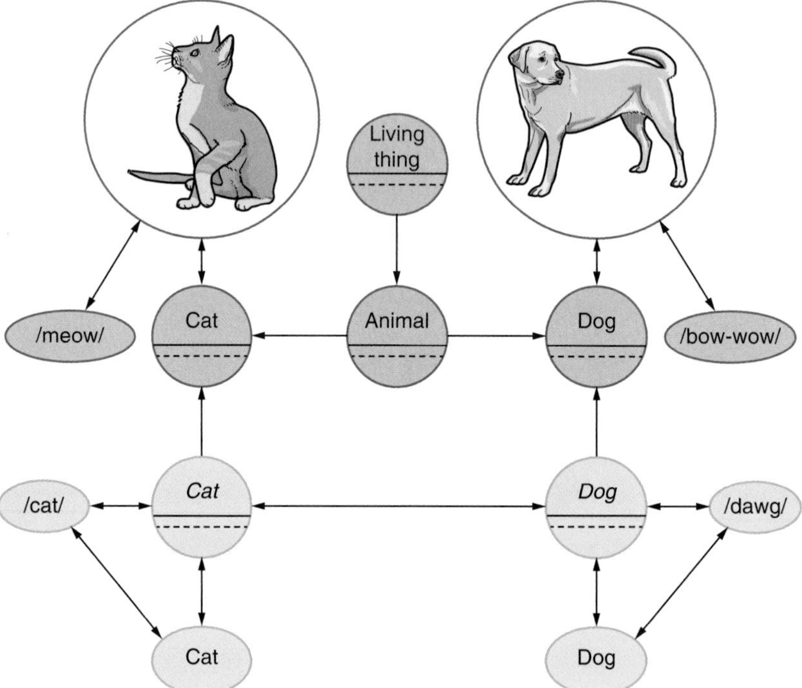

Figure 7.2 In this fragment of the semantic network, the nodes in orange are words and the nodes in purple are their meanings. Word response nodes are shown associated with their auditory(/dawg/) and visual (Dog) rerpresentations.

thing, animal, dog, and *cat* are shown. Relationships such as the one between *animal* and *dog* organize semantic concepts into a hierarchy. For example, *animal* is the category, and *dog* is an instance.

In the bottom half of the schematic are shown the representations of the words *dog* and *cat,* which are of course associated with the representations of dogs and cats in the upper half of the schematic. As shown in the figure, word representations also have response nodes. The response nodes for words are called **logogens**. Words provide an extremely useful means of gaining access to the information in semantic memory. They are especially useful for gaining access to the information of *someone else's* semantic memory. All you have to do to learn about cats from someone else is ask. Cognitive and social functions are therefore intertwined. Damage to both the anterior and posterior regions of the superior temporal cortex impairs lexical comprehension, leaving it unclear where logogens are found (Damasio *et al.*, 2004; Dronkers *et al.*, 2004).

Processing

The response nodes represent the point in the recognition process when a perceptual target is identified. When a perceptual representation is compared with a representation in memory, the more complete the match, the greater the increase in activation of the response node. When the activation of the response node exceeds its criterion, the target is recognized. Rapid visual serial presentation of pictures (Chapter 4) reveals that the visual recognition of familiar objects occurs in about one-tenth of a second. Potter (1975; 1976) and Intraub (1980; 1981) had students detect a target picture among a sequence of pictures presented for 114 milliseconds apiece, pressing a button when the target appeared. Sometimes the target was defined quite generally, such as a picture that is not house furnishings or decorations. Such a negative definition required the observer to identify every picture *except* the target as a furnishing or decoration. Hence, the observer identified *every* picture in the sequence as either an instance or non-instance of the specified category. Detection accuracy was almost perfect, demonstrating that a 114-millisecond exposure was sufficient to identify each picture in the sequence. Such high-speed recognition is what makes fast channel surfing possible when looking for something to watch.

When the activation of a response node exceeds its criterion and the activation levels of other nodes rise, these include the activation levels of other response nodes related to it in memory. Priming occurs between words in a variety of relationships. Meyer and Schvaneveldt (1971) were the first to find that, when associated words (such as *doctor, nurse*) are presented in rapid succession, the time to identify the second word is reduced. Fischler (1977) found the same effect for unassociated words that are related in meaning (such as *wife, nurse*). Unlike the priming of perceptual features (Chapter 5), associative and semantic primes must be visible (Abrams and Greenwald, 2000). (It is important to note that a subliminal input has an extremely limited effect on perception, hence on behavior, because people [such as Packard, 1957] have claimed otherwise, despite the convincing evidence that "subliminal perception" is extremely limited (Vokey and Read, 1985).)

The relationship between associative priming and semantic priming is unclear. It may be that associative primes are simply strong semantic primes or it may be that associative priming occurs at a different level of the recognition process from semantic priming. On the one hand, the magnitude of associative plus semantic priming is larger than the magnitude of semantic-only priming (Lucas, 2000). On the other hand, there is no evidence for pure associative (honeymoon) priming between semantically unrelated words (de Mornay Davies, 1998).

Semantic priming keeps someone oriented to his or her task by rapidly activating associated representations of things that are normally occur together, so that targets may be predicted, activated for comparison in advance of their detection, and rapidly identified when found. Usually the effect of semantic priming is not even noticed. But it can be made apparent through the use of ambiguous patterns that are perceived as different targets in different contexts. The central element of Figure 7.3 can be either the letter "B" or the number "13." In an unambiguous context you would never notice its other possible representation. Another well-known example illustrating this point is the ambiguous drawing shown in Figure 7.4 (Bugelski and Alampay, 1961). If you look at the picture carefully, you will see that it can be interpreted either as a rat or as a man's face. When the rat-man picture is presented alone, as in the figure, most people see it as a man. However, in the context of a series of unambiguous animal pictures, people see it as a rat. Presumably, cross-priming among animal response nodes increases their activation, giving the rat representation an advantage over the man representation.

People are remarkable in their ability to combine declarative and procedural knowledge in the performance of very sophisticated tasks. Beyond being able to search for a specific perceptual target (Chapter 4), people are able to search for a *kind of* instance, which does not have a single, definite, detailed description. Paleontologists can look for fossils and archeologists can look for fragments of civilization. In these cases, each possible target must be subjected to multiple comparisons with representations in memory at successively finer levels of detail. To get a sense of this task, try to identify the pictures in Figure 7.5. The pictures in Figure 7.5 have been degraded so that it is difficult to integrate the elements and perceive what they are. However, as shown in Figure 7.2, there is a pathway from the name of an object to its response node and from its response node to its visual representation. Reading the name of an unrecognized pictured object therefore activates its visual

12
A 13 C
14

Figure 7.3 The same input may be recognized as two entirely different things in different contexts.

Figure 7.4 Ambiguous drawing. Man or rat?

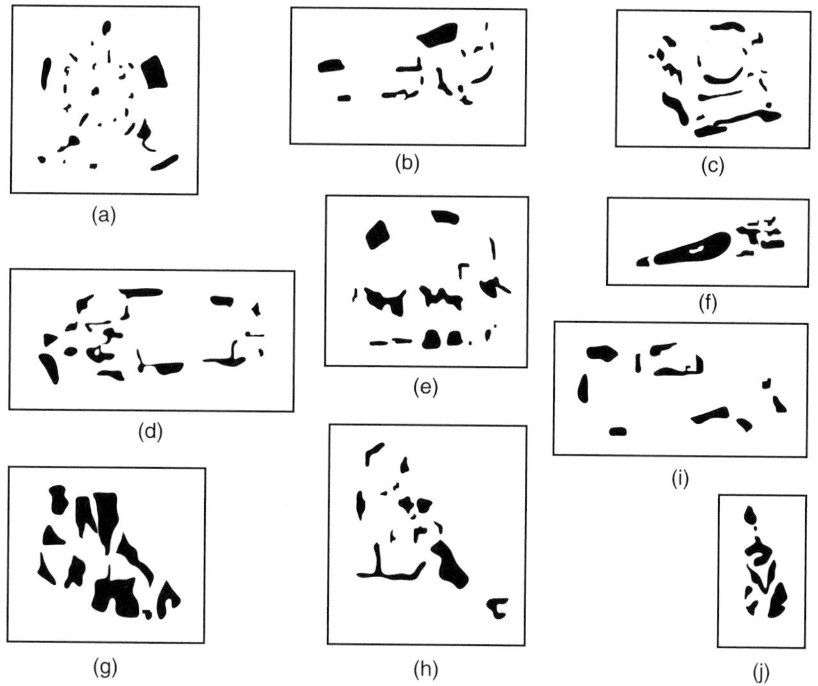

Figure 7.5 Figures used by Leeper (1935). (a) clock; (b) airplane; (c) typewriter; (d) bus; (e) elephant; (f) saw; (g) shoe; (h) boy with dog; (i) roadster; (j) violin.

representation, and a match with the picture causes its previously meaningless dark spots to snap into place as they are integrated into the organization of the matching visual representation.

Organization and expectation

Semantic memory makes task-relevant information rapidly available through two different mechanisms. The semantic priming that results from the spread of activation among response nodes in the temporal cortex is fast, automatic, and involuntary. Television shows make use of semantic priming by beginning a show with a few scenes from previous weeks. This reminder makes it possible for the viewer to immediately follow the action in the latest episode. There is also the early and late selection that results from target specification and inhibition from the prefrontal cortex directed to the temporal cortex (Chapter 4). When you channel-surf, looking for a show that you know is on when you are unsure of the channel, the target image pops out from the distracter images of other shows. In a classic experiment, Neely (1977) demonstrated the significance of both semantic priming and target specification in the speed of target identification by putting them in conflict. He found that activation spreads through the temporal cortex before inhibition reaches it from the temporal cortex, so semantic priming is faster than target specification, but, given sufficient time (three-quarters of a second), the prefrontal cortex (and hence the target it specifies) takes control of the processing.

In Neely's (1977) task, observers were asked to determine as rapidly as possible whether a string of letters was a word (such as *door*) or a nonword (such as *dook*). The letter string

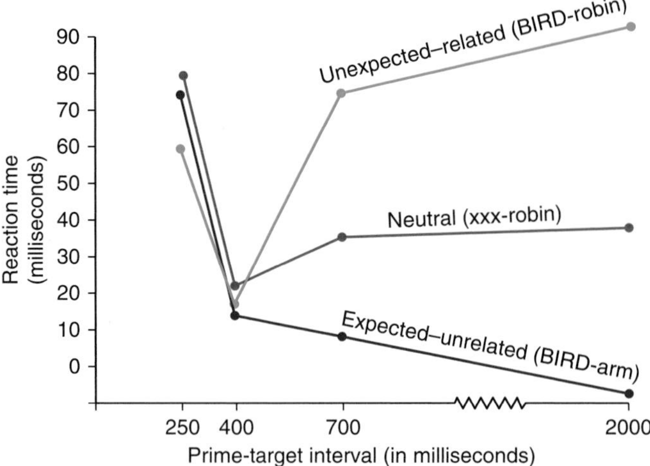

Figure 7.6 In a lexical decision task, at an SOA of 250 milliseconds an unexpected–related prime produces the fastest decision for a related target. At an SOA of 700 milliseconds or longer, an expected–unrelated prime produces the fastest decision for an expected target and inhibits decisions about related targets (Neely, 1977).

was preceded by a cue that was sometimes a word (such as *BODY*). When *BODY* appeared, the observers in the experiment knew that most of the time the word that followed (if the string was, in fact, a word) would be a building part (such as *door*) and that occasionally it would be a body part (*arm*) or unrelated (*robin*). Hence the observers were *not* expecting a body part after they saw the prime (*BODY*). However, as shown in Figure 7.6, when the word followed the semantic prime by only 250 milliseconds, body parts were identified more rapidly than building parts. So, 250 msec was all the time that was needed for *BODY* to automatically semantically prime body parts. In contrast, when the target followed *BODY* by 700 msec, building parts were identified more rapidly than body parts. The 700 msec were a sufficient interval for a person's expectations to reduce the time to recognize building parts, while suppressing the recognition of body parts and other unexpected words.

7.2 Speech and language

Language comprehension requires more than merely the recognition of familiar words. A sentence is a *sequence* of words that serve as cues to guide the construction of an episode that constitutes the meaning of the sentence. The ability to construct the meanings of sentences requires the integration of instrumental and habit control of action (Lum *et al.*, 2012).

Auditory system

Figure 7.7 shows the main brain structures involved in auditory processing and Figure 7.8 shows the same structures schematically (Rouiller, 1996). In some general ways the auditory processing system parallels the visual processing system, as shown in Table 7.1. Visual

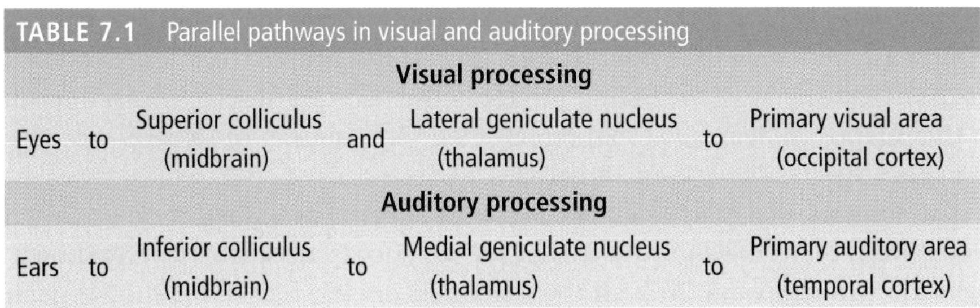

TABLE 7.1 Parallel pathways in visual and auditory processing

			Visual processing			
Eyes	to	Superior colliculus (midbrain)	and	Lateral geniculate nucleus (thalamus)	to	Primary visual area (occipital cortex)
			Auditory processing			
Ears	to	Inferior colliculus (midbrain)	to	Medial geniculate nucleus (thalamus)	to	Primary auditory area (temporal cortex)

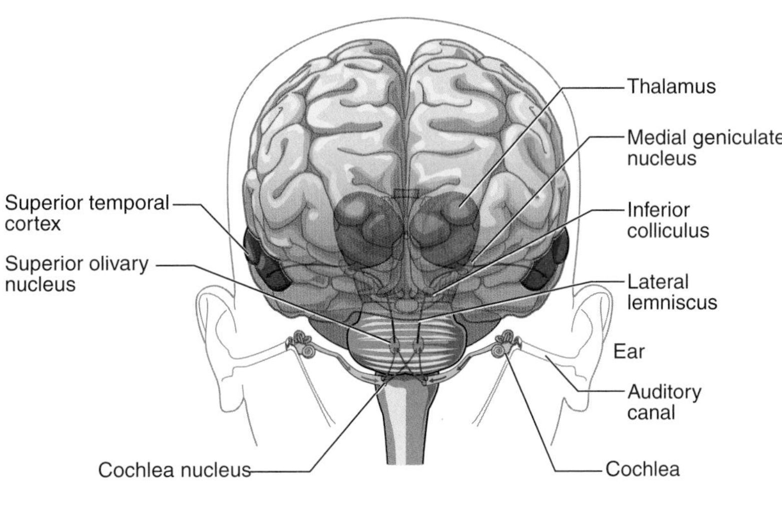

Figure 7.7 The auditory pathways combine the monaural signals from the right and left ears (red and blue arrows) to construct a binaural signal (purple arrows) that locates the sound in space.

processing consists of registration, feature analysis, and construction stages (Chapter 6), and so does auditory processing. For sensory registration, sound vibrations cause the movement of nerve ends in the cochlea of the ear, which converts them into the sensory input sent to the pair of **cochlear nuclei** at the base of the brain stem. From the cochlear nucleus, the auditory pathway divides into three main contralateral sub-pathways, to the **superior olivary complex** (in the brain stem), the lateral lemniscus, and the inferior colliculus (in the midbrain). In addition, an ipsilateral pathway goes to the superior olivary nucleus, and from there binaural and monaural pathways extend to the lateral lemniscus at the base of the inferior colliculus and from there into the inferior colliculus.

Feature analysis begins in the superior olivary complex in the brainstem. **Binaural** processing, combining the auditory output of both ears, is a major function of **superior olivary complex** neurons. The binaural properties of the superior olivary complex suggest that they play a role in the localization of a sound source in space. Binaural cues for location consist of the disparity of intensity between the two ears, and the temporal disparity difference between the two ears.

The binaural pathway is much larger, and at each stage the monaural pathway becomes smaller. The **lateral lemniscus** refines the binaural representation. The vast majority of the pathways originating in the cochlear nucleus, superior olivary complex, and lateral lemniscus terminate in the inferior colliculus. Furthermore, the inferior colliculus represents the principal source of ascending inputs to the auditory thalamus. An important function of the inferior colliculus is tonal representation. A quarter of its cells receive contralateral, monaural inputs. The rest are binaural.

The auditory thalamus receives its ascending pathway mainly from the inferior colliculus and sends it on to the auditory area of the superior temporal cortex. As shown in Figure 7.8, there are two pathways through the thalamus, one by way of the medial geniculate nucleus and the other by way of the posterior nucleus. These pathways divide further and carry information for three different subsystems: the **tonotopic** system, for tones; the **diffuse** system, for stress and rhythm; and the **polysensory** system, which integrates auditory information with information from other sensory modalities (Table 7.2). Because visual processing is binocular and auditory processing is binaural, both construct three-dimensional representations within their respective sensory modalities.

However, there is an important difference between the visual and auditory systems. The visual system is symmetrical with respect to the hemispheric processing of most visual inputs. That is why visual agnosia is the result of bilateral damage to the corresponding areas in both hemispheres. But the left hemisphere dominates the production and perception of speech and language. The schematic in Figure 7.8 shows the additional left hemisphere areas involved in the perception and production of speech. The corresponding anatomical pathways for speech processing are shown in Figure 7.9 (Friederici, 2012; Hickok and Poeppel, 2004; Scott and Wise, 2004).

Evolution of the speech and language systems

Our human ancestors had available at least two non-linguistic methods of communication to make social interaction possible. First, they shared with many other mammals the ability to make and recognize emotional utterances and (visual) expressions. This ancient ability does not even require the cortex. The recognition of negative emotions such as fear is available through pathways from the superior and inferior colliculus to the amygdala (Adolphs *et al.*, 1999), though additional cortical pathways are involved in humans. Second, humans are unique among primates in the ability to communicate through gesture. However, the kind of information transmitted by emotion is extremely limited, and gesture interferes with other manual actions. Humans therefore evolved to rely on increasingly sophisticated verbal communication, culminating in brains that were ready for human language.

Human language is possible only because of five recent evolutionary changes in the human line. First, associative learning between sights and speech sounds makes word meaning possible. No other creature has the rich network of polymodal neuronal connections in the middle of the temporal cortex to make naming possible. A few other animals have the ability to learn a limited number of verbal commands. However, no other animal approaches humans for ease of learning and consequent size of vocabulary. However, the naming ability is only the ability to learn individual words. Second, the habit system provides the ability to encode word *sequences* in an adjacent area of the temporal cortex, making it possible to learn to construct and understand sentences. The ability to construct and interpret sequences of words that describe episodes provides the basis for language. However, in order for speech to be understood, it is also necessary to have in place the procedures necessary for recoding

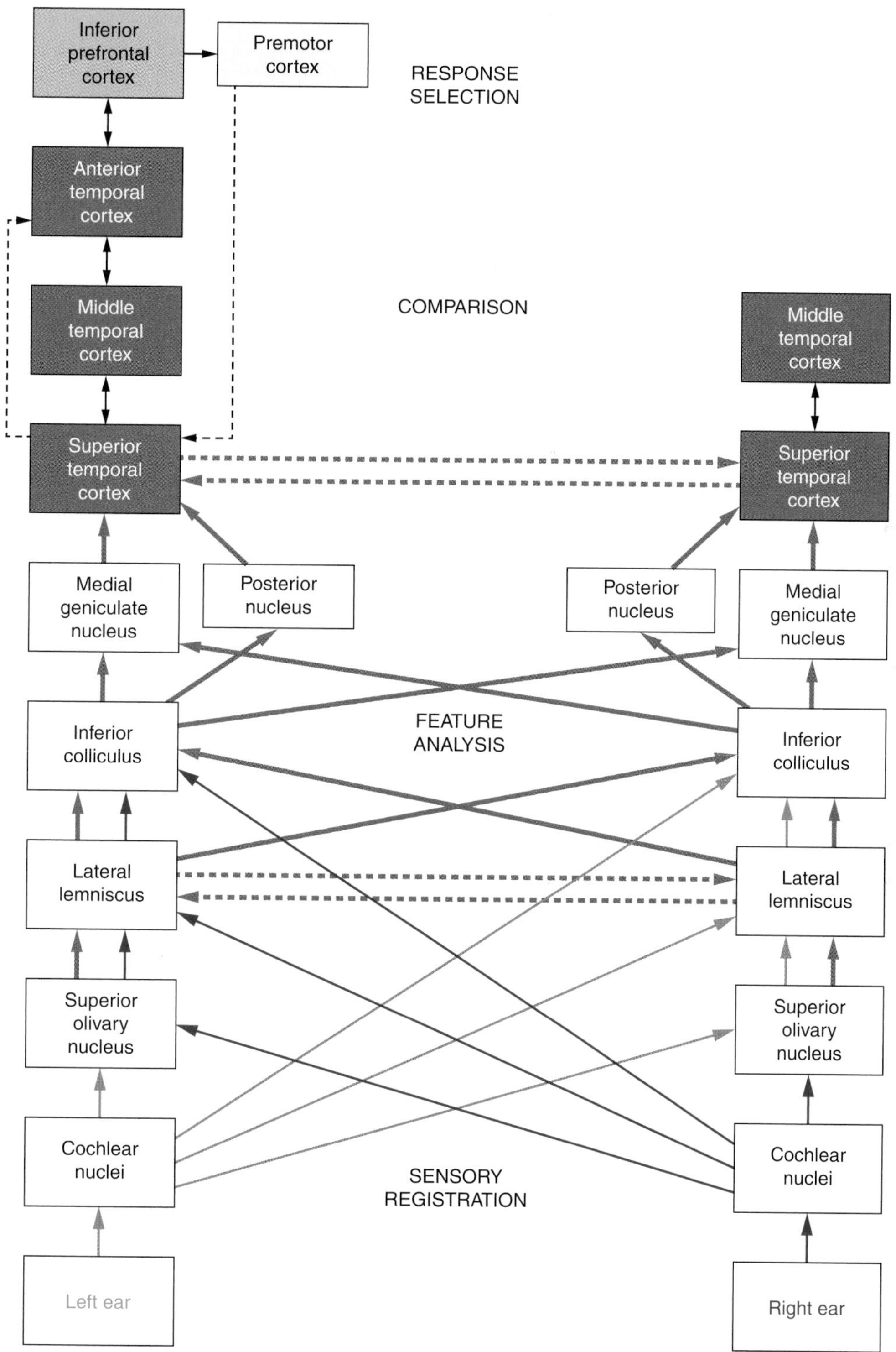

Figure 7.8 Schematic of auditory system showing additional processing of speech sounds in left hemisphere. Binaural pathways shown in purple and monaural pathways are shown in blue and pink. The binaural pathway is larger.

TABLE 7.2 Sub-pathways for auditory processing from inferior colliculus to medial geniculate nucleus (MGN) and posterior nucleus (PN) of thalamus (compare with Table 6.1)

System	Nucleus in Thalamus	Feature	Perceptual function
Tonotopic	PN Ventral MGN	Frequency	Tones
Diffuse	Dorsal MGN	Temporal	Stress, rhythm Variation in amplitude
Polysensory	Medial MGN	Polysensory input	Cross-modal integration

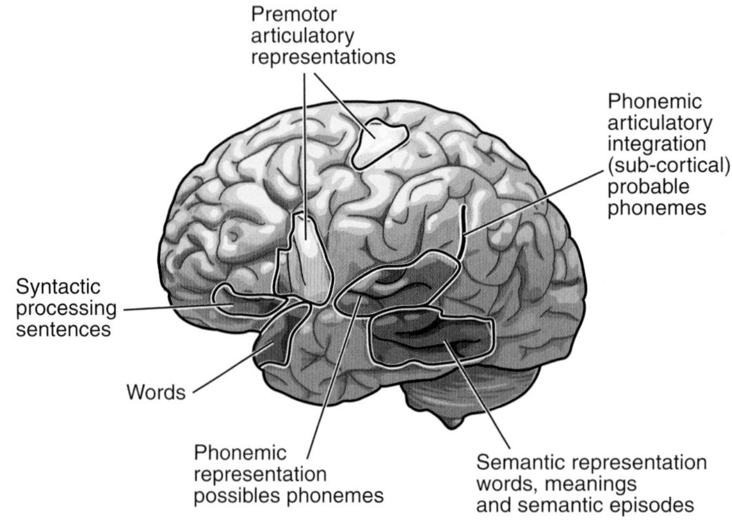

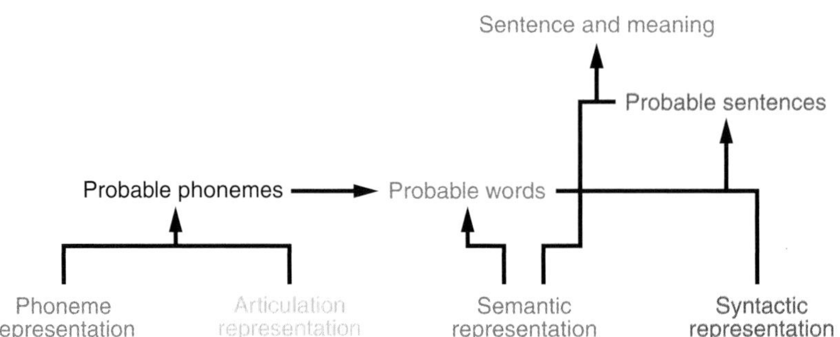

Figure 7.9 Cortical areas involved in speech processing in the left hemisphere include the superior medial temporal cortex for primary auditory processing with one pathway to the posterior inferior temporal cortex for semantic integration and one pathway into the area beneath the temporal- posterior parietal boundary and then forward to the frontal cortex for articulatory-phonemic integration (Hickok, and Poeppel, 2004). (Friederici, 2012).

auditory input into speech sounds. Three more evolutionary changes were necessary before language through speech was possible.

Larynx. The larynx is lower in the throats of humans than it is in other primates. The lower larynx creates a longer vocal cavity. The longer the vocal cavity, the more sounds it is physically possible to create, hence the greater variety of possible human speech sounds. The advantage of the longer vocal cavity presumably more than compensates for the one disadvantage of the human anatomy: only humans need an elaborate swallowing reflex to avoid food entering the lungs, causing them to choke on their own food. Infants make the limited kinds of sounds that we call baby speech precisely because their necks and vocal cavities are shorter (Miller, 1981: 47).

Specialized speech production areas. Control of the motor movements that produce speech is localized in specific areas of the frontal cortex and parietal cortex (Dronkers, 1996). How quickly people can speak determines the rate at which information is transmitted in a conversation. In turn, the rate at which people can speak depends on the number of different sounds they can make and the rate at which they can make them. The timing that is required for producing the sounds used in speech pushes the nervous system to its limit. A neuron takes about a millisecond to transmit an impulse. Speech requires successive motor acts that are only a few milliseconds apart. Localization in one hemisphere makes sound production faster than would be possible if control were shared between both hemispheres and required back and forth communication across the corpus callosum. If the control of speech were spread across two hemispheres, so that signals had to travel between them to coordinate their commands, the rate at which a person could speak would be significantly slowed. In fact, such slowed commands may be the cause of congenital stuttering, as "echo" commands from the right hemisphere produce the stutter. The phenomenon of stuttering suggests that it is the continuous planning of novel speech that most taxes the speech production system. Stuttering occurs only during spontaneous speech. It does not occur when reciting a rehearsed text. There are professional actors who took up acting as therapy for their stuttering. In addition, stuttering does not occur during singing.

Certain songbirds, including canaries, also have specialized hemispheres. The songs of these birds are under the control of the left hemisphere (Nottebohm, 1977), just as speech is in human beings. Of course, birds are very different from people. However, these findings for birds make salient the advantage of having the production of a complex vocal response lateralized. The need to learn complex vocalizations appears to be a task that requires hemispheric specialization. The birds with specialized hemispheres must learn to produce complex songs.

The need to create a specialized area for speech processing in the left hemisphere has had a knock-on effect that has resulted in one hemisphere or the other being specialized for the control of a variety of motor and emotional responses. Most human beings are right-handed. In this respect humans are unique, for we are the only animals to show any consistent hand preference as a population (Warren, 1977). The degree of linguistic lateralization is related to the degree of right-handedness (Newman, Malaia, and Seo, 2014). Non-right-handers tend to make better recoveries from aphasias caused by unilateral lesions in either hemisphere. Therefore, non-right-handers appear to be less likely to be completely lateralized for language (Rasmussen and Milner, 1977).

Specialized speech perception areas. However, even with these recent motor enhancements, the speech sounds that you actually make are run together and indistinct with respect to the sounds that you intend to make. This is because your muscles cannot keep up with the neural commands to the motor units. Accordingly, there is a specialized speech understanding area primarily, though not exclusively, in the left temporal lobe (Hickok and Poeppel, 2004; Scott and Wise, 2004) that makes it possible to recover phonemic intent.

Evidence of left hemispheric specialization for language

Five different kinds of observations of language processing provide independent evidence for the specialization of language processing in the left hemisphere.

Left hemisphere damage. Over 98 percent of all aphasias suffered by right-handed human beings result from injuries to the left hemisphere (Bogen and Bogen, 1976; Russell and Espir, 1961); for ambidextrous and left-handed individuals the percentage is somewhat less (Gloning, 1977; Russell and Espir, 1961). There may be right hemisphere damage as well.

Ambiguous sounds. A different sound can be presented to each ear by having a listener wear earphones and transmitting different sounds through the right earphone and left earphone. An artificial sound may be generated that is ambiguous between a speech sound and a non-speech sound. When an ambiguous sound that may be either a speech sound or a non-speech sound is presented simultaneously to the left and right ears, it is simultaneously heard as a speech sound in the right ear and a non-speech sound in the left ear (Best, Morrongiello, and Robson, 1981). For example, Rand (1974) split the syllable /ga/ into two components. One piece, the base, consisted of most of the segment, including its vowel. The other part was the portion of the very beginning that determines whether the entire segment is heard as /*g*a/ or /*d*a/. This segment sounds like a chirp in isolation. When the base segment was presented to one ear and the initial segment to the other, the listener simultaneously heard /*ga*/ in the base ear and a chirp in the other (see also Liberman, 1982; Liberman, Isenberg, and Rakerd, 1981). Hence, the same sound input was processed by one portion of the brain as a natural sound, then combined with the base by another portion of the brain and processed as a speech sound.

Ear dominance. Similarly, when different speech sounds are presented simultaneously to each ear (called **dichotic** presentation), there is a bias to hear the sound in the right ear (Kimura, 1961: 1967; but see also Bakker, 1970). In contrast, when Kimura (1974) presented listeners with brief excerpts of classical melodies dichotically, the results were reversed. The listeners heard the left ear (right hemisphere) melody more frequently. However, the results of further studies on the perception of music were quite complex. The advantage of one ear over the other depended on the precise nature of the task (Efron, Bogen, and Yund, 1977; Gordon, 1970; 1974; Robinson and Solomon, 1974) and on the musical experience of the listener (Bever and Chiarello, 1974; Gordon, 1980). So, the kind of judgment required determines which hemisphere controls the processing of a non-speech auditory input.

Wada test. Other clinical evidence comes from the Wada test. In this test, sodium amytal was injected unilaterally to anesthetize a hemisphere, and the effects on speech production were monitored. The test once was administered to determine speech dominance in epileptic patients before surgery. Loring *et al.* (1990) found that, of 103 patients (ninety-one right-handed and twelve left- or mixed-handed), seventy-nine had exclusively left hemisphere language representation (seventy-three right-handers) involving both production (counting) and comprehension (following simple commands). Only two patients had exclusive right hemisphere language representation (one right-hander). The remaining twenty-two participants (seventeen right-handers) had performance decrements after injections to each hemisphere.

Neuroimagining. Recall that functional magnetic resonance imaging is a measure of the oxygen use by neurons, hence of their level of activity. For most individuals, there is greater activity in those areas of the left hemisphere associated with speech perception and production, as measured by fMRI. The preponderance of individuals showing greater left hemisphere activity is greater for right-handers than for left-handers (Greve *et al.*, 2013).

In order to provide more oxygen, blood flow to the neurons increases. Using transcranial Doppler sonography, Knecht *et al.* (2000) reported that 95 percent of right-handers had a larger increase in blood flow in the left hemisphere when silently generating words starting with a particular letter. For the left-handers, the percentage of left dominance was 75 to 90 percent, depending on the degree of handedness.

The amount of blood flow to each area of the brain, hence its activity during a task, can also be measured by injecting into the blood a harmless amount of a radioactive isotope. In positron emission tomography (PET) scanning, the amount of radioactivity emitted by different brain areas is measured and used to construct a map of brain activity during a task. PET shows increased blood flow for the same areas in the left temporal and prefrontal lobes (all associated with speech perception and production) indicated by the other methods of neuroimaging (Xiong *et al.*, 1998). Different brain areas have different functions, so which areas show the most activity depends on the specific task being performed (Scott and Wise, 2003).

Split-brain individuals. Evidence of the specialized speech and language processing done by the left hemisphere was provided by a surgical procedure that is no longer used. Today epilepsy can be controlled by medication. However, in the recent past that was not always so. Information is transmitted between the hemispheres over a pathway called the corpus callosum. One surgical procedure used to control life-threatening seizures was to sever the corpus callosum in order to prevent the seizures from spreading. This operation greatly reduced the magnitude of the seizures, and it left the patients with their intellects and personalities intact. Recall from Chapter 6 that almost identical information about the entire visual field is transmitted to both hemispheres. Under normal viewing conditions, therefore, the left and right hemispheres both receive the same, complete information about the surrounding environment in split-brain patients.

However, the flow of information can be restricted to a single hemisphere by blindfolding the split-brain person when an object is placed in one hand or by presenting a visual input very rapidly to the right or left of the fixation point, which results in one hemisphere having control over the response to it. When these precautions are taken, the stimulus is effectively presented only to one hemisphere of the split-brain patient.

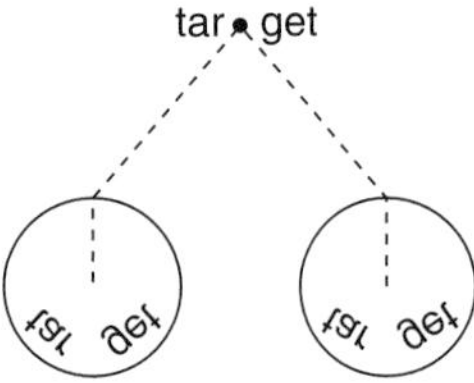

Figure 7.10 Hemispheric control. If the subject's gaze is fixed on the center of *target, tar* falls in the left visual field and *get* in the right.

When most inputs were presented to only a single hemisphere of a split-brain patient, either hemisphere could respond to it by making a motor response. The left hemisphere had good control of the right hand and poor control of the left hand, whereas the right hemisphere had good control of the left hand and poor control of the right. However, if forced to, either hemisphere could make gross movements with either hand. However, this equality of control did not extend to language. For example, because the connections between them were severed, different visual inputs could be presented simultaneously to each hemisphere of a split-brain patient. In a typical experiment, while the patient centers his or her gaze on a fixation point, a word is briefly presented so that half the letters fall to one side of the point and half the letters fall to the other side. As Figure 7.10 illustrates, if the word *target* was briefly presented, the letters *tar* would fall in the left visual field and be processed by the right hemisphere, while the letters *get* would fall in the right visual field and be processed by the left hemisphere. After such an input is presented, the patient is given a choice of four alternatives and asked to point to the one that was presented. For example, the alternatives might be *tar, get, cow,* and *pea.*

You might think that, since each hemisphere has processed different letters, the person would choose two alternatives and point to *tar* with the left hand and *get* with the right. However, this result did not occur when words were presented to most patients. Instead, they would point to the right visual field input (for example, *get*), whether asked to respond with the right or the left hand (Gazzaniga, 1970). Thus, the left hemisphere typically controls the response to conflicting linguistic inputs.

When the patient had a left hemisphere uninjured by the epilepsy, left hemisphere performance on linguistic tasks was essentially normal. For these patients, when a linguistic input, be it word or sentence, was presented in the right visual field (to the left hemisphere), the split-brain patient generally performed the task as well as he or she could prior to surgery. In other words, the person could understand sentences presented to just the left hemisphere and produce speech in response to them. However, the linguistic skills of the right hemisphere were often much less (Gazzaniga, 1983; Myers, 1984). When the same words and sentences were presented in the left visual field (to the right hemisphere), most patients were unable to indicate that they understood them in any way. Patients never produced any speech in response to an input just to the right hemisphere. Finally, when tested on Kimura's (1961; 1967) dichotic-listening task for speech sounds, performance for those speech sounds presented in the right ear was normal. In contrast, recognition of left-ear-presented speech sounds was near zero (Milner, Taylor, and Sperry, 1968; Sparks and Geschwind, 1968).

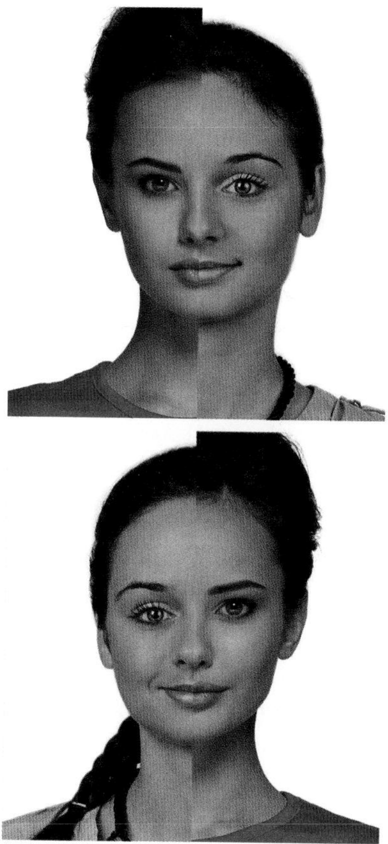

Figure 7.11 Chimeric face (Levy *et al.*, 1972).

When conflicting pictures were presented to the hemispheres, it was the right hemisphere that controlled the response. Levy, Trevarthan, and Sperry (1972) found that the right hemisphere determined the response to visual patterns such as the one shown in Figure 7.11. Such pictures, made up by putting the right and left halves of two different faces together, were flashed at each of four split-brain patients for 150 milliseconds. They were then asked to select which of three intact faces they had seen. None of these faces was the chimeric one actually presented. However, Levy, Trevarthan, and Sperry (1972) reported that patients failed to notice this fact. Instead, when the patients were asked to choose which face had been presented, the half shown in the left visual field (to the right hemisphere) was usually chosen. Patients made approximately the same responses whether asked to respond with the left or right hand, indicating that for this task the right hemisphere had taken control of the motor response mechanism. Similar results were obtained with nonsense shapes and pictures of common objects (Levy and Trevarthan, 1976; 1977).

This balance between the right and left hemispheres could be tipped one way or the other by the precise question asked. When the four split-brain patients were taught names for the three faces used in making up the two-faced stimuli and then asked to respond with the name of the face that had been presented, they most often responded with the name of the face corresponding to the right half of the picture (perceived by the left hemisphere). Similarly, when separate pictures were presented in the right and left visual fields, split-brain patients usually pointed to something visually similar to the left visual field input when asked to select what they had seen. However, when they were asked to point to a picture of something with a name that rhymed with that of something they had seen, they pointed to a picture with a name that rhymed with that of the picture presented on the right. Hence, the kind of judgment that must be made about the target determines the hemisphere that controls the response.

The work with split-brain patients stimulated the investigation of hemispheric control in normal human brains. In the normal brain, information presented to one hemisphere is rapidly transmitted across the corpus callosum to the other. However, the response to input should be a little faster if it is presented in the visual field of the hemisphere controlling the response, so that it does not have to be transmitted across the corpus callosum before a response is made. Whether reaction time was faster for left or right visual field presentation depended on the precise nature of the task (Bryden and Allard, 1976; Hellige, Cox, and Litvac, 1979). In general, linguistic tasks elicited faster responses with right visual field presentations, and visual pattern analysis tasks elicited faster responses with left visual field presentations (see also Hellige, 1980).

To summarize, the specialization of the left hemisphere for speech processing is the result of the special demands of speech production on cortical processing. First, speech production is localized in specific areas of the left frontal and temporal lobes because speech production requires the precise timing of vocal movements that cannot be achieved when control is shared between both hemispheres. Second, speech perception is localized in the left temporal cortex because the articulation of a speaker is imperfect and so the articulatory representations used to construct speech must be closely associated with the auditory representation that results in order to recognize the words with it.

Ambiguity and perception

Sentence understanding requires an articulatory representation as well as an auditory representation of the speech input because the purpose of speech perception is not to represent the sounds that a listener hears but the speech sounds that the speaker *intended to* produce. The role of memory looms so large in speech perception because what is important is not what sounds the speaker actually produced, or what sounds the listener initially registers, but what sounds the speaker intended to produce in the first place. The repeated comparison of the perceptual speech representation with representations of possible words and phrases in memory guarantees that the sound that reaches the listener's ears is ultimately heard as whatever speech sound makes the most sense in that context. So, when you hear speech, the sounds you hear may be closer to what the speaker intended to say than to what he or she actually produced!

Phoneme identification. Speech perception requires specialized processing because the speech that you actually produce is only a noisy approximation of the sounds you intend to produce. Special processing in a listener's brain is required to decode from the speech that was actually produced what the speaker intended to say in the first place. You may have learned as far back as elementary school that a word is made up of syllables, and syllables are made up of consonants and vowels. For example, the word *lady* contains the syllables /la/ and /dy/, which in turn contain the consonants /l/ and /d/ and the vowels /a/ and /e/. These vowels and consonants of English (or any other language) are called **phonemes**. (Slightly more technically, a phoneme is the smallest part of the speech input that makes a difference in a word's meaning.) When you speak, your intention is to produce distinct words made up of phoneme sequences. Furthermore, when you listen to someone speak, most of the words sound distinct – that is, each word is perceived as having a definite beginning and ending. The words do not blend into one another. However, that is not what you have actually produced. When you attempt to make a single speech sound, you must adjust your lips, teeth, tongue, vocal cords, and lungs in unison. When you try to speak, the neural commands for all the successive, distinct muscle movements come too rapidly for the vocal apparatus to react separately to each one. Instead, the movements for the various sounds become jumbled up and compromised. As a result, the actual speech produced is not the way it would be if each phoneme were separately articulated.

When the sound input is examined, it does not contain clean breaks of silence between the individual words of a sentence. For instance, Figure 7.12 is a **speech spectrogram** of the sentence "The steward dismissed the girl." A spectrogram is a visual record of the physical wave pattern you produce when you speak. All the information that the auditory system uses to construct a speech representation is contained in the speech spectrograph. The vertical axis represents frequency (roughly, the pitch of the sound pattern), and the horizontal axis represents time. The darkness of a point on the spectrogram represents the amplitude of that frequency (roughly, its loudness). As you can see from the spectrogram, there are some relatively white areas. The white areas represent moments of relative silence, and you therefore might imagine that they correspond to breaks between words. However, if you examine the bracketing at the bottom of the figure, you will see that they do not. The bracketing shows approximately where one word ends and another begins. Notice that the first word *the* blends into the word *steward* in the higher-frequency ranges. There is no break between the words at all. The first blank area occurs within the word *steward*. Similarly, *steward* blends into *dismissed*, which itself contains two white areas, and the second *the* blends into *girl* in the low-frequency ranges. Moments of relative silence are as likely to occur within words as between them. The breaks and pauses you hear when you listen to speech do not directly correspond to changes in the physical signal at all. Yet, in less than a tenth of a second of

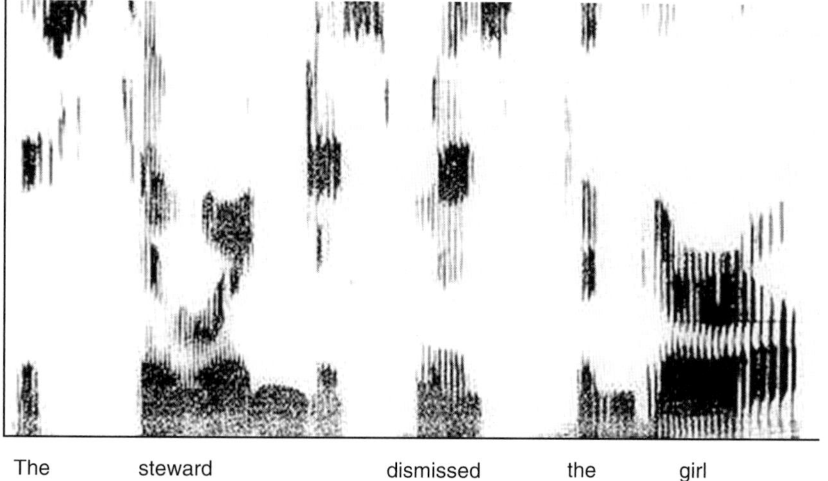

Figure 7.12 Spectrogram of "The steward dismissed the girl."

processing, the continuous input of speech sound is transformed into a representation of discrete words that are combined with their semantic representations into meaningful sequences in the next tenth of a second of processing (Friederici, 2012).

To understand spoken language, first the possible phonemes must be identified. Speech processing begins in the auditory area of the superior temporal cortex, as shown in Figure 7.9 (red area). For example, when you produce a /p/or /t/, you momentarily close your vocal tract and stop the flow of air from your lungs. (For this reason /p/ and /t/ are called **stop consonants**.) This stoppage produces a moment of silence in the speech signal. Hence, a moment of silence produces the perception of a /p/, /t/, or some other stop consonant when it is part of a speech segment (Liberman, 1982). How the silence is perceived depends on the pattern that contains it. Speech perception can be studied by generating synthetic speech and then determining how different segments are perceived in different contexts and in no context at all. If the speech input is segmented into small pieces, so that the temporal context is lost, a single segment may not sound like a speech sound at all but like a non-speech sound, such as a whistle (Liberman *et al.*, 1967). Furthermore, when the beginnings of different syllables containing the same consonant are played, they sound different from each other. For example, the beginning of the tape for /di/ sounds like a rising whistle, while the beginning of the tape for /du/ sounds like a falling whistle (Lieberman *et al.*, 1967). Thus, two different sound patterns may be perceived as the same consonant, depending on the following vowel. Moreover, the same sound pattern may be perceived as different consonants when the vowel context is changed. For example, the identical initial sound will produce /pi/ when paired with /i/ and /ka/ when paired with /a/ (Schatz, 1954).

Another way to put this is to say that speech perception is categorical, as all the input sounds are sorted into a number of discrete phoneme categories. There is a universal set of phoneme categories for all languages, and each actual language makes use of a subset of the universal set of possible phonemes. The same speech sound may therefore sound different to people who know different languages. The same two speech sounds that may be placed in the same phonemic category in one language may be placed in two different categories in another language. Native speakers of Japanese, a language that does not distinguish between the English phonemes /r/ and /l/, have great difficulty hearing this distinction.

Syntax

About 60,000 years ago a family invented modern human language in Africa at the end of the last ice age. Human language was invented once, and all languages spoken today are a variation of it (Atkinson, 2011). The defining characteristic of human language is to create novel but meaningful sentences that are cues for constructing episodes in semantic memory. How any particular speech segment is heard depends on the entire sequence of sounds forming the sentence, including what comes before and after it. The processing of successively longer speech segments to disambiguate them occurs in both the temporal–parietal boundary (Figure 7.9, black) and the anterior temporal cortex (Figure 7.9, purple).

The initial analysis of the speech input into phonemes occurs in the primary auditory cortex in the superior temporal cortex (Figure 7.9, purple). The representations of brief segments of speech are ambiguous as to the phonemes they represent. The initial comparison process between the speech input and representations in memory often produces several different matches for short segments of the speech input. The possible phoneme sequences are forwarded to the auditory–motor interface at the temporal–parietal border (Figure 7.9, black), where they are compared with the articulatory representations of actual words. As shown in Figure 7.9, the possible phonemic representations activated in the primary auditory cortex (purple) are compared with articulatory representations of actual words generated in the premotor cortex (yellow). Those phoneme sequences that do not match words are inhibited.

However, this is often not the end of the ambiguity, because two different representations of phoneme sequences constructed from the same auditory input may match different sequences of words, which have been encoded through response–effect learning by the habit system (Chapter 5). An inflection in a word or function word between words cues a semantic relationship between them. In the phrase *Fred's radio* the possessive relation is indicated by the inflection *-s* on *Fred*. Alternatively, in the phrase *the radio of Fred*, the function word *of* marks the possessive relationship between *the radio* and *Fred*. All languages use some mixture of inflections and function words for marking the relationships between words. Since a language contains fewer than 100 common inflections and functions, the same inflections and function words necessarily occur over successive sentences. Furthermore, the transitional probabilities between certain words are high, and these can be used to identify segments of speech (Hay *et al.*, 2011). The **transitional probabilities** between a pair of words are the probability that the one word will be followed by another in a sequence of words.

Function words and inflections reduce the number of different representations that match a word sequence. Hence, they reduce the number of comparisons to find a representation of the entire sentence and make it easier to understand. Word sequence representations that include function words or inflections that are associated with some component of an episode are called **syntactic** representations. Syntactic representations associated with a component of an episode are called **phrases**, and syntactic representations that are associated with an entire episode are called **clauses**. When a clause does not contain a function word that connects it with another clause, it is called a **sentence**.

Alternative representations of word sequences are forwarded to the phrase construction stage in the anterior temporal cortex (Figure 7.9, purple), where possible word sequences are compared with actual syntactic representations in the language and the possible syntactic representations are compared with word sequences that are meaningful phrases. Those word sequences that do not match meaningful phrases are inhibited. So, the auditory input is first compared with speech and then meaning representations in memory, until a single representation of the entire phrase is selected. To summarize, Figure 7.9 shows that the speech-processing system is at least a two-path heterarchy. The speech and meaning pathways construct different representations in parallel that are combined to generate a single representation of the sentence.

Figure 7.13 outlines some of the steps in the processing of the sound sequence that comprises *John's a man*. As shown in Figure 7.13 (a), the sequence /j/, /ahn/ matches the auditory representation for the word *John*; however, /j/ is not a word, so the word *on* is inhibited as a possible representation of /ahn/ in this context. As Figure 7.13 (b) shows, the beginnings of two different phrase descriptions match the sequence /j/, /ahn/, /z/. Phrase representations are indicated by the square nodes in the figure. Recall from Figure 7.2 that the circular nodes are logogens. As shown in the figure, two different syntactic representations encode a logogen followed by the sound /z/. One is for a possessive noun phrase (POS NP) (shown in violet). The one on the left is a description for a contraction of the noun phrase (NP)/verb phrase (VP) pair, *John is* (shown in blue). As is shown in Figure 7.14, the sound sequence /

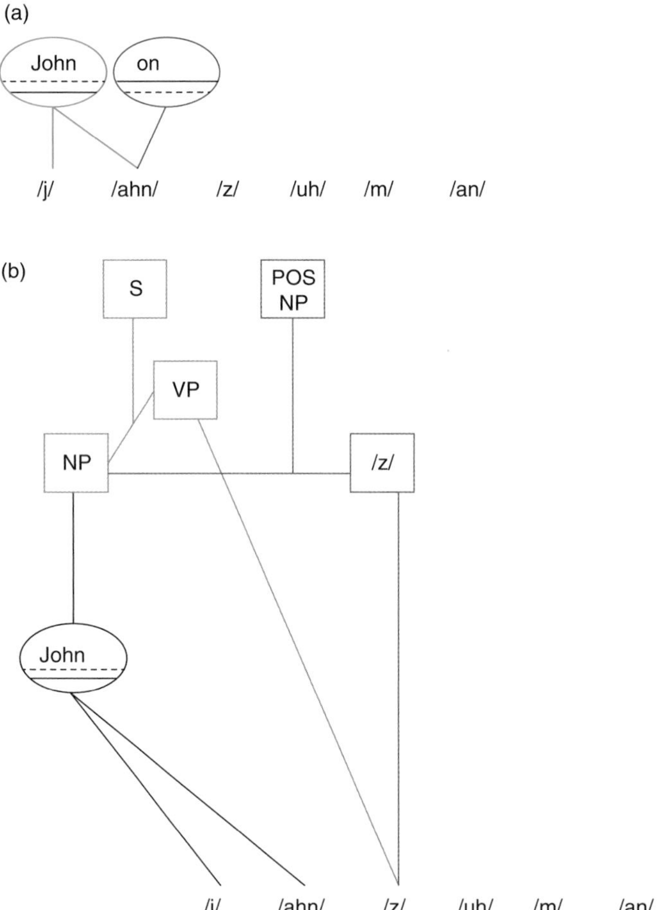

Figure 7.13 Processing of speech input (a): logogens matching initial speech input. (b): two syntactic representations for *John's* are shown in violet and blue.

uh/, /m/, /ahn/ matches the representation of a noun phrase. So the sounds are perceived as grouped according to the organization of that phrase.

Phonemic restoration. One powerful demonstration of how word representations and syntactic representations combine to influence speech perception is the **phonemic restoration effect**. This effect was first demonstrated by Richard Warren in 1970, and subsequently it has been investigated in detail by him and his colleagues (Obusek and Warren, 1973; Warren and Obusek, 1971; Warren and Warren, 1970). In one experiment Warren presented twenty people with a recording of the sentence "The state governors met with their respective legi*latures convening in the capital city." The asterisk indicates a 0.12-second portion of the recorded speech that had been carefully removed and replaced with the sound of a cough. The subjects were asked if there were any sounds missing from the recording. Just as people see an occluded object as complete (Chapter 6), they hear an occluded word as complete. Nineteen of the twenty subjects said there was no missing sound, and the other subject identified the wrong sound as missing. In fact, Warren himself heard the missing

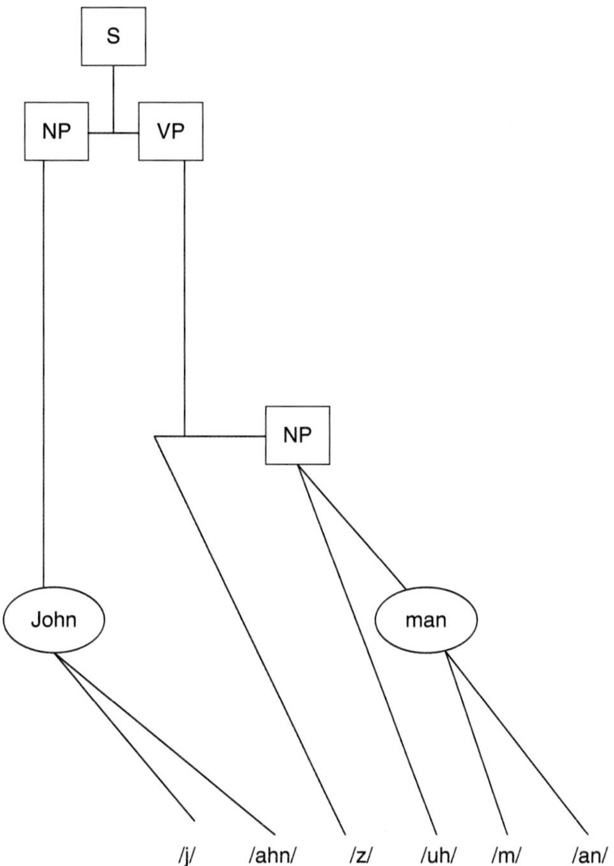

Figure 7.14 Processing speech input: syntactic structural description of *John is a man*.

sound. When the logogen of a word responds, the listener hears the entire word, not just whatever phonemes were matched with the input, when the presence of another sound indicates that the missing phonemes were drowned out. However, the missing portion was noticed if it was replaced simply with silence. The phonemic restoration effect is an extreme case of the general effect of noise on speech perception. If recorded speech is filtered to reduce the frequency range it contains, hence the amount of information about phonemes, the intelligibility of the speech is reduced. However, if noise is added to this reduced input, the intelligibility of both sentences and monosyllabic word lists is *increased* (Warren *et al.*, 1997). Apparently, the noise signals to the auditory system that some of the information in the speech input has been drowned out. In reaction, the criterion for a response is lowered, and less perceptual information is required for the listener to hear the words and sentences.

Speech is sufficiently redundant that, when the speech input is split down the middle into high-frequency and low-frequency halves, either half is sufficient to understand what is being said. This wonderful redundancy makes it possible to understand distant speech in a noisy world that has had to pass through sound barriers such as walls, so that only a small part of the original output remains. The redundancy also had an important influence on the development of technology. Alexander Graham Bell's original telephone transmitted only a small part of a speaker's frequency output, yet it was sufficient to understand what was being said.

Semantics. Of course, the purpose of language is to communicate information. Each clause describes an episode. The fact that clauses have meaning further restricts the word sequences that are likely to occur. Warren and Warren (1970) used the phonemic restoration task to demonstrate the effect of semantic context on speech perception. They presented different people with one of the following four sentences.

It was found that the *eel was on the axle.
It was found that the *eel was on the shoe.
It was found that the *eel was on the table.
It was found that the *eel was on the orange.

The string **eel* indicates a buzzing sound at the beginning of "eel."

The only difference between these sentences was the final word spliced onto the end of the tape: *axle*, *shoe*, *orange*, or *table*. Depending on the version people listened to, **eel* was perceived as *wheel*, *heel*, *meal*, and *peel*, respectively. Hence, even the meanings of words that follow it can influence the perception of a speech sound. So, just as semantic priming aids the perception of a degraded visual input, as seen above, it also aids in the perception of a degraded speech input. Since speech inputs are more likely to be degraded than visual inputs, the role of semantic priming in speech perception is correspondingly greater than it is in visual perception. Other studies also suggest that, when a word is mispronounced, people hear what the speaker intended to say (Cole, 1973; Marslen-Wilson, 1975; Marslen-Wilson and Welsh, 1978); people often do not even perceive the mispronunciation. When the speech input is processed, each input-sound is matched with one of the phonemes of the language that the listener knows. As a result, even if the match is less than perfect between a particular input and the representation of a particular phoneme in memory, the input is heard as that phoneme if it does not match any other phoneme more closely.

The process that converges on a single perceptual representation through the comparison of ambiguous auditory representations with different syntactic and semantic descriptions until a word sequence that describes an episode is found is called **analysis by synthesis** (Townsend and Bever, 2001).

Comprehension

Matching the auditory representation to a sequence of speech sounds does not always completely resolve the process of comprehension. The same sequence of speech sounds may match more than one sequence of words, and a word may label components of different episodes – that is, have more than one meaning. So, words and phrases may activate more than one semantic representation. As language processing moves from word construction to phrase and clause construction, therefore, further comparison and selection are required.

Lexical ambiguity. Many words are ambiguous. This is called **lexical ambiguity**. Normally, when you hear an ambiguous word in a sentence, you do not recognize that it is ambiguous; you are aware only of the meaning that fits the sentence. For example, for the sentence "They need a new sink," you perceive only the noun meaning of *sink* and not the verb meaning. However, Tanenhaus, Leiman, and Seidenberg (1979) showed that both meanings of an ambiguous word are initially activated, and then the appropriate one is selected and integrated into the sentential representation. Tanenhaus, Leiman, and

Seidenberg found that, if the word *swim* immediately follows "They need a new sink," its reading time is still primed. However, if *swim* follows "They need a new sink" by 200 milliseconds, it is no longer primed. Already, one meaning has been selected (see also Seidenberg *et al.*, 1982).

Notice that Tanenhaus, Leiman, and Seidenberg's (1979) findings for language comprehension are consistent with Neely's (1977) lexical decision results mentioned above. The two sets of findings neatly illustrate the complementary roles that the temporal cortex and prefrontal cortex play in attention and comprehension. Any word that might be relevant to the target, and hence the task at hand, is rapidly activated in the semantic network in the anterior temporal cortex. At the same time, the episode designated by the entire sequence of words is generated by the prefrontal cortex. Any association of a word in the sequence that does not designate the episode is inhibited. Comprehension thus occurs through a two-stage process of activation and selection.

If both meanings of *sink* are accessed then the next question to ask is whether they are accessed together or in a particular order. The answer is that the various meanings of an ambiguous word are accessed in an order determined by the frequency of each meaning and the context in which it occurs (MacDonald, Pearlmutter, and Seidenberg, 1994). As we saw above, a particular meaning may be activated through semantic priming from earlier phrases and sentences so that it is the first one accessed. When the wrong meaning is at first selected, a **garden path** misinterpretation occurs. In one study of the detection and resolution of inconsistencies, Carpenter and Daneman (1981) had subjects read "garden path" passages such as the following:

> The young man turned his back on the rock concert stage and looked across the resort lake. Tomorrow was the annual, one-day fishing contest and fishermen would invade the place. Some of the best bass guitarists in the country would come to this spot. The usual routine of the fishing resort would be disrupted by the festivities.

When they read this passage aloud, most people initially pronounced the ambiguous word *bass* in accord with its *fish* meaning, which had been primed by the preceding references to fishing. However, the *fish* interpretation is inconsistent with the immediately following word *guitarists*, which forces the interpretation related to low musical notes. Carpenter and Daneman measured subjects' eye fixations as they read the passage, and they found that people kept their gaze on *guitarists* a relatively long time as the inconsistency was detected, and then they regressed to reread the word *bass*. People thus use the context both to select meanings and to detect inconsistencies as early as possible.

Syntactic and semantic ambiguity. A central problem for human communication is that there are indefinitely many things to talk about but only a finite number of words. The usual purpose of communication is to communicate new information to the listener, which means the ad hoc construction of an episode described by a clause. This problem is solved by communicating not through individual familiar words but through novel sequences of familiar words. Even with short sequences, it is possible to generate as many different sequences as there are things to talk about. You know over 1,000 adjectives and way over 1,000 nouns, so (using scientific notation) you can recognize as noun phrases many more than $10^3 \times 10^3 = 10^6$ adjective noun combinations. This is over a million two-word combinations. In general, if a word sequence has n words and there are more than 10^3 instances in each category, then there are 10^{3n} different sequences. For n greater than three, the number is more word sequences than you can hear in your entire lifetime. Throughout your life, therefore, many of the word sequences that you say or hear you have not said or heard previously.

Each sequence must contain features that may be combined with the words by the language-processing system to designate an episode. Human language has two such features. As mentioned above, the local features are inflections and function words. The global feature is word order. These two features are combined to designate a specific relation. Consider the possessive noun phrase *Fred's radio*. The phrase *radio Fred's* means something entirely different. All languages use some mixture of word order, inflections, and function words for marking the relationships between words. Recall that an episode contains an action, target, context, and result. When a person represents his or her actions, he or she is implicitly the actor. However, when a person represents another's actions, the episode also includes an actor. The basic clause of all human languages contains an actor (subject), action (verb), and target (object). In some languages word order is more variable than in others, but every language has at least a preferred order for the two nouns representing the subject and object and a verb in the basic agent–action–target relationship. The different human languages each rely on one of three different orders, which are named for the grammatical relations of the sentence – subject (S), verb (V), object (O) – rather than the semantic relations of the episode it represents: agent, action, target. The orderings known to exist in different human languages are agent–action–target (SVO), agent–target–action (SOV), and action–agent–target (VSO) (Greenberg, 1963; Pullum, 1977).

A language has about 100 function words or inflections that define relationships between words, and these represent different kinds of semantic relations in different kinds of episodes. Consider the meaning of *went to* in the following three sentences:

Laurie went to the store.
Arthur went to get a pencil.
Lillie went to sleep.

Because the semantic relationship among the words of a phrase is constrained by the syntax of the phrase, even absurd statements such as "Bicycles push people" can be understood (Slobin, 1966). That people can understand even absurd sentences in a predictable way is a great advantage. It makes possible the creative figurative use of language through metaphor and poetry that expands the kinds of things that can be said and understood.

Verbal memory

When speech is comprehended, a sequence of sounds that forms a word or clause is compared with representations in memory until a single matching representation is found. As the phonemic restoration effect demonstrates, the entire sequence of sounds is literally not heard until a single semantic representation is selected. Once an ambiguity is resolved, a single phrase or clause is heard, and an episode is constructed, there is no reason to remember the words, and so the representation of the previous clause is inhibited when the next clause is processed. When people who listened to a passage wrote as much of the end of it as they could remember exactly, Jarvella (1970; 1971) found that people remembered the last clause verbatim 86 percent of the time and the second-to-last clause 54 percent of the time when the two clauses were part of the same sentence. When the second-to-last clause was not in the same sentence as the final clause, people recalled it verbatim only 20 percent of the time. Similarly, it took less time to respond if a word had appeared in a sentence when it occurred in the final (uninhibited) clause compared with the previous (inhibited) clause (Caplan, 1972). For example, subjects were faster to report that *oil* had appeared in

Now that artists are working fewer hours, oil prints are rare

than in

Now that artists are working in oil, prints are rare.

Disambiguation. There is a limit to the length of a phonemic string that may be retained while being disambiguated. When the length is exceeded, the most likely representation activates a response. When this response is the wrong one, so that the following words cannot be integrated with the representation, the sequence becomes incomprehensible (Warner and Glass, 1987). For example,

When the boys strike *the dog* kills

contains an ambiguity at *the dog*. The noun phrase *the dog* can be the end of the clause preceding it or the beginning of a new clause. The verb *strike* is usually followed by the object that has been struck, making this interpretation more likely. Nevertheless, in the sentence above, the second interpretation is selected by the following word, *kills*, and most listeners interpret it in this way. The sentence

Before the boy kills *the man* the dog bites strikes

contains the same ambiguity at *the man*. This time the second interpretation is not confirmed until four words later, by the word *strikes*. In this case, listeners interpreted *the man* as the end of a clause, consequently finding the word sequence incomprehensible in its entirety and rating it ungrammatical.

Novelty. Sentences encode information precisely because they are novel, hence partly unpredictable. Ad hoc voluntary action is necessary to construct the episode designated by a novel sentence. Because only one voluntary action can be performed at a time, Daneman and Carpenter (1983) found that performing a second memory task at the same time reduced performance in a sentence comprehension task. Furthermore, they found that performance on the combined task predicted reading comprehension even when a second task was not required. This result suggests that one factor influencing reading comprehension is the ability to engage in voluntary action when an unexpected element is encountered. For example, Daneman and Carpenter (1983) found that poor readers have a great deal of difficulty recovering from a garden path sequence such as "There is also one sewer near our home. He makes terrific suits."

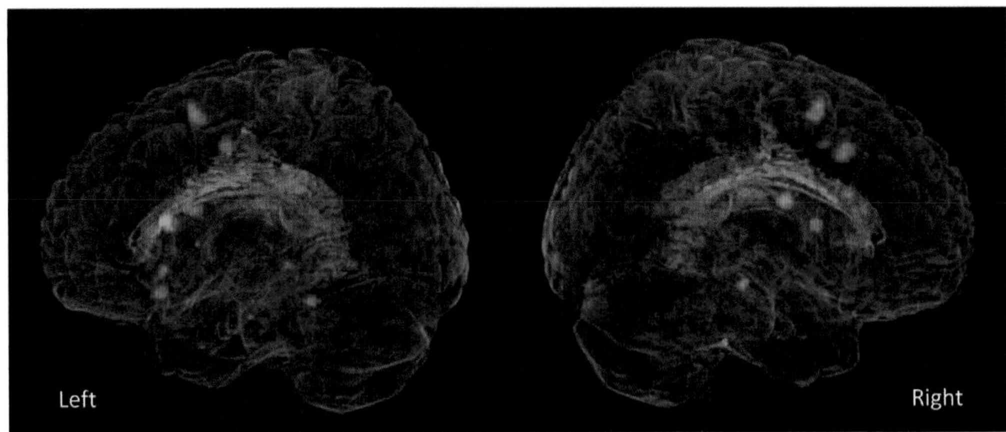

Figure 7.15 Bilingual influence on brain function and structure. Transparent brains show the left and right hemispheres. Green voxels depict grey matter regions showing high activation during bilingual language switching in a meta-analysis. Red–yellow voxels indicate regions of higher white matter integrity in bilingual older adults relative to monolinguals. Together, the functional and structural data indicate that neural correlates of bilingualism are observed in the frontal lobes, generally responsible for higher cognition such as executive functions (Bialystock *et al.*, 2012).

Bilingualism. Most people in the world speak more than one language. and bilingualism is another challenge to language processing (Kroll, Bobb, and Hoshino, 2014). Recall the Stroop effect from Chapter 5; word reading is automatic, so the word's pronunciation interferes with any other verbal response required, such as naming the color of the ink. For a bilingual individual, life is one big Stroop task. Whenever the individual utters a name or a sentence, its referent activates a different response for each language the bilingual knows, and all but one of them must be inhibited. Cognates are words whose form and meaning are similar across two languages (such as *piano* in Spanish and English), whereas interlingual homographs are words with similar forms but different meanings (for example, *pie* in Spanish means *foot* in English). Many studies have demonstrated that bilinguals recognize cognates more quickly but interlingual homographs more slowly than control words (see, for example, Dijkstra, Grainger, and van Heuven, 1999). Over time the two languages influence the understanding of each other's sentences and the pronunciation of each other's words (Ameel *et al.*, 2005). The necessity for constant inhibition during language comprehension and production has a large *positive* effect on the functioning of the prefrontal cortex, as well as other areas of the frontal cortex (Figure 7.15), including the caudate nucleus of the striatum, anterior cingulate gyrus, and the areas of the left hemisphere involved in language production (Bialystok, Craik, and Luk, 2012). Consequently, the performance of bilinguals on *non-language* tasks that require the ignoring of irrelevant information is generally superior to that of monolinguals (Bialystok, Craik, and Luk, 2012; Kroll, Bobb, and Hoshino, 2014). A long-term consequence of the additional routine inhibition required of the bilingual brain is a brain that maintains function when damaged by disease better than a monolingual brain (Bialystok, Craik, and Luk, 2012; Kroll, Bobb, and Hoshino, 2014).

Verbal agnosia. Damage to connections with the auditory cortex in the temporal lobe can cause **verbal agnosia** (Geschwind, 1970). Verbal agnosia is when sounds are still heard but speech sounds are no longer recognized. This is also called **pure word deafness**. Even though the person cannot understand spoken language, he or she can still understand written language. The precise symptoms depend on the location of the damage to the process of representing the sequence of sounds as a clause and then using it to construct an episode. For example, if the representation of the speech sequence is intact but the construction of the episode is impaired, a verbal agnosic may accurately repeat a word or sentence he or she cannot understand, as long as the pathway from the auditory representation to the motor representation for pronunciation is intact. This is similar to the ability of a visual agnosic to draw a picture of an object he or she cannot recognize (Chapter 5). In contrast, the opposite disorder also occurs. When only the pathway from the phonological representation to the articulatory representation for pronouncing it is severed, the person cannot repeat words and sentences that he or she can nevertheless understand, which is a form of apraxia (Chapter 3).

Schemas, story understanding, and pragmatics

Sentences are not understood in isolation but are related to one another in longer narratives. In stories, often a sequence of sentences more completely describes an episode than would be possible by a single sentence. Haberlandt, Berian, and Sandson (1980) studied how schemas are constructed by measuring the times needed to read individual sentences of simple stories. Each story consisted of a setting (S) and two episodes, with each episode consisting of a beginning (B), reaction (R), goal (G), attempt (A), outcome (O), and ending (E). An example is:

> Once upon a time there was a king. The king had three lovely daughters. The king's daughters went for a walk in the woods every day (S). One afternoon a dragon came into the woods and kidnapped the daughters (B). They were frightened by the dragon (R). So they planned to escape from the dragon (G). The daughters tried to distract the dragon by singing songs (A). But they remained the dragon's prisoners (O). The daughters cried desperately (E). Three knights heard the cries (B). They took pity on the daughters (R). They wanted to free the daughters (G). The knights attacked and fought the dragon (A). Finally they killed the fierce monster (O). The knights had saved the king's daughters (E).

Reading times were longest at the beginnings and ends of the episode and declined for sentences in the middle. Haberlandt, Berian, and Sandson suggested that, at the beginning of an episode, the schema activates a new node for integrating the next episode. At the end of the episode the individual sentence propositions are combined into a single proposition for the entire episode, which involves such operations as deleting redundant elements. Cirilo and Foss (1980) found a similar effect on sentence time for somewhat longer and more interesting stories.

You are so practiced at integrating information across sentences that you don't realize how meaningless individual sentences can be if connections cannot be made. However, Bransford and Johnson (1973) demonstrated this by ripping some sentences from their contexts. Consider:

The notes were sour because the seam was split.
The haystack was important because the cloth ripped.

Understanding them is difficult, because you are unable to connect the sentences to anything you already know. But a single word can provide a referent that makes each sentence perfectly comprehensible. The words are *bagpipes* and *parachute*, respectively.

Finally, the ability to understand language in a social setting, such as a restaurant, is facilitated because the sentences refer to the episode defined by the social situation, such as being seated, ordering, and paying for a meal. If you call to make a dinner reservation at a restaurant and the host asks "Do you want smoking or nonsmoking?" the correct answer is not "Yes." The contribution of the social setting to language understanding is called **pragmatics**.

Aphasia

An impairment of the ability to understand language is called **aphasia**. Word-finding difficulty, which is called **anomia**, is always a symptom of aphasia. Anomia is caused by damage to logogen–episode connections in semantic memory within the left temporal cortex. An anomic patient has difficulty identifying the referents of words. For example, when asked to touch an ankle, he or she may not know what to do or may touch his or her leg instead (Goodglass and Geschwind, 1976). Anomic patients also have difficulty naming objects. When asked the name of a familiar object, such as a spoon, they may be unable to respond, or may call it a knife. Even if they produce the correct answer, they may take excessive time and be unsure that they are right. Anomia can be assessed by showing the patient pictures of objects that vary in familiarity. Some individuals with aphasia will have normal comprehension of simple sentences, such as "The boy is jumping," but all individuals with aphasia will have impaired comprehension for complex sentences, such as "The girl is kissing the boy that the clown is hugging" (Dronkers *et al.*, 2004).

If the only language impairments an individual has are anomia and impaired sentence comprehension then the individual is said to have **anomic aphasia**. The patient recognizes people and objects, is aware of his or her impairment, and can make him- or herself understood through a combination of speech (for example, by saying "this one") and pointing. Even though performance on systematic tests, such as word associations, similarity judgments, and picture naming, is below normal it nevertheless is well above chance, indicating that some comprehension is retained. Notice that impaired comprehension of both spoken and written words and sentences is really a syndrome rather than a single disorder.

Dronkers *et al.* (2004) identified specific cortical areas, shown in Figure 7.16, in which left hemisphere damage causes aphasia by correlating the areas of cortical damage in a large number of patients with their specific impairments. The comparison of Figure 7.16, compiled on the basis of the effects of specific brain damage, and Figure 7.9, compiled on the basis of neuroimaging during task performance, provides converging evidence of the areas involved in speech and language processing.

Beyond anomia, cases of aphasia can be classified with respect to the kinds of additional symptoms that an individual may have, depending on which speech or language area is damaged and what specific function it has. The three most common forms of aphasia, conduction aphasia, Wernicke's aphasia, and Broca's aphasia, are described below. In older texts, Broca's aphasia is said to result from damage to an area in the frontal cortex called, appropriately, Broca's area, and Wernicke's aphasia is said to result from damage to an area in the

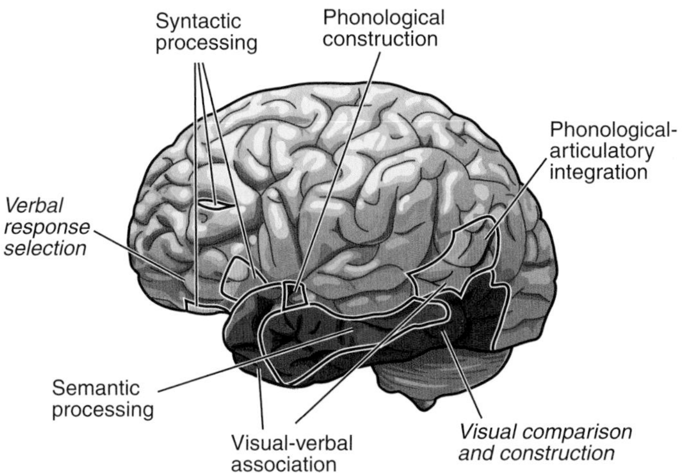

Figure 7.16 Cortical areas involved in language and semantic processing as indicated by whether damage causes aphasia or agnosia. Damage to areas labeled in upright case produce aphasia. The phonological construction area causes anomia. Damage to the phonological - articulatory integration areas causes conduction aphasia. The three prefrontal areas are associated with syntactic deficits (Broca's aphasia). Damage to the semantic processing area causes Wernicke's aphasia. Damage to areas labeled in italics produce impairment in picture naming but do not produce aphasia.

temporal cortex called Wernicke's area. Neither of these areas is shown in Figure 7.16, because it has subsequently become clear that the aphasias once attributed to damage exclusive to these areas resulted from extended damage that included these areas and the adjacent language areas shown in the figure.

Conduction aphasia. An aphasic individual who has lost the ability to repeat sentences is said to have **conduction aphasia**. Conduction aphasia is the result of damage to the phonological–articulatory integration area at the temporal–parietal border (Figure 7.16). The phonological–articulatory pathway makes verbal rehearsal possible. With verbal rehearsal impaired, sentence repetition is no longer possible. A person can still understand simple sentences, but when asked to repeat them gives a paraphrase instead.

Wernicke's aphasia. If the retrieval of information during comprehension is disrupted by widespread damage that includes the middle left temporal cortex then the result is a type of aphasia called **Wernicke's aphasia**. In Wernicke's aphasia, speech is fluent, though meaningless. Hence the disorder is also called **fluent aphasia**. The patient has poor or no understanding of language. Unsurprisingly, Wernicke's aphasia is often associated with visual agnosia, since this disorder is caused by bilateral damage to the adjacent visual processing area in the temporal cortex. Wernicke's aphasia is also called **semantic dementia**. The term "Wernicke's aphasia" is used when a head injury results in an immediate, obvious, impairment in meaningful speech production and comprehension, which may not get completely better but at least does not get worse. The term "semantic dementia" is used when some disease process gradually destroys the temporal cortex, so that initially imperceptible symptoms gradually become worse. Semantic dementia is a variant of **fronto-temporal dementia**, which afflicts the frontal cortex, the temporal cortex, or both.

If you casually heard a Wernicke's aphasic speak, you would have the impression that you were listening to someone articulate, amiable, and loquacious. His or her speech would seem to come out rapidly and effortlessly, with normal rhythm and intonation. However, if you listened more closely, your impression would quickly change. The first thing you would note is that the patient's speech was utterly devoid of content. The patient has difficulty finding words, especially concrete nouns. At best, such speech is filled with pronouns that do not refer to anything (such as "He went over there, and did that, and came over here and did this," etc.). At worst, the speech is filled with misused content words and nonsense words, run together very rapidly but with normal intonation, so that the speech sounds grammatical but is utterly meaningless. For example, the patient might say (Gardner, 1976: 68):

> Boy, I'm sweating, I'm awfully nervous, you know, once in a while I get up, I can't mention the tarripoi, a month ago, quite a little, I've done a lot well, I impose a lot, while, on the other hand, you what I mean, I have to run around, look it over, trebbin and all that sort of stuff.

The comprehension of a patient tends to mirror his or her production in severity. Patients with meaningless speech demonstrate little or no ability to comprehend anything. They exhibit overall poor performance on systematic tests. For example, when Zurif *et al.* (1974) asked aphasic patients to sort words into categories, severe Wernicke's patients did not appear to be sensitive to even the basic semantic distinction between humans and animals. Thus, destruction of the semantic associations seems to be the major component of the disorder. Not only do severe Wernicke's aphasic patients perform very poorly on comprehension tests but they also have anosognosia (Chapter 5); they appear to be largely unaware of their disability. As a result, their responses to situations are frequently inappropriate. The moods of different patients vary from jovial to paranoid.

Alzheimer's disease is the best known of the progressive dementias. It attacks other parts of the brain besides the temporal cortex but it includes semantic dementia in the later stages of the disorder. Progressive semantic dementia is characterized by a progressive loss of semantic knowledge, including both verbal and nonverbal material, resulting in severe impairments of naming and word comprehension. Warrington (1975) found that knowledge of subordinate categories (such as the name of a specific animal) was more impaired than knowledge of common superordinate categories (such as animals or birds). Similar findings were obtained by Snowden, Goulding, and Neary (1989) and Hodges *et al.* (1992). When attacked by a degenerative disease, the parts of semantic memory that were (Graham, Lambon Ralph, and Hodges, 1997) or are (Snowden, Griffiths, and Neary, 1995) used most often are the ones that survive the longest. Perceptual and reasoning abilities and memory for events are relatively well preserved early in the disorder. As semantic memory degenerates, all the symptoms of Wenicke's aphasia develop. Speech becomes increasingly empty and lacking in substantives, but output is fluent, effortless, and grammaticality correct (Kopelman, 2002).

Broca's aphasia. Broca's aphasia is most often a syndrome consisting of two distinct deficits. The first principal symptom of Broca's aphasia is halting and labored speech. The person's speech is filled with pauses and stutters (Goodglass, 1968; 1976; Goodglass and Berko, 1960; Goodglass, Fodor, and Schulhoff, 1967; Goodglass, Quadfasel, and Timberlake, 1964). Broca's aphasia is also called **expressive** or **nonfluent** aphasia, after this most obvious symptom (Dronkers, 1996). If damage is restricted to the surface of the neocortex then an individual's articulation may be impaired for a brief period following the injury. The impairment rapidly improves (Moss, 1972). However, if the damage extends below the surface then the articulation deficit persists (Alexander, Benson, and Stuss, 1989; Mohr, 1973). The patient may initially lose all language use, gradually improving to some permanent level of impairment. In general, the more severe the initial disorder is, the more severe the long-term disorder is likely to be (Mohr, 1976).

The other principal symptom of Broca's aphasia is difficulty with understanding clause and multi-clause representations. As shown in Figure 7.16, injury to any one of three distinct areas in the frontal cortex, produces this disorder (Dronkers *et al.*, 2004). This difficulty greatly reduces the syntactic complexity of the speech that Broca's aphasics can understand and produce. They are dependent on word meanings when interpreting complex sentences. When read a sentence that had one reasonable interpretation, on the basis of the words they selected the picture it described (Caramazza and Zurif, 1976). For example, even if one understands only the four main content words in "The bicycle that the boy is holding is broken," about the only thing the sentence can mean is that the boy is holding the broken bicycle. In comparison, the sentence "The lion that the tiger is chasing is fat" might plausibly be interpreted in at least four ways if only the content words are understood: the tiger might be chasing the fat lion, the lion might be chasing the fat tiger, the fat tiger might be chasing the lion, or the fat lion might be chasing the tiger. With this type of sentence, patients were unable to select the correct picture any more often than would be expected by chance (see also Bradley, Garrett, and Zurif, 1980). The cause of this impairment may be in the clause to episode pathway. Schwartz, Saffran, and Marin (1980) also found that patients with Broca's aphasia were at chance at understanding who kissed who in sentences such as "John was finally kissed by Louise." But they were 85 to 100 percent accurate at judging which of the following sentences was grammatical:

John has finally kissed Louise.
*John was finally kissed Louise.

The patients retained the ability to recognize grammatical sentences even though they could not use this information to help themselves understand the sentences.

Impaired semantic priming by clauses provides further evidence of an impairment in the clause to episode pathway. For example, in the sentence "The gymnast loved the professor from the northwestern city who complained about the bad coffee" the position in the sentence after the word *who* is called a gap. This is because it refers back to the word *professor*. Normally, the comprehension process fills in the gap automatically by activating *professor* so you know who *who* refers to. One way to demonstrate this is in a priming task in which the listener/observer sees a letter string while hearing the sentence and responds whether the letter string is a word. When a word appears just after *who* is heard, the normal listener is faster to judge it to be a word if it is semantically related to *professor*, such as *teacher*, than if it is unrelated to *professor*, such as *address*. Zurif *et al.* (1993) studied four patients with Broca's aphasia and found that, unlike normal individuals, they were no faster at recognizing *professor* than *address*. However, the normal results were obtained with four patients who had moderate Wernicke's aphasia. So, despite the impairment of the semantic network in Wernicke's aphasia, there was still priming in a syntactic context, while in Broca's aphasia there was not.

The two principal symptoms of Broca's aphasia interact so that a person has more difficulty pronouncing function words and inflections than pronouncing content words (Gardner, 1976: 63; Geschwind, 1970). Furthermore, one inflection may be harder to produce than another, even when both consist of the same sound (Goodglass and Hunt, 1958; Myerson and Goodglass, 1972). For example, some patients still inflect nouns but not verbs. As a result, a person might produce "The boy eats beets" as "The boy eat beets." The final "s" would be dropped from the verb (*eat*) but not the noun (*beets*). The same types of errors usually appear when the patient tries to write (Gardner, 1976: 65).

Like all aphasia, Broca's aphasia includes word-finding difficulty. However, the Broca's aphasic patient retains concrete nouns the best, in contrast to the Wernicke's aphasic patient, who retains them the worst (Caramazza and Berndt, 1978). When Zurif *et al.* (1974) asked aphasic patients to sort words into categories, the Broca's aphasic patients grouped animal words somewhat differently from normal patients but honored most of the main category boundaries.

Severity. The degree of aphasic impairment varies over the widest range possible, from those individuals whose ability to speak and comprehend are so slightly impaired that it can be detected only by special testing to those who are mute and understand nothing. At the mild end of the scale, aphasia may manifest itself as a limit on the amount the person can comprehend at one time. For example, an aphasic person who can perform each of three simple commands perfectly (for example, "Put the key in the cup," "Open the door," and "Touch your head with your hand") when they are given separately may be unable to perform any when they are given in combination.

One difficulty frequently reported by formerly aphasic patients (Moss, 1972) is that other people seemed to speak to them too rapidly during the period of aphasia. Another common report is that the speech of other people was not quite comprehensible. Imagine that you are listening to a stream of speech that sounds awfully familiar but that you cannot quite understand. Often a more severe aphasia improves over time to a barely detectable disorder. Nevertheless, a formerly severely aphasic individual may remain uncomfortable in ordinary conversational situations that you take for granted. For example, Schuell (1974: 125), related the following sad story:

> I once saw a patient who entered the hospital for seizure control two years after a head injury incurred in the war. He showed no obvious aphasia, but an alert resident referred him for examination because there was a history of transient aphasia on his military record. I found a mild word-finding difficulty and a mild reduction of verbal retention span running through all language modalities. I told the patient what I found and said that it was the result of his head injuries. I told him that it was very mild and that I would not have detected it if I had not tested him. I also told him that there were things that he could do at home to improve it if he were interested. Then he began to talk.
>
> He said it would have made all the difference in the world to him if someone had told him this two years before. He said that he had never heard of aphasia before. He did not know he'd been aphasic after his injury. He said that he went back to his hometown, saw people he had known all his life, and could not remember their names. He could not remember addresses or telephone numbers that he had known most of his life. One night he played cards and found that he could not keep score. He tried to

balance his checkbook and found he was not able to do this. He read the paper and did not know what he had read. He listened to news on the radio and did not know what he had heard. He thought he was losing his mind and he lived in the terror that if someone discovered this he would most certainly be committed to an institution. He began to avoid people. He did not dare to get a job. He said that he had sat at home and watched television for two years.

7.3 Reading

About 50,000 years after the invention of spoken language, written language was invented about 5,000 years ago, first with the invention of idiographic (pictorial symbols for words) and then alphabetic language. Reading and writing provide additional pathways beyond speech for language comprehension and production.

Logogens

Beneath the surface of the temporal cortex the visual and auditory pathways intersect, so that words can have meaning and things can have names. A fragment of the semantic system in the temporal lobe showing the representation of a single word is shown in Figure 7.17. Morton (1969; 1979) called the word representations in semantic memory **logogens**, derived from the Latin *logos* (*word*) and *genus* (*birth*). A logogen includes verbal and print representations for recognition and pronunciation and manual-motor representations for production, so it is a **polymodal** representation for a word.

The circle with two lines through it, and the word *dog* in italics in it, represent the logogen for the word *dog*. The dotted line in the logogen representation shows the activation

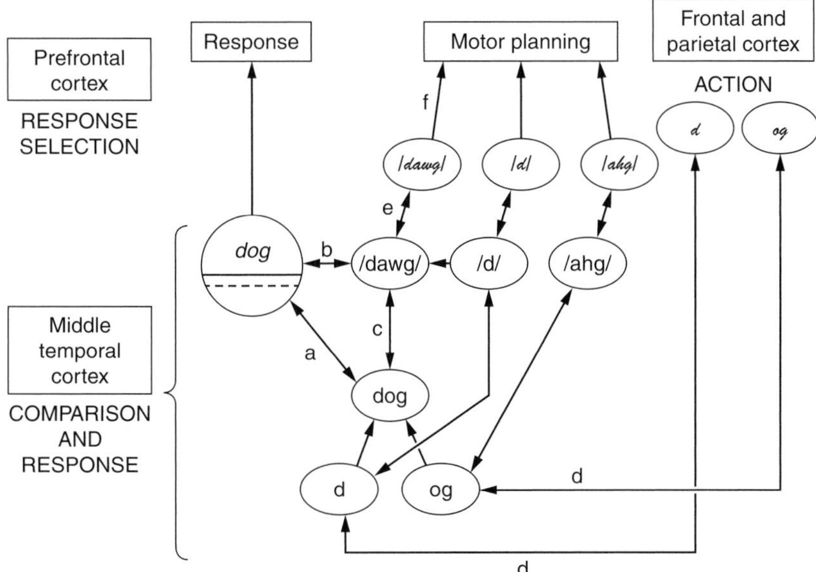

Figure 7.17 A fragment of the lexical component of semantic memory showing the pathways disrupted in agnosias and apraxias related to language: deep dyslexia (c), alexia (a, c), agraphia (d), verbal agnosia (b), and repetition failure (f) in conduction aphasia.

level of the logogen. The activation level depends on how well an associated perceptual representation matches the input. The area containing the visual representations of words is the inferior temporal area adjacent to the occipital cortex (Wandell, 2011). When a perceptual representation matches an input, activation increases in both other perceptual representations and the logogen connected to it. Recall from the discussion of visual scanning in Chapter 5 that, if the letter "d" of a three letter word is identified during an eye fixation, the activation of the letter sequence "og" (and other letter sequences that complete words that begin with "d") increases even before the comparison of the letter sequence with representations in memory is completed. Of course, the more of its perceptual representation that matches the input, the higher is the activation of the logogen, so, if "d" and "og" both match the input, its activation increases further. The solid line shows the criterion of the logogen for a response. When the activation level exceeds the criterion a response is transmitted to the prefrontal cortex, and the word is perceived and recognized. Your perception corresponds to the logogen that responded. For example, if a visual input causes the *dog* logogen to respond, then you see the word *dog*.

A subliminal presentation produces activation that does not exceed the criterion, so the word is not seen. However, this activation can accumulate over time. Haber and Hershenson (1965) presented letter strings so briefly (for ten milliseconds) that initially no letters could be seen at all. But, after several repetitions, the letters began to appear (see also Chastain, 1977). Presumably, each presentation of the input increased the activation of one or more letter representations in memory until they began to exceed the criterion. Haber and Hershenson called this the growth of the percept.

In Figure 7.17, lower-case letters, such as "d," indicate visual representations of printed letters, letter sequences, and words. The letters between the slash brackets (such as /d/) are auditory representations of consonants, syllables, and words. These **intra-modal** pathways are shown connected by single-headed arrows. The modality of a representation refers to its sensory origin, whether it is visual, auditory, motor, etc. "Intra" means within, so an intra-modal pathway is one within a modality. During reading, an intra-modal pathway goes from the visual representation of the printed word to its logogen. For example, when reading the word *dog*, successively, individual-letter (such as "d"), letter sequence (such as "og"), and whole-word ("dog") representations are activated by the input. **Inter-modal** (that is, between modality) pathways are shown as two-headed arrows. For example, the pathway between the visual representation of "d" and the manual-motor representation of "d" is shown. Motor representations are shown in mistral type font to distinguish them.

There are up to three parallel pathways for recognizing a printed word in the recognition heterarchy (Papp *et al.*, 1982). First, through the instrumental system (Chapter 2), the visual representation of a printed word can activate its meaning directly through a visual whole-word pathway. This is the dog to *dog* pathway in Figure 7.17. Second, the visual representation of the entire printed word can activate an auditory representation of the word, which activates its meaning through an auditory whole-word pathway. This is the dog to /dawg/ to *dog* pathway shown in Figure 7.17. Third, through the habit system (Chapters 2 and 5), the visual representations of the letters and letter strings activate their pronunciations, which are assembled by the pronunciation system into an auditory representation of the entire word. This pathway is not shown in Figure 7.17, because it does not exist for the irregularly pronounced word *dog*. Notice that, when a printed word is read, its meaning and pronunciation are activated together. It is *not* the case that the meaning is activated by pronouncing the word.

During reading, all existing pathways are activated in parallel and send inputs to the prefrontal cortex, where they arrive at slightly different times. Often, the three pathways converge on the same pronunciation and meaning, but this is not always the case. The letter sequence pathway is governed by spelling–sound correspondences that govern the pronunciation of most (for example, *barn, darn, mint, hint, gave, save, bog, fog*) but not all words. The pronunciation of exception words such as *warn, pint, have*, and *dog* does not follow the usual spelling–sound correspondences. Hence, the inputs from the auditory whole-word and letter sequence pathways to the pronunciation system are different, and only the input from the auditory whole-word pathway is correct. The conflicting information from the whole-word and letter sequence pathways must be resolved (usually by inhibiting the letter sequence pathway) before the word can be pronounced. Skilled readers are therefore slower to pronounce exception words than regular words. This **exception** or **regularity effect** is further qualified by word frequency. High-frequency words generally show little effect of exceptional spelling–sound correspondences. In contrast, low-frequency exception words are typically twenty-five to forty milliseconds slower, and more error-prone, than low-frequency regular words (Rastle and Coltheart, 1999a; Seidenberg *et al.*, 1984). This is because, for high-frequency words, the input of the whole-word pathway arrives at the pronunciation system before the letter sequence input, so there is no conflict. However, for low-frequency words, the input from the two pathways arrives together, and so the conflict must be resolved.

More generally, in the whole-word pathway all the letters of the word are activated in parallel, and every time the whole-word representation is matched to an input it is processed a little more quickly next time. In contrast, in the letter sequence pathway the word representation is constructed by serially scanning its letter sequence from left to right. The speed of construction is not determined by the frequency of the word but by the frequency and regularity of the component letter sequences. Thus, the word frequency affects the whole-word pathway but not the letter sequence pathway. The more often a particular word is seen, the less time it takes to recognize it (Forster and Chambers, 1973) and the more rapidly its particular pronunciation is activated (Baluch and Besner, 1991; McCann and Besner, 1987). In contrast, the number of letters in the word affects the letter sequence pathway, but not the whole-word pathway (Rastle and Coltheart, 1998; Weekes, 1997). Furthermore, since the representations in the letter sequence pathway are processed serially from left to right, it follows that the letter sequence pathway is more likely to produce a conflict with the whole-word pathway when the exceptional letter sequence occurs early in the word. In fact, this is what is found (Coltheart and Rastle, 1994; Rastle and Coltheart, 1999b).

Having redundant word recognition pathways is an advantage, because familiar exception words, such as *dog*, can be recognized rapidly through the visual whole-word pathway while a brand new word that is being encountered for the first time, such as *grog*, can still be pronounced through the letter sequence sound conversion pathway without ever having been heard beforehand. However, there is a slight downside to redundant pathways. As mentioned above, it may take a little longer to pronounce an exception word, and it also takes a little longer to detect a homophonic (sound-alike) error. **Homophones** are two different letter

Aoccdrnig to rscheearch at an Elingsh uinervtisy, it smotemeis deosn't mttaer in waht oredr the ltteers in a wrod are, the olny iprmoatnt tihng is taht the frist and lsat ltteer is at the rghit pclae. The rset can be a toatl mses and you can sitll raed it wouthit porbelm. Tihs is bcuseae we do not raed ervey lteter by it slef but the wrod as a wlohe.

Figure 7.18 Initial and final letters are the most important for word recognition (Rawlinson, 1976).

sequences that are pronounced the same way, such as *cellar* and *seller*, *work* and *werk*. When only one homophone is a word, the visual whole-word and auditory letter sequence pathways produce conflicting responses to the input. In a spelling error detection task, a homophone substitution such as *werk* for *work* was less likely to be noticed than a nonhomophone substitution such as *wark* for *work* (Corcoran, 1966; 1967; Corcoran and Weening, 1968; MacKay, 1968). Moreover, recall from Chapter 6 that the visual whole word pathway increases the difficulty of detecting spelling errors that preserve the overall shape of the word, such as *stud-cnt* (Healy, 1981).

The robustness of word recognition during reading is demonstrated by the text in Figure 7.18. Even though only the first and last letter of each word is in its correct place, the text can still be read. As each logogen becomes active, the letter string activating it is perceived as a misspelled word rather than as a meaningless letter string, because the response of the logogen determines how the letter string is perceived.

Alexia and dyslexia

Several visual agnosias are specific to reading. Figure 7.17 shows the associations disrupted by specific agnosias. **Deep dyslexia** is the result when the connection between the phonemic and visual representations of a word is severed (c). A person can still understand familiar visual words but loses the ability to pronounce them. Such patients may make semantic substitutions when asked to repeat words. For example, a patient might repeat *boat* as *ship*. When both pathways by which the visual representation of a word is recognized are severed (a, c), the result is **alexia**. The person can no longer recognize printed words but can still understand spoken language normally. Since perceptual representations and motor representations are distinct, production may be spared. Alexia is the most common visual agnosia that is specific to one kind of target. In alexia without **agraphia**, people can still write to dictation, because pathways b, a, and d from the auditory representation of the word to the motor representation for writing it are intact. But they cannot read their own writing! Conversely, if only pathway d is severed, then they suffer from pure agraphia, which is a form of apraxia. Reading is possible but writing is not. Verbal agnosia can also occur without agraphia if pathways c and d from the auditory representation of the word to the motor representation for writing it are intact. Sufferers can still write to dictation, though they don't understand what is being said (Ellis, 1984; Kohn and Friedman, 1986).

SUMMARY

- Semantic memory consists of
  - interrelated response nodes that designate components of episodes as the associated perceptual and motor representations of the targets and actions of the episodes; and
  - response nodes for words, called logogens, that designate targets and actions.
- The encoding and feature analysis stages of auditory processing
  - are anatomically parallel and functionally similar to the corresponding stages of visual processing; and
  - make a distinction between speech (left hemisphere) and nonspeech (right hemisphere) sounds, for which there is no analogy in vision.
- The speech- and language-processing system includes the superior temporal cortex, middle temporal cortex and prefrontal cortex.
- Speech sounds and the subsequent word and sentence representations require substantial computation.
  - Speech input tends to be ambiguous – that is, small segments of the input approximately match the representations of several different speech sounds.
  - The speech-processing system makes use of syntactic representations of meaningful word sequences, along with other knowledge, to constrain the representations of the input to those that are meaningful.
  - Speech recognition is therefore performed through a process of comparison (temporal cortex) and response selection (prefrontal cortex), called analysis by synthesis.
- The purpose of speech communication is the construction of a semantic representation that represents the meaning of the sentence. This is called comprehension. There is considerable ambiguity in the meanings of individual phrases, which is resolved through concatenation with
  - the meanings of adjacent phrases;
  - the nonlinguistic context of the utterance; and
  - the general knowledge of the listener.
- During reading there are three redundant pathways for word recognition:
  - a visual whole-word pathway;
  - an auditory whole-word pathway; and
  - a letter sequence pronunciation pathway.

Some 60,000 years ago semantic memory gave humans an enormous advantage in communicating with each other. Within an immediate context, a word could be used to indicate a specific action or target of an action. So, within the immediate context, words could guide actions. However, words alone are useless outside an immediate context. Words alone are insufficient to describe an event to a non-participant. When all you have are words such as *rock* and *throw*, there is no way to tell someone who wasn't there who did what to whom. This limitation was brilliantly overcome through the invention of language, specifically through the use of word order as a global feature to encode actor–action–object relations. Once word order had meaning independent of the words, so that "John kissed Mary" meant something different from "Mary kissed John," it became possible to tell someone who wasn't there what happened. The tasks of learning and routinely using language required the full range of human instrumental and habit abilities and taxed them to their limits. It took years of effort for a human to become proficient in the production and comprehension of language. However, the benefits were transformative. Planning became possible. Storytelling became possible. Autobiographical memory, the remembered self-authored story of one's own life, became possible. The inter-generational accumulation of knowledge became possible. Humans were no longer another kind of animal but distinct from animals. Through the accumulation of this knowledge, human civilization became much more complex and sophisticated, and the descendants of the family that invented language conquered the entire world.

About 5,000 years ago the invention of writing again transformed human civilization. However, until the last century only a tiny fraction of humans ever learned to read. Today, the time and effort spent learning to read proficiently is shaping the mature brains of the entire species. Furthermore, it is possible that new technology is transforming the nature of language in ways that will have consequences for cognition and civilization. Therefore, it is fortunate that in this century we have begun to have an understanding of how language is produced and understood, so that we can consider how transforming it may affect human cognition.

QUESTIONS

1. What daily task requires, or is at least influenced by, semantic priming?
2. What can be communicated by sentences that cannot be communicated by words alone?
3. What is the purpose of speech perception?
4. What is the longest single sentence that a person can immediately repeat after hearing it once?
5. What animals have left hemispheres specialized for functions not provided by the right hemisphere? Why is this specialization necessary?

FURTHER READING

Fitch, W. T. (2010). *The Evolution of Language*. Cambridge University Press.

Lum, J. A. G., Conti-Ramsden, G., Page, D., and Ullman, M. T. (2012). Working, declarative and procedural memory in specific language impairment. *Cortex*, 48, 1138–54.

Newman, S., Malaia, E., and Seo, R. (2014). Does degree of handedness in a group of right-handed individuals affect language comprehension? *Brain and Cognition*, 86, 98–103.

Spivey, M. J., McRae, K., and Joanisse, M. F. (eds.) (2012). *The Cambridge Handbook of Psycholinguistics*. Cambridge University Press.

8 Infant learning and language learning

Carolyn Rovee-Collier gave birth to her first son while she was a graduate student. She was faced with the difficulty of taking care of a newborn and writing a dissertation at the same time. As she attempted to write at her desk, her son was in the crib by her side. Hanging from the crib was a mobile that was intended to hold his attention. However, every time she tried to write a sentence, her son would cry, and she would have to stop writing to shake his mobile for him, which quieted him. Was there any way that she could get her son to entertain himself, so that he would stop interrupting? After all, she was a psychologist. She should be able to think of something.

What she thought of was to tie a ribbon from her son's ankle to the mobile hanging over the crib (Figure 8.1, top). Now, when the boy squirmed and moved his leg, the mobile moved as well. The movement instantly caught his attention, distracting and quieting him. Within a few minutes he learned that he could make the mobile shake by moving his leg. This delighted him no end. Transfixed, he would give his leg a quick jerk, observe the result, and laugh. Soon he laughed and squealed even before he kicked, anticipating what was going to happen. This left his mother free to complete her work. What was more remarkable was that, when Rovee-Collier attached the ribbon to his foot the next day, he started kicking straight away. He remembered how to make the mobile move.

This simple tale of infant learning illustrates the close connection between learning and action. From infancy, people remember the consequences of their actions. Then, in similar circumstances, it is possible to act effectively. After his initial discovery, every time Rovee-Collier's son saw the mobile to which he had been tethered he tried to move it with a kick.

This discovery of the learning ability of a newborn (Rovee and Rovee, 1969) was a major surprise. Anyone who has ever taken care of a newborn can be excused for considering it to be little more than a digestive tract. However, in fact the following applies:

- Shortly after birth an infant
  - is already able to make emotional responses, such as cries, and to selectively process novel targets;
  - can learn to move a mobile attached by a ribbon to its ankle by kicking its foot;

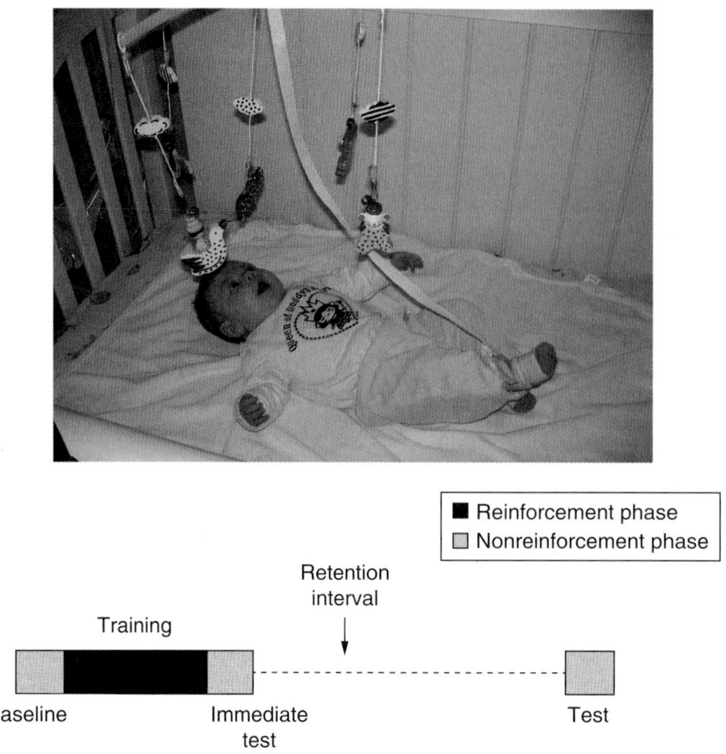

Figure 8.1 An ankle ribbon tied to a three-month-old infant's foot is strung to the hook suspending the mobile. When the infant kicks, the mobile moves (Rovee and Rovee, 1969).

  - encode detailed visual representations; and
  - generalize responses.
- During the first six months the infant
  - encodes episodes that allow it to recognize basic things that organize daily life, such as its caregiver and home;
  - learns the perceptual and motor skills that make efficient declarative learning possible; and
  - becomes able to remember routine episodes indefinitely as the result of distributed reminding.
- After six months the infant is able to
  - reach for and grasp objects, sit up, then crawl, and finally walk, enabling it to explore the world and learn about it; and
  - learn through the imitation of actions it has observed.

By two months of age the task of learning a spoken language has begun. The initial difficulties in establishing communication through speech are daunting and require specialized brain areas. Normal speech is a jumble of sounds that must be decoded on the basis of knowledge of the language being spoken. But the infant has no such knowledge.

- Speech is learned in the context of social communication between the infant and caregiver through emotional utterances, so the infant is already focused on the speech input and using it for communication.

- The infant is aided in segmenting the speech when the speaker speaks slowly with extra emphasis and pauses to aid segmentation.
  - By five months of age infants can discriminate the stress pattern of their own language from the stress patterns of other languages.
  - Over the second six months of life infants detect transitional probabilities between syllables and can recognize some isolated words.
  - By ten and a half months they are segmenting these words correctly when they are heard in fluent speech.
  - The serial learning of word sequences is probably aided by the infant's imitation of speech.
- Over the next two years the infant is actively learning language. Once the infant gets the idea that things have names, and, more generally, that words have meaning, perceptual, social, and emotional cues all guide the infant to the speaker's intent.
  - After the first few hundred, most words are learned the first time they are heard, and there is explosive growth in vocabulary.
  - At age four, nonword repetition is a predictor of vocabulary growth.
- Grammar learning begins when there is sufficient knowledge of different word forms.
  - The acquisition of the dominant word order of the language is a gradual process, involving generalization from examples.
  - As knowledge of word order stabilizes, verbal learning becomes an additional tool for learning the meanings of words.
- Reading is initially learned through letter–sound conversion, which makes English particularly difficult, but then the direct visual whole-word route is added, as early as the first year of primary school.
  - Reading results in a greatly expanded vocabulary. By the time a student enters college he or she knows about 50,000 words, which means that, from the age of six, he or she has learned about ten new words a day.
  - People differ in their ability to learn to comprehend language. This difference is evident only in academic settings, where unexplained difficulty in reading comprehension is called dyslexia. However, the most common cause of dyslexia is a general problem with language processing, called specific language impairment (SLI).
- Some infants are born without normal emotions or lose them after a year of life. These deficits result in a profound social impairment, which in turn causes cognitive and language impairments that may vary from mild to severe and are collectively called the autistic spectrum disorder (ASD).

8.1 Infant learning

There is one way that the learning experience is different for the infant from what it is for anyone else. As discussed in Chapters 4 through 6, beyond infancy, perceptual representations are compared with representations in memory. However, for the first few months of life many experiences are entirely new. For the newborn there are few if any representations in memory to compare with the perceptual representations of their necessarily new experiences. To compensate for his lack of knowledge, the infant is born with some abilities that make it possible to begin to learn without knowledge of the world. To begin with, the infant has innate emotional responses that allow it to communicate with its caregiver from birth and that provide an evaluation, good or bad, of the consequences of its actions. The infant also has a perceptual system that selects novel targets, and the perception of a novel target stimulates the learning system. So, the infant has an inborn tendency to learn about what is new in its world. The infant has an instrumental learning system that creates episodes representing ad hoc voluntary actions to novel targets. It also has a habit learning system that creates long-term episodes for routine actions to familiar targets. All this cognitive machinery would be of little value if infants were abandoned in the wild to be raised by wolves. However, social interaction with a doting caretaker provides both the opportunity and incentive for an infant to exploit all its abilities.

Emotion

As mentioned in Chapter 2, humans are the most social of all animals. In humans, the emotional system has a communicative function in addition to an evaluative one. MacLean (1993) suggested that a critical step was taken in the evolution of emotion when animals began to care for their children for an extended period of time, since a special "attachment-dependency" emotional system evolved to regulate the interactions between parents and children. According to MacLean, human emotional development begins with the attachment-dependency relationship between a mother and her infant that characterizes all mammals. This relationship exists because of the utterly helpless state of the infant and its complete dependence on the mother. In order for emotions to serve their social function, they must be expressed as well as felt. Within seconds of birth the human baby makes its first emotional communication: a cry. In the early months of life innately specified vocal and visible expressions of emotion enable infants and parents to communicate.

When adults speak to infants their voices always have vocal expression of emotion. This is in contrast to speech to other adults, in which the emotion is usually filtered out (Trainor, Austin, and Desjardins, 2000). Cohn and Tronick (1983) found that, when mothers address their three-month old infants with normal emotion, the infants are likely to cycle between play, positive expressions, and monitoring. But, when the mothers were instructed to address their infants with flat affect, the positive expressions decreased and the infants showed more wary expressions and made more protests. Fernald (1993) found that, from the age of five months, infants can discriminate affective messages indicating approval or prohibition, either in their parents' language or in a language that their parents do not speak. Infants showed more positive affect to approvals and more negative affect to prohibitions. By two or three months infants appear to smile to express happiness and to make distressed expressions in appropriate circumstances. Lewis, Alessandri, and Sullivan (1990) placed infants that were two, four, six and eight months old in an infant seat and attached a string to their arms. Pulling the string turned on music for a brief period of time. The infants quickly learned to pull the string to make the music and smiled when the music came on. But, when the apparatus was disconnected so that pulling the string no longer initiated the music, the infants made sounds of distress.

A system of reflexes causes people, including infants and adults alike, to literally show their emotions on their faces. By seven months babies can match facial and vocal expressions. Walker-Andrews (1986) showed them filmed expressions of happiness and anger along with adult voices expressing the same or a different emotion. The babies spent longer looking at the film clips of visual expressions that matched the sounds than at expressions that did not match. However, the facial expressions of fear, surprise, and anger are not well differentiated as late at eight to twelve months of age (Hiatt, Campos, and Emde, 1979; Lewis, Alessandri, and Sullivan, 1990). All we can say, therefore, is that, throughout the first year of life, infants express, recognize, and undoubtedly feel both happiness and distress in appropriate situations.

Beginning in the second year of life, as situational learning occurs, the distress emotion becomes differentiated into four distinct negative emotions: sadness, disgust, anger, and fear (Ekman, 1992; Izard, 1994). Happiness and surprise also become differentiated. Evidence for the set of six basic adult emotions comes from the ability of adults across different cultures to recognize facial expressions of each of these six emotions.

The perception of different emotions is associated with different brain areas, as revealed by the effects of injuries on adult perceptions. Hornak, Rolls, and Wade (1996) found that patients with aberrant behavior following orbitofrontal cortex lesions were generally impaired in their recognition of facial and vocal emotional expressions. Damage to specific parts of the emotional system results in impairments in the recognition of the facial expression of specific emotions. As reviewed by Blair and Curran (1999), damage to the amygdala impaired the recognition of fear, damage to the basal ganglia impaired the recognition of disgust, and suppression of the functioning of the **orbitofrontal** cortex, through the administration of Valium, impaired the recognition of anger.

Target selection

There are not many voluntary actions that a young infant can perform, but one thing it can do is look. One technique for assessing what targets an infant selects for further processing is to show it a pair of pictures or objects, one familiar and one novel, and record which it looks at longer (Fantz, 1958). Typically, immediately after a short study trial, the infant looks more at the familiar item, whereas after a long study trial it looks longer at the novel one (Bahrick and Pickens, 1995). The number of seconds of study time required to produce a novelty preference decreases with age (Rose *et al.*, 1982). One way of explaining this pattern is that, if the study time has been short, the infant has not finished examining and so continues to look at the study item when a novel item is placed next to it. But, if the study time has been sufficient to examine the study item and encode a presentation of it, then the perceptual system picks out the novel item, and that is now the one the infant examines. The selection of novel targets by the perceptual system is an aid to learning, because it makes the infant aware of new things in the world. Furthermore, when a novel target is selected for a response, the processing of it continues until a representation of it in memory is constructed.

As the retention interval between study and test is increased, the infant's preference for the novel over the familiar item disappears and then reverses. Over retention intervals of one day to two weeks, looking time is divided equally between items moving in a familiar and a novel pattern (Bahrick and Pickens, 1995) and listening time is divided equally between familiar and novel nursery rhymes (Spence, 1996). At a retention interval of three months the infant looks longer at the familiar items in the familiar motion. The change in the distribution of looking times has been explained by assuming that the infant will examine a picture for which there is an initial feeling of familiarity until a complete representation of the picture has been retrieved from memory. At three months it takes so long to retrieve the representation of the familiar picture that more time is spent looking at it than the novel picture (Bauer, 2002). Therefore, the extended examination of a familiar target after a long retention interval is an aid to retrieval. Furthermore, as we shall see below, distributed experience with a target over long intervals is also an aid to retention.

Infant learning

By two months of age an infant enjoys making things happen, such as pulling a string to make music (Lewis, Alessandri, and Sullivan, 1990) or kicking to move a mobile hanging above her crib (Rovee and Rovee, 1969). The infant encodes complete episodes of these enjoyable experiences, including detailed representations of the target, context, action, and result. It was Rovee-Collier who first found a way to test the long-term retention of an infant's memory by taking the mobile away and bringing it back at a later time. If the infant began to kick when he merely saw the mobile again then the kicking demonstrated that he had remembered it. Figure 8.1 (middle) shows how infant memory was measured. The baseline is a measure of how often the infants kicked to the mobile before they had ever been connected to it. During baseline one end of a ribbon was tied around their ankle and the end was tied around the side of the crib. So, when they kicked, the mobile didn't move. The baseline measure of kick rate was collected over an interval of one to two minutes. During training the end of the ribbon previously tied to the side of the crib was tied to the mobile, so then the infants made the mobile move when they kicked. The infants almost immediately noticed this, and began to do it straight away. So, a training session was set at two to four minutes. During the immediate and long-term retention tests, the ribbon was again tied to the side of the crib and did not move the mobile. If the infants kicked more often during the test than during baseline it demonstrated that they remembered moving the mobile during training and were still trying to do so. Furthermore, if the infants kicked as often during the long-term test as in the immediate test (measured by the retention ratio), this suggested that no forgetting had occurred during the retention interval. Of course, a test session is frustrating for the infants, so testing was kept from thirty seconds to a minute. As shown in Figure 8.1 (bottom), two-month-old infants remember how to move the mobile for a day, three-month-old infants remember for a week, and six-month-old infants remember for two weeks.

Visual target. Infants that have learned that they can move a specific training mobile will kick only when they see that specific training mobile. Therefore, the amount of detail in the infants' memory of the training mobile can be determined by showing them a very similar but novel mobile that differs in some specific detail from the training mobile. If the infants do not kick to the novel mobile then we can conclude that their representation of the training mobile contains the detail that discriminates between the training and novel mobiles.

Overall, the results of many experiments demonstrate that, shortly after birth, infants are remembering detailed representations of visual targets. At two to six months of age, infants did not respond twenty-four hours later to a test mobile even slightly different from the training mobile (Hartshorn *et al.*, 1998). Neither two- nor three-month-olds kicked to a five-block mobile when more than a single block on it was different from the training mobile (Fagen, Rovee, and Kaplan, 1976; Hayne *et al.*, 1986). They could even detect a mobile that differed by only a single block when it was sufficiently different in color to pop out from the others (Gerhardstein, Renner, and Rovee-Collier, 1999).

In other experiments all the blocks on the novel mobile were painted differently from the test mobile, but the difference was quite small. Infants did not kick to a test mobile with characters just 25 percent different in size from those on the blocks of the training mobile. Three-month-old infants did not kick to a seven-block test mobile with pluses ("+"s) on the blocks when trained a week earlier on mobile blocks with "T"s and "L"s, and vice versa (Adler and Rovee-Collier, 1994; Bhatt, Rovee-Collier, and Weiner, 1994). Finally, when three-month-old infants were trained with mobiles that had red "A"s painted on yellow blocks, they did not kick to a mobile that had red "2"s painted on yellow blocks, or a mobile with black "A"s painted on yellow blocks, or a mobile that had red "A"s painted on green blocks. So, both the size and specific visual features of the blocks are part of the training mobile's representation. Moreover, when trained with a mobile with red "A"s painted on yellow blocks, they did not kick to a test mobile that had yellow "A"s painted on red blocks (Bhatt and Rovee-Collier, 1994). The ability to discriminate a similar novel mobile from the training mobile demonstrates that, even in the first months of life, infants encode detailed visual representations. The ability to encode such detailed visual representations is obviously of great value in learning about the world. The infant can encode a detailed enough representation to recognize its own caregiver, and to represent objects in the world to which the caregiver refers.

Contexts. Furthermore, even at three months of age, an infant that learns to move a mobile remembers the entire episode, including the complete context of the target mobile. Recognition of the target mobile is therefore highly context-dependent. The infant would not kick to the training mobile at test if the liner of its crib was different from the training session (Butler and Rovee-Collier, 1989; Rovee-Collier, Griesler, and Earley, 1985), if the mobile was shown in a different room from the training room, or if the infant was in a different crib from the training crib (Hayne, Rovee-Collier, and Borza, 1991). Infants remember not just detailed visual representations but also a great many details about their environment.

However, infants can generalize a response to a target that appears in more than one context. Context dependence occurs only when a distinctive context is uniquely associated with a distinctive learning event. When infants were trained on the same mobile in two different contexts they kicked to it in a third context (Amabile and Rovee-Collier, 1991; Rovee-Collier and Dufault, 1991).

Exploration, emotion, and imitation

After six months of age, infants can reach for and grasp objects, sit up, then crawl, and finally walk, enabling them to explore the world and learn about it. Because there are more things that infants can do, there are more opportunities for them to learn and more opportunities to test what they can remember. Since the entire point of learning is the subsequent control of action (Chapter 2), it is unsurprising that, by six months of age, infants remember a toy that they have played with longer than a toy that they have merely seen. Diamond (1995) found that, when a six-month-old infant was merely shown a toy, the infant remembered the toy for no more than three minutes, but, when given the opportunity to play with the toy, it was remembered for at least ten minutes.

Distributed training. Recall from Chapter 2 that, because of encoding by the habit system, better long-term retention following distributed rather than massed training is ubiquitous across species. Recall from Chapter 3 that Baddeley and Longman (1978) found that, because of encoding by the habit system, distributed training was superior for the (*procedural*) perceptual-motor skill of typing. Hartshorn *et al.* (1998) found that distributed training was also superior for long-term (*declarative*) recognition memory of a mobile by three-month-old infants. Hartshorn *et al.* (1998) gave three-month-old infants three training sessions and tested retention twenty-one days after the final session. Infants that received training on days 0, 1, and 2 did not recognize the training mobile at test. But infants that received training on days 0, 2, and 8 did recognize the training mobile at test. Only the distributed training produced retention at an interval of twenty-one days. Of course, there is a limit to how far apart training sessions can be spaced in the distributed condition. When they are spread so far apart that the last session is forgotten before the next one occurs, there is no cumulative effect from the training sessions. Infants that received training on days 0, 4, and 8 did not recognize the training mobile at test. By the time of the second training session, on day 4, the training on day 0 was forgotten.

Notice that the distributed training schedule used by Hartshorn *et al.* (1998) was different from and more efficient than the one used by Baddeley and Longman (1978). Baddeley and Longman provided training sessions at equal intervals. In contrast, Hartshorn *et al.* provided training sessions at systematically increasing intervals. Each training session more than doubled the retention interval over which the mobile was remembered. This is a very useful property of distributed training, because a few, intermittent experiences can produce very long, and even permanent, retention.

Once children are six months old they can sit up in a high chair. So, instead of a mobile, Hartshorn and Rovee-Collier (1997) placed a toy train before children that they could make move by pressing a large paddle (Figure 8.2). Bar presses replaced foot kicks as evidence of remembering, but otherwise the task remained the same. With the same amount of training, older children were able to remember the train for a longer period of time (the black squares in Figure 8.3).

Figure 8.3 shows just how much longer a memory is retained following a distributed reminder compared with a massed reminder for the train task, in which infants were able to make the train move by repeatedly pressing a paddle. The black squares show for how many weeks the train task is remembered after a single session as a function of the infants' age. The red diamonds show for how many weeks the train task is remembered after a second session one day after the first. The green circles show for how many weeks the train task is remembered when the second session occurs at the end of the time window over which a single session is remembered. For example, previous research (the black squares in Figure 8.3) showed that a six-month-old remembered the train task for a week after a single session, so the second session was one week later, resulting in five-week retention (green circle). A nine-

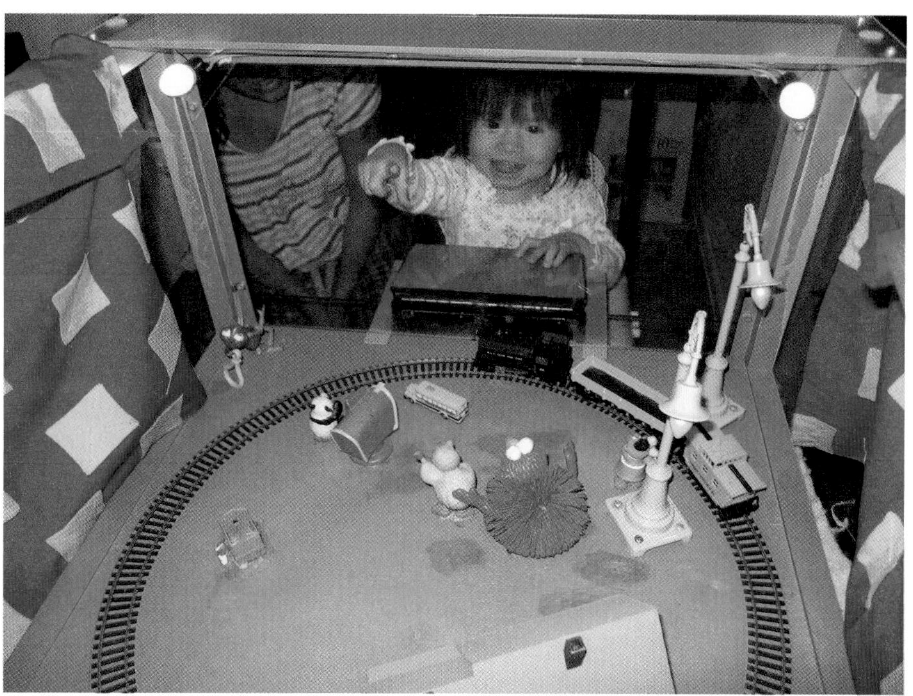

Figure 8.2 Train task, shown here with a six-month-old, is taught to children 6 months old and up. Each lever press moves the toy train for one to two seconds during training.

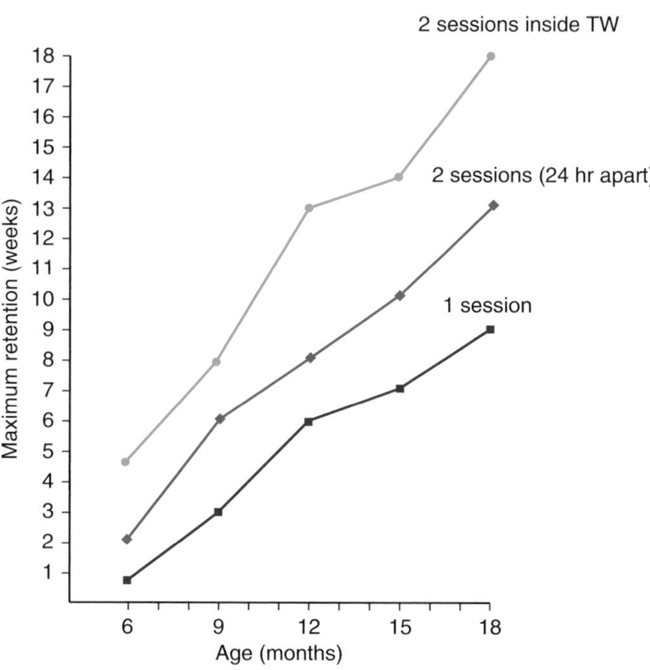

Figure 8.3 Effect of age, number of sessions, and inter-session interval on retention of the train task (Hsu, 2010).

month-old remembered the train task for three weeks after a single session, so the second session was three weeks later, resulting in eight-week retention (green circle). The distributed intervals for twelve-, fifteen-, and eighteen-month-olds were determined in the same way.

Emotion. When children become ambulatory, their emotional system develops along with their motor system to keep them safe from harm. What distresses infants changes over the first year of life. Scarr and Salapatek (1970) exposed infants between two months and two years of age to a variety of things that might distress them, including a jack-in-the-box, a moving toy dog, loud noises, a visual cliff, strangers, and someone wearing a mask. They found that the items fell into three categories with regard to the ages at which they distressed children. Few children under seven months showed marked expressions of fear or distress to anything. Their fear of a loud or sudden movement and of unfamiliar toys began at around seven months, reached a peak at the end of the first year, and then declined in intensity. Moreover, beginning at seven months, the infants showed fear of strangers and masks. Wariness of strangers was associated with distress on separation from the caregiver. Separation distress peaked between fifteen and eighteen months and then declined, so that by three years of age very distressed reactions to separation were rare. In addition, after twelve months children not only express distress but respond to another's distress by comforting, bringing a parent, or offering an object, thus clearly demonstrating that they experience the emotion themselves (Zahn-Waxler *et al.*, 1992).

Fear of the visual cliff also began at seven months of age, and by one year all children feared the visual cliff. The **visual cliff** is simply a clear plate extending over the edge of a table, so it looks as if one is stepping out into empty space. Obviously, once an infant is ambulatory, fear of stepping off a cliff is life-saving. Beyond ten months, an infant may look at a parent's face for emotional information before taking action with respect to an ambiguous elicitor (Walden and Ogan, 1988). For instance, Sorce *et al.* (1985) exposed one-year-old babies to a visual cliff adjusted to a height that did not evoke clear avoidance. Almost three-quarters (74 percent) of babies crossed when their mother showed a happy expression but none crossed when their mother showed a fearful expression. So, at one year of age, emotional expression was still a basis of communication between caregiver and infant.

Imitation. Recall from Chapter 3 that mirror neurons in the frontal cortex respond when a person performs or observes an action. Infants can learn through the imitation of other's actions as well through their own actions (Meltzhoff, 1988). If infants see one puppet taking a mitten off of another puppet and finding a bell, then they are likely to repeat the novel action when given the puppet with the glove. Furthermore, they can remember and perform the action even if they are not given the toy until the next day (Barr, Dowden, and Hayne, 1996). In contrast to the immobile infant, who tends to see the same thing in a single context, the toddler can see or perform the same action to similar targets in many contexts. So, once children become toddlers, their memories are no longer context-dependent. By eighteen months infants that see a novel action performed with a rabbit puppet in a day care center will repeat the same action with a mouse puppet at home (Hayne, Boniface, and Barr, 2000).

Reenactment and reminding. When people repeat an action that they have previously performed, this is called **reenactment**. Figure 8.3 shows that distributed reenactment results in long-term retention. This is a very useful property of memory, because, even if some routine task is only performed over long intervals, it is not forgotten. Another useful property of memory is the effect of a **reminder**. A reminder is some part of an episode that activates the entire episode in the memory and so prepares the appropriate action. The effect of a reminder was tested by showing infants the target mobile or target train that they had previously been able to move for a brief period of time without actually giving them the opportunity to move it. Although a reminder did not always produce as great an increase in long-term retention as reenactment, it was nevertheless very effective. The subjects were children who had previously learned to move a mobile (three months) or a train (six to eighteen months) by kicking or pressing a paddle repeatedly. As shown in Figure 8.4, after they had forgotten the target object, a brief look at it, moving, was all that it took to remind them of how they could get it moving. Furthermore, the recovered memory remained available for nearly as long as the original memory (Hsu and Rovee-Collier, 2006). Similarly, when the puppet task is reenacted one day after it is seen, it is remembered on day 10, then reenactment on day 10 preserves it to day 30, and reenactment on day 30 preserves it to day 70. If on any of these days the puppet is shown as a reminder without the opportunity for reenactment, the memory of the task is preserved just as long (Barr, Rovee-Collier, and Campanella, 2005).

The effect of distributed reminding on long-term retention is another useful property of memory. Long-term retention is the result of a dynamic process that preserves memories

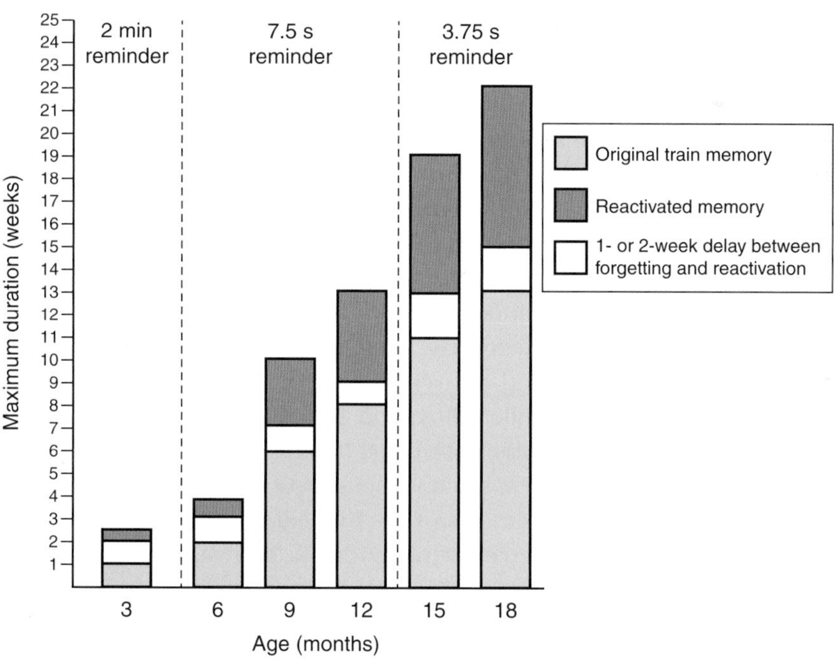

Figure 8.4 Children had previously learned to move a mobile (three months) by kicking or a train (six to eighteen months) by pressing a paddle. After they had forgotten the target object, a brief look at it, moving, was all that it took to remind them of how they could get it moving. Furthermore, the recovered memory remained available for nearly as long as the original memory (Hsu and Rovee-Collier, 2006).

through reminding. A human, including a human infant, has only to do something once to remember it forever. Afterwards, a reminder, such as the target of the action, or its context, may activate the entire episode, and this has the same qualitative effect as a reenactment in creating a longer-lasting memory. Reminding becomes even more useful when the child knows enough language to be reminded of episodes by words. Something done once can be remembered a lifetime through verbal reminders (Barr, Rovee-Collier, and Campanella, 2005).

Context and association. Recall from Chapter 2 that an episode includes not only the target but also its context. Actions are often useful only in specific contexts. Sometimes the target of one action is the context of another. For example, the infant manipulates a puppet in the context of a train it has moved or moves a train in the context of a puppet. In daily life these kinds of intersections, though largely unnoticed, undoubtedly occur all the time. When they do occur, another useful property of memory revealed by infant research is that the most memorable object in the context, rather than just the target object, determines the memorability of the entire episode.

If six-month-old infants press a paddle to make a train move two days in a row, they will remember the task for two weeks. If the infants imitate a puppet finding a bell in the glove of another puppet, they will remember the task for one day. However, if they perform the puppet task in the presence of the train they have learned to move then they also remember the puppet task for two weeks (Barr, Vieira, and Rovee-Collier, 2001; 2002). Similarly, if six-month-old infants press a paddle to make a train move on two occasions a week apart it is remembered for four weeks, and if the two occasions are two weeks apart it is remembered for eight weeks. When infants perform the puppet task in the presence of these better-remembered trains, it is remembered for four and six weeks, respectively (Barr, Rovee-Collier, and Learmonth, 2011). The same extension of retention for the less well remembered episode is obtained when the puppet is more memorable than the train. When six-month-olds learned the train task in a single session, so that it would normally be remembered for five days, in the presence of two previously repeatedly associated puppets that would be remembered for four weeks they remembered the train task for four weeks as well.

Once children begin to move around and do things, an occasional reenactment or reminder, including a verbal reminder, makes it possible for them to remember an action performed at different times indefinitely. Hudson and Sheffield (1998) varied the interval between immediate imitation and reenactment to compare the effects of massed with distributed reenactments and reminders. Boys and girls approximately eighteen months of age saw an adult perform eight activities with target objects in a playroom, such as find fish food and shake it over a fish tank. More spontaneous repetition eight weeks after training resulted from reenactment at two weeks than from immediate reenactment. Reenactment eight weeks after training resulted in perfect retention six months after training. Reenactment influenced retention whether it was spontaneous or elicited by a verbal reminder.

Object permanence and perseveration

The ability of infants to form long-term memories demonstrates that the habit system is functioning no later than shortly after birth. On the other hand, as children age, the same amount of experience results in longer retention (Figure 8.3), indicating that the effectiveness of the two systems – instrumental and habit – increases over the first year of life, possibly as a result of the maturation of neural pathways after birth. Two kinds of behaviors indicate the degree of control that each system has over learning during the first year of life.

Perseveration. As mentioned above, by six months of age infants can sit up and reach for an object. When given a choice between a pair of objects in view, infants reach for the one indicated by the caregiver. If the caregiver hides the object in the view of infants in an accessible location, they will still reach for the now hidden object in that location. When the task is repeated and the same location is always indicated, infants repeatedly reach for it in that location, correctly. However, suppose that, after six trials of reaching for the object on one side (for example, the left), the object on the other side (the right) is indicated. In this case, even when both objects are in plain view, and infants clearly see the one they are invited to reach for on that trial, they continue to reach for what is now the wrong one on the left (Smith *et al.*, 1999). This inability to alter a previously correct response when a new response is called for is called **perseveration**. Infants even make the previous response when it results in reaching for an empty location instead of a desirable toy (Bremner and Bryant, 2001).

The earliest age at which any infants can be found who can sit up and reach for an object is five months. Infants that could perform the task described above, which is called the "A-not-B" task, were tested at five, six, seven, and eight months of age. At the switch of location on the seventh trial, infants perseverated the previous response 15, 58, 72, and 85 percent of the time, respectively (Clearfield *et al.*, 2006). Recall that the habit and instrumental systems cooperate in the control of a mammal's response to a target. The initial ad hoc response is under the control of the instrumental system but after practice the response comes under the control of the habit system. Perseveration occurs when the balance of control between the habit and instrumental systems is disrupted, so that, when the instrumental system must assume control to initiate a new response, the habit system maintains control and makes an old one. The perseveration that emerges in the A-not-B task at the end of the first year demonstrates that the habit system matures more rapidly than the instrumental system.

Object permanence. Converging evidence for the immaturity of the instrumental system during the first year of life comes from the object permanence task, which is almost identical to the A-not-B task but measures a different factor that influences infants' behavior. In this task, a desirable toy is placed in one of two wells that are in view of infants and in easy reach of them, but so that it is hidden from view when it is in the well. When they are allowed to respond immediately, infants almost always reach for the well with the toy (Diamond, 1985). However, at seven and a half months of age, if infants' response is prevented for as little as two seconds then they are much less likely to make the correct response. Between seven and a half and twelve months the delay over which infants remember where the toy is increases from two to nearly ten seconds. Recall from Chapter 2 that the instrumental system includes the ability to construct mental maps, which makes it possible for an animal to find a hidden target. Infants' performance on the object permanence task demonstrates that this ability emerges slowly over the first year of life. It may be that an area in the dorsolateral prefrontal cortex must mature for the task. Rhesus monkeys could remember the location of the hidden target for ten seconds, but when an area in the dorsolateral prefrontal cortex (Figure 8.5) was damaged this ability deteriorated (Diamond and

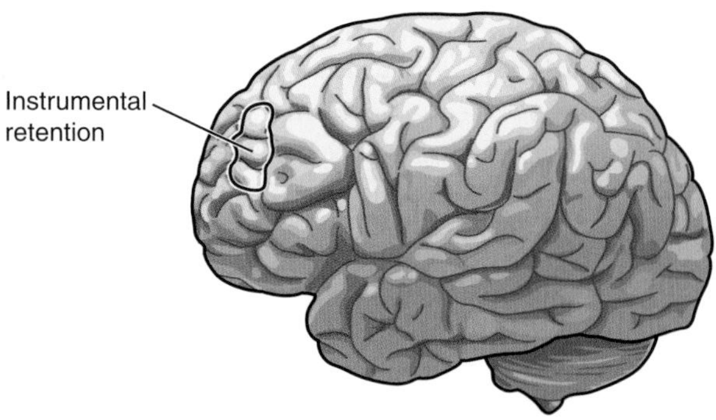

Figure 8.5 Damage to an area in the dorsolateral prefrontal cortex in rhesus monkeys reduces the interval over which the location of a hidden target is remembered. Shown above is the corresponding area in the human brain.

Goldman-Rakic, 1989). During the second of year of life infants' ability to remember objects not in view increases to the point of effortlessness and becomes an important part of language learning, as discussed below.

Finally, the fact that infants no longer reach for a hidden object is not definitive evidence that it is not remembered at all. Diamond (1995) assessed memory by letting infants see a toy for a period of time and then removing it. After a delay they were shown the old toy next to a new toy. Infants have a preference for novelty, and they will tend to look at the new toy. If they look more at the new toy than an old one it implies, of course, that the old toy has been remembered. Diamond found that four-month-old infants looked at the novel toy 70 percent of the time after a retention interval of ten seconds. Six-month-old infants looked at the novel toy 70 percent of the time after a retention interval of three minutes. By nine months, infants looked at the novel toy 70 percent of the time after ten minutes.

8.2 Language learning

After six months infants can follow pointing gestures (Butterworth and Itakura, 2000). After eight to ten months infants have developed fine enough motor control to use the thumb and forefinger in a pincer grip to lift things, and begin to point to communicate as well (Franco and Butterworth, 1996). Communication through pointing leads to communication through spoken language. The age of pointing onset predicts both the number of gestures produced and the number of sounds comprehended at fourteen months (Butterworth and Morissette, 1996). Pointing eventually gets incorporated into language as **deictic** words, such as *this* and *that*. Nonverbal communication skills at thirteen months predict language ability up to five years of age (Ulvund and Smith, 1996).

When newborn infants are laid down to rest, most of them turn their heads to the right (Turkewitz and Birch, 1971). Furthermore, infants and adults both show more electrical activity in the left hemisphere for some speech inputs but more electrical activity in the right hemisphere for some visual inputs, as measured by EEG recordings (Molfese *et al.*, 1976; Wade, 1977). So, even before language is learned, a specialized speech-processing mechanism begins to develop within the left hemisphere. The ratio of aphasias caused by left hemisphere versus right hemisphere lesions is almost as large for children as it is for adults

(Woods and Teuber, 1978). However, children make much fuller recoveries from aphasia than adults usually do. In fact, in general, children make much better recoveries from brain damage than adults do. When the brain is still young, another section can apparently take over the function of a part that has been lost. Dennis and her colleagues examined the limits of cortical plasticity by comparing the effects of left and right hemidecortication on children (Dennis, 1980; Dennis and Kohn, 1975; Dennis and Whitaker, 1976). In this operation, most of the cortex of either the right or left hemisphere is removed. They found that, after the removal of either cortex, the children's acquisition of language still approached normal limits. Therefore, the right hemisphere does have the capacity to acquire language, if necessary. Although the specialization of the left hemisphere facilitates language learning, it is not essential for it.

The social context of learning to understand speech

Around five or six months of age the learning of spoken language begins in the context of nonverbal communication. Furthermore, infants actively engage in conversation even before they understand what is being said. In many cultures, babies that are still too young to talk are often treated as if they can carry on a conversation. A parent may carry on a "dialog" with an infant in which the adult does all the talking, while treating the baby's burps, yawns, and smiles as "turns" in the conversation (Snow, 1977). By the time the child is a year old, he or she will actually be using one-word utterances in conversational context. On the other hand, language learning is not possible outside a social context supporting nonverbal communication. When deaf parents have a child who hears normally, they may leave their radio or TV on constantly so that the child will be exposed to speech. However, such children typically know much less language than other children do at the time they enter school, although they will quickly catch up (Sachs and Johnson, 1976). Similarly, a study of Dutch children who watched German television every day found that they knew virtually no German (Snow *et al.*, 1976).

Attempts to teach chimpanzees human-like language also make the role of conversation salient. Savage-Rumbaugh and her colleagues (Savage-Rumbaugh, Shanker, and Taylor, 1998) have devoted many years to the study of the communication skills of bonobos (which are very similar in appearance to chimpanzees). Since bonobos do not have the vocal skills of humans, they are taught to place colored shapes on a magnetic board to form meaningful expressions. Bonobos are human-like in their use of eye contact and their willingness to temporarily give up the care of infants to friends and relatives. Thus, when Metata gave birth to her son Kanzi, she willingly handed him over to a graduate student to play with in her presence during her lessons using the shape board for communication. The graduate student played with Kanzi in the same way as with a human infant, including responding to what she took as indications of his desires. Of course, as it turned out, the prodigy who best mastered the shape board was the ever-curious little "boy" Kanzi, who was exposed to it from birth. Kanzi became the first nonhuman to use the shape board to spontaneously communicate requests to his human friends, rather than merely responding to commands with nonverbal actions. Subsequently, other bonobos began to communicate with humans, and were able to learn spoken words as well as visual symbols. Together, the negative example of the Dutch children watching television and the positive example of bonobos demonstrate that language learning requires a social interaction in which the language is being used purposefully by both the caregiver and the infant.

Making sense of adult speech

Recall from Chapter 7 that fluent speech does not contain clear word boundaries. Normal speech is a jumble of sounds that must be decoded on the basis of knowledge of the language being spoken. But the infant has no such knowledge. So the infant's first task is to learn to segment speech input into individual words. Several cues together make it possible for infants to learn to pick out individual words from speech. The ability of infants to learn to segment the continuous stream of speech sounds ultimately depends on the fact that the speaker must breathe in order to speak. Breathing in and then out to produce sound inevitably produces a characteristic stress pattern for language that is an important segmentation cue. The rhythmic breathing, along with the motor movements of the mouth and throat, produce the consonant–vowel (CV) sequences of all languages. Four-day-old infants could discriminate CVCV utterances (such as *kepa*) from CVCVCV utterances (such as *mazopu*). To demonstrate this, Bijeljac-Babic, Bertoncini, and Mehler (1993) presented a sequence of two-CV utterances and then introduced a three-CV utterance. An infant sucking on a pacifier sucked harder when change occurred, demonstrating that it was noticed.

Another convenient methodology for studying what infants hear is the head turn preference task. The researcher turns on a light that is located to one side of infants. Their attention is attracted by the light, and when they turn their head towards it a speech passage begins to play from that direction. The infants' interest is measured by how long it is before they turn away for at least two seconds. It turns out that infants will listen longer to a familiar passage than to an unfamiliar one (just as they will look at a familiar object longer, as mentioned above). Therefore, to determine whether infants can hear the word *dog*, it is played over and over in the study phase of the experiment. Then, in the test phase, if infants spend more time listening to a passage that contains repetitions of the word *dog* than a passage that does not, it implies that they recognized the word, which implies that they could hear it in the first place.

All human languages are spoken in one of three rhythmic patterns. English, in which alternate vowels are stressed, is called stress-timed. French, in which each syllable receives equal stress, is called syllable timed. In Japanese, the stress unit is a speech segment called a mora, which may be either syllabic or subsyllabic in English; it is called mora-timed. By two months of age infants can discriminate their own language from one with a different stress pattern. In fact, infants exposed to two different languages in the womb may be able to distinguish them at birth (Byers-Heinlein, Burns, and Werker, 2010). By five months of age infants have sufficient knowledge of the stress pattern of their own language to discriminate it from any other language (Nazzi, Jusczyk, and Johnson, 2000). In English, it's most often the case that the first syllable of a word is stressed, and infants become sensitive to this pattern between six and nine months of age. At seven and a half months of age they begin to segment words with initial stress on the first syllable from fluent speech. Over the rest of the first year of life the transitional probabilities between speech segments are encoded and subsequently used to find words in the speech stream (Chapter 7). Furthermore, bilingual infants are able to distinguish both languages they are hearing from languages that they are not hearing as well as from each other (Bialystock, Craik, and Luk, 2012).

Other segmentation cues are very high frequency words (such as *a*, *the*). Frequent, distributed repetition is an important determinant of learning. By six months of age some infants may know isolated words. Tincoff and Juscyk (1999) showed twenty-four six-month-old infants side-by-side videos of their parents while listening to the words "mommy" and "daddy." The infants looked significantly more at the video of the named parent. Infants shown videos of unfamiliar parents did not adjust their looking patterns in response to "mommy" and "daddy." By eight months infants can detect frequently repeated words (Saffran, 2001; Saffran, Alsin, and Newport, 1996) and words segmented by stress (Johnson and Jusczyk, 2001) within the speech stream. By ten and a half months they are segmenting these words correctly when they are heard in fluent speech (Jusczyk, Houston, and Newsome, 1999). Finally, a feature of the speech signals a syntactic boundary. Because the speaker is running out of breath, there is falling pitch, followed by a pause, at the end of a clause. Infants learn to detect these cues (Jusczyk, 2002).

Since the task of segmenting the speech input requires infants to discriminate different sounds that occur in rapid succession, those that are better at rapid auditory discrimination have an advantage in learning spoken language. Benasich and Tallal (2002) tested seven-and-a-half-month-old infants on their ability to determine whether two tones were the same or different. The interval between the tones was reduced from 500 milliseconds to eight milliseconds to find the minimal interval at which infants could discriminate them. Those that could discriminate the tones at the shortest intervals were the most advanced in language learning at three years of age. The ability to discriminate sounds, including speech sounds, may be influenced by subcortical feature analysis. The response of the auditory brainstem in a click discrimination task at six weeks predicted language abilities at nine months (Chonchaiya *et al.*, 2013).

Infants are aided in the speech segmentation task by how they are spoken to. Speakers addressing young children go to great lengths to get them to attend to what is being said. They use the child's name frequently, particularly at the beginning of an utterance (Shatz and Gelman, 1973). Adults also tend to speak to young children in particularly high-pitched voices (Shute and Wheldall, 2001), and they frequently touch them as they start to talk. People also simplify their speech when addressing children (Broen, 1972; Phillips, 1973; Sachs, Brown, and Salerno, 1976). They speak more slowly and distinctly, with extra pauses. They use short sentences, with few complex syntactic constructions. Sentence frames such as "Look at...," "That's a...," and "Here comes..." are repeated over and over. In addition, adults tend to repeat themselves when giving instructions to children, as in the following example (Snow, 1972: 563).

> Pick up the red one. Find the red one. Not the green one. I want the red one. Can you find the red one?

While speaking to an infant or young child, the speaker coordinates the name of an object with gestures indicating it, such as pointing, touching and picking up (Gogate and Bahrick, 2000). Coordinated gestures are more prominent when speaking to younger infants (five to eight months) but decline as the child gets older (twenty-one to thirty months).

The net effect of these various modifications is to greatly increase the number of short repeated patterns that are detected at the feature analysis stage, so that they are perceived as separate word phrases in working memory. This increases the comprehensibility of speech. A psychologist who knew French only imperfectly described this effect from experience (Taylor, 1976: 231):

> I observed a French woman talking to a 10-month-old baby. She would say slowly and clearly, "red," "yellow," "orange," or "look, this one has a hole," holding appropriately colored and shaped toy objects. Furthermore, she repeated the whole sequence two or three times. I could understand everything she said in French to the baby, but could catch only odd words or messages when she was talking to the baby's mother in rapid, normal French.

Social interaction with a caregiver does more than provide an infant with speech that is easier to segment. The social interaction is what initiates learning in the first place. As soon as infants come to recognize the phonemes of their own language, they become insensitive to the phonemes of other languages. By nine to ten months of age infants learning English do not discriminate among phonemes of Mandarin Chinese. Kuhl, Tsao, and Liu (2003) found that they could preserve the ability to discriminate among Mandarin phonemes by having native Mandarin Chinese speakers speak to the nine-month-old infants over twelve laboratory sessions. Interaction with humans was essential. When infants were exposed to the same foreign-language speakers via audiovisual recordings, without interpersonal interaction, there was no effect on their ability to segment Mandarin.

The representation in memory of an infant's language influences its own speech. At five months of age a cooing baby makes the simplest sounds of all languages. Babies universally begin to babble at about the age of six months. At this point the babbling consists only of the sounds of the language that the baby hears (Jakobson, 1968; Slobin, 1973). First the child produces vowel sounds, such as */ah/*, and then consonant–vowel combinations. The first consonant sounds are also highly regular. They are typically sounds such as */m/*, */b/*, and /p/, which are produced by modulating the air at the lips. In fact, in many unrelated languages the first words used as names for the parents sound something like the English *mama* and *papa*, which are easily pronounced by children. Both these English words illustrate another universal tendency of children: to produce reduplications of consonant–vowel combinations. It is no accident that the words parents are so anxious to hear are designed to be exactly what the infant is naturally most likely to produce.

Imaging of neural activity while infants listen to speech confirm that between six and and twelve months the speech- and language-processing system (Figure 7.17) becomes fully engaged in speech processing (Kuhl and Rivera-Gaxiola, 2008). Figure 8.6 shows that there is little activity in the speech-processing areas at birth but between six and twelve months not only does activity in these areas increase but it is temporally synchronized across areas. Beyond the first year of life, infant neural activity in response to language is the same as adult activity for those words and phrases the infant recognizes (Kuhl and Rivera-Gaxiola, 2008). Throughout the first year of life the cortical response to language becomes more lateralized. Near-infrared spectroscopy was used to measure blood concentration changes in the bilateral temporal cortices of infants in three different age groups: three to six months, seven to ten months, and eleven to fourteen-months. All three groups of infants were tested with continuous audiovisual speech in both the language they heard and another, unfamiliar language. Over time the left lateralized response to the familiar language increased in comparison with response to the unfamiliar language (Fava, Hull, and Bortfeld, 2014).

Recall from Chapter 5 that serial learning of a visual target sequence is response–effect learning: a sequence of voluntary actions to the targets. The learning of speech sequences may be driven, or at least aided, by a sequence of voluntary actions as well. As just

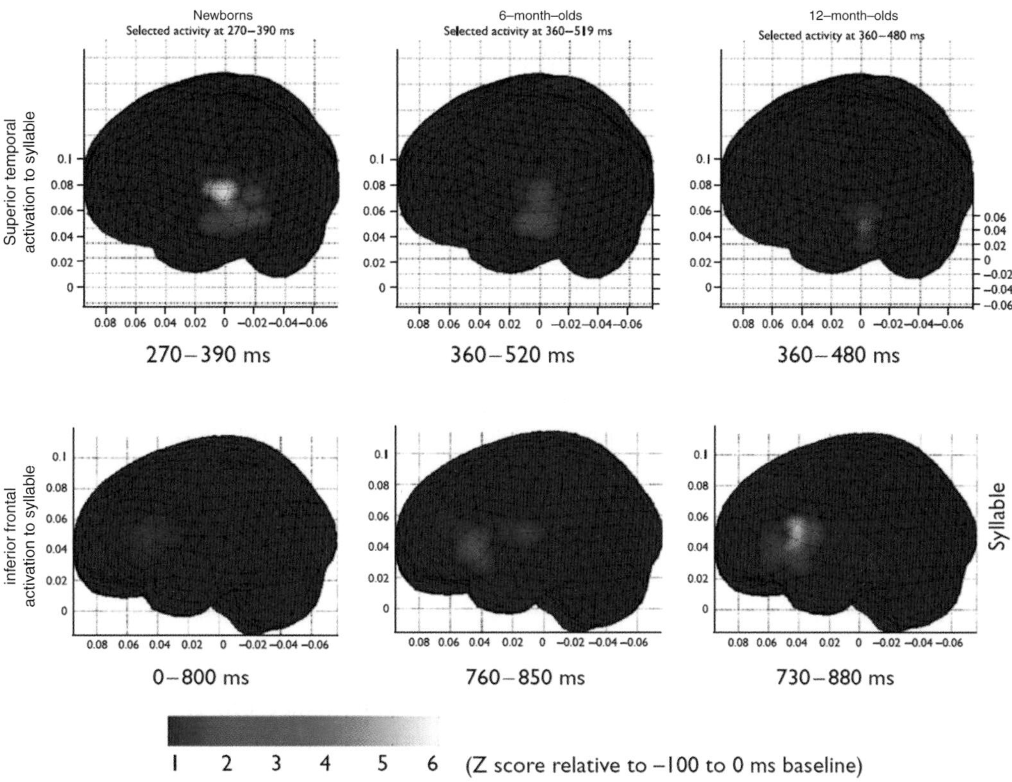

Figure 8.6 Imaging of neural activation in response to speech at the beginning of life. Top: activation of auditory area of temporal cortex. Bottom: activation of syntactic area of prefrontal cortex (Imada *et al*., 2006).

mentioned, when an infant begins to learn a language its speech progresses from cooing to babbling. At a minimum, this indicates that the infant has learned how to make the sounds of its language. By saying the word to itself, the infant both creates an articulatory representation of it and reactivates its auditory representation in memory. This action creates a permanent representation of the word, probably because articulation involves a sequence of actions, hence the construction of a long-term representation by the habit system (Chapters 3 and 5). Baddeley (1986) called this sequence of events the **phonological loop**. Gathercole and Baddeley (1989) found a task that children could perform that was a good measure of their ability to execute his phonological loop: repeating nonwords. Using this task, they found that, up until age five, the phonological loop plays a crucial role in learning new words. Nonword repetition ability at age four predicts vocabulary size at age five (Gathercole, 1995). Four-year-old children with better nonword repetition skills come to have a wider vocabulary, longer average utterances, and more syntactic constructions than children with poorer nonword repetition skills (Adams and Gathercole, 2000). Subsequently vocabulary knowledge becomes the major pacemaker in language development, and the influence of phonological memory on vocabulary subsides to a nonsignificant level (Gathercole *et al*., 1992). The critical cortical area for the phonological loop, where the phonological and articulatory representations are connected, is the angular gyrus in the posterior parietal cortex at the border with the temporal cortex (Figure 7.17).

It was mentioned above that an infant that is spoken to in more than one language can discriminate them. Nevertheless, as mentioned in the last chapter, knowledge of one language does affect the other. However, the effect is not an impediment to learning. In general, there is no substantial evidence for bilingual children acquiring speech sounds at a slower or faster rate than their monolingual peers when assessed with global acquisition scores. More detailed studies suggest that the acquisition of some sounds may be accelerated and others decelerated depending on interactions between specific language structures (Hambly *et al.*, 2013).

Learning vocabulary

Once infants get the idea that things have names, they face the formidable task of determining what the objects in their environment are called. Joint attention is critical for human social interaction and human social learning. At six months infants can pay attention to an object or a person. At nine months they begin to attend to the object that the adult is focused on. The **joint attention** of the adult and infant to the same target object make naming possible, because when the adult utters a new word the infant knows what is being named. The development of joint attention follows three steps (Carpenter, Nagell, and Tomasello, 1998), the first of which is gaze following. For the first six months the infant looks at the adult caregiver. Then the infant starts to follow the adult's gaze. Finally, at around nine months, the infant begins focusing on the same object fixated by the adult. It may be at this age that infants begin to associate objects with their names, even though they do not yet show any evidence of knowing the names of objects through head turning and reaching. When a person is surprised, the surprise is signaled by an increase in electrical activity in the brain 400 milliseconds after the surprising object appears (an N400 event-related potential [**ERP**] response). This was used to determine whether nine-month-olds expected to see a named object. Mothers spoke the name of an object that two-thirds of one-year-old children knew. Then an object appeared from behind a box on a computer screen for a second. When the object was not the named object, the infants' brains generated an N400 ERP, indicating that they know the names of some familiar objects three months before they have the motor skills to demonstrate that knowledge. By a year and a half, when an adult asks for a novel object with a novel name ("Give me the blicket"), infants hand him or her the one he or she is looking at.

At around ten months the second step in the development of joint attention emerges. Infants begin to point and to understand pointing. By fifteen months children will select the object being looked at by an adult when asked for something by a novel name (Baldwin *et al.*, 1996). By a year and a half, object memory is sufficiently developed for children to learn the name of an object no longer in view. Behne, Carpenter, and Tomasello (2005) found that, when an adult hid a toy in one of two buckets, children looked in the one to which the adult pointed. Joint attention tasks involving gaze and pointing can be performed by no other ape. In fact, they can be performed by no other animal except the one creature living in symbiosis with humans: dogs. The third step in the development of joint attention is imitation, which is central to the learning of many skills, though not to language learning.

In addition to the social cues of gaze and pointing, two other kinds of cues direct children to an object being named by an adult. These are the perceptual cue of the novelty of the object and the emotional cue of the emotional state of the adult. When an adult friend expressed excitement on seeing a child with two toys, a one-year-old child gave the adult the novel toy that the adult had not played with previously (Tomasello and Haberl, 2003). Akhtar, Carpenter, and Tomasello (1996) had two-year-olds play with three nameless objects that were later placed in a clear box along with a novel, nameless object. When an adult displayed excitement about the contents of the box and said a new word, the children selected the novel object as the referent of the word. Studies of slightly older children confirm the bias to associate new words with novel objects. Markman and Wachtel (1988) showed three-year-olds a familiar object (such as a cup) and an object that the children did not have a name for (such as tongs). The experimenter than asked the children: "Show me a dax." Children chose the object without a name (such as the tongs) approximately 80 percent of the time. Sixteen-month-old infants heard a speaker announce her intention to find an unknown object by using a new word. After rejecting one object with obvious disappointment she then gleefully picked up the target object. The infants selected the target object as the referent of the new word heard earlier (Tomasello, Strossberg, and Akhtar, 1996). By two years of age toddlers can combine social and emotional cues to learn words by overhearing others (Akhtar, Jipson, and Callanan, 2001).

Children's earliest use of language, when their expressive vocabulary is less than ten words, involves a variety of desires, concerns, and comments. These may include sound effects for animals and vehicles, social routines such as "Bye," "I," and "Uh-oh," and names for favorite people (Caselli, Casadio, and Bates, 1999). Figure 8.7 shows the growth of vocabulary between eight and sixteen months for English-learning infants in the United States and Italian-learning infants in Italy (Caselli *et al.*, 1995). Vocabulary was measured by having parents fill out a questionnaire on the words that their infants understood and produced. Notice from the figure that, early in life, comprehension is way ahead of production. Table 8.1 shows the forty words most frequently understood in this age group for American babies. As can be seen from the table, nouns predominate among the earliest understood words. Figure 8.8 shows the growth in vocabulary for a single child.

Figure 8.9 shows the growth of vocabulary between one and a half and two and a half years of age for English-learning infants in the United States and Italian-learning infants in Italy (Caselli *et al.*, 1999). The initial set of words an English- or Italian-speaking infant understands contains a high proportion of nouns. However, infants in other cultures, speaking different languages, tend to initially use different kinds of words. Korean (Gopnik and Choi, 1990) and Chinese (Tardiff, 1996) infants tend to produce more verbs than American infants do. The details of the child-rearing practices that produce these differences are not understood.

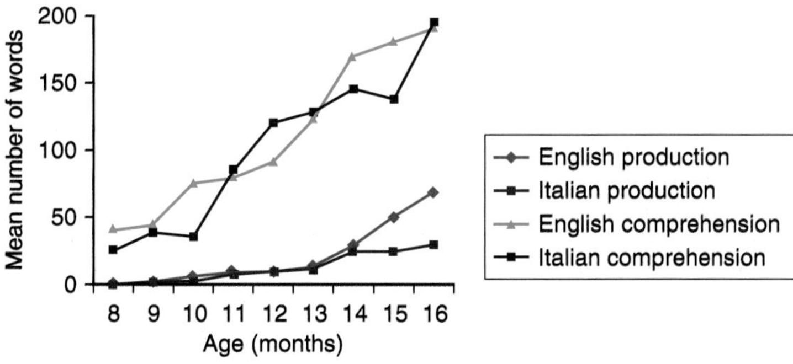

Figure 8.7 The growth in vocabulary over the first year in language learning (Caselli *et al.*, 1995).

TABLE 8.1 Most frequent words in comprehension of English for infants eight to sixteen months of age

Rank	Word	Percent of sample
1	Mommy (2)	95.0
2	Daddy (1)	93.5
3	Bye (3)	88.6
4	No (9)	86.3
5	Peekaboo	84.3
6	Bath (40)	76.2
7	Ball (7)	75.0
8	Bottle (10)	75.0
9	Hi (4)	74.0
10	Allgone	71.9
11	Dog (8)	70.8
12	Book (17)	68.7
13	Night-night (22)	68.5
14	Diaper	67.4
15	Kiss	66.2
16	Uh-oh (5)	65.1
17	Pattycake	62.6
18	Juice (28)	61.9
19	Shoe (24)	61.9
20	Baby (12)	61.6
21	Grandma (30)	61.3
22	Outside	61.0
23	Car (44)	60.1
24	Eat	59.7
25	Kitty (15)	58.8
26	Drink	58.1
27	Keys (41)	56.3
28	Don't	55.8
29	Comb	55.4
30	Nose (35)	55.4
31	Hug	54.9
32	Banana (26)	54.4
33	Cookie (34)	54.2
34	Bathtub	53.2
35	Balloon (20)	52.9
36	Milk	52.9
37	Cat (21)	52.7
38	Cracker (37)	52.7
39	Telephone	52.6
40	Yes (45)	52.6

Note: The figures in parentheses are the rank order in the list of words produced by infants in this age range.

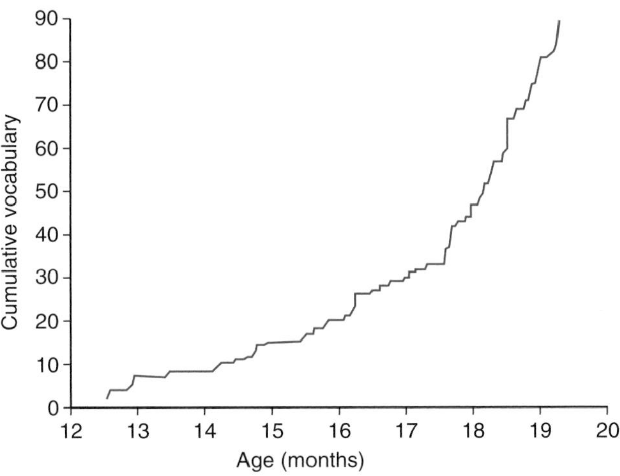

Figure 8.8 The growth in vocabulary for a single English-speaking child (Ganger and Brent, 2004).

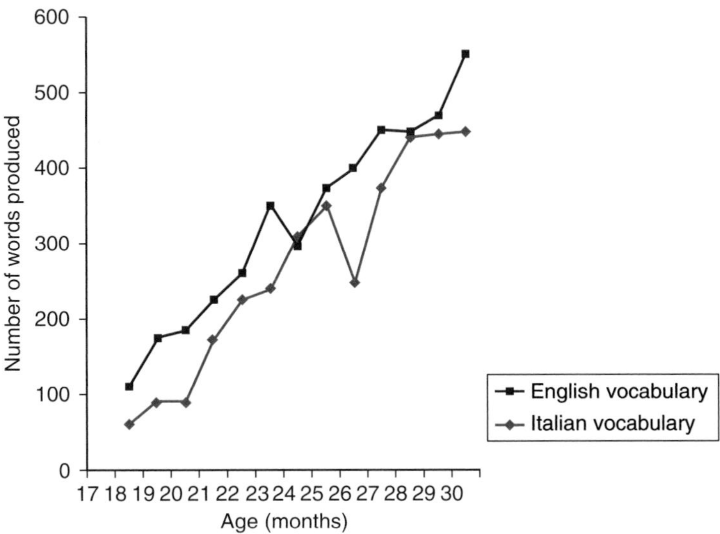

Figure 8.9 Vocabulary size as a function of age in English and Italian children between one and a half and two and a half years of age (Caselli *et al.*, 1999).

Learning syntax

As infants' vocabulary grows, the length and grammatical complexity of their utterances increase as well. Vocabulary size, length of utterance, and syntactic complexity are all closely connected, because syntactic sequences cannot be learned until a sufficient number of words have been learned to notice the repeated inflections and function words that define them. Children begin by repeating phrases they have heard previously as functional units. Lieven *et al.* (2003) conducted a longitudinal study of one two-year-old child. They recorded the child for five hours a week during six weeks. They found out that about two-thirds of the produced utterances on the target day were exact repetitions of utterances the child had produced earlier. Among the novel utterances, three-quarters consisted of a repetition of some part of previously produced utterances.

Some of the kinds of advances in grammatical complexity likely to occur during this period of life are shown in Table 8.2, which shows the simpler and more complex forms of utterances expressing the same grammatical function. Table 8.3 contains some two-word utterances of children a few months older than one year. Figure 8.10 shows grammatical

TABLE 8.2 Sample items from grammatical complexity checklist

Simple	Complex
1. Two shoe	Two shoes
2. Daddy car	Daddy's car
3. I make tower	I making tower
4. Kitty go away	Kitty went away
5. You fix it?	Can you fix it?
6. Where mommy go?	Where did mommy go?
7. Don't read book	Don't want you read that book
8. I want that	I want that one you got
9. We made this	Me and Paul made this

TABLE 8.3 Functions of two-word utterances in children's speech

Function	Example
Locate, name	There book
	That car
	See doggie
Demand, desire	More milk
	Give candy
	Want gum
Negate	No wet
	No wash
	Not hungry
Describe	Bambi go
	Mail come
	Hit ball
Possession	My shoe
	Mama dress
Modify	Pretty dress
	Big boat
Question	Where ball?

Source: Slobin (1979).

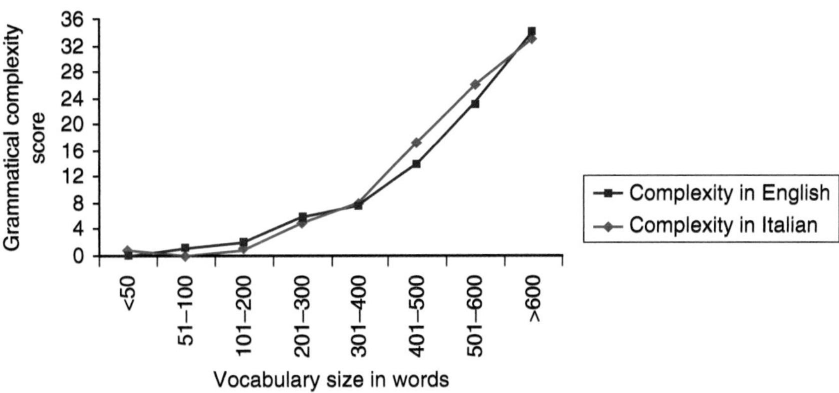

Figure 8.10 Grammatical complexity as a function of vocabulary size (Caselli *et al.*, 1999).

complexity as a function of vocabulary size for English- and Italian-speaking infants, whose data are also shown in Figure 8.10. Grammatical complexity was measured using a standardized scale in which the mother indicates whether her child is likely to produce the simpler or more complex grammatical construction for pairs, including those shown in Table 8.2. Figure 8.10 demonstrates why human language is beyond animal capabilities. Only a few individual animal prodigies have learned even 200 words. Figure 8.10 shows that it is only at 300 words that there begins a rapid increase in the length and syntactic complexity of the phrases produced and understood. Children must know at least 300 words to recognize sufficiently long word sequences to compute the transitional probabilities between words necessary for inferring the representations of phrases and clauses.

Children may use correctly whole words and even whole phrases that they hear frequently, including such high-frequency irregular verbs as *came, broke,* and *did.* High-frequency inflections are detected and encoded. Newport, Gleitman, and Gleitman (1977) found that growth in children's use of noun inflections (such as the plural marker "s") was positively related to the frequency of deictic utterances in maternal speech – for example, "That's a truck." Furthermore, there is cross-priming between related words and phrases (such as *boys* and *girls, talked* and *walked*). Therefore, children generalize inflections across similar words (Maratsos and Chalkley, 1980). One consequence of this awareness is the phenomenon of overregularization. Children will sometimes regularize an irregular verb. So words such as *camed, comed, goed, broked,* and *breaked* are all sometimes produced (Marcus *et al.*, 1992).

As their knowledge of vocabulary and grammar increases, children are increasingly able to use this knowledge to identify the meaning of a new word. Hall, Lee, and Belanger (2001) showed that, by two years of age, toddlers could recognize a novel word as a proper name by its grammatical context and use it to select the appropriate novel object. The children learned a novel label for a doll or stuffed animal ("This is Zav" or "This is a zav"). The object was then moved to a new location in front of the children and an identical object was placed nearby. The children's task was to choose which of the two identical objects the zav was. The children who heard the proper-name version were significantly more likely to select the named object than the children who heard the count-noun version of the utterance (see also Jaswal and Markman, 2001).

After three years of age, children begin to use clauses, which include an agent, action, and target in an order that defines each component of the episode for that language. The dominant word order of the language is learned through the production of many different examples. To study this process, Akhtar (1999) taught English-learning children in three age groups, two-, three-, and four-year-olds, one novel verb in each of three sentence positions: SVO, SOV, and VSO. The younger children were equally likely to produce the learned non-SVO order as to change it to SVO when they used the verb in speech, whereas the four-year olds consistently corrected to the SVO order.

Categorization

Infants also are born with direct knowledge of social kinship categories, such as caregiver or mother. As they learn about the world they learn functional categories, such as food. Finally, language provides a powerful tool for forming new categories through verbal labeling. All that is needed to create the category *bird* is to label some instances, such as a robin, canary, and pigeon, as birds and then leave it to the listener to infer the common properties of category members from these instances. Categorization provides a powerful learning tool, because, if you hear that a grackle is a bird, then you already know that it has feathers, a beak and lays eggs without ever seeing one. Gelman and Markman (1986) demonstrated that children as young as four years old make some use of language to direct their inference processes. Children who were asked questions such as whether a bird gave its baby mashed-up food or milk responded at the chance level, with about 50 percent selecting each of the two possible alternatives. Four-year-old children, therefore, did not know the answers to these questions.

Other children were presented with twenty triads of pictures, such as the triad shown in Figure 8.11. For this example the experimenter first told the child "This bird gives its baby mashed-up food" (pointing at the flamingo) and "This bat gives its baby milk" (pointing at the bat). Then the child was asked, "Does this bird (indicating the blackbird) give its baby mashed-up food or milk?" Even though the critical instance was always more similar visually to the out-of-category instance (the bat), on about 68 percent of test trials the children selected the answer corresponding to the instance of the same category (that is, they claimed that the new bird would feed its babies mashed-up food). Thus, even four-year-olds may

Figure 8.11 Pictures similar to the test pictures used by Gelman and Markman (1983).

know that instances of the same categories are likely to share properties that are not readily observable (see also Gelman and Markman, 1987).

One great advantage of language is that, even though it begins by naming concrete objects and actions, it comes to be used to name artifacts, events, intentional events, and emotions. Without language there would be no way to communicate about the invisible but nevertheless significant aspects of human life. Keil (1979) showed how young children extend the meanings of words, beginning with preschoolers as young as three years old and extending to children in kindergarten and the second, fourth, and sixth years at primary school. He asked whether sentences such as "The rabbit is sorry" and "The chair is awake" were "okay" or "silly." He used predicates that could be combined with different kinds of category concepts to examine children's understanding of the meaning of each word. For example, if a child agreed that either "A chair is heavy" or "A chair is light" were "okay," then Keil concluded that the child thought a chair was a physical object. Conversely, if the child thought that "A chair is alive" and "A chair is dead" were both "silly," Keil concluded that the child realized that a chair was not a living thing. Keil tested each child with a variety of nouns and predicates. The youngest children with the most primitive semantic development responded as if all concepts represented physical objects. For example, even if they used the word *idea*, they thought that an idea could be tall and heavy. The children distinguished between only two types of concepts: living (such as *girl*, *rabbit*) and nonliving (such as *chair, water, recess, fight, idea*). A comparison of the responses of younger and older children revealed the following sequence of steps in conceptual development:

(1) living and nonliving;
(2) artifacts (*chair*) and other nonliving physical objects (*water, thunderstorm, fight, love*);
(3) events (*thunderstorm, fight, love*) and physical objects (*water*);
(4) intentional events (*fight, love*) and other events (*thunderstorm*); and
(5) abstract concepts (*love*) and events (*fight*).

Reading

Reading is initially learned through letter–sound conversion, which makes English particularly difficult because there are no general pronunciation rules for letter sequences. However, as the printed words become familiar, the direct vision-to-meaning route is soon added, so that most of the time the visual representations of words access their meanings directly (Kleiman, 1975; Levy, 1978). Even children in the first year of primary school, just learning to read, do not appear to rely on the phonological recoding of print to determine meaning (Barron and Baron, 1977). Only when material is difficult is evidence of phonological recoding obtained (Hardyck and Petrinovich, 1970).

People can read much more quickly than they can speak, 300 versus 120 words a minute. Moreover, since writing can be crafted over an extended period of time but speech is spontaneous, writing can contain a much more complicated pattern of phrases than is ordinarily heard in speech. Finally, people must read a great deal to make their way first in school and then in the world. Much knowledge thus comes through reading. Literacy has a large effect on vocabulary growth, the development of grammar, and general cognitive functioning. By the time a student enters college he or she has learned about 50,000 words. Dividing the 50,000 words the student knows by the fewer than 5,000 days he or she has been alive during the ages of six to eighteen demonstrates that the student has learned about ten words a day every day. Because few new words are heard in daily conversation, most of these words must have been learned through reading. Even small differences among individuals in the ability to learn language are revealed and enhanced by the vast amount of language learning that literacy ordinarily entails. Recall from Chapter 3 that, as someone becomes skilled on a task, the area of the cortex devoted to that task increases. Students who improved the most in reading skill between the ages of five or six and eight or nine had the largest increase in the temporal-parietal region of the brain associated with reading (Myers *et al.*, 2014).

Difficulty in learning how to read is called **dyslexia**. Most children who read more poorly than their peers have a more general problem with language processing that is exaggerated by the demands of literacy (Benton, 1975; Mattis, French, and Rapin, 1975; Rourke, 1978; Rutter, 1978; Vellutino, 1979). This more general disorder, which is the most common cause of dyslexia, is called **specific language impairment. SLI** is a hereditary (Bishop, North, and Donlan, 1995), lifelong (Scarborough, 1984) disorder.

Autism

One of life's continuing tragedies demonstrates the contributions of social relations to learning language. Some infants are born without normal emotions or lose them after a year of life. The disorder these infants suffer from is called **autism**. Autism is associated with severely impaired language learning and profound cognitive deficits.

General description. **Early infantile autism** was first described by Kanner (1943). Beginning in infancy, there is an inability to develop normal social relations with people. If the child learns to speak at all, the speech is non-communicative and contains odd features, typically including pronominal reversal. Behavior includes repetitive and stereotyped play activities and a compulsive demand for the maintenance of sameness in the environment. Cognitively, there is a lack of imagination but a good rote memory (Dawson *et al.*, 2002; Schreibman, 1988; Sigman and Capps, 1997). Manifestations of the disorder range from subtle to marked to severe (Meyer and Minshew, 2002).

Arousal. Children with autism appear to suffer from wild fluctuations in arousal that make it impossible for them to selectively respond to informative events in a routine manner. This is evident by under- or overreaction to various inputs, or even to the same inputs on different occasions (Mundy and Sigman, 1989; Schreibman, 1988). For example, a child who fails to respond to his or her name or to loud noises may cover his or her ears and scream at the sound of a turning newspaper page or come running at the sound of a can being opened. This variability of responsiveness has led some researchers to refer to this pattern of responding as "apparent sensory deficit," to convey the idea that the deficit is apparent in behavior but not associated with known deficits at the receptor level (Mundy and Sigman, 1989; Ozonoff, Pennington, and Rogers, 1991; Schreibman, 1988).

Recall that there is a bias in the normal perceptual system to direct an observer's attention to a novel input, and that this is an important element in early learning. However, possibly because their large swings in arousal level make it unpleasant, autistic children shun novelty. They are very sensitive to specific arrangements and to order and may become very upset when the environment is altered. As young children they display limited and rigid play patterns that lack the variety and imagination displayed by normal children. For example, autistic children may play with blocks or toy cars only to the extent of lining them up in neat rows, perhaps by color and size, and become distressed if their orderly arrangement is disturbed. Even the smallest change in the environment or daily routine will be noticed and lead to a tantrum and/or attempts to return the situation to its former state (Schreibman, 1988).

Further evidence of an abnormal arousal level comes from the tendency for autistic children to engage in repetitive and even self-injurious behavior that seems to have no other reason than self-stimulation. This behavior is often viewed as a defining characteristic of autism, and was noted by Kanner (1943) in his original description of the disorder. The behavior has been variously labeled self-stimulation, stereotypic behavior, or disturbances in motility. At the gross motor level, typical behaviors include rhythmic body rocking, jumping, darting, or pacing, head bobbing, arm or hand flapping, or posturing (Klin *et al.*, 2002; Schreibman, 1988). At a more subtle level, the behavior may include gazing at lights, staring out of the corner of the eye, moving or rolling the eyes, tensing muscles, finger wiggling, waving fingers in front of the face, hair twirling, grimacing, and repeatedly uttering a phrase in a stereotypic, non-communicative manner. While much of this behavior provides kinesthetic feedback (such as rocking, jumping, flapping), a good deal involves visual and auditory feedback (such as gazing at flickering lights, repetitive vocal patterns, tapping objects, or straining to hear particular noises) (Schreibman, 1988). At the most extreme level, stereotypic behavior includes such self-injurious behavior as head banging and self-biting of hands or wrists. Other common self-injurious behaviors are elbow or leg banging, hair pulling or rubbing, face scratching, and self-slapping of face or sides (Siegel, 1996). Self-injury can vary in intensity, and the amount of damage incurred can range from slight to extremely severe.

Emotional and social deficits. Recall that MacLean (1993) suggested that human emotional development begins with the "attachment-dependency" relationship between a mother and her infant that characterizes all mammals. Severely autistic children completely lack the emotional ability to form this relationship with their parents. Kanner (1943) originally pointed to the autistic child's inability from the beginning of life to relate in a normal manner to people and situations. Numerous researchers have demonstrated that there is a definite lack of attachment to others and a failure to bond with parents (Klin *et al.*, 2002). Typically, the parents of autistic children say they feel the child does not "need" them in the true emotional sense. It has often been observed that autistic infants do not cry for attention, as do normal infants. Rather, they are perfectly content to lie alone in their crib, and seldom cry unless truly uncomfortable (that is, hungry or wet). They are frequently described as "good babies" because they are content to be left alone and rarely demand attention. They may not display the normal postural anticipation of being picked up when a parent is near and may even cry when approached (Schreibman, 1988). Another very early sign of social impairment, and one that persists throughout their lives, is the failure to establish social eye contact with others (Dawson *et al.*, 2002; Klin *et al.*, 2002). Not only do autistic children not show the normal social response of eye contact when interacting, they very often actively avoid it. This has been called **gaze aversion**. Consequently, face recognition is abnormal. Autistic individuals rely on individual facial features rather than processing the face as a whole (Meyer and Minshew, 2002).

Many children with autism also display an intolerance, or passive acceptance, of physical contact (Schreibman, 1988). In striking contrast to the intense, dependent, and affectionate emotional attachment demonstrated by non-autistic children, autistic children show minimal involvement with their parents or caregivers. This preference for being alone continues as they grow older. Autistic children usually avoid play situations with peers and, if in the same area, will engage in solitary activity. It is frequently reported that autistic children relate to people as "objects," and hence treat them as such. For example, an autistic child may stand on a parent's lap to reach a cookie jar but will do so without establishing eye contact or in any way acknowledging the parent as anything but a piece of furniture, a mere means to an end. A child might also lead people by the hand (without looking at them) to gain access to a desired object or activity.

Children with autism do not display appropriate emotions to situations. Their emotional behaviors may range from complete detachment, to giggling and hysterical laughter, to fury to inconsolable sobbing. These emotional responses often seem to be totally independent of environmental events, and the child can rapidly vacillate from one to the other without apparent reason (Klin *et al.*, 2002; Mundy and Sigman, 1989).

Speech and language. Given the severe impairments in arousal, emotions, and attachment, it should come as no surprise at this point that language learning is also severely impaired. Often it is the child's failure to acquire language that first alerts parents that something is wrong. Some children never begin to learn language. Other children begin to speak, learning to say "mama," or "dada," and other labels, but then suddenly lose the acquired speech and fail to progress linguistically. This language loss tends to occur between eighteen and thirty months of age (Schreibman, 1988). Approximately 50 percent of individuals with autism never develop functional speech, and those who do speak characteristically display speech that is qualitatively different from the speech of normal children and children with other language disorders (Schreibman, 1988). A speaking child usually receives an immediate positive response from an adult caregiver, which encourages the child to speak more often. Autistic individuals speak less to begin with, hence receive less encouragement from adults, and so receive much less practice in conversation (Warlaumont *et al.*, 2014).

Children with autism who do develop speech commonly display **echolalia**, the repetition of words or phrases spoken by others with no apparent intent to communicate. The only purpose appears to be self-stimulation through sensory feedback (Schreibman, 1988). It should be noted that echolalia is not peculiar to children with autism, nor is echoic responding necessarily pathological. However, when this echoing persists past the age of three or four years, it is considered to be pathological (Schreibman, 1988). **Pronominal reversal** is another distinctive characteristic of the speech of children with autism who do speak. Typically, the child will refer to him- or herself as "you" or by name. For example, a child named John who has sufficient speech for communicative purposes might ask for a glass of juice by saying "Do you want a glass of juice?" or "Want some juice, John?" This pronominal reversal is undoubtedly related to echolalia, and the reversal of pronouns is not surprising, in that other people typically refer to the child as "you" or by name. In the example above, it is likely that the child has heard his mother say "Do you want a glass of juice?" in a situation associated with obtaining juice (Schreibman, 1988). The speech of most speaking children with autism is characterized by **dysprosody**. The speech is characterized by inaccurate pitch, rhythm, inflection, intonation, pace, and/or articulation. The result is that even children who have relatively sophisticated language skills often sound abnormal when they speak (Schreibman, 1988).

Cognitive deficits. From 65 to 85 percent of children with autism are mentally retarded – that is, they test reliably below IQ 70 on conventional IQ tests (Gillberg and Coleman, 2000; Meyer and Minshew, 2002). (IQ tests are described in Chapter 15.) When examined in more detail, the cognitive impairment associated with autism presents itself in uneven cognitive profiles (Frith, 1991; Shah and Frith, 1992). For example, verbal abilities are usually poorer than performance skills; comprehension is quite often much more impaired than word production; and a variety of measures reflecting rote memory skills demonstrate good or even superior results while working memory may be impaired (Frith, 1991; Shah and Frith, 1992; Zelazo *et al.*, 2002).

Recall that Gelman and Markman (1986) and Keil (1979) found that, by age three, normal children could use language-defined categories to make inferences and, beginning with the living versus nonliving distinction, come to recognize successively more abstract categories. In contrast, many autistic children appear to lack any categorical structure or inferential ability at all (Happe and Frith, 1996; Klinger and Dawson, 2001).

SUMMARY

- Infant learning
  - Shortly after birth the infant is already able to
    - recognize its caregiver and home;
    - learn the basic perceptual and motor skills that make learning possible; and
    - use the emotional system for communication with the caregiver.
  - After six months the infant is able to
    - sit up, then crawl, walk, explore the world, and learn about it; and
    - reach for and grasp objects, and learn by imitation of actions.
- By two months of age the learning of spoken language begins.
  - Speech is learned in the context of communication through emotional utterances.
  - The infant is aided in segmenting the speech input into speech sounds by a number of adjustments made by the speaker and the context in which the speech is heard.
  - Once the infant gets the idea that things have names, and, more generally, that words have meaning, perceptual, social, and emotional cues all guide the infant to the speaker's intent.
  - Memory of a sequence of speech sounds plays a crucial role, because the child learns words by recoding a phonological representation as a long-term articulatory representation by repeating what he or she hears. At age four, nonword repetition is a predictor of vocabulary growth.
  - Grammar learning begins when there is knowledge of a sufficiently large vocabulary to compute transitional probabilities between words.
  - Reading is initially learned through letter–sound conversion, which makes English particularly difficult, but then the direct visual whole-word route is added as early as the first year of primary school.

QUESTIONS

1 How long can a three-month-old remember something when reminded at increasing intervals?
2 How early in life does an infant encode a detailed representation of a visual target?
3 How early in life does an infant begin to encode episodes?
4 At what age does language learning begin?
5 About how many words a week does a schoolchild learn?
6 What non-language behavior characterizes autism?

FURTHER READING

Elliott, J. G., and Grigorenko, E. L. (2014). *The Dyslexia Debate*. Cambridge University Press.
Nadel, J., and Butterworth, G. (eds.) (2011). *Imitation in Infancy.* Cambridge University Press.
Pauen, S. M. (2012). *Early Childhood Development and Later Outcome.* Cambridge University Press.
Tomasello, M. (1999). *The cultural origins of human cognition*. Cambridge, MA: Harvard University Press.
Willems, R. M. (ed.) (2015). *Cognitive Neuroscience of Natural Language Use.* Cambridge University Press.

9 Categorization and causal learning

Despite his scientific approach to detective work, Sherlock Holmes had a peculiar idea about human memory. Watson was surprised to discover that Holmes knew nothing of astronomy and was going to try to forget what Watson had told him. Holmes thought that humans could remember only a limited amount of information and that he shouldn't waste any space on facts irrelevant to solving crimes. In fact, there is no evidence that human memory ever becomes completed filled. Furthermore, as long as information is organized efficiently, it barely matters how much there is, as long as access is available to all of it rapidly. As children learn about the world, they organize the information into categories that make it possible to rapidly generalize actions to new targets in new contexts that share some features with old ones. Once knowledge of the world is organized by hierarchy of categories, it provides an efficient guide to learning ever more about the world, because new information is encoded by elaborating the existing representation.

Organization is essential to cognition. It turns mere information into knowledge. However, organization involves a choice. To organize one's knowledge of the world in a particular way that makes some relationships easy to comprehend necessarily makes other relationships difficult or impossible to comprehend. It is also difficult to begin a new topic and to start to learn about something you know nothing about. However, for different reasons, it may be just as difficult to learn something new about a topic you know a lot about. For example, at the end of my course on human cognition, I give my students the same final examination twice in a row. It is a multiple-choice exam. First, the students answer the questions without having access to their textbooks or notes. So, this test is a retrieval test, based on what the students learned during the semester in the course. Immediately after the first test the students again answer the same questions, but this time each question is accompanied with a paragraph that contains the answer. So, now it is a reading comprehension test. The proportion correct is exactly the same on both the retrieval test and the comprehension test (Glass and Sinha, 2012). Once you think you know something, it is difficult to accurately comprehend something that contradicts what you think you already know.

Human knowledge is organized by episode. First the infant, then the child, then the adult learns what effects their actions, including social actions, have upon the world. This kind of knowledge is called causal learning. Because humans are social creatures who can learn by observation, it includes knowledge of the actions of other actors. In addition, through the integration of visual and kinesthetic information, causal learning includes knowledge of cause and effect in the natural world.

Often the same action may be performed in similar contexts to many similar targets with the same result. There are many liquids people drink to quench thirst and many foods they eat to quench hunger. They wear different clothes for comfort and display. They have similar social interactions with family members, another set of social relations with relatives, and yet another set of social relations with friends. When the same action may be performed in similar contexts, to many similar targets, with the same result, the various targets are said to be **instances** of the same **category**. The ability to construct ad hoc actions is of little value without the knowledge necessary to direct those actions to successful conclusions. The organization of human knowledge is an important influence on thought and action. In the first half of this chapter the organization of targets into categories and its role in cognition is described. Categories may be defined by the following.

- Characteristic functions. A weapon, for example, is anything that can serve to inflict injury. Other categories defined by function are tools, furniture, clothing, and jewelry.
- Characteristic actions. For example, fish swim and birds fly.
- Social relations. Kinship terms, such as mother, father, and uncle, are all such categories.
- Occupations, such as doctor, lawyer, employee, and servant, are all of the above.

- Category learning
  - The perceptual similarity among instances is noticed.
  - Whenever the perceptual representation of a novel instance is as similar to the representation of the category instances as they are to each other, it may be classified as a category instance.
  - Verbal labels are assigned.
- Types of category learning
  - For natural categories, learning proceeds from the bottom up, when perceptual or functional similarities among instances are first noticed and then labeled.
  - For artificial categories, learning proceeds from the top down, when more than one instance is named as a member of the same category, inducing an observer to search for perceptual or functional similarities among them.

In the second half of this chapter causal learning and its role in cognition is described.

- Causal relations organize knowledge of the world.
  - Basic episodes organize knowledge of the physical world.
  - Complex episodes encoding beliefs and intentions encode knowledge of the social world.

9.1 Categorization and generalization

As mentioned in Chapter 7, infants learn to generalize, and when they are trained, on different occasions, to move two different mobiles through kicking they will kick to a third, novel mobile as well (Amabile and Rovee-Collier, 1991; Fagen *et al.*, 1984; Rovee-Collier and Dufault, 1991). An infant will kick to a novel mobile that shares a different feature with each training mobile, even if it is not highly similar to either one of them. Because the three training mobiles were given the same response they are represented in memory as instances of a common category: things that can be moved by kicking. Categories are of interest because effective action requires generalization. Throughout life an individual encounters many novel targets of possible actions, most of which are (perceptually) similar to a target encountered in the past. In each such encounter, the challenge to the individual is whether to perform the action that was successful with a previous similar target. When the similarity of the target and context are sufficiently similar to an episode representing previous experiences, the action specified by the episode is performed. Sometimes this challenge is trivial. One can be certain that identical cans of soda provide the identical experience, so one can generalize from drinking one can to another. Sometimes the challenge is significant, as when one is deciding whether to vacation in a place one has never been before.

When generalization is determined by the perceptual similarity of the new target to a set of old ones that all elicited the same response, three factors influence the perceived similarity to the set. The first is the similarity of the new target to the member of the set to which it is most similar. In the limit, if exactly the same target is repeated, the repetition of a response does not depend on how many other less similar targets have been previously encountered. How perceptual similarity is computed is far from settled (Medin, 1989). Medin and Schaffer (1978) proposed a detailed model of how the features of an instance are combined during the comparison with a category representation to assess similarity. Essentially, Medin and Schaffer assume that a single bad mismatch greatly diminishes similarity. For example, an ostrich is an atypical bird only because it is so large. Consider instances that can be represented by two feature values, as in Figure 9.1. Face (a) has a slightly smaller nose and ears

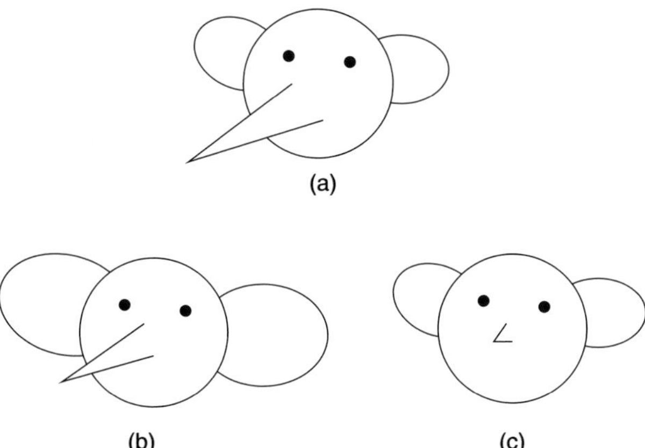

Figure 9.1 Instances of feature values: (a) large nose, medium ears; (b) medium nose, large ears; (c) small nose, medium ears. Face (a) differs from face (b) on two features (its ears are smaller and its nose is larger), and it differs from face (c) on only one feature (its nose). Yet face (a) looks more similar to face (b) (Medin and Schaffer, 1978).

than face (b), whereas it has the identical ears but a much larger nose than face (c). Medin and Schaffer's model correctly predicts that people judge face (a) to be more similar overall to face (b) than to face (c).

The second factor influencing the perceived similarity of a novel target to a set of old targets is its similarity to the entire set of targets. When all the features of a novel target are found in at least one member of the set, but none of its features are found in all the members of the set, the novel target may be similar to the entire set without being similar to any particular of the set. This point was first made by Wittgenstein (1953), who called these overlapping feature similarities "family resemblances." In experimental studies, Nosofsky and his colleagues (Nosofsky and Johansen, 2000; Palmeri and Nosofsky, 2001) confirmed that it is similarity to the entire set of old targets that influences the perceived similarity of a new target.

The third factor influencing the perceived similarity of a novel target to a set of old targets is the degree of similarity among the old targets. This factor influences the second factor. Only when previous instances were somewhat dissimilar to each other is it possible for the new instance to be similar to the group without being similar to any individual. The third factor also influences the criterion for inclusion within the category. The lower the similarity among old targets, the lower the criterion for the inclusion of a new target as a target of their response. Attneave (1957) anticipated the main conclusions of later work. He found that observers learn three characteristics of a category: (1) its central tendency; (2) the dimensions along which its members differ; and (3) the degree of variability among the category members. Posner and Keele (1968) found that categories based on more variable instances are initially harder to learn than categories based on less variable instances, but that observers are subsequently more likely to classify new inputs (especially highly distorted ones) as category members if the initial training instance is more variable (see also Homa and Vosburgh, 1976). Fried and Holyoak (1984) had subjects learn two categories of complex perceptual forms, one based on low-variability instances and one based on high-variability instances. In a subsequent transfer test, subjects were more likely to classify novel instances into the high-variability category, even for some patterns that were actually more similar to some instance of the low-variability category. The effect of instance variability on category judgment shows that people base category judgments on more than one remembered instance (Brooks, 1978; Elio and Anderson, 1981; Fried and Holyoak, 1984; Medin and Schaffer, 1978).

Perceptual similarity among targets provides a basis for generalization among targets even when the targets were not encoded as instances of a common category when they were first encoded. Even when examples of multiple categories are intermixed and subjects are not told the category to which any individual item belongs, distinctive categories can still be learned (Evans, 1967). Fried and Holyoak (1984) performed experiments in which instances of two categories of complex visual patterns were randomly intermixed, without category labels. Even though subjects were not told that they were in a category-learning task until after all the training instances had been presented, they were nonetheless able to classify novel instances in a manner indicating they had learned something about the central tendencies and variability of the categories. The **central tendencies** are what most category instances have in common. **Variability** is how the category instances differ from one another.

As will be described below, during a category-learning task participants attempt to create verbal definitions for the categories, and, when the definitions are simple enough, they

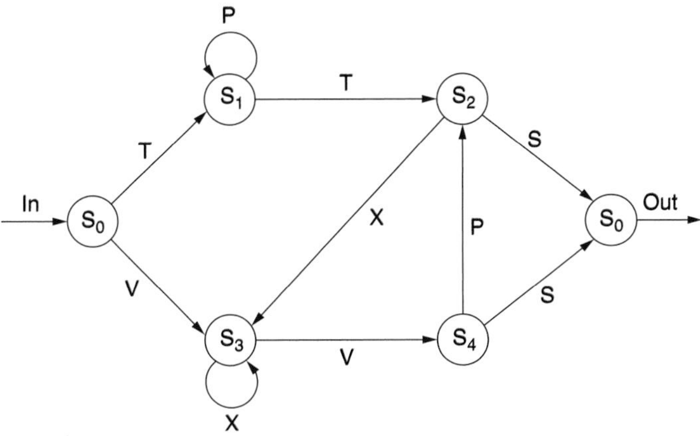

Figure 9.2 Finite-state grammar for generating artificial language (Reber, 1989).

often succeed. However, when given feedback after each judgment, even when the category definitions are too complicated to infer from the examples, people are still able to learn to categorize new examples on the basis of perceptual similarity to previously identified category members. Reber (1989) studied artificial category learning by using artificial "languages" composed of letter sequences. Such a language is defined by a grammar that determines which letter strings are category instances. Figure 9.2 illustrates one such grammar, represented in a special kind of flowchart called **a finite-state network**. Category instances are generated by following the arcs from node to node and producing the letter indicated on each arc as it is traversed. An arc that returns to the same node can be traversed any number of times in a row. The sequence always begins at the point labeled "In" and ends at the point labeled "Out." For example, for the network in Figure 9.2 the sequence TTS is a category instance, as are TPPPTXVS, VXVPS, and WS. In contrast, the sequences TVTS and VXXVP do not correspond to complete paths through the network, and hence they are not category instances. As you can see, such finite-state grammars can be quite complex. Participants could never spontaneously invent such a representation for it. Nonetheless, people who observed examples of category instances learned to make judgments about novel strings with reasonable accuracy. People were actually more successful in learning a category when they simply memorized sample strings rather than trying to figure out the rule system.

Finally, category learning based on perceptual features often influences the perceived similarity among and between category members. Imagine that members of one category have a particular shape and color whereas members of a different category have a different shape and color. In this case, shape and color would be relevant dimensions, while other dimensions, such as size and texture, would be irrelevant. After performing a category-learning task, participants are faster to perform same–difference judgments for pairs of objects that may differ along relevant dimensions than for pairs of objects that may differ along irrelevant dimensions (Folstein *et al.*, 2015).

Basic-level categories

One implication of this view that categorization is influenced by visual similarity is that there is a basic level at which people naturally divide the world into alternative categories on the basis of appearance (Rosch *et al.*, 1976). This is the object level of visual organization.

This level maximizes the perceptual similarities among instances of the same category, as well as maximizing the differences between instances of different categories, which match different structural descriptions. For example, consider the hierarchical sequence *kitchen table*, *table*, and *furniture*. *Furniture* is a functional category. It cannot be defined by a single structural description that is applicable to all instances. *Table*, on the other hand, has a clear visual structural description ("flat top," "usually four legs," etc.). Moreover, instances of table are quite distinct from instances of related categories, such as chair. What about *kitchen table*? It has a clear visual representation, but one that is very similar to the representation of close alternatives, such as living room table, which match the same structural description. So, *table* is a basic-level category. It is the concrete category level with a structural description that distinguishes it from alternative categories defined by different structural descriptions.

Rosch *et al.* (1976) found that people can classify pictures most quickly into basic-level categories. For example, suppose people are shown a photograph of a kitchen table. They can classify the photograph as a table more quickly than they can classify it as either a kitchen table or furniture. This result suggests that basic-level categories correspond to categories that people use in the recognition of objects. Rosch *et al.* also noted that basic-level categories are the earliest that children use to name or sort objects.

Even within a basic-level category, though all instances are similar to some other instances, some instances are similar to more of the other instances than others. An instance that is similar to many other instances is a **typical** member. An instance that is similar to only a few other instances is an **atypical** member. In fact, whereas typical instances are classified most quickly as members of the basic-level category, atypical instances are often classified more readily into subordinate categories. For example, although people can categorize a picture of a robin more quickly as a bird than as a robin, they can categorize a picture of an ostrich more quickly as an ostrich than as a bird (Jolicoeur, Gluck, and Kosslyn, 1984). Murphy and Smith (1982) replicated Rosch and her colleagues' (1976) natural-category results with categories for four basic kinds of unusual tools, which were invented especially for the experiment. They confirmed that people use visual representations to categorize instances. In their experiments they varied the level at which a single visual representation of the category best discriminated it from its alternatives, and they found that their pictures of tools were categorized most rapidly at this level.

Similarly, when people are asked to list instances of a category, they reliably produce typical instances both earlier and more frequently than atypical instances (Battig and Montague, 1969; Rosch, 1973). Both typicality ratings and frequency of production predict the speed with which people classify instances as members of a category. For example, people can verify the truth of the sentence "A robin is a bird" more quickly than they can verify "A goose is a bird" (Glass, Holyoak, and O'Dell, 1974; Rips, Shoben, and Smith, 1973; Wilkins, 1971). Nosofsky and his colleagues (Nosofsky and Johansen, 2000; Palmeri and Nosofsky, 2001) showed that typicality effects can be precisely accounted for by assuming that an instance is compared with many category members and its similarity is computed by averaging its similarity to all the individual category members. These experiments begin with subjects judging the similarity of pairs of instances. These judgments are used to construct a multidimensional model of how similar the instances are to each other. This measure of similarity predicts how typical each instance is rated. The typicality of each instance is its average similarity to all the other instances in the category.

Context

Even when a category is defined by its function, a possible new instance must be categorized on the basis of its appearance. Furthermore, the most typical instances of the category provide an alternative definition on the basis of appearance. For example, the most typical instances of the functional categories *glass*, *cup*, *vase*, and *bowl* all have distinctive shapes. However, through deliberate design, distinctive, hence atypical, instances are also created. A glass, for example, used to always be made of glass. But now a glass is often made of some other material, such as plastic. You might suspect that a cup is always distinguished by having a handle. But a Chinese teacup, for example, has no handle; neither does a Styrofoam cup. In addition, glasses tend to be used for cold liquids, cups for hot. But a "typical" cup (like a coffee cup) is still a cup even if you use it to drink cold lemonade.

Recall that the target's context is part of an episode and, when a target is ambiguous, the ambiguity is resolved by the context (Chapter 6). An object can be a certain type of container if it has either the right perceptual representation or the right functional properties. A familiar object will be recognized and named on the basis of its identifying perceptual features. However, an unfamiliar object will be named on the basis of how well it performs its function in a specific context. This distinction was nicely demonstrated in experiments by Labov (1973). He showed college students pictures of containers like the pictures in Figure 9.3 (a). All these drawings resemble cups to some degree, but some objects are rather strange. The cups numbered 10 through 19 illustrate a variety of shapes: cylindrical (10 to 12), conical (13 to 15), square (18), and triangular (19). Some of these objects might not always be called cup. Object 17, for example, with its long stem, might be referred to as a goblet. The cups of particular interest are numbered 1 through 9. Moving across the top from cup 1 to cup 4, the ratio of the width to the depth increases. The wider cups look more like bowls (with handles) than like cups. Similarly, the ratio of depth to width increases from cup 1 down the left column to cup 9. Here the taller cups look more and more like vases.

Labov set out to answer two questions. (1) How will these shape variations influence the names people use? (2) Will the function of the objects also influence naming? To answer these questions, he presented each of the drawings to his subjects in a random order and asked the subjects to name each object. He did this three times for each subject, and each time the subject was instructed to imagine the object in a different context. In the neutral context subjects were told to imagine the object in someone's hand. In the food context subjects were asked to imagine the object sitting on a dinner table and filled with mashed potatoes. In the flowers context they were told to imagine the object on a shelf, with cut flowers in it. Figure 9.3 shows the results. Figure 9.3 (b) gives the frequencies with which the drawings were called *cup* or *bowl* as the relative width increased. In the neutral context (solid lines) the most frequent name was *cup*, except for the very widest object. But the pattern was very different for the food context (dashed line). The frequencies for *cup* were quite a bit lower, while *bowl* was a frequent response for objects of medium or large width. Note that the very "best" cup (width-to-depth ratio of 1.0) was always called *cup*, even in the food context. But the names for the wider objects were heavily influenced by their imagined function. Figure 9.3 (c) shows that similar results were obtained for the use of *cup* versus *vase* in the neutral and flowers contexts. When subjects imagined the objects holding flowers, use of the name *cup* (actually, either *cup* or *mug*) greatly diminished, while use of the name *vase* greatly increased. But, again, the effect of context was much more pronounced for the

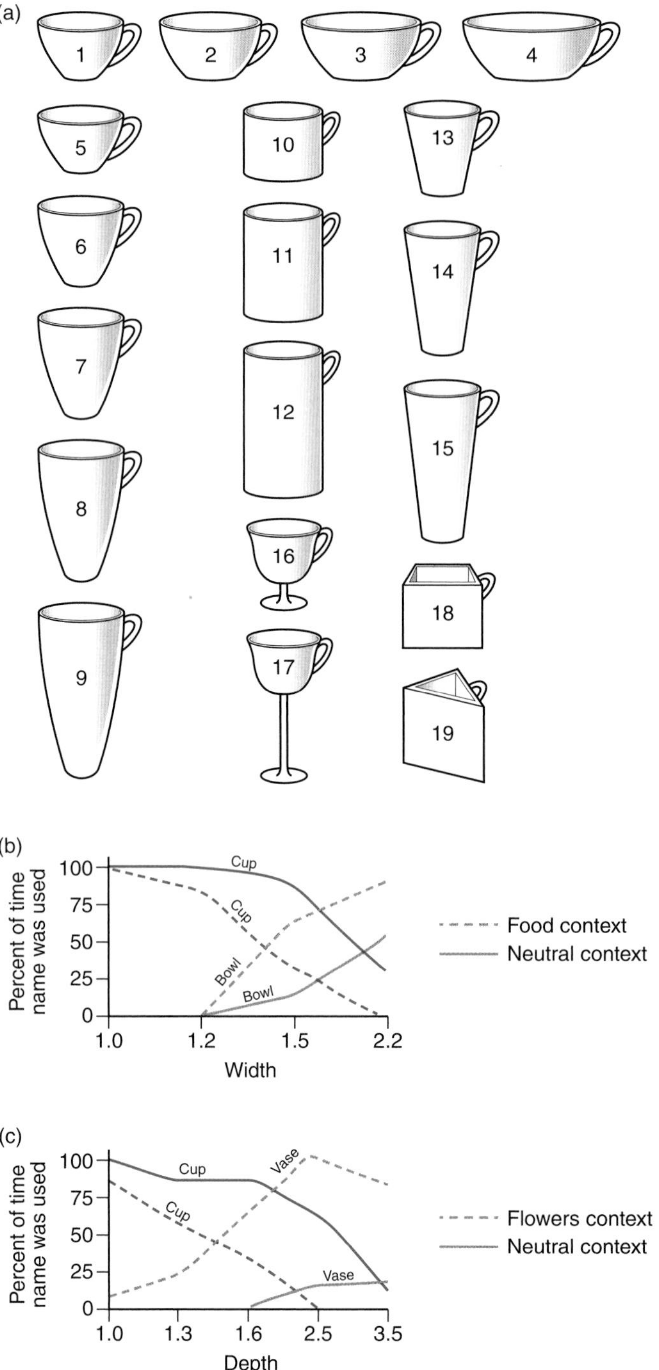

Figure 9.3 Cup-like objects (a); names applied to cuplike objects (b) and (c). (b) Use of names *cup* and *bowl* in food and neutral contexts; (c) use of names *cup* (or *mug*) and *vase* in flowers and neutral context (Labov, 1973).

relatively strange-looking objects (that is, the deepest ones), while the normal-shaped object was usually called a cup even if it held flowers.

Organization of color categories

It was mentioned that a typical instance is one that is similar to many other instances of the category. This explanation explains the typical instances of perceptual categories defined by their shapes but does not explain the organization of colors. Perceived color (more specifically, **hue**) is primarily a function of the wavelength of light. As the wavelength increases, the color of light moves through the categories of violet, blue, green, yellow, orange, and red, in that order. The boundaries of the color categories are difficult to judge. For example, there is a point on the spectrum at which it is uncertain whether the hue is better described as orange or red. Because the color spectrum is continuous, it cannot be the case that one color is similar to *more* other colors than another. Nevertheless, some colors are perceived as primary, and some shades of primary colors are perceived as more typical than others. There are two possible reasons for the organization of colors. One possibility is that it is culturally induced. Through joint attention, adults direct the attention of children to those uses considered primary. The other possibility is that primary colors are generated by the visual system, though color naming is culture-specific. The second explanation is the correct one, and it provides a window into how perceptual organization and naming interact in category formation.

Recall from Chapter 5 that cone cells in the fovea are sensitive to different frequencies that ultimately are perceived as colors. The opponent process theory of color vision (De Valois and Jacobs, 1968; Hering, 1964 [1920]; Jameson and Hurvich, 1955) postulates three types of color detectors: one for brightness (black versus white) and two for hue (red versus green and yellow versus blue). This system has six points of maximal response, corresponding to six of the eleven basic color terms: black, white, red, green, yellow, and blue. In the first months of life infants respond only to differences between these broad color categories (Bornstein, 1976).

Languages vary considerably in the number of major color categories they have. Berlin and Kay (1969) studied the distribution of color terms across languages. They then proceeded to map out the domain of the basic color terms in twenty languages by interviewing native speakers of each language. They showed each subject a set of 329 different-colored chips and asked the subject to answer two questions about each basic color term in his or her language.

(1) What chips would you be at all willing to call by this term?
(2) What chips are the best, most typical examples of the term?

The first question was designed to determine the boundaries of the color categories, while the second was designed to pick out the most central example, the focal color. People were not at all consistent in drawing boundaries between the basic terms. In contrast, speakers of different languages were very consistent in selecting the most typical shade of a color (that is, the best red, green, blue, etc.). Even though the boundaries of color categories varied from language to language, the most typical colors were universal. In fact, speakers of different languages showed no more variability in their placement of typical colors than did speakers of the same language. In addition, by matching typical colors across languages, Berlin and Kay discovered that all languages draw their basic color terms from a set of eleven. In English (which has all of them) these terms are black, white, red, green, yellow, blue, brown, purple, pink, orange, and gray. Furthermore, if a language has only two color terms, they correspond to white and black. If a language has three terms, they always correspond to white, black, and red. If a language has four color terms, the fourth will correspond to green, yellow, or blue. Note that the first six terms to appear are always the primary colors of the visual system.

Apparently, therefore, the typical instances of color categories are not determined by the specific language someone speaks. But can typical colors influence the cognition of people who do not have names for them? The Dani of New Guinea speak a language that has only two basic color terms: *mili* (roughly "dark") and *mola* (roughly "light"). Before they had much contact with other civilizations, Rosch (formerly Heider) performed a number of experiments to investigate the Dani memory for colors. She showed that the Dani remember typical colors better than atypical colors (Heider, 1972). The Dani could also learn names for the typical colors more quickly than they could for atypical colors (Rosch, 1973). Furthermore, the Dani judge the similarity of colors in very much the same way as English speakers do (Heider and Olivier, 1972). Rosch's results appeared to demonstrate that focal colors are primary in a way that does not depend on language. Unfortunately, Lucy and Schweder (1979) examined the set of color chips that Rosch had used in her experiments with the Dani and found that the atypical chips were less easily discriminated from others in the set than focal chips were, so her results on the role of perceptual categorization on memory are not definitive.

We still are left with the question of where the remaining five basic color terms come from. An elegant explanation of the development of the later terms was suggested by Kay and McDaniel (1978). Kay and McDaniel's explanation is illustrated in Figure 9.4. At the top of the figure, the graphs show the hypothetical goodness of the terms *yellow* and *red* when they are applied to a range of wavelengths. Each term applies best to its focal color (the

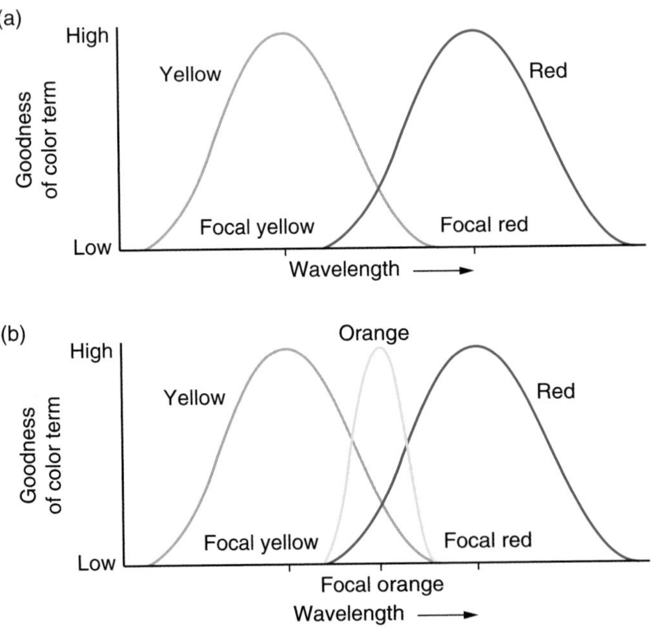

Figure 9.4 Hypothetical goodness of color terms with just *yellow* and *red* (top) and with the addition of *orange* (bottom) (Kay and McDaniel, 1978).

peaks of the bell-shaped curves), and it applies less and less well to colors further from the focal point. Now, if this hypothetical language could add one more color category, what would be the most useful point in the spectrum to name? Clearly, it is right in the middle of the "valley" between *yellow* and *red*. With only *yellow* and *red* in the color vocabulary, the language has no term that applies well in this region, and speakers would be unsure about what term to use. This situation is remedied at the bottom of Figure 9.4 with the addition of *orange* to the language. The new focal point is placed so that *orange* applies best at the very point where *yellow* and *red* apply worst. Note that *orange* is a relatively narrow category, one that fills the gap between *yellow* and *red* without competing in the regions in which *yellow* or else *red* applies well. Kay and McDaniel argued that the five later basic colors emerge in this way to fill gaps in the regions in which the first six terms do not apply well.

Verbal definition

Even though natural categories may be learned merely by viewing instances, when people are asked to sort instances into categories they often generate a verbal rule that describes the difference between the categories, and then use the rule to sort the instances (Medin, Wattenmaker, and Hampson, 1987; Wattenmaker, 1992). Once the rule has been generated, it may be used for classification rather than intuitions of perceptual similarity. For example, when people were asked to categorize vertical and horizontal rectangles like those in Figure 9.5, they were able to state the definitions of the categories after classifying instances of each. Once they were able to state the category definitions, their classifications became much faster. Presumably this was because they were no longer comparing the representation of each novel instance with several category instances but, instead, using the category definitions to check whether it was vertical or horizontal (Maddox and Ashby, 1993). However, even when categorization on the basis of perceptual similarity is accurate, if the features determining similarity are obscure then even a practiced observer may never be able to verbalize them. An example of such obscure categories is those formed by the bisected circles in Figure 9.6 (Maddox and Ashby, 1993). When the features determining category membership are obvious, the length of the verbal definition, measured by the number of "or" statements (for example, small green or large red), determines the time to learn the category (Feldman, 2003).

Once a category has a name, merely labeling an ambiguous instance as a category member influences its representation by determining the representation to which it is compared and possibly matched. Carmichael, Hogan, and Walter (1932) showed people ambiguous shapes like the one in the center of Figure 9.7 labeled as either a dumbbell or eyeglasses. People who received the dumbbell label were more likely to draw it later as shown on the right in Figure 9.7, while people who received the eyeglass label were more likely to draw it

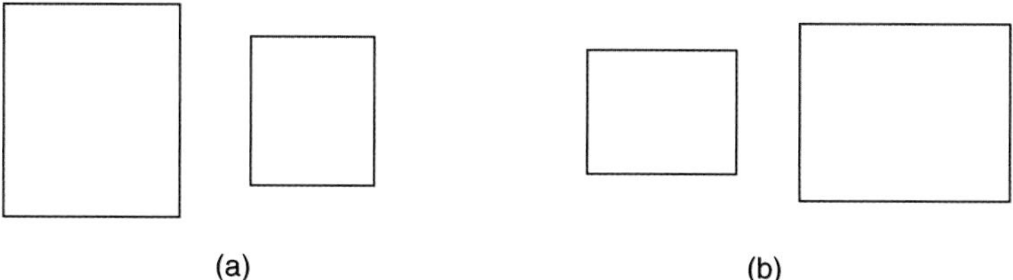

Figure 9.5 Two natural categories. Rectangles taller than wide (a) and rectangles wider than tall (b) (Maddox and Ashby, 1993).

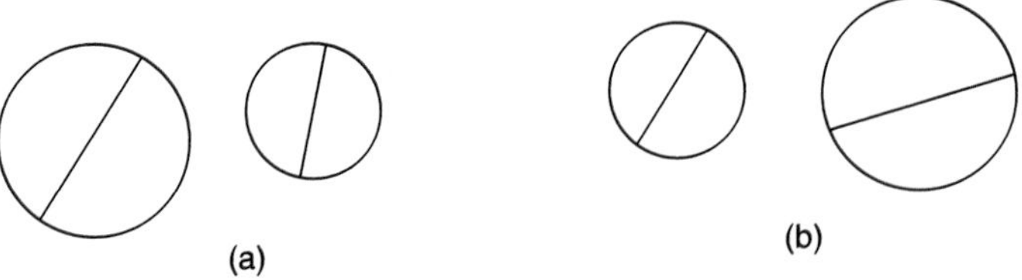

Figure 9.6 Two artificial categories. Size larger than tilt (a) and tilt larger than size (b) (Maddox and Ashby, 1993).

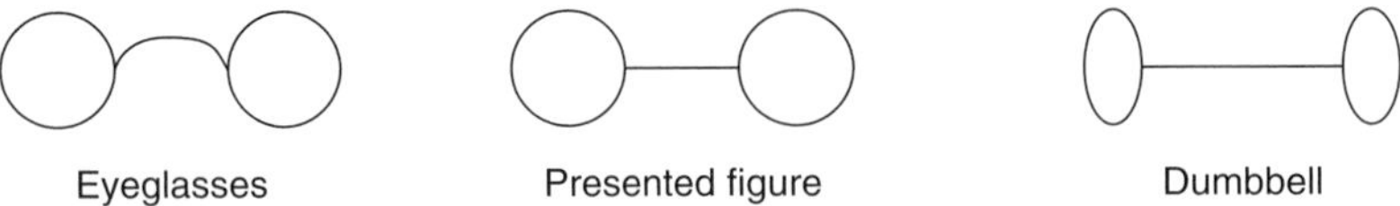

Figure 9.7 The effect of verbal labeling on reconstructive memory for line drawings (Carmichael *et al*., 1932).

later, as shown on the left in Figure 9.7. Bower and Holyoak (1973) showed the same thing for ambiguous sounds. Students heard ambiguous sounds, such as a heart beating or a ball bouncing, which were given an appropriate label either by the experimenter or by the subject. During a subsequent recognition test the students were also asked to provide a label for each sound. The students were more likely to recognize sounds to which they had given the same label that was associated with it at learning.

Social categories and theory of mind

Not all episodes are egocentric. This is implied by the structure of clauses, which include an actor, action and target (Chapter 6). Mammals, including humans, perceive the actions of others and represent them as episodes that contain an actor other than themselves as well an action, target, context, and result. Predators encode the episodes of prey behavior, and vice versa. One can see the role of episodes in how different animals hunt. A cat often relies on patience and speed. A cat can remain still for a long time until its prey gets close enough to pounce. Such behavior does not require any knowledge of the prey's behavior. However, dogs do not have such patience, though they do have speed. When a dog is chasing another animal, it often does not follow its path straight behind but runs at an angle to cut it off. So, the prey runs by the tree on one side and the dog goes past it on the other side. This behavior can occur only when the dog has an expectation of where the prey will run based on a representation of where it will run when chased. Several of the most obvious natural categories that humans encode – dogs, cats, birds, fish, etc. – are living creatures that are similar in appearance and action. Occupations, such as doctor, lawyer, and servant, are all categories defined by the functions of their actors.

Humans also encode episodes that represent themselves as actors. When an episode represents oneself as an actor, this is self-awareness. Such a representation is a representation of one's self as an actor. Since actual memories of one's own actions are egocentric, an episode in which one's self is the actor must be about the future. At a minimum, it is preparation for the future. However, in the case of a routine event that is expected at a particular time, the target and context components of the episode are a *belief* about the future, and the action component is an *intended* action consistent with the belief.

Not all episodes represent transitive actions. Episodes involving animal actors can include an emotional response of the actor rather than a motor action to a target. This makes it possible to feel sympathy, and, when the same emotion is invoked in oneself, empathy with another. Furthermore, emotions are mental responses rather than motor actions. The final step in the organization of human concepts is representing other actors as not only having emotions but intentions: a representation in which the action of an actor is an episode containing the actor, thus representing the actor's belief about the world and the actor's intention.

When an animal can represent the beliefs of another, it is said that the animal has a theory of mind. Except for a rudimentary capacity among some other primates, this is virtually an exclusively human ability. It emerges quite early in life. Suppose a four-year-old sees someone hide a toy in a box and leave. While the first person is gone, someone else removes the toy from the box. The child observer is asked whether the one who hid the toy still thinks it is in the box. A four-year-old answers this question correctly, that the one who hid it still thinks it is there (Baron-Cohen, Leslie, and Frith, 1985). The four-year-old understands that the one who originally hid the toy has a belief about where the toy is, and that this belief is false. Young children have understood that someone has a false belief in other situations. After manipulating a fake object (such as a sponge that looks like a rock), most four-year-olds expect a naive agent to be deceived by the object's misleading appearance (see, for example, Gopnik and Astington, 1988; Moore, Pure, and Furrow, 1990). Similarly, after being shown that a familiar, commercially available package holds unexpected contents (such as a candy box that holds pencils), four-year-olds typically expect a naive agent to falsely believe the package holds its usual contents (see, for example, Gopnik and Astington, 1988; Perner, Leekam, and Wimmer, 1987). Children younger than four are not skilled at giving verbal reports of the expectations. However, because they spontaneously engage in joint attention with another person (Chapter 7), they will look ahead to where they expect an adult they are observing to reach. After observing a false-belief-inducing scenario, children as young as thirteen months looked where the hidden object no longer was when watching the person who had originally hidden the moved object. Again, other situations provide evidence of false beliefs in very young children as well (Scott *et al.*, 2010).

Evidence of the elaboration of episodes in semantic memory (Chapter 6) to include actors and their beliefs is found in the areas that become active, as revealed by imaging, when tasks involving beliefs are performed. The posterior superior temporal region is active when someone views animate action. Right above it, the right temporal–parietal border becomes active when people read stories about other people's beliefs (Saxe and Baron-Cohen, 2006).

The ability to infer the beliefs and intentions of others makes the large number of social categories that organize daily life possible. Kinship terms, such as *mother*, *father*, *uncle*, are all categories. All social activities, such as buying, selling, and voting, and social instruments, such as money and ballots, are social categories.

In the twentieth century there was a great deal of discussion about the extent to which social and political interaction was influenced by the words that people used. Two influential books were *The Tyranny of Words* by Stuart Chase (1938) and *Nineteen Eighty-Four* by George Orwell (1949). The novel *Nineteen Eighty-Four* described a world in which words such as *liberty* and *freedom* were systematically expunged from language to make it harder to imagine what they represented.

Ad hoc categorization through naming

A limitless number of categories can be created by merely giving different instances the same name. Naming can be used to direct attention to instances whose similarity is not obvious. When people are asked to assign instances into categories and are given feedback whether their classifications are correct, they subsequently are able to perceive similarities among instances of a category that were not immediately apparent. Artificial categories can easily be created that a person can learn only with feedback (see, for example, McKinley and Nosofsky, 1995; Medin and Schwanenflugel, 1981). In other words, a person is told to sort instances into two or more categories. Every time an instance is placed in the wrong category, the person is told what category it belongs in. Once observers have seen enough instances of each category, with feedback they are able to identify new instances by matching them with representations of ones they have previously seen (Estes, 1986; Medin and Schaffer, 1978; Nosofsky, 1986). For example, Figure 9.5 and Figure 9.6 contrast pairs of obvious and nonobvious visually defined categories. The former are defined by whether height is greater than length and the later are defined by whether size is greater than tilt. Notice that, at an abstract level, the definitions of the pair of categories shown in Figure 9.5 and the pair of categories shown in Figure 9.6 are comparable. However, the pair of categories in Figure 9.5 are organized by the visual system into vertical and horizontal rectangles, since orientation is a basic visual feature and it defines the difference between the categories. People notice the difference between vertical and horizontal rectangles, therefore, even if they are not labeled as instances of different categories.

9.2 Causal learning

Perceptual causality

The organization of mammalian memory into episodes encodes the world in terms of causality. Within an episode, an action (that is, a cause) produces a result (that is, an effect). Recall from Chapter 4 that this representation is so central to memory that a sequence of actions to a sequence of targets is encoded as a sequence of response–effect pairs, despite the fact that there is no actual causal relation between each action and the following target. Another effect of encoding the world in episodes is the visual perception of motion. When an observer sees a moving square stop just as it touches a smaller square and the smaller square start to move away from the larger square at the moment of contact, the observer does not merely see one square stop moving and the other square start moving. Rather, the observer encodes the sequence within an episode and sees contact with the larger square *causing* the smaller square to move (Michotte, 1963). Finally, when a tone follows a key press, the interval between key press and tone is perceived as shorter than an equal interval for which the key press and tone were not causally related (Buehner and Humphreys, 2009).

Perceptual causality involves diverse neural systems in the brain. Woods *et al.* (2014) showed observers a video of one colored ball colliding with another and its effect. They varied the angle and temporal delay with which the second ball moved off after being struck by the first ball. The observers were asked whether the first ball caused the motion of the second ball, either on the basis of its angle of motion or its temporal reaction. While the

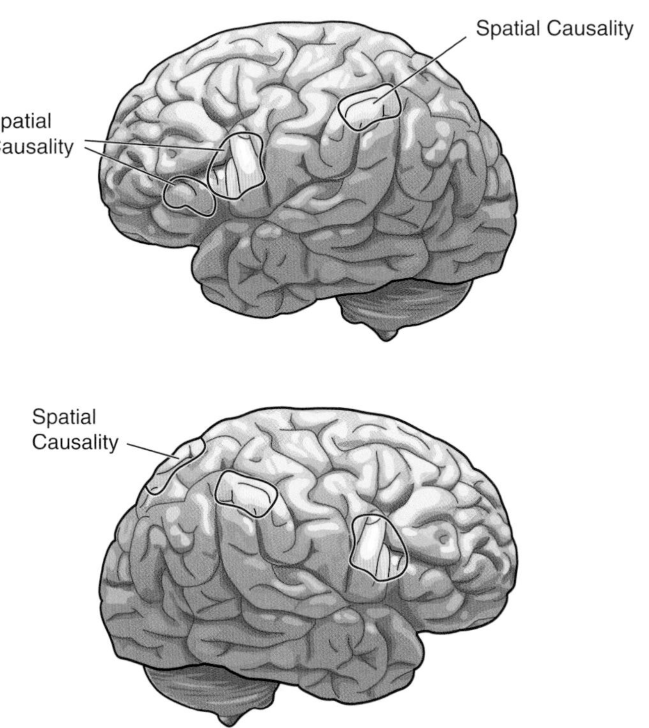

Figure 9.8 Brain activation for causal motion condition showing activation in inferior prefrontal cortex (IFG), superior parietal cortex (SPG), and inferior parietal cortex (IPG) (Woods *et al*., 2014).

observers made a judgment, fMRI showing the active areas of the brain was recorded. As shown in (Figure 9.8), when the observers focused on motion in the causal judgment, the inferior prefrontal cortex and parietal cortex were active. The activity of the parietal cortex is consistent with its role in guiding a voluntary action towards a moving target (Chapter 3). When the observers focused on time the medial structures (not shown in the figure) the cerebellum and hippocampus were active, areas involved in the timing of actions and events, respectively.

Physical causality

Furthermore, the encoding of the world in actor–action–result episodes means that all events are encoded as causal episodes embedded in larger causal narratives. People don't merely perceive snow melting on a sunny day. They perceive the sun melting the snow. Because all kinds of actions and effects are perceived causally, whether or not the cause is understood, people have the **illusion of explanatory depth**. People assume they understand the cause of something even when they do not (Rozenblit and Keil, 2002). The illusion of explanatory depth extends to how social policies work. People were unable to explain the causal change from policy implementation to intended effect for such proposals as raising the retirement age for social security, a single-payer healthcare system, and merit-based pay for teachers (Fernbach *et al*., 2013).

Social causality

As mentioned above, the episodic structure of semantic memory represents intentional as well as causal action. Consequently, even young children are able to perceive both causes and intentions and are able to learn from both. Children three years old to five years old observed someone removing a toy from a clear plastic apparatus, so that the causality of each action was obvious. The children imitated casually relevant actions whether or not they were intentional. However, when the apparatus was covered in black, so the causal effect of an action was opaque, the children imitated only intentional actions.

The intentions people have and attribute to others determine social causality. When someone intends to accomplish something and succeeds, the intention rather than the action is presumed to be the primary cause. So, individuals are presumed to cause the intentional consequences of acts but not the accidental consequences of their acts. Lagnado and Channon (2008) found that people rated intentional actions as more causal, and more blameworthy, than unintentional actions or physical events. There was also a strong influence of foreseeability: actions were rated as more causal and more blameworthy when they were highly foreseeable.

Sometimes a situation is ambiguous. The final outcome of a causal chain may be interpreted as intentional or an unintentional consequence. Suppose a train is about to run over and kill three individuals. Would you push a fourth individual to his death in front of the train if it resulted in saving the other three? Most people would not. Would you switch the train onto a side track to save the three individuals on the main line even if it resulted in killing one individual on the side track? More people agree to the switch scenario than the push scenario. Furthermore, when people hear the switch scenario before the push scenario, it has no effect on their lack of willingness to push someone onto the tracks. However, when people hear the push scenario before the switch scenario, they are less willing to switch the train onto the side track. Wiegmann and Waldmann (2014) found that this is because the switch scenario is ambiguous. The death of the one individual on the side track can be represented in the causal train as either intentional or as an unintended consequence of the switch of the train. Hearing the push scenario first eliminates the ambiguity by priming the intentional representation, because this representation is more similar to the representation of the push scenario itself. Similarly, Waldmann and Dieterich (2007) found that some people were willing to perform an action that would save five people even if, as a consequence, one other person would die, but were not willing to deliberately kill one person even if it resulted in five other people being saved.

Conclusion

Causal relations organize a person's understanding of both their physical world and their social world. The representation of both physical and social causal relations is implicit in the episode structure of semantic memory. The episode is the fundamental unit of narratives, which may describe causal chains. In planning future actions, people make use of episodes in mental simulations to assess the consequences of future actions (Sloman and Lagnado, 2015).

SUMMARY

- Common types of categories include:
  - functional; and
  - kinship.
- Category learning consists of the following.
  - The perceptual similarity among instances is noticed. A similar novel instance may be classified as a category member.
  - Verbal labels are assigned to category members.
  - An explicit verbal category definition may be constructed.
- Natural and ad hoc categories:
  - for natural categories, learning proceeds from the bottom up, when perceptual or functional similarities among instances are first noticed and then labeled;
  - for ad hoc categories, learning proceeds from the top down, when instances are named as members of the same category, inducing an observer to search for perceptual or functional similarities among them.
- Causal relations organize knowledge of the world.
  - Basic episodes organize knowledge of the physical world.
  - Complex episodes encoding beliefs and intentions encode knowledge of the social world.

QUESTIONS

1. How is causality represented in semantic memory?
2. What are examples of natural categories? What makes these categories natural?
3. When is feedback required for category learning?
4. How old are children before they attribute intentions to other individuals?
5. Is language necessary for category learning?

FURTHER READING

Pothos, E. M., and Wills, A. J. (2011). *Formal Approaches in Categorization*. Cambridge University Press.

Rozenblit, L., and Keil, F. C. (2002). The misunderstood limits of folk science: an illusion of explanatory depth. *Cognitive Science*, 26, 521–62.

Sloman, S. A., and Lagnado, D. (2015). Causality in thought. *Annual Review of Psychology*, 66, 223–47.

10 Semantic learning

I once heard two students talking after an exam. One student said to the other, "It's amazing how much clearer things are if you study when you are sober." The student had discovered an important fact about alcohol intoxication: its devastating effect on learning. However, it is also interesting that it took a sober episode to produce this insight. Often even good students have no insight into what makes learning easy or difficult.

As first described in Chapter 2, and repeatedly mentioned throughout the text, two distinct but integrated brain systems, the instrumental system and the habit system, make declarative learning possible. The human declarative learning system is remarkably sophisticated at remembering what is important and forgetting what is not. The representation of the immediate experience is immediately classified as familiar or novel. Novel experiences that may be important for future action are remembered but already familiar experiences that contain nothing new are not. Consequently, we all know how to order food from the drive-up speaker of a fast food restaurant without remembering every occasion on which we have done so.

Declarative learning begins with an initial encoding stage followed by either rapid forgetting or long-term retention. Long-term term retention of the episode is the result of the following.

- A novel event eliciting a strong emotional response is remembered because the instrumental system creates an enduring representation of it in memory.
- A routine mundane event is remembered when the event is repeated before it is forgotten because the habit system creates a more enduring representation of it.
- A novel mundane event may be deliberately remembered through a mnemonic action, which is an action that creates a more enduring representation. This action controlled by the instrumental system results in a more enduring representation being created by the habit system.

10.1 Initial encoding

As discussed in Chapter 7, people do not see colored shapes but familiar objects. Learning begins with recognizing objects in the immediate environment and sorting the immediate experience into what is familiar and what is novel. The task of the instrumental system is to encode and preserve what is novel about the experience. For example, when a visual display is a display of letters, what is novel is the precise set of letters in the display, so that is what must be encoded. The experiment described immediately below is an important one in the history of psychology because it provided a method for demonstrating what had been suspected: the amount of novel information that may be encoded in a brief period of time is quite limited, so what is remembered from a brief experience is often less than what was perceived. This was made possible by devising the two methods of reporting a brief display, described below: the full report procedure, which measured what could be remembered, and the partial report procedure, which measured how much was perceived.

Verbal recoding

When a visual display appears briefly, only those items of the display that were named during its appearance can be reported after the display is gone. For example, if the display contains letters, only those letters named while visible can be reported when the display is gone. Sperling (1960) found that, although nine letters of a visual display were perceived, only four or five letters could be reported. A display of up to twelve letters in three rows such as shown in Figure 10.1 (a) was presented briefly. In the whole- (or full-) report condition, the observer was simply told to report as many letters as could be recalled. As shown in Figure 10.1 (b), no matter how many letters were presented in the display, people in the whole-report condition were unable to correctly report more than four or five letters on average.

In the partial-report condition, immediately after the display was terminated the observer heard either a high tone, a medium tone, or a low tone. The tone indicated which row of let-

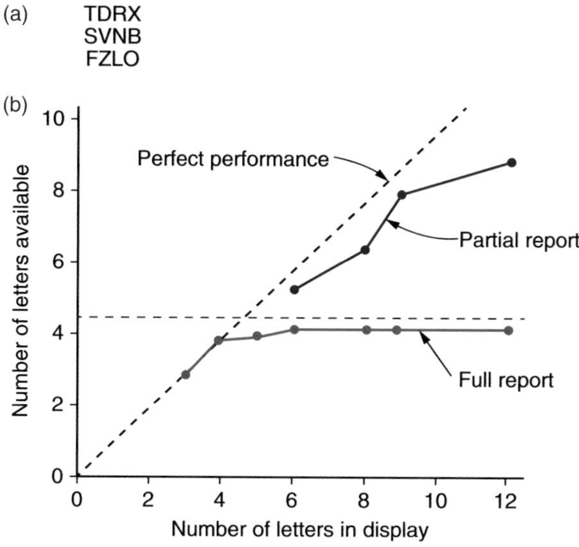

Figure 10.1 (a): kind of display used by Sperling (1960). (b): the partial-report procedure reveals that nine letters of the visual display are still available immediately after it has been terminated (Sperling, 1960).

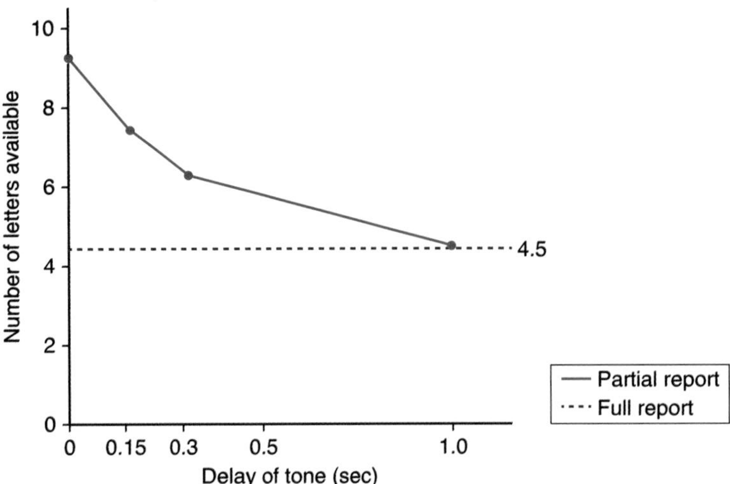

Figure 10.2 The number of letters available in the partial-report condition decreases with delay of the cue tone (Sperling, 1960).

ters had to be reported: high for top, medium for middle, and low for bottom. The observer never knew which row was to be reported until after the display was terminated. Thus, Sperling could use the number of letters reported correctly for the cued row to calculate the total number of letters available to the observer at the time that the cue was presented. The number of letters available is easy to calculate. For example, suppose there are four letters in each row, the second row is cued, and the observer is able to report three of the four letters. Since there were three rows in the display, and the observer presumably could have reported three letters from any one of them, the total number of letters available must have been 3 x 3 = 9. In other words, if the observer could report three out of four letters in one row, we can reasonably assume that nine of the twelve letters in the display were seen.

As illustrated in Figure 10.1 (b), Sperling's partial-report procedure revealed that an observer had been able to see more letters than the whole-report procedure had indicated. The reason that only four or five letters could be reported in the whole-report condition was presumably that the rest of the display had faded from consciousness by the time the names of four or five letters were spoken. This hypothesis was tested by varying the delay at which the tone followed the visual display. The display was presented for only fifty milliseconds, but, when the tone followed the display by up to about a third of a second, more letters were available in the partial-report condition than the whole-report condition (Figure 10.2). In other words, even though the display was presented for only 50 msec, an observer still saw it a little longer. But, if the cue was delayed for a second, the advantage of the partial-report condition disappeared, so by this point the visual input had faded from awareness. Thus, a perceptual target can be presented long enough to be recognized but not long enough to be verbally recoded for longer retention. If the target is not verbally recoded then it leaves no trace behind in declarative memory (Nelson and Batchelder, 1969).

Semantic learning

Even when the target picture is presented for longer than a brief instant, the verbal component of semantic memory plays a role in target memory. If a comment calls attention to a detail of a scene or picture, the observer is more likely to recognize that detail (Loftus and Kallman, 1979), to discriminate it from other pictures lacking the detail (Jorg and Hormann, 1978), and to recognize the similarity of other scenes that contain that detail (Bartlett, Till, and Levy, 1980). The influence of a label can be quite subtle. Jorg and Horman (1978) found that whether a picture was called a fish or a flounder influenced the **distracters** – that is, pictures not previously shown – from which it could be discriminated (see also Nagae, 1980; Warren and Horn, 1982).

Just as verbal labeling influences the memory of a picture, mental imaging of the object that a word names influences the memory of the word, increasing the probability that it will be remembered by activating its (long-term) representation in semantic memory. Any task that encourages the visual imaging of the referents of words or the naming of pictures increases learning (D'Agostino, O'Neill, and Paivio, 1977). Durso and Johnson (1980) had students perform either a verbal task (such as answering the question "What is the name of the item?") or an imaginal task (such as responding to the question "How long would it take to draw the object?") for words and pictures and then gave them a surprise memory task. They found that recognition and recall for words were both better following the imaginal task than the verbal task, but the reverse was true for pictures.

Emotion

Most episodes are fragile and do not survive in memory long. However, as mentioned in Chapter 2, a strong emotional response to an event indicates that it is worth remembering, so the stronger the emotional response to an event, the more robust is the episode created by the instrumental system. Cahill and McGaugh (1995) used a clever experimental technique to demonstrate the influence of emotional arousal on learning. College students were shown a sequence of a dozen slides while they were told a story about a mother taking her son to visit his father at work. Two versions of the story accompanied the slides. Half the students heard the emotionally neutral version of the story, in which the boy viewed an accident simulation in which make-up artists created realistic-looking injuries. The rest of the students heard an emotionally arousing story in which the boy was in an accident and surgeons reattached his severed feet. In a multiple-choice test given two weeks later, the group of students who had heard the emotionally arousing story performed better than the students who had heard the emotionally neutral story. Cahill and McGaugh (1995) also found that it was the release of adrenalin as part of the emotional response that signaled to the amygdala that the event was important. They found that blocking the release of adrenalin eliminated the effect of emotion on memory.

In contrast to strongly felt emotions of grief and joy, which make an event much more memorable, depression has a negative effect on information processing (Hasher and Zacks, 1979). Depressed people learn less in experimental situations (Watts, Morris, and MacLeod, 1987; Watts and Sharrock, 1987). In addition, profound depression in an elderly person may produce a pseudodementia (Wells, 1979), in which there is a generalized loss in the abilities to learn, recall, comprehend, and reason. Massman *et al.* (1992) compared depressed patients with amnesic patients suffering from Alzheimer's disease and Huntington's disease (described below) on a battery of memory tests. They were able to discriminate 70 percent of the patients from amnesics because their learning deficits were not as profound. However, the learning deficits of 30 percent of the depressed patients were indistinguishable from the deficits (described below) observed in patients with Huntington's disease, which results from deterioration of the striatum.

When learning is severely impaired strong emotion can produce little islands of memory in a sea of forgetting (Zola-Morgan and O'Berg, 1980). For example, I once tested an amnesic patient who had been brought in for testing by his family. The man did not know who had brought him to the office (his wife, son, and daughter), what year it was, or who was president. But he volunteered the information that he had been at the same hospital the previous Friday when his brother had died. This lone memory was accurate. Another amnesic man was institutionalized for years when he suffered carbon monoxide poisoning. One day his son and daughter-in-law came to visit, placed a baby in his arms, and told him the baby was his granddaughter. Ever after that he always remembered that child and always asked after her by name. However, he always thought of her as a little baby, even after she was a grown woman.

10.2 Long-term retention

When an experience is mundane, as most experiences are, the resulting episode in memory is fragile. If something else is encoded shortly afterwards, the construction of the new episode may result in the destruction of the old one. This negative effect of new learning on old is called **retroactive interference** (RI). Long ago, Müller and Pilzecker (1900) taught subjects two lists of syllables, one after the other. The subjects then had to recall the first list an hour and a half later. Recall of the first list was poorer when the second list was presented seventeen seconds after it than when the second list was presented six minutes after it (Lechner, Squire, and Byrne, 1999). Two factors cause retroactive interference. First, RI occurs when learning the second set of study materials means encoding responses that conflict with the responses encoded when the first set of study materials are learned. This interference is often made salient in the A-B, A-C experimental paradigm, designed to study RI. One set of context terms (called stimuli) is associated with one set of response terms the subject must learn in the first study list (such as car – wheel, house – roof, tree – root) and a second set of response terms in the second study list (such as car – drive, house – shelter, tree – grow). At recall, a subject is presented with the context term and must respond with the response term from the first study list. Learning the second set of response terms reduces recall of the first set of response terms. Second, as demonstrated by Müller and Pilzecker's result, RI occurs when the second study task is performed shortly after the first.

Despite the initial fragility of episodes of mundane events, routine events, regardless of how mundane they are, are well remembered. Strong emotion is sufficient but not necessary for long-term retention. An initially fragile mundane episode that is a representation of a routine event that requires a routine response will become more robust with each occurrence of the event, and will be retained in memory. The ability to respond appropriately to routine is, obviously, a useful one to any animal. So, it is not a surprise that distributed training improves the retention of conditioned reflexes, skills, and knowledge over a range of intervals and is supported by more than one neural mechanism. Distributed training increases the retention of conditioned reflexes in sea snails (Chapter 1), the retention of the procedural motor skill of typing by postal workers (Chapter 3), and declarative recognition of a mobile by an infant (Chapter 8). It makes memories of routine events available throughout an individual's lifetime.

Notice that repetition of a routine event creates a single robust episode of the event; it does not create a new episode every time an action is repeated. A person who travels to work five days a week has robust representations of the route map and the sequence of actions to follow it. The person does not have a separate memory for every time the route was traveled.

Because memory is a consequence of action, and people have the ability to perform ad hoc actions, people have the ability to take control of their memories and deliberately learn whatever is important, regardless of how mundane it is. You can learn a password regardless of how meaningless and uninteresting it is. Whether learning is incidental to an action or the intentional result of it, it is the actions performed, rather than their purpose, that determine what is learned. In the initial description of learning below, therefore, incidental as opposed to intentional learning will not be distinguished.

The first repetition

When being introduced to a bunch of people at a party, it is difficult to remember everyone's name and face. When the event is mundane (meeting someone new), its perceptual representation (face and/or name) within the instrumental system is fragile and may be destroyed by the processing of similar representations associated with different events. However, if the event is repeated before its perceptual representation is destroyed, it is marked as routine and a motor representation is generated by the habit system that is more robust. (Recall that this is also the case for procedural skill learning, as mentioned in Chapter 3.) Hence, in the transition from immediate forgetting to long-term retention, the first repetition of the target is critical.

To investigate the effect of the initial repetition, Madigan (1969) gave students two one-and-a-half-second presentations each of forty-eight words on a study list, after which they were asked to recall all the words they had seen. Figure 10.3 shows the percentage of words recalled after two presentations as a function of the number of items intervening between the two presentations of the same word, which varied from zero to forty. Figure 10.3 shows that the function showing the effect of lag can be partitioned into three different parts depending on whether the second repetition of the word was encoded as a continuation of an event, the repetition of a recent event, or the repetition of a no longer recent event. At a zero lag the two presentations of the word were encoded as a single event by a single episode and the word was recalled 30 percent of the time. At lags of two to eight the initial perceptual representation of the word was still available and the word was encoded as the

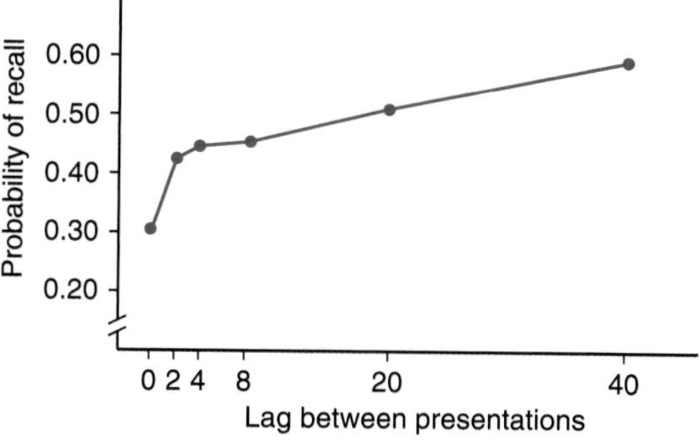

Figure 10.3 The probability of recalling a word increases with the lag between the two study presentations (Madigan, 1969).

repetition of a recent event by the instrumental system and was recalled 45 percent of the time. At lags of twenty and forty the initial perceptual representation of the word was no longer available, requiring the detection of the repetition through activation of the word's representation in semantic memory (Chapter 7), which began the process of creating a more robust, hence longer-lasting, articulatory representation by the habit system. The word was recalled 50 percent and 60 percent of the time, respectively. Cuddy and Jacoby (1982) found that the greater the similarity among the words on the study list, the shorter the lag that was required to increase the probability of recall. The more similar words caused the destruction of the initial perceptual representation as shorter lags, resulting in activation of the word's representation in semantic memory, in turn causing activation of the articulatory representation of the word, resulting in better recall.

Recall that, if a word is encoded at longer lags by articulating it, this action should interfere with another action that is a response to another target (Chapter 5). Johnston and Uhl (1976) used this prediction to confirm that only delayed repetition involves an articulatory representation encoded by the habit system. They had students do two tasks at the same time. The first task was to listen to a list of about 100 words presented at the rate of one every five seconds. The students heard the words in their right ear (by means of headphones). The students had to study and remember each list for a later recall test. Some of the words were repeated four times in the list. If a word was repeated, it could be presented four times in succession (massed) or at four separate times during the list (distributed). As we would expect, the students recalled more words after distributed than massed presentations. However, the real interest in the experiment involves the second task the students had to perform while studying the words. Their second task was to press a button as quickly as possible whenever they heard a faint tone presented to the left ear. Figure 10.4 shows the average time required to detect the tone when it occurred simultaneously with the first, second, third, or fourth presentation of a word. When the presentations were massed, the tone detection times decreased markedly with each successive presentation of a word, indicating an automatic perceptual process that did not interfere with tone detection. On the other hand, with spaced presentations the reaction times actually increased over repetitions, indicating that the comparison of the study word with long-term memory interfered with the detection of the tone.

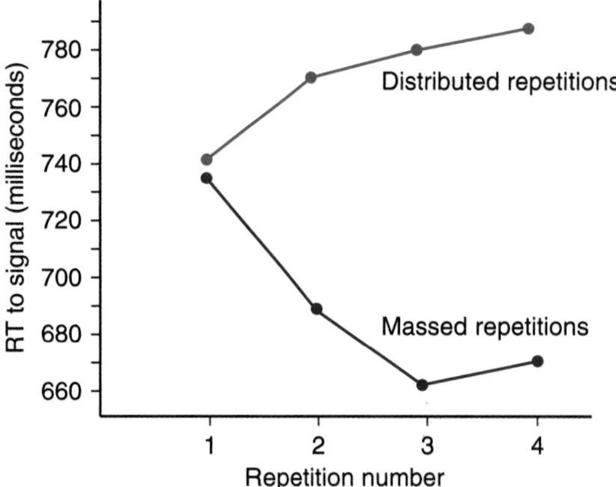

Figure 10.4 The time to detect a tone decreases over massed presentations of a word but increases over distributed presentations of a word (Johnston and Uhl, 1976).

A phonemic perceptual representation of a word within the instrumental system is sufficient for recognition; however, an articulatory representation of a word constructed by the habit system is required for recall. Melton (1967) used recognition versus recall to determine the role of the instrumental versus habit systems at shorter versus longer lags during study. At shorter lags subjects were more likely to *recognize* that the word was repeated, clearly implicating processing within the instrumental system, where recognition occurs. However, during the recall test at the end of the presentation of the study list, after longer lags subjects were more likely to *recall* the words, demonstrating that the encoding of an articulatory representation for generating a word was more likely to occur at these longer lags.

The increase in recognition and recollection that results from a long lag between the first and second presentation of a study item has practical implications for how teachers should teach and/or how students should study. Everything that will appear on a test should be taught and studied on two different occasions. Glass, Brill, and Ingate (2008) prepared students for their exams by asking each exam question once or twice prior to the exam. In a college general psychology course, during the four weeks of instruction before each exam the students answered all the multiple-choice questions that appeared on the exam and were told the correct response after they had answered. Answering the question once before had no effect on exam performance for that question, indicating that it had been completely forgotten. However, answering the same question twice beforehand improved exam performance on that question and on a related question that tested the same fact statement. The representation constructed by the instrumental system after answering the question once was too fragile to survive until the exam. However, the representation constructed by the habit system after answering the question twice was sufficiently robust to survive until the exam. This finding demonstrates how inefficiently good and bad students alike study. Most students do most of their studying the night before an exam. This massed studying results in short-term retention that improves immediate exam performance, followed by rapid forgetting. So the same material must be relearned if it is included on the final exam or any other course in the future. If the students could discipline themselves to study the material a few days before an exam, performance would be as good as following massed study and the material would not have to be relearned for the final.

The role of the habit system in learning from a repeated event was confirmed in a study with rats. On the first trial of an avoidance learning task in which stepping down from a platform is associated with a shock to the foot, the hippocampus alone plays a crucial in the rat learning not to step down. However, additional learning produced by a second training session in this task does not involve the hippocampus but, instead, the striatum (Cammarota *et al.*, 2005).

Long-term distributed repetition

Most experiments on distributed study have involved distributing study over intervals ranging from minutes to days and assessing the effect over intervals ranging from hours to weeks. Harry Bahrick was interested in performing an experiment in which the effect of distributed study over weeks was assessed over a retention interval of years. He was fortunate in being a very clever experimentalist and in having a family of psychologists who would participate, along with him, in the study (Bahrick *et al.*, 1993). The task was to learn pairs of words in which one word was in English and the other was in a language unknown to the participant (French or German, depending on the participant). Study was by the selective reminding method. Each study session began with the participant attempting to recall the English meaning of fifty words. After each word, the participant checked the meaning, and put aside the words he or she had gotten wrong. The participant successively retested all the words whose English meanings had not been recalled on the previous trial until every word's meaning had been recalled once. Each individual participated in six different schedules of training sessions. A different set of fifty words was used for each schedule. Three of the schedules consisted of thirteen sessions and three of the schedules consisted of twenty-six sessions. Intervals between training sessions were two, four, and eight weeks, respectively, for the three thirteen-session schedules and the three twenty-six-session schedules. The shorter the interval was between training sessions, the more English response words were recalled at the beginning of each session. This difference occurred across all training sessions. At the beginning of the last session, an average of forty-eight English response words were recalled for the two-week training interval, an average of forty-six English response words were recalled for the four-week training interval, and an average of forty-three English response words were recalled for the eight-week training interval. Recall of different words was tested at retention intervals of one, two, three, and five years. Since the results were the same at all retention intervals, the data shown in Figure 10.5 are collapsed over the retention interval and shown for each training schedule. The figure shows that both the number of training sessions and the length of the training interval increased recall. Again, the longer the interval was between study sessions, the longer was the retention of the word pairs.

REM sleep

As the brain has evolved to become more complex, sleep has acquired a variety of functions. These functions are marked by changes in neural activity and resulting motor activity during sleep. One stage of sleep in mammals is marked by rapid eye movements and so is called **REM** sleep. A newborn human infant spends approximately 70 percent of its total sleep time in REM sleep. The amount of REM sleep declines to 30 percent at six months of age. By eight years this has fallen further to 22 percent, then finally it drops to the adult percentage of 15 percent.

It has been hypothesized that sleep, especially REM sleep, aids in the process of making an episode more robust, called **consolidation** (Kavanau, 1996; Maquet, 2001; Vorster and Born, 2015), thus producing the advantage of distributing training over days. According to this theory, memory traces are vulnerable to interference until after the first post-exposure

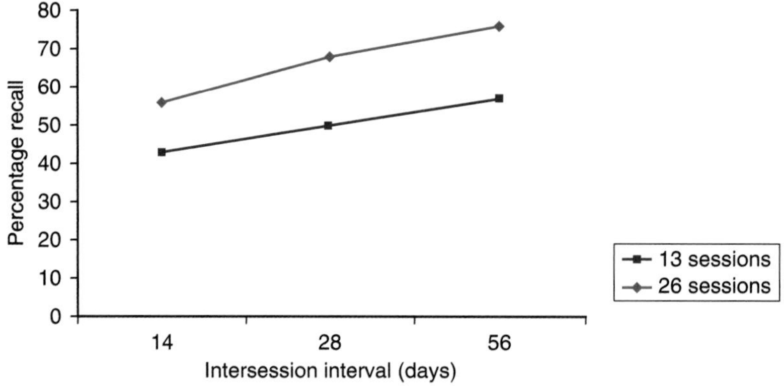

Figure 10.5 Recall of English translations of foreign words is a function of the interval between word – translation study sessions and the number of study sessions (Bahrick, 1993).

onset of sleep has occurred (Poe *et al.*, 2000). Stickgold, James, and Hobson (2000) found that, without any additional training sessions, performance on a visual discrimination task displayed maximal improvement forty-eight to ninety-six hours after an initial training episode. When participants were deprived of sleep for the first thirty-six hours after training and then allowed to have recovery sleep the next two nights, the improvement of performance on the task was no longer demonstrated. By allowing the participants at least six hours of sleep on the first night, participants were able to obtain maximal performance (Stickgold *et al.*, 2000). Thus, improvement in task performance is absolutely dependent on the first night of post-training sleep, and subsequent recovery sleep cannot compensate for this initial reduction in memory consolidation.

When recovering from sleep deprivation it has been noted that participants recover very little of stage one and two sleep (7 percent), while recovering 68 percent of slow-wave sleep and 53 percent of REM sleep (Kales *et al.*, 1970). These differential amounts of recovery sleep have led some researchers to focus on REM sleep as a possible stage in which memory consolidation occurs. In a perceptual learning task, animals that were deprived of REM sleep did not learn as well as those deprived of slow wave sleep (Karni *et al.*, 1994). Other researchers have proposed that non-REM–REM cycles, rather than the REM state, are essential for the consolidation of verbal information. Ficca *et al.* (2000) found that morning recall was impaired following a night of disrupted sleep cycles compared to a night with undisturbed sleep cycles. Both experimental groups had a similar amount of REM sleep. Salzarulo and Fagioli (1995) noted a positive correlation between sleep cycles and protein synthesis. A disruption in the sleep cycle could result in a decline of protein synthesis and thus impair processes for consolidating memory.

Resting while awake

Sleep may not be required for consolidation, as long as an individual is resting. Dewar *et al.* (2012) had participants read two stories; one story was followed by a ten-minute period of wakeful resting, the other by a ten-minute period during which participants played a spot-the-difference game. Wakeful resting led to better recall seven days later.

Expertise, knowledge, and brain size

Recall from Chapter 2 that learning involves the recruitment of new neurons to new representations and from Chapter 3 that procedural learning is associated with brain growth. The same effect occurs for declarative knowledge. London taxi drivers are required to learn a detailed map of London. This results in enlargement of the posterior hippocampus, which is critical for map learning. However, the more specific the skill or knowledge learned, the less generalization there is to other tasks, and it may actually impair performance on a similar novel task that competes for cortical resources. London taxi drivers were worse at learning *new* visual-spatial information than bus drivers (Maguire, Woollett, and Spiers, 2006) and performed more poorly than control subjects on an object search task not involving London, and had a smaller than normal anterior hippocampus (Wollett and Maguire, 2012).

Aging

One advantage of growing the brain through practice and study early in life is that it provides a buffer that preserves performance when the brain begins to shrink later in life. Figure 10.6 shows the result of a cross-sectional study in which the same tests were given to individuals of different ages (Park *et al.*, 2002). The graph shows that the change in test performance

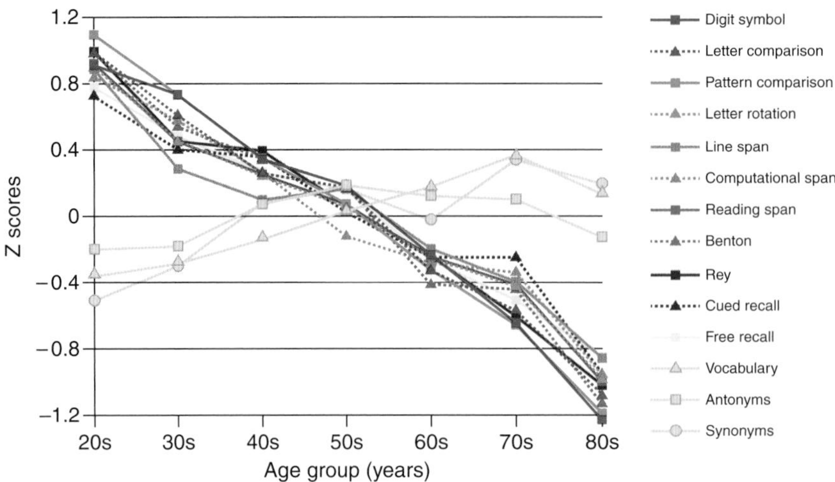

Figure 10.6 Cognitive performance declines on all tasks except knowledge of vocabulary (Park *et al*., 2002).

over time depends on the kind of test. For tests of general and vocabulary, performance improves. Such knowledge is called **crystallized intelligence** (Chapter 14). This improvement is not surprising. Older people have, necessarily, spent more total hours from their longer lives learning than younger people, so they should know more.

For all other tests, there is a decline in performance across the decades in cross-sectional studies. However, the apparent decline for all other kinds of tests that is shown in Figure 10.6 is misleading, as revealed by the results of another study shown in Figure 10.7 (Rabbitt, Lunn, and Wong, 2008). In this longitudinal study, the same tests were given to the *same* individuals every four years. At the start of the study 5,842 volunteers, 2,615 residents of Greater Manchester and 3,227 residents of Newcastle-upon-Tyne, United Kingdom, were all sufficiently healthy and motivated to travel independently to the University of Newcastle-upon-Tyne or the University of Manchester, where they were given cognitive tests in groups of ten to twenty. There were 1,711 men aged between forty-nine and ninety-three years and 4,131 women aged between forty-nine and ninety-two years. Again, the change in performance over time depended on the kind of test. Consistent with the findings shown in Figure 10.6, there was a slight increase in knowledge over the time period (not shown in Figure 10.7). Another kind of test given in the longitudinal study was a test involving a new task that the participants had not performed outside the study. Novel tasks are called tests of **fluid intelligence** (Chapter 14). These tasks test the ability of the instrumental system to generate ad hoc responses to novel situations. As shown on the left side of the figure, how well a person performed on a test of this kind, the Heim AH4-1 test of fluid intelligence, predicted how long the individual would participate in the study. Those who were still alive and participating twenty years later had no decline in performance, in direct contradiction to the results of the cross-sectional study in Figure 10.6. Rather, from the beginning of the study, people who were still enrolled twenty years later performed better than those who died after year 16, who in turn always performed better than those who died or dropped out after year 12, who in turn always did better than those who died or dropped out after year 8, who in turn did better than most of those who died or dropped out after year 4. Furthermore, there is a decline in scores for those people who are going to die in the next four years. The decline for most of the tests in Figure 10.6 is an artifact of the older groups of individuals containing more members who would die soon. It is illuminating to consider from Figure 10.8 how much your immediate mental status reflects long-term physical robustness and how your current performance on what appears to be a meaningless puzzle accurately predicts what will be the moment of your death. Nevertheless, the misleading evidence of decline in Figure 10.6 has provided a marketing opportunity for those unscrupulous enough to exploit it. This has led to an entire industry offering the opportunity to practice simple cognitive tasks, such as simple immediate recognition tasks described at the beginning of the next chapter, with the spurious promise that this practice will delay the decline (Thompson, 2014).

On the other hand, speed and accuracy decline on tasks requiring rapid responses as the result of a decline in processing speed with age from global changes in brain function, as

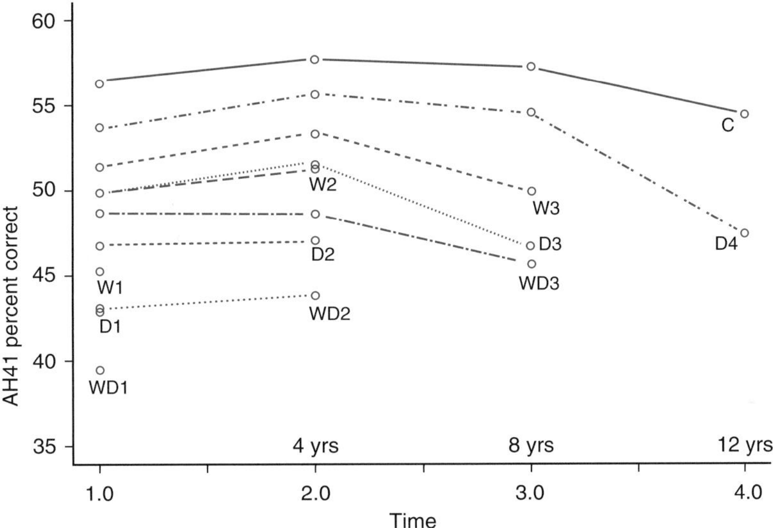

Figure 10.7 Profiles of percentage scores on the Heim AH4-1 test of fluid intelligence across testing sessions at four-year intervals for survivor (C), death (D), and dropout (W) groups every four years shows no decline in fluid intelligence for survivors (Rabbitt *et al.*, 2008).

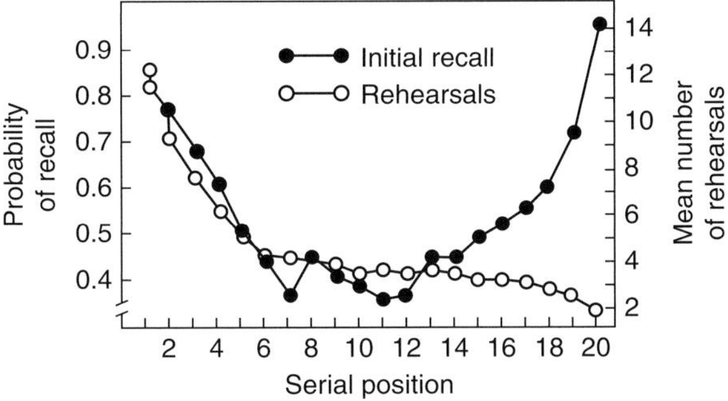

Figure 10.8 Serial position curves for immediate free recall and corresponding data on number of rehearsals given items at each position during presentation of list (Rundus, 1971).

measured by an increase in white matter lesions, loss of brain volume, and decrease in arterial blood flow. A decline in processing speed necessarily affects performance on any task performed under an explicit or implicit deadline. However, a decline in processing speed is not the complete explanation for age-related changes in cognition (Rabbitt *et al.*, 2007).

People are less successful at dividing attention among multiple inputs as they age (Craik, 1977), and so as you get older perhaps you will find it difficult to multitask between your cellphone and real life, and find this annoying. It is too early in the history of this technology to determine whether its skillful use will inevitably deteriorate with age. The one task in which the decline in performance has a noticeable effect on ordinary levels of performance is the encoding of new information, and many people become keenly aware of this decline as they age. As shown on the right side of Figure 10.7, even for the survivors of the longitudinal study there is a decline in performance in verbal learning only twelve years after the start of the study. Even when young and old subjects use exactly the same mnemonic strategies (Hulicka and Grossman, 1967; Hulicka, Sterns, and Grossman, 1967; Hultsch, 1971) or are given a recognition test, which eliminates any potential retrieval deficit (Erber, 1978; Kausler and Klein, 1978), or are instructed in a uniform study procedure (Sliwinski and Bushke, 1999), the young subjects remember more. However, as long as an older person is willing to put in the time (Hulicka and Wheeler, 1976; Treat and Reese, 1976), the ability to acquire new information remains more than adequate to keep up with changes in the environment and does not impair performance in most human endeavors.

Overall, as people age, while decline on all cognitive tasks is not inevitable, performance becomes more fragile, and so decline becomes more likely (Ghisletta *et al.*, 2012).

10.3 Rehearsal

As mentioned above, mundane events are often not remembered. However, a person can remember anything given sufficient time to actively study it. For example, you may have to memorize a password, or you may want to remember a funny joke you just heard so that you can tell it later. The most common human mnemonic for short-term and long-term retention is verbal rehearsal. **Verbal rehearsal** is the repetition of the same speech sequence, again and again. The sequence being rehearsed is in the immediate past, so rehearsal involves generating a sequence from memory.

Development of rehearsal strategies

You might think that rehearsal is such an obvious strategy that any child would automatically use it. However, children in the first year of primary school do not spontaneously rehearse (Flavell, Beach, and Chinsky, 1966). For example, Keeney, Cannizzo, and Flavell (1967) showed a group of first-year children a set of pictures of common objects. On each trial the experimenter pointed to several of the pictures (the number varied from three to five across trials). The children had to wait fifteen seconds (without looking at the pictures) and then had to point to the same pictures in the same order as the experimenter had used. One of the experimenters was a lip-reader and recorded any signs of verbalization during the delay interval. Several striking findings emerged in this study. Children who spontaneously rehearsed remembered the pictures more accurately than did the non-rehearsers. But, with a little instruction from the experimenter, the non-rehearsers could also be induced to rehearse;

when they did so, their accuracy rose to the same level as that of the spontaneous rehearsers. However, the effect of training was not long-lasting. More than half the children who had to be trained abandoned the rehearsal strategy, so their accuracy declined again. McGilly and Siegler (1989) found that children in kindergarten and the first and third years at primary school gradually begin to use rehearsal when asked repeatedly to perform a task benefiting from it. They had children try to recall three- and five-digit strings. The children alternated between three strategies: no rehearsal, a single rehearsal, and multiple rehearsals. Children would tend to again employ multiple rehearsals immediately after it had proved successful. They were thus beginning to develop **metamemory**, an understanding of their own memory abilities. Metamemory improves with experience, and particularly with schooling.

By the third year, schoolchildren rehearse three-quarters of the time. However, they tend to use inefficient massed rehearsal when distributed rehearsal is more effective. Ornstein, Naus, and Liberty (1975) asked children in years three, six, and eight to overtly rehearse lists of words that were presented for recall. After the words *yard*, *cat*, *man*, and *desk* had been presented an eighth-year child might be rehearsing "Desk, man, yard, cat," but third-year children would be rehearsing "Desk, desk, desk, desk."

Articulation and meaning

Even a single generation of a speech sequence has multiple and complex effects on memory. The individual articulates the speech representation, and as he or she articulates it the phonological representation is also generated. During rehearsal the phonological representation in turn may be used to guide articulation. Figure 7.17 shows the parietal area where the phonological and articulatory codes are integrated, hence making rehearsal possible. Articulating a speech sequence creates robust articulatory sub-sequences of the entire sequence (the associative stage of learning described in Chapters 3 and 5) that become longer with successive repetitions, until there is a single articulatory representation of the entire sequence (the autonomous stage described in Chapter 3). Furthermore, even a single articulation associates the sequence with a semantic representation, which may be as simple as the context in which it was articulated.

Span. For rehearsal to be useful, the first generation of the speech sequence must be accurate. The number of items in a speech sequence that may be repeated accurately is called its **span**. Span is increased when the sounds of the sequence name targets in semantic memory, so span is greater for a sequence of words of ones' own language than for unfamiliar words in another language. For a sequence of familiar items, the two factors that influence span are the sub-vocalization rate (how rapidly the members of the sequence can be said silently) and the set size from which members of the sequence are drawn (Standing *et al.*, 1980; Baddeley, 1992). For example, there are fewer digits than letters and an equal length digit sequence can be sub-vocalized more quickly than a letter sequence, so the average span is five to six for random letters and six to seven for random digits (Cavanaugh, 1972; Standing *et al.*, 1980) in English. So, even when the items are familiar, the length of a meaningless sequence that can be repeated perfectly the first time is quite short. In general, words that have similar articulatory representations are more difficult to articulate and take longer to do so. The extreme case of this is tongue-twisters. Digits take longer to articulate in Welsh and less time to articulate in Chinese than in English. Hence, average digit span is only six in Welsh but ten in Chinese (Ellis and Hennelly, 1980; Hoosain and Salili, 1988). When span for a sample from a large, diverse set of items, such as words, is considered, the phonological similarity among the words also influences the size of the span (Baddeley, 1992; Mueller *et al.*, 2003). When two words are too similar, the encoding of one may interfere with the representation of the other.

Recency. The separate effects of the articulatory and semantic representations are evident when a person attempts to repeat a list that exceeds his or her span. The solid circles in Figure 10.8 shows the probability of recall at each list position when students were asked to immediately recall a twenty-word list in any order. When recall is attempted immediately after the list is presented, people usually first attempt to recall the last four items. The resulting high probability of recall for the last four items is called the **recency effect**. As also shown in Figure 10.8, when someone must perform a verbal distracter task, such as counting backward before they recall the list, the recency portion of the recall curve is eliminated (Glanzer and Cunitz, 1966; Postman and Phillips, 1965).

Distributed rehearsal. When a list of words is presented that exceeds a person's span, and when the list is presented more slowly than a person can speak, a person trying to remember the list repeats some items more than once. To obtain a count of the number of rehearsals given each item, Rundus and Atkinson (1970) asked students to rehearse the words on a list aloud and tape-recorded their responses. The open circles in Figure 10.8 show how many times the words at each serial position were rehearsed. As shown in the figure, the early words on the list are given the most rehearsals. Since later words have more items competing for rehearsal at the same time, on average, they receive less total rehearsal than earlier words. In fact, the beginning and middle portions of the recall curve have virtually the same shape as the plot of the number of rehearsals (Rundus, 1971). The early list items, especially the first and second items, receive the most rehearsals and have a higher probability of being recalled than the middle items. This is called the **primacy effect**. Further experiments conducted by Modigliani (1980) indicated that what is important about the extra rehearsals that the early list items receive is not their number but where they occur. The later rehearsals for the early list items come in the middle and the end of the list. When subjects are free to rehearse as they please, immediate recall of a super-span list produces a U-shaped serial position function in which the recency portion is the articulation of the phonological representation of the last list items and the primacy portion represents retrieval from semantic memory of the meanings of the first list items, which received the most distributed rehearsals.

Whenever list recall is delayed and rehearsal is prevented during the delay, only the semantic memory of the early list items is available, so there is no recency, only primacy.

Distributed repetition has the same effect whether the repeated sequences are spontaneously generated by the learners or embedded in the study materials. The experimental findings accurately predict what people recall of partly learned and/or partly forgotten songs, poems, etc. that have repeated sequences. Hyman and Rubin (1990) cued seventy-six undergraduates with the title and first line of one of sixty-four different Beatles songs and asked them to write down the entire song. The probability of recalling each line was predicted by how early the line first appeared in the song and the number of times a line was repeated, thus exhibiting a primacy effect.

When people are encouraged or forced to distribute their rehearsals differently from the usual pattern, so that the first list items do not receive more distributed rehearsals, then the normal serial position function is disrupted. For example, a distinctive list item tends

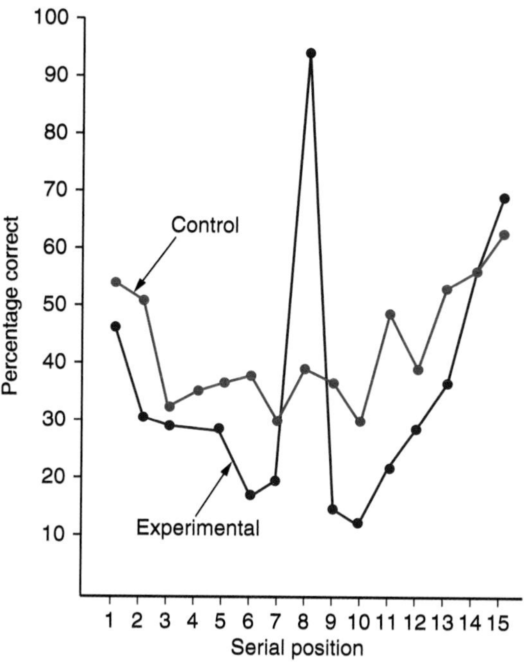

Figure 10.9 Percentage of correct recall by serial position shows a von Restorff effect for picture of nudes (Detterman and Ellis, 1972).

to be rehearsed more, which increases the item's memorability regardless of its list position. This result is known as the isolation or von Restorff (1933) effect, after its discoverer. In one demonstration Detterman and Ellis (1972) had students recall serially presented lists of line drawings of common objects (such as hat, pill, pencil sharpener). Half the lists contained, in the middle position, a photograph of a nude individual with exposed genitalia. Their results are shown in Figure 10.9. A dramatic von Restorff effect can be seen in the figure. In this effect, the distinctive item receives more rehearsals, at the expense of other list items.

Semantic association. When a subject engages in distributed rehearsal, the subject is not just repeating individual list items but is rehearing sub-span sequences of two or three words, so the initial items are repeated. Furthermore, each articulation of the sub-sequence activates not just its phonological and articulatory representations but the semantic representations of the words as well. Consequently, on successive recall attempts of the same list, the same sub-sequences or **clusters** of words are recalled and words tend to cluster semantically – that is, words similar in meaning are most likely to be repeated together (Buschke, 1973; 1976; 1977; Fuld and Buschke, 1976).

Rather than relying on spontaneous semantic clustering, word list learning can be facilitated by simply organizing the list by semantic category. For example, Bower *et al.* (1969) showed students four cards, each of which contained approximately twenty-eight words. The students studied each word set for about a minute and then tried to recall as many as possible of the 112 words. The students were then asked to study and recall the word sets three more times, for a total of four study test trials. One group (the hierarchical condition) saw the

TABLE 10.1 Two levels of organization

		Hierarchical condition		
		Minerals		
	Metals		Stones	
Rare	**Common**	**Alloys**	**Precious**	**Masonry**
Platinum	Aluminum	Bronze	Sapphire	Limestone
Silver	Copper	Steel	Emerald	Granite
Gold	Lead	Brass	Diamond	Marble
	Iron		Ruby	Slate
		Random condition		
		Knee		
	String		**Ruby**	
Drum	Arm	Lead	Percussion	Head
Flower	Slate	Instrument	Hand	Trumpet
Tuba	Foot	Maple	Rose	Marble
Neck	Piano	Toe	Birch	Aluminum
	Oak		Gold	Violin

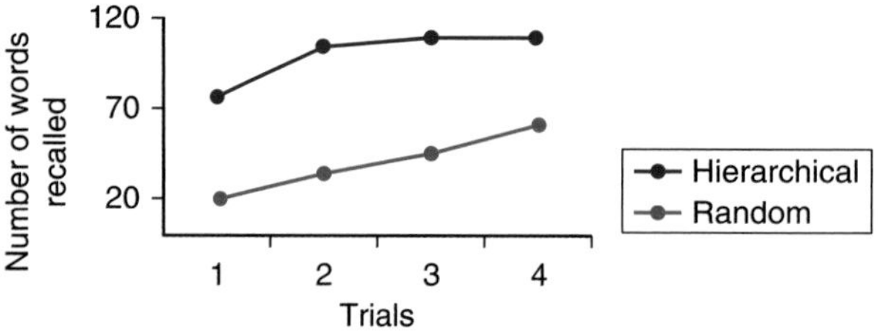

Figure 10.10 The effect of hierarchical and random organization on learning lists of words (Bower *et al*., 1969).

words on each card arranged in a hierarchical semantic classification scheme (see Table 10.1, top section). The other group (the random condition) saw each word set randomly scrambled (Table 10.1, bottom section). The recall results for the two conditions over the four trials are shown in Figure 10.10. As the figure shows, the students in the hierarchical semantic condition consistently recalled many more words than did students in the random condition.

Generation from memory. When a person rehearses a sequence, there are three separate effects of the rehearsal. First, the person is repeatedly recollecting the sequence from memory; second, the person is articulating the sequence; and, third, the articulatory representation activates the corresponding phonological representation. Glass, Krejci, and Goldman (1989) performed an experiment to determine how each of these three effects of rehearsal contributed to the learning of the sequence by varying both presentation and response conditions while college students heard a sequence of 150 digits. The entire sequence contained a sub-sequence of nine digits that was repeated five times at regular intervals in the sequence, as shown in Figure 10.11. In the **shadow response** condition, the students repeated every digit as it was heard. In the **continuous presentation** condition, the entire sequence was presented at the rate of one digit per second. Immediately following

Continuous Condition
I: ...2893105746102846395**786839210**065438924734089562**786839210**375862609...
*R: ...2893105746102846395**786839210**065438924 734089562**786839210**375862609...*

Segmented Condition
I: ...2893105746 102846395 **786839210** 065438924 734089562 **786839210** 375862609...
*R: ...2893105746 102846395 **786839210** 065438924 734089562 **786839210** 375862609...*

Rehearsal Condition
I: ...2893105746 102846395 **786839210** 065438924...
*R: 2893105746 102846395 **786839210** 065438924...*

Probability of recognition (chance = 0.33)
1
0.8
0.6
0.4
0.2
0
Continuous/ immediate
Segmented/ immediate
Segmented/ delayed
Rehearsal/ delayed
Study condition/retrieval interval

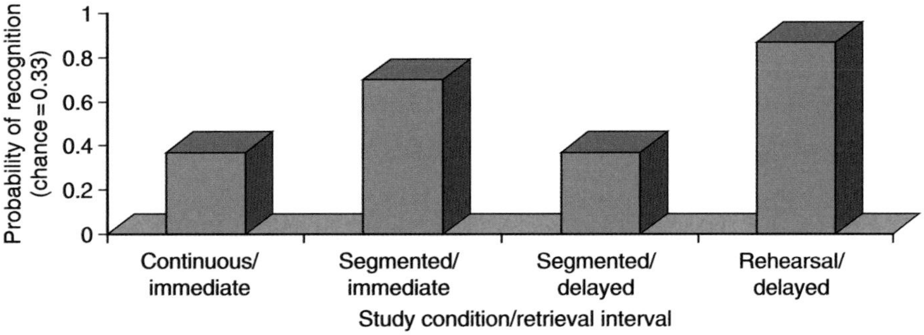

Figure 10.11 Experiment of Glass *et al.* (1989). Study sequence (I) is in regular type and responses (*R*) is in italics. The repeated string is shown in bold (top). Recognition is above chance only in segmented/immediate and rehearsal/delayed conditions.

shadowing of a continuous presentation, the students could not recognize the repeated sequence, indicating that merely hearing and saying a sequence of numbers over and over was not sufficient to encode a representation of a repeated sequence in declarative memory.

In the segmented presentation condition there was an additional one-second pause after every ninth digit in the sequence, as shown in Figure 10.11. This caused the auditory system to segment the sequence into strings of nine digits. As a result, representations of nine-digit strings were encoded. Immediately following shadowing of the segmented presentation of the entire 150-digit sequence, the students could recognize the repeated string. Shadowing a perceptually segmented string over and over was therefore sufficient to encode both an articulatory and a phonological representation of the string. But, if recognition was delayed an hour and the interval was filled with listening to other strings, the repeated string was not recognized. The representation of the repeated string was destroyed by listening to other strings of digits.

In the rehearsal condition there was a five-second pause after every ninth digit in the sequence, and the students had to try to repeat the most recent nine-digit string during the pause, as shown in Figure 10.11. The students recognized the repeated string even after an hour's delay filled with listening to other strings. So, it is necessary to generate a representation from semantic memory in order to construct within semantic memory an episode encoding a sequence.

Thus, the instrumental and habit systems both contributed to different components of declarative verbal knowledge. The perceptual organization of the sequence into nine-digit strings by the instrumental system resulted in the short-term perception of a repeated string as more *recent*. This representation was destroyed by subsequent perceptual processing. The mental act of repeatedly generating a nine-digit string from memory by the habit system resulted in the construction of an episode containing that string in semantic memory, which resulted in the long-term recollection of the string an hour later. Recency and recollection will be considered again in Chapter 11.

In the rehearsal condition, when a student articulated a string just heard, articulatory, phonological, and semantic representations of the string were constructed. The semantic representations constructed were not a by-product of the phonological–articulatory loop but were entirely independent of it. A rare disability demonstrated this independence between the semantic and speech representations. Baddeley, Papagno, and Vallar (1988) found a woman who did not have conduction aphasia (Chapter 7) but who had a lesion in the phonological–articulatory integration area (Figure 7.17), and so could no longer repeat what she heard, including random sequences of words and numbers. To further examine the effect of this lesion on learning they presented her with a list of pairs of words and then presented one member of each pair and asked her to respond with the other. When both words of the pair were familiar words with semantic representations, the woman learned the task normally despite the fact that she could not repeat what she had heard. But, when the response word was an unfamiliar nonword, she was unable to perform the task at all. So, a person can mentally generate a representation from semantic memory without actually saying it or hearing it. The most important function of the phonological–articulatory loop is in the learning of new words, as indicated by the predictive power of the nonwords repetition task for vocabulary growth (Chapter 8).

10.4 Visual imagery and knowledge

A person can also learn by engaging in visual imagery instead of or in addition to verbal rehearsal. Even more effectively than verbal rehearsal, visual imagery creates a semantic episode encoding a cluster of list items. Bower, Lesgold, and Tieman (1969) presented subjects with a list of twenty-four nouns in clusters of four at a time. One group of subjects imaged the same clusters of nouns during four successive presentations of the list, while another group imaged different clusters of the same nouns on each trial. Figure 10.12 presents the recall results for the two groups on the second, third, and fourth trials. As shown, recall improved much more over trials if the same nouns were clustered together on each trial.

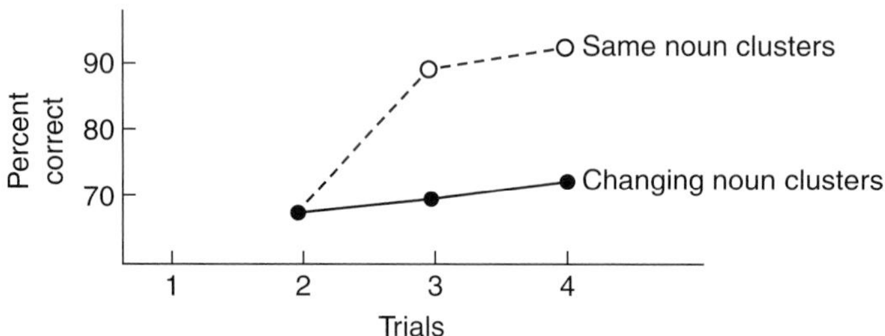

Figure 10.12 Imagery improves recall over trials much more when the same interactive images are repeated (Bower *et al.*, 1969).

Visual imagery more directly provides access to the semantic representations of words naming physical objects than rehearsing the words, and so has a larger effect on learning. High-imagery list items are more likely to be remembered than low-imagery list items even when explicit instructions to engage in visual imagery are not given. Words such as *tree* that refer to concrete, easily imaged objects are remembered better than words such as *thought*, which are abstract and do not refer directly to anything that can be imaged, whether the test is free recall (Stoke, 1929), recognition (Gorman, 1961), or paired-associate learning (Paivio, 1969). Bevan and Steger (1971) presented children and adults alike with a list consisting of a mixture of actual objects, pictures of objects, and names of objects. For both age groups, recall (always of the names) was best when the input was an object, next best for pictures, and poorest for words. When people are instructed to use imagery to learn high-imagery list items, recall is higher than for rehearsal instructions. Bower (1972) presented twenty consecutive pairs of nouns to students in a paired-associate task in which subjects had to recall the second word in each pair when given the first word as a cue. When the students were instructed to rehearse the pairs, they recalled only 33 percent correctly; but, when they were told to form interacting images for each pair, they recalled 80 percent.

Generally, tasks that require visual imagery increase the learning of the imaged items (Johnson-Laird, Gibbs, and deMowbray, 1978; Ross, 1981). For example, Jacoby, Craik, and Begg (1979) found that people are better able to recognize and recall the names of animals if they are involved in a difficult mental size comparison (for example, deciding which is larger: a tiger or a donkey) than an easy comparison (for example, choosing the larger of a frog and a kangaroo). However, Bower and Winzenz (1970) showed that explicit imagery instructions do not have to be given to induce people to use imagery, and hence to improve recall. They presented two groups of subjects with thirty pairs of words, such as *frog – tree*. The subjects' task was to learn to produce the second word in each pair given the first word as a cue. One group was told to form a visual image of the two objects interacting in some way. The other group was told to think of a sentence that contained both words. The imagery group recalled 87 percent of the words and the sentence group 77 percent of the words. Notice that, despite the different instructions, the representation that is encoded when making up a linking sentence may be exactly the same as the representation of an interactive image. For example, the meaning of the linking sentence "The frog was sitting under a tree" may simply be an interactive image of a frog sitting under a tree.

Action versus perception. Just as Glass, Krejci, and Goldman (1989) found that generating a sequence from memory creates a more robust semantic representation than shadowing a sequence, Bobrow and Bower (1969) found that a linking sentence is a more effective learning tool when the student makes it up for him- or herself, which is a voluntary action. Bobrow and Bower had two groups of undergraduates learn word pairs through linking sentences. In the experimental group, each student had to make up his or her own linking sentence as each word pair was presented. In the control group, a yoked control subject was given each sentence that the experimental student made up. In the test, the first member of each word pair was presented, and the student had to respond with the second member. Students in the experimental group recalled 58 percent of the response words but students in the control group recalled only 29 pecent of the response words.

The better retention that results from action versus perception has an important application to instruction and study. Recall that Glass, Brill, and Ingate (2008) improved exam performance by repeatedly asking students questions about the material. Students remember material better and longer when they answer questions about it compared with studying it without questions. This includes multiple-choice questions. Even though students and teachers alike think of exams as a method of discovering what students have learned, the questions asked on the exams are the largest determinant of what the student remembers. So, exams are actually the most effective *instructional* methodology currently employed. Four months after the course ended, Glass, Ingate, and Sinha (2013) invited students to take a post-final exam. Half the questions appeared on the final exam and half might have but did not. The students would therefore have studied the material covering all the questions. Nevertheless, the students performed better on the questions that had appeared on the final exam.

Story learning. Consistent with the results of list-learning experiments, Bransford and his colleagues (Bransford, 1979) found that, when the sentences describe familiar episodes in semantic memory, most of the story is remembered. However, when the sentences do not describe familiar episodes and must be remembered as sequences of speech, memory for the story is poor. In a typical experiment, students were asked to read the following passage (Bransford and Johnson 1972: 722):

> The procedure is actually quite simple. First you arrange things into different groups. Of course, one pile may be sufficient depending on how much there is to do. If you have to go somewhere else due to lack of facilities that is the next step, otherwise you are pretty well set. It is important not to overdo things. That is, it is better to do too few things at once than too many. In the short run, this may not seem important but complications can easily arise. A mistake can be expensive as well. At first the whole procedure will seem complicated. Soon, however, it will become just another facet of life. It is difficult to foresee any end to the necessity for this task in the immediate future, but then one never can tell. After the procedure is completed one arranges the materials into different groups again. Then they can be put into their appropriate places. Eventually they will be used once more and the whole cycle will then have to be repeated. However, that is part of life.

After reading the passage, the students were asked to recall as much as they could. Try recalling the passage yourself right now. You will probably find it difficult to remember very much at all, which was also true for the students in the actual experiment. The passage is entitled "Doing the laundry." Try reading the passage again. You will find that it suddenly all makes sense. In the actual experiment, students who were given the title before they read the passage recalled more of it.

This clever study makes an important point. What you remember is determined by what you understand, and what you understand is determined by what you already know. Consequently, beyond infancy, virtually all learning is an elaboration of what you already know. A truly novel sequence is meaningless, hence difficult to learn and easy to forget. This is why security directors will never convince people to use meaningless random sequences as passwords; it is inherently too difficult to ever seem worth the effort.

10.5 Formal mnemonics

Long ago, before there was paper to write things down on, students were taught explicit methods for remembering things. Several formal mnemonics were created. Before the invention of paper, a mnemonic provided a means for the semantic encoding of a lengthy narrative such as a speech. Ironically, today these methods exist as curiosities for their use in *verbatim* encoding, a concept that didn't even exist until literacy became commonplace. All mnemonics operate on the same general principal of rapidly associating list items with a semantic narrative in memory because memory of a story is much better than memory of a meaningless list. Most mnemonics are material-specific. In other words, a mnemonic that is useful for words will be useless for digits or anything else.

The method of loci

The method of loci, or mental walk technique, is the oldest known mnemonic strategy. Its origin is told in Greek myth. Yates tells the story in *The Art of Memory* (1966: 3):

> The "method of loci" has been known in Western civilization since ancient Greek times. Cicero (in De Orotore) claimed that the method originated in an observation by a Greek poet, Simonides, about whom he told the following story:
>
> Simonides was commissioned to compose a lyric poem praising a Roman nobleman and to recite this panegyric at a banquet in his honor attended by a multitude of guests. Following his oration before the assembled guests, Simonides was briefly called outside the banqueting hall by a messenger of the gods Castor and Pollux, whom he had also praised in his poem; while he was absent, the roof of the hall collapsed, killing all the celebrants. So mangled were the corpses that relatives were unable to identify them. But Simonides stepped forward and named each of the many corpses on the basis of where they were located in the huge banquet hall. This feat of total recall is said to have convinced Simonides of a basic prescription for remembering – to use an orderly arrangement of locations into which one could place the images of things or people that are to be remembered.
>
> Cicero relates this story about Simonides in connection with his discussion of memory regarded as one of the phases of rhetoric. In ancient times rhetoric teachers provided memory instruction because, in those days before inexpensive paper and writing implements, public speakers had to memorize an entire speech, or at least the main sequence of topics. For this reason most references to the method of loci come down to us from treatises on rhetoric, such as Cicero's De Oratore, the anonymous Rhetorica ad Herennium, and Quintilian's Institutio oratoria.

Yates provides a detailed description of how the method of loci was used in ancient times:

> It is not difficult to get hold of the general principles of the mnemonic. The first step was to imprint on the memory a series of loci or places. The commonest, though not only, type of mnemonic place system used was the architectural type. The clearest description of the process is that given by Quintilian. In order to form a series of places in memory, he says, a building is to be remembered, as spacious and varied a one as possible, the forecourt, the living room, bedrooms, and parlours, not omitting statues and

> other ornaments with which the rooms are decorated. The images by which the speech is to be remembered...are then placed in imagination on the places which have been memorized in the building. This done, as soon as the memory of the facts requires to be revived, all these places are visited in turn and the various deposits demanded of their custodians. We have to think of the ancient orator as moving in imagination through his memory building whilst he is making his speech drawing from the memorized places the images he has placed on them. The method ensures that the points are remembered in the right order, since the order is fixed by the sequence of places in the building.

To summarize, the prescription for memorizing a series of items is (1) to memorize a list of "memory snapshots" of locations arranged in a familiar order; (2) to make up a vivid image representing, symbolizing, or suggesting each of the items of information that are to be remembered; and (3) to take the items in the sequence they are to be learned and to associate them one by one with the corresponding imaginary locations in memory. The associations are to be established by "mentally visualizing" the image of the items placed into the imaginary context of the locational snapshots. The same loci are used over and over for memorizing any new set of items. Without this feature – if an entire new set of loci had to be learned for each new list – the use of the method would be uneconomical.

Once cheap paper made written documents the substance of academic and commercial life, the most common use left to mnemonics was to make it possible to remember a list of items the very first time that it was seen or heard.

Other word mnemonics

The pegword method is extremely similar to the method of loci. The only difference is that, instead of learning a sequence of locations, it involves first learning a series of number–word rhymes. A possible set is as follows: one is a bun, two is a shoe, three is a tree, four is a door, five is a hive, six is sticks, seven is heaven, eight is a gate, nine is a line, and ten is a hen. After this set of rhymes has been thoroughly learned, quickly and accurately learning any new list of ten words is then possible. The technique from this point on is the same as the method of loci. As each new word is presented, you form a vivid image relating the word to one of the pegwords. For example, suppose you wanted to remember the elements in the order of their atomic weights. To memorize the first element, hydrogen, you might imagine a bun rising out of the mushroom cloud of an exploding hydrogen bomb. For the second element, helium, you might image a shoe suspended from a helium balloon, etc. To recall the list later, you would run through the pegwords in order and retrieve the word associated with each. A nice feature of the pegword method is that, because the items are numbered, overlooking an item is impossible. For example, when one comes to three–tree, one knows that there is some word that comes with it that must be recalled.

With a little practice, both the method of loci and the pegword method produce extremely accurate recall (Roediger, 1980). The methods are limited only by the number of loci or pegwords you have learned. In fact, you can learn several different lists by using the same loci and not confuse them, at least for relatively short retention intervals, just as you would not be likely to confuse events that occurred on two different trips to school (Bower and Reitman, 1972). In each case the new material to be learned is associated with a set of cues that can easily be generated in order. A distinctive retrieval cue for each item is therefore available at the time of recall. Bower and Clark (1969) found that an even simpler mnemonic worked nearly as well. Students learned twelve lists of ten nouns each, by linking all the words together in sentences that formed a story. After the students had been presented with all twelve lists, they recalled 93 percent of the 120 words that had been presented.

Nonword mnemonics

When the list items are not words, the strategy is to first associate them with words and then connect the words in sentences and stories, as described above. One such strategy is called natural-language mediation (Montague, Adams, and Kiess, 1966; Prytulak, 1971). Natural-language mediation involves encoding a term by thinking of a real-word association. For example, suppose you had to learn a set of nonsense pairs such as wis–op, cer–val, or klm–ptg. One way to encode the material is by allowing yourself to freely associate while you are studying in order to come up with a more meaningful representation. In our examples, wis–op might remind you of whistle-stop, cer–val might translate into Sir Valiant, and klm–ptg might result in Dutch airline/paper tiger.

In the keyword method, subjects are trained to connect a foreign word to its translation in two steps. First, the foreign word is linked to a similar-sounding word in the native language (the keyword). Then the keyword is linked to the translation by a mental image. For example, the Russian word for *building, zdanie,* is pronounced somewhat like "zdawn-yeh," with emphasis on the first syllable. One could therefore use *dawn* as the keyword and then form a mental image of the first light of dawn casting its glow over a large building. Students taught to use the keyword method show improved ability in recalling the definitions of foreign vocabulary items (Atkinson and Raugh, 1975; Kasper and Glass, 1982).

Number mnemonics

In a creative use of work study, Chase and Ericsson (1981), instead of putting work study students to work in the college office, let the subjects invent their own mnemonic strategies for the digit span task, in which subjects listen to a series of digits read at the rate of one digit per second and then immediately attempt to report the series in order. Two subjects practiced the digit span task for two years, completing well over 200 sessions. First, the students learned to chunk sequences of three or four digits by matching them to representations already stored in semantic memory. Both subjects were runners, and their primary coding device was to relate incoming digits to well-known times of races (for example, the sequence "3–5–1" was coded as the "old world record for the mile for a long time"). Second, the students developed a retrieval structure – a device for indexing information in memory, such as the memory locations used in the method of loci. The two subjects both learned to group their low-level digit chunks into larger super-groups, hierarchically organized as illustrated in Figure 10.13. When the series was being reported, the subjects tended to pause for a longer time between the major boundaries in the retrieval structure. Finally, extensive practice produced an increase in the speed with which the subjects could access the relevant information in semantic memory. Figure 10.14 plots the growth in their average digit span with practice. One of the subjects, Steve Faloon, began like any other naive subject, with an initial span of seven digits. Ultimately, he attained truly spectacular levels of recall ability, culminating in a peak performance of eighty-two digits!

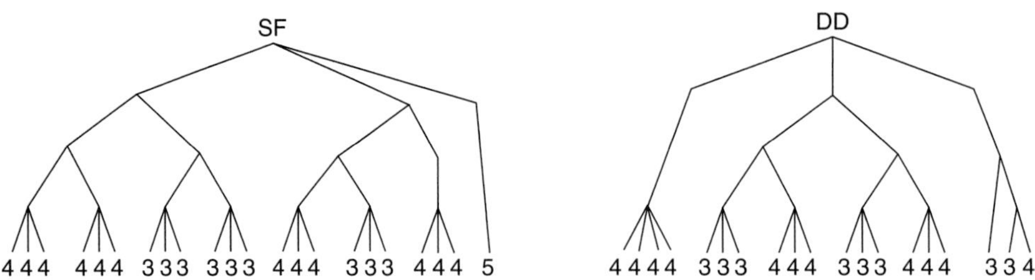

Figure 10.13 Hierarchical organizations used by two subjects in recoding digit strings (Chase and Ericsson, 1982).

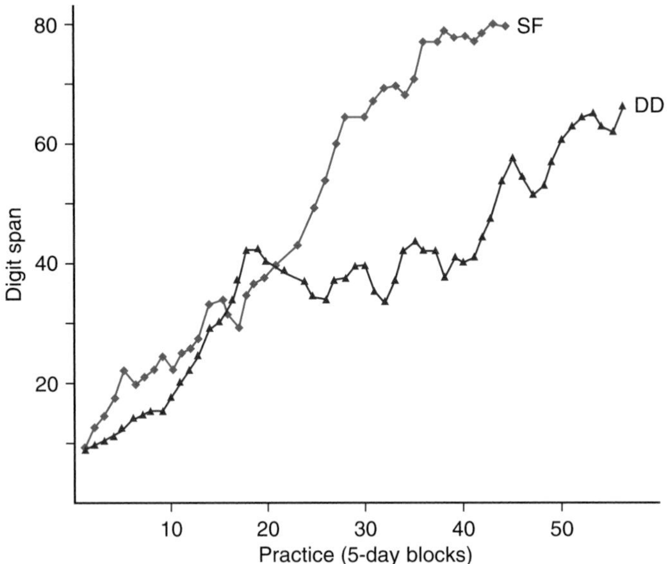

Figure 10.14 The increase in digit span for two subjects, SF and DD, is a function of practice with the recoding strategy (Chase and Ericsson, 1982).

Minds of the mnemonists

Throughout history, people with all kinds of backgrounds have become known for their ability to perform extraordinary memory feats. We will examine the memory feats of two individuals whose abilities were studied by psychologists: a history graduate student in Washington state and a reporter in the Soviet Union.

V. P. V. P. was born in Latvia but lived for many years in the United States. He was a very intelligent man (with an IQ of 136). V. P. was able to repeat seventeen digits in order (Hunt and Love, 1972). He also recalled a one-page story almost verbatim six weeks after being presented with it. V. P. apparently relied mainly on linguistic and semantic associations to elaborate what he was trying to remember. In doing so, he was aided by an extremely wide knowledge of languages (he could read almost all modern European languages). Since virtually all consonant sequences approximate a word in one language or another, he found it very easy to generate natural-language mediators for any nonsense syllable.

V. P. had his own views about how his skills developed. He regarded his memory abilities as the result of Jewish culture, which valued and encouraged rote memory. He viewed good memorizers such as himself as basically passive individuals who are prepared to devote their energies to encoding the presented material, without being particularly concerned with the purpose of remembering it.

S. was born a few miles from V. P.'s birthplace, shortly before the turn of the past century. In the 1920s he was a newspaper reporter in Russia. When the editor gave out assignments for the day, S. never took notes. One day the editor started to reproach him for being inattentive, but S. repeated the assignment word for word. The editor then sent him to a psychology laboratory. There he met the great Russian psychologist A. R. Luria. Luria studied S.'s memory abilities for almost thirty years, and he published his findings in an entertaining book called *The Mind of a Mnemonist* (1968). S.'s abilities were truly astounding. He could repeat seventy or more items in order without error, whether they were words, letters, nonsense syllables, or sounds. He could repeat the series either forward or backward. Furthermore, his recall of such lists was still perfect when tested after fifteen years, despite the fact that by that time S. had become a professional mnemonist, who had learned thousands of similar lists. To recall a particular list, he would carefully reconstruct the situation, as the following example demonstrates (Luria, 1968: 12):

> "Yes, yes... This was a series you gave me once when we were in your apartment... You were sitting at the table and I in the rocking chair... You were wearing a gray suit and you looked at me like this... Now, then, I can see you saying..." And then he would quickly recall the entire list.

S. relied on extraordinarily vivid visual imagery to encode material. For example, when S. was presented with a list of fifty digits, he reported that he could still "see" the numbers even after they were removed. As a result, he was able to rapidly read off the numbers by rows, columns, or diagonals of four. After four months he needed more time to "recapture the situation" before beginning to recall, but then he performed as quickly and accurately as ever. Part of S.'s encoding ability depended on an extreme form of synesthesia. **Synesthesia** occurs when an input evokes an image in a different sense modality. Many people experience synesthesia occasionally, as when a piece of music arouses visual images. But S. experienced synesthesia in response to virtually any input. For example, Luria reports S.'s reaction to a particular tone (1968: 23): "S. saw a brown strip against a dark background that had red, tongue-like edges. The sense of taste he experienced was like that of sweet and sour borscht, a sensation that gripped his entire tongue." His synesthesia allowed S. to easily form visual images of essentially anything – words, numbers, or nonsense material. Here, for example, is how S. imaged digits (Luria, 1968: 31): "Take the number 1. This is a proud, well built man; 2 is a high-spirited woman; 3 is a gloomy person (why, I don't know); 6 is a man with swollen feet; 7 a man with a mustache; 8 a very stout woman."

S. did occasionally make errors, but these seemed to be not so much defects of memory as defects of perception. For example, a noise during the reading of a list might be imaged as "puffs of steam" or "splashes," which would make it difficult for S. to encode the table. During recall he might do something along the lines of "misreading" the digit "8" as a "3." He often used the method of loci, which he appeared to have rediscovered for himself. Sometimes, he would omit words during recall because he couldn't "see" them clearly in his image. For example, on one occasion he missed the words *pencil* and *egg* in recalling a list by the mental walk technique. Here is his explanation for the errors (Luria 1968: 36):

> I put the image of the pencil near a fence...the one down the street, you know. But what happened was that the image fused with that of the fence and I walked right on past without noticing it. The same thing happened with the word egg. I had put it up against a white wall and it blended in with the background. How could I possibly spot a white egg up against a white wall?

While S.'s amazing abilities were in some ways an extraordinary benefit, they were also an extraordinary burden. Because everything aroused a distinctive image, he had trouble with any task requiring the ability to think more abstractly. For example, he sometimes had difficulty recognizing faces or voices. For him, a different expression or tone would seem to change the face or voice entirely. His vivid imagery also interfered with his ability to understand metaphorical or abstract language. Each word would conjure up a specific image, and he would have difficulty in ignoring these images to get to the meaning of the entire sentence. For example, consider how much trouble he had with the apparently simple sentence "The work got under way normally" (Luria, 1968: 128):

> I read that "the work got under way normally." As for work, I see that work is going on...there's a factory... But there's that word normally. What I see is a big, ruddy-checked woman, a normal woman... Then the expression got under way. Who? What is all this? You have industry...that is, a factory, and this normal woman – but how does all this fit together? How much I have to get rid of just to get the simple idea of the thing!

The power of S.'s imagination was extraordinary. He was able, for example, to make the temperature of his left hand go up while making the temperature of his right hand go down. He did so by imagining his left hand on a hot stove and his right hand holding ice. But his mental powers also created problems. To a large extent he lived in his imagination. He changed jobs dozens of times, working as a reporter, vaudeville actor, efficiency expert, and professional mnemonist. Although his life was rather unstable, he always believed he would somehow achieve greatness. Although he did not really succeed, through Luria he has given us a fascinating look at a phenomenal memory.

Normal versus unusual memory. The strategies and resulting abilities of V. P. do not seem to be fundamentally different from those of the Carnegie Mellon student Steve Faloon, mentioned above. Moreover, both were highly practiced in using their knowledge to facilitate encoding. Many mnemonists appear to be of this type. S. is a different case. His extraordinary synesthesia is not the kind of thing we would expect to develop through practice. Although he used some standard mnemonic devices, such as the method of loci, his encoding processes were generally highly unusual. Instead of abstracting only certain critical features of a sensory input in order to construct a representation of it, as people normally seem to do, he apparently retained a virtually exact representation of the entire experience. As we have seen, this detailed type of encoding affected not only his memory but other aspects of his thought processes as well.

Acting and competition. There is no great practical benefit to being a mnemonist. There are no occupations that put great time pressure on individuals to learn study materials to a high degree of accuracy. Professional actors have to remember a varying number of lines, as well as bits of stage business, accurately. However, they are not under the time pressure to learn their lines during the first reading of the script. Noice (1992) asked seven actors to describe the procedures they used in preparing and learning a role. There was unanimous agreement among the actors that they did not memorize the lines in a rote-type fashion. Nor did they use any of the mnemonics described here. In fact, they did not try to learn their lines at all! Instead, they read the script many times, trying to infer the motivation behind each utterance. All the actors stressed the importance of identifying the underlying meaning and of explaining why the character said those exact words. This type of active role playing eventually produces verbatim recall and makes line-for-line memorizing unnecessary. The spoken words become part of the episode describing the entire event.

Today, there are few practical uses for mnemonics. Some restaurant servers find them useful for remembering orders. They are still used by students to learn the twelve cranial nerves in biology and are still taught to get students through professional exams in law and medicine. Virtually the only opportunities to perform feats of memory are the competitions that are now held. These are rarely opportunities to make money. However, after Joshua Foer won the 2006 United States Memory Championship in New York he received $1.2 million to write a book and movie about the experience (Dowd, 2011).

10.6 Anterograde amnesia

The ability to learn at will is an essential characteristic of humanity. It keeps you oriented to person, place and time. In other words, you almost always know who you are, where you are, and – at least approximately – the date and time. When learning is impaired, knowledge of where you are and the date rapidly slip away. This is an extremely distressing experience. The consequence of an impaired ability to learn is called anterograde amnesia. **Anterograde amnesia** is an inability to remember events that occurred after a brain injury. It is contrasted with **retrograde amnesia**, which is the inability to remember events that occurred before a brain injury. The temporal lobes are essential to the permanent storage of memory traces. The storage system is bilateral, which is fortunate, because damage to the medial temporal lobe of one hemisphere leaves, at worst, a mild deficit in the retention of either visual targets (if the right hemisphere is damaged) or auditory targets (if the left hemisphere is damaged). However, when there is bilateral damage to one of three areas of the brain – the hippocampus or surrounding area in the medial temporal cortex, the anterior nuclei of the thalamus that connect with the hippocampus, or the basal forebrain (Gade, 1982) – then anterograde amnesia results (Figure 2.2).

Temporary amnesia

Temporary amnesia is a common consequence of a shock to the brain that does not produce a permanent injury. A common cause is a blow to the head. A head injury may produce a temporary amnesia lasting from a few minutes to a few months. One common source of such head injuries is collisions during sports competitions. When Dick (1994) used the

National Collegiate Athletic Assciation surveillance system to uniformly evaluate head injuries in twelve intercollegiate sports he found a surprisingly uniform rate of head injury across sports, though there were some differences. Ice hockey had the highest percentage of head injuries, followed by football and field hockey, women's lacrosse, and men's soccer. An apparently minor head injury can produce a deficit in word list learning or digit span that can last for weeks (Ruff *et al.*, 1989). Otherwise, the individual is unimpaired in daily life. However, a learning deficit that is detectable only by testing may be quite significant if the athlete is a student!

A somewhat mysterious temporary amnesia, called **transient global amnesia,** may occur for from two to twelve hours, most commonly in middle-aged to elderly men. For most cases, the cause is unknown, but it may be the result of a temporary reduction of blood flow to the medial temporal region of the brain. In a minority of cases, the patient has apparently had a seizure. In these cases the disorder is called **transient epileptic amnesia** (Kopelman, 2002).

Sometimes transient epileptic amnesia is deliberately induced under ironic circumstances. Depression may be cured by **electronic convulsive therapy** (ECT). An electric shock is applied to the cortex, which induces a seizure. Recall that impaired learning is a symptom of depression. When ECT lifts the depression there is also a long-term improvement in learning. However, ironically, Squire (1981) showed that electric shock itself causes temporary anterograde amnesia. He compared patients who received electric shock with alcoholic Korsakoff patients on a "Yes"/"No" picture recognition task. Alcoholic Korsakoff's patients have a severe permanent amnesia. Yet Squire found that the patients receiving electric shock showed more forgetting between two- and thirty-two-hour tests than those with Korsakoff's syndrome. Similarly, lithium (which relieves manic-depressive mood swings) and the tricyclic antidepressants, such as Valium (Judd *et al.*, 1987), impair learning.

Although permanent amnesia before the end of life is rare, temporary amnesia is a common occurrence, which many college students get to experience, thanks to the effect of alcohol. While a person is drunk, the storage of information in memory is impaired (Hartley, Birnbaum, and Parker, 1978; Ryan and Butters, 1983). The most dramatic aspect of this impairment is the well-known blackout phenomenon. Later, when the individual sobers up, he or she is unable to remember what occurred while drunk. This short-term encoding impairment clears up after the alcohol passes through the system if there is only occasional drinking. But frequent drinking results in a deficit even when sober from the poisonous effects of the drug. The effect of alcohol is insidious. The change in memory from day to day is imperceptible. Furthermore, whatever skills people use in their daily activities remain unimpaired. Frequently, years of gradual mental decline go unnoticed. Hence, even a superficially healthy person who is addicted to alcohol – someone who may appear to be functioning as a businessperson, college professor, or student – may suffer from a memory disorder. The brains of even young alcoholics in their twenties and thirties show cortical atrophy. Their brains also show abnormal electrical activity during target detection (Ryan and Butters, 1984). These changes cause a variety of nonverbal cognitive deficits. Ryan and Butters (1980) found that detoxified alcoholics performed more poorly than age-matched controls on paired-associate learning tests of unrelated words, and of digits and unfamiliar symbols (see also Ryan and Butters, 1983). There are also deficits involving visuospatial reasoning (Jones and Parsons, 1972) and visuospatial attention (Becker *et al.*, 1983). If at some point the person stops drinking, then there is a gradual improvement in some cognitive functions, although the ability to store new information remains permanently impaired (Brandt *et al.*, 1983).

Permanent and progressive amnesia

Permanent damage can result from trauma, poisoning, anoxia, vascular disorders, or herpes encephalitis. The effect of the damage depends on its location, not what caused it. Table 10.2 contrasts the performance of patients with different types of amnesic disorders on a variety of cognitive tasks. The table reveals a double dissociation between damage to the hippocampus or thalamus on the one hand and damage to the striatum on the other. Damage to the hippocampus or thalamus, hence to the instrumental system (Chapter 2), impairs declarative learning and recognition but leaves procedural motor skill learning intact. In contrast, damage to the striatum, hence to the habit system (Chapter 2), destroys procedural motor skill learning but leaves recognition intact.

When damage is restricted to the medial temporal cortex, which includes the hippocampus and thalamus, only declarative learning is impaired; other cognitive abilities are intact, with the exception of some degree of retrograde amnesia. When a progressive disease process destroys more and more of the brain, more symptoms emerge, and so it is called a syndrome. Alzheimer's disease progressively damages many cortical and subcortical brain structures until death results. Along the way there is an increasingly severe semantic dementia (Chapter 7) as well as an increasingly severe amnesia. Alzheimer's disease is distinguished from medial temporal/diencephalic amnesia by impaired semantic tasks, such as word finding.

TABLE 10.2 Impairments that characterize different dementias

Disorder		Hippocampal amnesia	Korsakoff's dementia	Alzheimer's dementia	Huntington's dementia
Damaged area		Medial temporal	Medial temporal	Temporal	Striatum
Cognitive function	**Task**				
Motor skill	Pursuit rotor	Normal	Normal	Normal	Impaired
Semantic priming	Word completion	Normal	Normal	Impaired	Normal
Semantic memory	Verbal fluency	Normal	Normal	Impaired instance production	Impaired production
Long-term memory	List recognition	Impaired	Impaired	Impaired	Mildly impaired
Working and long-term memory	List recall	Impaired	Impaired	Impaired	Impaired

Huntington's disease is the result of progressive damage to the striatum (Chapter 3), which leads to the loss of voluntary movement in addition to an increasingly severe amnesia. Huntington's disease is distinguished from the other disorders by impaired motor skills and by less impaired recognition.

Medial temporal amnesia

The same dense learning deficit is caused by bilateral damage to either the hippocampus or to the anterior thalamic nuclei. Damage to the hippocampus is the result of rare misfortune but damage to the anterior thalamic nuclei is most often the result of willful self-abuse by the excessive consumption of alcohol.

The most famous amnesic individual to ever live was Henry Molaison (Carey, 2008). He was known in the world during his lifetime as H. M. He was a man of above-average intelligence who had parts of his hippocampus and the surrounding cortical tissue removed in 1953 to alleviate life-threatening epileptic seizures. He had almost total anterograde amnesia for all events since that time, as was described in detail over many decades of study by Milner and her colleagues (Milner, Corkin, and Teuber, 1968; Milner, 1975). A few other people have had disorders like those of H. M. Encephalitis damaged the hippocampus of an optical engineer (S. S.). R. B. was a postal worker who had the blood supply to his brain cut off as the result of an atrial tear that occurred while he was in the hospital recovering from coronary artery bypass surgery (Zola-Morgan, Squire, and Amaral, 1986). What was notable about all these individuals was normal and even above-normal cognitive abilities in the moment but no retention of the moment immediately afterwards. The disorder combines normal perceptual and motor learning (Corkin, 1968) with an almost complete absence of declarative learning. To get an idea of the disorder, imagine that you are introduced to a pleasant man. A few minutes of conversation indicate that the man is of above-average intelligence. To confirm this impression, you could administer an IQ test, on which he scores well above the normal range. You ask him about himself, and he tells you about his wife, children, and job. There is no apparent memory deficit. At this point you leave him. Five minutes later, you visit him again. He has no memory of you. Now imagine that you continue to meet with this man every day. You rapidly discover that at every meeting you must reintroduce yourself. He never has any memory of the previous meetings. Brenda Milner, and later Suzanne Corkin, met Henry Mollison hundreds of times over fifty years without him ever remembering either one. A good sense of what it is like to live with such a disorder is given by the fictional movie *Memento*.

Korsakoff's syndrome. When the anterior thalamic nuclei are destroyed, the resulting symptoms are called Korsakoff's syndrome. The most common form of the disorder is called alcoholic Korsakoff's syndrome. **Alcoholic Korsakoff's syndrome** represents the chronic state of what is known as the **Wernicke–Korsakoff disorder**. It is the result of a thiamine deficiency coupled with alcohol abuse. Alcohol consumption causes alcoholic Korsakoff's syndrome because the metabolism of alcohol uses up the supply of thiamine, which is an essential nutrient for neurons in the anterior thalamic nuclei. When excessive drinking is combined with a thiamine-poor diet, cells in the diencephalon begin to die. The onset of the syndrome is signaled by a single traumatic event. This phase is the Wernicke phase of the disorder, named after the German neurologist who first described it. In the initial, acute Wernicke's phase there is confusion and severe motor dysfunction in the eyes and limbs.

If the patient is not treated with large doses of thiamine he or she is in danger of fatal midbrain hemorrhage. If treated with thiamine promptly about 75 percent of patients enter the chronic Korsakoff's phase and about 25 percent recover their intellectual functioning (Butters and Stuss, 1989). The chronic Korsakoff phase of the syndrome is named after the Russian neurologist who first described it.

The learning deficit in Korsakoff's syndrome is indistinguishable from that in medial temporal amnesia. Although 75 percent of Korsakoff patients show a degree of improvement over time, learning ability does not return to a normal level (Kopelman, 2002). There are other changes in cognition as well. Not surprisingly, there is a deficit in selective attention (recall from Chapter 4 that selective attention requires the opening and closing of thalamic gates). There are also mood and personality changes. Even when there is a prior history of aggression, patients are described as apathetic, euphoric, and irritable. Finally, there are mild visuospatial deficits. The problem-solving, visuoperceptual, attention, and motivational changes that characterize Korsakoff patients are similar to those reported for patients with damage to the prefrontal cortex from alcoholism (Butters and Stuss, 1989). As a result, it may be that many alcoholic Korsakoff patients suffer from alcohol-induced dementia in addition to Korsakoff's syndrome.

Skill learning. Both medial temporal amnesia and diencephalic amnesia are characterized by a severe deficit in declarative learning and no deficit in procedural learning. The damage causing them is therefore restricted to the instrumental system; the habit system is spared. Individuals learn motor skills (Chapter 3) and perceptual skills (Chapter 5) normally. Patients improve on the pursuit rotor task, in which a stylus must be maintained on a moving target (Cermak *et al.*, 1973), and in the reading of mirror-imaged writing (Cohen and Squire, 1981; Martone *et al.*, 1983). Every day the mirror-tracing apparatus must be shown to the patient as if for the first time, and the patient must be reinstructed in its use. But, once he or she takes up the task, the patient shows the same increment in improvement over the previous day's performance as an individual whose memory is unimpaired. Hence, the patient learns the skill normally without having any memory of having ever performed it previously.

Priming. In medial temporal and diencephalic amnesia the semantic network is intact and logogen activation is normal. Priming (Chapter 7) occurs normally, as revealed in a word completion task, even in the absence of explicit declarative learning. If you ask patients to remember a word (such as *butter*) and ask them to recall it five minutes later, they cannot do so. If you give them a recognition test, their ability to select *butter* as the word they heard is at chance. However, if you ask them to say the first word they can think of that begins with the letter "b," they are about as likely to say *butter* as a normal individual who was asked to remember the word (Graf, Shimamura, and Squire, 1985).

The first demonstration of normal priming in alcoholic Korsakoff patients was provided by Warrington and Weiskrantz (1970; 1974). They found that amnesic patients (including alcoholic Korsakoff patients) could exhibit almost normal performance when fragmented words, fragmented pictures, and two-letter word stems were used to cue recall. For example, amnesics who were severely impaired in their intentional recall and recognition of common words from a study list nevertheless evidenced rapid, accurate identification when shown the first two letters of the word. They reported that this priming effect occurred twenty-four and seventy-two hours later. Warrington and Weiskrantz tested only with explicit memory instructions but Graf, Squire, and Mandler (1984) used both explicit and implicit procedures. The explicit instructions were to use the three-letter word stems to cue recall of the previously presented words; the implicit instructions were to complete the stems with the first words that came to mind. Alcoholic Korsakoff patients produced significantly fewer of the to-be-remembered words than control subjects with explicit instructions (as well as with free recall and recognition). However, the two groups generated the same number of study words in the implicit free-association condition. Another demonstration of intact priming in alcoholic Korsakoff patients was provided by Gardner *et al.* (1973). After subjects were presented with a list of common words (for example, *tennis*, *lettuce*), belonging to one of six general categories (for example, sports, vegetables), recall was assessed under three different conditions. In one condition the patients were simply asked to recall the words that had been read to them (that is, free recall); in another, intentional recall was cued by category (for example, "A few moments ago I asked you to remember some words. One of them was a sport. What was it?"); in the third condition the subjects were simply given a category name (such as vegetables) and asked to produce the first example of this category that came to mind. The results showed that, although the Korsakoff patients were significantly impaired in comparison with intact subjects on the first two recall conditions, they did not differ from them on the third (free association) condition. The alcoholic Korsakoff patients and intact controls both tended to produce previously presented words (such as *tennis*) when asked to freely associate to the category names (such as sports). Gardner *et al.* (1973) and Graf, Squire, and Mandler (1984) found that alcoholic Korsakoff patients produced the same number of responses with both implicit and explicit instructions but normal subjects produced fewer study items with implicit instructions.

If priming is the result of the activation of associations that already exist in semantic memory then amnesic patients should show normal priming for familiar targets whose representations are already a part of semantic memory but not for novel targets. Gooding, Mayes, and van Eijk (2000) conducted a meta-analysis of thirty-six studies describing fifty-nine separate measures of priming for familiar versus novel information in amnesic patients and healthy controls that produced results generally consistent with this hypothesis. For the twenty-three measures of priming for familiar information, controls performed better eleven times and patients twelve times, so there was no difference in priming for familiar information (such as words, famous faces). For the remaining thirty-six measures of priming in which the targets (for example, nonwords) or associations between them (for example, unrelated word pairs) were novel, controls performed better than patients twenty-seven times. The meta-analysis shows that amnesic patients generally show normal priming for familiar information but not for unfamiliar information; however, some studies have not found this result, possibly because, if the priming task is too easy or difficult, there cannot be a difference in performance between healthy controls and amnesic patients (Ostergaard, 1994).

Alzheimer's disease

Alzheimer's disease eventually comes to include damage throughout the temporal cortex and so includes both semantic dementia (Chapter 7) and anterograde amnesia among its symptoms. Alzheimer's disease occurs when bits of protein that should be broken down and discarded accumulate as tangles and plaques within and between neurons. The growth is progressive and irreversible and it eventually destroys brain cells. The pathological changes tend to appear first in the temporal region and then spread over the temporoparietal cortex, eventually reaching the prefrontal cortex. The occipital cortex and motor area of the frontal cortex remain largely intact. In the early stages of Alzheimer's disease most of the basal ganglia and thalamic structures remain relatively unaffected, but in the middle and later stages of the disease changes also occur in these subcortical structures. Some of the cognitive impairment is the result of swelling from the collection of fluid occurring around the plaques. An effective treatment for the early cognitive symptoms is ibuprofen or some other nonsteroidal medicine that reduces swelling, such as Advil and Motrin.

The severe anterograde amnesia associated with the disease is directly attributable to the fact that the disease affects the medial temporal cortex bilaterally. Indeed, often the first detectable symptom is anterograde amnesia, as measured by the cued category retrieval test (Buschke *et al.*, 1999). Typically, amnesia and problem-solving deficits are the first signs of the disorder, followed by anomic aphasia (Chapter 7), and still later by visuospatial deficits. Since there is damage to semantic memory, patients with Alzheimer's disease do not benefit from semantic priming. Therefore, they do not exhibit implicit memory when asked to complete word stems or recognize picture fragments named by words they have studied earlier (Butters, Heindel, and Salmon, 1990). The semantic dementia also causes poor performance on a verbal fluency task, which requires recalling instances of a category, such as things found in a supermarket. The breakdown has been described as "bottom up," because patients tend to lose instances while retaining category labels. For example, a patient asked to generate items found in a supermarket may report meat, vegetables, fruits, cereals, etc., but fail to mention instances such as steak, beef, potatoes, corn, etc. (Hodges, Salmon, and Butters, 1992). However, procedural memory, including motor and visuospatial skills, is preserved.

Huntington's disease

The learning disorder in Huntington's disease is different from the other learning disorders described above, as shown in Table 10.2. Because of the deterioration of the basal ganglia, the ability to make a voluntary response is impaired. Motor skill learning is therefore impaired. Figure 10.15 shows the performance of normal controls, amnesics, Alzheimer's patients, and

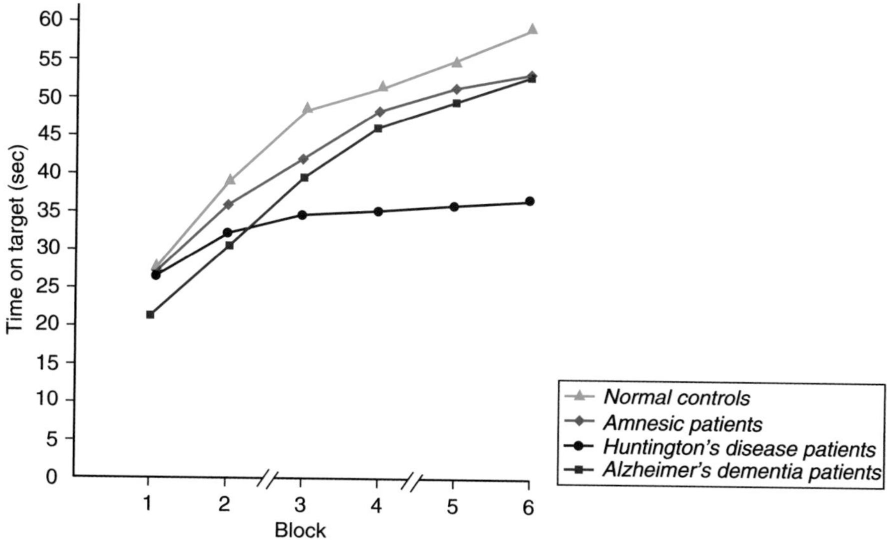

Figure 10.15 Performance of Alzheimer's dementia, Huntington's disease, and amnesic patients and normal controls on the pursuit-rotor task (Heindel *et al.*, 1988).

Huntington's patients on a pursuit rotor task, in which a stylus must be held on a dot on a rotating turntable. As shown in the figure, all groups learn the task normally, except for Huntington's patients, who fail to learn the task at all (Heindel, Butters, and Salmon, 1988). The impairment in the ability to act impairs the sophisticated verbal rehearsal and visual imagery strategies necessary to promote recall. Hence, patients with Huntington's disease perform much more poorly on recall than recognition tasks. This dissociation is not true of other forms of anterograde amnesia. Since recall is impaired, Huntington's patients are impaired in verbal fluency. But, since they do not have anomia, unlike Alzheimer's patients they do not produce an abnormal preponderance of category labels over instances (Troster *et al.*, 1989).

SUMMARY

Learning and memory make us who we are. Fortunately, declarative knowledge is the product of a sophisticated system that retains what is important and forgets what is not important. The ability to control what we learn allows us to control who we become. It makes it possible to acquire vicarious knowledge through study instead of experience.

- Declarative learning is the result of the combined operations of the instrumental and habit systems.
  - The instrumental system creates novel episodes in semantic memory. These episodes comprise a person's declarative knowledge.
  - The instrumental system includes the thalamus, hippocampus, and ventral medial prefrontal cortex.
  - Novel episodes are made permanent, in one of three ways.
    - If the emotional system signals that it is important by associating the representation with a strong emotion, then the instrumental system encodes a robust episode.
    - If a mundane event is repeated before the episode in memory is destroyed, the repetition signals that the event may be routine, so the habit system encodes a robust episode.
    - A robust episode of any mundane event may be encoded through the deliberate use of a mnemonic.
- The most common mnemonic action is verbal rehearsal.
  - Verbal rehearsal is possible because of the phonological–articulatory circuit at the temporal–parietal interface.
  - Rehearsal creates a new episode in semantic memory.
    - The robustness of a semantic representation increases with the number of distributed rehearsals. Early list items receive more distributed rehearsal and are better remembered. This is the primacy effect.
    - The phonological representation of the last four items can be used to generate them. This is the recency effect.
    - Since there is both a primacy effect and a recency effect, immediate recall is best for the beginning and end of a list, so immediate recall is a U-shaped function of list position.

- Visual imagery influences learning.
  - Generating visual images increases learning.
  - High-imagery words and nameable pictures are easily learned.
- When the purpose of a voluntary action is to learn something, it is called a mnemonic.
  - Two well-known mnemonics for words are:
    - the method of loci; and
    - the pegword method.
  - The extraordinary abilities of mnemonists are based on their use of special encoding strategies to exploit extraordinary knowledge. Mnemonists illustrate the general point that learning depends on knowledge.
- Anterograde amnesia is the inability to learn new things. It results from bilateral damage to the interior of the temporal cortex, especially the hippocampus or to connecting areas in the thalamus.
  - Declarative memory is impaired.
  - Perceptual-motor skill learning is normal.

QUESTIONS

1. What are the two systems that comprise the human learning system?
2. Is the ability to recognize someone an example of declarative or procedural knowledge?
3. How does long-term retention of an experience occur?
4. How does rehearsal cause long-term retention?
5. How do mnemonists learn?
6. What skill is preserved in medial temporal amnesia?
7. What skills are lost in Huntington's disease?

FURTHER READING

Altarriba, J., and Isurin, L. (eds.) (2014). *Memory, Language, and Bilingualism: Theoretical and Applied Approaches*. Cambridge University Press.

Corkin, S. (2013). *Permanent Present Tense*. New York: Basic Books.

Foer, J. (2011). *Moonwalking with Einstein: The Art and Science of Remembering Everything*. New York: Penguin Books.

Lieberman, D. A. (2012). *Human Learning and Memory*. Cambridge University Press.

11 Recognition

Ever since Superman first appeared in 1938, a running joke in the comic has been that, when he puts on a pair of glasses and a hat, he is no longer recognizable as Superman. However, as will be discussed below, a hat and glasses together do reduce recognition. The disguise posited in Action Comics #1 was not silly, therefore, but prescient. The human recognition ability is more than adequate for its primary task, to recognize kin and friends. However, outside its central social role, recognition is much less robust.

As described in Chapter 7, the match between the perceptual target representation and an episode in semantic memory produces a semantic response. In other words, if the perceptual representation of a face on which you fixate matches the representation of your best friend's face, then it activates everything you know about your friend. The semantic response has three parts. The last time you saw your friend it was at a particular place and time. His or her representation was encoded as part of an episode describing that event; saying good night after going to the movies. If any part of that episode is activated by seeing the face again, this contextual information about when and where you saw him or her becomes part of the **recollection**. Furthermore, you have had many experiences with your friend, which have resulted in many episodes containing his or her face. Collectively, these episodes determine his or her **familiarity**. If you have just seen the same face moments before in the hall it will appear recent when you see it again in the classroom. As mentioned in Chapter 10, the short-term perceptual representation of the instrumental system is experienced as a feeling of **recency**.

Thus, recognition occurs when a perceptual target is compared with semantic memory and matched with one or more episodes.

- The process of recognition has several distinct stages.
  - Feature analysis and perceptual organization stage.
    - The features of a perceptual target determine its representation and the response node it activates – hence, what it is recognized as.
- Comparison stage.
  - The level of target and contextual detail determines the specificity of the recognition response. Face recognition requires a high level of detail, so only familiar faces are recognized.

- Response stage.
  - After the first year of life a response occurs immediately following a match. However, in early infancy, after a long retention interval a match can take days to produce a response.
- Three responses determine the recognition judgment.
  - The target and context of the matching episode are recollected.
  - Additional matching episodes determine the familiarity response.
  - Short-term temporal order information encoded by the instrumental system is experienced as the recency response.
- The amount of recollection and familiarity and the perception of recency are all continuous variables, but recognition tasks frequently force a choice between two alternatives: old or new. As a result, a decision procedure must set a criterion so that every item with sufficient recollection and familiarity to exceed the criterion is called "old" and every item below the criterion is called "new." For short-term recognition, recency also contributes to the information compared with the criterion.
  - The person's expectations influence the level at which the criterion is set.
  - The theory of signal detection compares correct recognitions with false alarms as a means of separately measuring a person's ability to discriminate old targets from new distracters and the criterion used for calling a test item old.
  - The role of the decision criterion in recognition memory has an important application in the evaluation of eyewitness testimony. Eyewitnesses are overconfident, and the criterion is influenced by task demands.
- Delusions demonstrate that the decision stage generating the recognition judgment is distinct from the three recognition responses.

11.1 Perceptual and semantic processing

Recognition orients a person to both time and place. Recognition is the declarative knowledge that you are in familiar surroundings, that the person before you is your friend, and that that book on the table is your own, and where you placed it a few minutes beforehand. Recall from Chapter 7 that the process of recognition involves both a comparison stage and a response stage. In the feature analysis stage, in the occipital cortex for vision and the temporal cortex for audition, a target is analyzed as a set of features and organized into successively more complex patterns. In the comparison stage, in the temporal cortex, the representation of the input is compared with many memory representations in parallel. In the response stage, a match activates some response node in the temporal cortex, which communicates the response to the prefrontal cortex, which results in an awareness of the target. Figure 7.17 is a schematic of how the comparison and response stages operate together to produce recognition for the word *dog*.

Comparison stage

As mentioned in Chapter 7, a perceptual representation is simultaneously compared with everything in semantic memory. Consequently, human beings have a phenomenal capacity to recognize perceptual targets that they have previously encountered. People can identify thousands of different pictures from just a single exposure. This is a remarkable ability, but, as will be discussed below, somewhat misleading with regard to the accuracy of recognition in daily life.

Visual recognition. Table 11.1 summarizes the results of seven different studies of picture recognition. In each experiment a single presentation of the study list was followed by presentation of target/distracter pairs. No matter how long the study list, immediate recognition was, essentially, perfect, and remained good for at least a week. Even after six months it remained a little above chance performance. So, if people are shown exactly the same picture they have seen once before, they have a very good chance of recognizing it. In the first five experiments shown in the table, the distracter picture was of an entirely different object

TABLE 11.1 Picture recognition

Observers	Study set size	Immediate retention	Up to one week	At least a month	Study
Four-year-olds	100	98%	90%	67%	Brown and Scott (1971)
Adults	612	97%	87%	58%	Shepard (1967)
Adults	2,500		91%		Standing, Conezio, and Haber (1970)
Adults	10,000		85%		Standing (1973)
Adults	2,800	93%			Konkle *et al.* (2010)
Adults	2,500	92%			Brady *et al.* (2008)
		88% (similar distracter)			
Adults	400	82%	72%		Vogt and Magnussen (2007)
		3- to 5-second presentation rate for adults			

from the target picture. Since people had no difficulty performing this task, in the last two experiments shown in the table the distracters were made more similar to the targets. Brady *et al.* (2008) compared target–distracter discrimination when they were instances of completely different categories to discrimination when the distracter was another instance of the same category, such as target and distracter both being television remotes, or two pictures of the same object in different orientations (Figure 11.1). As shown in the table, recognition declined only slightly, from 92 percent to 88 percent. Finally, Vogt and Magnussen (2007) ensured that all the targets and distracters were very similar by showing people 400 pictures

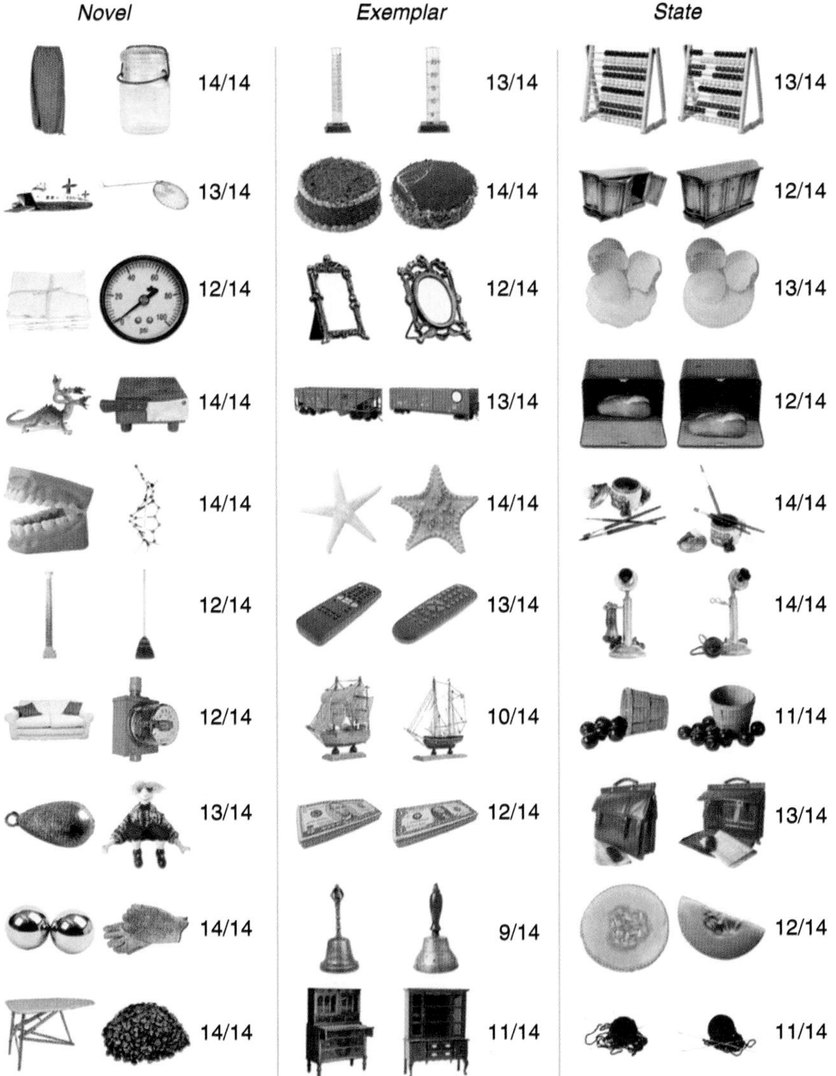

Figure 11.1 Example test pairs presented during the two-alternative forced-choice task with a dissimilar distracter (left column) and similar distracters (middle and right column). The number of correct responses out of 14 is shown for each pair (Brady *et al.*, 2008). Same picture set was used by Konkle *et al.* (2010) and Endress and Potter (2014).

of doors. As shown on the last row of the table, recognition was only 82 percent. However, remembering 400 pictures viewed once is an entirely artificial task. So, other than in experiments that make use of unnaturally similar targets and distracters, visual recognition of a picture seen only once before is excellent.

One reason that target–distracter discrimination was so accurate when the target and distracter were so similar was precisely because the target and distracter were so similar. Consequently, both members of the test pair could be compared to the same target representation in memory, and if only one had a critical feature in the target representation then that one had to be the target. Tulving (1981) demonstrated the importance of target–distracter similariy by rearranging the target–distracter pairs. To prepare his study materials, pictures were cut in half. One half-picture was in the study sequence, so one half-picture was the target and the other half-picture was the distracter at test. Recognition was better when the two half-pictures were together in the same test pair than when they were parts of different test pairs, as shown in Figure 11.2. When the two half-pictures were parts of different test pairs it was impossible to determine what the critical features were. However, when the two half-pictures were together in the same test pair and compared with the same target representation at the same time, the one matching a critical target feature was apparent.

Nonvisual recognition. Lawrence and Banks (1973) demonstrated a fairly impressive memory for common sounds. They had subjects listen to tape recordings of 194 common sounds (babies crying, dogs barking, a car starting, etc.). Their subjects were 89 percent accurate in recognizing the sounds that had been presented from a set including similar sounds

Figure 11.2 Examples of target–distracter pairs in which the distracter is extremely similar to a target: matched pairs (a), mismatched pairs (b) (Tulving, 1981).

that had not been presented. Engen and Ross (1973) found that immediate recognition of forty-eight smells was only 69 percent correct. However, memory for smell exhibits virtually no decline over fairly long time periods. In the Engen and Ross experiment students were 70 percent correct if the test was a week later and 68 percent correct if the test was given a month later. Subsequent studies using more familiar odors have obtained better initial recognition performance and confirmed the slow decline in performance over long retention intervals (Lawless and Cain, 1975; Rabin and Cain, 1984).

Verbal recognition. People's word recognition is also very good. Shepard (1967) showed people a sequence of 540 words and then tested them on sixty pairs of words in which one member of each pair had been shown in the inspection series. The subjects selected the target 88 percent of the time. Although people are good at recognizing both pictures and words, these are partly separate abilities. Woodhead and Baddeley (1981) selected people who had done either well (the good recognizers) or badly (the poor recognizers) on a facial recognition task and then gave them three more recognition tests: another involving faces, one involving paintings, and one involving visually presented words. The good recognizers performed better than the poor recognizers on the faces and paintings, but there was no difference between them on the words.

College students can also recognize passages they read one or two years previously. Recall from Chapter 5 that Kolers (1976) gave students two years of practice reading passages printed in inverted text. Kolers was interested in how much declarative learning also occurred during his procedural learning task. At the end of the experiment he gave the students all the passages they had read as well as some new passages they had never seen before. A passage could have been read at most twice, once during each year of the experiment. The students had to sort the articles into four categories: articles they had seen twice, articles they had seen only a year ago, articles they had seen only recently, and articles they had never seen before. Although they were not perfect, the students were able to sort the articles quite accurately (Table 11.2).

Familiar versus unfamiliar faces. On the basis of the results of picture recognition showing that people can remember thousands of pictures, you might be confident that you could recognize someone from a single photograph. However, you would be wrong. The task of recognizing the same face in two different photographs turned out to be different from and a far more difficult task than recognizing the same photograph of a face. The latter task requires the encoding and retention of a detailed visual representation of the photograph

TABLE 11.2 Actual occurrence of passage versus recognition response for inverted-text passages read once, twice, or never

Actual Occurrence	Both	Response Recent	Old	New
Both	0.49	0.29	0.17	0.05
Recent	0.30	0.55	0.08	0.07
Old	0.06	0.03	0.56	0.35
New	0.0	0.04	0.30	0.66

Source: Kolers (1976).

from a single brief viewing. The results in Table 11.1 show that this in fact occurs. The former task requires that the visual features of a face that remain constant over different orientations and variations in lighting and make-up be encoded from a single brief viewing. Bruce (1982) found that this does not happen. In her experiment, observers saw twelve pictures of the faces of people who worked in the same department as them and twelve pictures of the faces of strangers. The recognition test consisted of target–distracter pairs in which the target was a picture of one of the twenty-four individuals whose picture was part of the study list. The picture was either the same picture shown at study or a different picture that had been taken at the same time as the study picture. Pictures of the same individual differed on the expression of the individual, whether the pose was frontal or three-quarters, or both. The results are shown in Figure 11.3. The observers were virtually perfect at recognizing faces of familiar individuals whether the same picture or a different picture was shown. The observers were also virtually perfect at recognizing exactly the same picture of the face of a stranger. However, recognition of the face of a stranger from a different picture was only slightly above chance.

The encoding of the features necessary for recognition of the same face in different orientations, with different grooming, and at different ages requires the encoding of many faces over many years in order to extract those features (Chapter 6). On the one hand, people with ASD, who tend not to make eye contact, are impaired at face recognition because they choose not to encode all the features essential for recognition (Chapter 8). On the other hand, bilateral damage to the occipital cortex or temporal cortex impairs face recognition, because, once the neural-feature-encoding mechanisms are damaged, no amount of practice results in those features being encoded (Chapter 6). The long-term effect of practice encoding similar features is also evident in people's ability to recognize the faces of individuals of different races. Black and white American college students alike most accurately recognize the faces of the racial types with which they have had more experience (Bothwell, Brigham, and Malpass, 1989).

Even familiarity with a visually complex object is not a guarantee that all its features will be encoded, because only task-relevant information about a target is encoded, as demonstrated by inattention blindness (Chapter 4) and change blindness (Chapter 5).

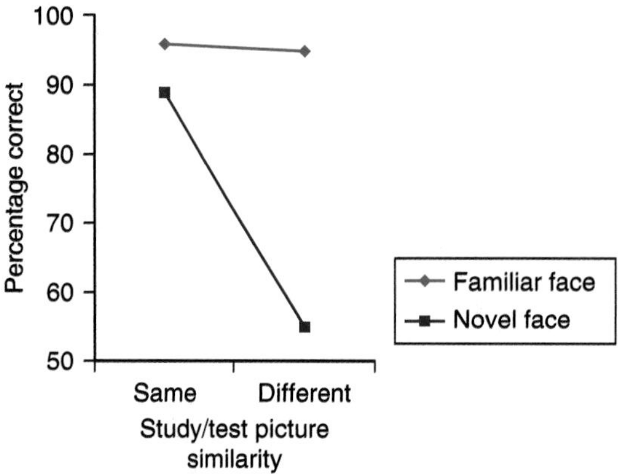

Figure 11.3 The recognition of familiar faces and repeated pictures is excellent. The recognition of novel test pictures of novel study faces is not different from chance (Bruce, 1982).

Nickerson and Adams (1979) examined the ability of American college students to recognize the appearance of an object they were extremely familiar with in the last century, before inflation and the widespread adoption of credit cards: the head side of a penny. They found that the students were quite poor in selecting the correct version of the coin when it was presented along with fourteen distracters in which various features were omitted or altered.

Response stage

Beyond the first year of life, a target is immediately perceived as either familiar or novel. However, long-term recognition is remarkably slow during the first three months of life. When Rovee-Collier trained three-month-old infants to move a mobile by kicking their feet she found that an infant remembered the mobile no more than a week (Figure 8.4). At longer retention intervals, when the infant saw the mobile there was neither a glint of recognition nor an immediate effort to get it moving through kicking. She wondered why that was. Was it because the representation of the mobile had been lost from the young memory, or was it because, after a week, a few minutes of looking were not enough time to gain access to it? To test the second possibility, Rovee-Collier (1993) decided to reactivate the memory of the mobile after thirteen days, well after it appeared to be forgotten. To do this she showed different groups of infants the training mobile as a reminder and then returned to test their memories after different intervals. Each infant was shown the training mobile for three minutes. The infant wasn't attached to the mobile, so the infant could not move it him- or herself. But the mobile was shaken to attract the infant's attention and perhaps remind the infant what he or she could once do. Then the mobile was taken away. With one group of infants, Rovee-Collier returned fifteen minutes later with the training mobile and attached it above them. Would they recognize the training mobile and kick to it? The infants did not. But maybe fifteen minutes was not enough time to retrieve the memory of the training mobile. She waited an hour after the reminder before returning with the training mobile for a second group of infants. But these infants also did not recognize or kick to it. But Rovee-Collier did not give up. She waited eight hours before returning with the mobile for a third group of infants. These infants kicked a little, but not enough to say that they remembered anything. So she waited twenty-four hours before returning with the training mobile for a fourth group of infants. These infants did recognize the mobile twenty-four hours after the reminder and kicked to try to move it, though not quite as much as during the original training session. However, Rovee-Collier was not done. With a fifth group of infants she waited seventy-two hours after the three-minute reminder before returning with the training mobile (Figure 11.4). The infants in this group recognized the mobile right away and kicked as vigorously as the last day of training, sixteen days previously! The infants' memories of the training mobile were perfect! After a single reminder, the forgetting function for the training mobile was exactly the same as after the original training session (Figure 11.5).

Consider what a remarkable result this is. A three-minute reminder was sufficient to reactivate the memory of a mobile an infant had learned to control at the age of three months. However, such a memory took a very long time to retrieve. It was fully seventy-two hours after the reminder had been shown that the memory was fully reactivated. In a further experiment, Rovee-Collier found that a reminder was effective at retrieving the memory of a training mobile formed at three months for up to twenty-seven days after the last training session. Furthermore, once the memory of the training mobile had been reactivated, it was

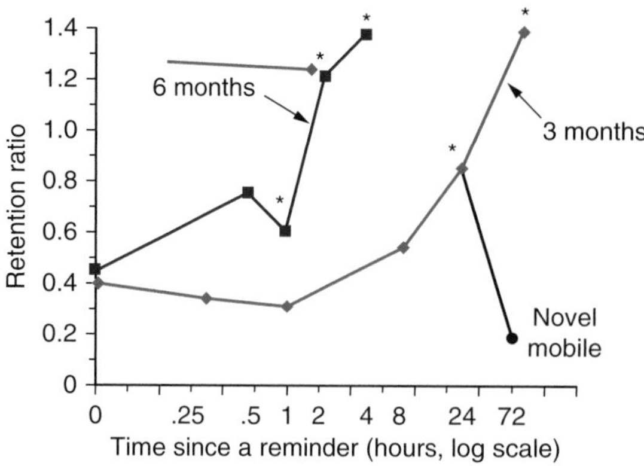

Figure 11.4 Rates of recovery of a forgotten memory at different delays after exposure to mobile reminder at 3 and 6 months. Asterisks indicate that retention was significant (Rovee-Collier, 1993). * = significant difference

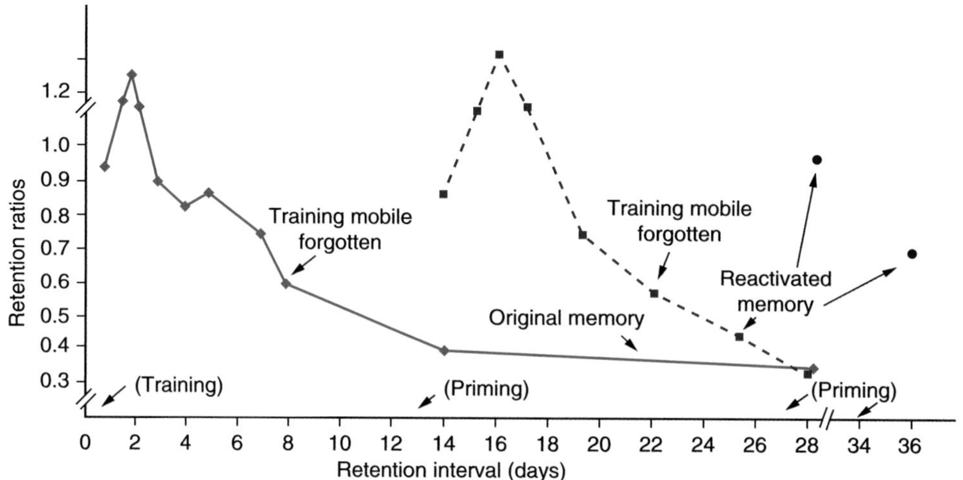

Figure 11.5 Retention ratio as a function of the retention interval after two days of training (original memory: solid line) or two days of training plus a reactivation treatment (reactivated memory: broken line). A single reactivation treatment (priming) occurred 13 days after training for all points connected by broken lines and on either 27 or 34 days after training for the single data points at the 28- and 35-day retention intervals. A retention ratio of 1.0 indicates perfect retention; rations of 0.6 and lower typically indicate complete forgetting. Infants whose memories had been forgotten days or weeks earlier exhibited perfect retention when their memories were primed the day before the two- or four-week long-term test, but a single prime before the five-week test did not alleviate forgetting. Each data point represents an independent group of at least five three-month-olds who were tested only once (Rovee-Collier, 1993).

forgotten at least as slowly as when the infant had first been trained to recognize it. When presented with a reminder twenty and twenty-seven days after training, an infant could recognize the training mobile forty-one days after training. Moreover, as an infant becomes older, retrieval becomes a much faster process. If a reminder is given for a training mobile that was first seen at six months, the training mobile is fully recognized four hours later. By the time a child is a year old, reactivation, or priming, takes less than a second (Hildreth and

Rovee-Collier, 1999). The extraordinarily long time to reactivate a three-month-old infant's memory after a retention interval of more than a week makes it clear that merely matching perceptual representation with a representation in memory is not sufficient to produce recognition, since this must have occurred when the reminder mobile was shown to the infant. The recognition response of the response node in semantic memory, which occurred three days later, is distinct from the match itself.

11.2 Continuous dual processes

Depending on the circumstances, you can make a variety of recognition judgments of varying degrees of specificity about when, where, and how often you have seen something beforehand. You can make a generic or identity judgment of an object (Chapter 7) – for example, "That's a jacket," or "That's my jacket." You can make a **familiarity judgment** about an object – for example, "I've seen you in that jacket before." You can make a **recency judgment** about an object (Chapter 10) – for example, "I just saw that jacket." You can **recollect** an **episode** – for example, "You wore that jacket when you came in."

There are three kinds of information generated by the recognition process on which these judgments are based. First, semantic information tells you what something is – that is, it makes a generic or identity judgment possible. Second, contextual information tells you that you have seen something previously – that is, it produces a **familiarity response**. So a penny looks familiar. Third, as described in Chapter 10, temporal order information from instrumental memory lets you know whether you have just seen or done something – that is, it produces a recency response. When channel-surfing, you recognize the shows you have just seen.

As discussed in Chapter 2, to control behavior, the instrumental system must keep track of a sequence of perceptual targets and the corresponding actions. When searching for something it is necessary to keep searching new locations and not search the same locations over and over. The instrumental system keeps track of targets by encoding a temporal tag with the episode containing the action. The activation of the tag declines over time; hence, its activation indicates how far back in the sequence of events it occurred. When a target is repeated, its temporal ordering is perceived as **recency**. The perirhinal cortex, adjacent to the hippocampus (Figure 11.6), is the part of the instrumental system that initially encodes recency (Suzuki and Naya, 2014) and transmits it to the prefrontal cortex. It responds to the repetition of a target, and the response declines over time. Recall from Chapter 10 that, in immediate list recall, the last four items are recalled first and with a high degree of probability of being recalled (the recency effect).

Recency and recollection provide alternative sources of information for making a recognition judgment. Experiments designed to isolate the effect of recency present targets at rates faster than one target per second. This provides insufficient time for encoding, hence subsequently recollecting, many details of the targets, thus requiring a subject on which to base recognition judgments on the perceived recency of the test item. When targets rarely repeat, the perception of recency is a useful indicator of which of two targets has occurred more recently. However, when members of the same small set of targets are repeatedly perceived, recency differences among them are reduced, so determining which one has occurred most recently becomes more difficult.

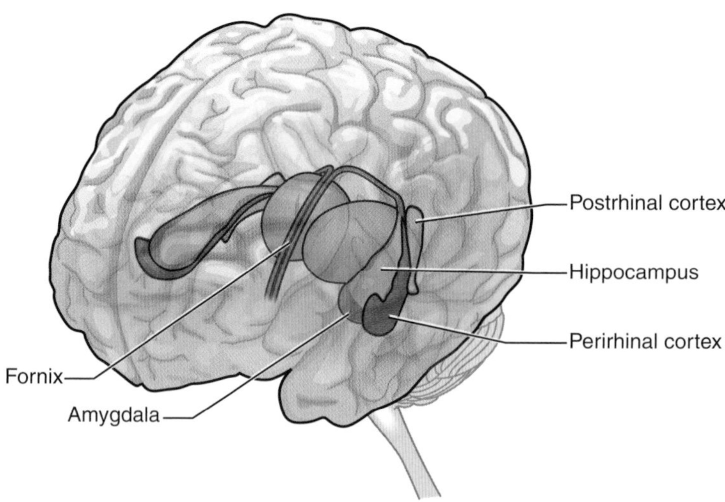

Figure 11.6 The perirhinal cortex is the part of the instrumental system that encodes recency (Suzuki and Naya, 2014).

Repeated targets

Consider the tasks shown in Figure 11.7. A simple study visual display is shown for a quarter of a second, followed by a blank inter-stimulus interval (**ISI**) for nine-tenths of a second, followed by a test display. The task is to determine whether the study display can be remembered accurately for less than a second in sufficient detail to notice whether the test stimulus display contains a difference. Four versions of the task are shown in Figure 11.7. In one version of the task the study and test displays have the same number of elements. In another version of the task the test display corresponds to only a part of the study display, so a part-to-whole comparison is made. The displays are typically meaningless novel spatial arrays of simple forms such as lines or circles. Both black and white and colored displays have been used. This does not seem like a difficult task, but when the items in the visual displays are all selected from the same small set of items – such as a small set of colored shapes – the specific items that comprise each successive test display can be retained only over the brief retention interval through rehearsal. Performance rapidly deteriorates over the first few trials, and only three or four features are recognized from the most recently presented display over an inter-stimulus interval of less than a second (Luck and Vogel, 1997; Oberauer, 2002). The effect of the earlier trials on the later trial is called proactive interference (**PI**). The amount of proactive interference in the visual comparison task is determined by two parameters: the degree of similarity among displays on successive trials (Makovski and Jiang, 2008) and the length of the interval between successive trials (Shipstead and Engle, 2013).

Similar results are found for a serial recall task called **running memory span**, in which a sequence of letter targets is presented one at a time, and the observer has to recall the order in which they were presented. There are various versions of this working memory task. Participants may strategically attempt to rehearse early targets at the expense of later targets. Therefore, a common procedure is to ask participants to recall the last seven members of a sequence of unknown length to encourage them to make the same response to each target. In one version of the task the test is verbal recall of the sequence. In another version of the task, at the end of the sequence a display containing all of the targets is presented, and the

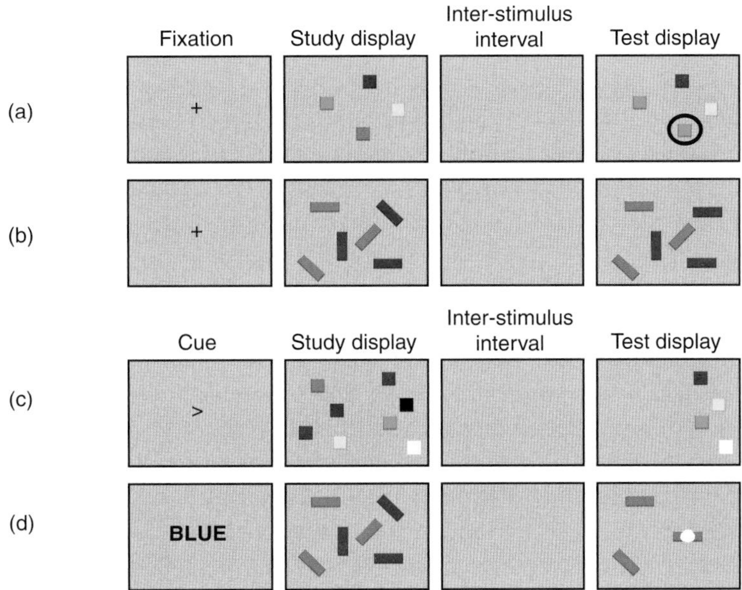

Figure 11.7 Examples of visual comparison tasks. Tasks (a) and (b) begin with fixation, which is followed by a study display, then an inter-stimulus interval (ISI). For (a) the test taker must indicate whether the encircled box in test display has changed colors. For (b) the test taker must indicate whether any box has changed its orientation. Tasks (c) and (d) begin with a cue that indicates the features defining the items in the study display that will also appear in the test display. This is followed by the study display. After ISI, the test display appears with only items with the cued feature. For (c) the test taker must indicate whether any box has changed color. For (d) the test taker must indicate whether the box with the white dot has changed orientation (Shipstead *et al.*, 2014).

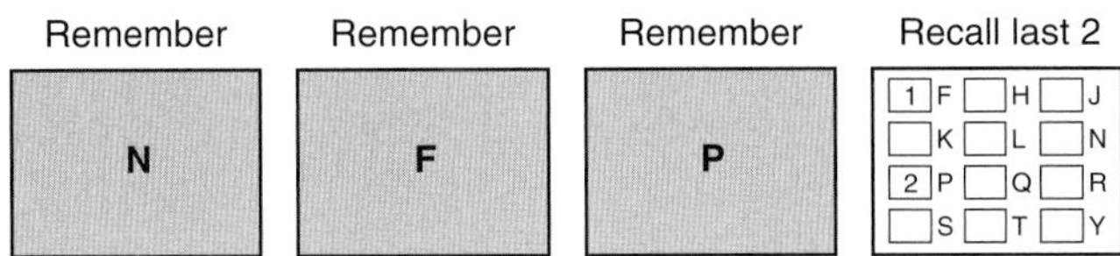

Figure 11.8 Example of the running memory span task. In this task a sequence of study items is displayed, one at a time. In this case, it is three letters. After the last item, the recall screen cues the test taker to report a recent sub-sequence of these letters. In this case it is the last 2 items (Shipstead *et al.*, 2014).

observer must mark the order in which they appear (Figure 11.8). The basic finding of running memory span tasks is only about three to four targets of the most recent sequence can be reported in the correct order. This is the limit reached by participants, who allow several items to accumulate in a single representation without attempting a response to any one item (Bunting, Cowan, and Saults, 2006).

On each successive trial the items of the test display that appeared on the immediately preceding study display must appear more recent than the items that did not appear on the immediately preceding display. Since all the items of the test display appeared on earlier study displays, it is necessary for the prefrontal cortex to inhibit the activation of the temporal tags, hence the perceived recency, derived from all study trials before the current one. The ability of the prefrontal cortex to inhibit mental activity is called attention control. An elaboration of the running span task called the **complex span** task was developed to further investigate how the prefrontal cortex inhibits competing representations. In between the presentation of each target in the sequence that the observer must remember, some other distracter task must be performed. For example, letters can alternate with addition problems in the sequence. As each addition problem appears, the participant must respond with the answer. At the end of the sequence, the observer must recall the order in which the letter targets appeared (Figure 11.9). The task measures the ability to inhibit the representations of the distracter task while building the representation of the target sequence (Unsworth and Spillers, 2010). The distracter task disrupts the perceptual target representations. Nevertheless, the instrumental system encodes the order of the targets by tagging their semantic memory representations (Unsworth and Engle, 2007; Unsworth and Spillers, 2010). So, the instrumental system can encode order at the semantic level.

Because all mental action is controlled by prefrontal inhibition, the performance of individuals on the various tasks described above, collectively called **working memory tasks**, is positively correlated with their performance on other cognitive tasks. Looking backwards, the correlations extend to selective attention, divided attention (Chapter 4), and continuous performance tasks (Chapter 5). Looking forwards, they extend to measures of intelligence (Shipstead *et al.*, 2014), which will be discussed in Chapter 14.

Novel targets

Endress and Potter (2014) used the RSVP task (Chapter 7) to compare retention of novel versus repeated targets. In three experiments, on each trial, participants saw a sequence of pictures of familiar everyday objects at a rate of a quarter of a second per picture. As shown in Figure 11.10, the sequences contained seven, twelve, or seventeen pictures in experiment 1, five, eleven, or twenty-one pictures in experiment 2, and twenty-five, fifty, or 100 pictures in experiment 3. Participants completed sixty trials per sequence size in experiments 1 and 2 and twelve trials per sequence size in experiment 3. Then, 1.7 seconds after the end of a

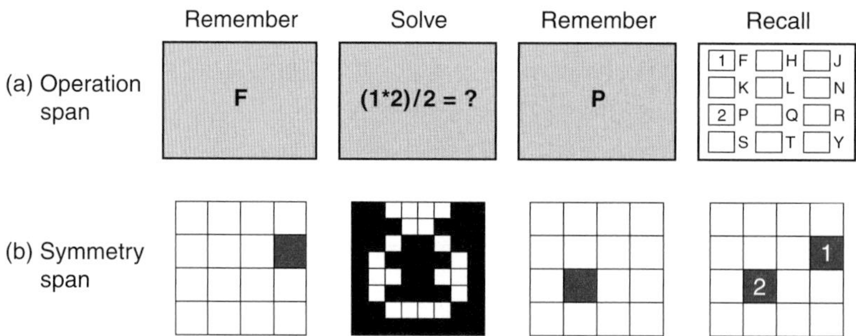

Figure 11.9 Examples of complex span tasks. Operation span (a) presents a letter, then requires a participant to solve a simple mathematical equation. After several such pairings, the test taker uses the "recall" screen to indicate the letters that had been presented, in the order that they were originally presented. The symmetry span (b) presents a spatial location on a grid, followed by a picture that must be judged as symmetrical or asymmetrical. Following several such pairings, the test taker uses the "recall" screen to indicate which locations had been presented, in the order that they were originally presented (Shipstead *et al.*, 2014).

sequence, an observer was shown a single test picture for four-fifths of a second and had to decide whether it had been presented in the sequence. On half the trials, it had been. From the percentage of times that an observer was able to recognize a target picture it was possible to compute the percentage of pictures in the sequence that had been retained at test. If the target was always recognized, it implied that all the pictures were retained; if the target was recognized half the time, it implied that half the pictures were retained; and so on. Furthermore, from the percentage of pictures retained and the number of pictures in the sequence it was possible to compute the number of pictures in the sequence that had been retained at test. For example, if a target picture were recognized half the time, this would imply that two or three pictures of a sequence of five were retained, three or four pictures of a sequence of seven were retained, and six pictures of a sequence of twelve were retained. The results are shown in Figure 11.10. Experiments 1 and 2 contained both a unique condition and a repeated condition. In the *unique* condition, all pictures were unique and were encountered only once in the experiment. In the *repeated* condition, the pictures on each sequence were selected from the same set of twenty-two pictures; participants thus saw the same pictures repeatedly across trials. A distracter at the end of a sequence was a picture from the set of twenty-two that had last been shown on an earlier trial. As shown in Figure 11.10, in the *repeated* condition, the number of pictures retained never reached five, which is consistent with the other studies using repeated items mentioned below. However, in the *unique* condition, in which proactive inhibition was low, the number of pictures retained reached thirty out of 100. Alternatively, the percentage retained was about 60 percent for sequences of five to seven pictures, 40 percent for sequences of twelve to fifty pictures, and 30 percent for a sequence of 100 pictures. The lower percentage of pictures recognized for longer sequences indicates that proactive interference from viewing earlier pictures affected recognition.

When an observer has more time to encode each picture, proactive interference from earlier pictures has less effect on its retention. Endress and Potter (2014) presented each picture for only a quarter of a second and found only 30 percent recognition for a sequence of 100 pictures. Brady *et al.* (2008) had subjects perform a continuous recognition task in which the observer saw a sequence of 2,896 pictures of familiar pictures at the rate of one picture every 3.8 seconds and had to indicate when a picture had been presented before. As shown

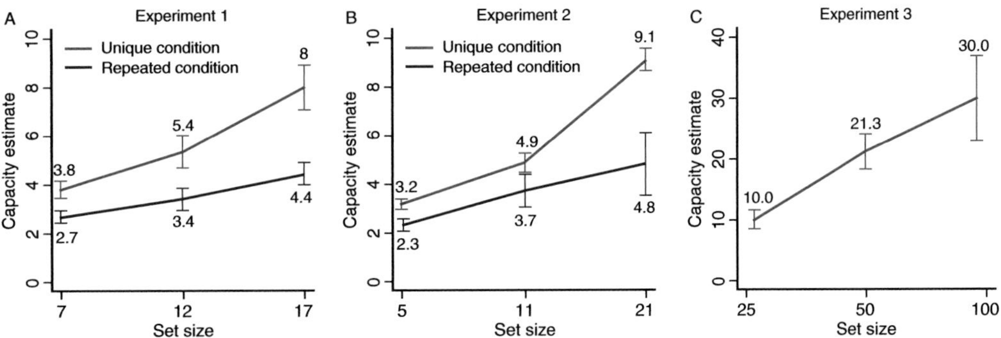

Figure 11.10 The number of items retained from a sequence of pictures of familiar objects presented at the rate of four pictures per second in three experiments in which study set size was varied. The red lines represent a sequence of pictures unique to that sequence and the blue lines represent a sequence of pictures that had appeared on previous sequences. Error bars represent the standard error of the mean (Endress and Potter, 2014).

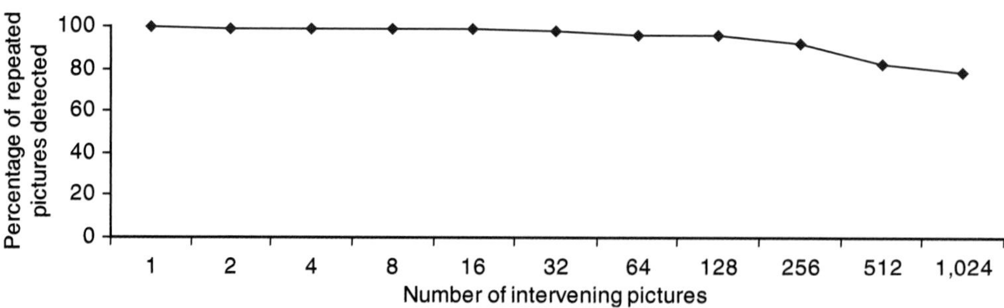

Figure 11.11 The number of intervening pictures has little effect on recognition of a repeated picture in a continuous recognition task (Brady *et al.*, 2008).

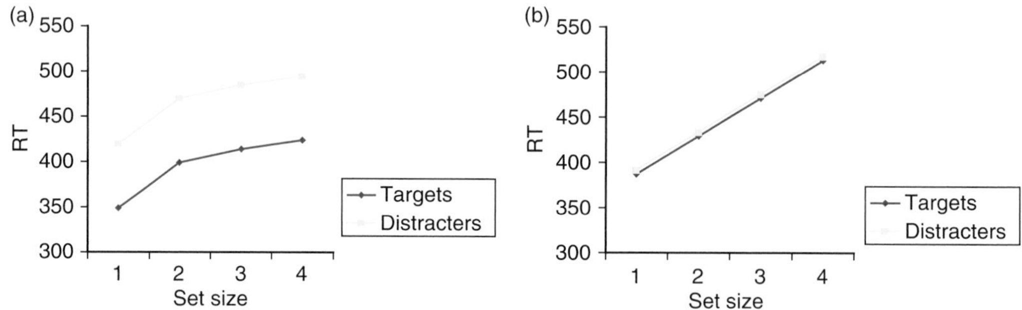

Figure 11.12 The effect of study set size on response times to targets and distracters in the varied category set condition (a) and the repeated category set condition (b) (Glass, 1993).

in Figure 11.11, after 128 intervening pictures recognition was still 96 percent, and even after 1,024 pictures recognition still stood at 79 percent.

Reaction time. Even when study times are long enough to ensure that there is short-term recollection, hence recognition, of every list item, the effect of recency on the recognition can be measured. Recency causes faster recognition than recollection does. Glass (1993) used a simple recognition task, introduced by Sternberg (1966), to measure the effect of recency on reaction time. On each trial an observer saw a set of from one to four letters or numbers and then a single test item. The study set consisted of either letters randomly drawn from the first ten in the alphabet, letters drawn from among the last ten in the alphabet, or digits. In the varied category set condition the category of set items was varied so that items from the same category were presented only once every third trial; beginning alphabet set, end of alphabet set, and digit set trials would be repeated in this order throughout the experiment. Response times as a function of study set size for targets and distracters are shown in Figure 11.12 (a) As shown in the figure, the increase in response time asymptotes at a study set size of four. This result indicates that an observer did not have to compare the test item with the study set one item at a time. Instead, it was possible to make a judgment of the test item's perceived recency, and this was only slightly affected by the size of the study set. Short-term recency judgments (over minutes) require unimpaired frontal lobe functioning. Milner (1995) showed that prefrontal damage impairs recency judgments. Patients with frontal damage who saw a sequence of pictures and then had to judge which of a pair had been seen more recently performed more poorly than patients with temporal damage (Milner, Corsi, and Leonard, 1991).

Recollection of a sequence. In the repeated category set condition of Glass's (1993) experiment, the category of set items was kept the same over a long sequence of trials. In the first third of the experiment all study sets were randomly drawn from the beginning of the alphabet; in the middle third of the experiment all study sets were randomly drawn from the end of the alphabet, and in the final third all study sets were randomly drawn from digits. As mentioned above, the amount of proactive interference in the visual comparison task is determined by two factors: the degree of similarity among displays on successive trials and the length of the interval between successive trials. When every study set was a subset of the same small set of items, the recency of an item was the same whether it was a target or distracter, because in either case it had been presented on many earlier trials. Consequently, the only way to determine whether the test item was a target or a distracter was to generate the most recent study set and compare it with the test item. The habit system generates a sequence of set items one item at at time (Checkosky and Baboorian, 1972). Response times as a function of study set size for targets and distracters are shown in Figure 11.12 (b). As shown in the figure, response time is a linear function of study set size, indicating that the study set was recollected one item at a time.

Familiarity and frequency judgments. Unlike short-term perceptual recency effects within the instrumental system, frequency is a long-term effect of experience involving recollection by the habit system. The more contexts that a representation is associated with, the more familiar the matching input appears. Since frequency influences familiarity, people base their frequency judgment on a feeling of familiarity (Harris, Begg, and Mitterer, 1980). Hasher and Chromiak (1977) found that students in the second, fourth, and sixth years and in college were only slightly more accurate at estimating the frequencies of words that appeared in a sequence when they were told they would have to make frequency judgments before viewing the sequence, suggesting that frequency information was accumulated in either case. Greene (1984) found that frequency judgments by college students were equally accurate regardless of whether the subjects were led to expect that they would have to make frequency judgments about words or simply that they would be given an unspecified memory test.

Word recognition. As mentioned in the subheading of this section, dual perceptual and semantic processing resulting in recency and recollection is called the dual-process model of recognition. In a normal recognition task, when an observer takes as much time as required to make a recognition response, recollection and recency are integrated within a single pathway for a single response node with a single criterion. Nevertheless, their separate effects on recognition can be distinguished by measuring the effects of different variables on different versions of the recognition task. Recall that recollection requires time (Checkosky and Baboorian, 1972), so forcing someone to make a rapid recognition response decreases the role of recollection, necessarily increasing the role of recency. In addition, when study items are pairs of unrelated words, recognizing the entire word pair requires recollection of the study pair (called **associative memory**) but recognizing a single word from the pair can be made on the basis of its perceived recency from its recent presentation. When the effects of the details of the study and test tasks on recognition are measured, a double dissociation is observed. Those study and test factors that affect recollection have their greatest effects on tasks in which the role of recollection is greatest – for example, associative memory – and those study and test factors that affect perception, hence recency, have their greatest effects on tasks in which the role of recency is greatest – for example, speeded recognition (Diana *et al.*, 2006; Yonelinas, 2002).

The effects of several task factors indicate the role of recollection in recognition. The recognition of low-frequency words is better than the recognition of high-frequency words whether the words appear in homogeneous or mixed-frequency lists (Chalmers, Humphreys, and Dennis, 1997; MacLeod and Kampe, 1996). Low-frequency words are perceived as more novel than higher-frequency words and so are more likely to be encoded in the episode representing the experience of learning the study list (Maddox and Estes, 1997). Consequently, at test a low-frequency word target is more likely to serve as a recollection cue for the episode for the study list. Furthermore, since recollection takes time, when recognition judgments were made under time pressure (500 to 800 milliseconds), there was no difference in hit rate for low-frequency and high-frequency words (Balota *et al.*, 2002; Joordens and Hockley, 2000). Furthermore, when study items were pairs of words, and distracters at test included two words from different study pairs, Rotello and Heit (2000) showed that incorrect responses to repaired items were greater under time pressure, presumably because participants had insufficient time to recollect the entire study pair.

Another way to ultimately affect recollection is to directly limit encoding. When Hirshman *et al.* (2002) reduced learning of the study words by administering the amnesia-producing drug Midazolam during study, the difference in hit rates between high- and low-frequency words was eliminated. Moreover, having subjects perform a distracter task along with the study task reduced the opportunity to encode, hence subsequently recollect, details of the target and its context. It had larger disruptive effects on memory of word voice tasks and word location tasks that required recollection than on recognition of the target, for which perceived recency is sufficient (Troyer *et al.*, 1999).

The effects of several other task factors indicate the role of recency in recognition. When subjects studied pairs of words, briefly flashing a word just prior to presenting it in a recognition test, visually presenting a word more clearly than other words in a test, revealing a word letter by letter compared to presenting the entire word, or presenting a word in a conceptually predictive compared to unrelated context, which all affect perception, hence perceived recency, influenced the recognition of individual study words but not of the entire study word pair (Cameron and Hockley, 2000). In addition, changing the perceptual modality of study items versus test items, hence reducing the perceived recency of targets, had larger effects on speeded compared with non-speeded tests (Toth, 1996). Finally, across thirty-two intervening items in a continuous recognition test, recognition memory for single items decreased significantly, whereas memory for associative recognition remained unchanged (Hockley, 1992), suggesting that recency, but not recollection, decreased across these delays. A similar pattern of disproportional forgetting for item recognition compared to associative recognition was also seen in procedures in which a study list is followed by a separate test list (Hockley, 1992).

Remember versus know judgments. Finally, people can distinguish between perceiving that something has just been seen from recollecting the context in which it has appeared. Tulving (1985) asked people making recognition judgments to categorize their recognition judgments into *remember* and *know* judgments. Gardiner (1988) suggested that people call recognition responses based on recollection *remember* judgments and recognition responses based only on recency *know* judgments. Alternatively, Donaldson (1996) suggested that people call high-confidence recognition responses *remember* judgments and low-confidence recognition responses *know* judgments. Low-confidence judgments are predominantly *know* judgments, so confidence does play a role in how recognition judgments are categorized. However, high-confidence recognition responses include both *remember* and *know* judgments. Furthermore, for equally high-confidence remember and know judgments, remember judgments are associated with more recollected information (Wixted and Mickes, 2010).

11.3 Hits versus false alarms

The head of Columbia Pictures movie studios, Harry Cohen, explained his negativity by saying that two-thirds of the ideas presented to him were terrible, so if he said "No" to everything he would be correct two-thirds of the time. Cohen unintentionally illustrated the fundamental insight of signal detection theory: his decision strategy provided no evidence of an ability to discriminate good ideas from bad ones. Using his strategy, he could honestly say that he rejected 100 percent of the bad ideas offered to him, of course ignoring the fact that he rejected 100 percent of the good ideas as well. The fundamental insight of signal detection theory is that, to determine whether someone can discriminate between two alternatives, two independent pieces of information are required.

Suppose you show two individuals ten pictures of people they went to high school with and ask them which they recognize. One individual selects eight pictures and the other selects four pictures. Does this mean that the individual who selected eight pictures performed better at recognition than the individual who selected four pictures? Does this mean that either individual can recognize anyone at all? In fact, this task provides no information that either individual can recognize any of his or her high school classmates. To determine whether they can, it is also necessary to include ten pictures of people they did not go to high school with. Correctly selecting the picture of a person who went to school with you is called a **hit**. Incorrectly selecting the picture of someone who did not go to high school with you is called a **false alarm**. If the person who had eight hits had no false alarms and the person who had four hits had one false alarm then the person who had eight hits (and no false alarms) was indeed better at recognizing old classmates than the person with four hits (and one false alarm). However, if the person who had eight hits also had eight false alarms and the person with four hits had four false alarms then neither individual could recognize any classmates. It was just that one individual chose to guess more often than the other.

The application of signal detection theory has been absolutely essential to describing and explaining recognition performance. This is because recognition is a continuous variable rather than an all-or-none variable. If you look at your high school yearbook and you went to a large high school, some faces will be familiar, some faces will be slightly familiar, and some faces will be unfamiliar. If you look at another high school yearbook, some faces will be at least slightly familiar, because they look like (though they are not) people you know. So, when the pictures from the two yearbooks are mixed together, you will not be able to select everyone in your old high school without making some false alarms as well. Thus, when recognition is based on a continous variable such as familiarity, not only a person's hit rate – the percentage of targets selected – but also the false alarm rate – the percentage of distracters selected – must be considered. When the hit rate is greater than the false rate, the observer has sorted old from new.

The results of a continuous recognition task performed by Konkle *et al.* (2010) demonstrated how recognition is influenced by the similarity among targets and distracters. The experiment was similar to that of Brady *et al.* (2008) mentioned above and made use of many of the same pictures. They had subjects perform a continuous recognition task in which the observer saw a sequence of 2,800 pictures of familiar objects at the rate of one picture every 3.8 seconds and had to indicate when a picture had been presented before. In the experiment of Brady *et al.* every object came from a different category, so when participants saw a picture of a television remote they had only to decide whether they had seen a picture of a television remote in the sequence. In contrast, in Konkle *et al.*'s experiment a sequence contained pictures showing different instances of the same category. So, when participants saw a picture of a television remote, they had to decide whether they had seen a picture of *that* television remote in the sequence. This was a more difficult recognition task. The participants made fewer hits (compare Figure 11.13 with Figure 11.11) and more false alarms (4 percent versus 1 percent) than in Brady *et al.*'s experiment. Figure 11.13 (b)

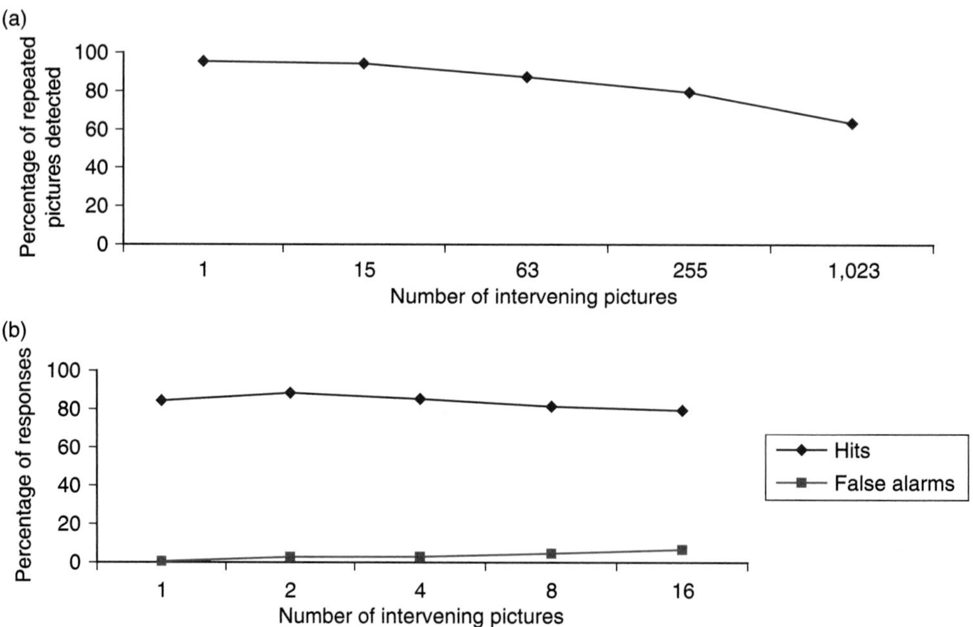

Figure 11.13 When distracters are similar, the percentage of repeated pictures detected declines as a function of the number of intervening pictures in a continuous recognition task (a). The hit rate declines and the false alarm rate increases as a function of the number of intervening pictures of similar objects (b) (Konkle *et al.*, 2010).

shows that the hit rate decreased and the false alarms increased as a function of the number of category instances previously seen.

If a test item appears more or less familiar, the observer must establish some criterion level of familiarity above which to respond that it has been seen beforehand. Recall from above the two hypothetical individuals who had to select pictures of former classmates. Someone who selects sixteen pictures from a pile of twenty had a more lenient familiarity criterion for recognition than someone who selects only eight pictures from the pile. To separate

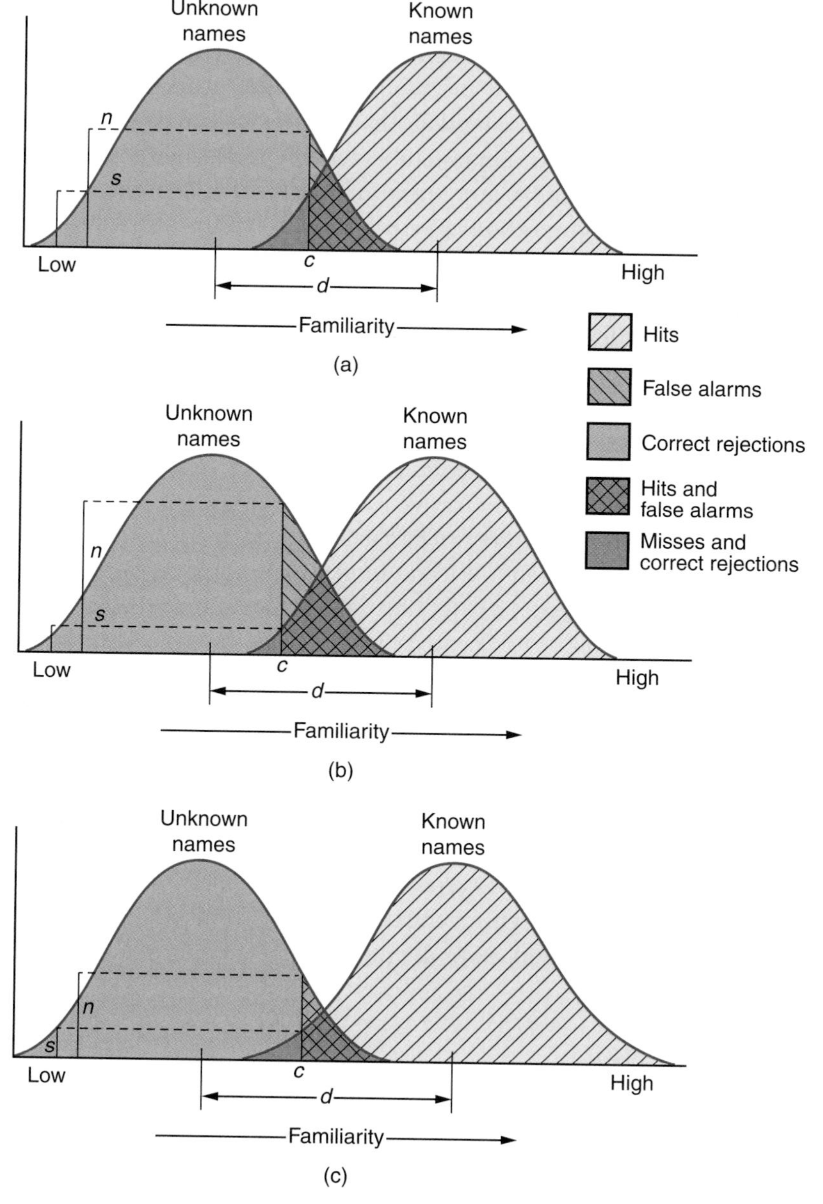

Figure 11.14 Signal detection analysis of two possible effects of extended study time on recognition: (a) baseline; (b) criterion shift; (c) increase in recency.

people's criterion from their sensitivity to familiarity, they may be asked to assign confidence ratings – such as certain, probability, just guessing – to their decisions. Then, by using the mathematical **theory of signal detection** (Banks, 1970; Swets, Tanner, and Birdsall, 1961), both how sensitive they are to differences between targets and distracters and their criterion for calling an item a target may be computed.

Figure 11.14 (a) shows how the ability to discriminate targets from distracters and the criterion used to identify a target are represented in signal detection theory. Figure 11.14 (a) shows the distributions of familiarity values for new and repeated pictures in the continuous recognition task described above. Both distributions are bell-shaped (a form that will be familiar to you if you have taken a statistics course). The familiarity distribution for repeated pictures is to the right of that for new pictures because the repeated pictures tended to be perceived as more familiar. However, the two distributions overlap, indicating that some new pictures were perceived as more familiar than some repeated pictures. In this situation perfect performance is impossible. Suppose obervers set a criterion at point c and respond "old" to all pictures more familiar and "new" for features less familiar. The shadings in Figure 11.14 (a) indicate the proportion of responses that will be of the four types logically possible: hits (correct responses to repeated pictures), correct rejections (no response to new pictures), misses (failure to respond to a repeated picture), and false alarms (an incorrect "old" response to a new picture).

Suppose that the speed of picture presentation in the continuous recognition task was slowed, giving an observer more time to view each picture. Figures 11.14 (b) and (c) illustrate two possible ways that giving a person more time might increase the proportion of hits. Figure 11.14 (b) depicts a pure criterion shift. The additional viewing time does not make the repeated pictures more familiar but makes viewers more confident, so they shift their criterion. The familiarity distributions are unchanged from those in Figure 11.14 (a), therefore, but the criterion c has been shifted to a lower level. The result is an increase in hits but also in false alarms. In contrast, Figure 11.14 (c) illustrates a pure change in sensitivity. The additional viewing time does make the repeated pictures more familiar. The criterion c is set at the same point as in Figure 11.14 (a), but the familiarity distribution for repeated pictures has been shifted to the right. As a result, the proportion of hits increases without any accompanying increase in false alarms.

In signal detection theory, difference in familiarity between the new and repeated pictures is measured by the distance between the means of the two distributions, which is called **d′**, and this distance can be calculated from the hit and false alarm rates. The criterion for identifying a picture as repeated is measured by the ratio of the height of the target distribution to the height of the distracter distribution at the criterion, a ratio that is called **ß** (Greek letter beta). Both d′ and ß can be computed from the hit and false alarm rates.

Eyewitnesses and lineups

One important application of signal detection theory is human eyewitness testimony. A person's expectations influence the level at which the criterion for recognition is set. If you expect to see your cousin at Thanksgiving dinner and you see someone similar to your cousin but radically different in weight, hair color, etc., the correct greeting is not "Who are you?" but "You look great!" More generally, people do not fail to recognize friends and places visited routinely or family and homes visited less often, so the high degree of confidence that people have in their recognition judgments is justified. However, in most ordinary recognition decisions it is someone or something familiar that is being recognized. Recall that Bruce (1982) found that recognition was considerably better for familiar than for other unfamiliar faces. In ordinary life it is the familiar people around you that you must recognize, so poor recognition for unfamiliar faces is not relevant. However, the one special circumstance in which an unfamiliar face must be recognized is when an eyewitness must select a perpetrator from a lineup. In this case the probability of a false alarm, calling a stranger the perpetrator, is of more than academic interest. The fundamental fairness of the criminal justice system requires that the false alarm rate be negligible. To study the accuracy of eyewitness identification, a crime wave hit psychology classrooms in the 1980s that has not abated to this day. In an influential study, students were assembled in a large lecture hall for a biofeedback demonstration (Malpass and Devine, 1981). During a pause in the demonstration a man entered the room, spoke with the instructor, and was asked to wait next to a rack of the apparatus. Instead, the man repeatedly changed settings on the rack, though asked by the instructor, with increasing anger, not to. The man responded to the last of these requests by shouting an obscenity, pushing the electronic rack to the floor, and escaping through a rear door. He had been visible to the audience for eighty-five seconds. Twenty minutes after the vandalism a state police officer arrived and interviewed faculty members and a few persons who were seated close to the vandalism. The audience was then told that the vandalism had been staged and that the vandal was a confederate of the investigators. Members of the audience were asked to volunteer to attend one of the lineups to be held on the following three evenings; 100 witnesses (seventy-four women, twenty-six men) appeared to view these lineups.

The lineup contained five individuals who were similar in height, body build, hair color and style, and dress. Two instructions, biased and unbiased, were given. The biased instructions read: "We believe that the person who pushed over the electronics equipment during the EEG demonstration is present in the lineup. Look carefully at each of the five individuals in the lineup. Which of these is the person you saw push over the equipment? Circle the number of his position in the lineup below." The eyewitnesses receiving this instruction were provided with five numbers (1 to 5) from which they could choose. Witnesses who wished to reject all five of the persons in the lineup had to ask how to indicate their judgment because no place was provided for such a response. Those witnesses who did ask were told that "if you believe that the vandal is not one of the people in the lineup, write that on the identification form." The unbiased instructions, however, explicitly provided the witnesses with a "No choice" option. It read: "The person who pushed over the electronics equipment during the EEG demonstration may be one of the five individuals in the lineup. It is also possible that he is not in the lineup. Look carefully at each of the five individuals in the lineup. If the person you saw push over the equipment is not in the lineup, circle 0. If the person is present in the lineup, circle the number of his position." The witnesses receiving this instruction were provided with six numbers from which to choose (0 to 5). On every other trial the perpetrator was absent and his place in the lineup was taken by a stand-in.

The lineup identifications under the various conditions are shown in Table 11.3. Under biased instructions, the misidentification rate was 78 percent when the perpetrator was absent and 25 percent when the perpetrator was present. Under unbiased instructions, the misidentification rate was 33 percent when the perpetrator was absent and 0 percent when

TABLE 11.3 Percentage of identifications for lineups with perpetrator present and absent under biased and unbiased instructions

	Perpetrator present		Perpetrator absent	
	Biased instructions	**Unbiased instructions**	**Biased instructions**	**Unbiased instructions**
Perpetrator	75	83		
Other lineup member	25	0	78	33
No choice	0	17	22	67

the perpetrator was present. With the perpetrator present under biased instructions all errors were false identifications, whereas under unbiased instructions all errors were failed recognitions. Confidence and accuracy were not related. When the instructions were unbiased and the perpetrator was actually present in the lineup, eyewitness identifications were reliable. However, even under unbiased instructions, if the perpetrator was not present in the lineup there was a 33 percent chance of a false identification. These results demonstrate how causing a witness to adopt a more lenient criterion through biased instructions can greatly increase the probability of a false identification.

Furthermore, face recognition is easily disrupted through disguise. Even just a hat and glasses influence recognition. Mansour *et al.* (2012) showed students a video of someone discussing a planned bank robbery, a planned burglary, or a plot to murder someone. The person was undisguised, wearing a soft brimless cap called a toque, wearing glasses, or wearing both a toque and glasses (Figure 11.15). Afterwards the witness saw a photo lineup of six pictures of undisguised individuals, presented either simultaneously or sequentially. When a photo of the person in the video was not in the lineup, false alarms were slightly higher with simultaneous presentation than with sequential presentation. When a photo of the person in the video was in the lineup, performance was better with simultaneous presentation than with sequential presentation. With simultaneous presentation, the undisguised individual was recognized 94 percent of the time, an individual wearing the cap was recognized 82 percent of the time, an individual wearing glasses was recognized 73 percent of the time, and an individual wearing both the cap and glasses was recognized 59 percent of the time.

Signal detection theory provides the framework for describing how the similarity of distracters and the instructions influence eyewitness performance when viewing a lineup. Instructions that cause shifts in criterion necessarily increase or decrease both hits and false alarms (Clark, Moreland, and Gronlund, 2014). In addition, a small detail of the testing procedure can influence the criterion, hence the probability of a false alarm. Some studies of photo lineups found more false alarms with simultaneous than with sequential presentation (Lindsay and Bellinger, 1999; Lindsay and Wells, 1985). In the case of lineups, the police already have a perpetrator in mind. Otherwise, an eyewitness may be asked to look through photos from a "mug book" in order to provide the police with investigative leads. When Stewart and McAllister (2001) compared one-at-a-time presentation to presentation of mug book photos in groups of twelve, they found fewer

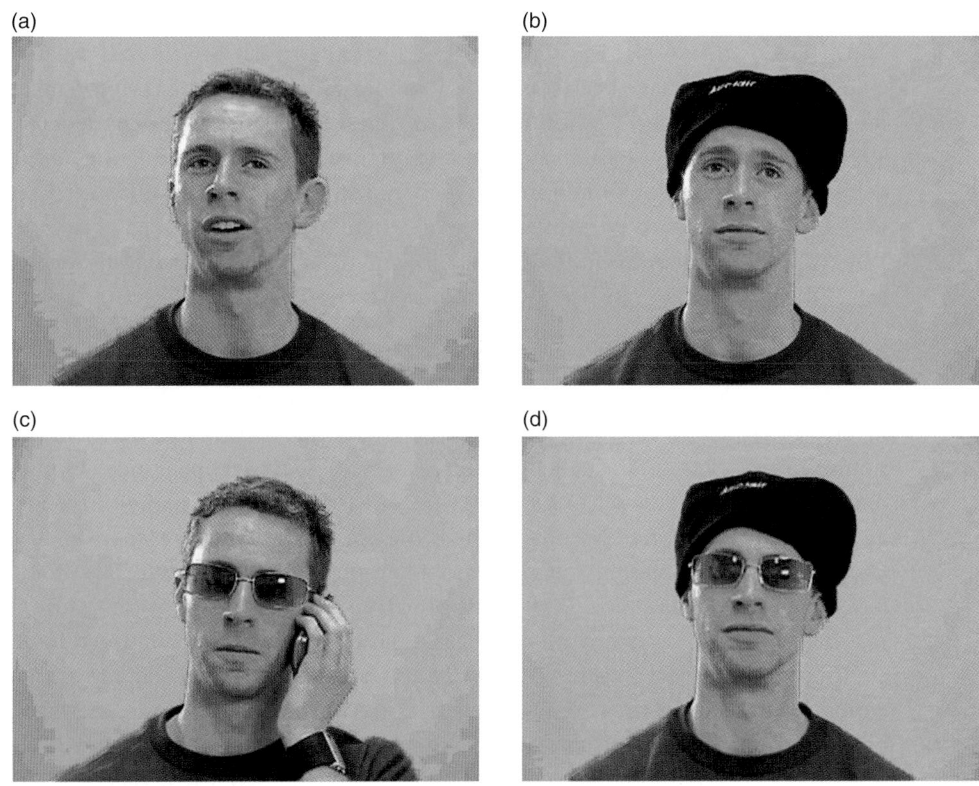

Figure 11.15 Examples of stimuli from experiment of (Mansour *et al*., 2012): (a) no disguise; (b) toque only disguise; (c) sunglasses only disguise; (d) toque and sunglasses disguise.

false alarms when the pictures were presented in groups. Eyewitnesses shown the pictures in groups tended to pick no more than one per page, but eyewitnesses shown the photos individually would say "Maybe" to photos less than twelve apart, resulting in the higher false alarm rate for individual presentation. The different results for photo lineups and mug books demonstrate how procedural details can influence recognition judgments, and the importance to the criminal justice system of understanding these details.

11.4 Delusions

In normal cognitive functioning, emotional, recency, and semantic information collects in the prefrontal cortex and then a recognition response is made. The feeling of knowing that characterizes the recognition response is based on the emotional, recency, and semantic information indicating how similar the target is to a representation in memory. However, the feeling of knowing is not the same as this information. In a variety of rare delusions, the perceived familiarity or novelty of a perceptual target becomes completely dissociated from the degree to which the perceptual target matches a representation in semantic memory.

These various delusions may occur in isolation or in combination (Hudson and Grace, 2000). The delusions also vary in severity. The patient may believe that a person or persons close to him or her have been replaced by robots (Silva and Leong, 1995). The delusions may result from brain injury (Box, Laing, and Kopelman, 1999), from schizophrenia (Edelstyn *et al.*, 1996; Oyebode *et al.*, 1998), or from mania (McEvedy, Hendry, and Barnes, 1996). When the delusion is the result of a brain injury, such as a stroke or head trauma as the result of an automobile accident, it usually dissipates over several weeks (Box, Laing, and Kopelman, 1999). When the delusion is associated with a psychiatric disorder it is usually alleviated by antipsychotic medication. The disorders result from an impairment in prefrontal functioning.

In **Capgras delusion** a person comes to believe that an exact duplicate has replaced someone close to him. Parents, a spouse, and in one instance even a pet dog have all been believed to be replaced by duplicates in different cases of the disorder. A person with Capgras delusion may say to his or her mother that she looks exactly like his or her mother but is not his or her mother. The belief is often restricted to visual appearance. Ramachandran (Ramachandran and Blakeslee, 1998) described a case in which a patient accepted his parents as his parents when he spoke with them on the phone, but not when he was with them. Capgras delusion is often associated with a flat, rather than a normal, emotional response to faces in general (Ellis *et al.*, 2000). **Reduplicative paramnesia** does for the home what Capgras delusion does for family members. The patient believes that a familiar location is in fact a duplicate of the real location. Hudson and Grace (2000) described a seventy-one-year-old woman who believed that her home was a duplicate of her real home. In Fregoli's syndrome patients come to believe that strangers they see are actually persons they know in disguise (Oyebode *et al.*, 1998; Edelstyn *et al.*, 1996). Of course, here the response is the opposite of that in Capgras syndrome. Perhaps the most extreme delusion is mirrored self-misidentification (Davies and Coltheart, 2000). Patients come to believe that their own reflection in the mirror is a different person who looks just like them and who silently follows them around. Patients may be aware of how odd their belief is, and quite frankly tell you that they would not believe such a story if told it by someone else. They may still remember what a mirror is and what a reflection is. Nevertheless, they may cover up the mirror in their bedroom so that the silent twin cannot look at their partner.

What all these delusions have in common is that a person's beliefs are no longer informed by perceptual or semantic information. The cognitive system representing social relations is partly independent of the semantic system. When it becomes completely separated, identity delusions result.

SUMMARY

- In a recognition task a perceptual target is compared with semantic memory and matched with one or more episodes.
- The process of recognition has distinct stages.
  - Comparison stage.
    - The level of target and contextual detail determines the specificity of the recognition response. Face recognition requires a high level of detail, so only familiar faces are recognized.

   - Response stage.
      - After the first year of life, a response occurs immediately following a match. However, in early infancy, after a long retention interval a match can take days to produce a response.
- Three responses determine the recognition judgment.
   - The target and context of the matching episode are recollected.
   - Additional matching episodes determine the familiarity response.
   - Short-term temporal order information encoded by the instrumental system is experienced as the recency response.
- The amount of recollection and familiarity and the perception of recency are all continuous variables, but recognition tasks frequently force a choice between two alternatives: old or new. As a result, a decision procedure must set a criterion so that every item with sufficient recollection and familiarity to exceed the criterion is called "old" and every item below the criterion is called "new." For short-term recognition, recency also contributes to the information compared with the criterion.
   - The person's expectations influence the level at which the criterion is set.
   - The theory of signal detection compares hits (correct recognitions) with false alarms as a means of separately measuring a person's ability to discriminate old targets from new distracters versus the criterion used for calling a test item "old."
   - The role of the decision criterion in recognition memory has an important application in the evaluation of eyewitness testimony. Eyewitnesses are overconfident, and the criterion is influenced by task demands.
- Delusions demonstrate that the decision stage generating the recognition judgment is distinct from the three recognition responses.

QUESTIONS

1. What are the different kinds of information that contribute to recognition?
2. Is recognition an all-or-none judgment or a continuous variable subject to a criterion?
3. According to signal detection theory, what two kinds of responses must be tabulated to measure recognition?
4. How does confidence influence eyewitness identification?
5. What is the Capgras delusion?

FURTHER READING

Konkle, T., Brady, T. F., Alvarez, G. A., and Oliva, A. (2010). Conceptual distinctiveness supports detailed visual long-term memory for real-world objects. *Journal of Experimental Psychology: General*, 139, 558–78.

Wixted, J. T., and Mickes, L. (2010). A continuous dual-process model of remember/know judgments. *Psychological Review*, 117, 1025–54.

12 Recall

Before we went to Paris, I suggested to my eight-year-old son that it would be fun to walk to the top of the Eiffel Tower. At first he was dubious, but when we got there he embraced the task with great enthusiasm. Soon he was bounding up the stairs at rapid clip, and we reached the top far in advance of the rest of our party, who waited for the elevator. Very much pleased with myself, when we returned home I asked him what he enjoyed most about the trip to Paris. He answered, unhesitatingly, "The Empire State Building."

Clearly, this was a retrieval error. It demonstrates that encoding the representation of an object or event is not sufficient to ensure an accurate memory later on. A recall task requires you to respond with information not in the question – for example, what you enjoyed best on your trip to Paris. In a recall task, the cue may be distinguished from the target response it elicits. In a question-and-answer format, the question is the cue, and the answer is the target of the recollection. In a navigation task, the goal is the cue, the location of the goal is the target, and the mental map containing the sequence of movements to the goal is the recollection.

Recall frees human thought and action from the constraints of the immediate environment. Recognition makes it possible to respond to whatever is immediately at hand (Chapter 10). However, self-cuing makes it possible to recall, hence think about, anything one has experienced.

- A recall task requires a response (answer) that is not included in the cue (question).
  - For example, "Who was the first president?" and "Name all the presidents" are recall tasks.
  - Sometimes the automatic recollection of information by the habit system is sufficient for a recall task. For example, "first president" activates "George Washington" as part of the response.
  - However, for a cue to be effective, it must be more strongly related to the information that needs to be recollected than to any other information. Retrieval failure occurs when similar targets have to be recalled, one right after the other, because there is no cue specific to any one target.
  - For many recall tasks, there must be repeated ad hoc cue generation by the instrumental system to initiate the repeated recollections necessary to fully respond to a task such as "Name all the presidents." So recall is produced through a two-stage generation and recollection process.

- In a recall task for a large number of targets, each cue may be used once and retrieves at most a small number of targets.
  - When instances of a very large category, such as animals, are retrieved, they are recalled in small clusters corresponding to distinct cues.
  - Over time fewer cues that retrieve new category members are generated, so fewer targets are retrieved.
  - Context-dependent memory is the result of the effect of environmental cues on recollection. More words can be recalled for a list when it is recalled where it is learned than are recalled in a different location. However, environmental context has no effect on recognition.
- In hierarchically organized lists, each cue uniquely retrieves two or three additional cues or targets.
  - The better that targets are organized in memory, the more targets one will be able to recall. When concepts form statements that form episodes that form stories, people can recall scores of details from a story they have heard once. Given a sufficient degree of organization, there is no limit on the number of concepts that can be recalled upon request.
  - The downside of associating information learned on different occasions in a single semantic network is losing the contextual details of when each piece of information was learned, causing source amnesia. The same associations that make a target easier to generate may make it less discriminable from distracters that may have been spontaneously generated during learning.
- When information is used to direct action, it becomes knowledge.
  - The application of information to action sometimes requires that an inference be made on the basis of an example or counterexample. When the generation of examples is incomplete, an error may be made.

12.1 Generation

The effectiveness of the cue at initiating recollection of the target depends on the specificity of the cue for the target. When the information automatically recollected in response to the cue is restricted to the target, the target has a high probability of being reported. As discussed in Chapters 3 and 6, a high degree of specificity is achieved because an area of the prefrontal cortex inhibits related representations when the target representation is activated. The area in the prefrontal cortex that inhibits distracter representations is shown in Figure 7.17, labeled "Verbal response selection." This area was identified by using a very simple recall task: saying what was done with a common object. For high-agreement objects, everyone gives the same response, such as knife – cut, but, for low-agreement objects, different people give different responses, such as pie – bake, eat, throw, etc. Both healthy individuals and individuals with damage to this area had to report the functions for objects that had high versus low levels of agreement. Low agreement across individuals implies that several of these responses are first activated by the picture and then one is selected by inhibiting the others. The individuals with damage to the selection area were not impaired in generating responses for high-agreement objects; but they were impaired at naming low-agreement objects (Thompson-Schill *et al.*, 1998).

Proactive interference

Recognizing all the members of a ten-word study sequence is easy (Chapter 10) but recalling them all is difficult (Chapter 9). The reason is retrieval failure. The learner does not have a different specific cue available within the episode describing the task for each list word, and a single cue is inadequate for all the list words. As will be discussed below, the cue *word list* is just too general.

Cue specificity in single-item recall. As discussed in Chapter 9, a list of items can be learned through rehearsal, which ultimately causes the construction of a single representation of the entire list that may be recollected through a single cue. Therefore, a distracter task is employed to prevent the learner from rehearsing so that each list item remains a distinct episode in memory. The task described here is sometimes called the Brown–Peterson paradigm, after the first investigators to perform this type of experiment (Brown, 1958; Peterson and Peterson, 1959). The task is performed as follows. A subject is presented with a consonant trigram, such as QBF. The person repeats it once and at the same time is presented with a three-digit number, such as 687. The person then has to immediately start counting backward by threes. The only purpose of the counting task is to prevent the person from rehearsing the trigram or using any other mnemonic to remember it. The counting also obliterates any temporal tag on the consonant trigram, so there is no recency effect (Chapters 9 and 10). After a specified period of time, which is usually three to eighteen seconds, the person is permitted to stop counting and is asked to recall the trigram. The series of events from the presentation of the consonant trigram until the subject is asked to recall it constitutes a single trial. A single experiment consists of many trials, with a different consonant trigram being presented on each one.

There is a lower probability of recalling the trigram on each successive trial, as shown in Figure 12.1 (Keppel and Underwood, 1962; Loess, 1964). As the figure shows, on the very first trial a person was almost certain to recall the trigram no matter how long he or she

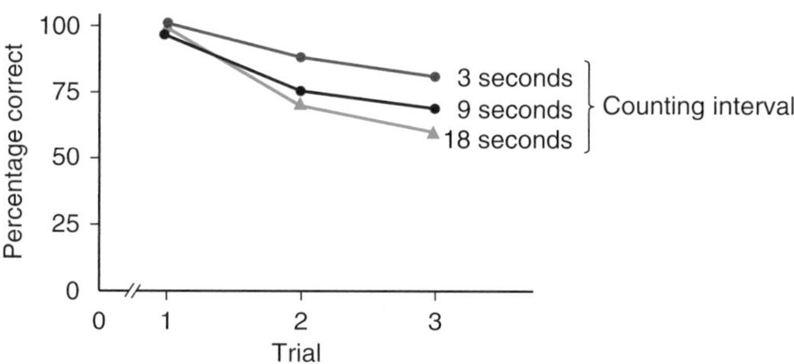

Figure 12.1 Experimental results when a distracter task follows a single study trigram. Performance deteriorates beginning with the second trial on the task (Keppel and Underwood, 1962).

first counted backwards. Virtually all the subjects who had counted backwards for three, nine, or eighteen seconds recalled their first trigram correctly. However, on the second trial performance begins to deteriorate, and performance is poorer the longer people have to count backwards before recalling the trigram. By the sixth trial, correct recall of the trigram averaged less than 50 percent after eighteen seconds of counting backwards. Consider what a really remarkable result this is. Three consonants are not very much information to remember. For example, memorizing someone's phone number, which contains seven digits, is quite easy. But the results in the distracter paradigm demonstrate that a relatively brief period of interference right at the time when a target would normally be associated with other information in memory has a very dramatic effect on later recall.

The distracter task prevents a subject from forming associations between the target and other information in memory that could serve as retrieval cues. So, when the subject is asked to recall the target at the end of the first trial, probably only one fact serves as a cue for the target: that it was a consonant trigram. However, since this association is recent and therefore strong, this one cue will probably be sufficient to generate the target. The memory structure on the first trial is depicted in Figure 12.2 (a). At the end of the second trial, when the subject has to recall the most recently presented trigram, the subject again only has a single cue: that a consonant trigram has been presented. But now the cue is associated with two recently presented trigrams, as shown in Figure 12.2 (b). As a result, there is a significant probability that, when the subject tries to use the cue to generate the trigram presented on the second trial, the trigram presented on the first trial will be generated instead. The retrieval cue has been overloaded. As the number of trials continues to increase, as Figure 12.2 (c) indicates, the recall cue will become associated with more and more trigrams, so the cue becomes increasingly useless. With each additional trial, generating the most recently presented trigram becomes more difficult. Recall from Chapter 10 that a retarding effect of earlier trials on performance is called proactive interference.

PI builds up only when items from the same category are studied on consecutive trials. If after several trials a study item from a different category is presented, recall on that trial will increase substantially. As shown in Figure 12.3, when Wickens, Born, and Allen (1963) had subjects recall consonant trigrams, there was the usual decline in recall over the first three trials. On the fourth trial half the subjects were given a digit trigram (such as 549) to recall. As Figure 12.3 shows, those subjects who were given a consonant trigram on the fourth trial continued to perform poorly, but the subjects given a digit trigram performed virtually as well as they had on the very first trial. Wickens and colleagues obtained the same result when they first presented digit trigrams and then shifted to consonants, and whether the

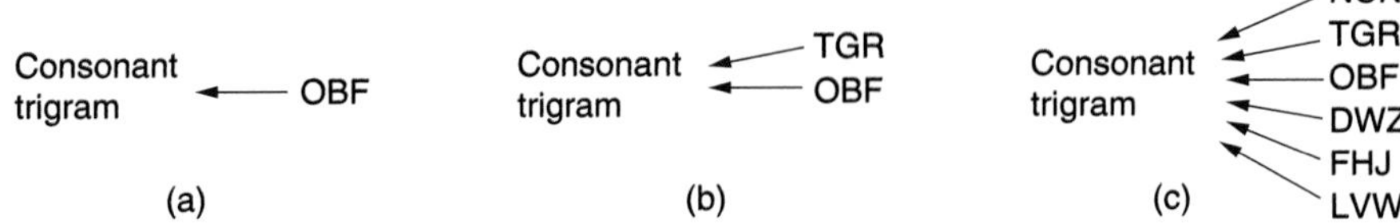

Figure 12.2 Cue target associations after one trial (a), two trials (b), and six trials (c) in the Brown–Peterson task (Keppel and Underwood, 1962).

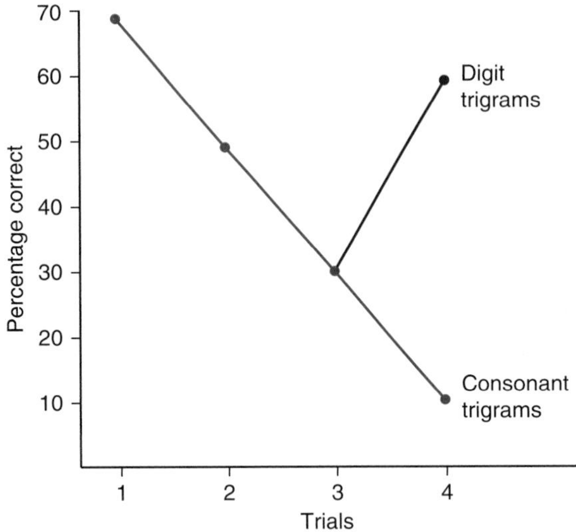

Figure 12.3 Recall in distracter paradigm. Recall deteriorates over trials, but it increases when the category of the input is changed (Wickens *et al*., 1963).

shift occurred on the fourth, seventh, or tenth trial. Performance always returned to the initial level of recall on the shift trial. In later studies Wickens (1972) showed that this effect is obtained with a wide variety of different shifts in inputs. In general, the more dissimilar the new category of targets was from the original category, the more recall improved.

A recall cue does not have to be noticed at study to be effective at recall. Gardiner, Craik, and Birtwistle (1972) demonstrated this by changing from one kind of target to another in a very subtle way and alerting the subject to the change at recall. The study was done in England, where gardening is a national hobby. Consequently, many people know the names of a great many flowers. When college students were presented with a series of trials on which the items were cultivated flowers (such as rose, carnation), followed by a critical trial on which the items were wildflowers (such as dandelion), recall did not improve. The students simply did not notice the subtle shift in category. But, when the experimenter provided the student at the time of recall on the last trial with the cue *wild*, release from PI occurred (Figure 12.4). Therefore, the critical factor causing improvement in recall seems to be the introduction of a new retrieval cue (Loftus and Patterson, 1975; Watkins and Watkins, 1975).

PI in list and category recall. The results of the Brown–Peterson paradigm demonstrate that even a just-presented trigram will not be recalled if there is not a cue for it in the subject's attempt to recall it. Furthermore, the high degree of specificity required for a cue to be

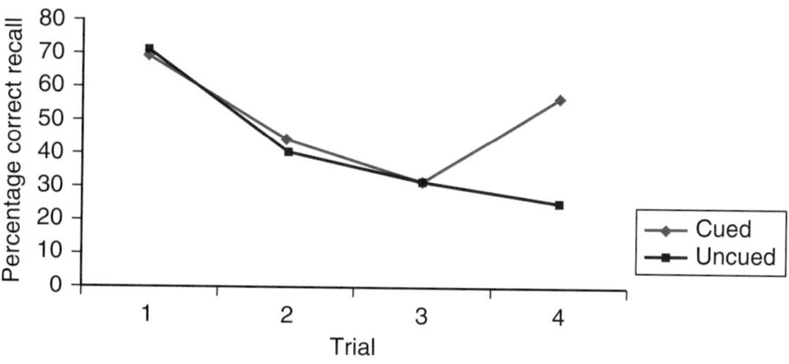

Figure 12.4 Even when the shift in category is not noticed at study, a recall cue causes release from PI (Gardiner *et al.*, 1972).

effective implies that a single cue can be effective for only a small number of targets. When we move from the recall of arbitrary list items to the recall of familiar things, the limitation on the number of items that may be generated from a single cue remains the same. Even though many Americans know the names of all fifty states, few can recall them all. The cue *state* results in the recollection of the names of only a small number of states. Furthermore, the logogens of whatever *state* names are initially recollected will have higher activation levels (Chapter 6) and so continue to be recollected to the same cue. As mentioned above, the repeated recollection of these state names will be associated with the inhibition of the names of all other states. Therefore, the cue *state*, or any cue, can be used only once.

Furthermore, once a cue has activated a target, a new cue related to both the old target and another, yet unrecalled, target will be more likely to cause recollection of the old target, because of its higher activation level. So, once a target or a distracter has been recalled, it blocks the retrieval of unrecalled targets. Brown (1968) required two groups of subjects to recall as many of the fifty states as they could. For one group he first read the names of twenty-five of the fifty states. This group naturally recalled more of the names of the twenty-five states that had been read aloud than did the group that had not heard the list. However, the former group of subjects recalled fewer of the twenty-five states that had not been read aloud than did the group that had no prior cuing. Slamecka (1968; 1969) introduced the part-list cuing paradigm for studying this effect systematically. Similarly, when people studied a list of words and were then given some of the list words and told to use them as cues to recall the remainder of the list, fewer list words not used as cues were recalled in this condition than in the condition in which subjects were not given any cues and simply told to freely recall the entire list (see also Anderson, Bjork, and Bjork, 1994; Roediger, 1978).

Release from PI through secondary recall cues. The limit on the number of responses that can be generated from a single cue places a limit on the number of similar targets that can be recalled at one time. For example, Battig and Montague (1969) asked college students to generate instances of fifty-six different categories (for example, flowers, diseases, ships, metals, toys). The students had thirty seconds to generate instances for each category. Each student was usually able to generate only five or six instances for a category within the thirty seconds. The greatest average number (eleven) of instances produced was for the category human body parts. Yet many of the categories obviously had more than 100 familiar instances (for example, female names, male names, cities).

To recall more than a few states, a person must use concepts other than *state* as recall cues. A person's knowledge of the world and cleverness in making use of this knowledge determine how many states will be recalled. One strategy might be to form a mental image of the map of the United States. Then the person could mentally scan the imaginary map and name each state as its location was encountered. Another strategy might be for the person to think of all the places he or she had visited. What both these strategies have in common is that potential targets are generated in a systematic fashion that prevents the person from using the same cues again and again. The additional recall cues are called **secondary recall cues**. When the target set is large, a person's skill at generating secondary recall cues may often be what determines how many targets are recalled (Rabinowitz, Mandler, and Patterson, 1977).

The recollection of targets from self-generated secondary recall cues during free recall produces a recall function that has four ubiquitous features. First, targets are generated in clusters of one to four items. Second, the items within a cluster are obviously related, usually semantically. Third, the interval between the generation of each cluster increases over time. Fourth, no target is ever reported more than once. For example, following Bousfield and Sedgewick (1944), Gruenewald and Lockhead (1980) gave students either fifteen or thirty minutes to generate all the instances of a category. Figure 12.5 shows that a continuous effort yields a lower and lower rate of production – that is, the curve increases less rapidly as the recall attempt progresses. Figure 12.6 shows that the instances are produced in clusters, and Figure 12.7 shows the distribution of cluster sizes. As shown in Figures 12.6 and 12.7, most clusters contain only one or two instances, but a few larger clusters are observed. As shown in Figure 12.5, the reason the rate of target production declines with time is that the rate of cluster production declines with time. As more and more targets are produced, there are fewer secondary recall cues that are most strongly related to an unrecalled target, so the person must generate more and more secondary recall cues before a new cluster is produced. As a result, the time between new clusters increases.

Because failure to free-recall list items is caused by an inability to generate secondary cues, suggesting a strategy for systematically generating secondary cues increases recall. After students saw that a study list containing 124 words could be hierarchically organized into four different categories they free-recalled the list. Then they were given the category headings

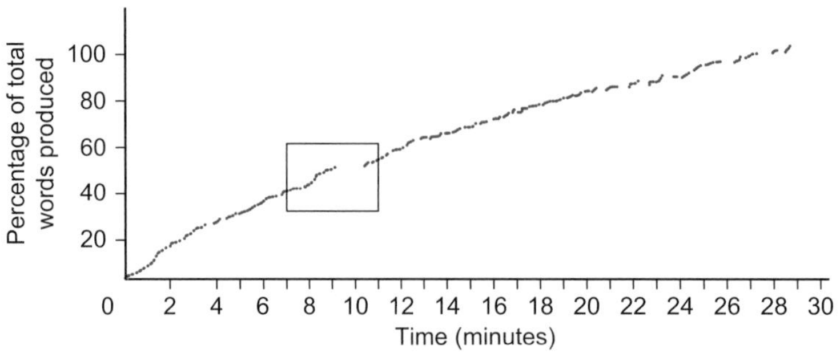

Figure 12.5 Cumulative number of animal names produced by a subject in a 30-minute session. The box shows those items detailed in Figure 12.6 (Gruenewald and Lockhead, 1980).

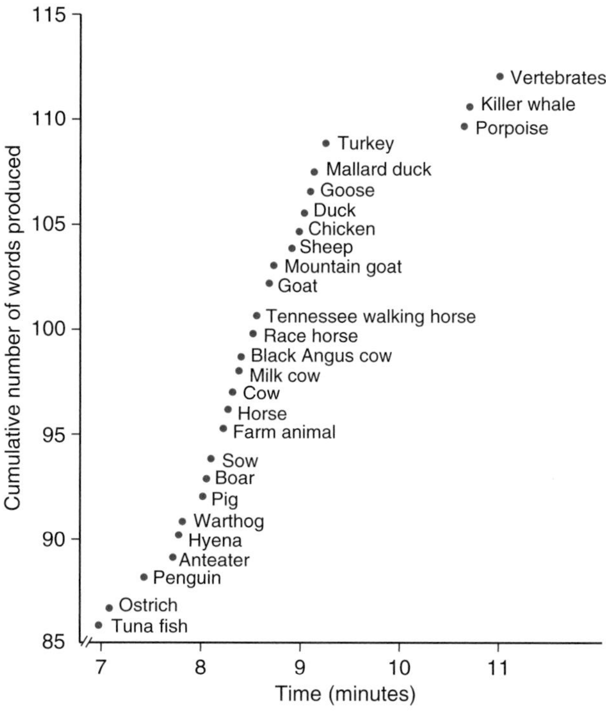

Figure 12.6 Items produced in a portion of the 30-minute animal recall task (Gruenewald and Lockhead, 1980).

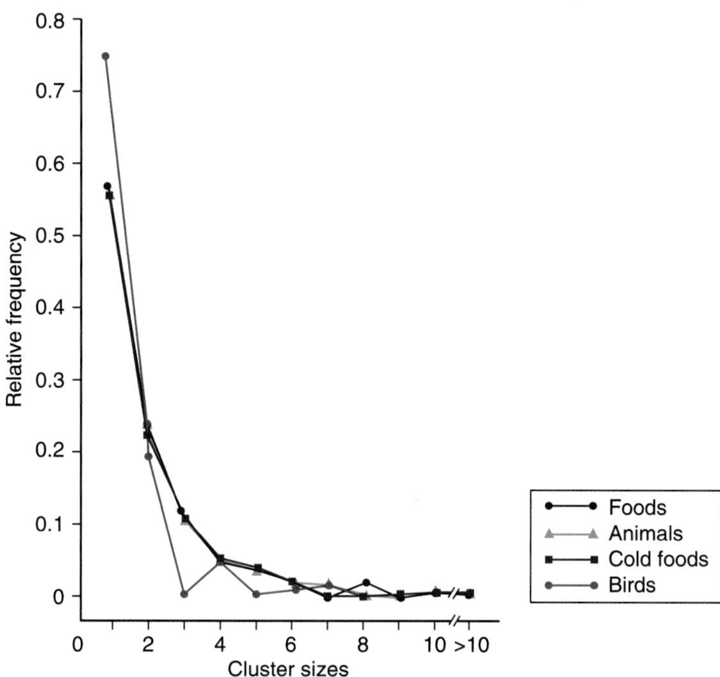

Figure 12.7 Frequency of occurrence of different sized clusters for four semantic categories (Gruenewald and Lockhead, 1980).

of the top three levels of each category. The category headings were either organized hierarchically:

Minerals
Metals Stones
Rare Common alloys Precious masonry

suggesting a strategy for generating a set of specific, hence effective, retrieval cues, or were organized randomly:

Rare
Precious Common
Masonry, alloys, stones Metals, minerals

When the students had studied a hierarchically organized list and received the hierarchically organized cues, they recalled nineteen more words when given the category headings arranged hierarchically. When the students studied a randomly organized list and received the hierarchically organized cues, they recalled ten more words. When the students studied a randomly organized list and received the randomly organized cues, they recalled only five more words (Santa *et al.*, 1975).

Generating semantically related items as possible targets does not guarantee accurate recall. When list words are closely related semantically, it results in confident false recall. First Deese (1959) and then Roediger and McDermott (1995) found that when a person was asked to recall a list of related words he or she might also recall or recognize a related word that was not on the list.For example, if a group of college students heard a list of words all related to *mountain*, such as *hill*, *valley*, *summit*, *peak*, over half the students recalled hearing *mountain* as well. Across several experiments, false recall and recognition for the similar distracter was often about as high as correct recall and recognition for words actually presented in the middle of the list. (Recall from Chapter 9 that words in the middle of the list are less well remembered than words at the beginning.) Two factors influenced the probabilty of both false recognition and false recall. The first factor was the probability of generating the distracter as an associate of the list item – for example, the probability of responding *mountain* when asked to give an associate to *hill*, *valley*, *summit*, etc. The higher the probability of generating the distracter as an associate of a list item, the more likely it was to be falsely remembered. The second factor was the overall level of recall of the list. The lower the level of list recall, the more likely the associated distracter was to be falsely remembered (Roediger *et al.*, 2001).

The first factor indicates that, when you see or hear a list of words, there is some probability that you will think of other associated words. So, if you hear *valley*, *hill*, *summit*, *peak*, etc., there is some probability that you will think of *mountain* as well (Goodwin, Meissner, and Ericsson, 2001). The automatic activation of associates is an aid to list learning because it provides a category (*mountain*) for organizing the list. But later, when you are asked to remember the list, you must discriminate those words you actually heard from those that you merely thought of. The second factor, the level of recall of the list, demonstrates that, when actual study items may be discriminated by either recency or the recollection of a distinguishing contextual feature, so recall is high, few false alarms will be made. However, when study items lack distinguishing features, not only will recall be lower but it will also be more difficult to discriminate targets from semantically related distracters.

Reminiscence and hypermnesia

The specific items of a long list or large category that are recalled on any specific attempt depend on their momentary activation levels and the generation strategy adopted on that occasion. If you try to recall the same list later you may think of a new generation strategy, and the activation levels of the targets will be different. So, you may generate targets that you didn't generate the first time. For example, Brown (1923) gave his college students two chances to recall all the states they could in five minutes. The two recall trials were half an hour apart. On their second try the students recalled about five states they had failed to recall on the first trial, but they also failed to recall about two states they had recalled previously. Buschke (1974) found a similar result with successive recall attempts of a list of randomly selected words. An even more striking increase in recall with time is observed with children. Ballard (1913) discovered that a partially learned poem studied by twelve-year-old London schoolchildren was not recalled as well immediately after the learning as it was a day or two later. Kasper (1983) obtained better performance on a later test in a paired-associate learning task in which twelve-year-old Brooklyn schoolchildren studied pairs of Spanish words and their English translations and then had to recall the translations when presented with the Spanish words. In all these studies, list items were recalled on a later test that were not recalled on an earlier test, which is called **reminiscence**. Moreover, on all these studies the total number of items recalled was higher on a later test than an earlier test, which is called **hypermnesia**.

Repeated recall attempts improve recall only when the list or category items can be recollected in a recognition task. As discussed in Chapter 10, long-term recognition for briefly presented pictures is better than long-term recognition for briefly presented words, so repeated attempts at recall of the names of pictured objects produce both reminiscence and hypermnesia. Erdelyi and Kleinbard (1978) presented subjects with sixty pictures of common objects (for example, watch, fish, feather) or with the names of the objects at the rate of a study item every five seconds. Afterwards, the subjects were asked to recall the list (always by writing the object names). The subjects then continued to try to recall the list, again and again over a period of a week. Figure 12.8 presents the average number of items recalled over time. When the items had been presented as words, average recall stayed fairly constant after the first hour. But, when the items were presented as pictures, recall continued to go up for about four days (see also Erdelyi and Becker, 1974). As discussed in Chapter 9, engaging in visual imagery during the study task increased the number of words that were remembered on a single retrieval test. Similarly, when subjects formed a visual image of each object as its name was presented, recall over successive tests increased (Erdelyi *et al.*, 1976). Instructions that focus attention on the meaning of the words produce similar effects when the words are easy to image (Roediger and Thorpe, 1978) but not when the words are abstract and hence difficult to image (Belmore, 1981). Successive testing causes increased recall even when there is PI from the learning of other lists (Gunawan and Gerkens, 2011).

Cue–target specificity

A cue is related to a target in one of the ways that a prime is related to a target. The perceptual representation of a **form cue** is similar to the perceptual representation of the target.

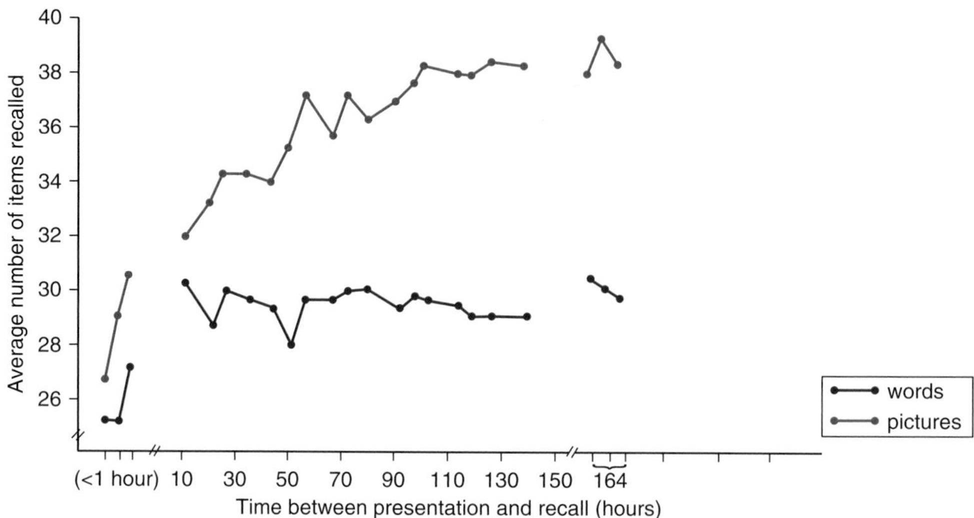

Figure 12.8 When there are multiple recall attempts, the number of items recalled increased over a longer period time for pictures than for words (Erdelyi and Kleinbard, 1978).

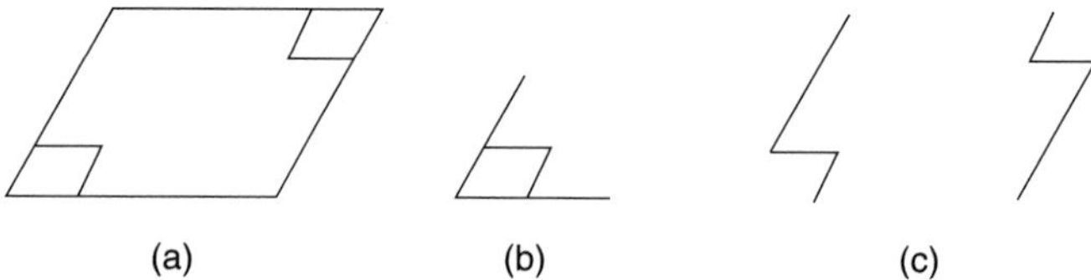

Figure 12.9 Study pattern (a), a part corresponding to a part of its representation (b), and a part that does not correspond to a part of its representation (c) (Bower and Glass,1976).

Hence, the target's representation is among those it activates. A semantic representation of a **semantic cue** is related in some way to the semantic representation of the target. For this reason, the semantic cue activates the semantic representation of the target. As mentioned above, the critical factor determining whether the cue will elicit recollection of the target is not the similarity between them but the specificity of the cue: whether the cue is more similar to the target than to anything else.

Form cues. When form cues are specific to their targets they are effective retrieval cues. Consider the pattern shown in Figure 12.9 (a). Most people perceive the features of this pattern as organized into three parts that form the entire figure – that is, they perceive this pattern as a parallelogram with boxes in the lower left and upper right corners. Therefore, the part of the pattern shown in Figure 12.9 (b) is a part of the representation of the pattern, whereas the part shown in Figure 12.9 (c) is not. Bower and Glass (1976) showed a group of undergraduates a series of patterns like the one shown in Figure 12.9 (a). The students were then given a piece of each pattern as a cue and asked to draw the complete patterns. If the cue was part of the representation of the pattern, then the students were able to recall the entire pattern about 90 percent of the time. But, if the part of the pattern presented as a cue was not a part of the representation, the pattern was recalled only about 20 percent of the time. Form cues mark the border between recall and recognition. When a form cue is used as a retrieval cue, the task can be described as either a part-to-whole recognition task or a cued recall task.

Form cues are also effective for word targets. Form cues for the unretrieved word may be effective in relieving the tip-of-the-tongue experience (Chapter 10). The first letter of the word (Freedman and Landauer, 1966; Gruneberg and Monks, 1974), a rhyming word (Kozlowski, 1977), and overall similarity, such as *goggle* for *gobble* (Brown, 1979) all sometimes help the person remember the word.

Semantic cues. Cohen and Granström (1970) showed people irregular visual patterns that they later had to either recognize or reproduce. The subjects were also asked to describe the forms in words. Cohen and Granstrom found that the patterns that could be described most accurately were most likely to be reproduced accurately. However, the accuracy of the description of the form had no influence on recognition performance. In another experiment, during a seven-second interval between study and test three names or three faces were presented for the subject to remember. The names interfered more with the reproduction task and the faces interfered more with the recognition task. The visual representation therefore determined visual recognition but the semantic representation controlled recall.

Semantic cues were more effective in visual recall when they were integrated with the target in a single meaningful episode. Figure 12.10 (a) depicts three separate objects; hence, each object is merely an associated cue for the others. Figure 12.10 (b) shows the same three objects in a single integrated representation; each object now is a semantic cue for the entire picture. Studies show that adults (Wollen, Weber, and Lowry, 1972) and children (Reese, 1965) alike are better at recalling integrated scenes than separate pictures from cues. Similarly, Bower (1970) found that interactive imagery instructions improved cued recall with respect to instructions to form separate images. In contrast, when recognition of the words was tested, instructions to form interactive images were no more effective than instructions to form separate images (see also Begg, 1978a). The fact that interactive imagery is superior only to separate imagery for recall, not to recognition, demonstrates that only the semantic cue primes the target through its semantic representation.

Partial recollection. Sometimes only partial recollection occurs and it is the verbal label that is missing. You know who someone is but cannot think of his or her name. This is called the **tip-of-the-tongue (TOT)** or **feeling of knowing (FOK)** state (Hart, 1965). Even five-year-olds can suffer the frustration of knowing they know something they cannot remember (Wellman, 1977). To induce the TOT experience, Brown and McNeill (1966)

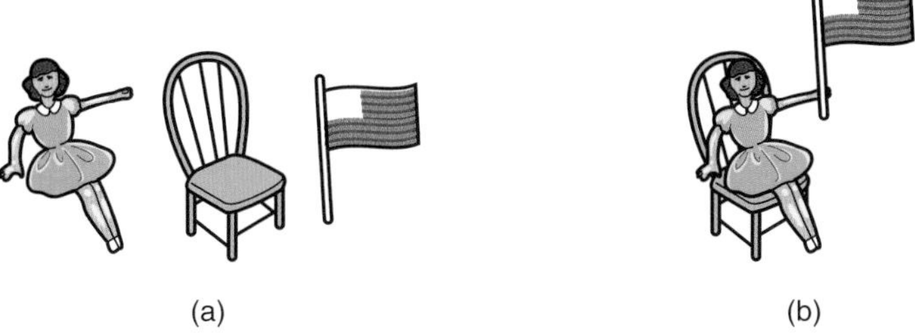

Figure 12.10 Visual representations not recalled as well separate (a) as integrated (b) (Bower, 1970).

read to students a large number of dictionary definitions, such as "an instrument used by navigators to measure the angle between a heavenly body and a horizon." Then, after reading each definition, they asked the students to indicate their ability to recall the defined word. Most students either recalled the word or were certain that they had no idea what the word might be. Brown and McNeill were not interested in either of these groups; instead, they focused on the few students who indicated that they were certain they knew the word but could not quite recall it. They expressed the feeling that the word was on the tips of their tongues. Whenever a student suggested that they were in a TOT state, Brown and McNeill proceeded to ask a variety of questions, such as "What is the first letter?" "How many letters does the word contain?" "How many syllables has it got?" and "Can you tell me what the word sounds like?" They found that students in the TOT state could often answer such questions quite accurately. For instance, they might know that the first letter was an "S," the word had two syllables, even that it had seven letters, but they still were unable to produce the name *sextant*. Instead, they might produce soundalikes, such as *secant* or *sextet*.

Context–target specificity

Recall that an episode encodes a target within its context and that, at three months of age, recognition of a target mobile is context-specific (Chapter 7). If an infant learns to kick to move a target mobile in a specific context then the infant recognizes only the mobile in that context.

However, the child soon learns to refine his or her recognition criterion to include only target features, and these alone are sufficient for excellent recognition (Chapter 10), so that any additional features provided by the context are irrelevant. However, for recall, when the cue itself is not a target feature, whatever additional cues are provided by the context influence recall (Smith, Glenberg, and Bjork, 1978).

Context-dependent recall. In a classic experiment (Godden and Baddeley, 1975), sixteen divers learned a list of forty unrelated words either on the shore or twenty feet under the sea. They were subsequently asked to recall the words in either the same or the alternative environment. Mean recall scores were as shown in Figure 12.11. As the figure shows, words were recalled more accurately in the environment in which they

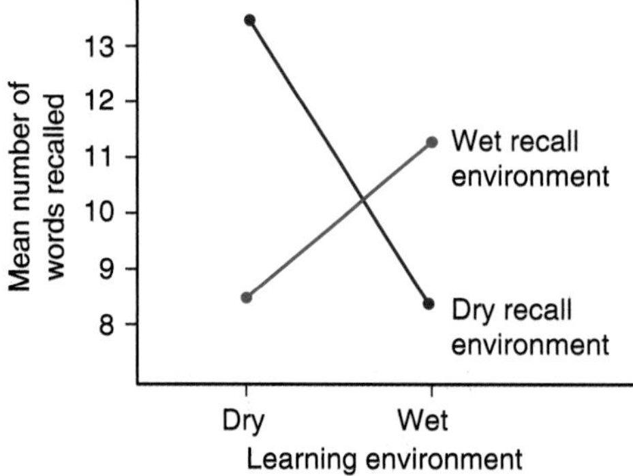

Figure 12.11 Godden and Baddeley (1975) found that word lists were recalled better in the same environment in which they were learned than they were in a different environment.

were originally learned. Godden and Baddeley also tested divers' recognition of words in different environments. A change in environmental context had no effect on recognition performance.

When people placed in a new environment were instructed to recall the original learning environment just prior to free recall of the list, their recall was as good in the new environment as in the original learning environment (Smith, 1979). So, when people are made aware of the learning context, it becomes a recall cue. Furthermore, just as in infancy, context-dependent memory in adulthood occurs only when a specific study list is learned in a single context. Smith (1982) found that context only facilitated recall when associating a context with a study list was a special event. He had college students perform different study tasks in different rooms of the college. When the students learned two different lists in two different rooms, context facilitated recall. When the number of rooms and study tasks was increased to five, recall was no longer facilitated by context.

State-dependent memory. A phenomenon that is related to context-dependent memory is state-dependent memory. This term originally was used to describe the casual observation that heavy drinkers, when sober, were unable to find money or alcohol they had hidden while drunk, but they remembered the hiding places when they were drunk again. To explain this result, researchers assumed that the physiological state of the person acted as a cue for the hiding place. The existence of this phenomenon was unclear until a thoughtful review by Eich (1980) showed that the tasks for which pharmacological-state-dependent retrieval is observed are the same as for context-dependent retrieval. In other words, state-dependent retrieval is generally observed with recall but not with cued recall (Eich and Birnbaum, 1982) or recognition. Apparently, in the latter cases the effects of the more salient retrieval cues obscure the effect of the state cue.

Mood congruency and depression. Related to but subtly different from state dependence is the mood dependent memory effect. A person recalls memories consistent with the mood he or she is in. For example, Clark and Teasdale (1982) asked patients who underwent mood swings to produce autobiographical memories in response to neutral words. The patients recalled fewer pleasant memories during their sad phase than their neutral phase. However, depressed patients recall fewer details of their lives in general than normal individuals do (Moore, Watts, and Williams, 1988). Nevertheless, Eich, Macaulay, and Lam (1997) again found mood dependence in people with bipolar mood swings. As was the case with context-dependent and state-dependent memory, mood-dependent memory may exist for recall but not for recognition (Eich, 1995) or cued recall (Eich and Birnbaum, 1982).

12.2 Knowledge

With the exception of dropping by a store to pick up a few needed items, recall tasks generally do not involve recalling lists of words as much as useful facts about the world, such as how to get to class, what the correct answers are to exam questions, and where you can find the phone number of someone you need to call. Furthermore, the purpose of recollection in such tasks is not the mere retrieval of information but the application of knowledge to direct action. The difference between information and knowledge is the relationship between a representation and the world. Any digit string, hence the representation of a digit string (in any modality), is information. However, knowing that a particular digit string is your phone number is **knowledge**.

Sentence verification

Inference plays an important role in the application of recollected information as knowledge. You can verify that a dog is an animal by recollecting from semantic memory that a dog is an animal (Collins and Quillian, 1969). But how do you know that a dog is not a cat? One falsification strategy is to determine that two concepts are mutually exclusive instances of the same superordinate category. Since dogs and cats are different kinds of animals, you can infer that a dog is not a cat when you retrieve that they are both animals. Supporting such a contradiction strategy, "false" decisions were made quickly when the two concepts shared a highly related superordinate, such as "A dog is a cat" (Holyoak and Glass, 1975). Holyoak and Glass also found that instances are used as counterexamples to disconfirm false generalizations such as "All birds are robins" (see also Lorch, 1978). Such sentences are rejected by retrieving an instance of the subject category that is not an instance of the predicate category. For example, a person could retrieve the fact that some birds are canaries; since canaries aren't robins, the canary is a counterexample to the claim "All birds are robins." Counterexamples can also be used to reject some false sentences about properties. For example, you could decide "All roses are red" is false by thinking of a yellow rose. However, as discussed above, there is no recall strategy that guarantees that all instances of a category will be recollected, so sometimes the search for a counterexample fails even when one exists. Holyoak and Glass (1975) found that most students agreed that all trees have leaves. However, pine trees have needles, not leaves, as the same students agreed when this was pointed out to them. Using a counterexample to determine that something is false is another example of making an inference. The ability to make inferences greatly expands the amount of information a hierarchical organization contains, since many positive and negative inferences can be drawn from it. You can infer that squirrels have hearts because they are animals and animals have hearts, but that squirrels do not have gills because they are not fish and only fish have gills – though you probably never thought about this beforehand.

Visual recall

Very few individuals possess the ability of Stephen Wiltshire to reproduce what he has seen (Chapter 5). As mentioned in Chapter 10, Nickerson and Adams (1979) found that American college students could not discriminate the head side of a penny from similar distracters. The students had even more difficulty when asked to draw the coin. Some of their rather lamentable efforts are displayed in Figure 12.12. Indeed, Rubin and Kontis (1983) found evidence that people base their recall of all coins on a single representation. Figure 12.13 (a) shows the American coins in use at the time of their study, and Figure 12.13 (b) shows versions based on the most frequent features subjects used in drawing each one. The striking result is that all the reconstructed coins tended to be the same except for the identity of the president depicted on each. The subjects appeared to know little about the specific details of each type of coin (except for its size and color, presumably), but they did seem to have a clear notion of what coins in general are like.

Figure 12.12 An American penny and drawings from students who attempted to reproduce it from memory (Nickerson and Adams, 1979).

Figure 12.13 Actual American coins (relative sizes not shown) (a) and coins reproduced from memory (b) (Rubin and Kontis, 1983).

Mental maps

In Chapter 1, the instrumental system was introduced in relationship to its ability to encode mental maps and use them to navigate an animal's environment. When human mental maps are examined, they are remarkably economical representations, to the point of oversimplification. The knowledge that allows a person to navigate his or her neighborhood is not represented in a single mental map but in several mental maps describing the pathways to familiar locations. These individual maps may contain distortions that make them inconsistent with each other. Moar and Bower (1983) had residents in Cambridge, England, estimate the angles formed by each of the three street intersections depicted in Figure 12.14. They found that the estimates were all biased towards 90 degrees. The consequence was that the sum of the three angels exceeded 180 degrees, which would be an impossible triangle.

Geographic knowledge

The study of personal navigation is difficult, because there is no easy way to ascertain the mental maps a person uses to navigate the local environment. Instead, it is much easier to investigate the common geographic knowledge that people have of distant cities and continents.

People again encode many simple maps and use the same inferential process described above to determine the relations among locations on different maps. Geographical regions are commonly represented as hierarchical structures. Thus, a building is in a city, which is in a state, which is in a country, etc. Because you know that the location of a superordinate constrains the location of all the regions within it, distortions caused by misalignment of the larger region are inherited by its subordinate locations (Tversky, 1981). Because most people, quite reasonably but mistakenly, align South America as south of North America, rather than as southeast of it, they infer that Miami, Florida, on the east coast of North America, is east of Lima, Peru, on the west coast of South America. But, as the map in Figure 12.15 reveals, the reverse is true. People are very prone to make such errors based on superordinate locations (Stevens and Coupe, 1978). As another example, most people believe that the Pacific terminus of the Panama Canal is west of the Atlantic terminus. But, as the map in Figure 12.16 reveals, the reverse is true. Most people do not have a visuospatial representation of the Panama Canal. However, they reason approximately as follows: the Pacific Ocean is west

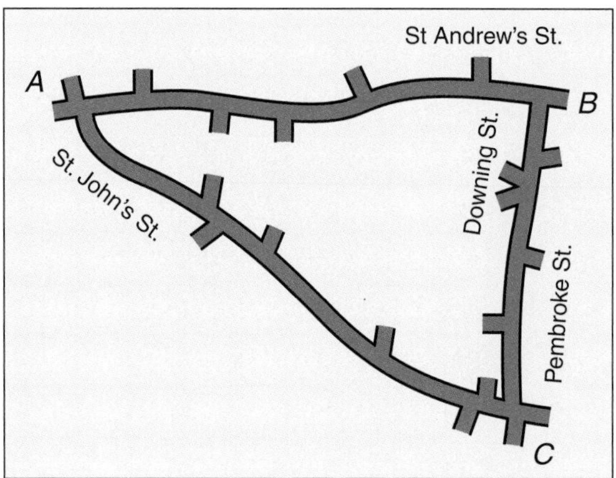

Figure 12.14 Intersections in Cambridge, England, for Moar and Bower's (1983) study.

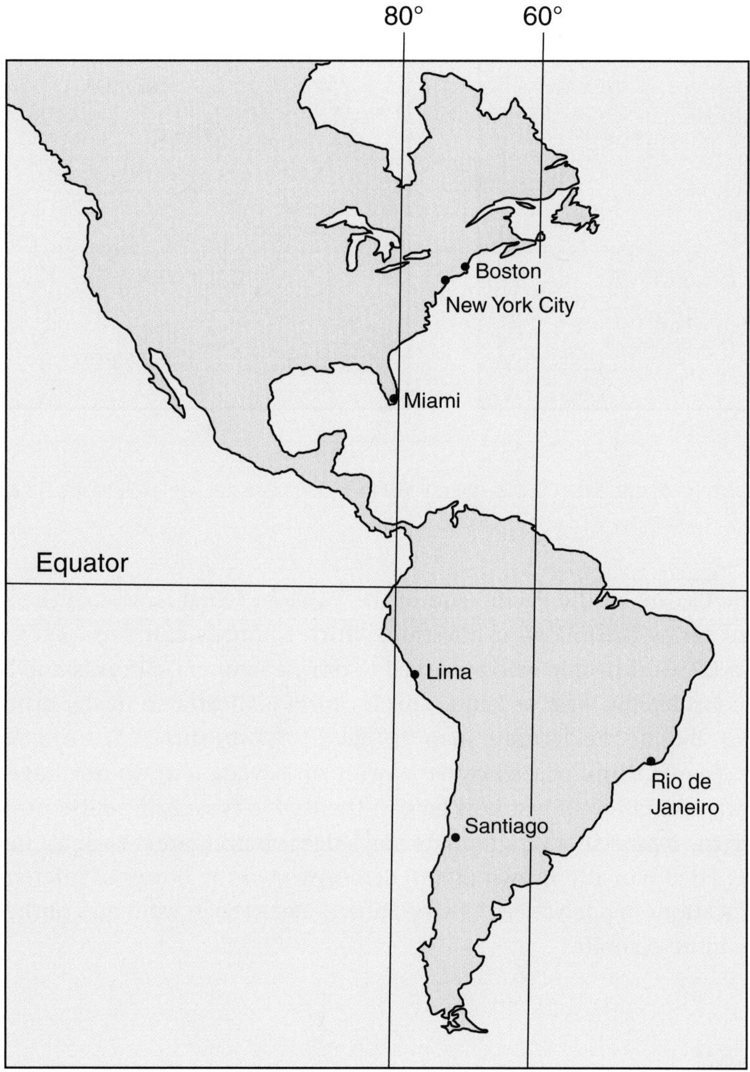

Figure 12.15 Correct map of Western hemisphere showing locations of cities.

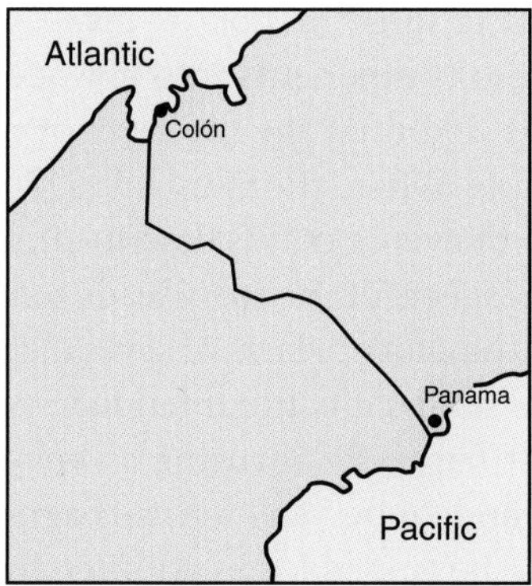

Figure 12.16 The Pacific end of the Panama Canal is east of the Atlantic end.

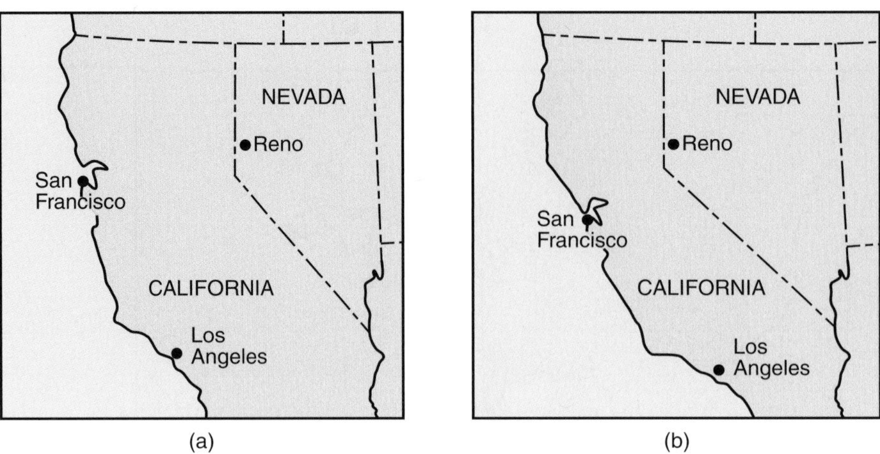

Figure 12.17 Geographical distortion: (a) mental location of Reno as east of Los Angeles; (b) actual location of Reno – west of Los Angeles.

of the Atlantic Ocean, so the Pacific end of the Panama Canal is west of the Atlantic end. Finally, try answering the following question: which is further east, Los Angeles, California, or Reno, Nevada? Most people who are asked to draw a map of California and Nevada place Los Angeles considerably west of Reno. This location is illustrated in the distorted map in Figure 12.17 (a). But, as the accurate map in Figure 12.17 (b) shows, Los Angeles is actually east of Reno. People think of California as west of Nevada and do not have an accurate visuospatial representation of just how far east the Pacific coast is in southern California. Of course, part of the reason that geographic knowledge is inaccurate is that, for most people, it is incomplete. Friedman and Brown (2000) demonstrated the power of inference by telling subjects the locations of a few "seed" cities. Subsequently, their estimates of the locations of all cities were more accurate.

12.3 Story recall

A simple story, called "Circle Island," was written by Dawes (1964), and used by him, Thorndyke (1977), and Buschke and Schaier (1979) to study story recall. The story is shown with each component of one of its episodes, actor, context, target, action, or result, numbered in Figure 12.18. The hierarchical organization of these components into episodes and of the episodes into the overall narrative is shown in the figure. At the top level of the hierarchy shown in Figure 12.18, the story divides into a setting (where the story takes place), a theme (the basic topic of the story), a plot (the sequence of events that is described), and a resolution (the eventual outcome). Each of these major aspects of the story leads to more specific information that fills in the details. For example, the plot consists of several episodes, each of which is elaborated to include a **sub-goal**. The sub-goal is the intended result of an action, hence the intention of an actor in the story (Chapter 8). Focusing on episode 2, we see that the sub-goal of this episode is specified in 25 and 26 by "The senators agreed to build a smaller canal." In a story schema, one episode may be embedded in another, so the attempt is described in 28 to 30 by "After starting construction on the smaller canal, the islanders

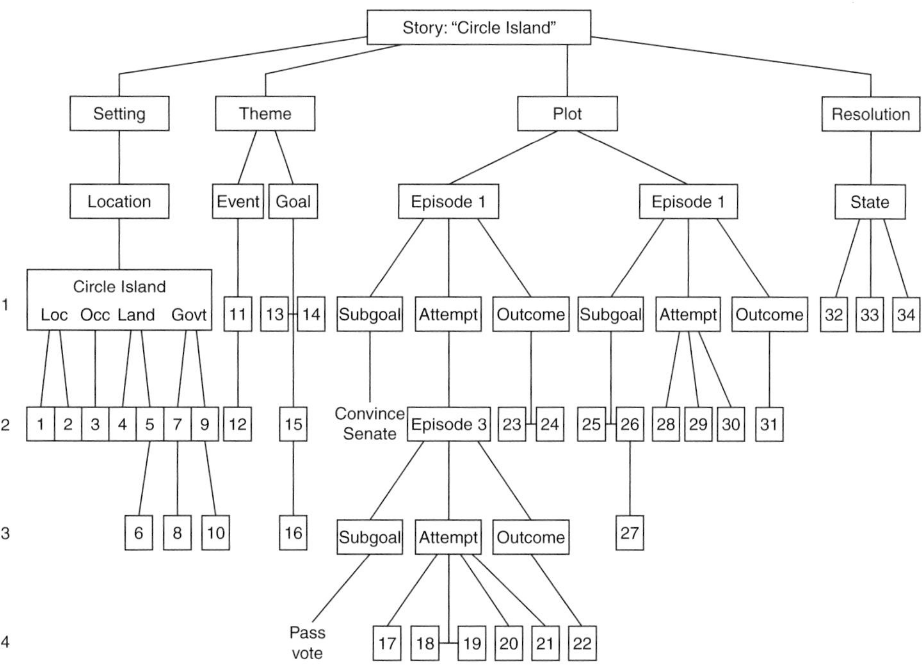

(1) Circle Island is located in the middle of the Atlantic Ocean, (2) north of Ronald Island. (3) The main occupations on the island are farming and ranching. (4) Circle Island has good soil, (5) but few rivers and (6) hence a shortage of water. (7) The island is run democratically. (8) All issues are decided by a majority vote of the islanders. (9) The governing body is a Senate, (10) whose job is to carry out the will of the majority. (11) Recently, an island scientist discovered a cheap method (12) of converting salt water into fresh water. (13) As a result, the island farmers wanted (14) to build a canal across the island, (15) so that they could use water from the canal (16) to cultivate the island's central region. (17) Therefore, the farmers formed a pro-canal association (18) and persuaded a few senators (19) to join. (20) The pro-canal association brought the construction idea to a vote. (21) All the islanders voted. (22) The majority voted in favor of construction. (23) However, the Senate decided that (24) the farmers' proposed canal was ecologically unsound. (25) The senators agreed (26) to build a smaller canal (27) that was two feet wide and one foot deep. (28) After starting construction on the smaller canal, (29) the islanders discovered that (30) no water would flow into it. (31) Thus the project was abandoned. (32) The farmers were angry (33) because of the failure of the canal project. (34) Civil war appeared inevitable.

Figure 12.18 Bottom: The Circle Island story with each statement labled. Top: The fact statements organized in a hierarchical story schema (Thorndyke, 1977).

discovered that no water would flow into it." Finally, the outcome of this episode is specified by proposition 31: "The project was abandoned."

The hierarchical organization of a narrative into a setting, theme, plot, and resolution applies to many different stories and is called a story **schema**. The hierarchical structure in Figure 12.18 determines both how people learn stories and how they recall them. To learn a story, its setting, theme, etc. are identified and the general story schema is elaborated with the information specific to that story. Without these relationships there would be no story. For instance, suppose someone took all the sentences of the story, wrote them on index cards, and then shuffled the cards. We certainly would not say that someone reading those index cards was reading the story.

The hierarchical story organization is also critical for accurate story recall. Someone trying to recall "Circle Island" will use his or her general knowledge of stories, encoded in a general story hierarchy, to generate general features such as setting and plot. These features, along with the specific cue "Circle Island," will be used to activate components of episodes at the top level of the "Circle Island" hierarchy. The context provided by the setting and theme at the highest level can be used to cue general episodes at the next lower level. From these general episodes, possible more specific episodes may be inferred and used to cue details of the story at the lowest level.

Notice that story recall is not self-limiting like the free recall of a list, described above. Each higher-level sub-goal provides a unique cue for the episode describing the attempt to achieve it immediately below it in the hierarchy, so there is relatively little cue overload. In addition, the sequence of episodes generated from the story hierarchy, such as goal–attempt–outcomes, provides a framework that reveals any important gaps in the recall and provides cues for filling those gaps. So, unlike the recall of list members, which approaches an asymptote after only a few minutes of effort, the recall of a story has no limit. In other words, there is no known limit to the length of a story that can be recalled in a single attempt.

If people actually use the hierarchical story structure in this way to cue information then a higher percentage of episode components high in the hierarchy than episodes low in the hierarchy should be recalled, because the recall of episodes low in the hierarchy is dependent on the prior recall of the sub-goals that dominate them. For example, episode 6 should not be recalled until 5 is first recalled and used as a cue to generate it. Consistent with this prediction, Thorndyke (1977) found that the percentage of information recalled at each level of the hierarchy decreased monotonically from level 1 to level 4.

With the sometime exception of those living in Neverland, children hear lots of stories, and so soon have a complete story schema represented in semantic memory. Fitzgerald, Spiegel, and Webb (1985) performed a clever investigation of whether children used a story schema to recall a simple story. The children read and recalled scrambled versions of stories (Figure 12.19) at the beginning of their fourth year at primary school and again at the beginning of the sixth year. They tended to recall the episodes of the story in the order of the original, not the scrambled order in which they were actually read. Furthermore, when older, their recall was closer to the order of the unscrambled story.

Long-term recall of a novel. Stanhope, Cohen, and Conway (1993) extended the study of the role of the hierarchical story schema on story recall from short, trivial stories to long-term recall of a novel originally studied as part of a university undergraduate course. Former students completed a test on Charles Dickens' *Hard Times* at three, fifteen, twenty-seven, or thirty-nine months after the course. A total of 50 percent of the reports of the most vivid and enduring memory were for the setting of the story, which is at the top of the schema hierarchy (Figure 12.18). As shown in Figure 12.20, for a free recall test of the names and roles of characters, retention initially declined quickly during the first few months to an asymptote and then remained stable, as was the case for typing skill (Figure 3.15). As also shown in Figure 12.20, retention of schematic knowledge (roles) was retained better than retention of non-schematic knowledge (names). Only role knowledge describes an actor in semantic memory, and so benefits from its organization at recall. Stanhope, Cohen, and Conway categorized events in the story as being of high, medium, or low importance depending on

	Original version	
	"The Wolf and the Bird with the Long Neck"	
	Setting	A Wolf was eating an animal he had killed
	Beginning	Suddenly, a small bone in the meat stuck in his throat. He could not swallow it.
	Reaction	He soon felt terrible pain in his throat.
	Goal	He wanted to stop the pain.
	Attempt	He tried to get everyone he met to take the bone out for him. "I would give anything," he said, "if you would take it out."
Outcome embedded	*Beginning*	At last a Bird with a long neck said he would try.
	Attempt	The Bird told the Wolf to lie down on his side. He had him open his mouth as wide as he could. Then the Bird put its long neck down the Wolf's throat. With its beak the Bird pulled on the bone
	Outcome	At last the Bird got the bone out.
	Ending	"Will you please give me the reward you said I could have?" said the Bird with the long neck. The Wolf grinned. He showed his teeth and said: "Be happy. You have put your head inside a Wolf's mouth and taken it out again safely. That is all the reward you will get."

Scrambled version

"The Wolf and the Bird with the Long Neck"

He soon felt terrible pain in his throat. He wanted to stop the pain. Suddenly, a small bone in the meat stuck in his throat. He could not swallow it. The Bird told the Wolf to lie down on his side. He had him open his mouth as wide as he could Then the Bird put its long neck down the Wolf's throat. With his beak, the Bird pulled on the bone. At last the Bird got the bone out. At last a Bird with a long neck said he would try. "Will you please give me the reward you said I could have?" said the Bird with a long neck. The Wolf grinned. He showed his teeth and said: "Be happy. You have put your head inside a Wolf's mouth and taken it out again safely That is all the reward you will get." A Wolf was eating an animal he had killed. He tried to get everyone he met to take the bone out for him. "I would give anything," he said, "if you would take it out."

Figure 12.19 The original and scrambled version of a story. Scrambled version read and recalled by fourth graders and sixth graders (Fitzgerald *et al.*, 1985).

whether they were at the top, in the middle, or at the bottom of the story schema. Statements describing the events were mixed with altered statements that incorrectly described events, and the former students had to identify which statements were true. Figure 12.21 (top) shows that recognition was better for more important events, again consistent with hierarchical organization. Figure 12.21 (top) does not show the usual initial decline in performance; however, this was because of the insensitivity of the accuracy measure. Figure 12.21 (bottom) shows confidence ratings for the correct responses plotted in the top of the figure. The response time data show the usual initial decline to a long-term asymptotic level of performance.

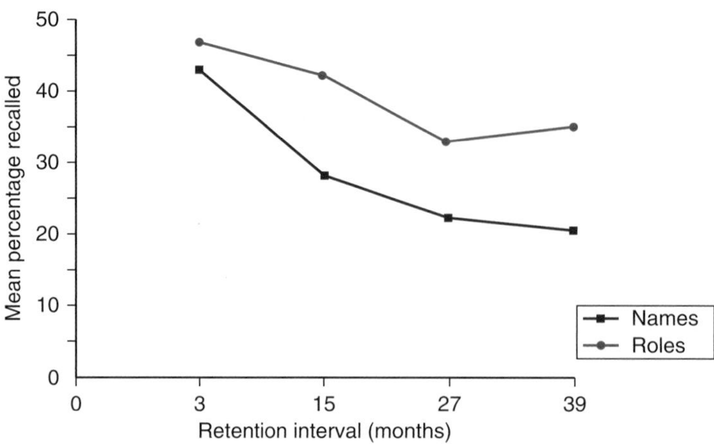

Figure 12.20 Mean percent recall for names and roles in *Hard Times* (Stanhope *et al*., 1993).

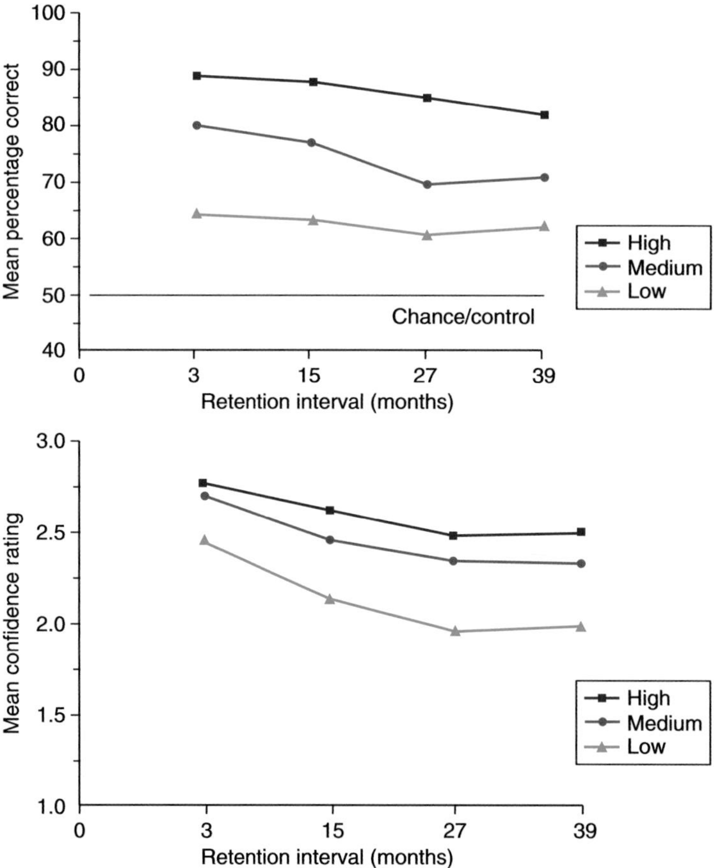

Figure 12.21 Mean percent correct recognition of high, medium, and low importance events and facts (top) and response times for correct responses (bottom) for *Hard Times* (Stanhope *et al*., 1993).

General knowledge. Both comprehending and recalling a story involve more than using a story schema to organize the story statements into a hierarchy. Virtually any part of a person's knowledge may be involved in understanding the causal relations in the story. This requires integrating the story statements with a person's general semantic knowledge. Recall that in Chapter 10 merely adding the title "Doing the laundry" was all that was required to connect a reader's general knowledge with a rather abstract passage, making the passage more comprehensible and more memorable. When a reader uses general knowledge to understand a story, when he or she tries to recall the story it may be difficult to discriminate what was in the story and what was already known. Sulin and Dooling (1974) showed that, when people integrate what they are learning with what they already know, they are soon unable to discriminate the new knowledge from the old. They had one group of students read the following passage, entitled "Carol Harris's need for professional help" (Sulin and Dooling, 1974: 256):

> Carol Harris was a problem child from birth. She was wild, stubborn, and violent. By the time Carol turned eight, she was still unmanageable. Her parents were very concerned about her mental health. There was no good institution for her problem in her state. Her parents finally decided to take some action. They hired a private teacher for Carol.

A second group of students read exactly the same passage, except for one change: the name "Helen Keller" was substituted for "Carol Harris." After reading the passage, all the students were given a recognition test. They were presented with a series of sentences and asked to judge whether or not each had been included in the passage. The most interesting part of the experiment focused on the responses given to one critical test sentence: "She was deaf, dumb, and blind." Since this sentence was not in the passage, everyone should have rejected it. In fact, students who had read the Carol Harris version did exactly that; not one of them claimed that the sentence had been presented. However, 20 percent of the students who read the Helen Keller version erroneously indicated that they had read the critical sentence. This difference in mistaken recognition was even more dramatic if the recognition test was postponed a week. Only 5 percent of the Carol Harris subjects misrecognized the critical sentence, but a whopping 50 percent of the Helen Keller students indicated that they had read it (see also Kozminsky, 1977).

SUMMARY

- A recall task requires a response (answer) that is not included in the cue (question).
  - For many recall tasks there must first be a stage in which potential targets, such as the possible names of presidents, must be generated. Recall responses are therefore often produced through a two-stage – generate and recollect – process.
- In a recall task, potential targets are generated by cues. Each cue may be used once and retrieves at most a small number of targets.
  - Hence, as instances of a very large category, such as animals, are retrieved, they are recalled in small clusters corresponding to distinct cues.
  - Over time fewer cues that retrieve new category members are generated, so fewer targets are retrieved.

- In a hierarchically organized list, each cue uniquely retrieves two or three additional cues or targets.
  - When concepts form statements that form episodes that form stories, people can recall scores of details from a story they have heard once. Given a sufficient degree of organization, there is no limit on the number of concepts that can be recalled upon request.
  - The downside of associating information learned on different occasions in a single semantic network is losing the contextual details of when each piece of information was learned. The same associations that make a target easier to generate may make it less discriminable from distracters that may have been spontaneously generated during learning.
- When information is used to direct action, it becomes knowledge.
  - The application of information to action sometimes requires that an inference be made on the basis of an example or counterexample. When the generation of examples is incomplete, an error may be made.

QUESTIONS

1. Why does recall of a single trigram fail in the Brown–Peterson task?
2. What are the characteristics of clustering in free recall?
3. On the basis of what is known about context-dependent memory, does it make any difference where a student studies for a multiple-choice exam?

FURTHER READING

Bartlett, F. C., and Kintsch, W. (1995). *Remembering: A Study in Experimental and Social Psychology*. Cambridge University Press.

Eich, E. (1995). Searching for mood-dependent memory. *Psychological Science*, 6, 67–75.

13 Autobiographical memory

The psychologist Jean Piaget began his book on memory with a story from his own life. When he was a young boy, he remembered when he had nearly been kidnaped in the park except for the alertness of his nanny. The one problem with this dramatic event is that it never happened. Years later the nanny admitted that she had made it up to explain a bruise he had received while playing. Piaget's vivid memory of an event that had not occurred makes an important point about the relationship between confidence and accuracy in autobiographical memory. The core of what we mean by *memory* is our own autobiographies, which we carry around with us all the time and are constantly updating. You may forget what you learned in school today but there is almost no chance that you will forget who you are. People have tremendous confidence in the accuracy of many of the autobiographical details that we all can recall. However, autobiographical memory is not a fixed record of the past but constantly subject to revision from the incorporation of post-event information.

- Autobiographical memory is organized by intentions and actions. Recall of life events is a process of reconstruction and storytelling that makes use of cues from a person's current intentions and general rules of how events are ordered to provide a coherent justification for recent and planned actions. The prefrontal cortex makes use of available cues to initiate recollection from the temporal cortex.
- The recollection of autobiographical memories makes use of both the instrumental system, to generate perceptual representations and an emotional response, and the habit system, to generate meaningful details. New details may be added to the semantic system at any time. Consequently, autobiographical memory is constantly being revised through the addition of post-event information to semantic memory.
- The long-term retention of semantic knowledge is remarkably good for the purposes of daily life.
  - Recognition of the names and faces of classmates, and the subject matter of topics studied over a few years, remains at a high level for a lifetime.
- The long-term recall of autobiographical events is described by a three-part function that reflects the roles of both the instrumental system and the habit system. When people are given cues and asked to recall a relevant life event, the following happens.
  - There is an overall recency effect. More recent autobiographical memories are more likely to be recalled than less recent autobiographical memories. The habit system plays a role in

    recollecting semantic information for autobiographical memories. The influence of the instrumental system, hence the amount of perceptual information, is strongest for the most recent events but declines and may be non-existent for older events.
  - However, there may be one or more reminiscence bumps for important, novel or first-time life events, which may be recalled regardless of when they occurred. The reminiscence bump is associated with the lingering influence of the instrumental system.
  - Finally, there is childhood amnesia for memories below the age of four. No autobiographical memories are reported from this period.
- Retrograde amnesia is the failure to retrieve memories that were encoded normally. There are two entirely different disorders of this type.
  - In psychogenic amnesia, an individual is oriented to time and place but doesn't know who he or she is. This disorder is very rare and highly controversial, since it is associated with lying on the part of the patient.
  - More common is organic retrograde amnesia, as the result of bilateral damage to the medial temporal cortex.
    - The individual knows who he or she is but has forgotten everything for some time period up to the moment of the injury. Hence, the patient is not oriented to time or place.
  - There are three distinct forms of organic retrograde amnesia, depending on the area of the brain impaired:
    - medial temporal cortex and thalamus damage causes most recent memories to be selectively impaired, because of selective damage to the instrumental system;
    - temporal cortex damage causes older memories to be more severely impaired, because of damage to semantic memory; and
    - prefrontal damage causes impairment of all autobiographical memories, because of damage to the system of cueing details and constructing a representation.
  - If there is also damage to the prefrontal cortex then the patient may also suffer from confabulation: entirely false memories may take the place of real ones.

13.1 Encoding autobiographical memory

The story that you know best is the story of your own life. But you are never finished learning this story, and it is constantly being revised. How the story of your life is organized during encoding determines what you are able to remember about yourself. Your autobiography is not a recording of things you observed. Rather, it is the story of the effect of your actions on the world, encoded in episodes in memory (Chapter 2). Whenever past experience must be consulted, an ad hoc autobiographical memory is constructed by the prefrontal cortex from different sources of information in the temporal, parietal, and occipital cortex. Semantic information fills in familiar details and locates events in time. In addition, visual representations and an emotional response by the amygdala make it somewhat possible to re-experience the past. Together, the perceptual and semantic information make it possible to construct a complete autobiographical memory, including the "When?", "Where?", and "Why?" of an experience, as well as perceptual and emotional detail of the experience itself (Conway and Pleydell-Pearce, 2000).

The brain areas revealed by fMRI to be involved in the construction of autobiographical memories and their functions are shown in Figure 13.1 (Cabeza and St. Jacques, 2007). The lateral prefrontal cortex initiates the recollection of episodes in the temporal cortex. These include both specifically autobiographical and general semantic memories. The prefrontal cortex identifies those episodes that represent personal experiences. For example, when people viewed photos of familiar locations, the medial prefrontal cortex was more active when participants recognized photos taken by themselves than photos taken by other participants.

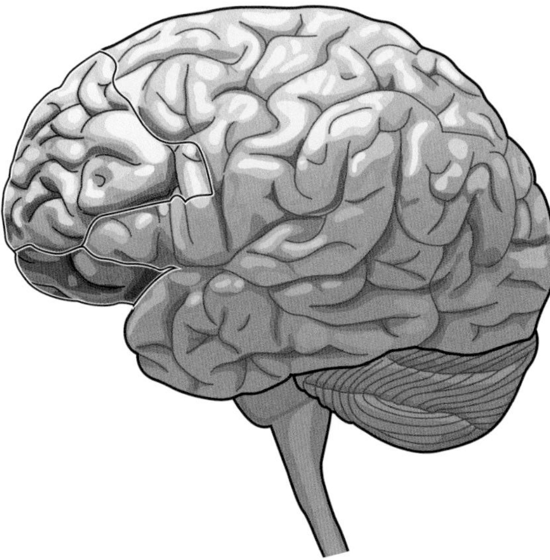

Figure 13.1 The prefrontal cortex evaluates perceptually-detailed episodes and associated emotions transmitted from the semantic system and constructs an autobiographical recollection of a past experience that is consistent with the narrative component of autobiographical memory (Cabeza and St. Jacques, 2007).

The orbitofrontal cortex integrates these personal reminiscences with associated emotions and generates the feeling of rightness or recognition of the memory. This area is impaired when abnormal confabulations occur in retrograde amnesia, as described below. These areas in the prefrontal cortex activate the hippocampus and the amygdala, which together activate the semantic episode for the autobiographical experience, an emotional response, and visual details (Figure 13.1).

Although autobiographical memory is retrospective, it is used prospectively. Episodes describing past events guide future actions. Your memory of past classes guides your plan to attend class during the coming week. To this end, there is not a fixed autobiographical record somewhere in semantic memory. Because autobiographical memory is used to navigate the presence and predict the future, it must be continuously updated. To perform an action at a specific day and time in a specific place one must know what time it is. The episodes in memory provide this information. By repeatedly comparing them with perceptual information from the immediate environment, people remain oriented to time and place. Students were able to get to class long before cellphones were invented that had clocks and GPS-enabled maps. Cues around you constantly update your awareness of the day and time.

Continuous updating

Evidence of the organization of the mental calendar comes from how long it takes to answer the question "What day of the week is today?" As Figure 13.2 shows, this question was answered most quickly on the weekends and most slowly in the middle of the week, suggesting that students use the weekend as a landmark for keeping track of the days (Koriat and Fischoff, 1974; Shanon, 1979). Consistent with the organizing effect of weekends, for questions asked at noon, at the beginning of the week people were faster to answer "What day of the week was yesterday?" than "What day of the week is tomorrow?", but the reverse was true for the end of the week. Evidence of continuous updating is that people were faster to answer "What day of the week was yesterday?" than "What day of the week is tomorrow" in the morning, but the reverse was true for the afternoon. In the morning we are still reflecting on yesterday's events, while by the afternoon we are already planning tomorrow's activities. Furthermore, the amount that is remembered from the recent past influences its perceived duration. The more distinct events that are remembered, the longer is the perceived duration (Ornstein, 1969).

Intentions, actions, and internal source amnesia

Your memory is organized into episodes by what you do (Chapter 2). Raye, Johnson, and Taylor (1980) found that students were more accurate at estimating the frequencies with which they had generated words than at estimating the frequencies with which they had studied words. Furthermore, judgments of internally generated words impaired estimates of environmental word frequency more than environmental frequency impaired judgments of internally generated words.

Recall that voluntary action has two components: the plan and the performance of the motor movement (Chapter 3). When an action does not have a memorable consequence, discriminating between a memory of what you actually did and what you intended to do can be difficult. Examples are remembering that you intended to mail a letter, lock the door,

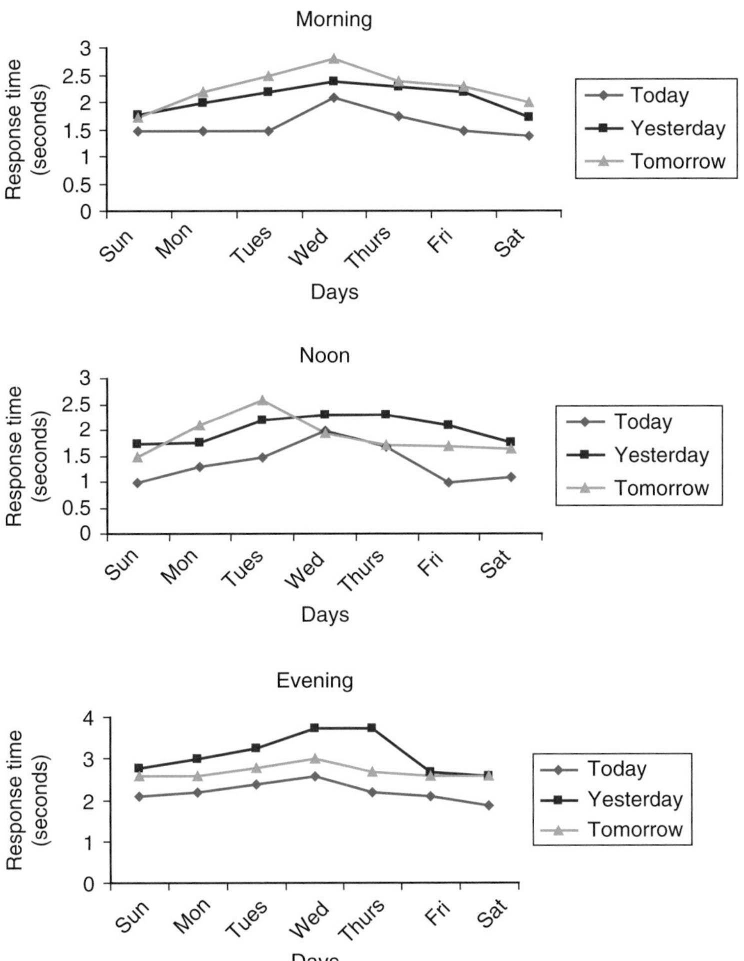

Figure 13.2 Time to respond to the question "What day of the week is it?" (Shannon, 1979).

or turn out the lights but not remembering whether you did it. Discriminating between having thought about saying something and actually having said something – that is, discriminating between an intention and an action – is more difficult than distinguishing between having said something and having heard something – that is, distinguishing between an action and a perception (Johnson and Foley, 1984; Johnson and Raye, 1981). Being unable to distinguish whether one merely thought of or actually did something is called **internal source amnesia** (Johnson, Hashtroudi, and Lindsay, 1993).

In social situations, when a memory of who said or failed to say what to whom may result in hurt feelings, internal source amnesia can have important ramifications. If someone is planning to make a suggestion that someone else makes first, both individuals may remember making the suggestion. Alternatively, through priming (Chapter 7), someone may repeat another's comment without awareness that it has already been said. Saying something without being aware that some else has said it earlier is called **cryptomnesia** (Brown and Murphy, 1989).

Perspective at recall

Even when source amnesia is not an issue, autobiographical recall may be influenced in other ways. When one is attempting to recall events, one's intention influences the cues available, hence the information about the event that is retrieved. After college undergraduates read a story about two boys playing hooky from school at one of their homes, they were instructed to take the perspective of either a burglar or a person interested in buying a home (Anderson and Pichert, 1978). Some of the information in the story was particularly relevant to a would-be burglar, whereas other information was particularly relevant to a homebuyer. For example, the color TV in the house was more relevant to a burglar, and the damp basement was more relevant to a homebuyer. As Figure 13.3 indicates, when they subsequently recalled the story, those students who had taken the burglar perspective recalled more burglar information than students who had taken the homebuyer perspective, whereas those who had taken the homebuyer perspective recalled more homebuyer information than those students who had taken the burglar perspective.

The students were asked to recall the story a second time, and some were told to maintain the same point of view, whereas others were now told to shift – for example, taking the perspective of a homebuyer instead of a burglar. Those subjects who changed perspective on the second recall attempt recalled an additional 7 percent of the information related to their new point of view and 7 percent less of the information related to their former view. A shift in perspective appeared to alter the cues available for the story information and hence systematically altered the likelihood of recalling different aspects of the story. A person's perspective at retrieval determined what they recalled regardless of their perspective at encoding (Kardash, Royer, and Greene, 1988).

Similarly, when you are attempting to recall past thoughts and intentions, recalling the thoughts most consistent with current beliefs is easier. Current thoughts and beliefs cue memories of consistent actions. Consequently, your actions will seem to you to be more consistent with your current beliefs than they actually were (Greenwald, 1980). When attitude change was induced in students by having them write an essay in favor of the opposing

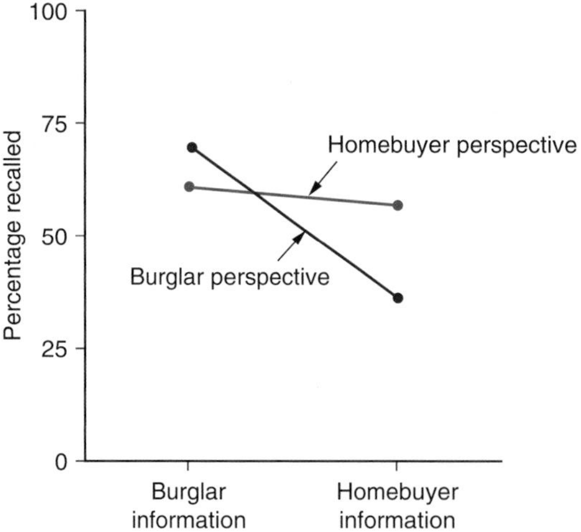

Figure 13.3 Proportion of perspective-relevant and perspective-irrelevant information recalled on the first and second tests (Anderson and Pichert, 1978).

side, they remembered their old opinion as having been consistent with their new one (Bem and McConnell, 1970; Wixon and Laird, 1976).

Post-event information and external source amnesia

Semantic memory is repeatedly elaborated through the integration of new information (Chapters 8, 9, and 10) into existing episodes. A consequence of elaboration is **external source amnesia**. The process of integrating all the facts of Abraham Lincoln's life into a single narrative in memory does not preserve when and where each fact was read or heard. Sometimes this effect is insidious. When undergraduates read texts about historical topics and then watched clips from popular films on the same topics that contained information that contradicted the text, about a third of the undergraduates recalled the false information in the movie as having been read in the text (Umanath, Butler, and Marsh, 2012).

While believing something false about a historical figure is regrettable, it will not necessarily lead to poor personal decisions. However, autobiographical memory is by definition experiential, so it is of great consequence if a personal memory of a foiled kidnapping as a child was something you actually experienced or instead heard about afterwards from your nanny. The source is inextricably linked to the truth of the memory. However, even when an autobiographical narrative is elaborated, the new source is often not preserved. First, three- and four-year-old children were given the opportunity to interact with Mr. Science, and then three months later the children heard their parents read a story about Mr. Science. In subsequent interviews, 41 percent of the children spontaneously reported that Mr. Science had done something during their meeting that had actually been mentioned only in the story (Poole and Lindsay, 1995).

The consequences of source amnesia for autobiographical memories are exacerbated when the post-event information contradicts details of the original experience. In fact, source amnesia has a much more profound effect on an incidental memory of an experience than on a memory of something that has been intentionally studied. There is a primacy effect in the permanent narratives in semantic memory, so later information does not retroactively interfere with the retrieval of information learned earlier. Nothing new you learn about Abraham Lincoln today is going to decrease your ability to recollect that he was president during the American Civil War and issued the Emancipation Proclamation to free the slaves. Learning new information does not make people confused about their names, addresses, phone numbers, passwords, or what they studied for exams as the result of subsequent experiences. Once a person has made the strategic decision to preserve what he or she has learned by encoding a plan for generating it through the habit system, merely hearing or reading contrary information will not distort it. However, there is a recency effect in the ever-changing set of cues that are used to recollect autobiographical memories. New information can retroactively interfere with the recollection of old information.

Consequently, whether a narrative is studied for recall and receives a crystallized representation by the habit system or is read as a description of a recent life experience and receives a fluid representation determines its susceptibility to alteration by post-event information. In an informative experiment, Spiro (1980) compared the effect of an incidental comment on the memory of a story that students were asked to remember versus the memory of a description of a real relationship they would be asked to comment on later. All the students in the experiment read the same story and then recalled it two days, three weeks, or six weeks later. The story is below. Half the students read the version with the happy ending and half the students read the version with the sad ending.

> This is a story about Bob and Margie. When they met they were both twenty years old and beginning their senior year in college. Bob was majoring in political science and Margie in history. They didn't know each other until they were introduced at a party in a mutual acquaintance's apartment. Since neither of them was particularly extraverted and they knew very few people at the party, they seemed glad to have each other to talk to. They found some interests they had in common, and hit it off fairly well. They soon began to see each other regularly.
>
> After several months, Bob began to think he would like to marry Margie. He felt he loved her and he believed the feeling was reciprocated. Still, he was not sure how she would react. Finally he asked her to marry him. She agreed and they happily began making plans for their marriage and life together.
>
> However, Bob's happiness was clouded by his awareness that there was something important he had to discuss with Margie – his strong feeling that he did not want to have children. He avoided bringing the subject up because he didn't want anything to hurt their relationship. However, he soon realized that he could not put off the discussion forever. Filled with apprehension, he told Margie he had a very important matter to discuss with her. He anxiously related to her his strong feelings against having children and awaited her response.
>
> **Happy ending:** Margie was elated. Because she wanted to have a career she had also felt that she didn't want to have children. They rejoiced in the dissolution of what would have been a very serious problem for them. A long discussion of the status of their relationship followed.
>
> **Sad ending:** Margie was horrified. She had always wanted to be a mother and had her heart set on having many children. They argued bitterly over what had become a very serious problem for them. A long discussion of the status of their relationship followed.

Students were either told that they were in a recall experiment (memory group) or an experiment in which they would have to react to a real-life event at a later time (interactive group), so that the story they were reading was true. After some of the students had read the story, the experimenter, while collecting the consent forms about eight minutes later, sometimes mentioned either that Bob and Margie had or had not gotten married. This information was either consistent or inconsistent with what the students had read, depending on whether they had read the happy or sad ending to the story. A third of the time Bob and Margie were not mentioned during the collection of the consent forms.

All the subjects had to write down exactly what they had read two days, three weeks, or six weeks later. The results are shown in Figure 13.4. Almost all the students who had been told that they were in a memory experiment and would have to recall the story did not make intrusion errors (adding or changing a proposition), even six weeks later. Similarly, almost all the students who had been told that the story was true but were not exposed to inconsistent information did not make intrusion errors. In contrast, some students who had been told that the story was true and exposed to inconsistent information made intrusion

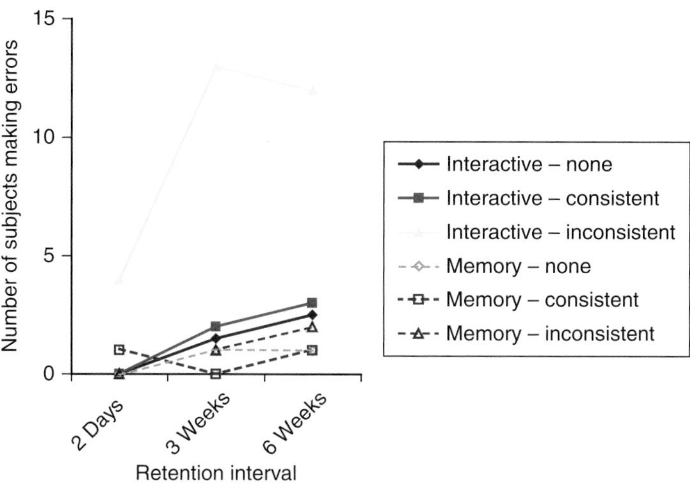

Figure 13.4 Effect of no, consistent, and inconsistent post-event information on story memory under memory and interactive instructions. Errors were made only when inconsistent post-event information was presented for a story believed by participants to describe an actual event (Spiro, 1980).

errors when tested only three weeks later. For example, two students who read the unhappy ending but heard that Bob and Margie had married wrote down the following.

(1) They separated but realized after discussing the matter that their love mattered more.
(2) They discussed it and decided they could agree on a compromise: adoption.

Two students who read the happy ending but heard that Bob and Margie had separated wrote down the following:

(1) There was a hassle with one or the other's parents.
(2) They disagreed about having children.

Thus, people are perfectly capable of remembering things they learned with the intention of recalling them later and are not easily confused by post-event information. However, stories about ordinary life events, even about other people, are subject to revision on the basis of post-event information. As a result, a person can have a false memory – that is, a memory of something that didn't happen. A false memory is called a **confabulation**. People are said to **confabulate** – that is, generate false memories.

Eyewitness testimony

No comfort about the accuracy of autobiographical memory may be taken from the fact that Spiro's experiment involved memory of a brief story. Eyewitness testimony may be influenced by a post-event question. The degree of distortion in eyewitness testimony is of particular importance, since the fairness of our justice system depends in large part on its accuracy. Leading questions as well as other forms of post-event information can influence the testimony of children and adults alike.

Child eyewitness testimony. Children are not always unreliable witnesses (Ceci and Bruck, 1993). False information rarely appears in preschoolers' spontaneous free recall of a past experience (Goodman and Reed, 1986). However, the effect of leading questions on eyewitness testimony is exacerbated when the eyewitness is a young child. Young children usually try to please adults with the right answer to a question, and, to the child, that means the answer the child thinks the adult wants. When children were asked the same question more than once in a way that implied to them that the previous answer was not what the adult wanted to hear, they often changed their answers. Cassel, Roebers, and Bjorklund (1996) asked primary schoolchildren about a bicycle theft. When presented with a misleading question, such as "The girl was wearing shorts, wasn't she?" when in fact she was wearing jeans, most children rejected the false information. When these children were asked a second misleading question, "Don't you remember that the girl was wearing shorts?", children in the second year and older continued to reject it. But 42 percent of kindergarten children changed their answer and now agreed with the false information.

Research on the reliability of child witnesses took on special urgency at the end of the twentieth century. In a few sensational cases, nursery school teachers were convicted of child abuse and served long prison terms (before ultimately successful appeals) on the basis of the often fantastic testimony of preschool children, despite a lack of physical evidence against the defendants or spontaneous accusations against them. Instead, the charges emerged only after the children had been repeatedly questioned by agitated parents and prosecutors whose initial reason for the questioning proved irrelevant to the ultimate prosecution. The key elements for obtaining a false allegation for a child five to seven years of age appears to be reinforcement of the allegations through social approval and validation of the allegations by referring to the testimony of other witnesses. These interviewing techniques, derived from transcripts of the infamous McMartin preschool case, induced 58 percent of the children interviewed to make false accusations against a classroom visitor, compared with 17 percent of the children who received leading questions (Garven *et al.*, 1998). Even when being questioned about fantastic events, such as being taken from school in a helicopter, children receiving social reinforcement made 52 percent false allegations, compared with 5 percent made by controls. In a second interview children repeated the allegations even when the reinforcement had been discontinued (Garven, Wood, and Malpass, 2000).

Adult eyewitness testimony. Although they are not as malleable as kindergarten students, adults are also susceptible to incorporating false details suggested by post-event questioning into memories of events (Mitchell, Johnson, and Mather, 2003). After witnessing a film of a collision between two cars, students were asked one of two questions: "About how fast were the cars going when they hit each other?" or "About how fast were the cars going when they smashed into each other?" Subjects gave higher estimates of the speed when the question contained the word *smashed* instead of *hit*. In addition, after a one-week delay the subjects who had been asked the question containing *smashed* showed a greater tendency to report erroneously that there had been broken glass at the accident scene (Loftus and Palmer, 1974). In this case, the question itself influenced how the person reconstructed a description of the original event. The post-event information does not have to be a question to be incorporated into the memory of an event. Adults who saw pictures alleged to be of scenes in a previously viewed video sometimes subsequently reported having witnessed those scenes in the video (Schacter *et al.*, 1997).

When sufficiently coercive techniques are combined with social approval, it is possible to implant false memories in adults. Even when a false response is initially coerced, it may subsequently affect the memory of an event. Zaragoza *et al.* (2001) showed college students an eight-minute excerpt from the Disney movie *Looking for Miracles*, which depicts the adventures of two brothers at summer camp. The clip was filled with action and drama, including a fight among the campers and an encounter with a deadly snake. Immediately thereafter, participants were individually interviewed and asked to respond to fourteen questions about the film. Of these, four were false-event questions about events that had obviously not been depicted in the video. Thus, in order to answer the false-event questions, participants had to make up, or confabulate, answers. In fact, students in the control group refused to answer the false-event questions and did not show evidence of distorted memories later. However, students in the forced group were told that they had to provide an answer to every question and were explicitly instructed to guess if they did not know an answer. For the forced group, each student received neutral feedback about responses to two false-event questions, such as "Okay," and confirmatory feedback about responses to two false-event questions, such as "That's right, knee is the correct answer." For example, the following is the transcript of the interview for a false-event question with confirmatory feedback for a student in the forced group.

INTERVIEWER: After he fell, where was Delaney bleeding?
PARTICIPANT: He wasn't. He was? I didn't see any blood.
INTERVIEWER: What's your best guess?
PARTICIPANT: Where was he bleeding?
INTERVIEWER: Yeah.
PARTICIPANT: But he wasn't bleeding. Oh...I don't have a best guess. I didn't think he was bleeding. His knee?
INTERVIEWER: Okay, his knee.
PARTICIPANT: It's not his knee!
INTERVIEWER: That's actually the right answer.
PARTICIPANT: Is it? I was just thinking: kid falling, hit his knee on the chair – you know.

One week later participants were met by a different experimenter, who informed them that the earlier interviewer had made some mistakes and had asked them questions about events that never happened in the video. Their task, they were told, was to indicate which things were in the video and which were not. This was done to eliminate social pressure to respond consistently across test sessions. All students were asked twenty-three yes/no questions of the form "When you watched the video, did you see...?" For the forced group, 27 percent of the false-event questions that received neutral feedback received "Yes" responses, and 55 percent of the false-event questions that received confirmatory feedback received "Yes" responses. Some of the students returned four to six weeks later to free-recall the video. The students incorporated 13 percent of the false events that received neutral feedback and 27 percent of the false events that received confirmatory feedback in their free recalls.

13.2 Remembering your life

When considering long-term and lifetime memories, there is the dissociation between semantic memory and autobiographical memory that was observed in Spiro's (1980) experiment on the recall of the romance of Bob and Margie. Semantic recall remains unchanged for a lifetime but autobiographical memories are always subject to change.

Lifetime recall of general knowledge

Harry Bahrick and his colleagues (Bahrick, 1983; 1984; Bahrick, Bahrick, and Wittlinger, 1975) pioneered research on the lifetime retention of different kinds of declarative knowledge. They all conformed to the same function (consistent with that for skill learning shown in Figure 3.15). When there was sufficient distributed study or experience, there was an initial period of forgetting; however, whatever was remembered a few years later was retained for a lifetime.

Bahrick, Bahrick, and Wittlinger (1975) asked groups of alumni to recognize names and pictures from their high school yearbook after intervals ranging up to almost fifty years after their graduation. The results are depicted by the top two lines in Figure 13.5. As the figure shows, the ability to recognize classmates' names showed no decline after fourteen years, and the ability to recognize classmates' pictures showed no decline after thirty-four years. In contrast, the ability to recall the names of classmates, even when cued by their pictures (not plotted in Figure 13.5), remained constant for only three years before beginning a steady decline with time. Moreover, reassuringly, students remember much of what they study in college for many years afterwards. Figure 13.6 shows the retention of students who studied Spanish in college.

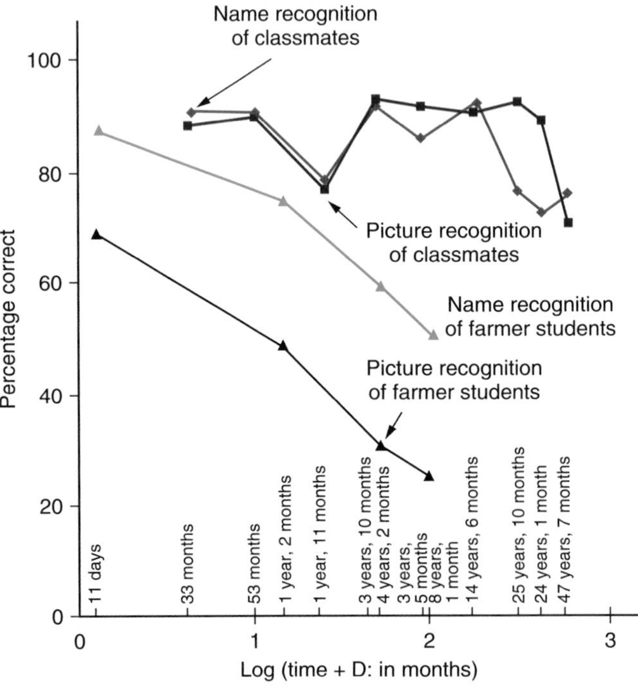

Figure 13.5 Long-term recognition of pictures of high school students by classmates does not change for more than 30 years. In contrast, recognition by their teachers declines within a year (Bahrick, 1984).

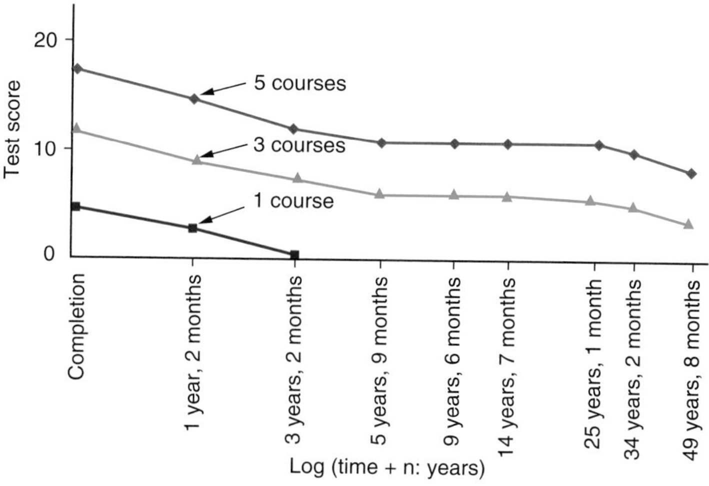

Figure 13.6 Long-term recall of Spanish as a function of initial learning. After an initial decline over the first five years there is no decline for the next 20 years (Bahrick, 1984).

Unsurprisingly, given the emotion associated with it, former students tend to remember how well they did in their courses. One to fifty-four years after graduating, 276 alumni correctly recalled 3,025 of 3,967 college grades. They free-recalled 65 percent of the courses and grades they had had in college. Then they were shown a list of their courses and asked to recall the remaining grades. The usual long-term asymptote in long-term performance was observed. After an initial decline, there was no decline in recall from seven to fifty-four years. One point of interest was whether the grades at the extremes of the scale, which might be presumed to have elicited stronger emotions when they were received, would be recalled more accurately. This was the case. The alumni recalled 91 percent of their "F" grades and 85 percent of their "A" grades (Bahrick, Hall, and Da Costa, 2008).

Autobiographical retention function

When you recall an episode in your life, you often reconstruct it through the use of rules and temporal landmarks that serve as cues for details of the episode (Shum, 1998). One way to study autobiographical memory is to examine the age distribution of memories that are recalled to general semantic cues as a function of retention interval. For example, suppose someone is given the cue word *fireworks* and asked to describe a specific event associated with fireworks. Will he or she mention the last time he or she saw them, or the first time? Will the event recalled be weeks, or months, or years old? Figure 13.7 shows the distribution of the ages of many events recalled in response to different cue words (Rubin, Wetzler, and Nebes, 1986). The function has three main features. First, older memories are less likely to be recalled than more recent ones. Hence, there is a strong recency effect. Second, contrary to this general recency trend, there are points in a person's life when more memories are recalled than predicted by their degree of recency. These are called reminiscence bumps (Koppel and Berntsen, 2015; Rubin, 2015). A common reminiscence bump is for the large number of memories coming from ages ten to thirty, particularly between fifteen and twenty-five. Third, there is childhood amnesia for the early years of life.

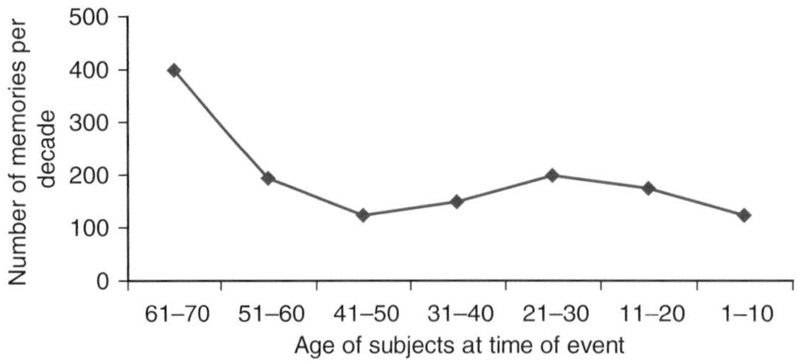

Figure 13.7 Long-term autobiographical memory consists of recency and reminiscence components. In addition, not shown in the figure is early childhood amnesia (Rubin *et al*., 1986).

Recency. Moving backwards in time, from the present to the past, the first part of the autobiographical retention function is the recency segment. When people are asked to recall things or events from throughout their lives, a greater number of recent events are recalled (Crovitz and Quina-Holland, 1976; Crovitz and Schiffman, 1974; Franklin and Holding, 1977; Squire and Slater, 1975; Warrington and Sanders, 1971). Different cues are most effective for memories of different ages (Robinson, 1976; Rubin, 1982), and perceptual cues are more likely to recollect recent memories. Furthermore, the recollection of some older memories is benefited by, first, the recollection of newer memories as cues. When Whitten and Leonard (1981) asked college students to name teachers from each of grades one through twelve, more students who were told to search backwards from grades twelve to one completed the task than students who were told to search forwards from grades one to twelve. Thus, older memories can be recovered best through a secondary cuing strategy that successively activates older and older memories. When adults reported their self-characteristics and autobiographical memories, current self-characteristics were reflected in individuals' memories. Recent memories were more frequently linked to current self-characteristics than were earliest memories (Demiray and Bluck, 2011).

Although the recency effect in autobiographical memory is ubiquitous, it is not quite universal. When all autobiographical memories are systematically organized in semantic memory, virtually everything is remembered, and so the recency effect is obliterated. The first person to announce that she remembered virtually her entire life was Jill Price (Parker, Cahill, and McGaugh, 2006; Price and Davis, 2008). Price made copious records of the events of her life in the form of recordings and kept a detailed diary from ages ten through thirty-four. She could remember the precise dates and days of the week of events from every day of her life from the age of twelve, including details of television shows she had watched.

After the report on Price, other individuals then reported highly superior autobiographical memory (LePort *et al.*, 2012). Most individuals with highly superior autobiographical memory exhibited a degree of obsessive-like behavior. Nine of the eleven participants reported that they hoarded items, need organization in their physical environment, and/or were germ-avoidant. They expressed significantly greater than normal obsessional tendencies. These tendencies may have contributed to their superior autobiographical memory. Although the participants were unequivocally superior in the recall of autobiographical events, their performance was normal on other memory tasks: digit span, verbal-paired associates, and visual reproduction. Nevertheless, LePort *et al.* concluded that intentional rehearsal was not the sole means by which individuals with highly superior autobiographical memory achieved their rich repertoire of memories. Instead, the investigators concluded that the individuals had an inherent ability to retain and retrieve vast amounts of public and autobiographical events.

Price and her fellow mnemonists represent one end of the autobiographical memory spectrum. A highly organized semantic memory makes it possible to specifically recollect almost any autobiographical memory in rich semantic and perceptual detail. At the other end of the spectrum are individuals who were unfortunate to suffer severe damage to the hippocampus earlier life. In adults, this produces severe anterograde amnesia (Chapter 10). Fortunately, if the damage occurs early in life then the consequence is different. Recall from Chapter 2 that, during the encoding of a novel experience into an episode, from the very beginning the instrumental system and the habit system encode in parallel, even though the instrumental system controls the initial response. When there is damage to the hippocampus at nine years or younger, the habit system by itself operates well enough for the child to learn language, recognize friends, family, and familiar surroundings, and learn the typical academic subjects (reading, writing, arithmetic, etc.) in normal school. However, there is no recollection of the perceptual information that normally differentiates individual autobiographical experiences, so there is no autobiographical memory at all. The individual is oriented to time and place in his or her daily life but cannot remember any individual events from that life (Vargha-Khadem *et al.*, 1997)!

Reminiscence bump. The second segment of the autobiographical retention function is the reminiscence bump. One reason that a reminiscence bump occurs is because of the large number of first-time experiences that occur between fifteen and thirty years of age. First-time and unique experiences generate stronger emotions, and hence are more memorable. A total of 93 percent of vivid life memories are either unique events or first-time experiences (Rubin, Wetzler, and Nebes, 1986). When alumni were asked to recall four memories from their first year of college, more than twenty years previously, 41 percent of the memories came from September.

Even more important, the adolescent/young adult reminiscence bump marks the period of life when a person's autobiographical memory becomes relatively stable and comes to define his or her identity (Conway, Singer, and Tagini, 2004; Habermas and Bluck, 2000). Berntsen and Rubin (Berntsen and Rubin, 2004; Rubin and Berntsen, 2003) found that only positive memories exhibited a reminiscence bump, indicating that they were more likely to become part of an individual's autobiography. Furthermore, memories not only were positive but also were characterized by high perceived control and high perceived influence on later development (Glück and Bluck, 2007).

Early childhood amnesia. The final segment of the autobiographical retention function is amnesia for early childhood. There is childhood amnesia for at least the first three years of life but by age four there is evidence of long-term retention, given sufficient cuing (Sheingold and Tenney, 1982; West and Bauer, 1999; but see also Eacott and Crawley, 1998). Children who received a medical procedure at the age of two had no memory of it eight to sixty-nine months later (Quas *et al.*, 1999). Two weeks after an emergency school evacuation of three- and four-year-old children there were no significant differences in the amount of information remembered by them. Seven years later, when the children were required to respond to forced-choice questions about the event, the younger children were at chance but the older children were 86 percent correct (Pillemer, Picariello, and Pruett, 1994).

However, the paucity of early childhood memories later in life does not imply that young children cannot remember events over long periods of time. Hamond and Fivush (1991) found that four-year-old children could remember a trip to Disney World taken when they were two and a half years old. However, very young children are not skilled enough at storytelling to weave their experiences into their autobiographies, which do not become a permanent part of their knowledge until around the age of four. In support of this hypothesis, children of mothers who frequently engage in conversations about the past provide rich descriptive information about previous experiences, and invite their children to participate in stories about the past, have earlier autobiographical memories than other children (Mullen, 1994; Reese, Haden, and Fivush, 1993). By helping their children engage in storytelling and life events, the mothers help the children to create stories of their own experiences. Conversations about past events between seventeen mother–child dyads were recorded by Jack *et al.* (2009) on multiple occasions between the children's second and fourth birthdays. When these children were aged twelve to thirteen years they were interviewed about their early memories. Adolescents whose mothers used a greater ratio of elaborations to repetitions during the early childhood conversations had earlier memories than adolescents whose mothers used a smaller ratio of elaborations to repetitions.

It may be that early memories are not forgotten all at once, but there is a recency effect (as there is for later memories). When children as young as two years old were shown a magic shrinking machine once and interviewed about it one day later, they remembered the machine six years later (Jack, Simcock, and Hayne, 2012). However, only a few cues may provide access to the earliest memories (Richardson and Hayne, 2007). Over the years, as new events are added, the cues that were originally specific to the early memories become associated with later experiences, so that the earliest memories are lost through retroactive inhibition. Adults remember fewer early events than children and adolescents and are less likely to memory an event from the first three and a half years of life (Tustin and Hayne, 2010).

On the other hand, your memories of your early childhood may be added to by the stories you hear about your earliest experiences afterwards rather than the experiences themselves. Pezdek and Hodge (1999) found that 36 percent of children aged five to twelve claimed to remember an event alleged to have occurred when they were four years old that had been made up by the experimenter. Recall from the beginning of the chapter that even children who grow up to be psychologists may incorporate a story into an autobiographical memory.

Reconstruction and accuracy

As mentioned above, autobiographical memory exhibits external source amnesia, because, when new information is integrated with old, the context in which each detail was seen or heard is often not encoded. Consequently, people sometimes incorporate in their autobiographies events they had heard about rather than experienced. When Sheen, Kemp, and Rubin (2001) asked twenty pairs of young adult twins to recall life events in response to cue words they found convincing evidence of false autobiographical memories. Both members of fourteen of the pairs recalled at least one adolescent event that only one of them had actually experienced! Some of these events are mentioned in Table 13.1. The fourteen pairs of

TABLE 13.1 Descriptions of memories in response in cue words that were disputed between twins

Age at test	Age at memory	Cue word	Description of memory
21	5	Bicycle	Both believe they were pushed off bike by their cousins
21	11	Fair	Both think they came 12th in an international cross country race
21	14	Restaurant	Who went for lunch with their mum and had a worm in her meal
21	12	Boat	Who was in boat with father when they saw a tiger shark
20	8	Accident	Who got nail in their foot
20	8	Accident	Both say the other ate half the contents of mustard jar and got sick
17	9	Car	Who on a trip in a car threw up on everyone
16	9	Fair	Who went on a roller coaster at a fairground

twins disputed a total of thirty-six events, because seven pairs of twins had more than one disputed memory. In fact, one pair of twins had fourteen disputed memories! The reason why identical twins shared so many memories was that the common memories were consistent with both their autobiographies. People who have led similar lives do not have to be twins to construct parallel autobiographies. A further experiment found disputed memories between non-twin siblings and friends, as well.

More generally, in the absence of a definite memory about a source, people's memories are influenced by their beliefs about the world. Frenda *et al.* (2013) asked 5,269 participants about their memories for three true and one of five fabricated political events. Each fabricated event was accompanied by a photographic image purportedly depicting that event. Approximately half the participants incorrectly remembered that the false event had happened, with 27 percent remembering that they saw the events happen on the news. Conservatives were more likely to falsely remember seeing Barack Obama shaking hands with the president of Iran, and liberals more likely to remember George W. Bush vacationing with a baseball celebrity during the Hurricane Katrina disaster.

Flashbulb memories. Even though a significant, high-emotion event is unlikely to be forgotten (Cahill and McGaugh, 1998), as mentioned in Chapter 10, emotional memories of important life events are as susceptible to alteration by post-event information as are mundane memories. Memories of events that evoked strong emotions and are recalled with special vividness are called **flashbulb memories**. It is difficult to study flashbulb memories of personal events because there are not detailed records of them. This is not a problem for public events. In 1977 every American remembered where they were on November 22, 1963, when they heard that President John F. Kennedy had been assassinated (Brown and Kulik, 1977). In the modern world, a particularly emotional public event can become the common memory of an entire generation, such as the Kennedy assassination, the Challenger space shuttle explosion, or the destruction of the twin towers on 9/11. You might think that anything worth remembering was worth remembering well, and so flashbulb memories would be immune from the changes caused by the incorporation of post-event information. People tend to remember flashbulb memories with a high degree of confidence. However, just because someone is confident does not necessarily mean that the person is accurate. For a long time Ulric Neisser had wondered about the accuracy of flashbulb memories. When the Challenger space shuttle exploded on take-off he had his chance. Within twenty-four hours of the explosion he and Nicole Harsch were interviewing students at Emory University about how they had heard of the explosion. They then reinterviewed the students up to two and a half years later. While the students remained confident in their recollections, the recollections remained accurate only for a year. After two and a half years, for 40 per cent of the students, the recollections had changed (Neisser and Harsch, 1992; Schmolck, Buffalo, and Squire, 2000). Several other studies confirmed these results. McCloskey, Wible, and Cohen (1988) also studied recall of the Challenger disaster. Conway *et al.* (1994) investigated recall of the resignation of Margaret Thatcher as prime minister in the United Kingdom. Neisser *et al.* (1996) looked at memory for the Loma Pieta earthquake in California. For about a year perceptual information is recoverable through the instrumental system, and the representation that is constructed remains consistent with the experience. Beyond a year the original perceptual information is no longer subject to recollection, and post-event semantic information is available for integration into subsequent reconstructions of the experience.

When two airplanes crashed into the twin towers of the World Trade Center on September 11, 2001, experimental psychologists were ready to exploit the tragedy. A team of sixteen investigators in different locations (Hirst *et al.*, 2009) interviewed more than 3,000 individuals from seven US cities on their memories of learning of the terrorist attacks (notification memory), as well as details about the attack, one week, eleven months, and/or thirty-five months after the assault (event memory). Event memory included details of the attack and notification memory included details of when, where, and how the individual first became aware of it. Event memory and notification memory both exhibited a normal forgetting function, approaching an asymptotic level of remembering at thirty-five months. Notification memory was personal and inaccuracies tended to be repeated as the memory became stable, since there was no way to correct them. In contrast, event memory became more accurate as the result of post-event information. The investigators pointed out that the degree of forgetting of flashbulb memories is heavily influenced by the degree of public discussion of the event. Event memories remain accurate because the post-event discussion is consistent with the original experience. There is no evidence that a high degree of emotion associated with the episode preserves it from elaboration, hence alteration, by post-event information.

Post-traumatic stress disorder. Notice that the flashbulb memories that have been studied all involved memories of tragedies. Emotions such as fear and distress are generated by the amygdala, which initiates an animal's avoidance responses. The benefit of a permanent memory of a fear-evoking experience on an animal's behavior is obvious. It helps the animal avoid a dangerous situation in the future. It is easy to see the effect of fear on memory in the behavior of animals. I have a dominant husky who rules the territory around his home and is known to every dog in the neighborhood. Nearly every dog has ventured onto his territory once and been knocked down by the husky. No dog has ever ventured onto his territory twice. However, when a human suffers through a terrible experience that will never happen to him or her again, there is no advantage to having a strong memory of that experience that is constantly brought to awareness by fortuitous cues in daily life. When the memory becomes so intrusive that it disrupts daily life, the resulting disability is called **post-traumatic stress disorder (PTSD)**. PTSD is the result of an unexpected horrifying or terrifying event, such as a car crash, flood, or violent attack. The disorder is found among war veterans, attack victims, and the survivors of natural disasters. The most prominent complaint is of an intrusive, vivid memory of the precipitating event that interferes with normal memory and attention, thus disabling normal daily activity (Bower and Sivers, 1998; Brewin, 1998; Witvliet, 1997). Such memories can persist for months or years. There is more to PTSD than the intrusive memory. PTSD patients have much in common with depressed patients in general. Like other depressed patients, PTSD patients recall fewer details of autobiographical events other than the precipitating event (Harvey, Bryant, and Dang, 1998). Like PTSD patients, depressed patients in general tend to report an intrusive memory of a distressing event (Reynolds and Brewin, 1999). However, just because the precipitating event is intrusive and vivid does not mean that its recall is particularly accurate. There is no evidence that the intrusive memories of PTSD individuals are more detailed to begin with or less susceptible to post-event information than other memories.

Brainwashing rationalized as therapy. The evidence of the existence of false memories has raised concern that some people may construct memories of events that never happened at the repeated suggestion of and reinforcement by a therapist in clinical settings. Recall how Zaragoza *et al.* (2001) were able to induce a false memory of a video clip only a week later through repeated questioning and social approval. Similarly, ten-year-old children who were shown a doctored photo of them in a hot air balloon and asked over three sessions to recall the ride eventually confabulated a memory of it (Strange, Hayne, and Garry, 2008).

Consider instead the power of a respected therapist to induce a false memory of an event that allegedly took place years earlier through repeated questioning, suggestion, and reinforcement, over many counseling sessions. This is especially the case when hypnosis is used as a therapeutic technique, because hypnosis seems to be a particularly powerful technique for implanting false memories. The use of repeated suggestion and reinforcement to control thought was first called "brainwashing" by Edward Hunter in 1953. It included getting an individual to remember something that he or she initially did not (Hunter, 1962). At that time brainwashing was not considered to be a good thing. However, the repeated interrogation methodology was reintroduced in the 1980s as a legitimate clinical technique for recovering repressed memories of trauma, particular by the best-selling *The Courage to Heal: A Guide for Women Survivors of Child Sexual Abuse* (Bass and Davis, 1988). This rationale flew in the face of the overwhelming evidence from PTSD that memories of traumatic events are not and cannot be repressed. To the contrary, memories of traumatic events are intrusive precisely because they are difficult to forget.

The combination of repeated interrogation and approval is effective for generating new memories regardless of the actual experiences of the individual doing the remembering. When the repeated interrogation technique is used clinically a patient who "recovers" a memory always remembers the kind of event that the therapist expects to find, regardless of how implausible or even impossible it may be. Therefore, clients of therapists who believe that people repress memories of sexual abuse recover only memories of sexual abuse. However, clients of therapists who believe that past lives are disturbing them recover memories of past lives. Finally, clients of therapists who believe that a memory of an alien encounter has been repressed recover memories of their encounter with aliens (Lindsay and Read, 1994; Spanos, Burgess, and Burgess, 1994).

13.3 Retrograde amnesia

Although autobiographical memory changes over time, it rarely contains substantial gaps and even more rarely disappears altogether. Retrograde amnesia for an extended period of the past is much more common in movies and novels than in real life. **Retrograde amnesia** refers to the inability to retrieve information learned normally prior to a brain injury. There are two kinds of retrieval disorders: psychogenic amnesia, resulting from emotional distress, and organic retrograde amnesia, resulting from bilateral damage to the medial cortex.

Psychogenic amnesia

Sometimes retrograde amnesia is the result of **motivated forgetting** caused by a personal crisis, such as a marital or financial crisis that is avoided by forgetting it. This is also called a **fugue state**. A fugue state consists of a sudden loss of personal identity and is usually associated with a period of wandering, which lasts a few hours or days and for which there is a virtually complete amnesic gap upon recovery. The individual may be oriented to time and place but either fails to recall his or her identity or confabulates a false identity. Although individuals know the date and where they are, they deny knowing who they are. Kopelman *et al.* (1994) reported the following case history.

A. T. reported that she "came round" on the London Underground railway between Liverpool Street and Bethnal Green stations. On video-tape a month later, she explained:

> I woke up on the tube at the Liverpool Street station. The train was just pulling into the Liverpool Street station. It seemed as if I'd been asleep because I woke up and found myself on the train and I didn't know where I was – where I was going, or where I was supposed to be, and everyone was getting off and I was alone. It was almost midnight, and I was very frightened. When we got to the Bethnal Green station, I got out. I asked the ticket agent if there was a phone I could use to call the police department and he told me that it was just about 50 yards down the road, so I walked over there and they eventually got someone to get me in hospital.

She did not know who she was. She was carrying a bag, and at the police station it was opened and found to contain a few clothes and an envelope addressed to Alice Thornton. She was admitted to the Royal London Hospital on 13 March 1990. Two weeks later she was oriented in time and place and had apparently retrieved a number of memories, usually of a macabre quality – for example, that her ex-husband and son had been killed in a traffic accident the previous December. The administration of 500mg of sodium amytal produced a flow of memories, almost all of which turned out to be false. Subsequently A. T. was discharged from hospital and seen as an outpatient. She proved to be very resourceful. She soon had paid employment and a boyfriend. She had a North American accent, and so the United States and Canadian embassies were contacted.

A. T. was identified on July 24, 1991, after her relatives in the United States had sent Scotland Yard a missing person poster. In fact, she had a living husband and three children. After a second amytal administration on September 16, 1991, she recalled a considerable amount of her past, including her name, her home town, and the names and ages of her three children. She subsequently reported: "[My husband] would drink quite heavily and he'd get very violent with his drinking... I think that I – I would if I were in that kind of a situation, now I would, I would try and get out of it somehow." She said that the last thing that she could recall was taking her children to school and dropping them off. "I remember being very sad, but I don't know why, unless maybe that's when I was planning to leave, I don't know." After her identification A. T. obtained a divorce from her husband and married her English boyfriend. She consistently reported complete amnesia for the period from March 6 to March 13, 1990 – the time from her disappearance in the United States to her appearance in the London tube.

Because fugue states are rare and frequently associated with criminal activity or some degree of dishonesty, whether they should be considered a genuine disorder is controversial (Coons, 1999). It later emerged that, three months after her arrival in Britain, when she was disclaiming all knowledge of her identity, A. T. had written to her eleven-year-old daughter in the United States saying that she had cancer of the cervix and that she had left home to spare the family the misery of her illness. A year later she sent the family a typewritten letter, apparently from a friend, saying that she had died and had been buried in Devon, England. Kopelman *et al.* (1994) concluded their report of A. T. as follows: "Finally, readers may care to note that the travel agency from which A. T. purchased her airline ticket was called 'Great Escapes Travel' and, perhaps appropriately, it carried a hot air balloon as its emblem."

Organic retrograde amnesia

Retrograde amnesia results from bilateral injury to the medial temporal cortex. If a person receives some kind of shock to the brain, such as a severe blow, he or she may forget events that occurred during some time period leading up to the moment of the trauma. Although no longer oriented to place and/or time, the person remembers his or her identity. In general, the more severe the shock, the longer is the time period that is forgotten. Football players who are stunned by a hard tackle may forget a few seconds of their lives. A patient who receives electroconvulsive shock treatment (ECT) in a hospital or a survivor of a severe auto accident with a major head injury may forget months or even years.

Immediately after the shock some memories that will later be lost are still available. Lynch and Yarnell (1973) attended football practices and games in the hopes that they would be in attendance when players received head impacts. When players appeared dazed, Lynch and Yarnell would immediately ask them the play they had just run. Players could usually recall the play at this point, but three to twenty minutes later they usually could not. Retrograde amnesia therefore seems to develop after a blow, but it does not appear to be an instantaneous consequence of the blow.

Medial temporal damage. Recall from Chapter 10 that a bilateral injury to the medial temporal cortex or thalamus impairs learning. Damage to the medial temporal cortex also impairs recall. Damage to the medial temporal cortex, like retroactive interference in general (Chapter 10), has the greatest effect on the memory of the event causing the injury and of the events immediately preceding the injury. However, unlike retroactive interference from a similar task, whose effect rarely extends beyond a few minutes into the past, the retroactive interference caused by a head injury can extend back in time over years. The more severe that the injury is, the further back in time is the extent of its effect. In the first half of 1974 Squire and his colleagues (Squire and Slater, 1975; Squire, Slater, and Chace, 1975) gave depressed patients a multiple-choice recognition test for television shows that had been on for only one season between 1957 and 1972. The tests were given before and after

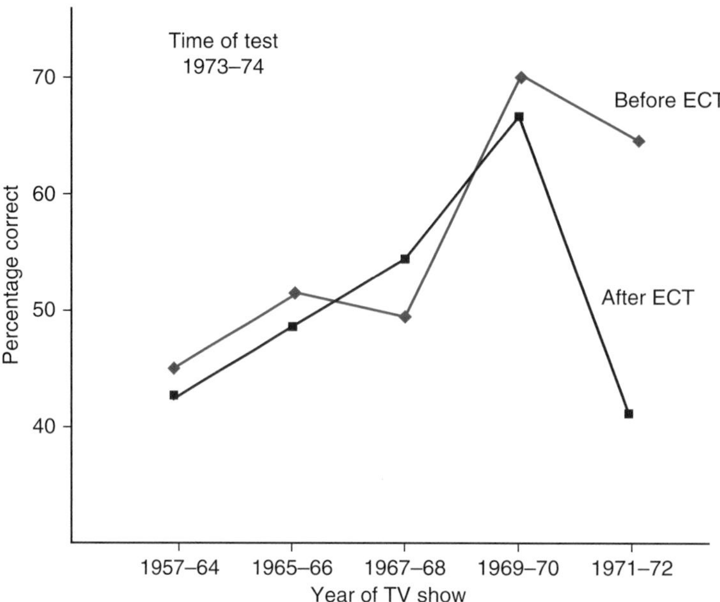

Figure 13.8 Results of TV show questionnaire administered to depressed psychiatric patients receiving a course of bilateral ECT. Testing was done before the first treatment and one hour after the fifth treatment (Squire *et al*., 1975).

an electroconvulsive shock was administered. The results are shown in Figure 13.8. Before ECT the patients showed the normal recency effect: the most recent shows were among the best remembered. After ECT recognition of shows seen two years previously was severely depressed, but recognition of older shows remained unchanged.

If there is recovery from the injury, it begins with memories for the oldest events affected by the injury and progresses to more recent events. Recovery often ends with a gap in memory for whatever was experienced and learned immediately prior to the injury. In rare cases a large temporal gap never closes, and the person in effect loses a few years from his or her life. In a particularly striking case, a thirty-six-year-old, college-educated man suffered a skull fracture that initially caused severe impairments in motor movements, language, learning, and memory. In particular, he could remember something for only a few minutes, so he could not recall where he was. The patient maintained that he was sixteen to eighteen years old and mentioned his parents' address as his address. He revealed no knowledge of his subsequent life history, his marriage, children, or past employment. His command of general information was equally impaired (Goldberg *et al*., 1982).

During the next two years the motor, linguistic, and learning deficits virtually disappeared. The patient again began orienting to the world and became aware of events since the injury from newspapers and television. However, he had no parallel recovery from the twenty-year-long retrograde amnesia. Although he was told about his past, he did not remember it. He also failed to recall anything he had learned during the period within the gap. He could not answer questions such as "Who wrote Hamlet?" or "What is the capital of France?"

The dementia associated with alcoholic Korsakoff's syndrome includes a retrograde amnesia that produces a reversed recency effect; more recent memories are forgotten. The results

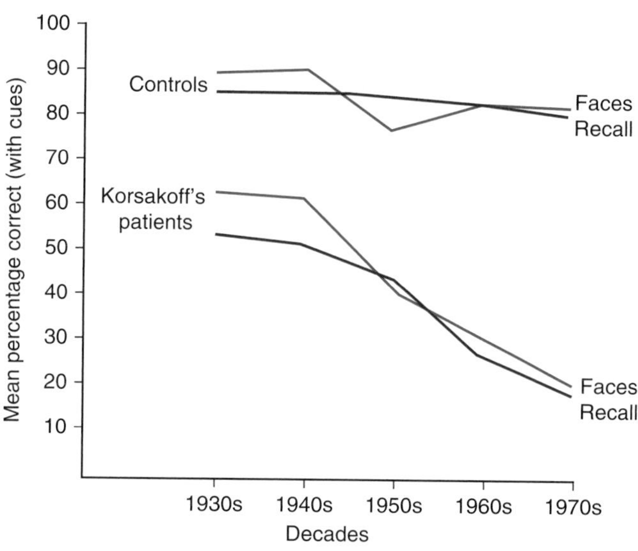

Figure 13.9 Overall performance of alcoholic Korsakoff's syndrome patients and normal controls on famous faces test and verbal recall questionnaire compared with control subjects. More recent memories are more severely impaired (Albert *et al.*, 1979).

for sixty-year-old patients with alcoholic-Korsakoff's syndrome and for normal subjects on face and verbal recall tests for people famous in different decades throughout their lifetimes are shown in Figure 13.9 (Albert, Butters, and Levin, 1979). (The tests were scaled so that normal individuals would achieve equal recall scores for all decades.) A similar but milder gradient was observed for the recognition task.

Alcoholics who do not have Korsakoff's syndrome are also impaired on facial and verbal recall in comparison with normal controls (Albert, Butters, and Brandt, 1981a; 1981b). However, the severe memory loss observed in Korsakoff's syndrome is not primarily the result of a lifetime of drinking but a consequence of the sudden, extreme damage that occurs at the onset of the disease (Chapter 10). This was established through the study of an individual who left a detailed record of what he remembered at the time of the onset of the disorder (Butters, 1984).

This patient (P. Z.) was an eminent scientist who developed alcoholic Korsakoff's syndrome at the age of sixty-five. He had written several hundred research papers and numerous books and book chapters, including an extensive autobiography written three years prior to the acute onset of the disorder in 1982. P. Z.'s amnesia was assessed through the construction of two special tasks: a famous scientists test and an autobiographical information test. The famous scientists test consisted of the names of seventy-five famous investigators and scholars in P. Z.'s scientific specialty, all of whom should have been well known to P. Z. The vast majority of these names were mentioned prominently in one or more of P. Z.'s books or major scholarly papers. Other names were chosen because of their documented professional interactions with P. Z. Twenty-eight of these scholars were prominent before 1965, twenty-four made major contributions before and after 1965, and twenty-three attained visibility after 1965. P. Z. was presented with each name and asked to describe the scholar's area of interest and major contribution. P. Z.'s recognition failure rate doubled from about 40 to 80 percent from the pre-1965 names to the post-1965 ones.

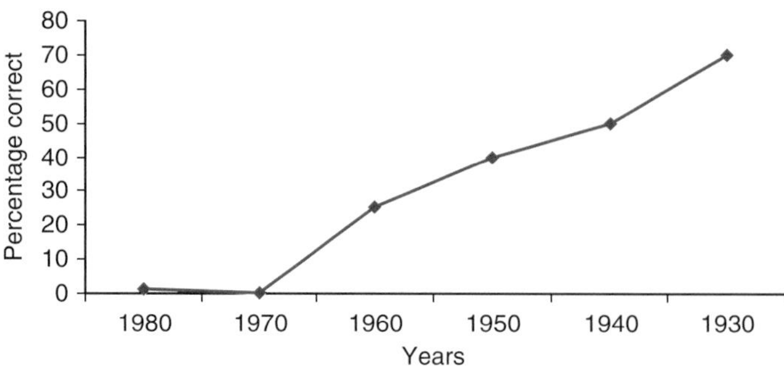

Figure 13.10 P. Z.'s recall of information from autobiography. More recent memories are more severely impaired (Butters, 1984).

The autobiographical information test consisted of questions about relatives, colleagues, collaborators, conferences, research assistants, research reports, and books mentioned prominently in P. Z.'s autobiography. The results, shown in Figure 13.10, show a steeply graded retrograde amnesia, which cannot be the result of a failure of original learning. The fact that all questions were drawn from P. Z.'s autobiography eliminates the possibility that the information was never acquired. Just three years prior to the onset of the Korsakoff's syndrome, P. Z. could retrieve this information and considered it to be important in his professional and personal life.

Memories of older events are more dependent on the long-term habit system for recollection, and this system is not impaired to the same degree as the instrumental system. Different cues are most effective for recent versus remote events (Robinson, 1976; Rubin, 1982). The shock disturbs the cues for recent events while leaving the cues for remote events intact.

Frontal and temporal damage. Recall that three areas of the brain contribute to the recollection of semantic and autobiographical memories: the prefrontal cortex, the middle temporal cortex, and the medial temporal cortex. As mentioned above (Figure 13.1), specific areas of the prefrontal cortex control recollection. In response, the hippocampus in the medial temporal cortex activates the visual components of recent memories. In contrast, the middle temporal cortex is involved in the storage and activation of semantic episodes in general (Chapter 7). Selective damage to each of these three areas produced three distinctive forms of retrograde amnesia (Kopelman, Stanhope, and Kingsley, 1999; Piolino *et al.*, 2003).

Alzheimer's disease begins with the deterioration of the medial temporal cortex; the temporal variant of frontal–temporal dementia is the atrophy of the anterior end of the temporal lobe, causing semantic dementia (Chapter 7); and the frontal variant of frontal–temporal dementia is the atrophy of the frontal lobe, damaging the control of recollection. The effects of damage to different cortical regions are summarized in Table 13.2. Damage to the medial temporal region results in the loss of recent memories having a large perceptual component. However, older memories are preserved, producing the reverse recency effect mentioned above. In contrast, in semantic dementia, the normal autobiographical memory function, recency-modulated by reminiscence bumps, is found, albeit at a much reduced level of performance because of the loss of semantic information. In frontal dementia, the inability to use ad hoc retrieval cues or to engage in ad hoc construction results in a general loss of autobiographical memory across all time periods.

TABLE 13.2 Retrograde amnesia as a function of location of brain impairment

Cause		Encephalitis or hypoxia	Korsakoff's syndrome	Alzheimer's disease	Semantic dementia	Frontal dementia
		Medial temporal cortex	Thalamus	Medial temporal cortex	Temporal cortex	Prefrontal cortex
Epoch	Most recent 12 months	Most impaired	Most impaired	Most impaired	Least impaired	Impaired
	More than 12 months	Gradient of less impairment for older memories	Gradient of less impairment for older memories	Gradient of less impairment for older memories	Recency modulated by reminiscence bumps	Impaired

Sources: Columns 1 to 2 derived from Kopelman *et al.* (1999); 3 to 5 derived from Piolino *et al.* (2003).

Recovery from retrograde amnesia

When amnesia is the result of a head injury rather than a disease process, there is the possibility that, as the brain heals, the amnesia will dissipate. When the memories of a person suffering from severe retrograde amnesia begin to return, the pattern in which they do so is quite disorganized. At first only a few memories are recovered (Kapur and Abbott, 1996), and the person may be unable to place them in the right temporal order. Two separate events may be combined into one. As more and more events are recalled, the person is able to create islands of remembering – that is, a series of related events may be placed together in their correct chronological order. As more events are recalled, the islands become bigger and the gaps between them become smaller, until finally the islands merge and the complete episodic record is restored. The process by which an amnesic gradually reconstructs autobiographical memory reveals the construction in normal autobiographical memory.

Confabulation

As described above, a certain amount of confabulation is a part of the functioning of normal autobiographical memory. One cause is when the general information about a routine event is used to fill in the gaps in an episode about a specific occurrence of the event. In retrograde amnesia, in which there is less information available about recent specific events and so more general information is filled in, there is a corresponding increase in normal confabulation. Normal confabulation produces a plausible memory that neither the speaker nor the listener has any reason to doubt.

In contrast, damage to the orbitofrontal cortex that produces delusions (Chapter 11) also produces an abnormal confabulation that is a kind of delusion. Abnormal confabulation produces an implausible false memory whose implausibility is apparent to a normal listener but not to the individual producing it. Implausible confabulations do not require severe retrograde amnesia. In fact, one confabulating patient had quite good recognition inabilities (Dab *et al.*, 1999). Rather, damage to the orbitofrontal cortex (Figure 13.1) produces confabulations (Mattioli, Miozzo, and Vignolo, 1999; Papagno and Baddeley, 1997; Schnider and Ptak, 1999; Schnider *et al.*, 2000). Causes of confabulation include anything that is likely to damage the prefrontal cortex, including alcoholism and damage to the anterior communicating artery, which supplies this region of the brain with blood (Brun and Andersson, 2001; Shallice, 1999).

Recall that the prefrontal cortex is involved in both recency and familiarity judgments. One source of confabulation is an impaired sense of familiarity and recency, so that episodes that occurred long ago are perceived as recent and details from episodes that occurred at different times are combined. Extreme temporal dislocation is called **spontaneous confabulation**, to distinguish it from normal confabulation, which results from retrieving insufficiently specific details. Examples are provided by Schnider (2001: 151):

> A 58-year-old woman hospitalized following rupture of an anterior communicating artery aneurysm was convinced that she was at home and had to feed her baby; but her "baby" was over 30 years old at the time… [A] tax accountant with extensive traumatic destruction of the orbitofrontal cortex inadvertently left the hospital in the conviction that he had a meeting with the county's financial director…

People who suffer from spontaneous confabulation often have no comprehension of their memory loss, or of their dissociation from current reality. Thus, the mother was agitated – not relieved – on being told her "baby" was actually thirty, and calmed down only when she was told that someone else was caring for it while she remained in the hospital.

To demonstrate that patients with spontaneous confabulation have impaired perceptions of familiarity and recency, Schnider and Ptak (1999) presented randomized sequences of pictures to patients and asked them to respond when they saw a target picture. The presentations were repeated after five minutes and after thirty minutes. The targets changed for each run, while the overall set of pictures remained the same. The patients who had shown spontaneous confabulation were more likely to indicate previous targets as current targets than were non-confabulating amnesiacs and healthy controls, especially in the runs that occurred after a lapse of time. In addition, Schnider (2000) asked patients to indicate which square of two on a computer screen stayed dark longer. He varied independently when each square turned dark and returned to light. So, observers had to track and remember two different durations that did not have a common onset or offset. Spontaneous confabulators were worse at choosing which square stayed dark longer.

However, impaired perceptions of familiarity and recency cannot be the sole source of all abnormal confabulations (Shallice, 1999). First, semantic knowledge, which does not depend on recency or familiarity, may also be confabulated (Diamond, DeLuca, and Fisher, 2000; Moscovitch and Melo, 1997). Second, some confabulations do not appear related to past events in the patients' lives. Johnson and Raye (1998: 140) listed several examples of patient confabulation:

> Benson et al. reported a patient who gave detailed descriptions of conversations with physicians that she had never met and trips she had made out of the hospital that had not occurred. Stuss et al. reported a patient who fabricated a story of a drowning accident in which he rescued one of his children and another patient who fabricated stories about how members of his family had been killed before his eyes.

Furthermore, some confabulations are too unrealistic to be based on memories of real events, such as a memory of being a space pirate. Therefore, there is not merely an inability to discriminate on the basis of familiarity or recency but a complete breakdown in the ability to assess the plausibility of a recollection as a possible life event. Anything the patient has ever read or seen or imagined becomes a possible confabulation. Third, although the retrograde amnesia of the patient remains unchanged, his or her confabulation is often a transient disorder, which improves along with tests of frontal lobe functioning (Benson *et al.*, 1996; Fischer *et al.*, 1995). Fourth, some confabulations include a compulsion to do something. Examples are the patient who believed she had to feed her baby (Schnider, 2001) and the patient who believed he had to go somewhere that required him to dress formally every morning (Shallice, 1999). At some point confabulations become false beliefs – that is, delusions.

SUMMARY

- One story that everyone knows is the story of his or her own life. This story is called autobiographical memory.
- Autobiographical memory is organized by intentions and actions. The recall of life events is a process of reconstruction and storytelling that makes use of cues from a person's current intentions and general rules of how events are ordered to provide a coherent justification for recent and planned actions. The prefrontal cortex makes use of available cues to initiate recollection from the temporal cortex.
- The recollection of autobiographical memories makes use of both the instrumental system, to generate perceptual representations and an emotional response, and the habit system, to generate meaningful details. New details may be added to the semantic system at any time. Consequently, autobiographical memory is constantly being revised through the addition of post-event information.
    - Autobiographical memories of past events may be transformed through contradictory post-event information.
    - Eyewitness testimony may be influenced by post-event questioning.
- The long-term retention of semantic knowledge is remarkably good for the purposes of daily life.
    - Recognition of the names and faces of classmates, and the subject matter of topics studied over a few years, remains at a high level for a lifetime.
- The long-term recall of autobiographical events is described by a three-part function that reflects the roles of both the instrumental system and the habit system. When people are given cues and asked to recall a relevant life event, the following occurs.
    - There is an overall recency effect. More recent autobiographical memories are more likely to be recalled than less recent autobiographical memories. The influence of the instrumental system, and so the amount of perceptual information, is strongest for the most recent events, but declines and may be non-existent for older events.
    - However, there may be one or more reminiscence bumps for important, novel, or first-time life events, which may be recalled regardless of when they occurred. The reminiscence bump is associated with the lingering influence of the instrumental system.

    - PTSD occurs whenever an unforgettable traumatic memory interferes with performance in daily life.
  - Finally, there is childhood amnesia for memories below the age of four. No autobiographical memories are reported from this period.
- Autobiographical memory is constantly being revised through the addition of post-event information to episodes representing past events.
  - Even memories for highly emotional and unforgettable events change over time.
  - Because of the effect of post-event suggestion, repeated interrogation may generate entirely false memories.
- Retrograde amnesia is the failure to retrieve memories that were encoded normally. There are two entirely different disorders of this type.
  - In psychogenic amnesia, an individual is oriented to time and place but doesn't know who he or she is. This disorder is very rare and highly controversial, since it is associated with lying on the part of the patient.
  - More common is organic retrograde amnesia, as the result of bilateral damage to the medial temporal cortex.
    - The individual knows who he or she is but has forgotten everything for some time period up to the moment of the injury. Hence, the patient is not oriented to time or place.
  - There are three distinct forms of organic retrograde amnesia, depending on the area of the brain impaired.
    - Medial temporal cortex or thalamus: the most recent memories are the most impaired, because the instrumental system no longer generates perceptual representations.
    - Temporal cortex: the most recent memories are the least impaired, because only semantic memories have been lost.
    - Prefrontal cortex: all memories are impaired, because of the impairment of cueing and construction.
  - If there is also damage to the prefrontal cortex then the patient may also suffer from confabulation: entirely false memories may take the place of real ones.

QUESTIONS

1. What is the purpose of autobiographical memory?
2. What kinds of memories last a lifetime?
3. What brain areas contribute to autobiographical memory?
4. What causes the construction of false memories?
5. What form of retrograde amnesia causes a loss of personal identity?

FURTHER READING

Berntsen, D., and Rubin, D. C. (2012). *Understanding Autobiographical Memory: Theories and Approaches*. Cambridge University Press.

Draaisma, D., Pomerans, A., and Pomerans, E. (2006). *Why Life Speeds Up as You Get Older: How Memory Shapes Our Past*. Cambridge University Press.

14 Reasoning

You know a lot of things that you have never learned. If a pair of jeans are too small for you, then you will try on a larger size, not a smaller size, because you know that an even smaller size cannot fit you. Such a deduction is obvious, but it is not trivial. After all, it provides you with a strategy for finding a pair of jeans that fit. Deductive reasoning greatly expands what an individual knows about the world by making explicit information that is implicitly encoded in semantic memory. Reasoning involves both visual and verbal representation. The visual representation provides the intuitions that make many inferences possible, such as which jeans might fit.

Deductive reasoning may be contrasted with inductive reasoning. Inductive reasoning is based on the intuition that things that are similar in some ways are similar in other ways as well, so that any one golden retriever will be as friendly as any other. As this example indicates, inductive reasoning is often used to predict behavior, and so is a core social skill.

Human reason is directed by the prefrontal cortex. This should be obvious, since the prefrontal cortex directs all forms of cognitive processing, and human deduction and induction are forms of voluntary (mental) action. The decision system in the prefrontal cortex supplies the "Why?" to the "What?" of the instrumental system and the "How?" of the habit system.

Human reason provides information about the world that supports effective voluntary action. A decision is a choice among different actions.

- Human reason involves both visual and verbal inference. Visual representation is essential even for what appear to be verbal tasks.
- Deduction about the truth of a statement often involves recollecting or generating an example or counterexample.
  - Tasks that require recollecting an example or counterexample from semantic memory for a familiar situation rapidly produce a usually accurate answer. This is the availability heuristic.
  - Tasks that require the generation of all possible examples for a novel situation require both rehearsal and divided attention, and are difficult because it is hard to keep track of all the cases.

- The basic decision strategy of induction is to recall a similar episode and predict the same result for the current target or episode. This is called the representativeness heuristic.
  - A fundamental weakness of human decision making based on the similarity of the current event to a previous episode is that it is based on an entirely causal representation of the world. Effects of random statistical variability go unrepresented in semantic memory; as a result, they go unnoticed when reasoning.
  - Furthermore, the determination of similarity is itself a heuristic process that is subject to distortion.
- Inductive inferences guide future action by predicting the behavior of others from their past behavior and predicting the consequences of a person's own future actions by the consequences of similar actions performed by oneself or others.
  - Human inductive inferences are based on a causal representation and so can lead to a wrong decision when relevant statistical information, such as the base rate, is excluded.
- Many decisions in life are risky. There is some probability of a gain but also some probability of a loss. Prospect theory describes how people make decisions under uncertainty. When people make such decisions most people, guided by the emotional system, make decisions to avoid loss. Moreover, the subjective magnitude of a probable gain or loss is less than its objective magnitude, so a probable gain of $200 is not perceived as twice as large as a certain gain of $100. Together, loss aversion and subjective magnitude explain human decision making under uncertainty.
  - Depending on whether a choice is framed as a gain or loss influences which choice is selected, because emotion guides opposite choices for gains versus losses.
  - Framing can influence a variety of life decisions in a variety of ways by controlling the information available for the decision and how that information is represented.

14.1 Neural system

Human reason is the final step in the evolution of the control of action by the prefrontal cortex and parietal cortex. Initially, they evolved to make ad hoc physical action possible (Chapters 1 and 3). Then, the control extended to perception, to make intentional looking and listening possible (Chapters 4 and 5). Next, the control extended to semantic memory, making recollection possible (Chapter 12). Finally, reasoning is pure mental action, including the construction of possible courses of action, the representation of their possible consequences, and a choice between them, before any physical action is taken.

Figure 4.1 and Figure 14.1 show that the prefrontal cortex and the parietal cortex are responsible for both perceptual skills and reasoning. Recall from Chapter 5 that the anterior cingulate gyrus is activated by a mismatch between prediction and event, indicating that an ad hoc response is required. As shown in Figure 14.1, the reasoning involved in selecting an ad hoc response is activated by a signal from the anterior cingulate gyrus.

Verbal reasoning and visual reasoning are both possible. As shown on the left of Figure 14.1, in blue, speech areas in the left prefrontal and temporal cortex together construct novel verbal and semantic sequences, such as when cards are counted. Alternatively, as shown on the right of Figure 14.1, in red, the right superior parietal cortex generates a visuospatial representation, such as one for size comparison. The remainder of the neural decision system operates bilaterally. As shown in Figure 14.1 in purple, the inferior parietal cortex manipulates components of semantic representation to access those components relevant to the decision task, and then the medial frontal cortex associates those components in a new representation. Finally, as shown in Figure 14.1, the dorsolateral prefrontal cortex generates the deductive or inductive inference on the basis of the new representation.

Human reason is limited by the absence of one kind of information that is not encoded as a component of the episodes that comprise semantic memory, and so is not an intuitive part of declarative knowledge. The episode does not have a component that encodes the frequency with which an event has occurred, which in turn may be used to predict the probability that it will occur again in a similar context. People do have some ability to encode the likelihood of an event that might possibly recur in a similar context because the robustness of the representation encoded by the habit system increases with each distributed repetition (Chapters 2 and 10), providing a mechanism for encoding the events frequency (Knowlton, Mangels, and Squire, 1996). However, as discussed in Chapter 3, information encoded in the habit system is generally not available as declarative knowledge. For example, a person may have a particularly foreboding intuition that rain is likely on a particular day beyond the general knowledge that rain falls from dark clouds, but the intuition that rain might come is not associated with knowledge of the number of events on which it is based, nor transferable to any other context (Shohamy *et al.*, 2008). As will be discussed below, because many decisions are made about uncertain events, the lack of intuitions about probability sometimes leads human reason into error.

14.2 Visual inference

As described in Chapter 12, inference is what turns information into knowledge. Knowledge retrieved from semantic memory makes it possible to answer questions about the world correctly. For example, is a cow bigger than a mouse? One way to answer the question is to

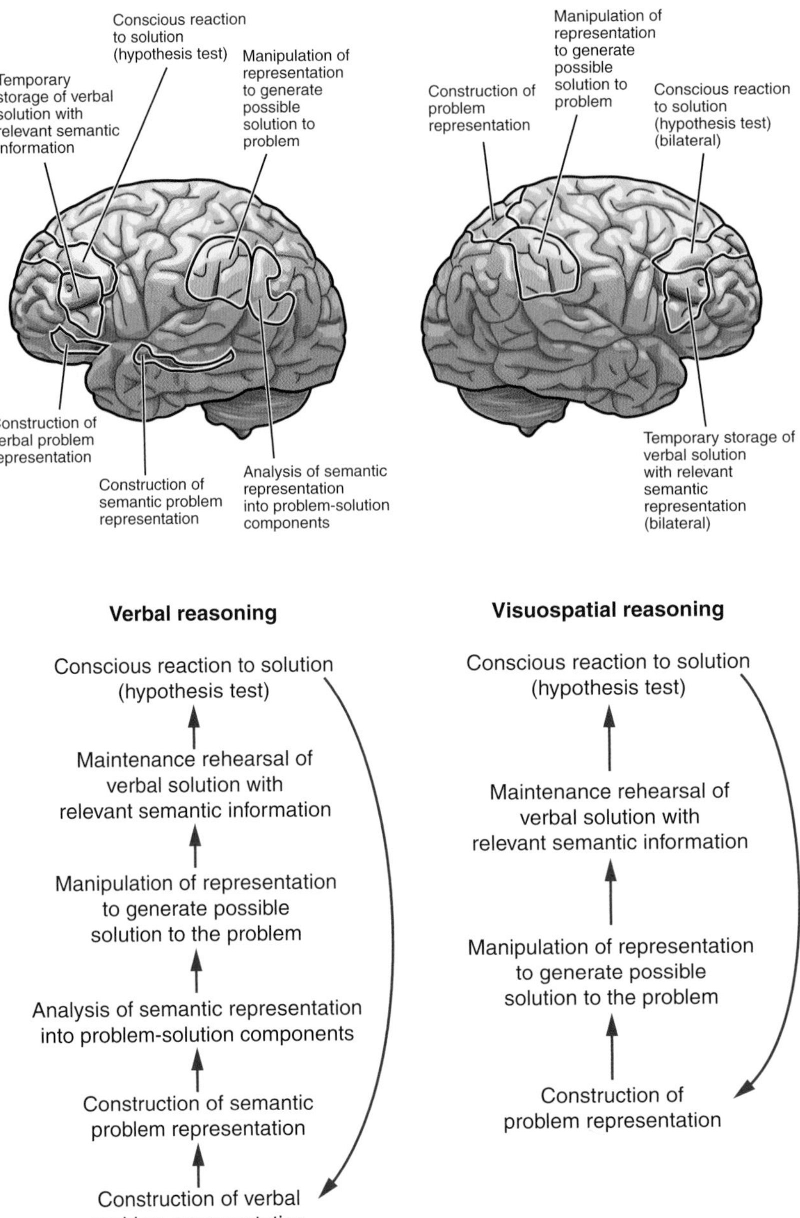

Figure 14.1 The cortical maps show the areas involved in verbal and visual reasoning and the schematic shows the pathways between them. The pathways show the flow of information from task initiation to decision (Baldo *et al.*, 2010; Jung and Haier, 2007; Prabhakaran, Rypma, and Gabrieli, 2001; Prabhakaran *et al.*, 1997; Rosenbloom, Schmahmann, and Price, 2012; Tanji and Hoshi, 2008).

generate mental images of a cow and a mouse and notice that the cow is bigger. In this case, both visual representation and visual inference would be involved in generating the answer. Another way to answer the question is to recall that a cow is a big animal and that a mouse is a small animal. In this case, the question would be answered semantically on the basis of

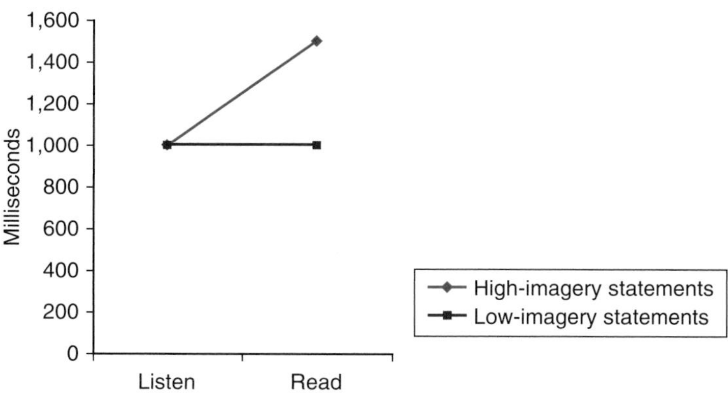

Figure 14.2 Glass *et al.* (1985) found that high-imagery statements took longer to verify when read than heard but there was no difference for low-imagery statements.

the meanings of the words *large* and *small*. Visual imagery would not be involved at all. To determine whether visual representation is involved in answering a question, the effect of answering the question on the perception or memory of a visual target is measured. Recall from Chapter 4 that generating a visual representation selectively interferes with a visually directed response. Glass, Eddy, and Schwanenflugel (1980) found that, when students had to remember a visual pattern while responding to whether statements were true or false, high-imagery statements such as "A cigarette is bigger than a pencil" interfered more with their memory of the pattern than low-imagery statements such as "Salt is used more often than pepper" did. In addition, Glass *et al.* (1985) found that high-imagery statements took longer when read than heard but that there was no difference for low-imagery statements (Figure 14.2).

Distance effects

People are faster to choose the larger animal of the pair *horse* and *cat* than of the pair *horse* and *goat* (Moyer, 1973). This is the result predicted by visual representation, because, the larger the size difference between visual targets, the faster is the visual difference between the two targets detected. So, people would also be faster to judge that a bear is bigger than a squirrel when they were judging pairs of actual animals in front of them. However, if size judgments were made by searching through a list of animals ordered by size then judgments would be faster for the animals closest in size, hence closest together in the list. So, the relationship between size difference and response time indicates that they are based on visual representation.

This is unsurprising for a visual feature such as size, especially because people have visual representations containing size information for many things. However, across many different types of concepts, reaction time measures show a **symbolic distance effect**: the further apart the items are on the relevant dimension, the more quickly a comparative judgment can be made. People are faster to choose the larger digit of the pair "2" and "8" than of the pair "2" and "3" (Moyer and Landauer, 1967). Symbolic distance effects have also been found in judgments of animal intelligence (Banks and Flora, 1977); for example, people can decide that horses are smarter than sheep.

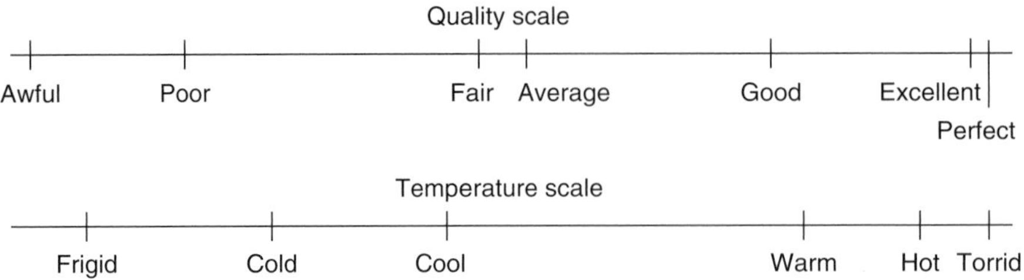

Figure 14.3 Scales showing psychological differences among terms for quality and for temperature (Holyoak and Walker, 1976).

Distance effects also occur for arbitrary orderings. Potts (1972; 1974) first taught subjects an arbitrary ordering by presenting them with sentences describing the relation between pairs of adjacent items, such as "Bill is taller than Dave," "Dave is taller than Bob," etc. After subjects had learned the ordering, they made true or false judgments about sentences describing all possible pairs of items. The reaction time actually decreased with the distance between the items. Sentences based on a pair of remote items (such as "Bill is taller than Pete") were evaluated more quickly than the sentences based on adjacent items (such as "Dave is taller than Bob"), even though only the latter sentences had actually been presented during learning. Even children as young as five years old seem to be able to use mental arrays to represent the relations between ordered items and hence make transitive inferences (Trabasso, Riley, and Wilson, 1975).

Memory for subjective magnitude can be quite detailed. Holyoak and Walker (1976) had subjects perform mental comparisons with pairs of words from semantic orderings, such as quality terms (for example, *poor, fair*) and temperature terms (for example, *cool, hot*). One group of subjects was asked to rate the psychological distance between the terms in each ordering. These ratings were used to derive a scale for each set of terms. Figure 14.3 shows how the quality and temperature terms were placed. As the figure shows, the terms are not spaced evenly. For example, the two central terms in the quality scale, *fair* and *average*, are very close. In contrast, the central terms in the temperature scale, *cool* and *warm*, are very far apart (that is, people feel that the temperature difference between *cool* and *warm* is greater than that between, say, *cold* and *cool*).

A different group of subjects then performed a reaction time task in which they chose the better of each possible pair of quality terms and the warmer of each possible pair of temperature terms. A symbolic distance effect was found for each scale: the greater the distance between the terms, the more rapidly the comparison was made. The exact spacing of the terms affected decision time. For example, the "close" pair *fair–average* was compared very slowly, whereas the more "distant" pair *cool–warm* was compared rapidly. These results indicate that not only does the order of the terms matter but also the psychological distance between them on the scale.

Williams syndrome

As the symbolic distance effect indicates, visual representation plays a central role in human reasoning. People with Williams syndrome cannot generate visual images. Consequently, their general reasoning ability is severely impaired (Bellugi *et al.*, 2000).

Children with Williams syndrome have excellent visual recognition skills, as measured by standardized face recognition tests. Their performance is just below, or even above, normal performance (Rossen *et al.*, 1995). Although language learning is initially delayed, children with Williams syndrome rapidly catch up for a while to same-age normal children in terms of vocabulary (Karmiloff-Smith *et al.*, 1997). The preserved abilities of Williams syndrome children result in an atypical pattern of language learning and, ultimately, an uneven level of linguistic performance (Bishop, 1999; Paterson *et al.*, 1999). When asked to produce instances of a category such as *animals* (the verbal fluency test) they produce more words than age-matched controls and more rare words than age-matched controls (Bellugi *et al.*, 2000). Furthermore, they show good understanding of the words they know. In addition, the syntactic complexity of their spontaneous speech is excellent and knowledge of syntax is generally good (Bellugi, Klima, and Wang, 1996; Karmiloff-Smith, 1998). Ultimately, the distribution of vocabulary scores for individuals with Williams syndrome is below that for normal individuals (Bellugi *et al.*, 2000). However, general conversational communication is excellent, and individuals with Williams syndrome are excellent storytellers (Jones *et al.*, 2000). Many become avid readers (Howlin, Davies, and Udwin, 1998).

In contrast, the performance of children with Williams syndrome on any task that requires any degree of visualization is extremely poor. When asked to compare a standard with a set of lines in different orientations, they cannot find the line in the same orientation as the standard (Bellugi *et al.*, 2000). Their ability to copy a pattern or picture is also poor. The contrast between drawing and storytelling ability is shown in Figure 14.4. Drawing does not exceed the level of a normal five-year-old. Even their use of spatial prepositions is impaired. Prepositions such as *on, in, in front of*, etc. may be misused in describing scenes, despite otherwise appropriate syntactic and semantic constructions (Bellugi *et al.*, 2000). The effect of this deficit on cognitive development is severe. On general cognitive tasks, individuals with Williams syndrome rank in the mild to moderate mentally retarded range (Bellugi *et al.*, 1996). Adults have a conceptual understanding of basic biological categories of living things such as people, animals, and plants that is equivalent only to that of normal six-year-olds (Carey, 1985).

Individuals with Williams syndrome have severely deficient computational skills. Only a few master addition. Fewer still master subtraction and division. Finally, the ability to make

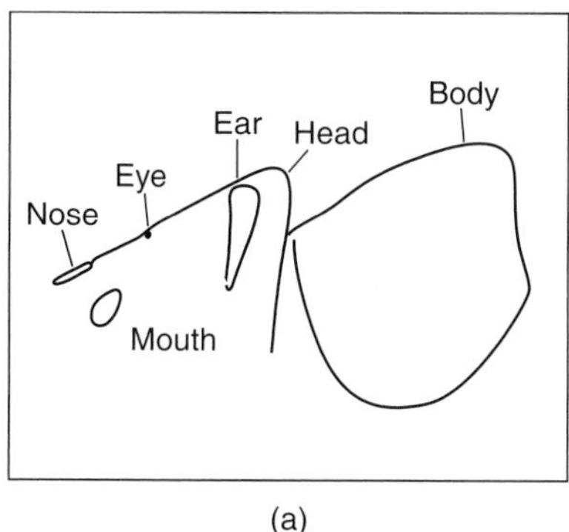

(a)

And what an elephant is, it is one of the animals. And what the elephant does, it lives in the jungle. It can also live in the zoo, And what it has, it has long gray ears, fan ears that can blow in the wind. It has a long trunk that can pick up grass, or pick up hay.... If they're in a bad mood it can be terrible... If the elephant gets mad it could stomp; it could charge like a bull can charge. They have long big tusks. They can damage a car... It could be dangerous. When they're in a pinch, when they're in a bad mood, it can be terrible. You don't want an elephant as a pet. You want a cat or a dog or a bird...

(b)

Figure 14.4 The contrast between the visuospatial and language abilities of an 18-year-old woman with Williams syndrome whose IQ is 49. On the left is her drawing of an elephant (a) and on the right is her verbal description of an elephant (b).

inferences is absent. When asked to estimate the sizes of familiar objects, many responses were far off the mark. The length of a dollar bill was estimated to be five feet by an eighteen-year-old and one inch by a twenty-year-old. The length of a bus was estimated at thirty inches by a twelve-year-old (Kopera-Frye, Dehaene, and Streissguth, 1996). Since much of daily conversation requires the making of what are normally obvious inferences, this leaves individuals with Williams syndrome with an inordinately concrete view of the world. A twenty-one-year-old woman with Williams syndrome had read several books on her favorite topic: vampires. When she was asked what a vampire is, she responded that a vampire is "a man who climbs into ladies' bedrooms at night and sinks his teeth into their necks." When asked why vampires do that, she thought for a bit, and then said, "Vampires must have an inordinate fondness for necks" (Johnson and Carey, 1998).

Verbal role in visual inference

In contrast, even five-year-olds could infer from "Ann is taller than Beth" and "Beth is taller than Carol" that "Ann is taller than Carol" (Trabasso, Riley, and Wilson, 1975). When the order of the statements is reversed, so we have "Beth is taller than Carol" and "Ann is taller than Beth," you must find the two no longer adjacent terms that are identical and use that information to reorder the two statements. You therefore detect the identical terms through a recency judgment and then reorder the statements through verbal rehearsal. Nevertheless, children could draw the correct conclusion from the reversed statements beginning at the age of five (Halford, 1984). So they could use verbal rehearsal to assist in the construction of a visual representation.

This integration of verbal rehearsal and visual representation is directed by the prefrontal cortex, as shown in Figure 14.1. Adults who had the frontal variant of frontal-temporal dementia (Chapter 13), and so had brain damage restricted to the prefrontal cortex, were tested on transitive chains of up to four premises by Waltz *et al.* (1999). The individuals were in the early stage of the dementia and so still had normal intelligence and memory. They could still make deductions for the transitive chains when they were ordered from largest to smallest:

Ann is taller than Beth;
Beth is taller than Carol;
Carol is taller than Debby;
Debby is taller than Eve.

However, they were unable to make the correct deduction when the order of the premises was scrambled. Human deduction is just a voluntary action. All but the simplest deduction requires the construction of a novel representation

Visual intuition versus semantic knowledge

Visual representation is only as accurate as the information it is based on. Consider the task of predicting the flight path of an object that had rolled out the end of a tube. Everyone has seen moving objects, so the task is not difficult. However, how and why they move is not open to observation. It was not until Isaac Newton codified the laws of motion that people had a system for computing the paths of moving objects. These laws are taught in a physics course. However, these abstract verbal laws are entirely apart from the visual representations

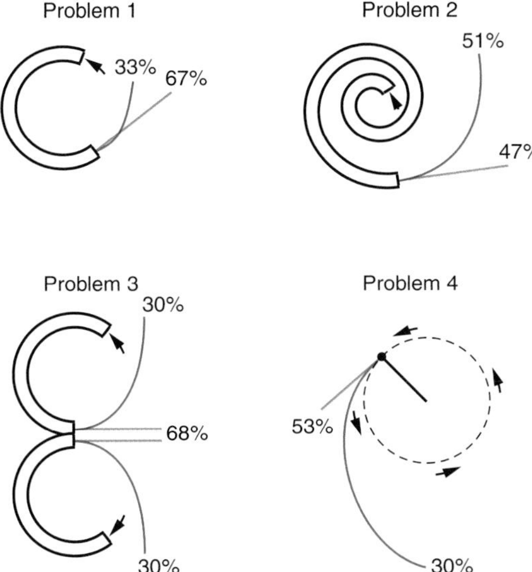

Figure 14.5 Four motion problems given to students who completed a college physics course. In problems 1 to 3 a ball is shot through a tube. In problem 4 a string swinging the ball breaks. The correct response and the percentage of students making it is shown in green. The most common incorrect response and the percentage of students making it is shown in red. (McCloskey *et al.*, 1980).

that generate visual intuition. McCloskey, Caramazza, and Green (1980) were interested in how often a knowledge of physics would be used in a task designed to cue visual inference. So they gave Johns Hopkins students who had just studied physics a test on the motion of objects. Students were shown three pictures of a ball that had just rolled through a tube and one of a ball that had just broken loose of a string and asked to draw its path (Figure 14.5). They asked the students to draw the trajectory of a ball shot through the tube at high speed. Figure 14.5 shows the two most common responses: the correct, straight path, specified by Newtonian physics, is shown in green; and the incorrect, curved path is shown in red, along with the percentage of students who selected each path. As can be seen from the figure, for each problem at least a third of the students could not overcome their visual intuition that balls fly in a curving path. In a subsequent study, McCloskey and Kohl (1983) found that, even when students had the opportunity of interacting with actual objects, such as a puck, exiting from a curved tube, many still indicated that it followed a curved path when it exited the tube.

14.3 Deduction from an example or counterexample

Recall from Chapter 12 that people confirm or disconfirm statements by recollecting an example or counterexample, such as disconfirming that all roses are red by recollecting a yellow rose. Notice that a single counterexample can disconfirm a statement; however, no number of examples can confirm a statement with absolute certainty unless one can be certain that all examples have been recollected. Moreover, as discussed in Chapter 12, regardless of the size of a category, because of proactive interference only a few instances may be generated in a brief period of time. This precludes the possibility of giving a definite answer to a question that requires recollecting all the members of a category – for example, how many or what percentage of animals have tails? Instead, people rely on the heuristic of **availability**. A **heuristic** is a decision procedure that usually gives the correct answer, but is not guaranteed to do so. Frequency decisions are made on the ease of generating an example. If retrieval is easy and fluent, the category will be judged to be large. For example, Tversky and Kahneman (1973) had students listen to a list of names of celebrities in which either the men or women were more famous. The list contained more names of one sex than the other, and afterwards the students were asked to report which sex had more names on the list. They incorrectly reported the sex with the more famous names had more names on the list even though there were fewer of them.

Availability affects risk assessment. Risks that one hears about more often are perceived as higher. Lichtenstein *et al.* (1978) found that people overestimate the frequency of well-publicized causes of death while underestimating the frequency of less notorious causes. For example, they found that homicides are judged to be about as frequent as death by stroke in the United States, whereas in fact stroke is over ten times more common than homicide as a cause of death.

Confirmatory bias. Questions about generalizations are often cues for positive examples, but not for negative examples. The statement "All roses are red" is a cue for red roses, so it is easier to recollect roses that are red than roses of any other color. The greater availability of positive examples is called **confirmatory bias**. For example, trainee counselors were shown a video of a client–counselor interaction and were asked to propose a possible diagnosis for the client. When asked to recall behaviors from the video, 64 percent were confirmatory of the diagnosis, 21 percent were neutral, and only 15 percent were disconfirming (Haverkamp, 1993).

Confirmatory bias can interfere with logical intuition itself. So far we have only considered deduction informally. To describe human reason in more detail, a more formal description is necessary. A logical syllogism consists of **premises** and a **conclusion** that is deduced from them. For example, from the **premises** "Some flowers are roses" and "Roses are red," one can deduce the **conclusion** "Some flowers are red." A deduction is **valid** when it is the case that, if the premises are true, then the conclusion must be true. To state this generalization, we replace the specific instances in the premises with abstract variables.

Some X are Y
Y are Z
———————
Some X are Z

is a valid syllogism.

People have limited intuitions about validity. Consequently, when asked whether a syllogism is valid, they resort to generating a concrete example. For example, from the premises "All men are humans" and "Some humans are Americans," can one deduce the conclusion "Some men are Americans"? When I posed this question to my students, most decided that this syllogism is valid. They reached this incorrect conclusion because the example reduces the availability of a counterexample. Although it is true that some men are Americans, this conclusion does not follow from the premises that were given. This can easily be seen when different instances are substituted in the syllogism. From the premises "All men are humans" and "Some humans are women," one cannot deduce the conclusion "Some men are women."

Anchoring effect. From general knowledge of the world, people can give quantitative estimates about the size of almost anything in their experience, from the length of the Mississippi river to how long it takes to place a call on a cellphone. To begin, an **anchor value** is generated that is not too large or too small when considering what is known about the target. Then, this value may be adjusted on the basis of whatever additional information is recollected about the target. In this task, availability also produces the **anchoring effect**. The anchor value that is generated may be primed by an unrelated cue. Students spun a (rigged) wheel numbered from "1" to "100" that always came up "10" or "65." They were then asked whether the percentage of African nations was larger or smaller than that number and what they thought the correct number was. Obviously, the number on the wheel bore no relation to the question. Nevertheless, the average guesses were 25 percent and 45 percent for the numbers "10" and "65," respectively (Kahneman, 2011: 119).

Hindsight bias. Finally, availability produces **hindsight bias**. The probability of an event is judged as greater after it occurs. Moreover, people overestimate their previous knowledge; for example, people overestimated the number of questions they answered correctly on an exam, once they knew what the correct answers were (Gros and Bayen, 2015). Hindsight bias plays an important role in the construction of autobiographical memories (Sanna and Schwarz, 2006). When people recollect past experiences they do not recollect them as a sequence of surprises but, rather, embed them in a causal narrative. As discussed in the last chapter, autobiographical memory is useful for future action. This means that it is more important to remember the correct answers to the questions on the last exam (which may be asked again in the final) than to remember the answers you actually put. Furthermore, the more you know now, the more you will infer you knew at the time of the exam.

Generating examples and counterexamples

Sometimes, when selecting a possible action, it is possible to deduce the most probable state of the world or result of each action in advance from what is already known. This is an important test of human reason. Can a person deduce the correct conclusion when all the relevant information is available? When such tasks are posed, it turns out that human reason is not perfect. Recall from Chapter 12 that the length of a novel sequence that can be immediately recalled is quite short. Most people cannot recall a digit sequence longer than a phone number. Similarly, when trying to determine a course of action, it is extremely difficult to systematically consider even a small list of possible cases or examples, because PI from whatever case is considered first interferes with generating all the remaining cases. Therefore, not all the possibilities are imagined.

Three-card problem. The failure to imagine all the possibilities is often what leads to error in deduction. Suppose you are told that there are three cards in a hat. One card is red on both sides (the all-red card). One card is white on both sides (the all-white card). One card is red on one side and white on the other (the red/white card). You close your eyes, pick a single card randomly, and put it down on the table. The drawn card has a red side up. What is the probability that this is the all-red card? If your answer is one-half then you responded like thirty-five of fifty-three of students in an experiment by Bar-Hillel and Falk (1982). Most people reason as follows. The red face means that we can exclude the all-white card from consideration. This means that the card can either be the all-red or the red/white one, each with a fifty–fifty chance. However, this response is incomplete, and leads to the wrong conclusion. There are three possible surfaces that are red. Two of these are on the all-red card and one on the red/white card. So, the correct answer is two-thirds.

Three-door problem. The three-door problem is impressively difficult because of its simplicity and because, even after it has been explained, the answer may be difficult to understand. Even a lot of experience with a problem will not necessarily guarantee the correct representation or the correct answer. For many years a popular show on television was *Let's Make a Deal*. At the end of the show a contestant was given a choice of three doors by the host, Monty Hall. Behind one door was a valuable prize, behind a second door a lesser prize, and behind one door a prize of little or no value. Suppose that the contestant chose door number 1. Sometimes Hall would increase the suspense by showing that the booby prize was behind door number 3 and then giving the contestant the chance to switch from door number 1 to door number 2 if he or she wished. Should you switch doors? On September 9, 1990, this problem appeared in Marilyn Vos Savant's column in *Parade* magazine, asking: "Is it to your advantage to switch your choice?"

What happened next was quite remarkable. Vos Savant gave the correct answer, that contestants should switch. Contestants have only a one-third chance of their initial choice being the one with the big prize, since they selected from among three doors. But, if they did not select the correct door, then the one that remains must have the big prize, since the one that was eliminated did not. Hence, if contestants stick with their original door, they have only a one-third chance of winning the big prize; but, if they switch, they have a two-thirds chance of winning it. In response came a cascade of mail from readers of all levels of education arguing that Vos Savant was wrong and it made no difference whether contestants stayed or switched. Vos Savant replied as follows:

> Yes, you should switch. The first door has a 1/3 chance of winning, but the second door has a 2/3 chance. Here's a good way to visualize what happened. Suppose there are a million doors, and you pick door No. 1 then the host, who knows what's behind the door and will always avoid the one with the prize, opens them all except for door No. 777,777. You'd switch to that door pretty fast, wouldn't you?

The difficulty appears to be the same in both the three-card and three-door problems. The statement of the problem encourages a person to collapse two of the possible outcomes together, so that what should be visualized as three outcomes is imagined as only two.

Wason selection task. The Wason (1966; 1968) selection problem is another deceptively simple but difficult problem. Wason presented his subjects with four cards, which were placed in front of them, showing symbols such as the following:

A M 6 3

If a card has a vowel on one side then it has an even number on the other side.

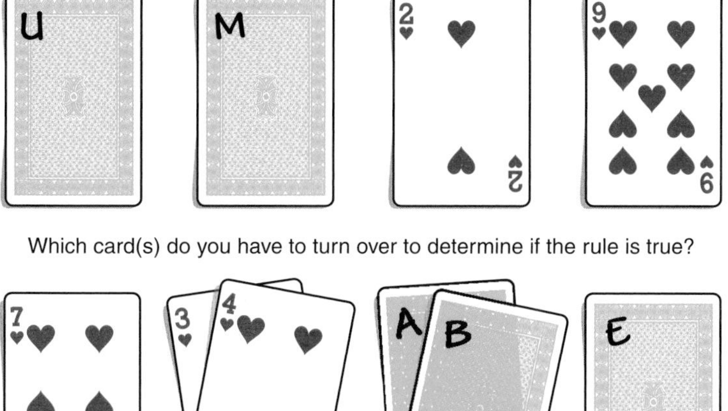

Figure 14.6 Top shows initial sides of cards and statement of problem. Bottom shows that the first and fourth cards could be disconfirming and so must be turned over. However, the second and third cards cannot disconfirm the rule whatever is on the other side, and so do not have to be turned over (Wason, 1966; 1968).

They were told that each card had a letter on one side and a number on the other. Then they were given a rule: "If a card has a vowel on one side, then it has an even number on the other side." The subjects' task was to name those cards, and those cards only, that needed to be turned over in order to determine whether the rule was true or false.

What do you think the correct answer is? Almost all the subjects in Wason's experiment said either "A and 6" or "only A." But the correct answer is "A and 3." Figure 14.6 (a) shows why this answer is correct. Card "6" is incorrect because, even if there isn't a vowel on the other side, it would not falsify the rule. The rule says only that, if a card has a vowel, then it will also have an even number. But the "3" is a critical card, because if a card with an odd number turns out to have a vowel on the other side then the rule will have been falsified.

To sum up, in the Wason selection task, there are four possible cards. Three are consistent with the rule and one is a counterexample to it.

Part of the difficulty of the Wason selection problem is that quite a lot of information must be represented in memory. The conditional statement "If a card has a vowel on one side, then it has an even number on the other side" is consistent with three cards: (1) vowel/even number; (2) consonant/even number; and (3) consonant/odd number. Few, if any, individuals begin by imagining these three possibilities. Rather, they consider each of the four pictured cards in conjunction with the verbal statement and construct a part of the mental model of the statement for each card (Gigerenzer and Hug, 1992; Manktelow and Over, 1991). Consequently, some examples are missed, and correct performance is 10 percent. When Staller, Sloman, and Ben-Zeev (2000) included the three cards described by the rule in the statement of the problem so that an individual could compare each card in the problem with each of the three positive examples of the rule, correct performance increased to 50 percent.

Negation. Conside the following two syllogisms, called by the Latin names *modus ponens* and *modus tollens*, respectively.

Modus ponens is:

If p, then q.
p.
Therefore q.

Modus tollens is:

If p, then q.
Not q.
Therefore not p.

Both these rules are valid. For example, suppose our initial premise is "If it is Wednesday, then we have psychology." *Modus ponens* then gives the following. If it is Wednesday, then we have psychology. It is Wednesday. Therefore we have psychology today.*Modus tollens* gives the following:If it is Wednesday, then we have psychology. We do not have psychology today. Therefore it is not Wednesday.

However, while both rules are valid, you have probably already noticed that they do not seem equally obvious. *Modus ponens* is immediately obvious, whereas *modus tollens* seems to require careful thought. In fact, studies have shown that, whereas virtually all college students endorse *modus ponens* as valid, a substantial proportion fail to endorse *modus tollens* (Taplin, 1971; Taplin and Staudenmayer, 1973). Seemingly, *modus ponens* is an intuitive rule of logic, but *modus tollens* is not.

Modus ponens can be verified through a straightforward matching strategy. If the second premise matches the first term of the first premise, then the conclusion is true. However, *modus tollens* involves negation, which inevitably increases processing difficulty (Clark and Chase, 1972). Probably the clearest justification of *modus tollens* is to reason as follows (using our example).

I know that, if it is Wednesday, then we have psychology. I also know that we do not have psychology today. Now, suppose it were Wednesday. Then (by *modus ponens*) we would have psychology today. But that contradicts the fact that we do not have psychology today. So my supposition must be false: it is not Wednesday.

Although most people find this justification of *modus tollens* compelling, it clearly involves several inference steps. In contrast, the simple matching operation for *modus ponens* is easily applied, so that the deduction is immediately recognized as valid. This discussion suggests that *modus ponens* is part of our cognitive repertoire of rules for everyday reasoning, whereas *modus tollens* is not.

To solve a logical reasoning problem you imagine a scene consistent with the premises and then scan the scene to determine what is true about it. This heuristic works for positive assertions but not for negative ones. First consider *modus ponens*. You imagine p and check for q. Next consider *modus tollens*. How can you make an image of "not q"? How would this image be different from the image of "not p" or "not r"? So, instead, you have to fall back on the extended verbal reasoning described above. To make a negated statement meaningful one must generate all the instances that contradict it. As mentioned above, this is a difficult task.

The bead problem. Because *modus ponens* is easy to visualize, its transitive nature is apparent. If we add the premise "If we have psychology, then we meet in Cattell auditorium" to the premises above, then it obviously follows from "Today is Wednesday" that we meet in Cattell auditorium. In contrast, if even two arguments having negation in them, hence requiring *modus tollens* to evaluate, are combined, the resulting problem requires such a long train of reasoning that, for most individuals, it is initially unsolvable.

Consider the following problem.

Only one of these two statements is true:

"At least some of the plastic beads are not red."

"None of the plastic beads are red."

Is it possible that none of the plastic beads are red?

What do you think the answer is? A total of 77 percent of the responses of Princeton University undergraduates were "Yes." But the answer is "No." If the answer is "Yes," and so none of the beads are red, then the second statement, "None of the plastic beads are red," is true, which means that the first statement, "At least some of the plastic beads are not red," is true, which contradicts the premise "Only one of these two statements is true."

What made this problem so difficult for the poor muddled Princeton undergraduates? The situation described by the premises cannot be imagined because only positive cases, not negative cases, can be imagined (Yang and Johnson-Laird, 2000). Furthermore, errors of reasoning increase with the number of details that must be maintained through rehearsal to solve the problem (O'Brien, Braine, and Yang, 1994).

14.4 Representativeness

The basic decision strategy for explaining the world is to represent events as episodes, which consist of actors, actions, targets, contexts, and results. Within an episode, an action causes a result. Because actions and their results are causally related, the episode usually provides an accurate description of an event. Because the strategy is to represent the world as it usually is, the strategy is called **representativeness**. However, an episode is an entirely causal representation of the world. Consequently, effects of random statistical variability go unrepresented in semantic memory, and so they go unnoticed. Representativeness is therefore a heuristic.

Sample size

The probability of drawing all marbles of the same color from an urn with an equal number of red and white marbles is 12.5 percent for a sample of four but only 1.56 percent for a sample of seven. A sample's size therefore has a large effect on its representativeness. The smaller the sample is, the more likely that it will be unrepresentative. People have no intuitions about the effect of sample size on representativeness. Even members of the Mathematical Psychology Group were found to lack such intuitions (Tversky and Kahneman, 1971). As a result, people intuitively think of large samples and small samples as equally representative. For example, suppose you kept track of all the days in a year in which 60 percent or more of the babies born in a hospital were boys. Would there be more such days for a large hospital or a small one? The answer is the small one. To stretch the example a little further, in which hospital would you expect more days of the year in which 60 percent or more of the babies born were girls? Would it be the small hospital that had more days with 60 percent boy babies or the large hospital with fewer days with 60 percent boy babies? The answer would be the small hospital, which would have more days in the year with 60 percent boy births *and* more days in the year with 60 percent girl births. Sometimes, in a consideration of how the world works, sample size is important. Wainer and Zwerling (2006) mentioned that the Gates Foundation spent $1.7 billion to break up big schools into small schools, because schools with the best average test scores were small schools. However, the schools with the worst average test scores were, necessarily, small schools as well.

Sequence probability

Correct intuitions about causality induce false intuitions about the results of a random process. When a sequence is generated randomly, such as for the order in which boys and girls are born on a given day in a hospital, all sequences are equally likely. However, representative sequences appear more plausible, hence more probable, than less plausible sequences. So, even though the following sequences are equally likely, most people perceive the third sequence to be most likely (Kahneman, 2011: 115):

BBBGGG
GGGGGG
BGBBGB

The sole reliance on representativeness blinds individuals to other natural relationships, such as set inclusion. Suppose a dice with four red and two green faces was rolled repeatedly, and you were given a choice of the three sequences below. If the one you selected was rolled, you would win $25. Which dice sequence would you select?

RGRRR
GRGRRR
GRRRRR

Tversky and Kahneman (1983) found that most people selected the middle sequence; however, the correct answer is the first one. The middle sequence contains the first sequence. Hence, if the first sequence were selected then, every time the middle sequence was selected, the $25 would be paid, as it would be paid on any sequence that contained it.

Sampling probability. There is also a surprising failure on the part of some individuals to compute even obvious probabilities. A red marble wins a prize. Which urn would you chose to select one marble from?

Urn A contains ten marbles, of which one is red.
Urn B contains 100 marbles, of which 8 are red.

Various studies have found that 30 to 40 percent of students selected urn B (Kirkpatrick and Epstein, 1992; Miller, Turnbull, and McFarland, 1989).

Similarity

To summarize, the basic strategy for understanding the world is that similar actions to similar targets will have similar results. A second limitation of this strategy, beyond its blindness to statistical effects, is the biases inherent in the human perception of similarity. Perceived similarity depends on the amount of information available about each target as well as the overlap. Consequently, the perceived similarity of a pair of targets depends on how they are compared (Tversky, 1977). Arizona may be more similar to California than California is to Arizona.

Figure 14.7 depicts the relation between the features of two representations in semantic memory, A and B, using Venn diagrams. The features of each representation are represented by a circle. The features can be partitioned into three sets. The area where the circles overlap represents the shared features of the representations. This set is referred to as "A ∩ B" (read "A and B"); in other words, these are features that are true of both A and B. The other two sets represent distinctive features. "A – B" is the set of distinctive features of representation A – that is, those true of A but not of B; similarly, "B – A" is the set of distinctive features of representation B.

The three types of features affect similarity judgments in the following way:

(1) Increasing A ∩ B increases similarity.
(2) Increasing A – B decreases similarity.
(3) Increasing B – A decreases similarity.

In other words, increasing the shared features of two representations increases their similarity, whereas increasing their distinctive features decreases their similarity. When a target representation is compared with another representation, called the referent representation, in memory the distinctive features of the target are usually given more weight than the distinctive features of the referent. Put differently, similarity is reduced more by the unique features of the target than by the unique features of the referent.

In addition, the more a person knows about something, the more weight its distinctive features are given. Tversky and Gati (1978) selected pairs of countries in which one was more familiar than the other (for example, China and North Vietnam, Belgium and Luxembourg, Russia and Poland). They asked two groups of college students to rate how similar each pair of countries was. For each pair, one group was asked to compare the more familiar country with the less familiar one (for example, "How similar is Russia to Poland?"), whereas the other group was asked to compare the less familiar country with the more familiar one (for example, "How similar is Poland to Russia?"). The less familiar country was usually judged to be more similar to the familiar country than vice versa.

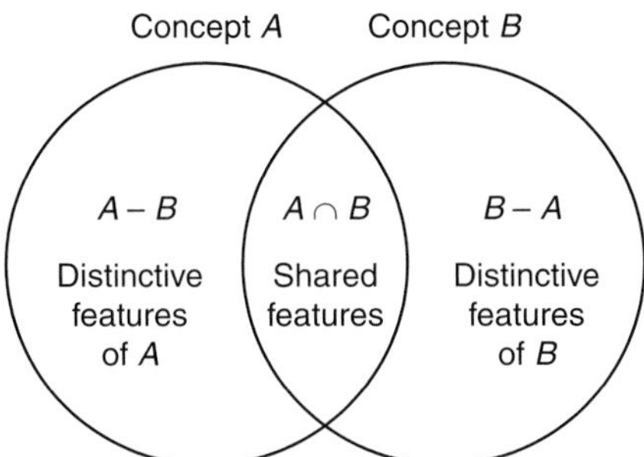

Figure 14.7 A graphical illustration of the relations between the features of two concepts (Tversky, 1977).

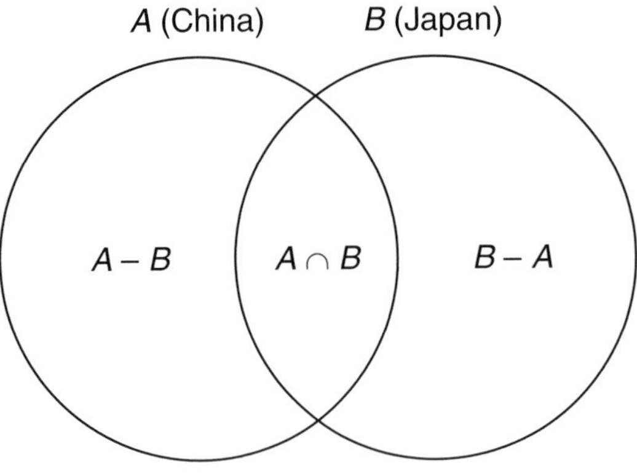

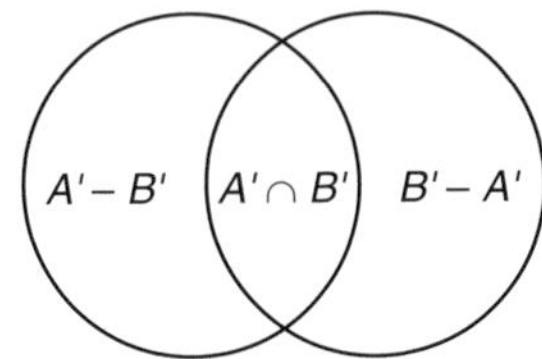

Figure 14.8 Similarity versus differences. China and Japan are perceived as both more similar to and more different from each other than Myanmar and Nepal are similar to or different from each other (Tversky and Gati, 1978).

Furthermore, it is possible for one pair of items to be both more similar and more different than another pair. China and Japan are two prominent countries that most people know a lot about. As a result, each country has many features. On the other hand, Myanmar and Nepal are two countries that most people know relatively little about. As a result, as shown in Figure 14.8, the two prominent countries have more shared features than do the less prominent ones (that is, A ∩ B is larger than A' ∩ B'). However, in addition, the more prominent countries also have more distinctive features (that is, A – B plus B – A is larger than A' – B' plus B' – A'). In other words, people can think of many similarities between Japan and China, and also many differences. But, since people do not know very much about Myanmar and Nepal, those countries do not seem either as similar or as different as Japan and China.

14.5 Induction and prediction

Inductive inferences guide future action. Inductive tasks involve predicting the behavior of others from their past behavior and predicting the consequences of a person's own future actions by the consequences of similar actions performed by oneself or others. The purpose is to guide future action. The memory system is designed to recollect all the information relevant to a decision. Relevance is defined by the context. This usually leads to a better decision. It is especially useful in social decisions, which are context-dependent.

As demonstrated above by the three-card problem, the three-door problem, the Wason selection problem, and the bead problem, human reasoning is challenged by tasks in which an ad hoc representation of a novel problem must be generated. Errors result from errors in representing all the features of the problem accurately and from maintaining all the features while dividing attention between the representation and the deductions from it. Recall that only 10 percent of college students made the correct choices in the Wason selection task. When exactly the same problem is restated as a familiar task for which a representation already exists in semantic memory, so there is no longer any need to construct or rehearse an ad hoc representation, the probability of an error is greatly reduced. The context specificity of human reason is demonstrated by the improvement in performance on the Wason selection task that resulted when it was described in a familiar framework. Performance on the task can be radically altered by varying the description of the rule. Figure 14.9 illustrates two versions of selection problems studied by Johnson-Laird, Legrenzi, and Legrenzi (1972). The abstract version of the role, shown at the bottom of the figure, was analogous to the rule that Wason (1966; 1968) had previously studied: "If a letter has a 'D' on one side, then it has a '5' on the other." Except for calling the components "letters" instead of "cards" and specifying "D" and "5" instead of "consonant" and "odd number," its representation was the same as in Figure 14.6. In the meaningful version of the rule, the subjects were told to imagine they were postal workers engaged in sorting letters. They were to decide if the following rule was being followed: "If a letter is sealed, then it has a 5d stamp on it." (The experiment was conducted in the United Kingdom prior to decimalization, when "d" was the symbol for "pence.") The choices were the four envelopes shown at the top of Figure 14.9: a closed envelope (p), an open envelope (not p), a 5d stamp (q), and a 4d stamp (not q).

The rule was exactly the same in both the meaningful and the abstract conditions. The two relevant cases to check were always p and not q – that is, the closed envelope and the 4d stamp in the meaningful version, and the "D" and the "4" in the abstract version. However, performance on the two versions was strikingly different. In the meaningful condition twenty-one of the twenty-four subjects were correct, whereas in the arbitrary condition only two of the same twenty-four subjects were correct. Moreover, no transfer occurred between the two conditions: Getting the correct solution to the meaningful version did not improve performance on the arbitrary version. The results of Johnson-Laird, Legrenzi, and Legrenzi

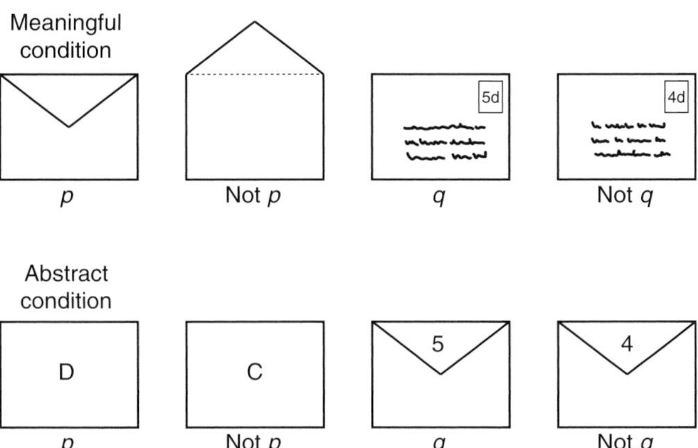

Figure 14.9 Materials used in meaningful and abstract conditions (Wason and Johnson-Laird, 1972).

(1972) thus indicated that people are much more successful at reasoning about a meaningful rule in a familiar context than a logically equivalent novel, abstract rule (Griggs, 1983; Wason, 1983). At the time of the original Johnson-Laird, Legrenzi, and Legrenzi study, there was, in fact, an actual British postal rule of this sort: a sealed envelope signified first-class mail, which required more postage. The postal rule version of the selection task was thus very similar to a rule with which the subjects were familiar. The importance of familiar context for the rule was confirmed by the findings of two later studies. Nearly ten years later, when the postal rule had been defunct for some time, Golding (1981) found that the postal rule version produced facilitation for older British subjects who were familiar with the rule but not for younger British subjects unfamiliar with it. Similarly, Griggs and Cox (1982) found that the postal rule version did not improve performance for American subjects, who were unfamiliar with it.

People are not entirely bound by experience. People can use a novel rule in a familiar situation as long as they are given a meaningful rationale that makes it possible to integrate the rule with the familiar representation. Cheng and Holyoak (1985) gave the postal rule problem both to students in the United States, who were unfamiliar with it, and to students in Hong Kong, where the post office still enforced such a rule. As would be expected given earlier results, the Hong Kong subjects selected the correct alternatives more often than did the American subjects. However, Cheng and Holyoak also tested conditions in which a rationale was provided along with the rule. Subjects in the rationale condition were simply told that the post office defined sealed mail as first class. When the rationale was provided, students in the United States performed just as well as Hong Kong students with prior familiarity with the rule.

Essentially, Cheng and Holyoak (1985) provided the students in the rationale condition with the method for deducing the conclusion. One thing people learn about regulations is how to check that they are followed. Many regulations, such as the postal rule, have the form "If a certain action [such as sealing an envelope] is to be taken, then a certain condition [such as providing adequate postage] must be met." If the action is taken, we need to check that the condition was met; and, if the condition wasn't met, we need to check that the action wasn't taken.

Concrete situations and rationales make the problem easier because they make the counterexample to the rule part of the person's representation. Using this principle, investigators have become highly inventive at creating versions of the selection problem that suggest a counterexample and hence are easy to solve. Almor and Sloman (1996) used the quality control rule "If the product breaks then it must have been used under abnormal conditions," and found that people were most likely to select the correct "p" and "not q" cards (the product broke and it was used under normal conditions). Presumably the quality control context elicited counterexamples: products that were bad despite correct usage (see also Green, 1995; Green and Larking, 1995; Sperber, Cara, and Girotto, 1995).

Causal versus statistical prediction

To summarize, when human logical intuition is combined with the causal semantic representations of specific tasks it provides a powerful engine for accurate social deduction and skilled decisions, in terms of acceptability, permission, and performance frameworks. However, causal representations are very much all-or-none representations. In an episode, an action is associated with a result in a specific context. The episode does not contain a component representing the probability that the result follows the action. Because context-specific, causal representations do not include the features of the context relevant to the calculation of probabilities, people do not take this information into account when using the representativeness heuristic to make predictions. For example, people know that the world changes, so they should be less confident predicting what someone will be doing five years from now than in predicting what that person will be doing tomorrow. However, distance into the future has almost no effect on confidence or any aspect of the prediction. Tversky and Kahneman (1974) presented subjects with several paragraphs, each describing the performance of a student teacher during a particular practice lesson. Some subjects were asked to evaluate the quality of the lesson. Other subjects were asked to predict the standing of each student teacher five years after the practice lesson. The judgments made under the two conditions were identical.

Base rates. In another experiment (Kahneman and Tversky, 1973) a group of sixty-five college students were presented with the following personality sketch:

> Tom W. is of high intelligence, although lacking in true creativity. He has a need for order and clarity, and for neat and tidy systems in which every detail finds its appropriate place. His writing is rather dull and mechanical, occasionally enlivened by somewhat corny puns and by flashes of imagination of the sci-fi type. He has a strong drive for competence. He seems to have little feel and little sympathy for other people and does not enjoy interacting with others. Self-centered, he nonetheless has a deep moral sense.

The subjects were asked to rate how similar Tom W. seemed to the typical graduate student in either computer science or the humanities. Overwhelmingly, they thought that Tom W. was more similar to a typical computer science student.

The same sketch was then given to a different group of 114 psychology students, along with the following additional information:

> The preceding personality sketch of Tom W. was written during Tom's senior year in high school by a psychologist, on the basis of projective tests. Tom W. is currently a graduate student.

Subjects were then asked to predict whether Tom W. was more likely to be in computer science or in the humanities. Overwhelmingly, they decided on computer science. Well, you might ask, what's surprising about that? After all, people think the sketch of Tom W. fits a computer science student. Three things make the result remarkable. First, yet another group of subjects simply estimated the relative percentages of the two types of graduate students. Humanities students were judged to be about three times more numerous. Therefore, the **prior odds,** the odds based on the percentage of computer science graduate students, were rather heavily against Tom W. being in computer science. Second, the same subjects who made the predictions were also asked how reliable they thought projective tests, such as ink blot tests, were. They thought that projective tests – the source of Tom W.'s personality sketch – were very unreliable. Third, even if the description were valid when Tom W. was in high school, everyone would agree he might well be very different by the time he was in graduate school. Seemingly, therefore, in making their predictions, subjects ignored the prior odds and based their decisions entirely on information they would readily admit was very likely wrong. The sketch was considered highly "representative" of the personality of a computer science student, and this high degree of representativeness appeared to overwhelm all other considerations.

Causal interpretation of prior odds. Prior odds are considered only in situations in which they seem to plausibly cause variations in the outcome (Ajzen, 1977; Tversky and Kahneman, 1978). Tversky and Kahneman told subjects that a particular town had two cab companies, the Blue Company and the Green Company. An accident had taken place, and a witness made an uncertain judgment about whether the cab involved was blue or green (visibility had been poor). One group of subjects was told that 85 percent of the cabs in town were blue and 15 percent were green. These subjects, like those in the studies discussed above, largely ignored the base rate percentage of each colored cab and based their decision about which company was involved in the accident primarily on the apparent reliability of the witness. A second group received base rate information in a different way. They were told that, although the blue and green cabs were equal in number, 85 percent of all accidents involving cabs were due to blue cabs and only 15 percent were due to green cabs. In this case, the prior odds had a clear causal interpretation: The drivers of the blue cabs were more careless. This second group of subjects was heavily influenced by the base rate information.

Set inclusion. Linda the feminist bank teller demonstrates that use of the representativeness heuristic may blind someone to logical relations, such as set inclusion, that are relevant to a prediction. Increasing the specificity of an event or outcome can only decrease its probability. For example, the probability that a person is both a lawyer and a tennis player must be less than the probability that the person is a lawyer. The probability that condition A and condition B are both met can only be less than the probability of meeting condition A alone. Even though this principle is intuitive, Tversky and Kahneman (1983) demonstrated that college students – including statistically sophisticated graduate students in the Stanford Business School – systematically violated it when using the representativeness heuristic. One of Tversky and Kahneman's demonstrations involved having subjects read the following brief personality sketch:

> Linda is 31 years old, single, outspoken, and very bright. She majored in philosophy. As a student, she was deeply concerned with issues of discrimination and social justice, and also participated in anti-nuclear demonstrations.

After they had read the description, the subjects were asked to rank-order the probabilities that various statements about Linda were true. Among these statements were the following two:

(1) Linda is a bank teller.
(2) Linda is a bank teller and active in the feminist movement.

The second of these statements, which is a conjunction that includes the first statement, can only be less probable. However, over 80 percent of the students Tversky and Kahneman (1983) tested said that the conjunctive statement was more probable. Students with statistical training were just as prone to this conjunction fallacy as were students who lacked such training.

Linda is more similar to a typical feminist than to a typical bank teller. As a result, students rated her as more similar to the compound "feminist bank teller" than to "bank teller." Apparently, then, the students who made probability judgments based their assessments on implicit similarity judgments; in other words, since Linda was viewed as more similar to a feminist bank teller than to a bank teller, students judged the conjunction to be more probable.

Generalization fallacy. Relying on representativeness can also make a generalization to a larger category seem more plausible than to a smaller category that it contains. Osherson *et al.* (1990) had people judge which of two generalizations they thought followed more strongly from an observation. They found that, when people were told "Robins secrete uric acid crystals," they thought that the generalization "All birds secrete uric acid crystals" followed more strongly than "Ostriches secrete uric acid crystals." It is easy to see where these intuitions come from. When you think of birds you think of typical birds such as robins, so the similarity between the robin and other instances is highlighted. However, ostriches have several salient differences from robins that lower the strength of the generalization. Nevertheless, since the category "All birds" includes ostriches, it makes no logical sense for the generalization to all birds to be stronger than the generalization for ostriches alone. Similarly, Sloman (1993) found that people prefer to generalize from animals to mammals than from animals to reptiles, though anything true of animals is obviously equally true of both mammals and reptiles. Moreover, Sloman (1998) found that people prefer to generalize from birds to sparrows than from animals to sparrows, though anything true of either animals or birds must be true of sparrows.

Causality. Because episodes are causal representations, more causally plausible scenarios are considered more probable than those without a plausible cause. Two different groups judged the probability of the following two events:

> A massive flood somewhere in North America next year, in which more than 1,000 people drown.
> An earthquake in California sometime next year, causing a flood in which more than 1,000 people drown.

Tversky and Kahneman (1983) found that the second statement was rated more probable even though the event it describes is included among the events described by the first statement, and so must be less probable.

Experts versus regression functions

Since the accuracy of the representativeness heuristic depends on knowledge of a specific context, one would expect that, the more experience one had with a context, so the more one knew about it, the better would be the prediction. For many tasks, experts do make more accurate predictions than novices. This is one reason why students are required to attend medical school and then be trained in a residency before practicing as doctors. However, there is a broad class of tasks, including medical diagnosis, for which there is something better than human expertise. Some results are the joint effect of many different causes. Several different academic and social factors influence school performance, and so several different measures of these factors, such as current grades and number of extracurricular activities, are correlated with school performance. Therefore, one way to predict school performance is to collect all the measures known to correlate with it and then use a regression equation to compute the level of academic performance jointly predicted by the levels of all the measures. This is what large universities do when deciding whom to admit, if for no other reason than it is impossible to give every applicant much individual attention.

Another way to predict school performance is to rely on the judgment of admissions officers, who have had years of experience examining applications. All schools also use admissions experts to some extent, if for no other reason than the applicants prefer being evaluated by a human rather than having their fate entirely determined by an impersonal equation. As mentioned above, semantic memory does not contain much information about the probabilities; nor does it contain any procedure for combining them. Consequently, it has been known for a long time that, when probabilities have to be combined to make a prediction, expert judgment is inferior to a regression equation (Meehl, 1954). For many people, their birth is the first time that their lives are determined by a numerical score. Five simple measures of newborns' well-being are made at birth, and then the Apgar score is used to determine whether the infant is in distress (Apgar, 1953; Finster and Wood, 2005).

14.6 Gain, loss, and uncertainty

Many decisions in life are risky. There is some probability of a gain but also some probability of a loss. **Prospect theory** describes how people make decisions under uncertainty. When people make such decisions, most people, guided by the emotional system, make decisions to avoid loss. Moreover, as Kahneman and Tversky (1979) found, people tend to perceive small probabilities as greater than they actually are and large probabilities as less than they actually are. Thus, a 50 percent chance of a gain of $200 is not perceived as twice as wonderful as a 100 percent chance of a gain of $100. Together, loss aversion and subjective probabilities explain human decision making under uncertainty.

Loss aversion

Most people exhibit loss aversion. For each of these choices, which one do you chose?

Get $900 for sure or have a 90 percent chance to get $1,000.

Lose $900 for sure or have a 90 percent chance to lose $1,000.

For the first pair of alternatives, the gain scenario, most people select the 100 percent chance to get $900. They are risk-averse. They are not going to risk a sure thing for a 10 percent chance of getting nothing. For the second pair of alternatives, the loss scenario, most people select the 90 percent chance to lose $1,000. They are risk-seeking. When people face a loss the amygdala is active and there is a strong emotional response of anxiety at the prospect of the loss (Damasio, 1994). Rather than resign themselves to a certain loss of $900, they seize at the 10 percent chance to lose nothing (Novemsky and Kahneman, 2005).

Endowment effect. Loss aversion causes the endowment effect. Neither sales personnel nor store owners feel a loss when they sell a store good. It is different when individuals sell a personal possession that gives pleasure, such as a painting that hangs on their wall. When faced with the loss of a cherished possession, the amygdala is active and there is a strong emotional response of anxiety at the prospect of the loss. The seller makes the buyer pay for this emotional pain. So, a person will sell a possession only for more than he or she would be willing to pay for it if he or she didn't own it.

Novemsky and Kahneman (2005) demonstrated the endowment effect by giving half the students in a group some very nice mugs with the college seal on it. They were then asked how much they would be willing to sell the mugs for, and the remaining students were asked how much they would pay for the mugs. The average offer price was half the average sale price. In another experiment, the half of the students who did not get the mugs were given a choice between the mug and a sum of money, and asked how much money would be preferred to the mug. The average selling price of the students possessing the mugs was $7.12. However, the average compensation preferred by students not possessing the mug was $3.12. **Framing.** Whether a choice is framed as a gain or loss scenario influences which choice is selected, because emotion guides opposite choices for gains versus losses, as described above. Consider the following problems to different groups of subjects by Kahneman and Tversky (1979):

> Problem 1. You are given $1,000. In addition, you may choose between (a) a 50% chance of an additional $1,000 or (b) a 100% chance of an additional $500.
> Problem 2. You are given $2,000. However, you must choose between (c) a 50% chance of losing $1,000 or (d) a 100% chance of losing $500.

Notice that outcome (a) is the same as outcome (c): a 50 percent chance each of either $1,000 or $2,000; and that outcome (b) is the same as outcome (d): a 100 percent chance of $1,500. Nevertheless, most people selected (b) over (a), and also selected (c) over (d). Most people preferred sure gains and also preferred to avoid sure loses. A change in the selection is called **preference reversal**.

According to prospect theory, the values of possible outcomes are represented as gains or losses from what you have before you act. The amount you have before you act is the **zero reference point**. How a problem is framed determines the zero reference point, and so how the outcomes are valued. In Problem 1 the participant has $1,000, so the zero point is here, and 84 percent of the participants selected the sure gain of $500. In Problem 2 the participant has $2,000, so the zero point is here, and 69 percent of the participants selected the 50 percent chance of a $1,000 loss, hence avoiding the sure loss of $1,000.

This one example illustrates the effect of subjective magnitude, the effect of framing, and the effect of loss aversion. Because of the effect of subjective magnitude, a 100 percent chance of a $500 gain or loss is perceived as larger than a 50 percent chance of a $1,000 gain or loss. Because of the effect of framing, problem 1 is perceived as a gain scenario and problem 2 is perceived as a loss scenario. Because of loss aversion, the sure gain of $500 is usually preferred in problem 1, and avoiding the sure loss of $500 is preferred in problem 2.

Framing and other context-specific effects are not restricted to financial gambles but generally influence life decisions as well. Public health decisions also may involve gains and losses. Tversky and Kahneman (1981) were able to restate the framing of an outcome as a gain or a loss as public health outcomes.

> Problem 1. Imagine that the United States is preparing for the outbreak of an unusual Asian disease, which is expected to kill 600 people. Two alternative programs to combat the disease have been proposed.
>
> If program A is adopted, 200 people will be saved.
>
> If program B is adopted, there is a one-third probability that 600 people will be saved, and two-thirds probability that no people will be saved.
>
> Which of the two programs would you favor?

> Problem 2. Imagine that the United States is preparing for the outbreak of an unusual Asian disease, which is expected to kill 600 people. Two alternative programs to combat the disease have been proposed.

If program C is adopted, 400 people will die.
If program D is adopted, there is a one-third probability that no people will die, and two-thirds probability that 600 people will die.
Which of the two programs would you favor?

Again, notice that program A is the same as program C: a 100 percent chance of 200 people living and 400 people dying; and program B is the same as program D: a one-third chance of all 600 people living and a two-thirds chance of all 600 people dying. Nevertheless, 72 percent of the participants selected program A over program B, but 78 percent of the participants selected program D over program C. Again, most people preferred sure gains and also preferred to avoid sure losses.

The demonstration of preference reversal in examples such as these fundamentality altered the understanding of human rationality. Before prospect theory was devised and the effect of framing demonstrated, a fundamental assumption was that human preferences were consistent, so that if a person liked ice cream more than pie then he or she liked pie less than ice cream. This was a fundamental assumption of all theories of economics, as well as

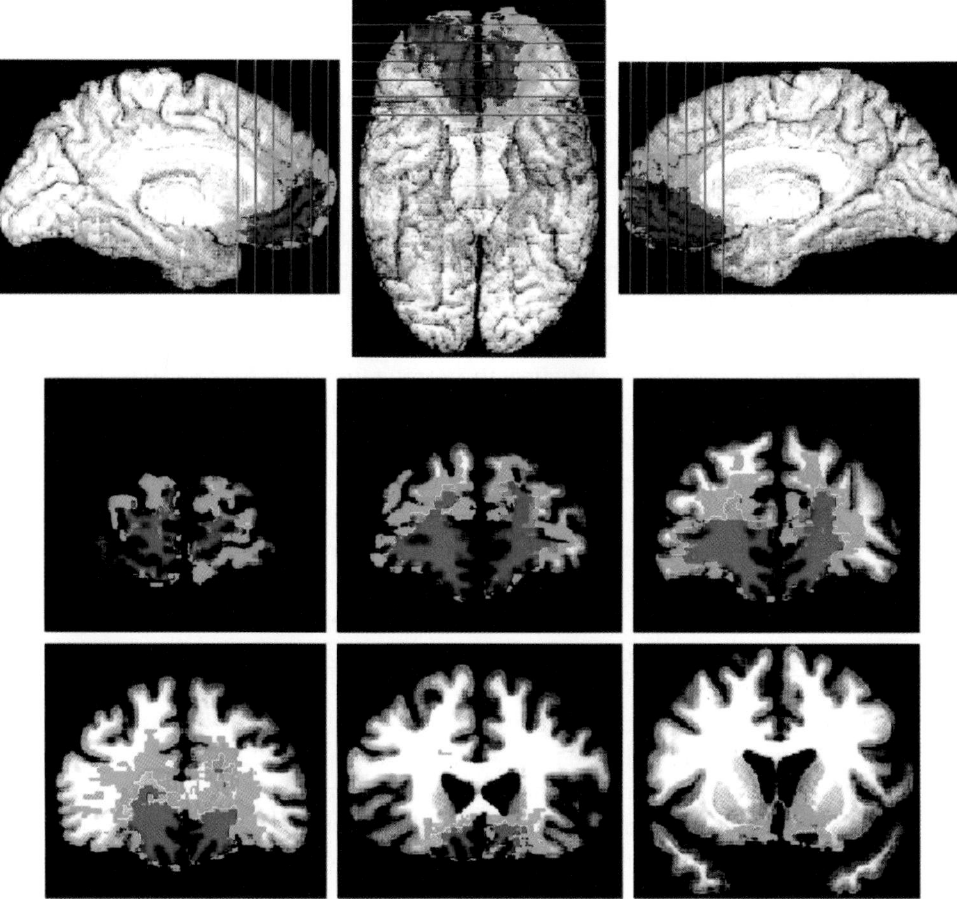

Figure 14.10 Overlap of lesions in the orbitofrontal cortex of 13 individuals that eliminated the effect of emotion on decision making. The red area shows the overlap of four or more lesions (Bechara *et al.*, 2000).

of theories of ethics, as in the public health example above. The demonstration of preference reversal for the problems above shows that this fundamental assumption is not true. What a person prefers depends on how the question is asked, and different frames cause preferences that are inconsistent with each other. Consequently, to adequately describe human reasons, the available choices must be described within the contexts that they are offered.

Emotion and loss aversion. Studies of brain activation while choosing among risky alternatives and studies of the effect of brain injury on choice among risky alternatives indicate that people do not routinely compute probabilities when faced with uncertainty. Rather, uncertainty produces anxiety, anxiety produces loss aversion, and loss aversion determines the choice. Activation is transmitted from the amygdala to the orbitofrontal cortex, where the decision among alternatives is made (Bechara, Damasio, and Damasio, 2000).

Without the guidance of emotional cues, individuals are unable to accurately evaluate the value of the outcomes of their actions, and undertake risky actions that they otherwise would not. Bechara *et al.* (1999) found that, when the amygdala was damaged, individuals no longer felt anxiety before making a risky choice. When the orbitofrontal prefrontal cortex was damaged, individuals still felt anxiety but it no longer affected their decision (Figure 14.10). Bechara, Tranel, and Damasio (2000) found that individuals whose responses were not influenced by loss aversion could not learn from gains and losses over many trials how to play a card game to ensure long-term gains. Bechara, Damasio, and Damasio (2000) found that, when the connection between the amygdala and the prefrontal cortex was severed, judgment was severely impaired.

SUMMARY

Reasoning is the ability to deduce the state of the world from separate pieces of evidence and to predict the results of future actions on the basis of experience.

- The neural decision system is bilateral but includes the specialized areas in the left hemisphere for language and the right hemisphere for imagery that make verbal and visual reasoning possible.
- Visual inference is an essential component of human reason.
  - Selective interference with visual perception demonstrates the role of visual inference.
  - One consequence of visual representation is the symbolic distance effect.
  - People with Williams syndrome cannot generate visual images, and so they cannot make visual inferences. Consequently, their general reasoning ability is severely impaired.
- Deductive decisions about the world are made on the basis of recollecting an example or a counterexample.
  - Frequency decisions are made on the ease of generating an example, which is called the availability heuristic. If retrieval is easy and fluent, the category will be judged to be large. Availability affects risk assessment. Risks that one hears about more often are perceived as higher.
  - Confirmatory bias occurs because, while the question is an obvious cue for positive instances, there is no cue for negative instances.

  - Availability also produces the anchoring effect. The size of something is computed by adjusting a value that may be primed by a related or unrelated cue.
  - Finally, availability produces hindsight bias. The probability of event is judged as greater after it occurs.
- Deductive decisions for novel problems are made on the basis of generating an example for each possible condition. It is extremely difficult to systematically consider even a small list of possible cases or examples because of PI from previous cases. Inferences involving negation are particularly difficult because they cannot be solved by generating a single, obvious counterexample.
- The basic decision strategy for explaining the world is to represent events as episodes, which consist of actors, actions, targets, contexts, and results, and to assume that, if the same action were repeated in the same context, it would produce the same result. Because the strategy is to represent the world as it usually is, the strategy is called the representativeness heuristic. This recollection of a target-specific, context-specific, causal representation (the episode) excludes information such as the frequency of occurrence. Effects of random statistical variability go unrepresented in semantic memory; hence, they go unnoticed when reasoning.
  - In explaining variability, false causal explanations are considered because the effect of small samples in producing extreme unrepresentative instances is not noticed.
  - Intuitions about causality induce false intuitions about the results of a random process. For example, some randomly generated sequences are perceived as more likely than others.
  - More generally, the sole reliance on representativeness blinds individuals to other natural relationships, such as set inclusion.
  - Furthermore, the determination of similarity is itself a heuristic process that is subject to distortion.
- Inductive inferences guide future action by predicting the behavior of others from their past behavior and predicting the consequences of a person's own future actions by the consequences of similar actions performed by oneself or others. The Wason selection problem becomes easy when framed as a social decision, so that it can be solved through recollection.
  - As described above, human inductive inferences can lead to a wrong decision when relevant statistical information, such as the base rate, is excluded.
  - Because episodes are causal, more causally plausible scenarios are considered more probable.
  - Because representativeness ignores probabilities, whenever a variety of indicators have independent correlations with an outcome, a regression equation performs better than expert intuition at predicting the outcome.
- Many decisions in life are risky. There is some probability of a gain but also some probability of a loss. Prospect theory describes how people make risky decisions. When people make such decisions, most people, guided by the emotional system, make decisions to avoid loss. In addition, the subjective magnitude of small probabilities is greater than the objective value, and the objective magnitude of large probabilities is less than their objective value, so a likely gain or loss of $200 is perceived as less than a sure gain or loss of $100. Together, loss aversion and subjective magnitude explain human decision making under uncertainty.
  - Consequently, depending on whether a choice is framed as a gain or loss influences which choice is selected, because emotion guides opposite choices for gains versus losses.
  - Framing is not restricted to financial gambles. Other life decisions, including medical decisions, are influenced by framing choices as gains or losses.

QUESTIONS

1 What parts of the cortex are involved in inference?
2 What parts of the cortex are involved in decisions involving risk?
3 How does the availability heuristic affect frequency judgments?
4 What kind of information is ignored when the representativeness heuristic is used?
5 Suppose A and B are any two things. Is it generally the case that A is as similar to B as B is to A?

FURTHER READING

Bechara, A., Damasio, H., and Damasio, A. R. (2000). Emotion, decision making, and the orbitofrontal cortex. *Cerebral Cortex*, 10, 295–307.

Dhami, M. K., Schlottmann, A., and Waldmann, M. R. (2013). *Judgment and Decision Making as a Skill*. Cambridge University Press.

Kahneman, D. (2011). *Thinking, Fast and Slow*. New York: Farrar, Strauss, & Giroux.

Meehl, P. (1954). *Clinical versus Statistical Prediction: A Theoretical Analysis and a Review of the Evidence*. Minneapolis: University of Minnesota Press.

Smith, K., Shanteau, J., and Johnson, P. (2011). *Psychological Investigations of Competence in Decision Making*. Cambridge University Press.

Thaler, R. H., and Sunstein, C. R. (2008). *Nudge: Improving Decisions about Health, Wealth, and Happiness*. New Haven, CT: Yale University Press.

Weber, E. U., Baron, J., and Loomes, G. (2011). *Conflict and Tradeoffs in Decision Making.* Cambridge University Press.

15 Problem solving and intelligence

At an intuitive level, everyone knows what kinds of tasks require problem solving. All problem-solving tasks have a goal, which is a description of what would constitute a solution to the problem. What makes a problem a problem is that the statement of the goal does not act as a cue for its own solution. If your friend asks you to get her a can of diet Coke from the refrigerator in your room, that is not a problem. But, if your friend asks you to get her something to drink, that is a problem statement, because there are several ways that you can formulate and solve your task. Problems vary in the extent to which they are well defined (Newell, 1969; Reitman, 1964; Simon, 1973). In a well-defined problem, such as solving a crossword puzzle or selecting a good chess move, the set of possible actions and the goal are all completely specified. In ill-defined problems there may be uncertainty concerning the possible actions that can be taken, and a variety of solutions may therefore be possible. Despite the slightly negative ring to the term "ill-defined," many ill-defined problems are very creative tasks, such as painting a picture, designing a house, and writing a story. Virtually all real-life problems, from preparing dinner to losing weight, are ill-defined in some way. In a crime story, both planning a murder and solving it describe solutions to ill-defined problems.

Problem solving is a special case of decision making tasks requiring reasoning, which were described in general in Chapter 14. What all problems have in common is that an ad hoc action must be taken in a novel situation. The neural decision-making system described in Figure 14.1 engages in the reasoning necessary for problem solving.

The process of solving a problem has three major steps (Figure 15.1). The first step is forming an initial representation of the problem. The second and third steps are the same as described for physical action in Chapter 3: planning and execution. The second step is generating and evaluating potential solutions. The third step is executing a procedure to carry out the planned solution that appears to be correct. The execution of a plan has already been described in Chapters 3, 4, and 5. Here, the first and second steps are described.

- Forming an initial representation of the problem.
  - Some problems require visuospatial representation and some problems require verbal representation. If the wrong representation is selected then the problem may be unsolvable.
  - Even if the correct type of representation is selected, implicit constraints in the statement of the problem may make it difficult or unsolvable.

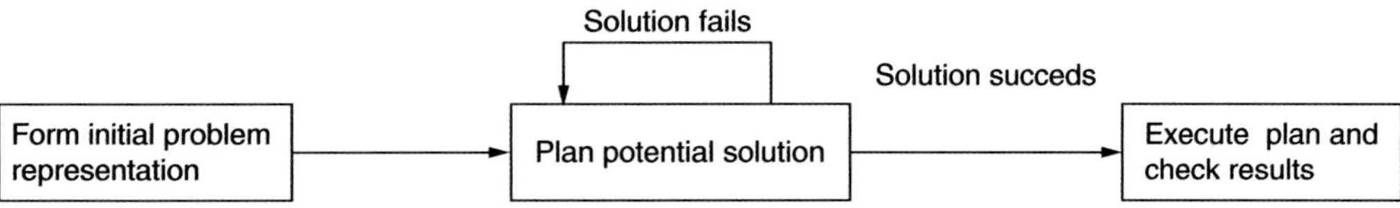

Figure 15.1 Schematic outline of problem-solving process.

    - Since individuals are not aware of self-imposed constraints, they rarely escape them. How some individuals become aware of another possible representation is not clear. Presumably, it includes an ability to inhibit the constraining one.
- Generating and testing potential solutions.
  - Generating the correct solution is difficult for some problems, because the description of the problem cues possible solutions that cannot work. The resulting proactive interference makes generating the correct solution more difficult.
    - Problem-solving set.
    - Functional fixedness.
  - Generating the correct solution is difficult for some problems because there are so many possible solutions that they cannot be exhaustively examined. Novices and experts differ in their ability to solve these problems.
    - Novices have two possible avenues to a solution.
      - Task analysis in sub-goals and the generation and testing of possible solutions to sub-goals.
      - Analogy to other tasks. However, novices are poor at finding analogies, because they are more likely to retrieve a representation with common superficial features instead of one for a structurally similar problem with a similar solution.
    - Experts narrow the search space by considering only solutions to structurely similar problems that have worked in the past.
  - Generating the correct solution is difficult for some problems because the solution requires the construction of a novel sequence of sub-goals.
    - Novices and experts differ in their ability to solve these problems because experts have knowledge of heuristics or algorithms for generating solutions, so they do not have to keep track of a novel sequence of sub-goals.
    - Moreover, the need to generate sub-goals may create a large number of possible solutions. The heuristics and algorithms that experts use narrow the search space.
- Intelligence. When people perform a variety of different tasks, task performance is positively correlated across tasks.
  - One possible explanation is that there is a single general ability, g, that is applied in all tasks.
    - g is associated with the role of the prefrontal cortex in the control of ad hoc action.
  - Intelligence tests were designed to predict academic performance in schools.
    - Since intelligence tests are collections of subtests, they are good measures of g.

15.1 The prefrontal cortex

The representation of the problem and the generation of a solution are performed by the neural system for reasoning described in Figure 14.1. The prefrontal cortex directs the sequence of voluntary actions required for problem solving. The ability to find a solution to a problem may require the consideration of several possible solutions. Each possible solution must be constructed, evaluated, and replaced by another possible solution if it is found inadequate. If a possible solution is rejected then its representation must be inhibited, so that another solution can be generated in its place. Furthermore, it is necessary to be able to keep track of which solutions have already been tried.

Even though it is not a problem-solving task, the importance of generation, inhibition, and the judgment of recency are all illustrated by the **verbal fluency task**. The task is to generate as many instances of a category as possible in a specified time period. For example, in Chapter 12, the generation of animal names was described. Another version of the task requires the generation of words that begin with a particular letter, such as the letter "f." Obviously, people who cannot generate the names of animals or words that begin with the letter "f" will be impaired at generating ad hoc solutions to problems. Generation, inhibition, and the judgment of recency are all directed by the frontal cortex. Impairment of any one of these three functions ultimately impairs the number of examples that are generated, and so also the number of possible solutions to the problem.

Recollection in response to a cue is impaired by damage to the left prefrontal cortex, and so is used to assess its functioning. Damage produces a failure to respond – that is, the patient produces one or two responses – for example *fix, fish*, but no more (Tucha, Smely, and Lange, 1999; Baldo and Shimamura, 1998).

Inhibition is impaired by damage to the prefrontal cortex. When it cannot be inhibited, there is **perseveration** of the initial response – for example, *fix, fish, fix, fix* (Crowe, 1992).

Finally, when generating instances of a category it is necessary to keep track of which ones have already been generated. However, damage to the prefrontal cortex impairs this ability. Recall from Chapter 11 that patients with prefrontal damage performed poorly in judging which of a pair of pictures they had seen more recently (Milner, Corsi, and Leonard, 1991). Even when generation and inhibition are preserved, a person who cannot perceive recency may repeat the same example over and over. When the frontal cortex is not functioning properly, the results are more catastrophic than an inability to generate lists of words. Potential solutions to a problem cannot be systematically constructed and considered.

15.2 Forming an initial representation

Often how a problem is represented determines whether or not the problem can be solved. As discussed in Chapter 14, the neural decision-making system encompasses both verbal and visuospatial representation. Some problems have both visual and verbal representations.

Consider the following well-defined problem:

> The price of a notebook is four times that of a pencil. The pencil costs 30¢ less than the notebook. What is the price of each?

This problem is presented in a purely verbal form. However, this form is not a very good representation for solving it. If you are like most people who have learned algebra, you will probably translate the problem into an algebraic representation and then apply numerical operations as follows:

> Let n = notebook and let p = pencil.
> Initial state: n = 4p, and p = n – 30; hence, by adding 30 to both sides, p + 30 = n.
> Substitute for n: p + 30 = 4p.
> Subtract p from both sides: 30 = 3p.
> Divide each side by 3: 10 = p.
> Substitute for p in n = 4p: n = 4*10 = 40.
> Therefore p = 10 and n = 40.

An algebraic representation makes use of both the verbal and the visuospatial representations to bring into play a set of operations for manipulating equations, making the problem quite simple to solve. Algebra makes use of naming to identify variables, but it also makes use of the visuospatial code in substituting variables and moving them from one side of the equation to the other. Some individuals can also translate the verbal representation directly into the visuospatial code. When this problem was given to S., the remarkable mnemonist studied by Luria (Chapter 10), S. reported imagining a series of visual equations, as illustrated in Figure 15.2. In Figure 15.2 (a) he imagined a notebook beside four pencils. Then in Figure 15.2 (b) he mentally pushed three pencils aside and replaced them with 30¢, since one pencil plus 30¢ equals the value of the notebook. Since 30¢ therefore is equivalent to three pencils, S. immediately realized (presumably by simple arithmetic) that one pencil was worth 10¢ and the notebook was worth 40¢. Some of S.'s major problem-solving operations were thus manipulations of visual images.

The example of the algebra problem illustrates that some problems can have both visual and verbal representations that lead to solutions. Other problems require visuospatial representation and still other problems require verbal representation. If the wrong representation is selected then the problem may be unsolvable.

Visual-only and verbal-only problem solving

An otherwise difficult problem that has a naive intuitive visual solution is the Buddhist monk problem. This problem, like many of those commonly discussed by psychologists, originated with the gestalt psychologists of the early twentieth century (in this case, Karl Duncker). The problem is as follows.

One morning, exactly at sunrise, a Buddhist monk began to climb a tall mountain. A narrow path, no more than a foot or two wide, spiraled around the mountain to a glittering temple at the summit. The monk ascended at varying rates of speed, stopping many times along the way to rest and eat dried fruit he carried with him. He reached the temple shortly

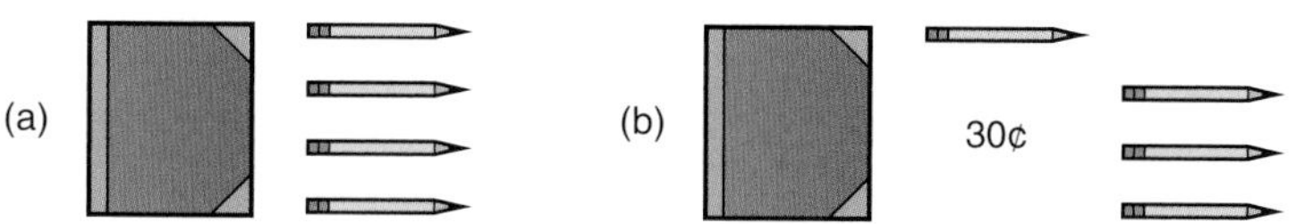

Figure 15.2 Visual equations that S. used to solve pencil and notebook problem: (a) original equation; (b) substituting 30 cents for three pencils (Luria, 1968).

before sunset. After several days of fasting and meditation he began his journey back along the same path, starting at sunrise and again walking at variable speeds, with many pauses along the way. His average speed descending was, of course, greater than his average climbing speed. Show that there is a spot along the path that the monk will occupy on both trips at precisely the same time of day.

People who think about this problem verbally or algebraically are unlikely to solve it. They may conclude that it would be an improbable coincidence for the monk to find himself at the same spot at the same time on two different days. But one can actually visualize the solution, as the following report by a young woman suggests (Koestler, 1964: 184):

> I tried this and that, until I got fed up with the whole thing, but the image of the monk in his saffron robe walking up the hill kept persisting in my mind. Then a moment came when, superimposed on this image, I saw another, more transparent one, of the monk walking down the hill, and I realized in a flash that the two figures must meet at some point in time – regardless of what speed they walk and how often each of them stops. Then I reasoned out what I already knew: whether the monk descends two days or three days later comes to the same; so I was quite justified in letting him descend on the same day, in duplicate so to speak.

Figure 15.3 provides a somewhat more abstract, visual solution to the problem. This graph plots the altitude of the monk on the mountain as a function of time of day, for both his ascent and his descent. We see that the two paths must cross, regardless of the monk's variable rates of progress. The point of intersection is the point on the path that the monk will occupy at the same time of day on both trips.

In the report quoted above the problem solver experiences a flash of insight when she visualizes the solution. Insight, a concept stressed by gestalt psychologists who investigated problem solving, seems to involve a sudden awareness of a new problem representation that precedes finding a solution.

The successful visual solution to the Buddhist monk problem can be contrasted with the solution to the following mental paper-folding problem (Adams, 1974: 63):

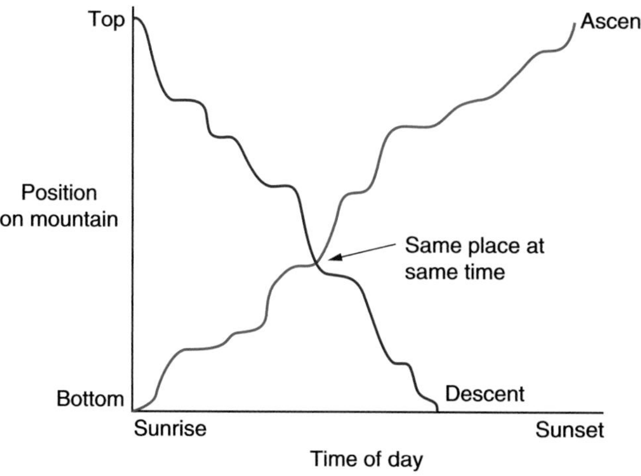

Figure 15.3 Graphical solution to Buddhist monk problem.

> Picture a large piece of paper, 1/100 of an inch thick. In your imagination, fold it once (now having two layers), fold it once more (now having four layers), and continue folding it over on itself 50 times. It is true that it is impossible to fold any actual piece of paper 50 times. But for the sake of the problem, imagine that you can. About how thick would the 50-times-folded paper be?

At first glance this problem might seem like another problem requiring a visual solution. But, in fact, a visual solution is impossible. Note that the first fold will result in two times the original thickness, while the second fold will result in 2 x 2 = 4 times the original thickness. In fact, each fold increases the thickness by a factor of two. So, fifty folds will increase the paper's thickness by a factor of two multiplied by two exactly fifty times, or 2^{50}. This number works out to about 1,100,000,000,000,000 – a number so large that the resulting thickness of the folded paper would approximate the distance from the Earth to the Sun. Obviously, visual imagery cannot produce this result. People who try to visualize a few folds and then extrapolate to estimate the thickness resulting from fifty folds invariably wildly underestimate the correct answer. In this case, only a mathematical representation can easily produce an accurate solution.

Reformulating problem representations

Even if the correct type of representation is selected, cues or implicit constraints in the statement of the problem may make it difficult or unsolvable. As described in Chapter 14, some students failed to recognize a physics problem when it was presented visually and mathematical psychologists failed to recognize statistical problems when presented as descriptions of possibly causal events. An example of how visual presentation can imply a constraint that makes the problem impossible is the nine-dot problem. The problem is to draw four straight lines through all the nine dots depicted in Figure 15.4 (a) without lifting the pencil from the paper. People see a square boundary around the nine dots. As a result, when most people are given this problem, they tend to assume that the four lines can't go outside the imaginary boundary. In fact, the problem can be solved only by extending some of the lines beyond the boundary, as in Figure 15.4 (b). Once exposed to the original version of the problem, constructing a new representation is not easy. Weisberg and Alba (1981) instructed some subjects, after they had made several unsuccessful attempts, that it was necessary to draw lines outside the boundary to solve the problem. Only 25 percent of the subjects eventually solved the problem.

Knoblich, Ohlsson, and Raney (2001) used three matchstick Roman numeral arithmetic problems, shown in Figure 15.5, to study how an implicit constraint makes problem solving

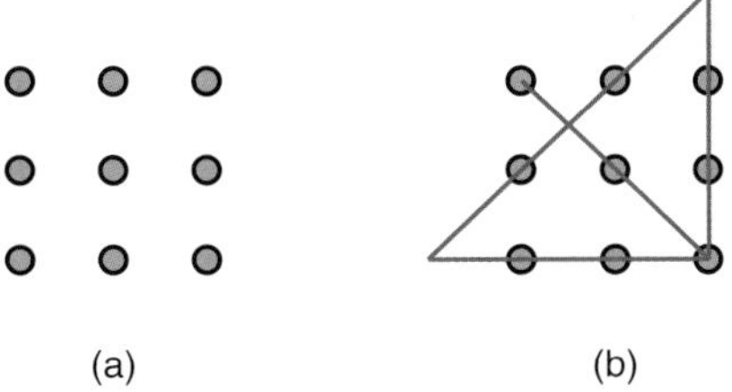

Figure 15.4 Nine-dot problem: (a) configuration of nine-dots; (b) solution.

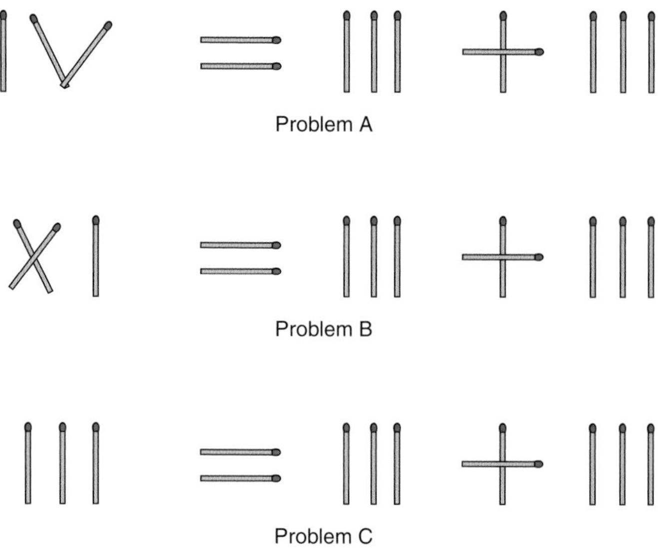

Figure 15.5 Make each arithmetic statement correct by moving one matchstick (Knoblich *et al*., 2001).

difficult. In matchstick arithmetic the problem solver is faced with an incorrect arithmetic statement expressed in Roman numerals constructed out of matchsticks. The goal is to correct the arithmetic statement by moving a single matchstick from one position in the statement to another. Try to solve the problems before going on. Problem A is the easiest of the three. The matchstick in the "4" is moved to the right of the "V" to form a six and solve the problem. In problem B one stick in the "X" must be moved to change it to a "V." Knoblich, Ohlsson, and Raney (2001) suggested that this problem was more difficult because the reformulation involved decomposing what is normally taken as a "chunk," the presentation of the "X," as a single character.

The first two problems induce a **problem-solving set** in the problem solver. A problem-solving set is a strategy for finding a solution that is highly available because it has recently been successfully used to solve similar problems. In problem C one stick in the plus sign must be moved to change it to an equals sign, giving "3 = 3 = 3." This reformulation is difficult because it requires not just the decomposition of a chunk but the reformulation of constraints. The problem solver must focus on an operator.

15.3 Generating a problem solution

Even when the correct representation is selected, there are several mental barriers to a solution. A problem solver may know too much. and so get blocked from the correct novel solution by the availability of an incorrect solution, or the problem solver may know too little. and so may be lost in a maze of many possible solutions.

Proactive interference

As the flowchart in Figure 15.1 indicates, the second step of the problem – trying to plan a potential solution – may be repeated multiple times. If the plan of a potential solution fails then an attempt will be made to construct another possible solution, so the second step will be repeated. Once a successful plan is constructed, it can be executed. In this section, consider how a possible solution plan can be generated.

Recall from Chapter 12 that the availability of a previously generated representation makes the generation of a similar but novel representation difficult, because cues for both representations will bring to mind only the one previously recollected. Proactive interference from the earlier, discarded, potential solutions makes reformulating a problem difficult. Generating the first possible solution is usually easy, but then thinking of new possibilities becomes quite difficult, because discarded solutions are likely to be associated with many of the same cues as new solutions. In problem solving, PI manifests itself in two ways, called the problem-solving set and functional fixedness.

Problem-solving set. As described above, a problem-solving set is a tendency to repeat a solution process that has been previously successful. The classic demonstration of a problem-solving set was a series of experiments by Luchins (1942; Luchins and Luchins, 1950). Luchins tested over 9,000 subjects, ranging in age from elementary school children to adults, on water jar problems. A typical series of problems is shown in Table 15.1. The subject was asked to imagine three jars of various specified capacities and told to find a way to get a required amount of water. For the first problem in Table 15.1 the solution is to fill jar B, then to take out the volume of jar A, and then to take out the volume of jar C twice. The series of problems was set up so that this same general solution (B – A – 2C) worked for the first five problems. This series was designed to establish a problem-solving set.

On trials 6 and 7 there were two possible solutions: the previously successful formula and also a simpler one. One measure of the effect of a set is how often people discover the simpler solution. Finally, trial 8 was a problem for which the earlier formula wouldn't work but a simpler one (A – C) would. Luchins found that subjects very often failed to notice the

TABLE 15.1 Typical series of water jar problems

	Capacity of given jars (in quarts)			
Problem	**A**	**B**	**C**	**Amount of quarts to get**
1	21	127	3	100
2	14	163	25	99
3	18	43	10	5
4	9	42	6	21
5	20	59	4	31
(B – A – 2C is the solution to the first five problems)				
6	23	49	3	20
	(A – C also works)			
7	15	39	3	18
	(A + C also works)			
8	28	76	3	25
(A – C works, but B – A – 2C doesn't)				

Source: Luchins (1942).

simpler solutions to problems 6 and 7 and sometimes failed to solve problem 8 at all. An initially successful solution blocks the discovery of alternative solutions.

Functional fixedness. Duncker (1945) presented subjects with several objects lying on a table and asked them to find a way to use them to support a board. The available objects included two iron joints and a pair of pliers. The solution to the problem was to use the iron joints to support one end of the board and the pliers to support the other. In one condition the subject first had to use the pliers to free the board. Duncker found that the subjects who began the experiment by using the pliers to free the board were less likely to find the solution of using the pliers as a support. He called this phenomenon **functional fixedness**: If an object has one established use in a situation, subjects have difficulty in using the object in another way.

Functional fixedness is a tendency to think of past uses of an object to the exclusion of novel potential uses. The most familiar functions of objects are directly stored with the objects in a single episode in the semantic memory; for example, the concept *pliers* might be associated with the function "used for grasping objects." These familiar uses are the most available ones. But the perceptual attributes of an object (such as its shape, size, or weight) are compatible with other potential uses, sometimes called affordances (Gibson, 1966). A pair of pliers can therefore be used as a support and as a conductor of electricity. However, these potential uses are harder to think of than defining functions stored in memory.

Saugstad showed that success in generating a problem solution can be predicted by measures of the availability to the problem solver of the functions required for a solution. Saugstad (1955) showed fifty-seven college students objects to be used later in a problem in which some hollow tubes and putty had to be used to blow out a candle six feet away. Nothing was mentioned of the problem itself. Subjects were simply instructed to list all the possible functions that the objects might serve. All thirteen subjects who listed functions for the objects that were later necessary to solve the problem did, in fact, solve the problem. In contrast, only 58 percent of the remaining subjects solved the problem. In another experiment, Saugstad and Raaheim (1960) demonstrated the functions of some objects, which turned out to be critical to the solution of a problem, to twenty male high school students. Nineteen of the boys later solved the problem. In contrast, only ten out of forty-five boys who had not seen the demonstration were able to solve the problem.

Another task that illustrates functional fixedness is the so-called candle problem (Duncker, 1945). In this problem, subjects are given the task of affixing a candle to a wall and lighting it. The objects available for use are some matches, a candle, and a matchbox filled with thumbtacks. The optimal solution, as defined by Duncker, is to use the tacks to fix the matchbox to the wall, put the candle on the box, and then light it with the matches. Duncker found that more subjects used the box as a candle holder when it was presented empty than when it was full of tacks. Seeing the box as a container for tacks made it difficult for subjects to see it also as a platform. Presenting it empty made it easier for them to perceive the box as a candle holder.

Glucksberg, Weisberg, and their colleagues (Glucksberg and Danks, 1968; Glucksberg and Weisberg, 1966; Weisberg and Suls, 1973) showed that cueing the function of the box as a platform increased the probability that the candle problem would be solved. Sometimes the experimenter would name the box while giving instructions to the subject, while sometimes he named only the tacks. More subjects solved the problem by using the box as a platform (the box solution) when the box itself was labeled. Glucksberg and Danks (1968) also described a task in which hearing the name of an object interfered with noticing its task-relevant function. In this experiment the subject's task was to complete an electric circuit. The objects provided were batteries, a bulb, a switch, and a wrench. The solution was to use the wrench to complete the circuit. In this case subjects were more likely to find the solution when they were required to refer to the wrench by a nonsense name, such as vorpin, rather than by the familiar name: wrench.

Functional fixedness is a result of experience with an object's typical use. When given a box of tacks that had to be used as a support to solve a problem, six-year-old children showed functional fixedness, but five-year old children did not. The five-year-old children were insufficiently familiar with the typical use of the tack box for it to impair their performance (German and Defeyter, 2000).

Problem-solving behavior requires such extensive conscious manipulation of representations that only a few animals engage in anything that closely resembles human problem-solving behavior. Kohler (1925) demonstrated that chimpanzees can sometimes overcome functional fixedness. In one sequence the chimp Sultan was in a cage and noticed a banana lying outside, out of reach. In the cage was a bushy tree. Sultan suddenly went to the tree, broke off a branch, ran back to the bars, and used the branch to bring the banana into reach. What was at first not even a separate object was suddenly recognized as a potential tool.

Insight. Fortunately, when a problem becomes familiar, the PI caused by problem-solving set and functional fixedness is eventually overcome in a flash of insight. Siegler and Stern (1998) gave primary schoolchildren in their second year seven sessions of practice over as many weeks on sets of arithmetic problems that included inversion problems – problems that included the same term added and subtracted, such as 28 + 36 – 36. For problems such as this, it is not necessary to do the addition and subtraction of the repeated term because it does not change the result. Over the seven sessions 90 percent of the pupils had this insight and stopped performing the extraneous addition and subtraction. This resulted in a reduction in the time to solve the problem. When the extra addition and subtraction were performed it took at least eight seconds to record the answer but when they no longer performed them it took no more than four seconds. Once the pupils were familiar with the problems they were increasingly effective cues for their answers, so that the pupils could see ahead to the answers even before they computed them. When this occurred they could see that the earlier and later states were the same and stopped computing the intermediate additions. Each session, Siegler and Stern had the pupils report how they were solving the problems. Most reported not computing the extraneous one or two sessions only after their response times had revealed that they had stopped computing. So, the insight was not the result of deliberation but, instead, followed the recognition of a regularity that became possible when all the steps of the problem could be perceived together as a single narrative.

Novice problem solving

Some problems are impossible to solve because there are so many possible solutions that it is impossible to test them all. The process of generating a problem solution can be viewed as a search through a space of possible solutions (Newell and Simon, 1972). A problem can be made difficult by making the search space enormous. This feature is the principle behind the use of alphanumeric passwords. If a password has eight characters then there are 36^8 possible passwords. The sheer size of the search space will protect an online account from a thief who tries to use the generate-test method to discover the correct combination. People do get better at solving problems because they learn task-specific knowledge. Experts therefore solve problems differently from novices. For a plumber, fixing a leaky faucet is not a problem at all but a routine action. For a person with average general knowledge, fixing a leaky faucet is a difficult problem-solving task. Novices have available general strategies to solve novel problems: task analysis and analogical reasoning.

Task analysis. Task analysis refers to conceptualizing a problem as a hierarchy of the simpler problems that comprise it. Each problem begins with a **goal**. In order to solve the problem it may be necessary to break it down into smaller, well-defined, problems, each with is own **sub-goal**. Many everyday tasks, such as preparing a meal, may require sub-goals. Before you can eat, you must decide what to make, and where to obtain the ingredients and utensils to make it. Keeping track of sub-goals is also necessary for all kinds of problems including simple mathematics problems. Passolunghi, Cornoldi, and De Liberto (1999) divided fourth year primary schoolchildren into good and poor problems solvers on the basis of their ability to perform simple mathematics word problems such as:

> On Pascoli Street there are 45 shops. 3/5 of them sell clothes. How many clothes shops are there on Pascoli Street?

In general, poor problem solvers were less able to inhibit the task-irrelevant information in the word problems. When a problem requires keeping track of sub-goals, the overall task is comprised of the sub-tasks of rehearsing the goals and sub-goals as well as performing whatever action is required to reach a sub-goal. When a problem solver cannot inhibit irrelevant information, it may interfere with accurate recollection of the sub-goal. So the poor problem solvers' had difficulty performing both the ad hoc actions for reaching the sub-goals and the ad hoc actions (that is, the rehearsal) for recollecting them. Consequently, the poor problem solvers also performed more poorly on the Daneman and Carpenter (1983) task, in which the second task, the memory task, influenced sentence comprehension (Chapter 7). When the prefrontal cortex is not functioning properly, it is not possible to keep track of sub-goals. When it is impossible to keep track of sub-goals, even simple problems, such as cooking or shopping (Shallice and Burgess, 1991), become impossible.

An example of a problem requiring task analysis is the problem of winning a game of chess. The course of a chess game can be represented as a tree similar to the one shown in Figure 15.6. The top node in the tree represents the initial position on the chessboard. Each of the possible alternative moves will lead to a different new position. At an average choice point a chess player may have twenty or thirty possible alternatives; for simplicity, only three alternatives are shown at each choice point in the figure. At the second level in the tree the opponent will select a move, again changing the board position. The first player then chooses one of the next set of possible moves, etc. As Figure 15.6 illustrates, the final positions at the bottom of the tree determine how the game ends – whether the first player wins, ties, or loses. The dark line in the figure shows a path through the tree (that is, a sequence of moves) that leads to a win. Only a few of the possible paths are shown in Figure 15.6, and all the paths are just four moves long. An actual chess game will often be fifty or more moves long.

There is a clear way to win a game that can be represented as a decision tree, as in Figure 15.6. This method is to explore every possible path in the tree to determine its final

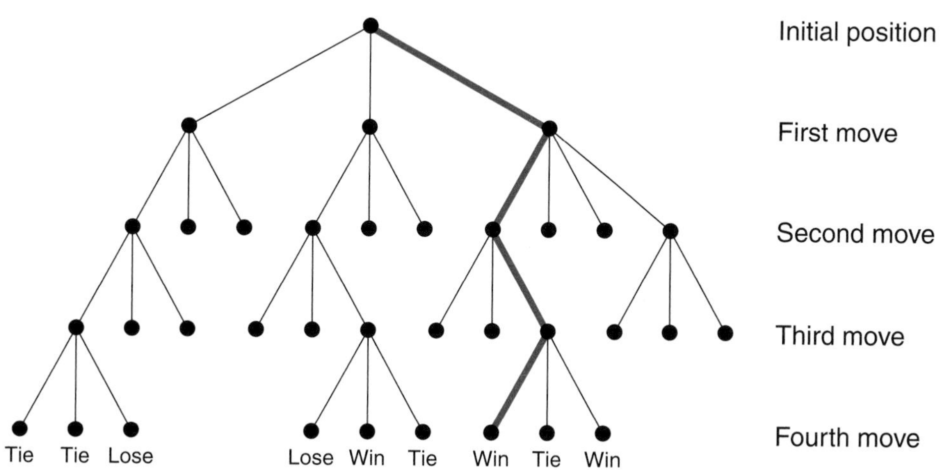

Figure 15.6 Hypothetical decision tree for a game of chess showing path of moves leading to win for first player.

outcome, and then to always select a move that sends the game along a path that cannot end in a win for the opponent.

There are two fatal defects to the task analysis approach to problem solving. The first is that it is necessary to keep track of the goal, and possibly multiple sub-goals, through verbal rehearsal while generating and evaluating a solution to each sub-goal. As discussed in Chapter 10, even without performing a second task involving generation and evaluation, rehearsal can be used to maintain a representation of only a short novel string, which would be equivalent to a limited number of sub-goals.

The second problem with task analysis is that, for many tasks, the number of paths that would have to be considered at each choice point is astronomical. An astronomical number will certainly arise in a complex game such as chess, in which the tree of possible moves is both very wide (many alternatives at each choice point) and very deep (many moves to complete a game). As a result, the only effective way to play a good chess game is to use a problem-solving method that sharply restricts the search space.

Noticing and applying analogies. Another way an unfamiliar problem may be solved is by recollecting a solution to an analogous problem. The solution to the known problem is used to plan a solution to the new one. Useful analogies can sometimes be found between situations that are superficially very different because the same target–action–results relationship can exist for very different targets. Analogies to familiar situations are potentially a rich source of heuristics and algorithms for solving novel problems. Unfortunately, Gick and Holyoak (1980; 1983) found that analogies from other knowledge domains are only occasionally useful in reformulating problems, because the problem solver rarely notices their relevance. They studied the ability of problem solvers to find analogies to the radiation problem made famous by Duncker (1945). The problem runs as follows:

> Suppose you are a doctor faced with a patient who has a malignant tumor in his stomach. To operate on the patient is impossible, but unless the tumor is destroyed, the patient will die. A kind of ray, at a sufficiently high intensity, can destroy the tumor. Unfortunately, at this intensity the healthy tissue that the rays pass through on the

way to the tumor will also be destroyed. At lower intensities the rays are harmless to healthy tissue but will not affect the tumor, either. How can the rays be used to destroy the tumor without injuring the healthy tissue?

This problem is reasonably realistic, since it describes a situation similar to what actually arises in radiation therapy. Gick and Holyoak (1980) wanted to find out whether college students could use a remote analogy to solve the problem. To provide the students with a potential analogy, the experimenters first had them memorize a story about the predicament of a general who wished to capture a fortress located in the center of a country. Many roads radiated outward from the fortress, but these roads were mined such that, although small groups could pass over them safely, any large group would detonate the mines. However, the general needed to get his entire large army to the fortress in order to launch a successful attack. Thus, the general's situation was analogous to that of the doctor in the radiation problem.

The correspondences between the convergence version of the military story and the radiation problem are shown in Table 15.2. Even though the particular objects involved (soldiers

TABLE 15.2 Correspondences between two convergence problems and their schema
Military problem
Representation
Goal: use army to capture fortress
Resources: sufficiently large army
Operators: divide army, move army, attack with army
Constraint: unable to send entire army along one road safely
Solution plan: send small groups along multiple roads simultaneously
Outcome: fortress captured by army
Radiation problem
Representation
Goal: use rays to destroy tumor
Resources: sufficiently powerful rays
Operators: reduce ray intensity, move ray source, administer rays
Constraint: unable to administer high-intensity rays from one direction safely
Solution plan: administer low-intensity rays from multiple directions simultaneously
Outcome: tumor destroyed by rays
Convergence schema
Representation
Goal: use force to overcome a central target
Resources: sufficiently great force
Operators: reduce force intensity, move source of force, apply force
Constraint: unable to apply full force along one path safely
Solution plan: apply weak forces along multiple paths simultaneously
Outcome: central target overcome by force

Source: Gick and Holyoak (1983).

and rays, a fortress and a tumor) are very different, the basic relations that make the convergence solution possible are present in both. The goal, resources (and other objects), operations, and constraints are structurally similar, and they can be matched, or "mapped," from one problem to the other. Because the military story provides clear operations (such as "divide army"), subjects are able to use the mapping to construct corresponding operators (such as "reduce ray intensity") that can be used to solve the ray problem. The abstract structure common to the two problems is described at the bottom of Table 15.2.

After the students had memorized the story of the general's predicament, they were given the ray problem to solve. Twelve students were given the hint that the story they memorized would help them solve it. Eleven of these students found the analogy and suggested the simultaneous application of weak rays to solve the ray problem. However, only one of the fifteen students who did not receive the hint thought of this solution. One way in which the difficulty of noticing distant analogies can be overcome is by encouraging abstraction of the underlying general similarities. Gick and Holyoak (1983) demonstrated this by having subjects first read two convergence stories, such as the military story and a story about fire fighting (for example, a story in which the hero extinguished an oil well fire by using multiple small hoses). The subjects were asked to describe ways in which the stories were similar, thus encouraging them to combine the common elements into a single prototype. When such subjects subsequently attempted to solve the radiation problem, they were much more likely to generate the parallel solution even without a hint than were subjects who had received just one prior story.

Expert problem solving

Experts narrow the search space by considering only solutions to structurally similar problems that have worked in the past. In some cases they have knowledge of heuristics or algorithms for generating solutions so that they do not have to keep track of a novel sequence of sub-goals. In domains such as physics, in which knowledge is highly systematized, the role of specialized algorithms is especially apparent (Larkin *et al.*, 1980). A major factor differentiating experts from novices is that experts can rapidly classify problems as to the relevant solution procedure. When Chi, Feltovich, and Glaser (1981) asked novices and experts in the domain of physics problems to sort problems into clusters on the basis of similarity, novices tended to form categories based on relatively surface features of the problem statements (for example, inclined-plane problems). In contrast, experts sorted the problems with respect to applicable physical laws (for example, problems solvable by the principle of the conservation of energy). If you compare the problem pairs depicted in Figure 15.7, which were grouped together by novices, with those depicted in Figure 15.8, which were grouped by experts, you will get a sense of the greater degree of abstraction involved in the experts' problem categories. The experts were able to articulate the explicit solution procedures for problems of a given type. The novices' protocols, on the other hand, even when they mentioned abstract problem features, usually did not reveal knowledge of the appropriate algorithms to solve the problems.

Lightning calculator. An extreme form of expertise is lightning calculation. Some people have exceptional abilities to perform numerical calculations in their heads. Hunter (1962; 1977) presented an interesting case study of one such "lightning calculator," Professor A. C. Aitken of Edinburgh University. Here is one example of his prodigious skill. He was given the task of expressing 4/47 in decimals. After an initial pause of four

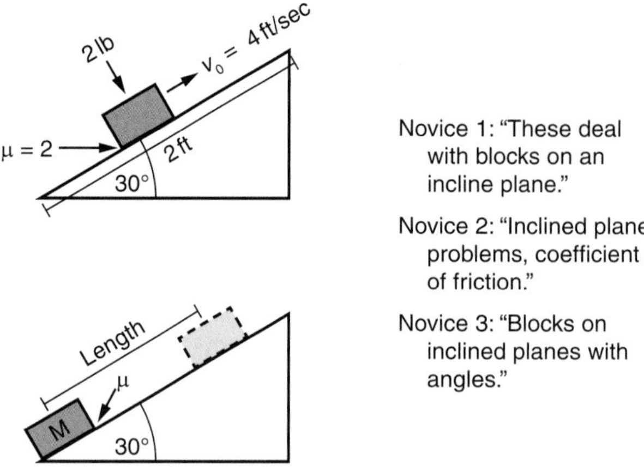

Figure 15.7 Diagrams of two problems categorized together by novices and samples of explanations given (Chi *et al.*, 1981).

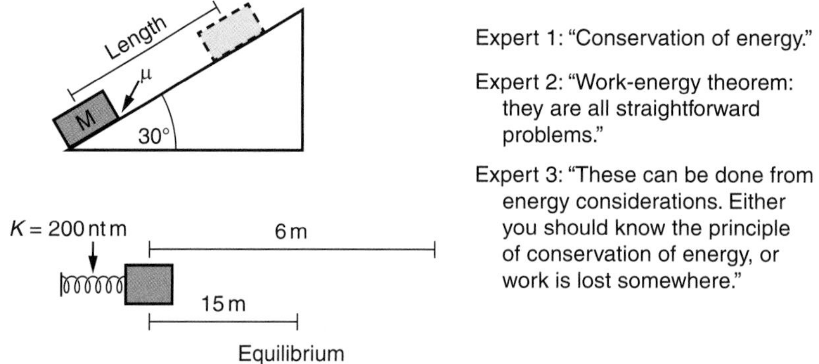

Figure 15.8 Diagrams of two problems categorized together by experts and samples of explanations given (Chi *et al.*, 1981).

seconds, he began to produce the answer at the rate of about one digit every four seconds: ".08510638297872340425531914... [a pause of about one minute], 191489... [a five-second pause] 361702127659574458." At this point he stopped and announced that the decimal pattern repeats itself. Aitken's ability depended on two essential types of knowledge. First, he simply knew an enormous number of facts about numbers. Second, he had many alternative strategies for performing calculations. These strategies in turn relied on the number of facts that Aitken knew. He worked a calculation in two steps. First, he examined the problem and decided upon a plan of attack. In doing so, he might translate the problem into a different form that was easier to handle. Second, he actually implemented the method and generated the answer. Consider a second example, for which Aitken described how he arrived at the solution. The problem was to express 1/851 in decimals. The first thing he did was recall that 851 equals 23 x 37 (a number fact). Then he also recalled that 1/37 equals 0.027027027..., recurring. As a result, his chosen plan of attack was to divide 1/37 by 23. At this point Aitken began to produce the answer in the following way:

23 into 0.027 = 0.001 with remainder 4;
23 into 4027 = 175 with remainder 2;
23 into 2027 = 88 with remainder 3;
23 into 3027 = 131 with remainder 14;
23 into 14,027 = 609 with remainder 20; etc.

In addition, Aitken could easily calculate how far the solution would go before repeating. He knew that 1/37 repeats after three places and that 1/23 repeats after twenty-two places. As a result, 1/851 must start to repeat after 3 x 22 = 66 places.

Aitken's plan of attack was always to minimize the amount of conscious processing he had to do at any one time. Most of us have great difficulty with such mental calculations, because we have to compute and remember so many partial results as we go along. Aitken minimized this problem of limited capacity by using his enormous repertoire of number facts that were already stored in memory and could be retrieved without computation. We all know, for example, that 8 / 4 = 2. But Aitken also knew all the prime numbers up to 1,000 and the factors of all the nonprimes (such as 851 = 23 x 37). When the year 1961 was mentioned, for example, he commented that 1961 was 37 x 53, also 44 squared + 5 squared, as well as 40 squared + 19 squared.

Unlike most of us, Aitken thought of large numbers as single chunks rather than as combinations of digits. He said that all numbers up to 1,000 seemed like "one idea," while numbers from 1,000 to 1 million seemed (regrettably) like "two ideas." As a result of having such compact chunks for numbers, Aitken had no trouble repeating fifteen digits either forward or backward when they were read out to him at the rate of five per second (Baddeley, 1976: 367).

Before the age of electronic calculators and computers, lightning calculation was a very valuable skill for a mathematician. Today it is a dying art. One of the saddest days in Professor Aitken's life was in 1923, when he first used a mechanical calculator. After that first encounter he lost interest in extending his abilities any further, and he believed that his skills deteriorated.

Chess. De Groot (1965) investigated the knowledge and skills that make a master chess player better than a weaker player. He collected protocols from some of the best chess players in the world as they selected chess moves. The master chess players did not search through more possible moves than ordinary players before selecting one. In fact, if anything, the masters considered fewer alternatives than did ordinary players. The difference was that the masters explored particularly good moves, whereas weaker players spent more time considering bad moves. The good moves seemed to be immediately apparent to the master players.

The most striking difference between masters and weaker players emerged in a test of perceptual and memory abilities. In this test a chess position, such as the middle game (the board position in the middle of an actual game) shown in Figure 15.9 (a), was displayed for five seconds and then removed. The player then had to reconstruct the board position from memory. Chase and Simon (1973) performed this experiment with a master player (an expert), a class A player (a very good player), and a beginning (B) player. Figure 15.9 (c) plots the number of pieces correctly recalled by each player over seven trials. As shown, memory performance is ordered in the same way as the level of chess skill: the master recalled the most pieces, followed by the class A player, then the beginner. Chase and Simon also performed the memory test with positions in which the pieces were arranged randomly, as in Figure 15.9

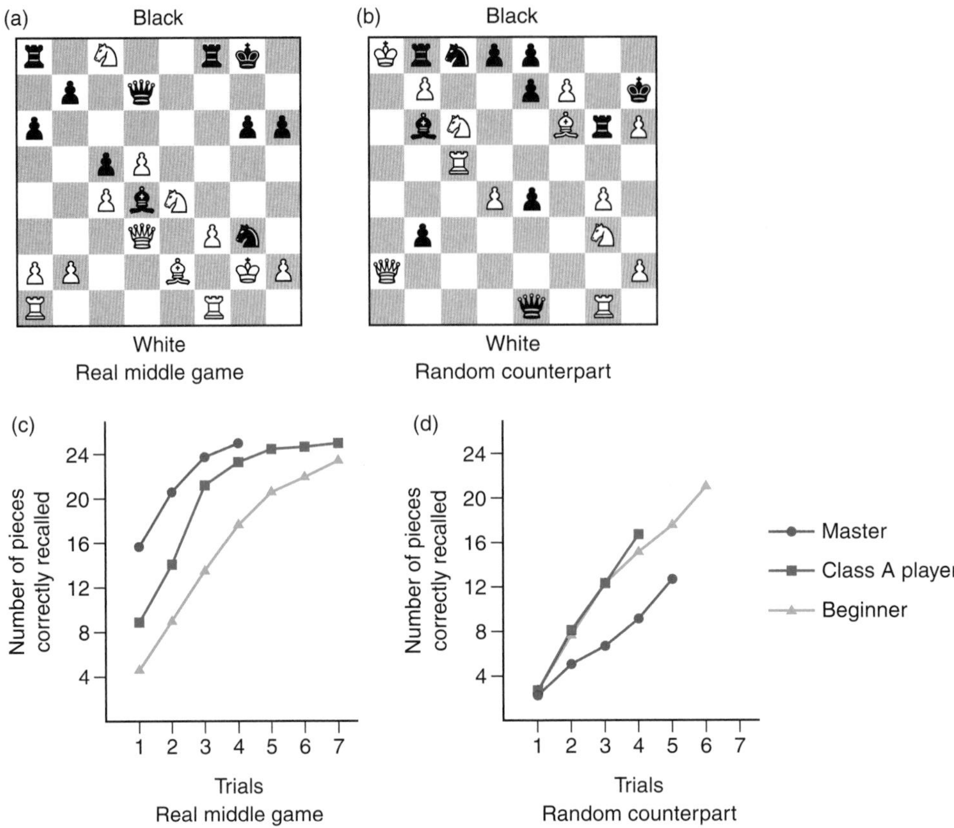

Figure 15.9 Examples of chess configurations: real middle game (a); random counterpart (b); number of pieces recalled correctly by master, class A player, and beginner over trials for actual board positions (c) and for random board positions (d) (Chase and Simon, 1973).

(b). With these random games the superiority of the master player completely disappeared. In fact, as Figure 15.9 (d) indicates, the master actually tended to recall fewer correct pieces than the weaker players.

Apparently, then, the master players are especially good at a very specialized task: encoding actual chess positions. To confirm that master players perform so well because they can recognize large meaningful chunks in board positions, Chase and Simon (1973) defined **chunks** on the basis of chess relations and then measured how long it took master players to recall them.

Two pieces were part of the same chunk when they were related in some way that was important to the game. Chase and Simon examined five relations between two pieces that are important in chess:

(1) One piece can attack another.
(2) One piece can defend another.
(3) Two pieces can be on adjacent squares.
(4) Two pieces can have the same color.
(5) Two pieces can be of the same type (for example, both pawns).

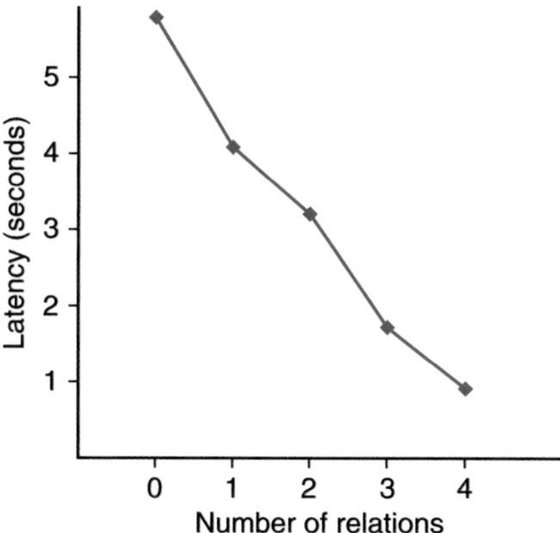

Figure 15.10 Average latency between two pieces as a function of number of relations between them (Chase and Simon, 1973).

Figure 15.10 plots the length of the pause between the recall of one piece and the next as a function of the number of relations between them. As the figure shows, the more relations there were between the two pieces, the shorter was the pause.

Chase and Simon (1973) also timed how long subjects paused between each placement of a piece as they recalled the positions on the first trial. If the pause was less than two seconds long, the two successive pieces were defined as belonging to the same chunk. If the pause was longer than two seconds, the two pieces were defined as belonging to different chunks. Chase and Simon found that pieces belonging to the same chunk tended to be recalled together on both the first and second trials, even though the order of recall within a cluster varied. This result suggests that each chunk is stored in memory as a single compound representation. Master players recalled larger chunks and more chunks than weaker players. This result suggests that the master is able to perceive associations among more pieces, and so encode larger chunks, and to perceive relations among chunks that form a narrative of the game, so that one chunk can serve as a retrieval cue for another.

Britton and Tesser (1982) hypothesized that, if experts activated more knowledge when performing a problem-solving task, they would be slower to detect a target that was part of a secondary task. Expert and novice chess players alike were given chess problems to solve, but they were also told to press a telegraph key when they heard a click. The experts took longer than the novices to respond to the clicks. Finally, Gobet and Simon (1996) also found evidence that a chess master automatically recognizes useful game positions. They rated the performance of the world chess champion Garry Kasparov both in normal chess matches and when playing multiple opponents. They reasoned that going from an average time of three minutes to thirty seconds per move should disrupt a deliberative generation process more than it would automatic recognition. They found only a small reduction in Kasparov's performance in the multiple matches, which they interpreted as supporting the automatic recognition hypothesis.

Simon and Gilmartin (1973) developed a computer program that simulated the way chess players store board positions in memory. The program contained information about many familiar patterns of pieces. Simon and Gilmartin used the performance of their program to estimate how many patterns a master chess player has stored in memory. Their estimate was

30,000. This is less than the number of words that a good reader can recognize (Chapter 8). A master chess player will have spent as much time studying chess positions as a good reader will have spent reading. In fact, the most basic requirement for becoming a master player appears to be an incredible amount of practice: as many as 50,000 hours spent working with chess positions. As a result of this practice, the master is able to recognize complex chess patterns as chunks, just as a skilled reader recognizes words as chunks. Because skilled chess players have their knowledge of board positions organized into large perceptual chunks, they know immediately after looking at a board what the best move is. Perception of a familiar perceptual chunk leads directly to an appropriate action.

Evidence for the effect of knowledge has been found with another complex board game: the oriental game of go. The game involves placing black and white stones on a grid and fighting for territory on the board. A player can capture an enemy stone by surrounding it with his or her own pieces. Reitman (1976) studied a go master and a beginner, using the kinds of memory tests used with chess players. As in chess, the go master player showed superior memory for real go positions but not for random positions. The go master also tended to recall pieces in clusters. Figure 15.11 shows several examples of board positions (labeled "A" through "D") that were presented to the master. The circles show how the master himself partitioned the pieces into chunks. Notice that the go master saw the chunks as overlapping in many different ways. In other words, the same piece was often included in several different clusters. The numbers on the pieces in Figure 15.11 give the order in which the pieces were recalled on that trial (if there is no number, the piece was not recalled). As shown, pieces that were part of the same pattern had a very strong tendency to be recalled together. The study of chess and go reveals that the perceptual skills that support expertise in problem solving rely on the same kinds of operations and procedures as other perceptual skills, such as reading (Chapter 5) and face recognition (Chapter 6).

Planning

Some solutions are unlikely to be imagined because they involve an unexpected or even counterintuitive operation. The only way to solve such a problem is to plan a sequence of operations so that it can be seen that an action that moves the components of the task to a state further from the goal is necessary to ultimately obtain a solution. An example is the Tower of Hanoi puzzle depicted in Figure 15.12. A number of disks (three in Figure 15.12) must be moved from peg A to peg C. Only one disk (the top disk on a peg) can be moved at a time, and no disk can ever be placed on top of a disk smaller than itself. This puzzle derives its name from a legend that a group of monks near Hanoi are working on a version of the puzzle that uses sixty-four disks. The legend says that the world will end when they finish the puzzle, which, at the rate of one perfect move every second, will take them about a trillion years (Raphael, 1976).

The three-disk version of the puzzle is considerably more tractable, but it still requires generating sub-goals that will bring the problem closer to a solution. For example, clearly the solution to the puzzle in Figure 15.12 requires that the largest disk (disk 3) be placed on peg C first. (This approach is an illustration of working backwards from the goal to solve a problem.) Therefore, we begin by setting up a sub-goal of getting disk 3 to peg C. It is also clear that disks 1 and 2 have to be moved from disk 3 before the latter can be moved. This step results in a further sub-goal of moving disks 1 and 2, which in turn sets up a sub-goal of first moving disk 1.

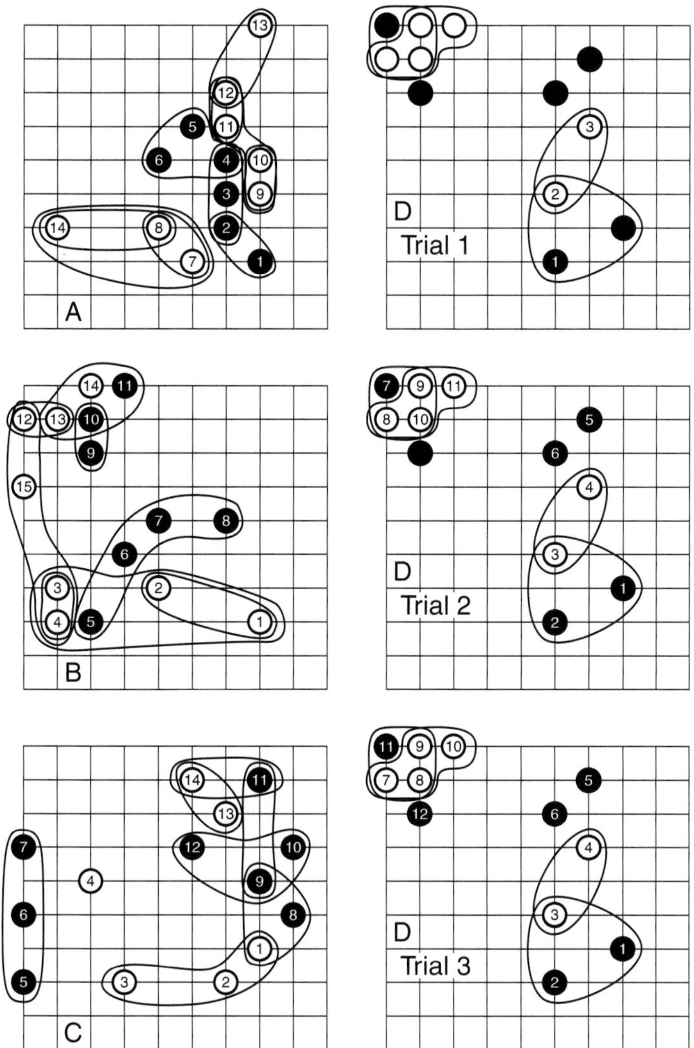

Figure 15.11 Examples of go master's penciled partitioning of meaningful patterns and orders in which he recalled elements (Reitman, 1976).

However, should disk 1 go to peg B or peg C? Here looking ahead a few moves will help. For, if we move disk 1 to peg B, then disk 2 will have to go on peg C. But then disk 3 won't be able to go on peg C. On the other hand, if we begin by moving disk 1 to peg C, the following sequence will accomplish the sub-goal of moving disk 3 to peg C:

disk 1 to peg C;
disk 2 to peg B;
disk 1 to peg B;
disk 3 to peg C.

Having completed the initial sub-goal, we can set up the next sub-goal: getting disk 2 onto peg C. This step is easily accomplished:

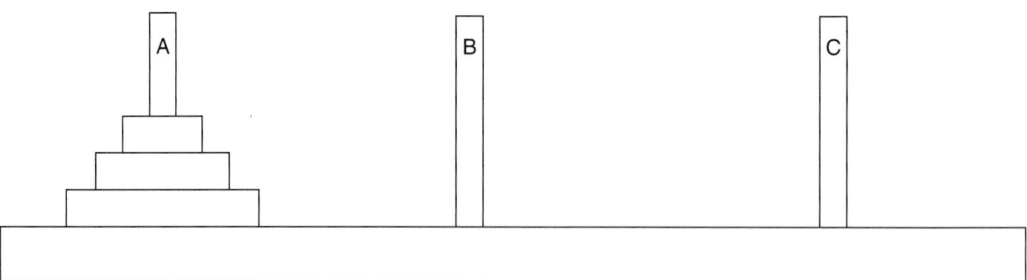

Figure 15.12 Initial state for three-disk Tower of Hanoi problem.

disk 1 to peg A (which undoes the previous move of disk 1);
disk 2 to peg C.

Then a final move (disk 1 to peg C) completes the puzzle.

Notice that this approach to the Tower of Hanoi puzzle involves formulating a hierarchy of sub-goals (for example, the sub-goal "move disk 3 to peg C" generates the sub-goal "move disk 2 off disk 3," which in turn generates the sub-goal "move disk 1 off disk 2"). This puzzle becomes increasingly difficult when more disks are used, because the sub-goal hierarchies get deeper. Thinking far enough ahead in planning moves and remembering how all the sub-goals that are generated relate to each other becomes very difficult. Egan and Greeno (1974) observed subjects as they worked on a six-disk Tower of Hanoi problem. They found that the probability of a subject's making an error on a move increased with the number of sub-goals that had to be set up between moves. Ward and Allport (1997) found that the most difficult moves in the development of a solution were those that initiated a sub-goal when there were alternative moves available. In addition to the Tower of Hanoi puzzle (Egan and Greeno, 1974), the water jugs puzzle (Atwood and Polson, 1976), and the missionaries and cannibals puzzle (Jeffries *et al.*, 1977), as well as chess problems, have been used to study planning.

15.4 Intelligence

The modern concept of intelligence as a general ability that can be measured is only about 100 years old. The modern concept of intelligence would not exist without the mathematical procedure for computing a correlation. A correlation is a measure of the relationship between two sequences of numbers. The correlation between any sequence and itself is 1.0. If there is no relationship in the order of two sequences then the correlation is zero. By computing their correlation, the relationship between any two things in the world that can be measured, hence assigned a number, can be measured. Furthermore, correlations can be computed among groups of measures.

When the mathematical procedure for computing correlations was first invented, psychologists used it to compute the relationships among measures of performance on a variety of perceptual, memory, language, and reasoning tests. The results were surprising. In general, across all kinds of cognitive tests, Spearman (1927) found that the correlations were positive. Some people tended to do better than average on all the tests and other people tended to do worse than average on all the tests. Similarly, students tend to do about the same in all their subjects in school. An "A" student tends to get, mostly, "A" grades, and a "B" student tends to get, mostly, "B" grades, etc. Spearman attributed the correlation in test performance to some general ability, g, that some people had more of than others. Of course, each test also required specific abilities: s_1, s_2, etc. According to Spearman's theory, performance on a specific test was determined both by a person's general ability and whatever specific ability, s_i, was required for that test.

Whether g reflects a single cognitive ability or the effects of several abilities has always been controversial. Thurstone (1938) defined intelligence by seven primary abilities: verbal comprehension, verbal fluency, number, space, memory, inductive reasoning, and perceptual speed. Many modern theorists have also redefined intelligence as sets of specialized abilities, rather than as a single general ability (Ceci, 1996; Gardner, 1983; Sternberg, 1985; 1988). Regardless of whether g measures the effect of a single ability or a small set of abilities, many findings provide evidence of a general ability that is associated with the control of cognition by the prefrontal cortex. Tests that require higher levels of g are associated with a higher level of activity in the lateral prefrontal cortex (Duncan *et al.*, 2000). The general ability appears to be the ability of the lateral prefrontal cortex to inhibit irrelevant processing when performing a working memory task that requires the rehearsal of a novel perceptual sequence, as discussed in detail in Chapter 11. This ability is the basis of **fluid intelligence** (Chapter 10), which is especially evident in performance on novel tasks. So, fluid intelligence describes the performance of the instrumental system, whose entire purpose is to construct ad hoc actions to perform novel tasks. Fluid intelligence remains stable in healthy individuals but is fragile and often impaired, as shown in Figure 10.7.

Intelligence tests

Intelligence tests do not directly measure g, and have entirely different purposes. The tests that are today called intelligence tests have two origins (Tuddenham, 1962). At the beginning of the twentieth century the Binet–Henri test was a collection of simple tests of the skills needed to perform academic tasks, developed as a predictor of scholastic achievement to determine which French schoolchildren required special education. This test was translated into English by Lewis B. Termin of Stanford University and hence is known in the United States as the Stanford–Binet (the Stanford revision of the Binet test). Since then it has been translated and used around the world as a good predictor of academic performance. The variety of tests used around the world to predict academic performance, such as the Scholastic Aptitude Test (SAT), are all similar to intelligence tests, and scores on these tests are correlated with intelligence scores (Frey and Detterman, 2004).

The term "IQ" stands for "intelligence quotient." The test was used to measure the pupil's intellectual age, which was represented as the age at which at least half the pupils achieved that level of performance. So, if at least a half of eight-year-old pupils performed at a certain level, then the intellectual age for that level of performance would be 8. The intelligence quotient was defined as:

IQ = (pupil's intellectual age / pupil's chronological age) x 100.

When applying this formula to a student's performance, when the student's performance was no better than that of younger children then the ratio between intellectual age and chronological age would be less than 1 and so the IQ would be less than 100. When the student's performance was better than that of older children then the ratio would be greater than 1 and so the IQ would be greater than 100. From the time this formula was first created the problems with it were obvious. Students who had exactly the same performance on the test after the same number of years of schooling but were of different ages would be assigned different IQs by the formula. In addition, the formula did not generate meaningful scores for adults. Accordingly, a better definition of IQ was created, as described below. However, the original name, IQ, was too popular and well understood to discard.

David Wechsler was a clinical neuropsychologist who had the task of evaluating whether people brought to Bellevue Hospital in New York City were mentally competent. He collected the scores of normal adults on a battery of simple cognitive tests, measuring such things as vocabulary, analogies, and arithmetic, similar to the tests given to schoolchildren as part of the Stanford–Binet. However, the Wechsler Adult Intelligence Scale (WAIS) test gave a **deviation score**. The score indicated how far the individual's score deviated (above or below) the mean of the normal population. The mean is set at 100. So, a score above 100 is better than average and less than 100 is worse than average. Since intelligence tests are collections of simple subtests, and performance on all these tests is influenced by g, they provide a good way of measuring g. However, intelligence tests do not measure learning ability or long-term retention. The functioning of the habit system is outside the scope of the exam.

The concept of a general ability, g, has long been bound up with the question of the extent to which g is determined by a person's heredity or environment. On the one hand, since intelligence tests measure performance on academic tasks learned in school, performance on those tests is necessarily influenced by what was taught in school, and so by the experiences of the student. Someone who has never learned to read or do arithmetic is not going to do very well. On the other hand, not everyone may develop the same skills and knowledge from the same experience, and how much is learned may depend on the control of the instrumental system when a novel experience requires ad hoc action. The influence of the instrumental system is observed in infancy, long before schooling begins. Recall from Chapter 8 that, when given a choice between a novel or familiar input, infants spend more time looking at the familiar input. In addition, when the same pattern is shown to an infant repeatedly, the infant spends less time looking at it on each trial. Infants differ in the amount of novelty preference they show. Fagan and Singer (1983) found that, the stronger an infant's novelty preference was at three to seven months, the higher its IQ score was up to seven years later (see also Bornstein and Sigman, 1986). These results suggest that some people from the very beginning of life are more interested in novelty, and so become more practiced at skills for responding to it, and this leads to a greater growth in IQ.

Regardless of an infant's innate tendencies, scores on intelligence tests do not become stable over time until school age. Furthermore, the correlation between the IQs of children and their biological parents is low at birth and does not become significant until sixteen years of age (Plomin *et al.*, 1997). Furthermore, as education improved in the twentieth century, the population mean on intelligence tests increased by about 3 points per decade (Flynn, 1987). Over the last eighty years the increase has occurred in both industrialized and developing nations and across the entire distribution of scores. All scores, from the lowest to the highest, have risen relative to previous decades. The increase has been greatest for tests involving problem solving on novel tasks and visuospatial reasoning (Wai and Putallaz, 2011).

Presumably, if whatever has been causing performance on intelligence tests to rise for eighty years could be identified then there would be a way of making people smarter. Recall that the short-term retention tasks described in Chapter 11 test prefrontal inhibition, and so performance on these tests are correlated with measures of fluid intelligence. One possibility that has been intensively investigated (and widely advertised and sold online as if it actually worked) is training on such short-term retention tasks, either to improve everyone's intelligence or to prevent the decline in fluid intelligence associated with age. The extensive research in this area has established that practice on such task does *not* improve fluid intelligence (Harrison *et al.*, 2013; Redick *et al.*, 2013).

The effect of experience causing the Flynn effect, whatever it is, does not rule out an effect of heredity on an individual's performance. Studies of adult identical twins reared together have found correlations of 0.80 in their test performance, which is higher than for nontwin siblings or for unrelated individuals (Bouchard *et al.*, 1990; Plomin and Loehlin, 1989). This works out to IQ being about 50 percent the result of genetics for whites living in the relatively homogeneous educational environments of the United States and the United Kingdom. The percent of the variance due to genetics is less among members of population groups living in less homogeneous educational and social environments (Ceci, 1996). Rowe, Jacobson, and Van den Oord (1999) compared the percentage of the variability in IQ attributable to genetics in adolescents raised by highly educated versus poorly educated parents. Presumably, all highly educated parents provide their children with rich educational environments, so the level of eduction that all the children in this group received was uniformly high. However, presumably, the levels of education that the poorly educated parents provided their children were more variable. For the adolescents raised by the highly educated parents, 79 percent of the variance was attributed to heredity and 0 percent to environment. But, for the adolescents raised by poorly educated parents, 26 percent of the variance was attributed to heredity and 23 percent to environment.

Sex differences in visuospatial ability

Recall from Chapter 14 that children with Williams syndrome, who have a severe deficit in basic visual comparison, are also severely deficient in mathematics and logical reasoning. After a lifetime of research, Witkin, Goodenough, and Oltman (1979) found that visual comparison was a necessary component of mathematical ability in all individuals. In their studies, people were consistent in their ability to detect or attend to camouflaged targets across a variety of tasks. People better at attending to targets in the presence of distracters were more likely to study math and science and were less sensitive to social inputs than people who were more influenced by the distracters. Males tended to perform better at selective visual attention tasks and at mathematics than females did. This difference was most noticeable at the highest levels of ability. Twenty years of research by Camilla Benbow and her colleagues (Benbow *et al.*, 2000) has confirmed that, at all ages, the top 1 percent of individuals on tests of mathematical reasoning ability are predominantly male. However, there are no differences in verbal ability. This difference accounts for the predominance of males in science and engineering.

Since the science, technical, engineering, and medical professions have become more important in society, the under-representation of women in the first three of these professions has become a matter of concern. Extensive training improves the performance of both men and women but does not eliminate the difference in performance between them (Uttal *et al.*, 2013).

Triarchic theory of intelligence

As discussed in Chapter 2, the ultimate purpose of the increase in human cognitive abilities has been to increase human social abilities. Success in human society depends on an individual's social skills. Academic skills may be considered an important subset of social skills because they are skills that make a person a useful member of society. However, they are not the only kinds of skills that people have. Taking the broad view, Sternberg (1985; 1988) argued that human intelligence is comprised of all the abilities that lead to success in human society, and divided them into three broad categories – analytical intelligence, creative intelligence, and practical intelligence – creating the triarchic theory of intelligence. **Analytical intelligence** is the use of a person's semantic knowledge and skills to solve problems in the world, requiring either fluid or crystallized intelligence. **Creative intelligence** is the ability to respond to novel tasks. It is similar to the concept of fluid intelligence but also includes musical and artistic talent. Analytical and creative intelligence are both conscious activities, involving declarative knowledge, that require the operation of both the instrumental and habit systems. Declarative knowledge is also the basis of the third category of intelligence, practical intelligence. **Practical intelligence** is the ability to accomplish one's own goals in daily life. Since this often involves understanding how others will act and persuading other individuals to take specific acts, a large component of practical intelligence is social intelligence. Because of the social component, practical intelligence relies more on emotional processing than the other kinds of intelligence, but otherwise it relies on the same neural systems.

Sternberg and his colleagues (Sternberg *et al.*, 2012) developed and evaluated a new test for predicting academic success at college based on the triarchic theory of intelligence. This test evaluated creative and practical intelligence, in addition to the measures of analytical intelligence included in the SAT and also measured by high school grades. One issue addressed by Sternberg's new test was the long-standing differences in the performance of different ethnic groups on tests of analytical intelligence such as the SAT. For the students who took this test in high school in addition to the SAT, prediction of the students' first-year university grade point average was substantially increased over that provided by SAT and high school grade point average. Moreover, ethnic group differences, relative to SAT, were reduced. Students admitted to college because of their creative or practical intelligence performed as well as or better than did other students, without the ethnic group differences typically observed in measures of crystallized intelligence. Enhanced prediction of active citizenship and leadership activities was also demonstrated through these measures.

SUMMARY

- The process of solving a problem has three major steps.
  - Forming an initial representation of the problem.
  - Generating and testing potential solutions (the generate-and-recognize strategy of recall is a special case). It has two steps:
    - (1) generate a candidate for a solution; and
    - (2) test to see whether it is actually a solution. If the candidate fails the test, another candidate is generated, and the cycle repeats until a solution is found.
  - Executing a procedure to carry out a planned solution and checking the results.
- The initial representation of the problem is different for novices as opposed to experts.
  - A novice may employ either of two strategies for representing the problem.
    - Task analysis, in which the overall problem is broken down into subproblems that the novice can solve.
    - Applying an analogy – that is, retrieving a representation of some other problem previously solved. However, novices are poor at finding analogies, because they are more likely to retrieve a representation with common superficial features instead of one for a structurally similar problem with a similar solution.
  - In contrast, experts are likely to retrieve the representation of a structurally similar problem that has a similar solution.
- Generation.
  - Problem-solving set; PI from previously generated potential solutions may emerge during generation.
  - Functional fixedness; superficial features can interfere with generating potential solutions.
  - The number of sub-goals that comprise the solution plan is limited by constraints on working memory.
- Intelligence. When people perform a variety of different tasks, task performance is positively correlated across tasks.
  - One possible explanation is that there is a single general ability, g, that is applied in all tasks.
    - g is associated with the role of the prefrontal cortex in the control of ad hoc action.
  - Intelligence tests were designed to predict academic performance in schools.
    - Since intelligence tests are collections of subtests they are good measures of g.
  - Performance on intelligence tests has been improving for the last eighty years, demonstrating the effect of experience.
  - However, innate ability also influences performance, as indicated by correlations in performance among family members.

QUESTIONS

1 What is an example of a problem-solving set?
2 What is an example of functional fixedness?
3 What are the strategies that novices use to solve problems?
4 What does "g" stand for and what is the evidence for it?
5 What task were intelligence tests originally designed for?

FURTHER READING

Davidson, J. E., and Sternberg, R. J. (2000). *The Psychology of Problem Solving*. Cambridge University Press.

Gallagher, A. M., and Kaufman, J. C. (2005). *Gender Differences in Mathematics: An Integrative Psychological Approach*. Cambridge University Press.

Marshall, S. P. (2007). *Schemas in Problem Solving*. Cambridge University Press.

Sternberg, R. J., and Pretz, J. E. (2004). *Cognition and Intelligence: Identifying the Mechanisms of the Mind*. Cambridge University Press.

BIBLIOGRAPHY

Abbott, L. F., and Kandel, E. R. (2012). A computational approach enhances learning in *Aplysia*. *Nature Neuroscience*, 15, 178–9.

Abrams, R. L., and Greenwald, A. G. (2000). Parts outweigh the whole (word) in unconscious analysis of meaning. *Psychological Science*, 11, 118–24.

Adams, A. M., and Gathercole, S. E. (2000). Limitations in working memory: implications for language development. *International Journal of Language and Communication Disorders*, 35, 95–116.

Adams, J. A. (1976). *Learning and Memory: An Introduction*. Homewood, IL.: Dorsey Press.

Adams, J. A., Goetz, E. T., and Marshall, P. H. (1972). Response feedback and motor learning. *Journal of Experimental Psychology*, 92, 391–7.

Adams, J. L. (1974). *Conceptual Blockbusting*. Stanford Alumni Association.

Adams, M. J. (1979). Models of word recognition. *Cognitive Psychology*, 11, 133–76.

Adler, S. A., and Rovee-Collier, C. (1994). The memorability and discriminability of primitive perceptual units. *Vision Research*, 34, 449–59.

Adolphs, R., Tranel, D., Hamann, S., Young, A. W., Calder, A. J., Phelps, E. A., Anderson, A., Lee, G. P., and Damasio, A. R. (1999). Recognition of facial emotion in nine individuals with bilateral amygdala damage. *Neuropsychologia*, 37, 1111–17.

Afifi, A. K., and Bergman, R. A. (1980). *Basic Neuroscience*. Baltimore: Urban & Schwarzenberg.

Ajzen, I. (1977). Intuitive theories of events and the effects of base-rate information on prediction. *Journal of Personality and Social Psychology*, 35, 303–14.

Akhtar, N. (1999). Acquiring basic word order: evidence for data-driven learning of syntactic structure. *Journal of Child Language*, 26, 339–56.

Akhtar, N., Carpenter, M., and Tomasello, M. (1996). The role of discourse novelty in early word learning. *Child Development*, 67, 635–45.

Akhtar, N., Jipson, J., and Callanan, M. A. (2001). Learning words through overhearing. *Child Development*, 72, 416–30.

Albert, M. S., Butters, N., and Brandt, J. (1981a). Memory for remote events in alcoholics. *Journal of Studies on Alcohol*, 41, 1071–81.

(1981b). Patterns of remote memory in amnesic and demented patients. *Archives of Neurology*, 38, 495–500.

Albert, M. S., Butters, N., and Levin, J. (1979). Temporal gradients in the retrograde amnesia of patients with alcoholic Korsakoff's disease. *Archives of Neurology*, 36, 211–16.

Alexander, M. P., Benson, D. F., and Stuss, D. T. (1989). Frontal lobes and language. *Brain and Language*, 37, 656–91.

Almor, A., and Sloman, S. A. (1996). Is deontic reasoning special? *Psychological Review*, 103, 374–80.

Altarriba, J., and Isurin, L. (eds.) (2014). *Memory, Language, and Bilingualism: Theoretical and Applied Approaches*. Cambridge University Press.

Amabile, T. A., and Rovee-Collier, C. (1991). Contextual variation and memory retrieval at six months. *Child Development*, 62, 1155–66.

Ameel, E., Storms, G., Malt, B. C., and Sloman, S. A. (2005). How bilinguals solve the naming problem. *Journal of Memory and Language*, 53, 60–80.

Andersen, R. A., Snyder, L. H., Bradley, D. C., and Xing, J. (1997). Multimodal representation of space in the posterior parietal cortex and its use in planning movements. *Annual Review of Neuroscience*, 20, 303–30.

Anderson, B. L., and Nakayama, K. (1994). Toward a general theory of stereopsis: binocular matching, occluding contours, and fusion. *Psychological Review*, 101, 414–45.

Anderson, J., and Revelle, W. (1982). Impulsivity, caffeine, and proofreading: a test of the Easterbrook hypothesis. *Journal of Experimental Psychology: Human Perception and Performance*, 8, 614–24.

Anderson, M. C., Bjork, R. A., and Bjork, E. L. (1994). Remembering can cause forgetting: retrieval dynamics in long-term memory. *Journal of Experimental Psychology: Learning, Memory, and Cognition*, 20, 1063–87.

Anderson, R. C., and Pichert, J. W. (1978). Recall of previously unrecallable information following a shift in perspective. *Journal of Verbal Learning and Verbal Behavior*, 17, 1–12.

Anzola, G. P., Bertoloni, G., Buchtel, H. A., and Rizzolatti, G. (1977). Spatial compatibility and anatomical factors in simple and choice reaction time. *Neuropsychologia*, 15, 295–302.

Apgar, V. (1953). A proposal for a new method of evaluation of the newborn infant. *Current Researches in Anesthesia and Analgesia*, 32, 260–7.

Apostolides, P. F., and Trussell, L. O. (2013). Regulation of interneuron excitability by gap junction coupling with principal cells. *Nature Neuroscience*, 16, 1764–74.

Aramideh, M., and Ongerboer de Visser, B. W. (2002). Brainstem reflexes: electrodiagnostic techniques, physiology, normative data, and clinical applications. *Muscle Nerve*, 26, 14–30.

Atkinson, Q. D. (2011). Phonemic diversity supports a serial founder effect model of language expansion from Africa. *Science*, 332, 346–9.

Atkinson, R. C., and Raugh, M. R. (1975). An application of the mnemonic keyword method to the acquisition of a Russian vocabulary. *Journal of Experimental Psychology: Human Learning and Memory*, 104, 126–33.

Attneave, A. (1957). Transfer of experience with a class schema to identification learning of patterns and shapes. *Journal of Experimental Psychology*, 54, 81–8.

Atwood, M. E., and Polson, P. G. (1976). A process model for water jug problems. *Cognitive Psychology*, 8, 191–216.

Azizi, A. H., Schieferstein, N., and Cheng, S. (2014). The transformation from grid cells to place cells is robust to noise in the grid pattern. *Hippocampus*, 24, 912–19.

Baddeley, A. D. (1972). Selective attention and performance in dangerous environments. *British Journal of Psychology*, 63, 537–46.

Baddeley, A. D. (1976). *The Psychology of Memory*. New York: Basic Books.

(1986). *Working Memory*. Oxford University Press.

(1992). Working memory. *Science*, 255, 556–9.

Baddeley, A. D., and Gathercole, S. E. (1998). The phonological loop as a language learning device. *Psychological Review*, 105, 158–73.

Baddeley, A. D., and Longman, D. J. A. (1978). The influence of length and frequency of training sessions on the rate of learning to type. *Ergonomics*, 21, 627–35.

Baddeley, A. D., Papagno, C., and Vallar, G. (1988). When long-term learning depends on short-term storage. *Journal of Memory and Language*, 27, 586–95.

Bahrick, H. P. (1970). Two-phase model for prompted recall. *Psychological Review*, 77, 215–22.

(1983). Memory and people. In J. Harris (ed.), *Everyday Memory, Actions, and Absentmindedness*, 19–34. New York: Academic Press.

(1984). Semantic memory content in permastore: fifty years of memory for Spanish learned in school. *Journal of Experimental Psychology: General*, 113, 1–29.

Bahrick, H. P., Bahrick, L. E., Bahrick, A. S., and Bahrick, P. E. (1993). Maintenance of foreign language vocabulary and the spacing effect. *Psychological Science*, 4, 316–21.

Bahrick, H. P., Bahrick, P. O., and Wittlinger, R. P. (1975). Fifty years of memory for names and faces: a cross-sectional approach. *Journal of Experimental Psychology: General*, 104, 54–75.

Bahrick, H. P., Hall, L. K., and Da Costa, L. A. (2008). Fifty years of memory of college grades: accuracy and distortions. *Emotion*, 8, 13–22.

Bahrick, L. E., and Lickliter, R. (2014). Learning to attend selectively: the dual role of intersensory redundancy. *Current Directions in Psychological Science*, 23, 414–20.

Bahrick, L. E., and Pickens, J. N. (1995). Infant memory of object motion across a period of three months: implications for a four-phase attention function. *Journal of Experimental Child Psychology*, 59, 343–71.

Bains, J. S., and Oliet, S. H. (2007). Glia: they make your memories stick! *Trends in Neuroscience*, 30, 417–24.

Bakker, D. J. (1970). Ear asymmetry with monaural stimulation: relations to lateral dominance and lateral awareness. *Neuropsychologia*, 8, 103–17.

Baldo, J. V., Bunge, S., Wilson, S., and Dronkers, N. F. (2010). Is relational reasoning dependent on language? A voxel-based lesion symptom mapping study. *Brain and Language*, 113, 59–64.

Baldo, J. V., and Shimamura, A. P. (1998). Letter and category fluency in patients with frontal lobe lesions. *Neuropsychology*, 12, 259–67.

Baldwin, D. A., Markman, E. M., Bill, B., Desjardins, R. N., and Irwin, J. M. (1996). Infants' reliance on a social criterion for establishing word–object relations. *Child Development*, 67, 3135–53.

Ballard, P. B. (1913). Oblivescence and reminiscence. *British Journal of Psychology Monograph Supplement*, 1, 1–82.

Balota, D. A., Burgess, G. C., Cortese, M. J., and Adams, D. R. (2002). The word-frequency mirror effect in young, old, and early-stage Alzheimer's disease: evidence for two processes in episodic recognition performance. *Journal of Memory and Language*, 46, 199–226.

Baluch, B., and Besner, D. (1991). Visual word recognition: evidence for strategic control of lexical and nonlexical routines in oral reading. *Journal of Experimental Psychology: Learning, Memory, and Cognition*, 17, 644–52.

Banks, W. P. (1970). Signal detection theory and human memory. *Psychological Bulletin*, 74, 81–99.

Banks, W. P., and Flora, J. (1977). Semantic and perceptual processes in symbolic comparisons. *Journal of Experimental Psychology: Human Perception and Performance*, 3, 278–90.

Barber, T. X. (1969). *Hypnosis: A Scientific Approach*. New York: Van Nostrand Reinhold.

Barber, T. X., and Glass, L. B. (1962). Significant factors in hypnotic behavior. *Journal of Abnormal and Social Psychology*, 64, 222–8.

Bar-Hillel, M., and Falk, R. (1982). Some teasers concerning conditional probabilities. *Cognition*, 11, 109–22.

Baron-Cohen, S. (1995). *Mindblindness: An Essay on Autism and Theory of Mind*. Cambridge, MA: MIT Press.

Baron-Cohen, S., Leslie, A. M., and Frith, U. (1985). Does the autistic child have a "theory of mind"? *Cognition*, 21, 37–46.

Barr, R., Dowden, A., and Hayne, H. (1996). Developmental changes in deferred imitation by 6- to 24-month-old infants. *Infant Behavior and Development*, 19, 159–79.

Barr, R., Rovee-Collier, C., and Campanella, J. (2005). Retrieval protracts deferred imitation by 6-month-olds. *Infancy*, 7, 263–83.

Barr, R., Rovee-Collier, C., and Learmonth, A. E. (2011). Potentiation in young infants: the origin of the prior knowledge effect? *Memory and Cognition*, 39, 625–35.

Barr, R., Vieira, A., and Rovee-Collier, C. (2001). Mediated imitation at 6 months of age: remembering by association. *Journal of Experimental Child Psychology*, 79, 229–52.

(2002). Bidirectional priming in infants. *Memory and Cognition*, 30, 246–55.

Barron, R. W., and Baron, J. (1977). How children get meaning from printed words. *Child Development*, 48, 587–94.

Barsalou, L. W. (2008). Grounded cognition. *Annual Review of Psychology*, 59, 617–45.

Bartlett, F. C., and Kintsch, W. (1995). *Remembering: A Study in Experimental and Social Psychology*. Cambridge University Press.

Bartlett, J. C., Till, R. E., and Levy, J. C. (1980). Retrieval characteristics of complex pictures: effects of verbal encoding. *Journal of Verbal Learning and Verbal Behavior*, 19, 430–49.

Bartolo, A., Cubelli, R., Della Sala, S., Drei, S., and Marchetti, C. (2001). Double dissociation between meaningful and meaningless gesture reproduction in apraxia. *Cortex*, 37, 696–9.

Bass, E., and Davis, L. (1988). *The Courage to Heal: A Guide for Women Survivors of Child Sexual Abuse*. New York: Harper & Row.

Battig, W. F., and Montague, W. E. (1969). Category norms of verbal items in 56 categories: a replication and extension of the Connecticut category norms. *Journal of Experimental Psychology*, 80, 1–46.

Bauer, P. J. (2002). Early memory development. In U. Goswami (ed.), *Blackwell Handbook of Childhood*

Cognitive Development, 127–46. Malden, MA: Blackwell.

Bay, M., and Wyble, B. (2014). The benefit of attention is not diminished when distributed over two simultaneous cues. *Attention, Perception, and Psychophysics*, 76, 1287–97.

Bechara, A., Damasio, H., and Damasio, A. R. (2000). Emotion, decision making, and the orbitofrontal cortex. *Cerebral Cortex*, 10, 295–307.

Bechara, A., Damasio, H., Damasio, A. R., and Lee, G. P. (1999). Different contributions of the human amygdala and ventromedial prefrontal cortex to decision-making. *Journal of Neuroscience*, 19, 5473–81.

Bechara, A., Tranel, D., and Damasio, H. (2000). Characterization of the decision-making deficit of patients with ventromedial prefrontal cortex lesions. *Brain*, 123, 2189–202.

Beck, D. M., Muggleton, N. G., Walsh, V., and Lavie, N. (2006). Right parietal cortex plays a critical role in change blindness. *Cerebral Cortex*, 16, 712–17.

Beck, D. M., Rees, G., Frith, C. D., and Lavie, N. (2001). Neural correlates of change detection and change blindness. *Nature Neuroscience*, 4, 645–50.

Becker, J. T., Butters, N., Hermann, A., and D'Angelo, N. (1983). A comparison of the effects of long-term alcohol abuse and aging on the performance of verbal and nonverbal divided attention tasks. *Alcoholism: Clinical and Experimental Research*, 7, 213–19.

Becker, W. (1991). Saccades. In R. H. S. Carpenter (ed.), *Vision and Visual Dysfunction*, vol. VIII, *Eye Movements*, 95–137. Boca Raton, FL: CRC Press.

Begg, I. (1978a). Imagery and organization in memory: instructional effects. *Memory and Cognition*, 6, 174–83.

(1978b). Similarity and contrast in memory for relations. *Memory and Cognition*, 6, 509–17.

Behne, T., Carpenter, M., and Tomasello, M. (2005). One-year-olds comprehend the communicative intentions behind gestures in a hiding game. *Developmental Science*, 8, 492–9.

Behrmann, M., Avidan, G., Marotta, J. J., and Kimchi, R. (2005). Detailed exploration of face-related processing in congenital prosopagnosia I: behavioral findings. *Journal of Cognitive Neuroscience*, 17, 1130–49.

Behrmann, M., Moscovitch, M., and Winocur, G. (1994). Intact visual imagery and impaired visual perception in a patient with visual agnosia. *Journal of Experimental Psychology: Human Perception and Performance*, 20, 1068–87.

Bellugi, U., Klima, E. S., and Wang, P. P. (1996). Cognitive and neural development: clues from genetically based syndromes. In D. Magnussen (ed.), *The Lifespan Development of Individuals: Behavioral, Neurobiological, and Psychosocial Perspectives: A Synthesis*, 223–43. New York: Cambridge University Press.

Bellugi, U., Lichtenberger, L., Jones, W., Lai, Z., and St. George, M. (2000). The neurocognitive profile of Williams syndrome: a complex pattern of strengths and weaknesses. *Journal of Cognitive Neuroscience*, 12 (supplement), 7–29.

Belmore, S. M. (1981). Imagery and semantic elaboration in hypermnesia for words. *Journal of Experimental Psychology: Human Learning and Memory*, 7, 191–203.

Bem, D. J., and McConnell, H. K. (1970). Testing the self-perception explanation of dissonance phenomena: on the salience of premanipulation attitudes. *Journal of Personality and Social Psychology*, 14, 23–31.

Benasich, A., and Tallal, P. (2002). Infant discrimination of rapid auditory cues predicts later language impairment. *Behavioural Brain Research*, 136, 31–49.

Benbow, C. P., Lubinski, D., Shea, D. L., and Eftekhari-Sanjani, H. (2000). Sex differences in mathematical reasoning ability at age 13: their status 20 years later. *Psychological Science*, 11, 474–80.

Benbow, C. P., and Minor, L. L. (1990). Cognitive profiles of verbally and mathematically precocious students: implications for identification of the gifted. *Gifted Child Quarterly*, 34, 21–6.

Benson, D. F., Djenderedjian, A., Miller, B., Pachana, N., Chang, L., Itti, L., and Mena, I. (1996). Neural basis of confabulation. *Neurology*, 46, 1239–43.

Benson, D. F., and Greenberg, J. P. (1969). Visual form agnosia. *Archives of Neurology*, 20, 82–9.

Benton, A. L. (1968). Differential behavioral effects in frontal lobe disease. *Neuropsychologia*, 6, 53–60.

(1975). Developmental dyslexia: neurological aspects. In W. J. Friedlander (ed.), *Advances in Neurology*, vol. VII, *Current Reviews of Higher Nervous System Dysfunction*, 1–47. New York: Raven Press.

Benton, A. L., and Tranel, D. (1993). Visuoperceptual, visuospatial, and visuoconstructive disorders. In K. M. Heilman and E. Valenstein (eds.), *Clinical*

Neuropsychology, 215–78. New York: Oxford University Press.

Bergum, B. O., and Lehr, D. J. (1964). Monetary incentive and vigilance. *Journal of Experimental Psychology*, 67, 197–8.

Berkinblit, M. B., Feldman, A. G., and Fukson, O. (1986). Adaptability of innate motor patterns and motor control mechanisms. *Behavioral and Brain Sciences*, 9, 585–638.

Berlin, B., and Kay, P. (1969). *Basic Color Terms: Their Universality and Evolution*. Berkeley: University of California Press.

Berntsen, D., and Rubin, D. C. (2004). Cultural life scripts structure recall from autobiographical memory. *Memory and Cognition*, 32, 427–42.

(2012). *Understanding Autobiographical Memory: Theories and Approaches*. Cambridge University Press.

Best, C. T., Morrongiello, B., and Robson, R. (1981). Perceptual equivalence of acoustic cues in speech and nonspeech perception. *Perception and Psychophysics*, 29, 191–211.

Bevan, W., and Steger, J. A. (1971). Free recall and abstractness of stimuli. *Science*, 172, 597–9.

Bever, T. G., and Chiarello, R. J. (1974). Cerebral dominance in musicians and nonmusicians. *Science*, 185, 137–9.

Beylin, A. V., Gandhi, C. C., Wood, G. E., Talk, A. C., Matzel, L. D., and Shors, T. J. (2001). The role of the hippocampus in trace conditioning: temporal discontinuity or task difficulty? *Neurobiology of Learning and Memory*, 76, 447–61.

Bhatt, R. S., and Rovee-Collier, C. (1994). Perception and 24-hour retention of feature relations in infancy. *Developmental Psychology*, 30, 142–50.

Bhatt, R. S., Rovee-Collier, C., and Weiner, S. (1994). Developmental changes in the interface between perception and memory retrieval. *Developmental Psychology*, 30, 151–62.

Bialystok, E., Craik, F. I. M., and Luk, G. (2012). Bilingualism: consequences for mind and brain. *Trends in Cognitive Sciences*, 16, 240–50.

Biederman, I. (1985). Human image understanding: recent research and a theory. *Computer Vision, Graphics, and Image Processing*, 32, 29–73.

Biederman, I., and Bar, M. (1999). One-shot viewpoint invariance in matching novel objects. *Vision Research*, 39, 2885–99.

Biederman, I., and Checkosky, S. F. (1970). Processing redundant information. *Journal of Experimental Psychology*, 83, 486–90.

Biederman, I., and Cooper, E. E. (1991). Priming contour-deleted images: evidence for intermediate representations in visual object recognition. *Cognitive Psychology*, 23, 393–419.

Biederman, I., Mezzanotte, R. J., and Rabinowitz, J. C. (1982). Scene perception: detecting and judging objects undergoing relational violations. *Cognitive Psychology*, 14, 143–77.

Bijeljac-Babic, R., Bertoncini, J., and Mehler, J. (1993). How do 4-day old infants categorize multisyllabic utterances? *Developmental Psychology*, 29, 711–21.

Binder, J. R., and Desai, R. H. (2011). The neurobiology of semantic memory. *Trends in Cognitive Sciences*, 15, 527–36.

Bishop, D. V. M. (1999). An innate basis for language? *Science*, 286, 2283–4.

Bishop, D. V. M., North, T., and Donlan, C. (1995). Genetic basis of specific language impairment: evidence from a twin study. *Developmental Medicine and Child Neurology*, 37, 56–71.

Bisiach, E., Capitani, E., Luzzatti, C., and Perani, D. (1981). Brain and conscious representation of outside reality. *Neuropsychologia*, 19, 543–51.

Bisiach, E., Rusconi, M. L., and Vallar, G. (1992). Remission of somatophrenic delusion through vestibular stimulation. *Neuropsychologia*, 29, 1029–31.

Black, J. B., and Bower, G. H. (1980). Story understanding as problem solving. *Poetics*, 9, 223–50.

Blair, R. J. R. (1995). A cognitive developmental approach to morality: investigating the psychopath. *Cognition*, 57, 1–29.

Blair, R. J. R., and Curran, J. V. (1999). Selective impairment in the recognition of anger induced by diazepam. *Psychopharmacology*, 147, 335–8.

Bobrow, S. A., and Bower, G. H. (1969). Comprehension and recall of sentences. *Journal of Experimental Psychology*, 80, 455–61.

Bogen, J. E., and Bogen, G. M. (1976). Wernicke's region: where is it? *Annals of the New York Academy of Sciences*, 280, 834–43.

Bornstein, M. H. (1973). Color vision and color naming: a psychophysiological hypothesis of cultural difference. *Psychological Bulletin*, 80, 257–85.

(1976). Infants' recognition memory for hue. *Developmental Psychology*, 12, 185–91.

Bornstein, M. H., and Sigman, M. D. (1986). Continuity in mental development from infancy. *Child Development*, 57, 251–74.

Botella, J., Privado, J., Gil-Gomez de Liano, B., and Suero, M. (2011). Illusory conjunctions reflect the time course of the attentional blink. *Attention, Perception, and Psychophysics*, 73, 1361–73.

Bothwell, R. K., Brigham, J. C., and Malpass, R. S. (1989). Cross-racial identification. *Personality and Social Psychology Bulletin*, 15, 19–25.

Bouchard, T. J., Lykken, D. T., McGue, M., Segal, N. L., and Tellegen, A. (1990). Sources of human psychological differences: the Minnesota study of twins reared apart. *Science*, 250, 223–8.

Bousfield, W. A., and Sedgewick, H. W. (1944). An analysis of sequences of restricted associative responses. *Journal of General Psychology*, 30, 149–65.

Bouton, M. E., and Bolles, R. C. (1979). Contextual control of the extinction of conditioned fear. *Learning and Motivation*, 10, 445–66.

Bower, G. H. (1970). Analysis of a mnemonic device. *American Scientist*, 58, 496–510.

(1972). Mental imagery and associative learning. In L. W. Gregg (ed.), *Cognition in Learning and Memory*, 51–88. New York: Wiley.

Bower, G. H., and Clark, M. C. (1969). Narrative stories as mediators for serial learning. *Psychonomic Science*, 14, 181–2.

Bower, G. H., Clark, M. C., Lesgold, A. M., and Winzenz, D. (1969). Hierarchical retrieval schemes in recall of categorized word lists. *Journal of Verbal Learning and Verbal Behavior*, 8, 323–43.

Bower, G. H., and Glass, A. L. (1976). Structural units and the reintegrative power of picture fragments. *Journal of Experimental Psychology: Human Learning and Memory*, 2, 456–66.

Bower, G. H., and Holyoak, K. J. (1973). Encoding and recognition memory for naturalistic sounds. *Journal of Experimental Psychology*, 101, 360–6.

Bower, G. H., Lesgold, A. M., and Tieman, D. (1969). Grouping operations in free recall. *Journal of Verbal Learning and Verbal Behavior*, 8, 481–93.

Bower, C. H., and Reitman, J. S. (1972). Mnemonic elaboration in multilist learning. *Journal of Verbal Learning and Verbal Behavior*, 11, 478–85.

Bower, G. H., and Sivers, H. (1998). Cognitive impact of traumatic events. *Development and Psychopathology*, 10, 625–53.

Bower, G. H., and Winzenz, D. (1970). Comparison of associative learning strategies. *Psychonomic Science*, 20, 119–20.

Box, O., Laing, H., and Kopelman, M. (1999). The evolution of spontaneous confabulation, delusional misidentification and a related delusion in a case of severe head injury. *Neurocase*, 5, 251–62.

Bradley, D. C., Garrett, M. F., and Zurif, E. B. (1980). Syntactic deficits in Broca's aphasia. In D. Caplan (ed.), *Biological Studies of Mental Processes*, 269–822. Cambridge, MA: MIT Press.

Brady, T. F., Konkle, T., Alvarez, G. A., and Oliva, A. (2008). Visual long-term memory has a massive storage capacity for object details. *Proceedings of the National Academy of Sciences*, 105, 14325–9.

Braitenberg, V. (1967). Is the cerebellar cortex a biological clock in the millisecond range? *Progress in Brain Research*, 25, 334–46.

Brandt, J., Butters, N., Ryan, C., and Bayog, R. (1983). Cognitive loss and recovery in long-term alcohol abusers. *Archives of General Psychiatry*, 40, 435–42.

Bransford, J. D. (1979). *Human Cognition: Learning, Understanding and Remembering*. Belmont, CA: Wadsworth.

Bransford, J. D., and Johnson, M. K. (1972). Contextual prerequisites for understanding: some investigations of comprehension and recall. *Journal of Verbal Learning and Verbal Behavior*, 11, 717–21.

(1973). Consideration of some problems of comprehension. In W. G. Chase (ed.), *Visual Information Processing*, 383–438. New York: Academic Press.

Brebner, J., Shephard, M., and Cairney, P. T. (1972). Spatial relationships and S–R compatibility. *Acta Psychologica*, 36, 1–15.

Bregman, A. S. (1981). Asking the "what for" question in auditory perception. In M. Kubovy and J. R. Pomerantz (eds.), *Perceptual Organization*, 99–118. Hillsdale, NJ: Erlbaum.

Bremner, A., and Bryant, P. (2001). The effect of spatial cues on infants' responses in the AB task, with and without a hidden object. *Developmental Science*, 4, 408–15.

Brewin, C. R. (1998). Intrusive autobiographical memories in depression and post-traumatic stress disorder. *Applied Cognitive Psychology*, 12, 359–70.

Britton, B. K., and Tesser, A. (1982). Effects of prior knowledge on use of cognitive capacity in three complex cognitive tasks. *Journal of Verbal Learning and Verbal Behaviour*, 24, 421–36.

Broadbent, D. E. (1958). *Perception and Communication*. London: Pergamon Press.

(1978). The current state of noise research: reply to Poulton. *Psychological Bulletin*, 85, 1052–67.

Broadbent, D. E., and Broadbent, M. H. P. (1987). From detection to identification: response to multiple targets in rapid serial visual presentation. *Perception and Psychophysics*, 42, 105–13.

Brockmole, J. R., Wang, R. F., and Irwin, D. E. (2002). Temporal integration between visual images and visual percepts. *Journal of Experimental Psychology: Human Perception and Performance*, 28, 315–34.

Broen, P. (1972). The verbal environment of the language-learning child. *Monographs of the American Speech and Hearing Association*, 17, 1–103.

Brooks, L. R. (1968). Spatial and verbal components of the act of recall. *Canadian Journal of Psychology*, 22, 349–68.

(1978). Nonanalytic concept formation and memory for instances. In E. Rosch and B. B. Lloyd (eds.), *Cognition and Categorization*, 3–170. Hillsdale, NJ: Erlbaum.

Brown, A. L., and Scott, M. S. (1971). Recognition memory for pictures in preschool children. *Journal of Experimental Child Psychology*, 11, 401–12.

Brown, A. S. (1979). Priming effects in semantic memory retrieval processes. *Journal of Experimental Psychology: Human Learning and Memory*, 5, 65–77.

Brown, A. S., and Murphy, D. R. (1989). Cryptomnesia: delineating inadvertent plagiarism. *Journal of Experimental Psychology: Learning, Memory, and Cognition*, 15, 432–42.

Brown, E. L., and Deffenbacher, K. (1979). *Perception and the Senses*. New York: Oxford University Press.

Brown, J. (1958). Some tests of the decay theory of immediate memory. *Quarterly Journal of Experimental Psychology*, 10, 12–21.

(1968). Reciprocal facilitation and impairment of free recall. *Psychonomic Science*, 10, 41–2.

Brown, R., and Kulik, J. (1977). Flashbulb memories. *Cognition*, 5, 73–99.

Brown, R., and Lenneberg, E. H. (1954). A study in language and cognition. *Journal of Abnormal and Social Psychology*, 49, 454–62.

Brown, R., and McNeill, D. (1966). The "tip of the tongue" phenomenon. *Journal of Verbal Learning and Verbal Behavior*, 5, 325–37.

Brown, W. (1923). To what extent is memory measured by a single recall? *Journal of Experimental Psychology*, 6, 377–82.

Bruce, V. (1982). Changing faces: visual and non-visual coding processes in face recognition. *British Journal of Psychology*, 73, 105–16.

Brun, A., and Andersson, J. (2001). Frontal dysfunction and frontal cortical synapse loss in alcoholism: the main cause of alcohol dementia? *Dementia and Geriatric Cognitive Disorders*, 12, 289–94.

Bryden, M. P., and Allard, F. (1976). Visual hemifield differences depend on typeface. *Brain and Language*, 3, 191–200.

Buehner, M. J., and Humphreys, G. R. (2009). Causal binding of actions to their effects. *Psychological Science*, 20, 1221–8.

Bugelski, B. R., and Alampay, D. A. (1961). The role of frequency in developing perceptual set. *Canadian Journal of Psychology*, 15, 205–11.

Bunting, M., Cowan, N., and Saults, J. S. (2006). How does running memory span work? *Quarterly Journal of Experimental Psychology*, 59, 1691–700.

Buschke, H. (1973). Selective reminding for analysis of memory and learning. *Journal of Verbal Learning and Verbal Behavior*, 12, 543–50.

Buschke, H. (1974). Spontaneous remembering after recall failure. *Science*, 184, 579–81.

(1976). Learning is organized by chunking. *Journal of Verbal Learning and Verbal Behavior*, 15, 313–24.

(1977). Two-dimensional recall: immediate identification of clusters in episodic and semantic memory. *Journal of Verbal Learning and Verbal Behavior*, 16, 201–15.

Buschke, H., Kuslansky, G., Katz, M., Steward, W. F., Sliwinski, M. J., Eckholdt, H. M., and Lipton, R. B. (1999). Screening for dementia with the Memory Impairment Screen. *Neurology*, 52, 231–8.

Buschke, H., and Schaier, A. H. (1979). Memory units, ideas, and propositions in semantic remembering. *Journal of Verbal Learning and Verbal Behavior*, 18, 549–63.

Butler, J., and Rovee-Collier, C. (1989). Contextual gating of memory retrieval. *Developmental Psychobiology*, 22, 533–52.

Butters, N. (1984). Alcoholic Korsakoff's syndrome: an update. *Seminars in Neurology*, 4, 226–44.

Butters, N., Heindel, W. C., and Salmon, D. P. (1990). Dissociation of implicit memory in dementia: neurological implications. *Bulletin of the Psychonomic Society*, 28, 359–66.

Butters, N., and Stuss, D. T. (1989). Diencephalic amnesia. In F. Boller and J. Grafman (eds.), *Handbook of Neuropsychology*, vol. III, 107–48. New York: Elsevier.

Butterworth, G., and Itakura, S. (2000). How the eyes, head and hand serve definite reference. *British Journal of Developmental Psychology*, 18, 25–50.

Butterworth, G., and Morissette, P. (1996). Onset of pointing and the acquisition of language in infancy. *Journal of Reproductive and Infant Psychology*, 14, 219–31.

Byers-Heinlein, K., Burns, T. C., and Werker, J. F. (2010). The roots of bilingualism in newborns. *Psychological Science*, 21, 343–8.

Cabeza, R., and St. Jacques, P. (2007). Functional neuroimaging of autobiographical memory. *Trends in Cognitive Sciences*, 11, 219–27.

Cahill, L., and McGaugh, J. L. (1995). A novel demonstration of enhanced memory associated with emotional arousal. *Consciousness and Cognition*, 4, 410–21.

(1998). Mechanisms of emotional arousal and lasting declarative memory. *Trends in Neurosciences*, 21, 294–9.

Cameron, T. E., and Hockley, W. E. (2000). The revelation effect for item and associative recognition: familiarity versus recollection. *Memory and Cognition*, 28, 176–83.

Cammarota, M. L., Bevilaqua, R. M., Kohler, C., Medina, J. H., and Izquierdo, I. (2005). Learning twice is different from learning once and from learning more. *Neuroscience*, 132, 273–9.

Camras, L. A. (1977). Facial expressions used by children in a conflict situation. *Child Development*, 48, 1431–5.

Caplan, D. (1972). Clause boundaries and recognition latencies for words in sentences. *Perception and Psychophysics*, 12, 73–6.

Caporale, N., and Dan, Y. (2008). Spike timing-dependent plasticity: a Hebbian learning rule. *Annual Review of Neuroscience*, 31, 25–46.

Caramazza, A., and Berndt, R. S. (1978). Semantic and syntactic processes in aphasia: a review of the literature. *Psychological Bulletin*, 85, 898–918.

Caramazza, A., and Zurif, E. B. (1976). Dissociation of algorithmic and heuristic processes in language comprehension: evidence from aphasia. *Brain and Language*, 3, 572–82.

Carbon, C., Gruter, T., Weber, J., and Lueschow, A. (2007). Faces as objects of non-expertise: processing of thatcherised faces in congenital prosopagnosia. *Perception*, 36, 1635–45.

Carew, T. J., and Kandel, E. R. (1973). Acquisition and retention of long-term habituation in *Aplysia*: correlation of behavioral and cellular processes. *Science*, 182, 1158–60.

Carew, T. J., Walters, E. T., and Kandel, E. R. (1981). Associative learning in *Aplysia*: cellular correlates supporting a conditioned fear hypothesis. *Science*, 211, 501–4.

Carey, B. (2008). H. M., an unforgettable amnesiac, dies at 82. *New York Times*, December 4.

Carey, S. (1985). *Conceptual Change in Childhood.* Cambridge, MA: MIT Press.

Carlsson, A. (1988). Speculations on the control of mental and motor functions by dopamine-modulated cortico-striato-thalamo-cortical feedback loops. *Mount Sinai Journal of Medicine*, 55, 6–10.

Carmichael, L., Hogan, H. P., and Walter, A. A. (1932). An experimental study of the effect of language on the reproduction of visually perceived form. *Journal of Experimental Psychology*, 15, 73–86.

Carpenter, M., Nagell, K., and Tomasello, M. (1998). Social cognition, joint attention, and communicative competence from 9 to 15 months of age. *Monographs of the Society for Research in Child Development*, 63, 1–143.

Carpenter, P. A., and Daneman, M. (1981). Lexical retrieval and error recovery in reading: a model based on eye fixations. *Journal of Verbal Learning and Verbal Behavior*, 20, 137–60.

Carruthers, P., and Chamberlain, A. (2000). *Evolution and the Human Mind: Modularity, Language and Meta-Cognition*. Cambridge University Press.

Caselli, M. C., Bates, E., Cadadio, P., Fenson, J., Fenson, L., Sanderl, L., and Weir, J. (1995). A cross-linguistic study of early lexical development. *Cognitive Development*, 10, 159–99.

Caselli, M. C., Casadio, P., and Bates, E. (1999). A comparison of the transition from first words to grammar in English and Italian. *Journal of Child Language*, 26, 69–111.

Cassel, W. S., Roebers, C. E. M., and Bjorklund, D. F. (1996). Developmental patterns of eyewitness responses to increasingly suggestive questions. *Journal of Experimental Child Psychology*, 61, 116–33.

Cavanaugh, J. P. (1972). Relation between the immediate memory span and the memory search rate. *Psychological Review*, 79, 525–30.

Ceci, S. J. (1996). *On Intelligence: A Bio-Ecological Treatise on Intellectual Development.* Cambridge, MA: Harvard University Press.

Ceci, S. J., and Bruck, M. (1993). Suggestibility of the child witness: a historical review and synthesis. *Psychological Bulletin*, 113, 403–39.

Cermak, L. S., Lewis, R., Butters, N., and Goodglass, H. (1973). The role of verbal mediation in performance of motor tasks by Korsakoff patients. *Perceptual and Motor Skills*, 37, 259–62.

Chalmers, K. A., Humphreys, M. S., and Dennis, S. (1997). A naturalistic study of the word frequency effect in episodic recognition. *Memory and Cognition*, 25, 780–4.

Chase, S. (1938). *The Tyranny of Words*. New York: Harcourt, Brace.

Chase, W. G., and Ericsson, K. A. (1981). Skilled memory. In J. R. Anderson (ed.), *Cognitive Skills and Their Acquisition*, 141–89. Hillsdale, NJ: Erlbaum.

Chase, W. G., and Simon, H. A. (1973). The mind's eye in chess. In W. G. Chase (ed.), *Visual Information Processing*, 215–81. New York: Academic Press.

Chastain, G. (1977). Feature analysis and the growth of a percept. *Journal of Experimental Psychology: Human Perception and Performance*, 3, 291–8.

Checkosky, S. F., and Baboorian, N. (1972). Memory search for CVC and CCC trigrams. *Journal of Experimental Psychology*, 96, 158–63.

Cheng, P. W., and Holyoak, K. J. (1985). Pragmatic reasoning schemas. *Cognitive Psychology*, 17, 391–416.

Cherry, E. C. (1953). Some experiments on the recognition of speech, with one and two ears. *Journal of the Acoustical Society of America*, 25, 975–9.

Chi, M. T. H., Feltovich, P. J., and Glaser, R. (1981). Categorization and representation of physics problems by experts and novices. *Cognitive Science*, 5, 121–52.

Chomsky, N. (1975). *Reflections on Language*. New York: Pantheon Books.

Chonchaiya, W., Tardif, T., Mai, X., Xu, L., Li, M., Kaciroti, N., Kileny, P. R., Shao, J., and Lozoff, B. (2013). Developmental trends in auditory processing can provide early predictions of language acquisition in young infants. *Developmental Science*, 16, 159–72.

Christian, K. M., and Thompson, R. F. (2003). Neural substrates of eyeblink conditioning: acquisition and retention. *Learning and Memory*, 11, 427–55.

Cirilo, R. K., and Foss, D. J. (1980). Text structure and reading time for sentences. *Journal of Verbal Learning and Verbal Behavior*, 19, 96–109.

Clark, D. M., and Teasdale, J. D. (1982). Diurnal variations in clinical depression and accessibility of memories of positive and negative experiences. *Journal of Abnormal Psychology*, 91, 87–95.

Clark, H. H., and Chase, W. G. (1972). On the process of comparing sentences against pictures. *Cognitive Psychology*, 3, 472–517.

Clark, S. E., Moreland, M. B., and Gronlund, S. D. (2014). Evolution of the empirical and theoretical foundations of eyewitness identification reform. *Psychonomic Bulletin and Review*, 21, 251–67.

Clearfield, M. W., Diedrich, F. J., Smith, L. B., and Thelen, E. (2006). Young infants reach correctly in A-not-B tasks: on the development of stability and perseveration. *Infant Behavior and Development*, 29, 435–44.

Cohen, N. J., and Squire, L. R. (1981). Retrograde amnesia and remote memory impairment. *Neuropsychologia*, 19, 337–56.

Cohen, R. L., and Granström, K. (1970). Reproduction and recognition in short-term visual memory. *Quarterly Journal of Experimental Psychology*, 22, 450–7.

Cohn, J. F., and Tronick, E. Z. (1983). Three-month-old infants' reaction to simulated maternal depression. *Child Development*, 54, 185–93.

Cohn, N. B., Dustman, R. E., and Bradford, D. C. (1984). Age-related decrements in Stroop color test performance. *Journal of Clinical Psychology*, 40, 1244–50.

Colavita, F. B. (1974). Human sensory dominance. *Perception and Psychophysics*, 16, 409–16.

Cole, R. A., (1973). Listening for mispronunciations: a measure of what we hear during speech. *Perception and Psychophysics*, 11, 153–6.

Collins, A. M., and Loftus, E. F. (1975). A spreading-activation theory of semantic processing. *Psychological Review*, 82, 407–28.

Collins, A. M., and Quillian, M. R. (1969). Retrieval time from semantic memory. *Journal of Verbal Learning and Verbal Behavior*, 8, 240–8.

Coltheart, M., and Rastle, K. (1994). Serial processing in reading aloud: evidence for dual route models of reading. *Journal of Experimental Psychology: Human Perception and Performance*, 20, 1197–211.

Comalli, P. E., Wapner, S., and Werner H. (1962). Interference effects of Stroop color–word test in childhood, adulthood, and aging. *Journal of Genetic Psychology*, 100, 47–53.

Conrad, R. (1964). Acoustic confusion in immediate memory. *British Journal of Psychology*, 55, 75–84.

Conway, M. A., Anderson, S. J., Larsen, S. F., Donnelly, C. M., McDaniel, M. A., McClelland, A. G. R., and Rawles, R. E. (1994). The formation of flashbulb memories. *Memory and Cognition*, 22, 326–43.

Conway, M. A., Collins, A. F., Gathercole, S. E., and Anderson, S. J. (1996). Recollections of true and false autobiographical memories. *Journal of Experimental Psychology: General*, 125, 69–95.

Conway, M. A., and Haque, S. (1999). Overshadowing the reminiscence bump: memories of a struggle for independence. *Journal of Adult Development*, 6, 35–44.

Conway, M. A., and Pleydell-Pearce, C. W. (2000). The construction of autobiographical memories in the self-memory system. *Psychological Review*, 107, 261–88.

Conway, M. A., Singer, J. A., and Tagini, A. (2004). The self and autobiographical memory: correspondence and coherence. *Social Cognition*, 22, 491–529.

Cook, R., and Bird, G. (2013). Do mirror neurons really mirror and do they really code for action goals? *Cortex*, 49, 2944–5.

Coons, P. M. (1999). Psychogenic or dissociative fugue: a clinical investigation of five cases. *Psychological Reports*, 84, 881–6.

Cooper, A. C. G., and Humphreys, G. W. (2000). Coding space within but not between objects: evidence for Balint's syndrome. *Neuropsychologia*, 38, 723–33.

Corcoran, D. W. J. (1966). An acoustic factor in letter cancellation. *Nature*, 210, 658.

(1967). Acoustic factor in proofreading. *Nature*, 214, 851–2.

Corcoran, D. W. J., and Weening, W. J. (1968). Acoustic factors in visual search. *Quarterly Journal of Experimental Psychology*, 20, 83–5.

Corkin, S. (1968). Acquisition of motor skills after bilateral medial temporal-lobe excision. *Neuropsychologia*, 6, 255–65.

(2013). *Permanent Present Tense*. New York: Basic Books.

Craik, F. I. M. (1977). Age differences in human memory. In J. E. Birren and K. W. Schaie (eds.), *Handbook of the Psychology of Aging*, 384–420. New York: Van Nostrand Reinhold.

Crossman, E. R. F. W. (1959). A theory of the acquisition of speed-skill. *Ergonomics*, 2, 153–66.

Crovitz, H. F., and Quina-Holland, K. (1976). Proportion of episodic memories from early childhood by years of age. *Bulletin of the Psychonomic Society*, 7, 61–2.

Crovitz, H. F., and Schiffman, H. (1974). Frequency of episodic memories as a function of their age. *Bulletin of the Psychonomic Society*, 4, 517–18.

Crowder, R. G. (1982). *The Psychology of Reading: An Introduction*. Oxford University Press.

Crowe, S. F. (1992). Dissociation of two frontal lobe syndromes by a test of verbal fluency. *Journal of Clinical and Experimental Neuropsychology*, 14, 327–39.

(1996). The performance of schizophrenic and depressed subjects on tests of fluency: support for a compromise in dorsolateral prefrontal functioning. *Australian Psychologist*, 13, 204–9.

Cubelli, R., Marchetti, C., Boscolo, G., and Della Sala, S. (2000). Cognition in action: testing a model of limb apraxia. *Brain and Cognition*, 44, 144–65.

Cuddy, L. J., and Jacoby, L. L. (1982). When forgetting helps memory: an analysis of repetition effects. *Journal of Verbal Learning and Verbal Behavior*, 21, 451–67.

Currie, C. B., McConkie, G. W., Carlson-Radvansky, L. A., and Irwin, D. E. (2000). The role of the saccade target object in the perception of a visually stable world. *Perception and Psychophysics*, 62, 673–83.

Cutting, J. (1976). Auditory and linguistic processes in speech perception: inferences from fusions in dichotic listening. *Psychological Review*, 83, 114–40.

Dab, S., Claes, T., Morais, J., and Shallice, T. (1999). Confabulation with a selective descriptor process impairment. *Cognitive Neuropsychology*, 16, 215–42.

D'Agostino, P. R., O'Neill, B. J., and Paivio, A. (1977). Memory for pictures and words as a function of level processing: depth or dual coding? *Memory and Cognition*, 5, 252–6.

Dagenbach, D., Carr, T. H., and Wilhelmsen, A. (1989). Task-induced strategies and near-threshold priming: conscious influences on unconscious perception. *Journal of Memory and Language*, 28, 412–43.

Dahaene, S., Posner, M. I., and Tucker, D. M. (1994). Localization of a neural system for error detection and compensation. *Psychological Science*, 5, 303–5.

Dalrymple-Alford, E. C., and Budayr, D. (1966). Examination of some aspects of the Stroop color–word test. *Perceptual and Motor Skills*, 23, 1211–14.

Daneman, M., and Carpenter, P. A. (1983). Individual differences in integrating information between and within sentences. *Journal of Experimental Psychology: Learning, Memory, and Cognition*, 9, 561–84.

Darley, C. F., and Glass, A. L. (1975). Effects of rehearsal and serial list position on recall. *Journal of Experimental Psychology: Human Learning and Memory*, 104, 453–8.

Damasio, A. R. (1994). *Descartes' Error: Emotion, Reason, and the Human Brain*. New York: G. P. Putnam.

Damasio, H., Tranel, D., Grabowski, T., Adolphs, R., and Damasio, A. R. (2004). Neural systems behind word and concept retrieval. *Cognition*, 92, 179–229.

Daoudal, G., and Debanne, D. (2003). Long-term plasticity of intrinsic excitability: learning rules and mechanisms. *Learning and Memory*, 10, 456–65.

Davidson, J. E., and Sternberg, R. J. (2000). *The Psychology of Problem Solving*. Cambridge University Press.

Davidson, R. J. (1993). Neuropsychology of emotion and affective style. In M. Lewis and J. M. Haviland (eds.), *Handbook of Emotions*, 143–54. New York: Guilford Press.

Davies, D. R., and Tune, G. S. (1969). *Human Vigilance Performance.* New York: Elsevier.

Davies, M., and Coltheart, M. (2000). Introduction: pathologies of belief. In M. Coltheart and M. Davies (eds.), *Pathologies of Belief*, 1–46. Malden, MA: Blackwell.

Davies, S. P. (2000). Memory and planning processes in solutions to well-structured problems. *Quarterly Journal of Experimental Psychology*, 53A, 896–927.

Dawes, R. (1964). Cognitive distortion. *Psychological Reports*, 14, 443–59.

Dawson, G., Webb, S., Schellenberg, G. D., Dager, S., Friedman, S., Aylward, E., and Richards, T. (2002). Defining the broader phenotype of autism: genetic, brain, and behavioral perspectives. *Development and Psychopathology*, 14, 581–611.

De Groot, A. D. (1965). *Thought and Choice in Chess*. The Hague: Mouton.

De Mornay Davies, P. (1998). Automatic semantic priming: the contribution of lexical- and semantic-level processes. *European Journal of Cognitive Psychology*, 10, 389–412.

De Valois, R. L., and Jacobs, G. H. (1968). Primate color vision. *Science*, 162, 533–40.

Deese, J. (1959). On the prediction of occurrence of particular verbal intrusions in immediate recall. *Journal of Experimental Psychology*, 58, 17–22.

Demiray, B., and Bluck, S. (2011). The relation of the conceptual self to recent and distant autobiographical memories. *Memory*, 19, 975–92.

Dennis, M. (1980). Capacity and strategy for syntactic comprehension after left or right hemi-decortication. *Brain and Language*, 10, 287–317.

Dennis, M., and Kohn, B. (1975). Comprehension of syntax in infantile hemiplegics after cerebral hemi-decortication: left hemisphere superiority. *Brain and Language*, 2, 475–86.

Dennis, M., and Whitaker, H. A. (1976). Language acquisition following hemi-decortication: linguistic superiority of the left over the right hemisphere. *Brain and Language*, 3, 404–33.

Dent, K., Allen, H. A., Braithwaite, J. J., and Humphreys, G. W. (2012). Parallel distractor rejection as a binding mechanism in search. *Frontiers in Psychology*, 3, article 278.

Deroost, N., Kerckhofs, E., Coene, M., Wijnants, G., and Soetens, E. (2006). Learning sequence movements in a homogeneous sample of patients with Parkinson's disease. *Neuropsychologia*, 44, 1653–62.

Deroost, N., and Soetens, E. (2006). Perceptual or motor learning in SRT tasks with complex sequence structures. *Psychological Research*, 70, 88–102.

Desimone, R., and Duncan, J. (1995). Neural mechanisms of selective visual attention. *Annual Review of Neuroscience*, 18, 193–222.

Desmedt, A., Marighetto, A., Garcia, R., and Jaffard, R. (2003). The effects of ibotenic hippocampal lesions on discriminative fear conditioning to context in mice: impairment or facilitation depending on the associative value of a phasic explicit cue. *European Journal of Neuroscience*, 17, 1953–63.

Detterman, D. K., and Daniel, M. H. (1989). Correlations of mental tests with each other and with cognitive variables are highest for low IQ groups. *Intelligence*, 13, 349–59.

Detterman, D. K., and Ellis, N. R. (1972). Determinants of induced amnesia in short-term memory. *Journal of Experimental Psychology*, 95, 308–16.

Dewar, M., Alber, J., Butler, C., Cowan, N., and Della Sala, S. (2012). Brief wakeful resting boosts new memories over the long term. *Psychological Science*, 23, 955–60.

Dhami, M. K., Schlottmann, A., and Waldmann, M. R. (2013). *Judgment and Decision Making as a Skill*. Cambridge University Press.

Diamond, A. (1985). Development of the ability to use recall to guide action, as indicated by infants' performance on A-not-B. *Child Development*, 56, 868–83.

Diamond, A. (1995). Evidence of robust recognition memory early in life even when assessed by reaching behavior. *Journal of Experimental Child Psychology*, 59, 419–56.

Diamond, A., and Goldman-Rakic, P. S. (1989). Comparison of human infants and rhesus monkeys on Piaget's A-not-B task: evidence for dependence on dorsolateral prefrontal cortex. *Experimental Brain Research*, 74, 24–40.

Diamond, B. J., DeLuca, J., and Fisher, C. (2000). Confabulation and memory in anterior communicating artery aneurysm. *Abstracts/Archives of Clinical Neuropsychology*, 15, 721–2.

Diana, R., Reder, L. M., Arndt, J., and Park, H. (2006). Models of recognition: a review of arguments in favor of a dual process account. *Psychonomic Bulletin and Review*, 13, 1–21.

Dick, R. W. (1994). A summary of head and neck injuries in collegiate athletics using the NCAA surveillance system. In E. F. Horner (ed.), *Head and Neck Injuries in Sports*, 13–19. Philadelphia: ASTM.

Dijkstra, T., Grainger, J., and van Heuven, W. J. B. (1999). Recognition of cognates and interlingual homographs: the neglected role of phonology. *Journal of Memory and Language*, 41, 496–518.

Donaldson, W. (1996). The role of decision processes in remembering and knowing. *Memory and Cognition*, 24, 523–33.

Dowd, M. (2011). Sexy ruses to stop forgetting to remember. *New York Times*, March 8.

Draaisma, D., Pomerans, A., and Pomerans, E. (2006). *Why Life Speeds Up as You Get Older: How Memory Shapes Our Past*. Cambridge University Press.

Drew, T., Võ, M. H., and Wolfe, J. M. (2013). The invisible gorilla strikes again: sustained inattentional blindness in expert observers. *Psychological Science*, 24, 1848–53.

Dronkers, N. F. (1996). A new brain region for coordinating speech articulation. *Nature*, 384, 159–61.

Dronkers, N. F., Wilkins, D. P., Van Valin, R. D., Redfern, B. B., and Jaeger, J. J. (2004). Lesion analysis of the brain areas involved in language comprehension. *Cognition*, 92, 145–77.

Druker, J. F., and Hagen, J. W. (1969). Developmental trends in the processing of task-relevant and task-irrelevant information. *Child Development*, 40, 371–82.

Duchaine, B. C., Germine, L., and Nakayama, K. (2007). Family resemblance: ten family members with prosopagnosia and within-class object agnosia. *Cognitive Neuropsychology*, 24, 419–30.

Dunbar, R. I. M. (2005). *The Human Story: A New History of Mankind's Evolution*. London: Faber & Faber.

Dunbar, R. I. M. (2013). An evolutionary basis for social cognition. In M. Legerstee, D. W. Haley, and M. H. Bornstein (eds.), *The Infant Mind: Origins of the Social Brain*, 3–18. New York: Guilford Press.

Dunbar, R. I. M., and Sutcliffe, A. G. (2012). Social complexity and intelligence. In J. Vonk and T. K. Shackelford (eds.), *The Oxford Handbook of Comparative Evolutionary Psychology*, 102–17. New York: Oxford University Press.

Duncan, J. (1980). The locus of interference in the perception of simultaneous stimuli. *Psychological Review*, 87, 272–300.

Duncan, J., and Humphreys, G. W. (1992). Beyond the search surface: visual search and attentional engagement. *Journal of Experimental Psychology: Human Perception and Performance*, 18, 578–88.

Duncan, J., and Nimmo-Smith, I. (1996). Objects and attributes in divided attention: surface and boundary systems. *Perception and Psychophysics*, 38, 1076–84.

Duncan, J., Sietz, R. J., Kolodny, J., Bor, D., Herzog, H., Ahmed, A., Newell, F. N., and Emslie, H. (2000). A neural basis for general intelligence. *Science*, 289, 457–60.

Duncker, K. (1945). On problem solving. *Psychological Monographs*, 58, 1–113.

Dunlap, G. L., and Dunlap, L. L. (1979). Manipulating the word frequency effect in free recall. *Memory and Cognition*, 7, 420–5.

Durso, F. T., and Johnson, M. K. (1980). The effects of orienting tasks on recognition, recall, and modality confusion of pictures and words. *Journal of Verbal Learning and Verbal Behavior*, 19, 416–29.

Dwyer, D. M., Lydall, E. S., and Hayward, A. J. (2011). Simultaneous contrast: evidence from licking microstructure and cross-solution comparisons. *Journal of Experimental Psychology: Animal Behavior Processes*, 37, 200–10.

Dwyer, J. (2009). Like a skyline is etched in his head. *New York Times*, October 28.

Dyer, F. N., and Severance, L. J. (1973). Stroop interference with successive presentations of separate incongruent words and colors. *Journal of Experimental Psychology*, 98, 438–9.

Eacott, M. J., and Crawley, R. A. (1998). The offset of childhood amnesia: memory for events that occurred before age 3. *Journal of Experimental Psychology: General*, 127, 22–33.

Easterbrook, J. A. (1959). The effect of emotion on cue utilization and the organization of behavior. *Psychological Review*, 66, 183–201.

Easton, R., and Moran, P. W. (1978). A quantitative confirmation of visual capture of curvature. *Journal of General Psychology*, 98, 105–12.

Edelstyn, N. M. J., Riddoch, M. J., Oyebode, F., Humphreys, G. W., and Forde, E. (1996). Visual processing in patients with Fregoli syndrome. *Cognitive Neuropsychiatry*, 1, 103–24.

Efron, R., Bogen, J. E., and Yund, E. W. (1977). Perception of dichotic chords by normal and commissurotomized human subjects. *Cortex*, 13, 137–49.

Efron, R., and Yund, E. W. (1974). Dichotic competition of simultaneous tone bursts of different frequency I: dissociation of pitch from lateralization and loudness. *Neuropsychologia*, 12, 149–56.

Egan, D., and Greeno, J. (1974). Theory of inductive learning: knowledge acquired in concept identification, serial pattern learning, and problem solving. In L. W. Gregg (ed.), *Knowledge and Cognition*, 43–103. Hillsdale, NJ: Erlbaum.

Egeth, H. E., and Sager, L. C. (1977). On the locus of visual dominance. *Perception and Psychophysics*, 22, 77–86.

Ehrlich, S. F., and Rayner, K. (1981). Contextual effects on word perception and eye movements during reading. *Journal of Verbal Learning and Verbal Behavior*, 20, 641–55.

Eich, E. (1980). The cue-dependent nature of state-dependent retrieval. *Memory and Cognition*, 8, 157–73.

(1995). Searching for mood-dependent memory. *Psychological Science*, 6, 67–75.

Eich, E., and Birnbaum, I. M. (1982). Repetition, cuing, and state-dependent memory. *Memory and Cognition*, 10, 103–14.

Eich, E., Macaulay, D., and Lam, R. W. (1997). Mania, depression, and mood-dependent memory. *Cognition and Emotion*, 11, 607–18.

Eichenbaum, H. (2008). *Learning and Memory*. New York: W. W. Norton.

Eijkman, E., and Vendrik, A. J. H. (1965). Can a sensory system be specified by its internal noise? *Journal of the Acoustical Society of America*, 37, 1102–9.

Einstein, G. O., and Hunt, R. R. (1980). Levels of processing and organization: additive effects of individual-item and relational processing. *Journal of Experimental Psychology: Human Learning and Memory*, 6, 588–98.

Ekman, P. (1992). Facial expressions of emotion: new findings, new questions. *Psychological Science*, 3, 34–8.

Elio, R., and Anderson, J. R. (1981). The effects of category generalizations and instance similarity on schema abstraction. *Journal of Experimental Psychology: Human Learning and Memory*, 7, 397–417.

Elliott, J. G., and Grigorenko, E. L. (2014). *The Dyslexia Debate*. Cambridge University Press.

Ellis, A. W. (1984). Introduction to Bramwell's (1897) case of word meaning deafness. *Cognitive Neuropsychology*, 1, 245–58.

Ellis, H. D., Lewis, M. B., Moselhy, H. F., and Young, A. W. (2000). Automatic without autonomic responses to familiar faces: differential components of covert face recognition in a case of Capgras delusion. *Cognitive Neuropsychiatry*, 5, 255–69.

Ellis, N. C., and Hennelly, R. A. (1980). A bilingual word-length effect: implications for intelligence testing and the relative ease of mental calculation in Welsh and English. *British Journal of Psychology*, 71, 43–52.

Endress, A. D., and Potter, M. C. (2014). Large capacity visual memory. *Journal of Experimental Psychology: General*, 143, 548–65.

Engen, T., and Ross, B. M. (1973). Long-term memory of odors with and without verbal descriptions. *Journal of Experimental Psychology*, 100, 221–7.

Enns, J. T., and Resnick, R. A. (1990). Sensitivity to three-dimensional orientation in visual search. *Psychological Science*, 1, 323–6.

Erber, J. T. (1978). Age differences in a controlled-lag memory test. *Experimental Aging Research*, 4, 195–205.

Erdelyi, M. H., and Becker, J. (1974). Hypermnesia for pictures: incremental memory for pictures but not words in multiple recall trials. *Cognitive Psychology*, 6, 159–71.

Erdelyi, M. H., Finkelstein, S., Herrell, N., Miller, B., and Thomas, J. (1976). Coding modality vs. input modality in hypermnesia: is a rose a rose a rose? *Cognition*, 4, 311–19.

Erdelyi, M. H., and Kleinbard, J. (1978). Has Ebbinghaus decayed with time? The growth of recall (hypermnesia) over days. *Journal of Experimental Psychology: Human Learning and Memory*, 4, 275–89.

Erickson, K. I., Boot, W. R., Basak, C., Neider, M. B., Prakash, R. S., Voss, M. W., Graybiel, A. M., Simons, D. J., Fabiani, M., Gratton, G., and Kramer, A. F. (2010). Striatal volume predicts level of video game skill acquisition. *Cerebral Cortex*, 20, 2522–30.

Ericsson, K. A., Krampe, R., and Tesch-Romer, C. (1993). The role of deliberate practice in the acquisition of expert performance. *Psychological Review*, 100, 363–406.

Eriksen, C. W., and Collins, J. F. (1967). Some temporal characteristics of visual pattern perception. *Journal of Experimental Psychology*, 74, 476–84.

Eriksson, P. S., Perfilieva, E., Bjork-Eriksson, T., Alborn, A. M., Nordborg, C., Peterson, D. A., and Gage, F. H. (1998). Neurogenesis in the adult human hippocampus. *Nature Medicine*, 4, 1313–17.

Estes, W. K. (1986). Array models for category learning. *Cognitive Psychology*, 18, 500–49.

Estes, W. K., Allmeyer, D. H., and Reder, S. M. (1976). Serial position functions for letter identification at brief and extended exposure durations. *Perception and Psychophysics*, 19, 1–15.

Evans, S. H. (1967). A brief statement of schema theory. *Psychonomic Science*, 8, 87–8.

Eysenck, H. J. (1967). *The Biological Basis of Personality*. Springfield, IL: Thomas.

Eysenck, M. W. (1982). *Attention and Arousal*. Berlin: Springer-Verlag.

Fagan, J. F., and Singer, L. T. (1983). Infant recognition memory as a measure of intelligence. *Advances in Infancy Research*, 2, 31–78.

Fagen, J. W., Morrongiello, B. A., Rovee-Collier, C., and Gekoski, M. J. (1984). Expectancies and memory retrieval in 3-month-old infants. *Child Development*, 55, 936–43.

Fagen, J. W., Rovee, C., and Kaplan, M. G. (1976). Psychophysical scaling of stimulus similarity in 3-month-old infants and adults. *Journal of Experimental Child Psychology*, 22, 272–81.

Fantz, R. L. (1958). Pattern vision in young infants. *Psychological Record*, 8, 43–7.

Farah, M. J. (1990). *Visual Agnosia: Disorders of Object Recognition and What They Tell Us about Normal Vision*. Cambridge, MA: MIT Press.

Fava, E., Hull, R., and Bortfeld, H. (2014). Dissociating cortical activity during processing of native and non-native audiovisual speech from early to late infancy. *Brain Sciences*, 4, 471–87.

Feldman, J. (2003). The simplicity principle in human concept learning. *Current Directions in Psychological Science*, 12, 227–32.

Feltenstein, M. W., and See, R. E. (2008). The neurocircuitry of addiction: an overview. *British Journal of Pharmacology*, 154, 261–74.

Fernald, A. (1993). Approval and disapproval: infant responsiveness to vocal affect in familiar and unfamiliar languages. *Child Development*, 64, 657–74.

Fernbach, P. M., Rogers, T., Fox, C. R., and Sloman, S. A. (2013).Political extremism is supported by an illusion of understanding. *Psychological Science*, 24, 939–46.

Ferrand, L., and Grainger, J. (1994). Effects of orthography are independent of phonology in masked form priming. *Quarterly Journal of Experimental Psychology*, 47A, 365–82.

Ficca, G., Lombardo, P., Rossi, L., and Salzarulo, P. (2000). Morning recall of verbal material depends on prior sleep organization. *Behavioural Brain Research*, 112, 159–63.

Fields, R. D. (2008). Oligodendrocytes changing the rules: action potentials in glia and oligodendrocytes controlling action potentials. *Neuroscientist*, 14, 540–3.

Finster, M., and Wood, M. (2005). The Apgar score has survived the test of time. *Anesthesiology*, 102, 855–7.

Fischer, B., and Breitmeyer, B. (1987). Mechanisms of visual attention revealed by saccadic eye movements. *Neuropsychology*, 25, 73–84.

Fischer, R., Alexander, M., D'Esposito, M., and Otto, R. (1995). Neuropsychological and neuroanatomical correlates of confabulation. *Journal of Clinical and Experimental Neuropsychology*, 17, 20–8.

Fischler, I. (1977). Semantic facilitation without association in a lexical decision task. *Memory and Cognition*, 5, 335–9.

Fitch, T. W. (2010). *The Evolution of Language*. Cambridge University Press.

Fitts, P. M. (1954). The information capacity of the human motor system in controlling the amplitude of movement. *Journal of Experimental Psychology*, 47, 381–91.

Fitts, P. M., and Deininger, R. L. (1954). S–R compatibility: correspondence among paired elements within stimulus and response codes. *Journal of Experimental Psychology*, 48, 483–91.

Fitts, P. M., and Posner, M. I. (1967). *Human Performance*. Belmont, CA: Brooks.

Fitts, P. M., and Seegar, C. M. (1953). S–R compatibility: spatial characteristics of stimulus and response codes. *Journal of Experimental Psychology*, 46, 199–210.

Fitzgerald, J., Spiegel, D. L., and Webb, T. B. (1985). Development of children's knowledge of story structure and content. *Journal of Educational Research*, 79, 101–8.

Flavell, J. H., Beach, D. H., and Chinsky, J. M. (1966). Spontaneous verbal rehearsal in a memory task as a function of age. *Child Development*, 37, 283–99.

Fleishman, E. A., and Parker, J. K. (1962). Factors in the retention and relearning of perceptual-motor skills. *Journal of Experimental Psychology*, 64, 215–26.

Flowers, J. H., Warner, J. L., and Polansky, M. L. (1979). Response and encoding factors in ignoring irrelevant information. *Memory and Cognition*, 7, 86–94.

Flynn, J. R. (1987). Massive IQ gains in 14 nations: what IQ tests really measure. *Psychological Bulletin*, 101, 171–91.

Foer, J. (2011). *Moonwalking with Einstein: The Art and Science of Remembering Everything*. New York: Penguin Books.

Folstein, J. R., Palmeri, T. J., Van Gulick, A. E., and Gauthier, I. (2015). Category learning stretches neural representations in visual cortex. *Current Directions in Psychological Science*, 24, 17–23.

Forster, K. I., and Chambers, S. M. (1973). Lexical access and naming time. *Journal of Verbal Learning and Verbal Behavior*, 12, 627–35.

Forster, K. I., and Davis, C. (1991). The density constraint on form-priming in the naming task: interference effects from a masked prime. *Journal of Memory and Language*, 30, 1–25.

Forster, K. I., and Taft, M. (1994). Bodies, antibodies, and neighborhood density effects in masked form priming. *Journal of Experimental Psychology: Learning, Memory, and Cognition*, 20, 844–63.

Franco, F., and Butterworth, G. (1996). Pointing and social awareness: declaring and requesting in the second year. *Journal of Child Language*, 23, 307–36.

Franklin, H. C., and Holding, D. H. (1977). Personal memories at different ages. *Quarterly Journal of Experimental Psychology*, 29, 527–32.

Franklin, S. S., and Erickson, N. L. (1969). Perceived size of off-size familiar objects under normal and degraded viewing conditions. *Psychonomic Science*, 15, 312–13.

Freedman, J. L., and Landauer, T. K. (1966). Retrieval of long-term memory: "tip-of-the-tongue" phenomenon. *Psychonomic Science*, 4, 309–10.

Frenda, S. J., Knowles, E. D., Saletan, W., and Loftus, E. F. (2013). False memories of fabricated political events. *Journal of Experimental Social Psychology*, 49, 280–6.

Frey, M. C., and Detterman, D. K. (2004). Scholastic assessment or g? The relationship between the scholastic aptitude test and general cognitive ability. *Psychological Science*, 15, 373–8.

Fried, L. S., and Holyoak, K. J. (1984). Induction of category distributions: a framework for classification learning. *Journal of Experimental Psychology: Learning, Memory, and Cognition*, 10, 234–57.

Friederici, A. D. (2012). The cortical language circuit: from auditory perception to sentence comprehension. *Trends in Cognitive Sciences*, 16, 262–8.

Friedman, A., and Brown, N. R. (2000). Reasoning about geography. *Journal of Experimental Psychology: General*, 129, 193–219.

Frith, U. (ed.) (1991). *Autism and Asperger Syndrome*. Cambridge University Press.

Fuld, P. A., and Buschke, H. (1976). Stages of retrieval in verbal learning. *Journal of Verbal Learning and Verbal Behavior*, 15, 401–10.

Gade, A. (1982). Amnesia after operations on aneurysms of the anterior communicating artery. *Surgical Neurology*, 18, 46–9.

Gallagher, A. M., and Kaufman, J. C. (2005). *Gender Differences in Mathematics: An Integrative Psychological Approach*. Cambridge University Press.

Ganger, J., and Brent, M. R. (2004). Reexamining the vocabulary spurt. *Developmental Psychology*, 40, 621–32.

Gardiner, A. K. (2014). Beyond irrelevant actions: understanding the role of intentionality in children's imitation of relevant actions. *Journal of Experimental Child Psychology*, 119, 54–72.

Gardiner, J. M. (1988). Functional aspects of recollective experience. *Memory and Cognition*, 16, 309–13.

Gardiner, J. M., Craik, F. I. M., and Birtwistle, J. (1972). Retrieval cues and release from proactive inhibition. *Journal of Verbal Learning and Verbal Behavior*, 11, 778–83.

Gardner, E. (1994). *Fundamentals of Neurology*. Philadelphia: Saunders.

Gardner, H. (1976). *The Shattered Mind*. New York: Vintage Books.

(1983). *Frames of Mind: The Theory of Multiple Intelligences*. New York: Basic Books.

Gardner, H., Boller, F., Moreines, J., and Butters, N. (1973). Retrieving information from Korsakoff patients: effects of categorical cues and reference to the task. *Cortex*, 9, 165–75.

Garven, S., Wood, J. M., and Malpass, R. S. (2000). Allegations of wrongdoing: the effects of reinforcement on children's mundane and fantastic claims. *Journal of Applied Psychology*, 85, 38–49.

Garven, S., Wood, J. M., Malpass, R. S., and Shaw, J. S. (1998). More than suggestion: the effect of interviewing techniques from the McMartin preschool case. *Journal of Applied Psychology*, 83, 347–59.

Gathercole, S. E. (1995). Is nonword repetition a test of phonological memory or long-term knowledge? It all depends on the nonwords. *Memory and Cognition*, 23, 83–94.

Gathercole, S. E., and Baddeley, A. D. (1989). Development of vocabulary in children and short-term phonological memory. *Journal of Memory and Language*, 28, 200–13.

Gathercole, S. E., and Broadbent, D. E. (1984). Combining attributes in specified and categorized target search: further evidence for strategic differences. *Memory and Cognition*, 12, 329–37.

Gathercole, S. E., Willis, C. S., Emslie, H., and Baddeley, A. D. (1992). Phonological memory and vocabulary development during the early school years: a longitudinal study. *Developmental Psychology*, 28, 887–98.

Gaveau, V., Pisella, L., Priot, A., Fukui, T., Rossetti, Y., Pélisson, D., and Prablanc, C. (2014). Automatic online control of motor adjustments in reaching and grasping. *Neuropsychologia*, 55, 25–40.

Gazzaniga, M. S. (1970). *The Bisected Brain*. New York: Appleton-Century-Crofts.

(1983), Right hemisphere language following brain bisection. *American Psychologist*, 38, 525–37.

Gazzaniga, M. S., Ivry, R. B., and Mangun, G. R. (1998). *Cognitive Neuroscience*. New York: W. W. Norton.

Gehring, W. J., Goss, B., Coles, M. G. H., Meyer, D. E., and Donchin, E. (1993). A neural system for error detection and compensation. *Psychological Science*, 4, 385–90.

Gelman, S. A., and Coley, J. D. (1990). The importance of knowing a dodo is a bird: categories and inferences in 2-year-old children. *Developmental Psychology*, 26, 796–804.

Gelman, S. A., and Markman, E. M. (1986). Categories and induction in young children. *Cognition*, 23, 183–209.

(1987). Young children's inductions form natural kinds: the role of categories and appearances. *Child Development*, 58, 1532–41.

Georgopoulos, A. P. (1995). Motor cortex and cognitive processing. In M. S. Gazzaniga (ed.), *The Cognitive Neurosciences*, 507–17. Cambridge, MA: MIT Press.

Gerhardstein, P., Renner, P., and Rovee-Collier, C. (1999). The roles of perceptual and categorical similarity in colour pop-out in infants. *British Journal of Developmental Psychology*, 17, 405–20.

German, T. P., and Defeyter, M. A. (2000). Immunity of functional fixedness in young children. *Psychonomic Bulletin and Review*, 7, 707–12.

Gescheider, G. A., Sager, L. C., and Ruffolo, L. J. (1975). Simultaneous auditory and tactile information processing. *Perception and Psychophysics*, 18, 209–16.

Geschwind, N. (1970). The organization of language and the brain. *Science*, 170, 940–4.

Ghisletta, P., Rabbitt, P. M. A., Lunn, M., and Lindenberger, U. (2012). Two thirds of the age-based changes in fluid and crystallized intelligence, perceptual speed, and memory in adulthood are shared. *Intelligence*, 40, 260–8.

Gibson, J. J. (1966). *The Senses Considered as Perceptual Systems*. Boston: Houghton Mifflin.

Gick, M. L., and Holyoak, K. J. (1980). Analogical problem solving. *Cognitive Psychology*, 12, 306–55.

(1983). Schema induction and analogical transfer. *Cognitive Psychology*, 15, 1–38.

Gigerenzer, G., and Hug, K. (1992). Domain-specific reasoning: social contracts, cheating, and perspective change. *Cognition*, 43, 127–71.

Gillberg, C., and Coleman, M. (2000). *The Biology of the Autistic Syndromes*, 3rd edn. Cambridge University Press.

Gilovich, T. (1981). Seeing the past in the present: the effect of associations to familiar events on judgments and decisions. *Journal of Personality and Social Psychology*, 40, 797–808.

Glanzer, M., and Cunitz, A. R. (1966). Two storage mechanisms in free recall. *Journal of Verbal Learning and Verbal Behavior*, 5, 351–60.

Glass, A. L. (1993). The role of generation in recognition. *Scandinavian Journal of Psychology*, 34, 255–67.

Glass, A. L., Brill, G., and Ingate, M. (2008). Combined online and in-class pre-testing improves exam performance in general psychology. *Educational Psychology*, 28, 483–503.

Glass, A. L., Eddy, J. K., and Schwanenflugel, P. J. (1980). The verification of high and low imagery sentences. *Journal of Experimental Psychology: Human Learning and Memory*, 6, 692–704.

Glass, A. L., and Holyoak, K. J. (1975). Alternative conceptions of semantic memory. *Cognition*, 3, 313–39.

Glass, A. L., Holyoak, K. J., and Kiger, J. I. (1979). Role of antonymy relations in semantic judgments. *Journal of Experimental Psychology: Human Learning and Memory*, 5, 598–606.

Glass, A. L., Holyoak, K. J., and O'Dell, C. (1974). Production frequency and the verification of quantified statements. *Journal of Verbal Learning and Verbal Behavior*, 13, 237–54.

Glass, A. L., Ingate, M., and Sinha, N. (2013). The effect of a final exam on long-term retention. *Journal of General Psychology*, 140, 224–41.

Glass, A. L., Krejci, J., and Goldman, J. (1989). The necessary and sufficient conditions for motor learning, recognition and recall. *Journal of Memory and Language*, 28, 189–99.

Glass, A. L., Millen, D. R., Beck, L. G., and Eddy, J. K. (1985). The representation of images in sentence verification. *Journal of Memory and Language*, 24, 442–65.

Glass, A. L., and Sinha, N. (2012). Providing the answers does not improve performance on a college final exam. *Educational Psychology*, 32, 1–32.

Gloning, K. (1977). Handedness and aphasia. *Neuropsychologia*, 15, 355–8.

Glück, J., and Bluck, S. (2007). Looking back across the lifespan: a life story account of the reminiscence bump. *Memory and Cognition*, 35, 1928–39.

Glucksberg, S., and Danks, J. (1968). Effects of discriminative labels and of nonsense labels upon availability of novel function. *Journal of Verbal Learning and Verbal Behavior*, 7, 72–6.

Glucksberg, S., and Weisberg, R. W. (1966). Verbal behavior and problem solving: some effects of labeling in a functional fixedness problem. *Journal of Experimental Psychology*, 71, 659–64.

Gnadt, J. W., Lu, S., Breznen, B., Basso, M. A., Henriquez, V. M., and Evinger, C. (1997). Influence of the superior colliculus on the primate blink reflex. *Experimental Brain Research*, 116, 389–98.

Gobet, F., and Simon, H. A. (1996). The roles of recognition processes and look-ahead search in time-constrained expert problem solving: evidence from grand-master-level chess. *Psychological Science*, 7, 52–5.

Godden, D. R., and Baddeley, A. D. (1975). Context-dependent memory in two natural environments: on land and underwater. *British Journal of Psychology*, 66, 325–32.

Godijn, R., and Theeuwes, J. (2002). Programming of endogenous and exogenous saccades: evidence for a competitive integration model. *Journal of Experimental Psychology: Human Perception and Performance*, 28, 1039–54.

Godwin, H. J., Reichle, E. D., and Menneer, T. (2014). Coarse-to-fine eye movement behavior during visual search. *Psychonomic Bulletin and Review*, 21, 1244–9.

Gogate, L., and Bahrick, L. (2000). A study of multimodal motherese: the role of temporal synchrony between verbal labels and gestures. *Child Development*, 71, 878–94.

Goldberg, E., Hughes, J. E., Mattis, S., and Antin, S. P. (1982). Isolated retrograde amnesia: different etiologies, same mechanisms? *Cortex*, 18, 459–62.

Goldberg, G. (1985). Supplementary motor area structure and function: review and hypothesis. *Behavior and Brain Science*, 8, 567–616.

Golding, E. (1981). The effect of past experience on problem solving. Paper presented at the annual conference of the British Psychological Society, Guildford, University of Surrey, April 12.

Goodale, M. A., Milner, M. D., Jakobson, L. S., and Carey, D. P. (1991). A neurological dissociation between perceiving objects and grasping them. *Nature*, 349, 154–6.

Goodglass, H. (1968). Studies on the grammar of aphasics. In S. Rosenberg and J. Kaplin (eds.), *Developments in Applied Psycholinguistic Research*, 177–208. New York: Macmillan.

(1976). Agrammatism. In H. Whitaker and M. A. Whitaker (eds.), *Studies in Neurolinguistics*, vol. I, 237–60. New York: Academic Press.

Goodglass, H., and Berko, J. (1960). Aphasia and inflectional morphology in English. *Journal of Speech and Hearing Research*, 10, 257–62.

Goodglass, H., Fodor, I., and Schulhoff, S. (1967). Prosodic factors in grammar: evidence from aphasia. *Journal of Speech and Hearing Research*, 10, 5–20.

Goodglass, H., and Geschwind, N. (1976). Language disorders (aphasia). In E. C. Carterette and M. Friedman (eds.), *Handbook of Perception*, vol. VII, *Speech and Language*, 389–428. New York: Academic Press.

Goodglass, H., and Hunt, J. (1958). Grammatical complexity and aphasic speech. *Word*, 14, 197–207.

Goodglass, H., Quadfasel, F. A., and Timberlake, W. H. (1964). Phrase length and the type and severity of aphasia. *Cortex*, 1, 133–58.

Gooding, P. A., Mayes, A. R., and van Eijk, R. (2000). A meta-analysis of indirect memory tests for novel material in organic amnesics. *Neuropsychologia*, 38, 666–76.

Goodman, G. S., and Reed, R. S. (1986). Age differences in eyewitness testimony. *Law and Human Behavior*, 10, 317–22.

Goodwin, K. A., Meissner, C. A., and Ericsson, K. A. (2001). Toward a model of false recall: experimental manipulation of encoding context and the collection of verbal reports. *Memory and Cognition*, 29, 806–19.

Gopnik, A., and Astington, J. W. (1988). Children's understanding of representational change and its relation to the understanding of false belief and the appearance–reality distinction. *Child Development*, 59, 26–37.

Gopnik, A., and Choi, S. (1990). Do linguistic differences lead to cognitive differences? A cross-linguistic study of semantic and cognitive development. *First Language*, 10, 99–215.

Gordon, H. W. (1970). Hemispheric asymmetries in the perception of musical chords. *Cortex*, 6, 387–98.

(1974). Hemispheric asymmetry and musical performance. *Science*, 189, 68–9.

(1980). Degree of ear asymmetries for perception of dichotic chords and for illusory chord localization in musicians of different levels of competence. *Journal of Experimental Psychology: Human Perception and Performance*, 6, 516–27.

Gorman, A. M. (1961). Recognition memory for nouns as a function of abstractness and frequency. *Journal of Experimental Psychology*, 61, 23–9.

Gould, E., Beylin, A., Tanapat, P., Reeves, A., and Shors, T. J. (1999). Learning enhances adult neurogenesis in the hippocampal formation. *Nature Neuroscience*, 2, 260–5.

Graf, P., Shimamura, A., and Squire, L. R. (1985). Priming across modalities and priming across category levels: extending the domain of preserved function in amnesia. *Journal of Experimental Psychology: Learning, Memory, and Cognition*, 11, 386–96.

Graf, P., Squire, L. R., and Mandler, G. (1984). The information that amnesic patients do not forget. *Journal of Experimental Psychology: Learning, Memory, and Cognition*, 10, 164–78.

Graham, K. R. (1977). Perceptual processes of hypnosis: support for a cognitive-state theory based on laterality.

Annals of the New York Academy of Sciences, 296, 274–83.

Graham, K. S., Lambon Ralph, M. A., and Hodges, J. R. (1997). Determining the impact of autobiographical experience on "meaning": new insights from investigating sports-related vocabulary and knowledge in two cases with semantic dementia. *Cognitive Neuropsychology*, 14, 801–37.

Grainger, J., and Ferrand, L. (1996). Masked orthographic and phonological priming in visual word recognition and naming: cross-task comparison. *Journal of Memory and Language*, 35, 623–47.

Grandstaff, N. W., and Pribram, K. H. (1975). Habituation: electrical changes in the visual system. *Neuropsychologia*, 10, 125–32.

Green, D. W. (1995). Externalization, counter-examples, and the abstract selection task. *Quarterly Journal of Experimental Psychology*, 48A, 424–46.

Green, D. W., and Larking, R. (1995). The locus of facilitation in the abstract selection task. *Thinking and Reasoning*, 1, 183–99.

Greenberg, J. H. (1963). Some universals of grammar with particular reference to the order of meaningful elements. In J. H. Greenberg (ed.), *Universals of Language*, 73–113. Cambridge, MA: MIT Press.

Greene, R. L. (1984). Incidental learning of event frequency. *Memory and Cognition*, 12, 90–5.

Greenwald, A. G. (1980). The totalitarian ego: fabrication and revision of personal history. *American Psychologist*, 35, 603–18.

Gregory, R. L. (1998). *Eye and Brain: The Psychology of Seeing*, 5th edn. Princeton University Press.

Greve, D. N., Van der Haegen, L., Cai, Q., Stufflebeam, S., Sabuncu, M. R., Fischl, B., and Brysbaert, M. (2013). A surface-based analysis of language lateralization and cortical asymmetry. *Journal of Cognitive Neuroscience*, 25, 1477–92.

Griggs, R. A. (1983). The role of problem content in the selection task and in the THOG problem. In J. St. B. T. Evans (ed.), *Thinking and Reasoning: Psychological Approaches*, 16–43. London: Routledge & Kegan Paul.

Griggs, R. A., and Cox, J. R. (1982). The elusive thematic-materials effect in Wason's selection task. *British Journal of Psychology*, 73, 407–20.

Grison, S., and Strayer, D. L. (2001). Negative priming and perceptual fluency: more than what meets the eye. *Perception and Psychophysics*, 63, 1063–71.

Gros, J., and Bayen, U. J. (2015). Hindsight bias in younger and older adults: the role of access control. *Aging, Neuropsychology, and Cognition*, 22, 183–200.

Groves, P. M., and Thompson, R. F. (1970). Habituation: a dual-process theory. *Psychological Review*, 77, 419–50.

Gruenewald, P. J., and Lockhead, G. R. (1980). The free recall of category examples. *Journal of Experimental Psychology: Human Learning and Memory*, 6, 225–40.

Gruneberg, M. M., and Monks, J. (1974). Feeling of knowing and cued recall. *Acta Psychologica*, 38, 257–65.

Gunawan, K., and Gerkens, D. R. (2011). The recovery of blocked memories in repeated recall tests. *British Journal of Psychology*, 102, 373–91.

Guridi, J., Rodriguez-Oroz, M. C., Lozano, A. M., Moro, E., Albanese, A., Nuttin, B., Gybels, J., Ramos, E., and Obeso, J. A. (2000). Targeting the basal ganglia for deep brain stimulation in Parkinson's disease. *Neurology*, 55 (Supplement 6), 21–8.

Haber, R. N., and Hershenson, M. (1965). The effects of repeated brief exposures on the growth of a percept. *Journal of Experimental Psychology*, 69, 40–6.

Haber, R. N., and Schindler, R. M. (1981). Error in proofreading: evidence of syntactic control of letter processing? *Journal of Experimental Psychology: Human Perception and Performance*, 7, 573–9.

Haberlandt, K., Berian, C., and Sandson, J. (1980). The episodic schema in story processing. *Journal of Verbal Learning and Verbal Behavior*, 19, 635–50.

Habermas, T., and Bluck, S. (2000). Getting a life: the emergence of the life story in adolescence. *Psychological Bulletin*, 126, 748–69.

Hadani, I., Ishai, G., Frisch, H. L., and Kononov, A. (1994). Two metric solutions to the three-dimensional reconstruction for an eye in pure rotations. *Journal of the Optical Society of America*, 11, 1564–74.

Hagen, J. W., Meacham, J. A., and Mesibov, G. (1970). Verbal labeling, rehearsal, and short-term memory. *Cognitive Psychology*, 1, 47–58.

Halford, G. S. (1984). Can young children integrate premises in transitivity and serial order tasks? *Cognitive Psychology*, 16, 65–93.

Hall, D. G., Lee, S. C., and Belanger, J. (2001). Young children's use of syntactic cues to learn proper names and count nouns. *Developmental Psychology*, 37, 298–307.

Hambly, H., Wren, Y., McLeod, S., and Roulstone, S. (2013). The influence of bilingualism on speech production: a systematic review. *International Journal of Language and Communication Disorders*, 48, 1–24.

Hamers, J. F., and Lambert, W. E. (1972). Bilingual interdependencies in auditory perception. *Journal of Verbal Learning and Verbal Behavior*, 11, 303–10.

Hammerton, M. (1963). Retention of learning in a difficult tracking task. *Journal of Experimental Psychology*, 66, 108–10.

Hamond, N. R., and Fivush, R. (1991). Memories of Mickey Mouse: young children recount their trip to Disneyworld. *Cognitive Development*, 6, 433–48.

Hanna, E., and Meltzoff, A. N. (1993). Peer imitation by toddlers in laboratory, home, and day-care contexts: implications for social learning and memory. *Developmental Psychology*, 29, 701–10.

Hansen, R. M., and Skavenski, A. A. (1985). Accuracy of spatial localization near the time of saccadic eye movements. *Vision Research*, 25, 1077–82.

Happe, F., and Frith, U. (1996). The neuropsychology of autism. *Brain*, 119, 1377–400.

Hardyck, C. D., and Petrinovich, I. F. (1970). Subvocal speech and comprehension level as a function of the difficulty level of the reading material. *Journal of Verbal Learning and Verbal Behavior*, 9, 647–52.

Harris, G., Begg, L., and Mitterer, J. (1980). On the relation between frequency estimates and recognition memory. *Memory and Cognition*, 8, 99–104.

Harris, P., Brown, E., Marriott, C., Whittall, S., and Harmer, S. (1991). Monsters, ghosts, and witches: testing the limits of the fantasy reality distinction in young children. *British Journal of Developmental Psychology*, 9, 105–23.

Harrison, T. L., Shipstead, Z., Hicks, K. L., Hambrick, D. Z., Redick, T. S., and Engle, R. W. (2013). Working memory training may increase working memory capacity but not fluid intelligence. *Psychological Science*, 24, 2409–19.

Hart, J. T. (1965). Memory and the feeling of knowing experience. *Journal of Educational Psychology*, 56, 208–16.

Hartley, J. T., Birnbaum, I. M., and Parker, E. S. (1978). Alcohol and storage deficits: kind of processing? *Journal of Verbal Learning and Verbal Behavior*, 17, 635–47.

Hartman, M., Knopman, D. S., and Nissen, M. J. (1989). Implicit learning of new verbal associations. *Journal of Experimental Psychology: Learning, Memory, and Cognition*, 15, 1070–82.

Hartshorn, K., and Rovee-Collier, C. (1997). Infant learning and long-term memory at 6 months: a confirming analysis. *Developmental Psychobiology*, 30, 71–85.

Hartshorn, K., Wilk, A. E., Muller, K. L., and Rovee-Collier, C. (1998). An expanding training series protracts retention for 3-month-old infants. *Developmental Psychobiology*, 33, 271–80.

Harvey, A. G., Bryant, R. A., and Dang, S. T. (1998). Autobiographical memory in acute stress disorder. *Journal of Consulting and Clinical Psychology*, 66, 500–6.

Hasher, L., and Chromiak, W. (1977). The processing of frequency information: an automatic mechanism? *Journal of Verbal Learning and Verbal Behavior*, 16, 173–84.

Hasher, L., and Zacks, R. (1979). Automatic and effortful processes in memory. *Journal of Experimental Psychology: General*, 108, 356–88.

Hatfield, E., and Rapson, R. L. (1993). Love and attachment processes. In M. Lewis and J. M. Haviland (eds.), *Handbook of Emotions*, 595–604. New York: Guilford Press.

Haverkamp, B. E. (1993). Confirmatory bias in hypothesis testing for client-identified and counselor self-generated hypotheses. *Journal of Counseling Psychology*, 40, 303–15.

Hay, J. C., Pick, H. L., and Ikeda, K. (1965). Visual capture produced by prism spectacles. *Psychonomic Science*, 2, 215–16.

Hay, J. F., Pelucchi, B., Estes, K. G., and Saffran, J. R. (2011). Linking sounds to meanings: infant statistical learning in a natural language. *Cognitive Psychology*, 63, 93–106.

Hayne, H., Boniface, J., and Barr, R. (2000). The development of declarative memory in human infants: age-related changes in deferred imitation. *Behavioral Neuroscience*, 114, 77–83.

Hayne, H., Greco, C., Earley, L. L., Griesler, P., and Rovee-Collier, C. (1986). Ontogeny of early event memory II: encoding and retrieval by 2- and 3-month-olds. *Infant Behavior and Development*, 9, 461–72.

Hayne, H., Rovee-Collier, C., and Borza, M. A. (1991). Infant memory for place information. *Memory and Cognition*, 19, 378–86.

Hayward, W. G., and Tarr, M. J. (1997). Testing conditions for viewpoint invariance in object recognition. *Journal of Experimental Psychology: Human Perception and Performance*, 23, 1511–21.

Healy, A. F. (1976). Detection errors on the word the: evidence for reading units larger than letters. *Journal of Experimental Psychology: Human Perception and Performance*, 2, 235–42.

(1980). Proofreading errors on the word the: new evidence on reading units. *Journal of Experimental Psychology: Human Perception and Performance*, 6, 45–57.

(1981). The effects of visual similarity on proofreading for misspellings. *Memory and Cognition*, 9, 453–60.

Heathcote, A., Brown, S., and Mewhort, D. J. K. (2000). The power law repealed: the case for an exponential law of practice. *Psychonomic Bulletin and Review*, 7, 185–207.

Heider, E. R. (1972). Universals in color naming and memory. *Journal of Experimental Psychology*, 93, 10–20.

Heider, E. R., and Olivier, D. (1972). The structure of the color space in naming and memory for two languages. *Cognitive Psychology*, 3, 337–54.

Heilman, K. M., Rothi, L. I., and Valenstein, E. (1982). Two forms of ideomotor apraxia. *Neurology*, 32, 342–6.

Heilman, K. M., Watson, R. T., and Valenstein, E. (1993). Neglect and related disorders. In K. M. Heilman and E. Valenstein (eds.), *Clinical Neuropsychology*, 279–386. New York: Oxford University Press.

Heindel, W. C., Butters, N., and Salmon, D. P. (1988). Impaired learning of a motor skill in patients with Huntington's disease. *Behavioral Neuroscience*, 102, 141–7.

Heit, E. (2000). Properties of inductive reasoning. *Psychonomic Bulletin and Review*, 7, 569–92.

Hellige, J. B. (1980). Effects of perceptual quality and visual field of probe stimulus presentation on memory search for letters. *Journal of Experimental Psychology: Human Perception and Performance*, 6, 639–51.

Hellige, J. B., Cox, P. I., and Litvac, L. (1979). Information processing in the cerebral hemispheres: selective hemisphere activation and capacity limitations. *Journal of Experimental Psychology: General*, 108, 251–79.

Henderson, J. M. (2003). Human gaze control during real-world scene perception. *Trends in Cognitive Science*, 7, 498–504.

Hering, E. (1964 [1920]). *Outlines of a Theory of the Light Sense*. Cambridge, MA: Harvard University Press.

Hiatt, S., Campos, J. J., and Emde, R. N. (1979). Facial patterning an infant facial expression: happiness, surprise, and fear. *Child Development*, 50, 1020–35.

Hickok, G., and Poeppel, D. (2004). Dorsal and ventral sreams: a framework for understanding aspects of the functional anatomy of language. *Cognition*, 92, 67–99.

Hildreth, K., and Rovee-Collier, C. (1999). Decreases in the response latency to priming over the first year of life. *Developmental Psychobiology*, 35, 276–90.

Hilgard, E. R., and Hilgard, J. R. (1975). *Hypnosis in the Relief of Pain*. Los Altos, CA: Kaufman.

Hinrichs, J., and Craft, J. L. (1971). Stimulus and response factors in discrete choice reaction time. *Journal of Experimental Psychology*, 91, 305–9.

Hirshman, E., Fisher, J., Henthorn, T., Arndt, J., and Passannante, A. (2002). Midazolam amnesia and dual-process models of the word-frequency mirror effect. *Journal of Memory and Language*, 47, 499–516.

Hirst, W., Phelps, E. A., Buckner, R. L., Budson, A. E., Cuc, A., Gabrieli, J. D. E., Johnson, M. K., Lustig, C., Lyle, K. B., Mather, M., Meksin, R., Mitchell, K. J., Ochsner, K. N., Schacter, D. L., Simons, J. S., and Vaidya, C. J. (2009). Long-term memory for the terrorist attack of September 11: flashbulb memories, event memories, and the factors that influence their retention. *Journal of Experimental Psychology: General*, 138, 161–76.

Hockley, W. E. (1992). Item versus associative information: further comparisons of forgetting rates. *Journal of Experimental Psychology: Learning, Memory, and Cognition*, 18, 1321–30.

Hodges, J. R., Patterson, K., Oxbury, S., and Funnel, E. (1992). Semantic dementia: progessive fluent aphasia with temporal lobe atrophy. *Brain*, 115, 1783–806.

Hodges, J. R.,.Salmon, D. P., and Butters, N. (1992). Semantic memory impairment in Alzheimer's disease: failure of access or degraded knowledge? *Neuropsychologia*, 30, 301–14.

Hoffman, R. R., Hancock, P. A., Scerbo, M. W., Parasuraman, R., and Szalma, J. L. (2014). *The Cambridge Handbook of Applied Perception Research*. Cambridge University Press.

Hoffmann, J., Sebald, A., and Stöcker, C. (2001). Irrelevant response effects improve serial learning in serial reaction time tasks. *Journal of Experimental Psychology: Learning, Memory, and Cognition*, 27, 470–82.

Holbrook, M. B. (1978). Effect of subjective interletter similarity, perceived word similarity, and contextual variables on the recognition of letter substitutions in a proofreading task. *Perceptual and Motor Skills*, 47, 251–8.

Holmes, D. S. (1984). Meditation and somatic arousal reduction: a review of the experimental evidence. *American Psychologist*, 39, 1–10.

Holmes, G. (1939). The cerebellum of man. *Brain*, 62, 1–30.

Holyoak, K. J., and Glass, A. L. (1975). The role of contradictions and counterexamples in the rejection of false sentences. *Journal of Verbal Learning and Verbal Behavior*, 14, 215–39.

Holyoak, K. J., and Walker, J. H. (1976). Subjective magnitude information in semantic orderings. *Journal of Verbal Learning and Verbal Behavior*, 15, 287–99.

Homa, D., and Vosburgh, R. (1976). Category breadth and the abstraction of prototypical information. *Journal of Experimental Psychology: Human Learning and Memory*, 2, 322–30.

Hongpaisan, J., and Alkon, D. L. (2007). A structural basis for enhancement of long-term associative memory in single dendritic spines regulated by PKC. *Proceedings of the National Academy of Sciences*, 104, 19571–6.

Hoosain, R., and Salili, F. (1988). Language differences, working memory, and mathematical ability. In M. M. Gruneberg, P. E. Morris, and R. N. Sykes (eds.), *Practical Aspects of Memory: Current Research and Issues*, vol. II, *Clinical and Educational Implications*, 512–17. Chichester, UK: Wiley.

Hornak, J., Rolls, E. T., and Wade, D. (1996). Face and voice expression identification in patients with emotional and behavioral changes following ventral frontal lobe damage. *Neuropsychologia*, 34, 247–61.

Horne, J. A. (1988). *Why We Sleep: The Functions of Sleep in Humans and Other Mammals*. Oxford University Press.

Horne, J. A., and Moore, V. J. (1985). Sleep EEG effects of exercise with and without additional body cooling. *Electroencephalography and Clinical Neurophysiology*, 60, 33–8.

House, E. L., and Pansky, B. (1967). *A Functional Approach to Neuroanatomy*. New York: McGraw-Hill.

Howlin, P., Davies, M., and Udwin, O. (1998). Cognitive functioning in adults with Williams syndrome. *Journal of Child Psychology and Psychiatry*, 39, 183–9.

Hsu, V. C. (2010). Time windows in retention over the first year-and-a-half of life: spacing effects. *Developmental Psychobiology*, 52, 764–74.

Hsu, V. C., and Rovee-Collier, C. (2006). Memory reactivation in the second year of life. *Infant Behavior and Development*, 29, 91–107.

Hudson, A. J., and Grace, G. M. (2000). Misidentification syndromes related to face specific area in the fusiform gyrus. *Journal of Neurology, Neurosurgery and Psychiatry*, 69, 465–8.

Hudson, J. A., and Sheffield, E. G. (1998). Déjà vu all over again: effects of reenactment on toddlers' event memory. *Child Development*, 69, 51–67.

Hulicka, I. M., and Grossman, J. L. (1967). Age-group comparisons for the use of mediators in paired-associate learning. *Journal of Gerontology*, 22, 46–51.

Hulicka, I. M., Sterns, H., and Grossman, J. L. (1967). Age-group comparisons of paired associate learning as a function of paced and self-paced association and response times. *Journal of Gerontology*, 22, 274–80.

Hulicka, I. M., and Wheeler, D. (1976). Recall scores of old and young people as function of registration intervals. *Educational Gerontology*, 1, 361–72.

Hultsch, D. F. (1971). Adult age differences in free classification and free recall. *Developmental Psychology*, 4, 338–42.

Humphreys, G. W., and Price, C. J. (1994). Visual feature discrimination in simultanagnosia: a study of two cases. *Cognitive Neuropsychology*, 11, 393–434.

Humphreys, G. W., and Rumiata, R. I. (1998). Agnosia without prosopagnosia or alexia: evidence for stored visual memories specific to objects. *Cognitive Neuropsychology*, 15, 243–77.

Hunt, E., and Love, T. (1972). How good can memory be? In A. W. Melton and E. Martin (eds.), *Coding Processes in Human Memory*, 237–50. Washington, DC: Winston.

Hunter, I. M. L. (1962). An exceptional talent for calculative thinking. *British Journal of Psychology*, 53, 243–58.

(1977). Mental calculation. In P. N. Johnson-Laird and P. C. Wason (eds.), *Thinking: Readings in Cognitive Science*, 35–45. Cambridge University Press.

Hyman, I. E., Husband, T. H., and Billings, F. J. (1995). False memories of childhood experiences. *Applied Cognitive Psychology*, 9, 181–97.

Hyman, I. E., and Rubin, D. C. (1990). Memorabilia: a naturalistic study of long-term memory. *Memory and Cognition*, 18, 205–14.

Hyona, J., and Bertram, R. (2004). Do frequency characteristics of nonfixated words influence the processing of fixated words during reading? *European Journal of Cognitive Psychology*, 16, 104–27.

Ifft, P. J., Lebedev, M. A., and Nicolelis, M. A. L. (2011). Cortical correlates of Fitts' law. *Frontiers in Integrative Neuroscience*, 5, article 85.

Imada, T., Zhang, Y., Cheour, M., Taulu, S., Ahonen, A., and Kuhl, P. K. (2006). Infant speech perception activates Broca's area: a developmental magnetoencephalography study. *NeuroReport*, 17, 957–62.

Intraub, H. (1980). Presentation rate and the representation of briefly glimpsed pictures in memory. *Journal of Experimental Psychology: Human Learning and Memory*, 6, 1–12.

(1981). Rapid conceptual identification of sequentially presented pictures. *Journal of Experimental Psychology: Human Perception and Performance*, 7, 604–10.

(1985). Visual dissociation: an illusory conjunction of pictures and forms. *Journal of Experimental Psychology: Human Perception and Performance*, 11, 431–42.

Iordanova, M. D., Good, M., and Honey, R. C. (2011). Retrieval-mediated learning involving episodes requires synaptic plasticity in the hippocampus. *Journal of Neuroscience*, 31, 7156–62.

Ivry, R. B., and Keele, S. W. (1989). Timing functions of the cerebellum. *Journal of Cognitive Neuroscience*, 1, 136–52.

Izard, C. E. (1994). Innate and universal facial expressions: evidence from developmental and cross-cultural research. *Psychological Bulletin*, 115, 288–99.

Jack, F., MacDonald, S., Reese, E., and Hayne, H. (2009). Maternal reminiscing style during early childhood predicts the age of adolescents' earliest memories. *Child Development*, 80, 496–505.

Jack, F., Simcock, G., and Hayne, H. (2012). Magic memories: young children's verbal recall after a 6-year delay. *Child Development*, 83, 159–72.

Jacoby, L. L., Craik, F. I. M., and Begg, I. (1979). Effects of decision difficulty on recognition and recall. *Journal of Verbal Learning and Verbal Behavior*, 18, 585–600.

Jakobson, R. (1968). *Child Language, Aphasia, and Phonological Universals*. The Hague: Mouton.

Jameson, D., and Hurvich, L. M. (1955). Some quantitative aspects of an opponent-colors theory: chromatic responses and spectral saturation. *Journal of the Optical Society of America*, 45, 546–52.

Jarvella, R. J. (1970). Effects of syntax on running memory span for connected discourse. *Psychonomic Science*, 19, 235–6.

(1971). Syntactic processing of connected speech. *Journal of Verbal Learning and Verbal Behavior*, 10, 409–16.

Jaswal, V. K., and Markman, E. M. (2001). Learning proper and common names in inferential versus ostensive contexts. *Child Development*, 72, 768–86.

Jeannerod, M. (1994). The representing brain: neural correlates of motor intention and imagery. *Behavioral and Brain Sciences*, 17, 187–245.

Jeffries, R., Polson, P., Razran, L., and Atwood, M. E. (1977). A process model for missionaries–cannibals and other river crossing problems. *Cognitive Psychology*, 9, 412–40.

Jerison, H. J. (1977). Vigilance: biology, psychology, theory, and practice. In R. R. Mackie (ed.), *Vigilance: Theory, Operational Performance, and Physiological Correlates*, 27–40. New York: Plenum Press.

Jersild, A. T. (1927). Mental set and shift. *Archives of Psychology*, 14, 5–82.

Johansson, F., Jirenhed, D.-A., Rasmussen, A., Zucc, R., and Hesslow, G. (2014). Memory trace and timing mechanism localized to cerebellar Purkinje cells. *Proceedings of the National Academy of Sciences*, 111, 14930–4.

Johnson, E. K., and Jusczyk, P. W. (2001). Word segmentation by 8-month-olds: when speech cues count more than statistics. *Journal of Memory and Language*, 44, 548–67.

Johnson, M. K., and Foley, M. A. (1984). Differentiating fact from fantasy: the reliability of children's memory. *Journal of Social Issues*, 40, 33–50.

Johnson, M. K., Hashtroudi, S., and Lindsay, D. S. (1993). Source monitoring. *Psychological Bulletin*, 114, 3–28.

Johnson, M. K., and Raye, C. L. (1981). Reality monitoring. *Psychological Review*, 88, 67–85.

(1998). False memories and confabulation. *Trends in Cognitive Sciences*, 2, 137–45.

Johnson, S. C., and Carey, S. (1998). Knowledge enrichment and conceptual change in folk biology: evidence from Williams syndrome. *Cognitive Psychology*, 37, 156–200.

Johnson-Laird, P. N., Gibbs, G., and de Mowbray, J. (1978). Meaning, amount of processing, and memory for words. *Memory and Cognition*, 6, 372–5.

Johnson-Laird, P. N., Legrenzi, P., and Legrenzi, M. (1972). Reasoning and a sense of reality. *British Journal of Psychology*, 63, 395–400.

Johnston, W. A. (1978). The intrusiveness of familiar nontarget information. *Memory and Cognition*, 6, 38–42.

Johnston, W. A., and Dark, V. (1986). Selective attention. *Annual Review of Psychology*, 37, 43–75.

Johnston, W. A., and Heinz, S. P. (1979). Depth of nontarget processing in an attention task. *Journal of Experimental Psychology: Human Perception and Performance*, 5, 168–75.

Johnston, W. A., and Uhl, C. N. (1976). The contributions of encoding effort and variability to the spacing effect on free recall. *Journal of Experimental Psychology: Human Learning and Memory*, 2, 153–60.

Johnston, W. A., and Wilson, J. (1980). Perceptual processing of nontargets in an attention task. *Memory and Cognition*, 8, 372–7.

Jolicoeur, P., Gluck, M., and Kosslyn, S. M. (1984). Pictures and names: making the connection. *Cognitive Psychology*, 16, 243–75.

Jones, B. M., and Parsons, O. A. (1972). Specific vs. generalized deficits of abstracting ability in chronic alcoholics. *Archives of General Psychiatry*, 26, 380–4.

Jones, W., Bellugi, U., Lai, Z., Chiles, M., Reilly, J., Lincoln, A., and Adolphs, R. (2000). Hypersociability in Williams syndrome. *Journal of Cognitive Neuroscience*, 12 (supplement), 30–46.

Joordens, S., and Hockley, W. E. (2000). Recollection and familiarity through the looking glass: when old does not mirror new. *Journal of Experimental Psychology: Learning, Memory, and Cognition*, 26, 1534–55.

Jorg, S., and Hormann, H. (1978). The influence of general and specific verbal labels on the recognition of labeled and unlabeled parts of pictures. *Journal of Verbal Learning and Verbal Behavior*, 17, 445–54.

Jouvet-Mounier, D., Astic, L., and Lacote, D. (1969). Ontogenesis of the states of sleep in rat, cat, and guinea pig during the first postnatal month. *Developmental Psychobiology*, 2, 216–39.

Judd, L. L., Squire, L. R., Butters, N., Salmon, D. P., and Paller, K. A. (1987). Effects of psychotropic drugs on cognition and memory in normal humans and animals. In H. Y. Meltzer (ed.), *Psychopharmacology: The Third Generation of Progress*, 1467–75. New York: Raven Press.

Julesz, B. (1971). *Foundations of Cyclopean Perception*. University of Chicago Press.

(1981). Textons, the elements of texture perception and their interactions. *Nature*, 290, 91–7.

(1995). *Dialogues on Perception*. Cambridge, MA: MIT Press.

Jung, R., and Haier, R. (2007). The parieto-frontal integration theory (P-FIT) of intelligence: converging neuroimaging evidence. *Behavioral and Brain Sciences*, 30, 135–187.

Jusczyk, P. W. (2002). How infants adapt speech-producing capacities to native-language structure. *Current Directions in Psychological Science*, 11, 13–18.

Jusczyk, P. W., Houston, D. M., and Newsome, M. (1999). The beginnings of word segmentation in English-learning infants. *Cognitive Psychology*, 39, 159–207.

Just, M. A., and Carpenter, P. A. (1980). A theory of reading: from eye fixations to comprehension. *Psychological Review*, 87, 329–54.

Justel, N., Pautassi, R., and Mustaca, A. (2014). Proactive interference of open field on consummatory successive negative contrast. *Learning and Behavior*, 42, 58–68.

Kahneman, D. (1973). *Attention and Effort.* Englewood Cliffs, NJ: Prentice Hall.

(2011). *Thinking, Fast and Slow*. New York: Farrar, Strauss, & Giroux.

Kahneman, D., and Tversky, A. (1972). Subjective probability: a judgment of representativeness. *Cognitive Psychology*, 3, 430–54.

(1973). On the psychology of prediction. *Psychological Review*, 80, 237–51.

(1979). Prospect theory: an analysis of decision under risk. *Econometrica*, 47, 263–91.

(1982). The simulation heuristic. In D. Kahneman, P. Slovic, and A. Tversky (eds.), *Judgment under Uncertainty: Heuristics and Biases*, 201–8. New York: Cambridge University Press.

Kales, A., Tan, T.-L., Kollar, E., Naitoh, P., Preston, T., and Malmastrom, E. (1970). Sleep patterns following 205 hours of sleep deprivation. *Psychosomatic Medicine*, 32, 189–200.

Kandel, E. R. (2006). *In Search of Memory: The Emergence of a New Science of Mind*. New York: W. W. Norton.

Kandel, E. R., Schwartz, J. H., and Jessell, T. M. (2000). *Principles of Neural Science*, 4th edn. New York: McGraw-Hill.

Kanner, L. (1943). Autistic disturbances and affective contact. *Nervous Child*, 2, 217–50.

Kapur, N., and Abbott, P. (1996). A study of recovery of memory function in a case of witnessed functional retrograde amnesia. *Cognitive Neuropsychiatry*, 1, 247–58.

Kardash, C. A., Royer, J. M., and Greene, B. A. (1988). Locus of schema effects on prose: encoding or retrieval? *Journal of Educational Psychology*, 80, 324–9.

Karmiloff-Smith, A. (1998). Development itself is the key to understanding developmental disorders. *Trends in Cognitive Sciences*, 2, 289–98.

Karmiloff-Smith, A., Grant, J., Berthoud, J., Davies, M., Howlin, P., and Udwin, O. (1997). Language in Williams syndrome: how intact is "intact?" *Child Development*, 68, 246–62.

Karnath, H.-O., and Perenin, M.-T. (2005). Cortical control of visually guided reaching: evidence from patients with optic ataxia. *Cerebral Cortex*, 15, 1561–9.

Karni, A., Tanne, D., Rubenstein, B., Askenasy, J., and Sagi, D. (1994). Dependence on REM sleep of overnight improvement of a perceptual skill. *Science*, 265, 679–82.

Kasper, L. F. (1983). The effects of linking sentence and interactive picture mnemonics on the acquisition of Spanish nouns by middle school children. *Human Learning*, 2, 141–56.

Kasper, L. F., and Glass, A. L. (1982). The role of the keyword method in the acquisition of Spanish nouns. *Human Learning*, 1, 235–50.

Kattler, H., Dijk, D.-J., and Borbély, A. (1994). Effect of unilateral somatosensory stimulation prior to sleep on the sleep EEG in humans. *Journal of Sleep Research*, 3, 159–64.

Kausler, D. H., and Klein, D. M. (1978). Age differences in processing relevant versus irrelevant stimuli in multiple-item recognition learning. *Journal of Gerontology*, 33, 87–93.

Kavanau, J. (1996). Memory, sleep, and dynamic stabilization of neural circuitry: evolutionary perspectives. *Neuroscience and Biobehavioral Reviews*, 20, 289–311.

Kay, P., and McDaniel, C. K. (1978). The linguistic significance of the meanings of basic color terms. *Language*, 54, 610–46.

Keeney, T. J., Cannizzo, S. R., and Flavell, J. H. (1967). Spontaneous and induced verbal rehearsal in a recall task. *Child Development*, 38, 953–66.

Keil, F. C. (1979). *Semantic and Conceptual Development: An Ontological Perspective*. Cambridge, MA: Harvard University Press.

Keller, C. M., and Keller, J. D. (2008). *Cognition and Tool Use: The Blacksmith at Work*. New York: Cambridge University Press.

Keppel, G., and Underwood, B. J. (1962). Proactive inhibition in short-term retention of single terms. *Journal of Verbal Learning and Verbal Behavior*, 1, 153–61.

Kiger, J. I., and Glass, A. L. (1983). The facilitation of lexical decisions by a prime occurring after the target. *Memory and Cognition*, 11, 356–65.

Kihlstrom, J. F. (1977). Models of posthypnotic amnesia. *Annals of the New York Academy of Sciences*, 296, 284–301.

Kim, J. G., and Biederman, I. (2012). Greater sensitivity to nonaccidental than metric changes in the relations between simple shapes in the lateral occipital cortex. *NeuroImage*, 63, 1818–26.

Kimura, D. (1961). Cerebral dominance and the perception of verbal stimuli. *Canadian Journal of Psychology*, 15, 166–71.

(1967). Functional asymmetry of the brain in dichotic listening. *Cortex*, 3, 163–78.

(1974). Left–right differences in the perception of melodies. *Quarterly Journal of Experimental Psychology*, 16, 355–8.

Kinney, J. A. S., and Luria, D. M. (1970). Conflicting visual and tactual-kinesthetic stimulation. *Perception and Psychophysics*, 8, 189–92.

Kirkpatrick, L. A., and Epstein, S. (1992). Cognitive-experiential self-theory and subjective probability: evidence for two conceptual systems. *Journal of Personality and Social Psychology*, 63, 534–44.

Kirsch, I., and Braffman, W. (2001). Imaginative suggestibility and hypnotizability. *Current Directions in Psychological Science*, 10, 57–61.

Kleiman, G. M. (1975). Speech recoding in reading. *Journal of Verbal Learning and Verbal Behavior*, 14, 323–9.

Klein, G. S. (1964). Semantic power measured through the interference of words with color-naming. *American Journal of Psychology*, 77, 576–88.

Kliegl, R., Nuthmann, A., and Engbert, R. (2006). Tracking the mind during reading: the influence of past, present, and future words on fixation durations. *Journal of Experimental Psychology: General*, 135, 12–35.

Klin, A., Jones, W., Schultz, R., Volkmar, F., and Cohen, D. (2002). Visual fixation patterns during viewing of naturalistic social situations as predictors of social competence in individuals with autism. *Archives of General Psychiatry*, 59, 809–16.

Klinger, L. G., and Dawson, G. (2001). Prototype formation in autism. *Development and Psychopathology*, 13, 111–24.

Kluver, H., and Bucy, P. C. (1937). "Psychic blindness" and other symptoms following bilateral temporal lobectomy. *American Journal of Physiology*, 119, 352–3.

Knecht, S., Dräger, B., Deppe, M., Bobe, L., Lohmann, H., Flöel, A., Ringelstein, E.-B., and Henningsen, H. (2000). Handedness and hemispheric language dominance in healthy humans. *Brain*, 123, 2512–18.

Knierim, J. J., and Van Essen, D. C. (1992). Neuronal responses to static texture patterns in area V1 of the alert Macaque monkey. *Journal of Neurophysiology*, 67, 961–80.

Knight, R. T., Hillyard, S. A., Woods, D. L., and Neville, H. J. (1981). The effects of frontal cortex lesions on event-related potentials during auditory selective attention. *Electroencephalography and Clinical Neurophysiology*, 52, 571–82.

Knight, R. T., Scabini, D., and Woods, D. L. (1989). Prefrontal cortex gating of auditory transmission in humans. *Brain Research*, 504, 338–42.

Knoblich, G., Ohlsson, S., and Raney, G. E. (2001). An eye movement study of insight problem solving. *Memory and Cognition*, 29, 1000–9.

Knopman, D., and Nissen, M. J. (1991). Procedural learning is impaired in Huntington's disease: evidence from the serial reaction time task. *Neuropsychologia*, 27, 245–54.

Knowlton, B. J., Mangels, J. A., and Squire, L. R. (1996). A neostriatal habit learning system in humans. *Science*, 273, 1399–402.

Koch, I., and Hoffman, J. (2000). The special status of locations in sequence learning. *Journal of Experimental Psychology: Learning, Memory, and Cognition*, 26, 863–82.

Koestler, A. (1964). *The Act of Creation*. New York: Macmillan.

Kohler, W. (1925). *The Mentality of Apes*. London: Routledge & Kegan Paul.

Kohn, S. E., and Friedman, R. B. (1986). Word-meaning deafness: a phonological–semantic dissociation. *Cognitive Neuropsychology*, 3, 291–308.

Kolb, B., and Whishaw, I. Q. (1980). *Fundamentals of Human Neuropsychology*. San Francisco: Freeman.

Kolers, P. A. (1976). Reading a year later. *Journal of Experimental Psychology: Human Learning and Memory*, 2, 554–65.

Konkle, T., Brady, T. F., Alvarez, G. A., and Oliva, A. (2010). Conceptual distinctiveness supports detailed visual long-term memory for real-world objects. *Journal of Experimental Psychology: General*, 139, 558–78.

Kopelman, M. D. (2002). Disorders of memory. *Brain*, 125, 2152–90.

Kopelman, M. D., Christensen, H., Puffett, A., and Stanhope, N. (1994). The great escape: a neuropsychological study of psychogenic amnesia. *Neuropsychologia*, 32, 675–91.

Kopelman M.D., Stanhope N., and Kingsley D. (1999). Retrograde amnesia in patients with diencephalic, temporal lobe or frontal lesions. *Neuropsychologia*, 37, 939–58.

Kopera-Frye, K., Dehaene, S., and Streissguth, A. P. (1996). Impairments of number processing induced by prenatal alcohol exposure. *Neuropsychologia*, 34, 1187–96.

Koppel, J., and Berntsen, D. (2015). The peaks of life: the differential temporal locations of the reminiscence bump across disparate cueing methods. *Journal of Applied Research in Memory and Cognition*, 4, 66–80.

Koriat, A., and Fischoff, B. (1974). What day is today? An inquiry into the process of time orientation. *Memory and Cognition*, 2, 201–5.

Kozlowski, L. T. (1977). Effects of distorted auditory and of rhyming cues on retrieval of tip-of-the-tongue words by poets and nonpoets. *Memory and Cognition*, 5, 477–81.

Kozminsky, E. (1977). Altering comprehension: the effect of biasing titles on text comprehension. *Memory and Cognition*, 5, 482–90.

Kroll, J. F., Bobb, S. C., and Hoshino, N. (2014). Two languages in mind: bilingualism as a tool to investigate language, cognition, and the brain. *Current Directions in Psychological Science*, 23, 159–63.

Kroll, N. E. A., Parks, T., Parkinson, S. P., Bieber, S. L., and Johnson, A. L. (1970). Short-term memory while shadowing: recall of visually and aurally presented letters. *Journal of Experimental Psychology*, 85, 220–4.

Krose, B. J. A., and Julesz, B. (1989). The control and speed of shifts attention. *Vision Research*, 29, 1607–19.

Kuhl, P. K., and Rivera-Gaxiola, M. (2008). Neural substrates of language acquisition. *Annual Review of Neuroscience*, 31, 511–34.

Kuhl, P. K., Tsao, F.-M., and Liu, H.-M. (2003). Foreign-language experience in infancy: effects of short-term exposure and social interaction on phonetic learning. *Proceedings of the National Academy of Sciences*, 100, 9096–101.

Labov, W. (1973). The boundaries of words and their meanings. In C.-J. N. Bailey and R. W. Shuy (eds.), *New Ways of Analyzing Variation in English*, 340–73. Washington, DC: Georgetown University Press.

Lagnado, D. A., and Channon, S. (2008). Judgments of cause and blame: the effects of intentionality and foreseeability. *Cognition*, 108, 754–70.

Lane, D. M. (1980). Incidental learning and the development of selective attention. *Psychological Review*, 87, 316–19.

Larkin, J. H., McDermott, J., Simon, D. P., and Simon, H. A. (1980). Expert and novice performance in solving physics problems. *Science*, 208, 1335–42.

Latash, M. L. (2012). *Fundamentals of Motor Control*. New York: Academic Press.

Lawless, H. T., and Cain, W. S. (1975). Recognition memory for odors. *Chemical Senses and Flavor*, 1, 331–7.

Lawrence, D. M. (1971). Two studies of visual search for word targets with controlled rates of presentation. *Perception and Psychophysics*, 10, 85–9.

Lawrence, D. M., and Banks, W. P. (1973). Accuracy of recognition memory for common sounds. *Bulletin of the Psychonomic Society*, 1, 298–300.

Lechner, H. A., Squire, L. R., and Byrne, J. H. (1999). 100 years of consolidation: remembering Müller and Pilzecker. *Learning and Memory*, 6, 77–87.

Lederman, S. J., and Abbott, S. G. (1981). Texture perception in studies of intersensory organization using a discrepancy paradigm and visual versus tactual psychophysics. *Journal of Experimental Psychology: Human Perception and Performance*, 7, 902–15.

LeDoux, J. E. (1993). Emotional networks in the brain. In M. Lewis and J. M. Haviland (eds.), *Handbook of Emotions*, 109–18. New York: Guilford Press.

Leeper, R. (1935). A study of a neglected portion of the field of learning: the development of sensory organization. *Journal of Genetic Psychology*, 46, 41–75.

LePort, A. K., Mattfield, A. T., Dickinson-Anson, H., Fallon, J. H., Stark, C. E., Kruggel, F., Cahill, L., and McGaugh, J. L. (2012). Behavioral and neuroanatomical investigation of highly superior autobiographical memory (HSAM). *Neurobiology of Learning and Memory*, 98, 78–92.

Levin, D. T., and Simons, D. J. (1997). Failure to detect changes to attended objects in motion pictures. *Psychonomic Bulletin and Review*, 4, 501–6.

Levinthal, C. F. (1983). *Introduction to Physiological Psychology*. Englewood Cliffs, NJ: Prentice Hall.

Levitt, D. R., and Teitelbaum, P. (1975). Somnolence, akinesia, and sensory activation of motivated behavior in the lateral hypothalamic syndrome. *Proceedings of the National Academy of Sciences*, 72, 2819–23.

Levy, B. A. (1978). Speech analysis during sentence processing: reading versus listening. *Visible Language*, 12, 81–101.

Levy, J., and Trevarthan, C. (1976). Metacontrol of hemispheric function in human split-brain patients. *Journal of Experimental Psychology: Human Perception and Performance*, 2, 299–312.

(1977). Perceptual, semantic and phonetic aspects of elementary language processes in splitbrain patients. *Brain*, 100, 105–18.

Levy, J., Trevarthan, C., and Sperry, R. W. (1972). Perception of bilateral chimeric figures following hemispheric deconnexion. *Brain*, 95, 61–78.

Lewis, M., Alessandri, S. M., and Sullivan, M. W. (1990). Violation of expectancy, loss of control and anger expressions in young infants. *Developmental Psychology*, 26, 745–51.

Liberman, A. M. (1982). On finding that speech is special. *American Psychologist*, 37, 148–67.

Liberman, A. M., Cooper, F. S., Shankweiler, D. P., and Studdert-Kennedy, M. (1967). Perception of the speech code. *Psychological Review*, 74, 431–61.

Liberman, A. M., Isenberg, D., and Rakerd, B. (1981). Duplex perception of cues for stop consonants: evidence for a phonetic mode. *Perception and Psychophysics*, 30, 133–43.

Lichtenstein, S., and Slovic, P. (1971). Reversals of preference between bids and choices in gambling decisions. *Journal of Experimental Psychology*, 89, 46–55.

Lichtenstein, S., Slovic, P., Fischhoff, B., Layman, M., and Combs, B. (1978). Judged frequency of lethal events. *Journal of Experimental Psychology: Human Learning and Memory*, 4, 551–78.

Lieberman, D. A. (2012). *Human Learning and Memory*. Cambridge University Press.

Lieven, E., Behrens, H., Spears, J., and Tomasello, M. (2003). Early syntactic creativity: a usage-based approach. *Journal of Child Language*, 30, 333–70.

Lindsay, D. S., and Read, J. D. (1994). Psychotherapy and memories of childhood sexual abuse: a cognitive perspective. *Applied Cognitive Psychology*, 8, 281–338.

Lindsay, R. C. L., and Bellinger, K. (1999). Alternatives to sequential lineup: the importance of controlling the pictures. *Journal of Applied Psychology*, 76, 796–802.

Lindsay, R. C. L., and Wells, G. L. (1985). Improving eyewitness identification from lineups: simultaneous versus sequential lineup presentation. *Journal of Applied Psychology*, 70, 556–64.

Loess, H. (1964). Proactive inhibition in short-term memory. *Journal of Verbal Learning and Verbal Behavior*, 3, 362–8.

Loftus, E. F., and Palmer, J. C. (1974). Reconstruction of automobile destruction: an example of the interaction between language and memory. *Journal of Verbal Learning and Verbal Behavior*, 13, 585–9.

Loftus, E. F., and Pickrell, J. E. (1995). The formation of false memories. *Psychiatric Annals*, 25, 720–5.

Loftus, G. R., and Kallman, H. J. (1979). Encoding and use of detail information in picture recognition. *Journal of Experimental Psychology: Human Learning and Memory*, 5, 197–211.

Loftus, G. R., and Patterson, K. K. (1975). Components of short-term proactive interference. *Journal of Verbal Learning and Verbal Behavior*, 14, 105–21.

Lok, C. (2011). Seeing without seeing. *Nature*, 469, 284–5.

Lopez, A. (1995). The diversity principle in the testing of arguments. *Memory and Cognition*, 23, 374–82.

Lorch, R. F. (1978). The role of two types of semantic information in the processing of false sentences. *Journal of Verbal Learning and Verbal Behavior*, 17, 523–37.

(1981). Effects of relation strength and semantic overlap on retrieval and comparison processes during sentence verification. *Journal of Verbal Learning and Verbal Behavior*, 20, 593–610.

Lorenz, K. Z. (1958). The evolution of behavior. *Scientific American*, 199, 67–83.

Loring, D. W., Meador, K. J., Lee, G. P., Murro, A. M., Smith, J. R., Flanigin, H. F., Gallagher, B. B., and King, D. W. (1990). Cerebral language lateralization: evidence from intracarotid amobarbital testing. *Neuropsychologia*, 28, 831–8.

Lubow, R. E. (1965). Latent inhibition: effects of frequency of nonreinforced preexposure of the CS. *Journal of Comparative and Physiological Psychology*, 60, 454–7.

Lucas, M. (2000). Semantic priming without association: a meta-analytic review. *Psychonomic Bulletin and Review*, 7, 618–30.

Luchins, A. S. (1942). Mechanization in problem solving. *Psychological Monographs*, 54, 1–95.

Luchins, A. S., and Luchins, E. (1950). New experimental attempts at preventing mechanization in problem solving. *Journal of General Psychology*, 42, 279–97.

Luck, S. J., and Vogel, E. K. (1997). The capacity of visual working memory for features and conjunctions. *Nature*, 390, 279–81.

Lucy, J. A., and Schweder, R. A. (1979). Whorf and his critics: linguistic and nonlinguistic influences on color memory. *American Anthropologist*, 81, 581–615.

Lum, J. A. G., Conti-Ramsden, G., Page, D., and Ullman, M. T. (2012). Working, declarative and procedural memory in specific language impairment. *Cortex*, 48, 1138–54.

Lupker, S. J. (1979). On the nature of perceptual information during letter perception. *Perception and Psychophysics*, 25, 303–12.

Lupker, S. J., and Katz, A. N. (1981). Input decision and response factors in picture–word interference. *Journal of Experimental Psychology: Human Learning and Memory*, 1, 269–82.

Luria, A. R. (1968). *The Mind of a Mnemonist*. New York: Basic Books.

Lynch, S., and Yarnell, P. R. (1973). Retrograde amnesia: delayed forgetting after concussion. *American Journal of Psychology*, 86, 643–5.

MacDonald, M. C., Pearlmutter, N., and Seidenberg, M. S. (1994). The lexical nature of syntactic ambiguity resolution. *Psychological Review*, 101, 676–703.

MacKay, D. G. (1968). Phonetic factors in the perception and recall of spelling errors. *Neuropsychologia*, 6, 321–5.

(1973). Aspects of the theory of comprehension, memory, and attention. *Quarterly Journal of Experimental Psychology*, 25, 22–40.

Mackie, R. R. (ed.) (1977). *Vigilance: Theory, Operational Performance, and Physiological Correlates*. New York: Plenum Press.

Mackworth, J. F. (1964). Performance decrement in vigilance, threshold, and high-speed perceptual motor tasks. *Canadian Journal of Psychology*, 18, 209–23.

Mackworth, N. H. (1948). The breakdown of vigilance during prolonged visual search. *Quarterly Journal of Experimental Psychology*, 1, 6–21.

MacLean, P. D. (1993). Cerebral evolution of emotion. In M. Lewis and J. M. Haviland (eds.), *Handbook of Emotions*, 67–83: New York: Guilford Press.

MacLeod, C. M. (1991). Half a century of research on the Stroop effect: an integrative review. *Psychological Bulletin*, 109, 163–203.

MacLeod, C. M., and Kampe, K. E. (1996). Word frequency effects on recall, recognition, and word fragment completion tests. *Journal of Experimental Psychology: Learning, Memory, and Cognition*, 22, 132–42.

Maddox, W. T., and Ashby, F. G. (1993). Comparing decision bound and exemplar models of categorization. *Perception and Psychophysics*, 53, 49–70.

Maddox, W. T., and Estes, W. K. (1997). Direct and indirect effects of stimulus frequency effects in recognition. *Journal of Experimental Psychology: Learning, Memory, and Cognition*, 23, 539–59.

Madigan, S. A. (1969). Intraserial repetition and coding processes in free recall. *Journal of Verbal Learning and Verbal Behavior*, 8, 828–35.

Maguire, E. A., Woollett, K., and Spiers, H. J. (2006). London taxi drivers and bus drivers: a structural MRI and neuropsychological analysis. *Hippocampus*, 16, 1091–101.

Makovski, T., and Jiang, Y. V. (2008). Proactive interference from items previously stored in visual working memory. *Memory and Cognition*, 36, 43–52.

Malley, G. B., and Strayer, D. L. (1995). Effect of stimulus repetition on positive and negative identity priming. *Perception and Psychophysics*, 57, 657–67.

Malpass, R. S., and Devine, P. G. (1981). Eyewitness identification: lineup instructions and the absence of the offender. *Journal of Applied Psychology*, 66, 482–9.

Manktelow, K. I., and Over, D. E. (1991). Social roles and utilities in reasoning with deontic conditionals. *Cognition*, 39, 85–105.

Mansour, J. K., Beaudry, J. L., Bertrand, M. I., Kalmet, N., Melsom, E. I., and Lindsay, R. C. L. (2012). Impact of disguise on identification decisions and confidence with simultaneous and sequential lineups. *Law and Human Behavior*, 36, 513–26.

Maquet, P. (2001). The role of sleep in learning and memory. *Science*, 294, 1048–52.

Maratsos, M., and Chalkley, A. (1980). The internal language of children's syntax: the ontogenesis and representation of syntactic categories. In K. E. Nelson (ed.), *Children's Language*, vol. II, 127–214. New York: Gardner Press.

Marcus, G., Pinker, S., Ullman, M., Hollander, M., Rosen, T. J., and Xu, F. (1992). Overregularization in language acquisition. *Monographs of the Society for Research in Child Development*, 57, 1–178.

Markman, E. M., and Wachtel, G. F. (1988). Children's use of mutual exclusivity to constrain the meaning of words. *Cognitive Psychology*, 20, 121–57.

Marshall, S. P. (2007). *Schemas in Problem Solving*. Cambridge University Press.

Marslen-Wilson, W. D. (1975). Sentence perception as an interactive parallel process. *Science*, 189, 226–8.

Marslen-Wilson, W. D., and Welsh, A. (1978). Processing interactions and lexical access during word recognition in continuous speech. *Cognitive Psychology*, 10, 29–63.

Martone, M., Butters, N., Payne, M., Becker, J. T., and Sax, D. S. (1984). Dissociations between skill learning and verbal recognition in amnesia and dementia. *Archives of Neurology*, 41, 965–70.

Massman, P. J., Delis, D. C., Butters, N., Dupont, R. M., and Gillin, J. C. (1992). The subcortical dysfunction hypothesis of memory deficits in depression: neuropsychological validation in a subgroup of patients. *Journal of Clinical and Experimental Neuropsychology*, 14, 687–706.

Mattioli, F., Miozzo, A., and Vignolo, L. A. (1999). Confabulation and delusional misidentification: a four year follow-up study. *Cortex*, 35, 413–22.

Mattis, S., French, J. H., and Rapin, I. (1975). Dyslexia in children and young adults: three independent neuropsychological syndromes. *Developmental Medicine and Child Neurology*, 17, 150–63.

McCann, R. S., and Besner, D. (1987). Reading pseudohomophones: implications for models of pronunciation and the locus of word frequency effect in word naming. *Journal of Experimental Psychology: Human Perception and Performance*, 13, 14–24.

McClain, L. (1983a). Effects of response type and set size on Stroop color–word performance. *Perceptual and Motor Skills*, 56, 735–43.

(1983b). Stimulus–response compatibility affects auditory Stroop interference. *Perception and Psychophysics*, 33, 266–70.

McCloskey, M., Caramazza, A., and Green, B. (1980). Curvilinear motion in the absence of external forces: naive beliefs about the motion of objects. *Science*, 210, 1139–41.

McCloskey, M., and Glucksberg, S. (1979). Decision processes in verifying category membership statements: implications for models of semantic memory. *Cognitive Psychology*, 11, 1–37.

McCloskey, M., and Kohl, D. (1983). Naïve physics: the curvilinear impetus principle and its role in interactions with moving objects. *Journal of Experimental Psychology: Learning, Memory, and Cognition*, 9, 146–56.

McCloskey, M., Wible, C. G., and Cohen, N. J. (1988). Is there a special flashbulb-memory mechanism? *Journal of Experimental Psychology: General*, 117, 171–81.

McConkie, G. W., and Rayner, K. (1975). The span of the effective stimulus during a fixation in reading. *Perception and Psychophysics*, 17, 578–86.

McEvedy, C. J. B., Hendry, J., and Barnes, T. R. E. (1996). Delusional misidentification: the illusion of Fregoli and a dog. *Psychopathology*, 29, 215–17.

McGilly, K., and Siegler, R. S. (1989). How children choose among serial recall strategies. *Child Development*, 60, 172–82.

McKinley, S. C., and Nosofsky, R. M. (1995). Investigations of exemplar and decision bound models in large-size, ill-defined category structures. *Journal of Experimental Psychology: Human Perception and Performance*, 21, 128–48.

McLean, J. P., Broadbent, D. E., and Broadbent, M. H. P. (1982). Combining attributes in rapid sequential visual presentations. *Quarterly Journal of Experimental Psychology*, 35A, 171–86.

Medin, D. L. (1989). Concepts and conceptual structure. *American Psychologist*, 44, 1469 –81.

Medin, D. L., and Schaffer, M. M. (1978). A context theory of classification. *Psychological Review*, 85, 207–38.

Medin, D. L., and Schwanenflugel, P. J. (1981). Linear separability in classification learning. *Journal of Experimental Psychology: Human Learning and Memory*, 1, 335–68.

Medin, D. L., Wattenmaker, W. D., and Hampson, S. E. (1987). Family resemblance, conceptual cohesiveness, and category construction. *Cognitive Psychology*, 19, 242–79.

Meehl, P. (1954). *Clinical versus Statistical Prediction: A Theoretical Analysis and a Review of the Evidence*. Minneapolis: University of Minnesota Press.

Melton, A. W. (1967). Repetition and retrieval from memory. *Science*, 158, 532.

Meltzhoff, A. N. (1988). Immediate and deferred imitation in fourteen- and twenty-four-month-old infants. *Child Development*, 56, 62–72.

Meyer, D. E., and Schvaneveldt, R. W. (1971). Facilitation of recognizing pairs of words: evidence of a dependence between retrieval operations. *Journal of Experimental Psychology*, 90, 227–34.

Meyer, J. A., and Minshew, N. J. (2002). An update on neurocognitive profiles in Asperger syndrome and high-functioning autism. *Focus on Autism and Other Developmental Disabilities*, 17, 152–60.

Meyerowitz, B. E., and Chaiken, S. (1987). The effect of message framing on breast self-examination attitudes, intentions, and behavior. *Journal of Personality and Social Psychology*, 52, 500–10.

Michotte, A. (1963). *The Perception of Causality*. London: Methuen.

Miller, B. L., Boone, K., Cumming, J. L., Read, S. L., and Mishkin, F. (2000). Functional correlates of musical and visual ability in frontotemporal dementia. *British Journal of Psychiatry*, 176, 458–63.

Miller, D. T., Turnbull, W., and McFarland, C. (1989). When a coincidence is suspicious: the role of mental simulation. *Journal of Personality and Social Psychology*, 57, 581–9.

Miller, E. A. (1972). Interaction of vision and touch in conflict and nonconflict form perception tasks. *Journal of Experimental Psychology*, 96, 114–23.

Miller, G. A. (1981). *Language and Speech*. San Francisco: Freeman.

Milner, A. D., and Goodale, M. A. (1995). *The Visual Brain in Action*. Oxford University Press.

Milner, B. (1975). Psychological aspects of focal epilepsy and its neurological management. *Advances in Neurology*, 8, 299–321.

(1995). Aspects of human frontal lobe function. *Advances in Neurology*, 66, 67–84.

Milner, B., Corkin, S., and Teuber, H. L. (1968). Further analysis of the hippocampal amnesic syndrome: 14 year follow-up study of H. M. *Neuropsychologia*, 6, 215–34.

Milner, B., Corsi, P., and Leonard, G. (1991). Frontal-lobe contributions to recency judgements. *Neuropsychologia*, 29, 601–18.

Milner, B., Taylor, L., and Sperry, R. W. (1968). Lateralized suppression of dichotically presented digits after commissural section in man. *Science*, 161, 184–5.

Mitchell, K. J., Johnson, M. K., and Mather, M. (2003). Source monitoring and suggestibility to misinformation: adult age-related differences. *Applied Cognitive Psychology*, 17, 107–19.

Moar, I., and Bower, G. H. (1983). Inconsistencies in spatial knowledge. *Memory and Cognition*, 11, 107–13.

Moates, D. R., and Schumacher, G. M. (1980). *An Introduction to Cognitive Psychology*. Belmont, CA: Wadsworth.

Modigliani, V. (1980). Immediate rehearsal and initial retention interval in free recall. *Journal of Experimental Psychology: Human Learning and Memory*, 6, 241–53.

Mohr, J. P. (1973). Rapid amelioration of motor aphasia. *Archives of Neurology*, 28, 77–82.

(1976). Broca's area and Broca's aphasia. In H. Whitaker and M. A. Whitaker (eds.), *Studies in Neurolinguistics*, vol. I, 201–36. New York: Academic Press.

Molfese, D. L., Nunez, V., Seibert, S. M., and Ramanaiah, N. V. (1976). Cerebral asymmetry: changes in factors affecting its development. *Annals of the New York Academy of Sciences*, 280, 821–33.

Montague, W. E., Adams, J. A., and Kiess, H. O. (1966). Forgetting and natural language mediation. *Journal of Experimental Psychology*, 72, 829–33.

Moore, C., Pure, K., and Furrow, D. (1990). Children's understanding of the modal expression of speaker certainty and uncertainty and its relation to the development of a representational theory of mind. *Child Development*, 61, 722–30.

Moore, J. J., and Massaro, D. W. (1973). Attention and processing capacity in auditory recognition. *Journal of Experimental Psychology*, 99, 49–54.

Moore, R. G., Watts, F. N., and Williams, J. M. G. (1988). The specificity of personal memories in depression. *British Journal of Clinical Psychology*, 27, 275–6.

Moore, V., and Wyke, M. A. (1984). Drawing disability in patients with senile dementia. *Psychological Medicine*, 14, 97–105.

Moray, N. (1959). Attention in dichotic listening: affective cues and the influence of instructions. *Quarterly Journal of Experimental Psychology*, 11, 56–60.

Moray, N., Fitter, M., Ostry, D., Favreau, D., and Nagy, V. (1976). Attention to pure tones. *Quarterly Journal of Psychology*, 28, 271–83.

Morris, J. S., DeGelder, B., Weiskrantz, L., and Dolan, R. J. (2001). Differential extrageniculostriate and amygdala responses to presentation of emotional faces in a cortically blind field. *Brain*, 124, 1241–52.

Morton, J. (1969). Interaction of information in word recognition. *Psychological Review*, 76, 165–78.

(1979). Facilitation in word recognition: experiments that cause changes in the logogen model. In P. A. Kolers, M. E. Wrolstad, and H. Bouma (eds.), *Processing of Visible Language*, vol. I, 259–68. New York: Plenum Press.

Moscovitch, M., and Melo, B. (1997). Strategic retrieval and the frontal lobes: evidence from confabulation and amnesia. *Neuropsychologia*, 35, 1017–34.

Moss, C. S. (1972). *Recovery with Aphasia*. Urbana: University of Illinois Press.

Moyer, R. S. (1973). Comparing objects in memory: evidence suggesting an internal psychophysics. *Perception and Psychophysics*, 13, 180–4.

Moyer, R. S., and Landauer, T. K. (1967). Time required for judgments of numerical inequality. *Nature*, 215, 1519–20.

Mueller, S. T., Seymour, T. L., Kieras, D. E., and Meyer, D. E. (2003). Theoretical implications of articulatory duration, phonological similarity, and phonological complexity in verbal working memory. *Journal of Experimental Psychology: Learning, Memory, and Cognition*, 29, 1353–80.

Mullen, M. K. (1984). Earliest recollections of childhood: a demographic analysis. *Cognition*, 52, 55–79.

Müller, G. E., and Pilzecker, A. (1900). Experimentelle Beitrage zur Lehre vom Gedachtnis. *Zeitung Psychologische Erganzungsband*, 1, 1–300.

Müller, H. J., and Rabbitt, P. M. (1989). Reflexive and voluntary orienting of visual attention: time course of activation and resistance to interruption. *Journal of Experimental Psychology: Human Perception and Performance*, 15, 315–30.

Mullin, J., and Corcoran, D. W. J. (1977). Interaction of task amplitude with circadian variation in auditory vigilance performance. *Ergonomics*, 20, 193–200.

Mundy, P., and Sigman, M. (1989). The theoretical implications of joint-attention deficits in autism. *Development and Psychopathology*, 3, 173–83.

Murphy, G. L., and Smith, E. E. (1982). Basic-level superiority in picture categorization. *Journal of Verbal Learning and Verbal Behavior*, 21, 1–20.

Murray, J. E., Yong, E., and Rhodes, G. (2000). Revisiting the perception of upside-down faces. *Psychological Science*, 11, 492–6.

Myers, J. J. (1984). Right hemisphere language: science or fiction? *American Psychologist*, 39, 315–20.

Myers, C. A., Vandermosten, M., Farris, E. A., Hancock, R., Gimenez, P., Black, J. M., Casto, B., Drahos, M., Tumber, M., Hendren, R. L., Hulme, C., and Hoeft, F. (2014). White matter morphometric changes uniquely predict children's reading acquisition. *Psychological Science*, 25, 1870–83.

Myerson, R., and Goodglass, H. (1972). Transformational grammars of three agrammatic patients. *Language and Speech*, 15, 40–50.

Nachreiner, F. (1977). Experiments on the validity of vigilance experiments. In R. R. Mackie (ed.), *Vigilance: Theory, Operational Performance, and Physiological Correlates*, 665–78. New York: Plenum Press.

Nadel, J., and Butterworth, G. (eds.) (2011). *Imitation in Infancy*. Cambridge University Press.

Nagae, S. (1980). Nature of discriminating and categorizing functions of verbal labels on recognition memory for shape. *Journal of Experimental Psychology: Human Learning and Memory*, 6, 421–9.

Nakayama, K., and He, Z. J. (1995). Attention to surfaces: beyond a Cartesian understanding of focal attention. In T. V. Papathomas, C. Chubb, A. Gorea, and E. Kowler (eds.), *Early Vision and Beyond*, 181–8. Cambridge, MA: MIT Press.

Napier, R. M., Mcrae, M., and Kehoe, E. J. (1992). Rapid reacquisition in conditioning of the rabbit's nictitating membrane response. *Journal of Experimental Psychology: Animal Behavior Processes*, 18, 182–92.

Nazzi, T., Jusczyk, P. W., and Johnson, E. K. (2000). Language discrimination by English-learning 5-month-olds: effects of rhythm and familiarity. *Journal of Memory and Language*, 43, 1–19.

Neal, M. (2012). "Acquired savant" Derek Amato becomes musical prodigy after hitting his head hard diving into shallow end of pool. *New York Daily News*, June 7.

Neely, J. H. (1977). Semantic priming and retrieval from lexical memory: role of inhibitionless spreading activation and limited capacity attention. *Journal of Experimental Psychology: General*, 106, 226–54.

Neill, W. T., and Joordens, S. (2002). Negative priming and multiple repetition: a reply to Grison and Strayer (2001). *Perception and Psychophysics*, 64, 855–60.

Neisser, U. (1963). Decision-time without reaction-time: experiments in visual scanning. *American Journal of Psychology*, 76, 376–85.

(1967). *Cognitive Psychology*. Englewood Cliffs, NJ: Prentice Hall.

Neisser, U., and Harsch, N. (1992). Phantom flashbulbs: false recollections of hearing the news about Challenger. In E. Winograd and U. Neisser (eds.), *Affect and Accuracy in Recall: Studies of "Flashbulb" Memories*, 9–31. New York: Cambridge University Press.

Neisser, U., Winograd, E., Bergman, E. T., Schreiber, C. A., Palmer, S. E., and Weldon, M. S. (1996). Remembering the earthquake: direct experience versus hearing the news. *Memory*, 4, 337–57.

Nelson, T. O., and Batchelder, W. H. (1969). Forgetting in short-term recall: all-or-none or decremental? *Journal of Experimental Psychology*, 82, 96–106.

Newell, A. (1969). Heuristic programming: ill-structured problems. *Progress in Operations Research*, 3, 361–413.

Newell, A., and Simon, H. A. (1972). *Human Problem Solving*. Englewood Cliffs, NJ: Prentice Hall.

Newman, S., Malaia, E., and Seo, R. (2014). Does degree of handedness in a group of right-handed individuals affect language comprehension? *Brain and Cognition*, 86, 98–103.

Newport, E. L., Gleitman, H., and Gleitman, L. R. (1977). Mother, I'd rather do it myself: some effects and noneffects of maternal speech style. In C. E. Snow and C. A. Ferguson (eds.), *Talking to Children: Language*

Input and Acquisition, 109–50. Cambridge University Press.

Nickerson, R. A., and Adams, M. J. (1979). Long-term memory for a common object. *Cognitive Psychology*, 11, 287–307.

Nissen, M. J., and Bullemer, P. (1987). Attentional requirements of learning: evidence from performance measures. *Cognitive Psychology*, 19, 1–32.

Nissen, M. J., Willingham, D., and Hartman, M. (1989). Explicit and implicit remembering: when is learning preserved in amnesia? *Neuropsychologia*, 27, 341–52.

Noice, H. (1992). Elaborative memory strategies of professional actors. *Applied Cognitive Psychology*, 6, 417–27.

Norman, D. A., and Bobrow, D. G. (1975). On data-limited and resource-limited processes. *Cognitive Psychology*, 7, 44–64.

Norman, D. A., and Rumelhart, D. E. (1975). *Explorations in Cognition*. San Franciso: Freeman.

Northdurft, H. C. (1993). The role of features in preattentive vision: comparison of orientation, motion, and color cues. *Vision Research*, 33, 1937–58.

Nosofsky, R. M. (1986). Attention, similarity, and the identification-categorization relationship. *Journal of Experimental Psychology: General*, 115, 39–57.

Nosofsky, R. M., and Johansen, M. K. (2000). Exemplar-based accounts of "multiple-system" phenomena in perceptual organization. *Psychonomic Bulletin and Review*, 7, 375–402.

Nottebohm, F. (1977). Asymmetries in neural control of vocalization in the canary. In S. Harnad, R. W. Doty, L. Goldstein, J. Jaynes, and G. Krauthamer (eds.), *Lateralization in the Nervous System*, 23–44. New York: Academic Press.

Notterman, J. M., and Tufano, D. R. (1980). Variables influencing outflow-inflow interpretations of tracking performance: predictability of target motion, transfer function, and practice. *Journal of Experimental Psychology: Human Perception and Performance*, 6, 85–8.

Novemsky, N., and Kahneman, D. (2005). The boundaries of loss aversion. *Journal of Marketing Research*, 42, 119–28.

Oberauer, K. (2002). Access to information in working memory: exploring the focus of attention. *Journal of Experimental Psychology: Learning, Memory, and Cognition*, 28, 411–21.

Obeson, J. A., Rodriguez-Oroz, M. C., Rodriguez, M., Macia, R., Alvarez, L., Guridi, J., Vitek, J., and DeLong, M. R. (2000). Pathophysiologic basis of surgery for Parkinson's disease. *Neurology*, 55 (Supplement 6), 8–12.

O'Brien, D. P., Braine, M. D. S., and Yang, Y. (1994). Propositional reasoning by mental models? Simple to refute in principle and in practice. *Psychological Review*, 101, 711–24.

Obusek, C. J., and Warren, R. M. (1973). Relation of the verbal transformation and the phonemic restoration effects. *Cognitive Psychology*, 5, 97–107.

Ockelford, A. (2007). A musical module in working memory? Evidence from the performance of a prodigious musical savant. *Musicae Scientiae*, 11, 5–36.

Ojemann, G. A. (1977). Asymmetric function of the thalamus in man. *Annals of the New York Academy of Sciences*, 299, 380–96.

O'Keefe, J., and Dostrovsky, J. (1971). The hippocampus as a spatial map: preliminary evidence from unit activity in the freely-moving rat. *Brain Research*, 34, 171–5.

Ophir, E., Nass, C., and Wagner, A. D. (2009). Cognitive control in media multitaskers. *Proceedings of the National Academy of Sciences*, 106, 15583–7.

Orne, M. T. (1959). The nature of hypnosis: artifact and essence. *Journal of Abnormal and Social Psychology*, 58, 277–99.

(1966). Hypnosis, motivation and compliance. *American Journal of Psychiatry*, 122, 721–6.

(1977). The construct of hypnosis: implications of the definition for research and practice. *Annals of the New York Academy of Sciences*, 296, 14–33.

Ornstein, P. A., Naus, M. J., and Liberty, C. (1975). Rehearsal and organizational processes in children's memory. *Child Development*, 46, 818–30.

Ornstein, R. E. (1969). *On the Experience of Time*. Baltimore: Penguin Books.

Orwell, G. (1949). *Nineteen Eighty-Four*. New York: Harcourt, Brace & World.

Osherson, D. N., Smith E. E., Wilkie, O., Lopez, A., and Shafir, E. (1990). Category-based induction. *Psychological Review*, 97, 185–200.

Ostergaard, A. L. (1994). Dissociations between word priming effects in normal subjects and patients with memory disorders: multiple memory systems or retrieval? *Quarterly Journal of Experimental Psychology A*, 47, 331–64.

Oyebode, F., Edelstyn, N. M. J., Booker, E., and Humphreys, G. W. (1998). Facial processing and the delusional misidentification syndromes. *Cognitive Neuropsychiatry*, 3, 299–314.

Ozonoff, S., Pennington, B. F., and Rogers, S. J. (1991). Executive function deficits in high-functioning autistic individuals: relationship to theory of mind. *Journal of Child Psychology and Psychiatry*, 32, 1081–105.

Packard, M. G. (2009). Anxiety, cognition, and habit: a multiple memory systems perspective. *Brain Research*, 1293, 121–8.

Packard, M. G., Hirsh, R., and White N. M. (1989). Differential effects of fornix and caudate nucleus lesions on two radial maze tasks: evidence for multiple memory systems. *Journal of Neuroscience*, 9, 1465–72.

Packard, M. G., and McGaugh, J. L. (1996). Inactivation of hippocampus or caudate nucleus with lidocaine differentially affects expression of place versus response learning. *Neurobiology of Learning and Memory*, 65, 65–72.

Packard, V. (1957). *The Hidden Persuaders*. New York: McKay.

Paivio, A. (1969). Mental imagery in associative learning and memory. *Psychological Review*, 76, 241–63.

Palmeri, T. J., and Nosofsky, R. M. (2001). Central tendencies, extreme points, and prototype enhancement effects in ill-defined perceptual categorization. *Quarterly Journal of Experimental Psychology*, 54A, 197–235.

Papagno, C., and Baddeley, A. (1997). Confabulation in a dysexecutive patient: implication for models of retrieval. *Cortex*, 33, 743–52.

Papp, K. R., Newson, S. L., McDonald, J. E., and Schvaneveldt, R. W. (1982). An activation-verification model for letter and word recognition: the word-superiority effect. *Psychological Review*, 89, 573–94.

Pardo, J. V., Pardo, P. J., Janer, K. W., and Raichle, M. E. (1990). The anterior cingulate cortex mediates processing selection in the Stroop attentional conflict paradigm. *Proceedings of the National Academy of Sciences*, 87, 256–9.

Parise, E., and Csibra, G. (2012). Electrophysiological evidence for the understanding of maternal speech by 9-month-old infants. *Psychological Science*, 23, 728–33.

Park, D. C., Lautenschlager, G., Hedden, T., Davidson, N. S., Smith, A. D., and Smith, P. K. (2002). Models of visuospatial and verbal memory across the adult life span. *Psychology and Aging*, 17, 299–320.

Parker, E. S., Cahill, L., and McGaugh, J. L. (2006). A case of unusual autobiographical remembering. *Neurocase*, 12, 35–49.

Pascalis, O., de Haan, M., and Nelson, C. A. (2002). Is face processing species-specific during the first year of life? *Science*, 296, 1321–3.

Passolunghi, M. C., Cornoldi, C., and De Liberto, S. (1999). Working memory and intrusions of irrelevant information in a group of specific poor problem solvers. *Memory and Cognition*, 27, 779–90.

Paterson, S. J., Brown, J. H., Gsodl, M. K., Johnson, M. H., and Karmiloff-Smith, A. (1999). Cognitive modularity and genetic disorders. *Science*, 286, 2355–8.

Pauen, S. M. (2012). *Early Childhood Development and Later Outcome*. Cambridge University Press.

Pavlov, I. P. (1927). *Conditional Reflexes: An Investigation of the Physiological Activity of the Cerebral Cortex*. Oxford University Press.

Penfield, W., and Rasmussen, T. (1950). *The Cerebral Cortex of Man: A Clinical Study of Localization and Function*. New York: Macmillan.

Perea, M., and Gotor, A. (1997). Associative and semantic priming effects occur at very short SOAs in lexical decision and naming. *Cognition*, 67, 223–40.

Perea, M., and Rosa, E. (2000). Repetition and form priming interact with neighborhood density at a brief stimulus onset asynchrony. *Psychonomic Bulletin and Review*, 7, 668–77.

Perner, J., Aichhorn, M., Kronbichler, M., Staffen, W., and Ladurner, G. (2006). Thinking of mental and other representations: the roles of left and right temporo-parietal junction. *Social Neuroscience*, 1, 245–58.

Perner, J., Leekam, S. R., and Wimmer, H. (1987). Three-year-olds' difficulty with false belief: the case for a conceptual deficit. *British Journal of Developmental Psychology*, 5, 125–37.

Peterson, L. R., and Peterson, M. J. (1959). Short-term retention of individual items. *Journal of Experimental Psychology*, 58, 193–8.

Pezdek, K., and Hodge, D. (1999). Planting false childhood memories in children: the role of event plausibility. *Child Development*, 70, 887–95.

Phillips, J. R. (1973). Syntax and vocabulary of mothers' speech to young children: age and sex comparisons. *Child Development*, 44, 182–5.

Pillemer, D. B., Picariello, M. L., and Pruett, J. C. (1994). Very long-term memories of a salient preschool event. *Applied Cognitive Psychology*, 8, 95–106.

Pilleri, G. (1979). The blind Indus dolphin, Platanista indi. *Endeavours*, 3, 48–56.

Pinsker, H. M., Hening, W. A., Carew, T. J., and Kandel, E. R. (1973). Long-term sensitization of a defensive withdrawal in *Aplysia*. *Science*, 182, 1039–42.

Piolino, P., Desgranges, B., Belliard, S., Matuszewski, V., Lalevee, C., De La Sayette, V., and Eustache, F. (2003). Autobiographical memory and autonoetic consciousness: triple dissociation in neurodegenerative diseases. *Brain*, 126, 2203–19.

Plomin, R., and Loehlin, J. C. (1989). Direct and indirect IQ heritability estimates: a puzzle. *Behavior Genetics*, 19, 331–42.

Plomin, R., Fulker, D. W., Corley, R., and DeFries, J. C. (1997). Nature, nurture, and cognitive development from 1 to 16 years. *Psychological Science*, 8, 442–7.

Poe, G., Nitz, D., McNaughton, B., and Barnes, C. (2000). Experience-dependent phase-reversal of hippocampal neuron firing during REM sleep. *Brain Research*, 855, 176–80.

Poltrock, S. E., Lansman, M., and Hunt, E. (1982). Automatic and controlled attention processes in auditory target detection. *Journal of Experimental Psychology: Human Perception and Performance*, 8, 37–45.

Pomerantz, J. R. (1981). Perceptual organization in information processing. In M. Kubovy and J. R. Pomerantz (eds.), *Perceptual Organization*, 141–80. Hillsdale, NJ: Erlbaum.

Poole, D. A., and Lindsay, D. S. (1995). Interviewing preschoolers: effects of nonsuggestive techniques, parental coaching, and leading questions on reports of nonexperienced events. *Journal of Experimental Child Psychology*, 60, 129–54.

Posner, M. I. (1994). Attention: the mechanisms of consciousness. *Proceedings of the National Academy of Sciences*, 91, 7398–403.

Posner, M. I., and Cohen, Y. (1984). Components of performance. In H. Bouma and D. Bouwhuis (eds.), *Attention and Performance*, vol. X, *Control of Language Processes*, 531–56. Hillsdale, NJ: Erlbaum.

Posner, M. I., and Keele, S. W. (1968). On the genesis of abstract ideas. *Journal of Experimental Psychology*, 77, 353–63.

Posner, M. I., Nissen, M. J., and Klein, R. M. (1976). Visual dominance: an information-processing accounts of its origins and significance. *Psychological Review*, 83, 157–71.

Posner, M. I., and Petersen, S. E. (1990). The attention system of the human brain. *Annual Review of Neuroscience*, 13, 25–42.

Postman, L., and Phillips, L. W. (1965). Short-term temporal changes in free recall. *Quarterly Journal of Experimental Psychology*, 17, 132–8.

Pothos, E. M., and Wills, A. J. (2011). *Formal Approaches in Categorization*. Cambridge University Press.

Potter, M. C. (1975). Meaning in visual search. *Science*, 187, 965–6.

(1976). Short-term conceptual memory for pictures. *Journal of Experimental Psychology: Human Learning and Memory*, 2, 509–22.

Potts, G. R. (1972). Information processing strategies used in the encoding of linear orderings. *Journal of Verbal Learning and Verbal Behavior*, 11, 727–40.

(1974). Storing and retrieving information about ordered relationships. *Journal of Experimental Psychology*, 103, 431–9.

Povel, D. J., and Collard, R. (1982). Structured factors in patterned finger tapping. *Acta Psychologia*, 2, 107–23.

Prabhakaran, V., Rypma, B., and Gabrieli, J. D. E. (2001). Neural substrates of mathematical reasoning: a fluid magnetic resonance imaging study of neocortical activation during performance of the necessary arithmetic operations test. *Neuropsychology*, 15, 115–27.

Prabhakaran, V., Smith, J. A. L., Desmond, J. E., Glover, G. H., and Gabrieli, J. D. E. (1997). Neural substrates of fluid reasoning: an fMRI study of neocortical activation during performance of Raven's progressive matrices. *Cognitive Psychology*, 33, 43–63.

Proteau, L., Marteniuk, R. G., and Levesque, L. (1992). A sensorimotor basis for motor learning: evidence indicating specificity of practice. *Quarterly Journal of Experimental Psychology*, 44A, 557–75.

Price, J., with Davis, B. (2008). *The Woman Who Can't Forget: The Extraordinary Story of Living with the Most*

Remarkable Memory Known to Science: A Memoir. New York: Free Press.

Pring, L., Woolf, K., and Tadic, V. (2008). Melody and pitch processing in five musical savants with congenital blindness. *Perception*, 37, 290–307.

Prinzmetal, W., and Silvers, B. (1994). The word without the tachistiscope. *Perception and Psychophysics*, 56, 495–500.

Proctor, R. W., and Van Zandt, T. (1994). *Human Factors in Simple and Complex Systems*. Needham Heights, MA: Allyn & Bacon.

Prytulak, L. S. (1971). Natural language mediation. *Cognitive Psychology*, 2, 1–56.

Psalta, L., Young, A. W., Thompson, P., and Andrews, T. J. (2014). Orientation-sensitivity to facial features explains the Thatcher illusion. *Journal of Vision*, 14, 1–10.

Pullum, G. K. (1977). Word order universals and grammatical relations. In P. Cole and J. M. Sadock (eds.), *Syntax and Semantics*, vol. VIII, *Grammatical Relations*, 249–77. New York: Academic Press.

Quas, J. A., Goodman, G. S., Bidrose, S., Piple, M., Craw, S., and Ablin, D. S. (1999). Emotion and memory: children's long-term remembering, forgetting, and suggestibility. *Journal of Experimental Child Psychology*, 72, 235–70.

Rabbitt, P. M. A. (1967). Time to detect errors as a function of factors affecting choice-response time. *Acta Psychologica*, 27, 131–42.

(1968). Three kinds of error-signaling responses in a serial choice task. *Quarterly Journal of Experimental Psychology*, 20, 179–88.

Rabbitt, P. M. A., Lunn, M., and Wong, D. (2008). Death, dropout, and longitudinal measurements of cognitive change in old age. *Journal of Gerontology: Psychological Sciences and Social Sciences*, 63, 271–8.

Rabbitt, P. M. A., Oemetse, M., Scott, M., Thacker, N., Lowe, C., Horan, M., Pendleton, N., Jackson, A., and Lunn, D. (2007). Effects of global atrophy, white matter lesions, and cerebral blood flow on age-related changes in speed, memory, intelligence, vocabulary, and frontal function. *Neuropsychology*, 21, 684–95.

Rabin, M. D., and Cain, W. S. (1984). Odor recognition: familiarity, identifiability, and encoding consistency. *Journal of Experimental Psychology: Learning, Memory, and Cognition*, 10, 316–25.

Rabinowitz, J. C., Mandler, G., and Barsalou, L. W. (1979). Generation-recognition as an auxiliary retrieval strategy. *Journal of Verbal Learning and Verbal Behavior*, 18, 57–72.

Rabinowitz, J. C., Mandler, G., and Patterson, K. E. (1977). Determinants of recognition and recall: accessibility and generation. *Journal of Experimental Psychology: General*, 106, 302–29.

Ramachandran, V. S. (1988). Perceiving shape from shading. *Scientific American*, 259, 76–83.

Ramachandran, V. S., and Blakeslee, S. (1998). *Phantoms in the Brain: Probing the Mysteries of the Human Mind*. New York: William Morrow.

Ramachandran, V. S., Rogers-Ramachandran, D., and Cobb, S. (1995). Touching the phantom limb. *Nature*, 377, 489–90.

Ramachandran, V. S., Rogers-Ramachandran, D., and Stewart, M. (1992). Perceptual correlates of massive cortical reorganization. *Science*, 258, 1159–60.

Rand, T. C. (1974). Dichotic release from masking for speech. *Journal of the Acoustical Society of America*, 55, 678–80.

Randich, A., and Lolordo, V. M. (1979). Associative and nonassociative theories of the UCS preexposure phenomenon: implications for Pavlovian conditioning. *Psychological Bulletin*, 86, 523–48.

Rapcsak, S. Z., Cimino, C. R., and Heilman, K. M. (1988). Altitudinal neglect. *Neurology*, 38, 277–81.

Raphael, B. (1976). *The Thinking Computer*. San Francisco: Freeman.

Rasmussen, T., and Milner, B. (1977). The role of early left-brain injury in determining lateralization of cerebral speech functions. *Annals of the New York Academy of Sciences*, 299, 355–69.

Rastle, K., and Coltheart, M. (1998). Whammies and double whammies: the effect of length on nonword reading. *Psychonomic Bulletin and Review*, 5, 277–82.

Rastle, K., and Coltheart, M. (1999a). Lexical and nonlexical phonological priming in reading aloud. *Journal of Experimental Psychology: Human Perception and Performance*, 25, 461–81.

(1999b). Serial and strategic effects in reading aloud. *Journal of Experimental Psychology: Human Perception and Performance*, 25, 482–503.

Raye, C. L., Johnson, M. K., and Taylor, J. H. (1980). Is there something special about memory for internally generated information? *Memory and Cognition*, 8, 141–8.

Rayner, K. (1975). The perceptual span and peripheral cues in reading. *Cognitive Psychology*, 7, 65–81.

(2009). Eye movements and attention in reading, scene perception, and visual search. *Quarterly Journal of Experimental Psychology*, 62, 1457–506.

Rayner, K., Liversedge, S. P., White, S. J., and Vergilino-Perez, D. (2003). Reading disappearing text: cognitive control of eye movements. *Psychological Science*, 14, 385–8.

Raz, A., Shapiro, T., Fan, J., and Posner, M. I. (2002). Hypnotic suggestion and the modulation of Stroop interference. *Archives of General Psychiatry*, 59, 1155–61.

Reber, A. S. (1989). Implicit learning and tacit knowledge. *Journal of Experimental Psychology: General*, 118, 219–35.

Reber, P. J., and Squire, L. R. (1998). Encapsulation of implicit and explicit memory in sequence learning. *Journal of Cognitive Neuroscience*, 10, 248–63.

Reder, L. M. (1982). Plausibility judgments versus fact retrieval: alternative strategies for sentence verification. *Psychological Review*, 89, 250–80.

Redick, T. S., Shipstead, Z., Harrison, T. L., Hicks, K. L., Fried, D. E., Hambrick, D. Z., Kane, M. J., and Engle, R. W. (2013). No evidence of intelligence improvement after working memory training: a randomized, placebo-controlled study. *Journal of Experimental Psychology: General*, 142, 359–79.

Reese, E., Haden, C. A., and Fivush, R. (1993). Mother–child conversations about the past: relationships of style and memory over time. *Cognitive Development*, 8, 403–30.

Reese, H. W. (1965). Imagery in paired associate learning in children. *Journal of Experimental Child Psychology*, 2, 290–6.

Reicher, G. M. (1969). Perceptual recognition as a function of meaningfulness of stimulus material. *Journal of Experimental Psychology*, 81, 275–80.

Reisberg, D., Baron, J., and Kemler, D. G. (1980). Overcoming Stroop interference: the effects of practice on distractor potency. *Journal of Experimental Psychology*, 81, 275–80.

Reitman, J. S. (1976). Skilled perception in go: deducing memory structures from inter-response times. *Cognitive Psychology*, 8, 336–56.

Reitman, W. R. (1964). Heuristic decision procedures, open constraints, and the structure of ill-defined problems. In M. W. Shelly and G. L. Bryan (eds.), *Human Judgments and Optimality*, 282–315. New York: John Wiley.

Remington, R. (1980). Attention and saccadic eye movements. *Journal of Experimental Psychology: Human Perception and Performance*, 6, 726–44.

Rescorla, R. A., and Heth, C. D. (1975). Reinstatement of fear to an extinguished conditioned stimulus. *Journal of Experimental Psychology: Animal Behavior Processes*, 104, 88–96.

Rescorla, R. A., and Wagner, A. R., (1972). A theory of Pavlovian conditioning: variations in the effectiveness of reinforcement and nonreinforcement. In A. H. Black and W. F. Prokasy (eds.), *Classical Conditioning*, vol. II, *Current Research and Theory*, 64–99. New York: Appleton-Century-Crofts.

Revelle, W., Humphreys, M. S., Simon, L., and Gilliland, K. (1980). The interactive effect of personality, time of day and caffeine: a test of the arousal model. *Journal of Experimental Psychology: General*, 109, 1–31.

Reynolds, B. (1945). The acquisition of a trace conditioned response as a function of the magnitude of the stimulus trace. *Journal of Experimental Psychology*, 35, 15–30.

Reynolds, M., and Brewin, C. R. (1999). Intrusive memories in depression and posttraumatic stress disorder. *Behavior Research and Therapy*, 37, 201–15.

Richardson, R., and Hayne, H. (2007). You can't take it with you: the translation of memory across development. *Current Directions in Psychological Science*, 16, 223–7.

Riggs, L. A. (1971). Vision. In J. W. Kling and L. A. Riggs (eds.), *Woodworth and Schlosberg's Experimental Psychology*, 3rd edn, 273–314. New York: Holt, Rinehart & Winston.

Rips, L. J., Shoben, E. J., and Smith, E. E. (1973). Semantic distance and the verification of semantic relations. *Journal of Verbal Learning and Verbal Behavior*, 12, 1–20.

Robinson, G. M., and Solomon, D. J. (1974). Rhythm is processed in the speech hemisphere. *Journal of Experimental Psychology*, 102, 508–11.

Robinson, J. A. (1976). Sampling autobiographical memory. *Cognitive Psychology*, 8, 578–95.

Rock, I. (1984). *Perception*. New York: Scientific American Books.

Rock, I., and Victor, J. (1964). Vision and touch: an experimentally created conflict between the two senses. *Science*, 143, 594–6.

Roda, C. (ed.) (2014). *Human Attention in Digital Environments*. Cambridge University Press.

Roediger, H. L. (1978). Recall as a self limiting process. *Memory and Cognition*, 8, 54–63.

(1980). The effectiveness of four mnemonics in ordering recall. *Journal of Experimental Psychology: Human Learning and Memory*, 6, 558–67.

Roediger, H. L., and McDermott, K. B. (1995). Creating false memories: remembering words not presented in lists. *Journal of Experimental Psychology: Learning, Memory, and Cognition*, 21, 803–14.

Roediger, H. L., and Neely, J. M. (1982). Retrieval blocks in episodic and semantic memory. *Canadian Journal of Psychology*, 36, 213–42.

Roediger, H. L., and Thorpe, L. A. (1978). The role of recall time in producing hypermnesia. *Memory and Cognition*, 6, 296–305.

Roediger, H. L., Watson, J. M., McDermott, K. B., and Gallo, D. A. (2001). Factors that determine false recall: a multiple regression analysis. *Psychonomic Bulletin and Review*, 8, 385–407.

Rogers, R. D., and Monsell, S. (1995). Costs of a predictible switch between simple cognitive tasks. *Journal of Experimental Psychology: General*, 124, 207–31.

Rosch, E. (1973). On the internal structure of perceptual and semantic categories. In T. E. Moore (ed.), *Cognitive Development and the Acquisition of Language*, 111–44. New York: Academic Press.

(1975). Cognitive representations of semantic categories. *Journal of Experimental Psychology: General*, 104, 192–233.

Rosch, E., Mervis, C. B., Gray, W., Johnson, D., and Boyes-Braem, P. (1976). Basic objects in natural categories. *Cognitive Psychology*, 8, 382–439.

Rose, S. A., Gottfried, A. W., Melloy-Carminar, P., and Bridger, W. H. (1982). Familiarity, novelty and preferences in infant recognition memory: implications for information processing. *Developmental Psychology*, 18, 704–13.

Rosenbaum, D. A. (2009). *Human Motor Control*, 2nd edn. New York: Academic Press.

Rosenbaum, D. A., Loukopoulos, L. D., Meulenbroek, R. G. J., Vaughn, J., and Engelbrecht, S. E. (1995). Planning reaches by evaluating stored postures. *Psychological Review*, 102, 28–67.

Rosenbaum, D. A., Meulenbroek, R. G. J., Vaughn, J., and Jansen, C. (2001). Posture-based motion planning: applications to grasping. *Psychological Review*, 108, 709–34.

Rosenkranz, K., Kacar, A., and Rothwell, J. C. (2007). Differential modulation of motor cortical plasticity and excitability in early and late phases of human motor learning. *Journal of Neuroscience*, 27, 12058–66.

Rosenbloom, M. H., Schmahmann, J. D., and Price, B. H. (2012). The functional neuroanatomy of decision-making. *Journal of Neuropsychiatry and Clinical Neurosciences*, 24, 266–77.

Ross, B. H. (1981). The more the better? Number of decisions as a determinant of memorability. *Memory and Cognition*, 9, 23–33.

Ross, H. A., Russell, P. N., and Helton, W. S. (2014). Effects of breaks and goal switches on the vigilance decrement. *Experimental Brain Research*, 232, 1729–37.

Rossen, M. L., Jones, W., Wang, P. P., and Klima, E. S. (1995). Face processing: remarkable sparing in Williams syndrome. *Genetic Counseling*, 6, 138–40.

Rotello, C. M., and Heit, E. (2000). Associative recognition: a case of recall-to-reject processing. *Memory and Cognition*, 28, 907–22.

Rothi, L. J. G., Ochipa, C., and Heilman, K. M. (1997). A cognitive neuropsychological model of limb praxis and apraxia. In L. J. G. Rothi and K. M. Heilman (eds.), *Apraxia: The Neuropsychology of Action*, 29–49. Hove, UK: Psychology Press.

Rothwell, J. C., Traub, M. M., Day, B. L., Obeso, J. A., Thomas, P. K., and Marsden, C. D. (1982). Manual motor performance in a deafferented man. *Brain*, 105, 515–42.

Rouiller, E. M. (1996). Functional organization of the auditory pathways. In E. Gunter and R. Roman (eds.), *The Central Auditory System*, 3–96. New York: Oxford University Press.

Rouleau, I., Salman, D. P., and Butters, N. (1996). Longitudinal analysis of clock drawings in Alzheimer's and Huntington's disease. *Brain and Cognition*, 31, 17–34.

Rourke, B. P. (1978). Neuropsychological research in reading retardation: a review. In A. L. Benton and D. Pearl (eds.), *Dyslexia: An Appraisal of Current Knowledge*, 141–71. New York: Oxford University Press.

Rovee, C., and Rovee, D. T. (1969). Conjugate reinforcement of infant exploratory behavior. *Journal of Experimental Child Psychology*, 8, 33–9.

Rovee-Collier, C. (1993). The capacity for long-term memory in infancy. *Current Directions in Psychological Science*, 2, 130–5.

Rovee-Collier, C., and Dufault, D. (1991). Multiple contexts and memory retrieval at three months. *Developmental Psychobiology*, 24, 39–49.

Rovee-Collier, C., Earley, L. A., and Stafford, S. (1989). Ontogeny of early event memory III: attentional determinants of retrieval at 2 and 3 months. *Infant Behavior and Development*, 12, 147–61.

Rovee-Collier, C., Griesler, P. C., and Earley, L. A. (1985). Contextual determinants of retrieval in three-month-old infants. *Learning and Motivation*, 16, 139–57.

Rovee-Collier, C., Hankins, E. M., and Bhatt, R. S. (1992). Textons, visual pop-out effects, and object recognition in infancy. *Journal of Experimental Psychology: General*, 121, 436–46.

Rowe, D. C., Jacobson, K. C., and Van den Oord, E. J. C. G. (1999). Genetic and environmental influences on vocabulary IQ: parental education level as moderator. *Child Development*, 70, 1151–62.

Rozenblit, L., and Keil, F. C. (2002). The misunderstood limits of folk science: an illusion of explanatory depth. *Cognitive Science*, 26, 521–62.

Rubin, D. C. (1982). On the retention function for autobiographical memory. *Journal of Verbal Learning and Verbal Behavior*, 21, 21–38.

(2015). One bump, two bumps, three bumps, four? Using retrieval cues to divide one autobiographical memory reminiscence bump into many. *Journal of Applied Research in Memory and Cognition*, 4, 87–9.

Rubin, D. C., and Berntsen, D. (2003). Life scripts help to maintain autobiographical memories of highly positive, but not highly negative, events. *Memory and Cognition*, 31, 1–14.

Rubin, D. C., and Kontis, T. C. (1983). A schema for common cents. *Memory and Cognition*, 11, 335–41.

Rubin, D. C., Wetzler, S. E., and Nebes, R. D. (1986). Autobiographical memory across the adult lifespan. In D. C. Rubin (ed.), *Autobiographical Memory*, 202–21. Cambridge University Press.

Ruff, R. M., Levin, H. S., Mattis, S., High, W. M., Marshall, L. F., Eisenberg, H. M., and Tabaddor, K. (1989). Recovery of memory after mild head injury: a three-center study. In H. S. Levin, H. M. Eisenberg, and A. L. Benton (eds.), *Mild Head Injury*, 176–88. New York: Oxford University Press.

Rumbaugh, D. (2003). *Intelligence of Apes and Other Rational Beings*. New Haven, CT: Yale University Press.

Rumelhart, D. E. (1977). Understanding and summarizing brief stories. In D. LaBerge and S. J. Samuels (eds.), *Basic Processes in Reading: Perception and Comprehension*, 265–303. Hillsdale, NJ: Erlbaum.

Rundus, D. (1971). Analysis of rehearsal processes in free recall. *Journal of Experimental Psychology*, 89, 63–77.

(1973). Negative effects of using list items as recall cues. *Journal of Verbal Learning and Verbal Behavior*, 12, 43–50.

Rundus, D., and Atkinson, R. C. (1970). Rehearsal processes in free recall: a procedure for direct observation. *Journal of Verbal Learning and Verbal Behavior*, 9, 99–105.

Russell, R., Duchaine, B. C., and Nakayama, K. (2009). Super-recognizers: people with extraordinary face recognition ability. *Psychonomic Bulletin and Review*, 16, 252–7.

Russell, W. R., and Espir, M. L. E. (1961). *Traumatic Aphasia: A Study of Aphasia in War Wounds of the Brain*. Oxford University Press.

Ruthruff, E., Pashler, H. E., and Klaassen, A. (2001). Processing bottlenecks in dual-task performance: structural limitations or strategic postponement? *Psychonomic Bulletin and Review*, 8, 73–80.

Rutter, M. (1978). Prevalence and types of dyslexia. In A. L. Benton and D. Pearl (eds.), *Dyslexia: An Appraisal of Current Knowledge*, 3–28. New York: Oxford University Press.

Ryan, C., and Butters, N. (1980). Learning and memory impairments in young and old alcoholics: evidence for the premature-aging hypothesis. *Alcoholism*, 4, 288–93.

(1983). Cognitive deficits in alcoholics. In B. Kissin and H. Begleiter (eds.), *The Biology of Alcoholism*, vol. VII, *The Pathogenesis of Alcoholism: Biological Factors*, 485–538. New York: Plenum Press.

(1984). Alcohol consumption and premature aging: a critical review. In M. Galanter (ed.), *Recent Developments in Alcoholism*, vol. I, 223–50. New York: Plenum Press.

Sachs, J. S., Brown, R., and Salerno, R. A. (1976). Adults' speech to children. In W. van Raffler Engel and Y. Lebrun (eds.), *Baby Talk and Infant Speech*, 240–5. Amsterdam: Swets & Zeitlinger.

Sachs, J. S., and Johnson, M. (1976). Language development in a hearing child of deaf parents. In W. van Raffler Engel and Y. Lebrun (eds.), *Baby Talk and Infant Speech*, 246–52. Amsterdam: Swets & Zeitlinger.

Saffran, J. R. (2001). Words in a sea of sounds: the output of infant statistical learning. *Cognition*, 8, 149–69.

Saffran, J. R., Aslin, R. N., and Newport, E. L. (1996). Statistical learning by 8-month-old infants. *Science*, 274, 1926–8.

Salzarulo, P., and Fagioli, I. (1995). Sleep for development or development for waking? Some speculations from a human perspective. *Behavioural Brain Research*, 69, 23–7.

Sanders, M. S., and McCormick, E. J. (1993). *Human Factors in Engineering and Design*. New York: McGraw-Hill.

Sanna, L. J., and Schwarz, N. (2006). Metacognitive experiences and human judgment: the case of hindsight bias and its debiasing. *Current Directions in Psychological Science*, 15, 172–6.

Santa, J. L., Ruskin, A. B., Snuttjer, D., and Baker, L. (1975). Retrieval in cued recall. *Memory and Cognition*, 3, 341–8.

Sarbin, J. R., and Coe, W. C. (1972). *Hypnosis: A Social Psychological Analysis of Influence Communication*. New York: Holt, Rinehart & Winston.

Saugstad, P. (1955). Problem-solving as dependent on availability of functions. *British Journal of Psychology*, 46, 191–8.

Saugstad, P., and Raaheim., K. (1960). Problem-solving, past experience and availability of functions. *British Journal of Psychology*, 51, 97–104.

Savage-Rumbaugh, S., Shanker, S. G., and Taylor, T. J. (1998). *Apes, Language, and the Human Mind*. New York: Oxford University Press.

Saxe, R., and Baron-Cohen, S. (2006). Editorial: The neuroscience of theory of mind. *Social Neuroscience*, 1, 1–9.

Scarborough, H. S. (1984). Continuity between childhood dyslexia and adult reading. *British Journal of Psychology*, 75, 329–48.

Scarr, S., and Salapatek, P. (1970). Patterns of fear development during infancy. *Merrill-Palmer Quarterly*, 16, 53–90.

Schacter, D. L., Koutstaal, W., Johnson, M. K., Gross, M. S., and Angell, K. E. (1997). False recollection induced by photographs: a comparison of older and younger adults. *Psychology and Aging*, 12, 203–15.

Schatz, C. D. (1954). The role of context in the perception of stops. *Language*, 30, 47–56.

Schiffman, H. R. (1967). Size estimation of familiar objects under informative and reduced conditions of viewing. *American Journal of Psychology*, 80, 229–35.

Schiller, P. H. (1966). Developmental study of color-word interference. *Journal of Experimental Psychology*, 72, 105–8.

Schindler, R. M. (1978). The effect of prose context on visual search for letters. *Memory and Cognition*, 6, 124–30.

Schmitt, V., and Davis, R. (1974). The role of hemispheric specialization in the analysis of the Stroop stimuli. *Acta Psychologica*, 18, 149–58.

Schmolck, H., Buffalo, E. A., and Squire, L. R. (2000). Memory distortions develop over time: recollections of the O. J. Simpson trial verdict after 15 and 32 months. *Psychological Science*, 11, 39–45.

Schneider, W., and Shiffrin, R. M. (1977). Controlled and automatic human information processing I: detection, search, and attention. *Psychological Review*, 84, 1–66.

Schnider, A. (2000). Spontaneous confabulations, disorientation, and the processing of "now." *Neuropsychologia*, 38, 175–85.

Schnider, A. (2001). Spontaneous confabulation, reality monitoring, and the limbic system: a review. *Brain Research Reviews*, 36, 150–60.

Schnider, A., and Ptak, R. (1999). Spontaneous confabulators fail to suppress currently irrelevant memory traces. *Nature Neuroscience*, 2, 677–81.

Schnider, A., Ptak, R., von Däniken, C., and Remonda, L. (2000). Recovery from spontaneous confabulations parallels recovery of temporal confusion in memory. *Neurology*, 55, 74–83.

Schouenborg, J. (2008). Action-based sensory encoding in spinal sensorimotor circuits. *Brain Research Reviews*, 57, 111–17.

Schreibman, L. (1988). *Autism*. London: Sage.

Schuell, H. (1974). *Aphasia Theory and Therapy: Selected Lectures and Papers of Hildred Schuell*. Baltimore: University Park Press.

Schumacher, E. H., Seymour, T. L., Glass, J. M., Fencsik, D. E., Lauber, E. J., Kieras, D. E., and Meyer, D. E. (2001). Virtually perfect time sharing in dual-task performance: uncorking the central cognitive bottleneck. *Psychological Science*, 12, 101–8.

Schvaneveldt, R. W., Durso, F. T., and Mukerji, B. R. (1982). Semantic distance effects in categorization tasks.

Journal of Experimental Psychology: Human Learning and Memory, 18, 1–15.

Schwartz, M. F., Saffran, E. M., and Marin, O. S. (1980). The word order problem in agrammatism I: comprehension. *Brain and Language*, 10, 249–62.

Schwenkreis, P., El Tom, S., Ragert, P., Pleger, B., Tegenthoff, M., and Dinse, H. R. (2007). Assessment of sensorimotor cortical representation asymmetries and motor skills in violin players. *European Journal of Neuroscience*, 26, 3291–302.

Scott, R. M., Baillargeon, R., Song, H., and Leslie, A. M. (2010). Attributing false beliefs about non-obvious properties at 18 months. *Cognitive Psychology*, 61, 366–95.

Scott, S. K., and Wise, R. J. S. (2003). PET and fMRI studies of the neural basis of speech perception. *Speech Communication*, 4, 7–21.

(2004). The functional neuroanatomy of prelexical processing in speech perception. *Cognition*, 92, 13–45.

Seidenberg, M. S., Tanenhaus, M. K., Leiman, J. M., and Bienkowski, M. (1982). Automatic access of the meanings of ambiguous words in context: some limitations of knowledge-based processing. *Cognitive Psychology*, 14, 489–537.

Seidenberg, M. S., Waters, G. S., Barnes, M. A., and Tanenhaus, M. K. (1984). When does irregular spelling or pronunciation influence word recognition? *Journal of Verbal Learning and Verbal Behavior*, 23, 383–404.

Selfe, L. (1977). *Nadia: A Case of Extraordinary Drawing Ability in an Autistic Child*. New York: Harcourt Brace Jovanovich.

(2011). *Nadia Revisited: A Longitudinal Study of an Autistic Savant*. New York: Psychology Press.

Sellers, H. (2010). *You Don't Look Like Anyone I Know*. New York: Riverhead Books.

Shah, A., and Frith, U. (1992). Why do autistic individuals show superior performance on the block design task? *Journal of Child Psychology and Psychiatry*, 34, 1351–63.

Shallice, T. (1999). The origin of confabulations. *Nature Neuroscience*, 2, 588–90.

Shallice, T., and Burgess, W. (1991). Deficits in strategy application following frontal lobe damage in man. *Brain*, 114, 727–41.

Shanon, B. (1979). Yesterday, today, and tomorrow. *Acta Psychologica*, 43, 469–76.

Shatz, M., and Gelman, R. (1973). The development of communication skills: modifications in the speech of young children as a function of listener. *Monographs of the Society for Research in Child Development*, 38, 1–38.

Shaver, P. R., Wu, S., and Schwartz, J. C. (1992). Cross-cultural similarities and differences in emotion and its representation. In M. S. Clark (ed.), *Review of Personality and Social Psychology*, vol. XIII, *Emotion*, 175–212. Newbury Park, CA: Sage.

Shaw, M. L. (1984). Division of attention among spatial locations: a fundamental difference between detection of letters and detection of luminance increments. In H. Bouma and D. Bouwhuis (eds.), *Attention and Performance*, vol. X, *Control of Language Processes*, 109–21. Hillsdale, NJ: Erlbaum.

Sheen, M., Kemp, S., and Rubin, D. C. (2001). Twins dispute memory ownership: a new false memory phenomenon. *Memory and Cognition*, 29, 779–88.

Sheingold, K., and Tenney, Y. J. (1982). Memory for a salient childhood event. In U. Neisser (ed.), *Memory Observed*, 201–12. New York: Freeman.

Shelton, P. A., Bowers, D., and Heilman, K. M. (1990). Peripersonal and vertical neglect. *Brain*, 113, 191–205.

Shepard, R. N. (1967). Recognition memory for words, sentences, and pictures. *Journal of Verbal Learning and Verbal Behavior*, 6, 156–63.

Shiffrin, R. M., and Schneider, W. (1977). Controlled and automatic human information processing II: perceptual learning, automatic attending, and a general theory. *Psychological Review*, 84, 127–90.

Shipstead, Z., and Engle, R. W. (2013). Interference within the focus of attention: working memory tasks reflect more than temporary maintenance. *Journal of Experimental Psychology: Learning, Memory, and Cognition*, 39, 277–89.

Shipstead, Z., Lindsay, R. B., Marshall, R. L., and Engle, R. W. (2014). The mechanisms of working memory capacity: primary memory, secondary memory, and attention control. *Journal of Memory and Language*, 72, 116–41.

Shohamy, D., Myers, C. E., Kalanithi, J., and Gluck, M. A. (2008). Basal ganglia and dopamine contributions to probabilistic category learning. *Neuroscience and Biobehavioral Reviews*, 32, 219–36.

Shokur, S., O'Doherty, J. E., Winans, J. A., Bleuler, H., Lebedev, M. A., and Nicolelis, M. A. L. (2013). Expanding the primate body schema in sensorimotor cortex by virtual touches of an avatar. *Proceedings of the National Academy of Sciences*, 110, 15121–6.

Shor, R. E., and Orne, E. C. (1962). *The Harvard Group Scale of Hypnotic Susceptibility: Form A*. Palo Alto, CA: Consulting Psychologists Press.

Shors, T. J. (2009). Saving new brain cells. *Scientific American*, 300, 46–52.

Shultz, S., and Dunbar, R. I. M. (2010). Species differences in executive function correlate with hippocampal volume and neocortex ratio across nonhuman primates. *Journal of Comparative Psychology*, 124, 252–60.

Shum, M. S. (1998). The role of temporal landmarks in autobiographical memory processes. *Psychological Bulletin*, 124, 423–42.

Shute, B., and Wheldall, K. (2001). How do grandmothers speak to their grandchildren? Fundamental frequency and temporal modifications in the speech of British grandmothers to their grandchildren. *Educational Psychology*, 21, 493–503.

Siegel, B. (1996). *The World of the Autistic Child: Understanding and Treating Autism Spectrum Disorders*. New York: Oxford University Press.

Siegler, R. S., and Stern, E. (1998). Conscious and unconscious strategy discoveries: a microgenetic analysis. *Journal of Experimental Psychology: General*, 127, 377–97.

Sigman, M., and Capps, L. (1997). *Children with Autism: A Developmental Perspective*. Cambridge, MA: Harvard University Press.

Silva, J. A., and Leong, G. B. (1995). Visual-perceptual abnormalities in delusional misidentification. *Canadian Journal of Psychiatry*, 40, 6–8.

Simon, H. A. (1973). The structure of ill-structured problems. *Artificial Intelligence*, 4, 181–201.

Simon, H. A., and Gilmartin, K. (1973). A simulation of memory for chess positions. *Cognitive Psychology*, 5, 29–46.

Simons, D. J., and Ambinder, M. S. (2005). Change blindness. *Current Directions in Psychological Science*, 14, 44–8.

Simons, D. J., and Chabris, C. F. (1999). Gorillas in our midst: sustained inattentional blindness for dynamic events. *Perception*, 28, 1059–74.

Simons, D. J., and Levin, D.T. (1997). Change blindness. *Trends in Cognitive Sciences*, 1, 261–7.

(1998). Failure to detect changes to people in a real-world interaction. *Psychonomic Bulletin and Review*, 5, 644–9.

Simonton, D. K. (1999). Talent and its development: an emergenic and epigenetic model. *Psychological Review*, 106, 435–57.

Sisti, H., Glass, A. L., and Shors, T. J. (2007). Neurogenesis and the spacing effect: learning over time enhances memory and the survival of new neurons. *Learning and Memory*, 14, 368–75.

Skavenski, A. A., and Hansen, R. M. (1978). Role of eye position information in visual space perception. In J. Senders, D. Fisher, and R. Monty (eds.), *Eye Movements and the Higher Psychological Functions*, 15–34. Hillsdale, NJ: Erlbaum.

Slachevsky, A., Pillon, B., Fourneret, P., Renie, L., Levy, R., Jeannerod, M., and Dubois, B. (2003). The prefrontal cortex and conscious monitoring of action: an experimental study. *Neuropsychologia*, 41, 655–65.

Slack, C. W. (1956). Familiar size as a cue to size in the presence of conflicting cues. *Journal of Experimental Psychology*, 52, 194–8.

Slamecka, N. J. (1968). An examination of trace storage in free recall. *Journal of Experimental Psychology*, 76, 504–13.

(1969). Testing for associative storage in multitrial free recall. *Journal of Experimental Psychology*, 81, 557–60.

Sliwinski, M., and Buschke, H. (1999). Cross-sectional longitudinal relationships among age, cognition, and processing speed. *Psychology and Aging*, 14, 18–33.

Slobin, D. I. (1966). Grammatical transformations and sentence comprehension in childhood and adulthood. *Journal of Verbal Learning and Verbal Behavior*, 5, 219–27.

(1973). Cognitive prerequisites for the acquisition of grammar. In C. A. Ferguson and D. I. Slobin (eds.), *Studies of Child Language Development*, 173–208. New York: Holt, Rinehart & Winston.

(1979). *Psycholinguistics*, 2nd edn. Glenview, IL: Scott, Foresman.

Sloboda, J. A., Hermelin, B., and O'Conner, N. (1985). An exceptional musical memory. *Music Perception*, 3, 150–70.

Sloman, S. A. (1993). Feature-based induction. *Cognitive Psychology*, 25, 231–80.

(1998). Categorical inference is not a tree: the myth of inheritance hierarchies. *Cognitive Psychology*, 35, 1–33.

Sloman, S. A., and Lagnado, D. (2015). Causality in thought. *Annual Review of Psychology*, 66, 223–47.

Slovic, P. (1975). Choice between equally valued alternatives. *Journal of Experimental Psychology: Human Perception and Performance*, 1, 280–7.

Smith, E. E., Shoben, E. J., and Rips, L. J. (1974). Structure and process in semantic memory: a featural model for semantic decisions. *Psychological Review*, 81, 214–41.

Smith, K., Shanteau, J., and Johnson, P. (2011). *Psychological Investigations of Competence in Decision Making*. Cambridge University Press.

Smith, L. B., Thelen, E., Titzer, R., and McLin, D. (1999). Knowing in the context of acting: the task dynamics of the A-not-B error. *Psychological Review*, 106, 235–60.

Smith, M. C., and Magee, L. E. (1980). Tracing the time course of picture–word processing. *Journal of Experimental Psychology: General*, 109, 373–92.

Smith, S. M. (1979). Remembering in and out of context. *Journal of Experimental Psychology: Human Learning and Memory*, 5, 460–71.

Smith, S. M. (1982). Enhancement of recall using multiple environmental contexts during learning. *Memory and Cognition*, 10, 405–12.

Smith, S. M., Glenberg, A., and Bjork, R. A. (1978). Environmental context and human memory. *Memory and Cognition*, 6, 342–53.

Smith, S. M., and Vela, E. (2001). Environmental context-dependent memory: a review and meta-analysis. *Psychological Bulletin and Review*, 8, 203–20.

Snow, C. E. (1972). Mothers' speech to children learning language. *Child Development*, 43, 549–65.

(1977). The development of conversation between mothers and babies. *Journal of Child Language*, 4, 1–22.

Snow, C. E., Arlman-Rupp, A., Hassing, Y., Jobse, J., Joosten, J., and Vorster, J. (1976). Mothers' speech in three social classes. *Journal of Psycholinguistic Research*, 5, 1–20.

Snowden, J. S., Goulding, P. J., and Neary, D. (1989). Semantic dementia: a form of circumscribed cerebral atrophy. *Behavioral Neurology*, 2, 167–82.

Snowden, J. S., Griffiths, H. L., and Neary, D. (1995). Autobiographical experience and word meaning. *Memory*, 3, 225–46.

Snyder, A. Z., Abdulleav, Y. G., Posner, M. I., and Raichle, M. E. (1995). Scalp electrical potentials reflect regional cerebral blood flow responses during processing of written words. *Proceedings of the National Academy of Sciences*, 92, 1689–93.

Somberg, B. L., and Salthouse, T. A. (1982). Divided attention abilities in young and old adults. *Journal of Experimental Psychology: Human Perception and Performance*, 8, 651–63.

Somers, D. C., and Sheremata, S. L. (2013). Attention maps in the brain. *WIREs Cognitive Science*, 4, 327–40.

Sorce, J. F., Emde, R. N., Campos, J., and Klinnert, M. D. (1985). Maternal emotional signaling: its effect on the visual cliff behavior of 1-year-olds. *Developmental Psychiatry*, 21, 195–200.

Spanos, N. P., Burgess, C. A., and Burgess, M. F. (1994). Past-life identities, UFO abductions, and satanic ritual abuse: the social construction of memories. *International Journal of Clinical and Experimental Hypnosis*, 42, 433–46.

Sparks, R., and Geschwind, N. (1968). Dichotic listening in man after section of neocortical commissures. *Cortex*, 4, 3–16.

Spearman, C. (1927). *The Abilities of Man*. New York: Macmillan.

Spector, A., and Biederman, I. (1976). Mental set and mental shift revisited. *American Journal of Psychology*, 89, 669–79.

Spence, M. J. (1996). Young infants' long-term auditory memory: evidence for changes in preference as a function of delay. *Developmental Psychobiology*, 29, 685–95.

Sperber, D., Cara, F., and Girotto, V. (1995). Relevance theory explains the selection task. *Cognition*, 57, 31–95.

Sperling, G. (1960). The information available in brief visual presentations. *Psychological Monographs*, 74, 1–29.

Sperling, G., and Weichselgartner, E. (1995). The episodic theory of the dynamics of spatial attention. *Psychological Review*, 102, 503–32.

Spiro, R. J. (1980). Accommodative reconstruction in prose recall. *Journal of Verbal Learning and Verbal Behavior*, 19, 84–95.

Spivey, M. J., McRae, K., and Joanisse, M. F. (eds.) (2012). *The Cambridge Handbook of Psycholinguistics*. Cambridge University Press.

Squire, L. R. (1981). Two forms of human amnesia: an analysis of forgetting. *Journal of Neuroscience*, 1, 635–40.

Squire, L. R., and Slater, P. C. (1975). Forgetting in very long-term memory as assessed by an improved questionnaire technique. *Journal of Experimental Psychology: Human Learning and Memory*, 1, 50–4.

Squire, L. R., Slater, P. C., and Chace, P. M. (1975). Retrograde amnesia: temporal gradient in very long-term memory following electroconvulsive therapy. *Science*, 187, 77–9.

Staller, A., Sloman, S. A., and Ben-Zeev, T. (2000). Perspective effects in nondeontic versions of the Wason selection task. *Memory and Cognition*, 28, 396–405.

Standing, L. (1973). Learning 10,000 pictures. *Quarterly Journal of Experimental Psychology*, 25, 207–22.

Standing, L., Bond, B., Smith, P., and Isely, C. (1980). Is the immediate memory span determined by subvocalization rate? *British Journal of Psychology*, 71, 525–39.

Standing, L., Conezio, J., and Haber, R. N. (1970). Perception and memory for pictures: single-trial learning of 2560 visual stimuli. *Psychonomic Science*, 19, 73–4.

Stanhope, N., Cohen, G., and Conway, M. (1993). Very long-term retention of a novel. *Applied Cognitive Psychology*, 7, 239–56.

Stensola, H., Stensola, T., Solstad, T., Froland, K., Moser, M., and Moser, E. I. (2012). The entorhinal grid map is discretized. *Nature*, 492, 72–8.

Sternberg, R. J. (1985). *Beyond IQ: A Triarchic Theory of Human Intelligence*. Cambridge University Press.

(1988). *The Triarchic Mind: A New Theory of Human Intelligence*. New York: Viking Press.

Sternberg, R. J., Bonney, C. R., Gabora, L., and Merrifield, M. (2012). WICS: a model for college and university admissions. *Educational Psychologist*, 47, 30–41.

Sternberg, R. J., and Pretz, J. E. (2004). *Cognition and Intelligence: Identifying the Mechanisms of the Mind*. Cambridge University Press.

Sternberg, S. (1966). High-speed scanning in human memory. *Science*, 153, 652–4.

Sternberg, S., Knoll, R. L., and Gates, B. A. (1971). Prior entry reexamined: effect of attentional bias on order perception. Paper presented at the annual meeting of the Psychonomic Society meeting, San Antonio, Texas, November 10.

Stevens, A., and Coupe, P. (1978). Distortions in judged spatial relations. *Cognitive Psychology*, 10, 526–50.

Stewart, H. A., and McAllister, H. A. (2001). One-at-a-time versus grouped presentation of mug book pictures: some surprising results. *Journal of Applied Psychology*, 86, 1300–5.

Stickgold, R., James, L., and Hobson, J. (2000). Visual discrimination learning requires sleep after training. *Nature Neuroscience*, 3, 1237–8.

Stickgold, R., Whidbee, D., Schirmer, B., Patel, V., and Hobson, J. (2000). Visual discrimination task improvement: a multi-step process occurring during sleep. *Journal of Cognitive Neuroscience*, 12, 246–54.

Stoke, S. M. (1929). Memory for onomatapes. *Journal of Genetic Psychology*, 36, 594–6.

Strange, D., Hayne, H., and Garry, M. (2008). A photo, a suggestion, a false memory. *Applied Cognitive Psychology*, 22, 587–603.

Stratton, G. M. (1897). Vision without inversion of the retinal image. *Psychological Review*, 4, 341–60.

Strayer, D. L., and Drews, F. A. (2007). Cell-phone-induced driver distraction. *Current Directions in Psychological Science*, 16, 128–31.

Strayer, D. L., Drews, F. A., and Albert, R. W. (2002). Negative priming and stimulus repetition: a reply to Neill and Joordens (2002). *Perception and Psychophysics*, 64, 861–5.

Strayer, D. L., and Grison, S. (1999). Negative identity priming is contingent on stimulus repetition. *Journal of ExperimentalPsychology: Human Perception and Performance*, 25, 24–38.

Strayer, D. L., and Johnston, W. A. (2001). Driven to distraction: dual-task studies of simulated driving and conversing on a cellular telephone. *Psychological Science*, 12, 462–6.

Stroh, C. M. (1971). *Vigilance: The Problem of Sustained Attention*. Oxford: Pergamon Press.

Stroop, J. R. (1935). Studies of interference in serial verbal reactions. *Journal of Experimental Psychology*, 18, 643–62.

Sulin, R. A., and Dooling, D. J. (1974). Intrusions of a thematic idea in retention of prose. *Journal of Experimental Psychology*, 103, 255–62.

Susilo, T., Germine, L., and Duchaine, B. C. (2013). Face recognition ability matures late: evidence from individual differences in young adults. *Journal of Experimental Psychology: Human Perception and Performance*, 39, 1212–17.

Susilo, T., Yovel, G., Barton, J. J. S., and Duchaine, B. C. (2013). Face perception is category-specific: evidence from normal body perception in acquired prosopagnosia. *Cognition*, 129, 88–94.

Suthana, N., Haneef, Z., Stern, J., Mukamel, R., Behnke, E., Knowlton, B., and Fried, I. (2012). Memory enhancement and deep-brain stimulation of the entorhinal area. *New England Journal of Medicine*, 366, 502–10.

Suzuki, A., Stern, S. A., Bozdagi, O., Huntley, G. W., Walker, R. H., Magistretti, P. J., and Alberini, C. M. (2011). Astrocyte–neuron lactate transport is required for long-term memory formation. *Cell*, 144, 810–23.

Suzuki, W. A., and Naya, Y. (2014). The perirhinal cortex. *Annual Review of Neuroscience*, 37, 39–53.

Swets, J. A., Tanner, W. P., and Birdsall, T. G. (1961). Decision processes in perception. *Psychological Review*, 68, 301–40.

Tanenhaus, M. K., Leiman, J. M., and Seidenberg, M. S. (1979). Evidence for multiple stages in the processing of ambiguous words in syntactic contexts. *Journal of Verbal Learning and Verbal Behavior*, 18, 427–40.

Tanji, J., and Hoshi, E. (2008). Role of the lateral prefrontal cortex in executive behavior control. *Physiological Reviews*, 88, 37–57.

Taplin, J. E. (1971). Reasoning with conditional sentences. *Journal of Verbal Learning and Verbal Behavior*, 10, 219–25.

Taplin, J. E., and Staudenmayer, H. (1973). Interpretation of abstract conditional sentences in deductive reasoning. *Journal of Verbal Learning and Verbal Behavior*, 12, 530–42.

Tardiff, T. (1996). Nouns are not always learned before verbs: evidence from Mandarin speakers' early vocabularies. *Developmental Psychology*, 32, 492–504.

Taylor, I. (1976). *Introduction to Psycholinguistics*. New York: Holt, Rinehart & Winston.

Teghtsoonian, R., and Teghtsoonian, M. (1970). Two varieties of perceived length. *Perception and Psychophysics*, 8, 389–92.

Thaler, R. H., and Sunstein, C. R. (2008). *Nudge: Improving Decisions about Health, Wealth, and Happiness*. New Haven, CT: Yale University Press.

Theeuwes, J., Kramer, A. F., and Atchley, P. (1998). Visual marking of old objects. *Psychonomic Bulletin and Review*, 5, 130–4.

(1999). Attentional effects on preattentive vision: spatial precues affect the detection of simple features. *Journal of Experimental Psychology: Human Perception and Performance*, 25, 341–7.

Theeuwes, J., Kramer, A. F., Hahn, S., and Irwin, D. E. (1998). Our eyes do not always go where we want them to go: capture of the eyes by new objects. *Psychological Science*, 9, 379–85.

Theeuwes, J., Kramer, A. F., Hahn, S., Irwin, D. E., and Zelinsky, G. J. (1999). Influence of attentional capture on oculomotor control. *Journal of Experimental Psychology: Human Perception and Performance*, 25, 1595–608.

Thompson, C. (2014). Can video games fend off mental decline? *New York Times, Sunday Magazine*, October 23.

Thompson, P. (1980). Margaret Thatcher: a new illusion. *Perception*, 9, 483–4.

Thompson, R. F. (1986). The neurobiology of learning and memory. *Science*, 233, 941–7.

Thompson-Schill, S. L., Swick, D., Farah, M. J., D'Esposito, M., Kan, I. P., and Knight, R. T. (1998). Verb generation in patients with focal frontal lesions: a neurolopsychological test of neuroimaging findings. *Proceedings of the National Academy of Sciences*, 95, 15855–60.

Thorndyke, P. W. (1977). Cognitive structures in comprehension and memory of narrative discourse. *Cognitive Psychology*, 9, 77–110.

Thurstone, L. L. (1938). *Primary Mental Abilities.* University of Chicago Press.

Tincoff, R., and Jusczyk, P. W. (1999). Some beginnings of word comprehension in 6-month-olds. *Psychological Science*, 10, 172–5.

Tipper, S. P. (2001). Does negative priming reflect inhibitory mechanisms? A review and integration of conflicting views. *Quarterly Journal of Experimental Psychology*, 54A, 321–43.

Tippett, L. J., Miller, L. A., and Farah, M. J. (2000). Prosopamnesia: a selective impairment in face learning. *Cognitive Neuropsychology*, 17, 241–55.

Titchener, E. B. (1908). *Lectures on the Elementary Psychology of Feeling and Attention.* New York: Macmillan.

Todd, T. P., Vurbic, D., and Bouton, M. E. (2013). Behavioral and neurobiological mechanisms of extinction in Pavlovian and instrumental learning. *Neurobiology of Learning and Memory*, 108, 52–64.

Tolman, E. C. (1932). *Purposive Behavior in Animals and Men*. Berkeley: University of California Press.

Toma, R. J., and Tsao, Y.-C. (1985). Interference effects in the picture–word Stroop task. *Perceptual and Motor Skills*, 61, 223–8.

Tomasello, M. (1999). *The Cultural Origins of Human Cognition*. Cambridge, MA: Harvard University Press.

Tomasello, M., and Haberl, K. (2003). Understanding attention: 12- and 18-month-olds know what's new for other persons. *Developmental Psychology*, 39, 906–12.

Tomasello, M., Strosberg, R., and Akhtar, N. (1996). Eighteen-month-old children learn words in non-ostensive contexts. *Journal of Child Language*, 23, 157–76.

Toth, J. P. (1996). Conceptual automaticity in recognition memory: levels-of-processing effects on familiarity. *Canadian Journal of Experimental Psychology*, 50, 123–38.

Townsend, D. J., and Bever, T. G. (2001). *Sentence Comprehension*. Cambridge, MA: MIT Press.

Trabasso, T., Riley, C. A., and Wilson, E. G. (1975). The representation of linear order and spatial strategies in reasoning: a developmental study. In R. Falmagne (ed.), *Reasoning: Representation and Process*, 201–29. Hillsdale, NJ: Erlbaum.

Trainor, L. J., Austin, C. M., and Desjardins, R. N. (2000). Is infant-directed speech prosody a result of the vocal expression of emotion? *Psychonomic Science*, 11, 188–95.

Treat, N. J., and Reese, H. W. (1976). Age, pacing, and imagery in paired-associate learning. *Developmental Psychology*, 12, 119–24.

Treffert, D. A. (2014). Savant syndrome: realities, myths, and misconceptions. *Journal of Autism and Developmental Disorders*, 44, 564–71.

Treisman, A. M. (1964). Verbal cues, language, and meaning in selective attention. *American Journal of Psychology*, 27, 215–16.

Treisman, A. M. (1991). Search, similarity, and the integration of features between and within dimensions. *Journal of Experimental Psychology: Human Perception and Performance*, 17, 252–76.

Treisman, A. M. (1992). Spreading suppression or feature integration? A reply to Duncan and Humphreys. *Journal of Experimental Psychology: Human Perception and Performance*, 18, 589–93.

Treisman, A. M., and Gelade, G. (1980). A feature-integration theory attention. *Cognitive Psychology*, 12, 97–136.

Treisman, A. M., and Gormican, S. (1988). Feature analysis in early vision: evidence from search asymmetries. *Psychological Review*, 95, 15–48.

Treisman, A. M., and Riley, J. G. A. (1969). Is selective attention selective perception or selective response? A further test. *Journal of Experimental Psychology*, 79, 27–34.

Treisman, A. M., and Schmidt, H. (1982). Illusory conjunctions in the perception of objects. *Cognitive Psychology*, 14, 107–41.

Tresilian, J. (2012). *Sensorimotor Control and Learning: An Introduction the Behavioral Neuroscience of Action*. Basingstoke, UK: Palgrave Macmillan.

Troster, A. I., Salmon, D. P., McCullough, D., and Butters, N. (1989). A comparison of the category fluency deficits associated with Alzheimer's and Huntington's disease. *Brain and Language*, 37, 500–13.

Troyer, A. K., Winocur, G., Craik, F. I. M., and Moscovitch, M. (1999). Source memory and divided attention: reciprocal costs to primary and secondary tasks. *Neuropsychology*, 13, 467–74.

Tseng, P., Hsu, T., Muggleton, N. G., Tzeng, O. J. L., Hung, D. L., and Juan, C. (2010). Posterior parietal cortex mediates encoding and maintenance processes in change blindness. *Neuropsychologia*, 48, 1063–70.

Tseng, W., Guan, R., Disterhoft, J. F., and Weiss, C. (2004). Trace eyeblink conditioning is hippocampally dependent in mice. *Hippocampus*, 14, 58–65.

Tsotsos, J. K. (1995). Toward a computational model of visual attention. In T. V. Papathomas, C. Chubb, A. Gorea, and E. Kowler (eds.), *Early Vision and Beyond*, 207–18. Cambridge, MA: MIT Press.

Tucha, O., Smely, C., and Lange, K. W. (1999). Verbal and figural fluency in patients with mass lesions of the left or right frontal lobes. *Journal of Clinical and Experimental Neuropsychology*, 21, 229–36.

Tuddenham, R. D. (1962). The nature and measurement of intelligence. In L. Postman (ed.), *Psychology in the Making*, 469–525. New York: Alfred A. Knopf.

Tulving, E. (1981). Similarity relations in recognition. *Journal of Verbal Learning and Verbal Behavior*, 20, 479–96.

Tulving, E. (1985). Memory and consciousness. *Canadian Psychologist*, 26, 1–12.

Turkewitz, G., and Birch, H. G. (1971). Neurobehavioral organization of the human newborn. In J. Hellmuth (ed.), *Exceptional Infant*, vol. II, 24–40. New York: Brunner.

Tustin, K., and Hayne, H. (2010). Defining the boundary: age-related changes in childhood amnesia. *Developmental Psychology*, 46, 1049–61.

Tversky, A. (1972). Elimination by aspects: a theory of choice. *Psychological Review*, 79, 281–99.

Tversky, A. (1977). Features of similarity. *Psychological Review*, 84, 327–52.

Tversky, A., and Gati, I. (1978). Studies in similarity. In E. Rosch and B. B. Lloyd (eds.), *Cognition and Categorization*, 79–98. Hillsdale, NJ: Erlbaum.

Tversky, A., and Kahneman, D. (1971). Belief in the law of small numbers. *Psychological Bulletin*, 76, 105–10.

(1973). Availability: a heuristic for judging frequency and probability. *Cognitive Psychology*, 5, 207–32.

(1974). Judgments under uncertainty: heuristics and biases. *Science*, 185, 1124–31.

(1978). Causal schemata in judgments under uncertainty. In M. Fishbein (ed.), *Progress in Social Psychology*, 49–72. Hillsdale, NJ: Erlbaum.

(1981). The framing of decisions and the psychology of choice. *Science*, 211, 453–8.

(1982). Evidential impact of base rates. In D. Kahneman, P. Slovic, and A. Tversky (eds.), *Judgment under Uncertainty: Heuristics and Biases*, 153–60. New York: Cambridge University Press.

(1983). Extensional versus intuitive reasoning: the conjunction fallacy in probability judgment. *Psychological Review*, 90, 293–315.

Tversky, A., Sattath, S., and Slovic, P. (1988). Contingent weighting in judgment and choice. *Psychological Review*, 95, 371–84.

Tversky, B. (1981). Distortions in memory for maps. *Cognitive Psychology*, 13, 407–33.

Tyler, C. W. (1995). Cyclopean riches: cooperativity, neurontropy, hysteresis, stereoattention, hyperglobality, and hypercyclopean processes in random-dot stereopsis. In T. V. Papathomas, C. Chubb, A. Gorea, and E. Kowler (eds.), *Early Vision and Beyond*, 5–15. Cambridge, MA: MIT Press.

Ulvund, S. E., and Smith, L. (1996). The predictive validity of nonverbal communicative skills in infants with perinatal hazards. *Infant Behavior and Development*, 19, 441–9.

Umanath, S., Butler, A. C., and Marsh, E. J. (2012). Positive and negative effects of monitoring popular films for historical inaccuracies. *Applied Cognitive Psychology*, 26, 556–67.

Unger, S. M. (1964). Habituation of the vasoconstrictive orienting reaction. *Journal of Experimental Psychology*, 67, 11–18.

Unsworth, N., and Engle, R. W. (2007). The nature of individual differences in working memory capacity: active maintenance in primary memory and controlled search from secondary memory. *Psychological Review*, 114, 104–32.

Unsworth, N., and Spillers, G. J. (2010). Working memory capacity: attention, memory, or both? A direct test of the dual component model. *Journal of Memory and Language*, 62, 392–406.

Uttal, D. H., Meadow, N. G., Tipton, E., Hand, L. L., Alden, A. R., Warren, C., and Newcombe, N. S. (2013). The malleability of spatial skills: a meta-analysis of training studies. *Psychological Bulletin*, 139, 352–402.

Van der Helm, P. A. (2014). *Simplicity in Vision: A Multidisciplinary Account of Perceptual Organization*. Cambridge University Press.

Vandenbossche, J., Deroost, N., Soetens, E., Coomans, D., Spildooren, J., Vercruysse, S., Nieuwboer, A., and Kerckhofs, E. (2013). Impaired implicit sequence learning in Parkinson's disease patients with freezing of gait. *Neuropsychology*, 27, 28–36.

Vargha-Khadem, F., Gadian, D. G., Watkins, K.E., Connelly, A., Van Paesschen, W., and Mishkin, M. (1997). Differential effects of early hippocampal pathology on episodic and semantic memory. *Science*, 277, 376–80.

Vellutino, F. R. (1979). *Dsylexia: Theory and Research*. Cambridge, MA: MIT Press.

Vingerhoets, G. (2014). Contribution of the posterior parietal cortex in reaching, grasping and using objects and tools. *Frontiers in Psychology*, 5, article 151.

Vogt, S., and Magnussen, S. (2007). Long-term memory for 400 pictures on a common theme. *Experimental Psychology*, 54, 298–303.

Vokey, J. R., and Read, J. D. (1985). Subliminal messages: between the devil and the media. *American Psychologist*, 40, 1231–9.

Von Noorden, G. K. (1995). *Binocular Vision and Ocular Motility: Theory and Management of Strabismus*, 5th edn. Toronto: Mosby.

Von Restorff, H. (1933). Über die Wirkung von Bereichsbildungen im Spurenfeld. *Psychologisch Forschung*, 18, 299–342.

Vorster, A. P., and Born, J. (2015). Sleep and memory in mammals, birds and invertebrates. *Neuroscience and Biobehavioral Reviews*, 50, 103–19.

Wade, J. A. (1977). Prelanguage and fundamental asymmetry of the infant brain. *Annals of the New York Academy of Sciences*, 299, 370–9.

Wagner, D. A. (1974). The development of short-term and incidental memory: a cross-cultural study. *Child Development*, 45, 389–96.

Wai, J., and Putallaz, M. (2011). The Flynn effect puzzle: a 30-year examination from the right tail of the ability distribution provides some missing pieces. *Intelligence*, 39, 443–55.

Wainer, H., and Zwerling, H. L. (2006). Evidence that smaller schools do not improve student achievement. *Phi Delta Kappan*, 88, 300–3.

Walden, T. A., and Ogan, T. A. (1988). The development of social referencing. *Child Development*, 59, 1230–40.

Waldmann, M. R., and Dieterich, J. H. (2007). Throwing a bomb on a person versus throwing a person on a bomb: intervention myopia in moral intuitions. *Psychological Science*, 18, 247–53.

Walker-Andrews, A. S. (1986). Intermodal perception of expressive behaviors: relation of eye and voice? *Developmental Psychology*, 22, 373–7.

Walsh, V., and Kulikowski, J. (2010). *Perceptual Constancy: Why Things Look as They Do*. Cambridge University Press.

Waltz, J. A., Knowlton, B. J., Holyoak, K. J., Boone, K. B., Mishkin, F. S., de Menezes Santos, M., Thomas, C. R., and Miller, B. L. (1999). A system for relational reasoning in human prefrontal cortex. *Psychological Science*, 10, 119–25.

Wandell, B. (2011). The neurobiological basis of seeing words. *Annals of the New York Academy of Sciences*, 1224, 63–80.

Wang, Q., Cavanaugh, P., and Green, M. (1994). Familiarity and pop-out in visual search. *Perception and Psychophysics*, 56, 495–500.

Ward, G., and Allport, A. (1997). Planning and problem-solving using the five disc Tower of London. *Quarterly Journal of Experimental Psychology*, 50A, 49–78.

Ward, R. D., Gallistel, C.R., and Balsam, P. D. (2013). It's the information! *Behavioural Processes*, 95, 3–7.

Warlaumont, A. S., Richards, J. A., Gilkerson, J., and Oller, D. K. (2014). A social feedback loop for speech development and its reduction in autism. *Psychological Science*, 25, 1314–24.

Warner, J., and Glass, A. L. (1987). Context and distance-to-disambiguation effects in ambiguity resolution: evidence from grammaticality judgments of garden path sentences. *Journal of Memory and Language*, 26, 714–38.

Warren, D. H., and Cleaves, W. T. (1971). Visual-proprioceptive interaction under large amounts of conflict. *Journal of Experimental Psychology*, 90, 206–14.

Warren, J. M. (1977). Functional lateralization of the brain. *Annals of the New York Academy of Sciences*, 299, 273–80.

Warren, L. R., and Horn, J. W. (1982). What does naming a picture do? Effects of prior picture naming on recognition of identical and same-name alternatives. *Memory and Cognition*, 10, 167–75.

Warren, R. M., Hainsworth, K. R., Brubaker, B. S., Bashford, J. A., and Healy, E. W. (1997). Spectral restoration of speech: intelligibility is increased by inserting noise in spectral gaps. *Perception and Psychophysics*, 59, 275–83.

Warren, R. M., and Obusek, C. J. (1971). Speech perception and phonemic restorations. *Perception and Psychophysics*, 9, 358–62.

Warren, R. M., and Warren, R. P. (1970). Auditory illusions and confusions. *Scientific American*, 223, 30–6.

Warrington, E. K. (1975). The selective impairment of semantic memory. *Quarterly Journal of Experimental Psychology*, 27, 635–57.

Warrington, E. K., and Sanders, H. (1971). The fate of old memories. *Quarterly Journal of Experimental Psychology*, 23, 432–42.

Warrington, E. K., and Weiskrantz, L. (1970). Amnesic syndrome: consolidation or retrieval? *Nature*, 228, 628–30.

(1974). The effect of prior learning on subsequent retention in amnesic patients. *Neuropsychologia*, 12, 419–28.

Wason, P. C. (1966). Reasoning. In B. M. Foss (ed.), *New Horizons in Psychology*, 135–51. Harmondsworth, UK: Penguin Books.

(1968). Reasoning about a rule. *Quarterly Journal of Experimental Psychology*, 20, 273–81.

(1983). Realism and rationality in the selection task. In J. St. B. T. Evans (ed.), *Thinking and Reasoning: Psychological Approaches*, 44–75. London: Routledge & Kegan Paul.

Watkins, O. C., and Watkins, M. J. (1975). Buildup of proactive interference as a cue-overload effect. *Journal of Experimental Psychology: Human Learning and Memory*, 104, 442–52.

Wattenmaker, W. D. (1992). Relational properties and memory-based category construction. *Journal of Experimental Psychology: Learning, Memory, and Cognition*, 15, 282–304.

Watts, F. N., Morris, L., and MacLeod, A. (1987). Recognition memory in depression. *Journal of Abnormal Psychology*, 96, 273–5.

Watts, F. N., and Sharrock, R. (1987). Cued recall in depression. *British Journal of Clinical Psychology*, 26, 149–50.

Weber, E. U., Baron, J., and Loomes, G. (2011). *Conflict and Tradeoffs in Decision Making*. Cambridge University Press.

Weeks, D. J., and Proctor, R. W. (1990). Compatibility effects for orthogonal stimulus–response dimensions. *Journal of Experimental Psychology: General*, 119, 355–66.

Weekes, B. (1997). Differential effects of number of letters on word and nonword naming latency. *Quarterly Journal of Experimental Psychology*, 50A, 439–56.

Weichselgartner, E., and Sperling, G. (1987). Dynamics of automatic and controlled visual attention. *Science*, 238, 778–80.

Weisberg, R. A., and Alba, J. W. (1981). An examination of the alleged role of "fixation" in the solution of several "insight" problems. *Journal of Experimental Psychology: General*, 110, 169–92.

Weisberg, R. A., and Suls, J. (1973). An information-processing model of Duncker's candle problem. *Cognitive Psychology*, 4, 255–76.

Weiskrantz, L. (1956). Behavioral changes associated with ablation of the amygdaloid complex in monkeys. *Journal of Comparative and Physiological Psychology*, 49, 381–91.

Weiskrantz, L., Warrington, E. K., Sanders, M. D., and Marshall, J. (1974). Visual capacity in the hemianopic field following a restricted occipital ablation. *Brain*, 97, 709–28.

Weitzenhoffer, A. M., and Hilgard, E. R. (1959). *Stanford Hypnotic Susceptibility Scale: Forms A and B*. Palo Alto, CA: Consulting Psychologists Press.

(1962). *Stanford Hypnotic Susceptibility Scale: Form C*. Palo Alto, CA: Consulting Psychologists Press.

Wellman, H. M. (1977). Tip-of-the-tongue and the feeling of knowing experience: a developmental study of memory monitoring. *Child Development*, 48, 13–21.

Wells, C. E. (1979). Pseudodementia. *American Journal of Psychiatry*, 136, 895–900.

Weltman, G., Smith, J. E., and Egstrom, G. H. (1971). Perceptual narrowing during simulated pressure-chamber exposure. *Human Factors*, 13, 99–107.

West, L. J. (1967). Vision and kinesthesis in the acquisition of typewriting skill. *Journal of Applied Psychology*, 51, 161–6.

West, T. A., and Bauer, P. J. (1999). Assumptions of infantile amnesia: are there differences between early and later memories? *Memory*, 7, 257–78.

Wheeler, D. D. (1970). Processes in word recognition. *Cognitive Psychology*, 1, 59–85.

Whiten, A., and Byrne, R. W. (1997). *Machiavellian Intelligence II: Extensions and Evaluations*. Cambridge University Press.

Whitten, W. B., and Leonard, J. M. (1981). Directed search through autobiographical memory. *Memory and Cognition*, 9, 566–79.

Wickens, D. D. (1972). Characteristics of word encoding. In A. W. Melton and E. Martin (eds.), *Coding Processes in Human Memory*, 191–215. Washington, DC: Winston.

Wickens, D. D., Born, D. G., and Allen, C. K. (1963). Proactive inhibition and item similarity in short-term memory. *Journal of Verbal Learning and Verbal Behavior*, 2, 440–5.

Wiegmann, A., and Waldmann, M. R. (2014). Transfer effects between moral dilemmas: a causal model theory. *Cognition*, 131, 28–43.

Wilkins, A. J., Binnie, C. D., and Darby, C. E. (1981). Interhemispheric differences in photosensitive epilepsy I: pattern sensitivity thresholds. *Electroencephalography and Clinical Neuropsychology*, 52, 461–8.

Wilkins, A. J., and Lewis, E. (1999). Covered overlays, text, and texture. *Perception*, 28, 641–50.

Wilkins, A. J., and Nimmo-Smith, M. I. (1987). The clarity and comfort of printed text. *Ergonomics*, 30, 1705–20.

Wilkins, A. T. (1971). Conjoint frequency, category size, and categorization time. *Journal of Verbal Learning and Verbal Behavior*, 10, 382–5.

Willems, R. M. (ed.) (2015). *Cognitive Neuroscience of Natural Language Use*. Cambridge University Press.

Willingham, D., Nissen, M. J., and Bullemer, P. (1989). On the development of procedural knowledge. *Journal of Experimental Psychology: Learning, Memory, and Cognition*, 15, 1047–60.

Windes, J. D. (1968). Reaction time for numerical coding and naming of numerals. *Journal of Experimental Psychology*, 78, 318–22.

Winner, E. (2000). Giftedness: current theory and research. *Current Directions in Psychological Science*, 9, 153–6.

Wise, L. A., Sutton, J. A., and Gibbons, P. D. (1975). Decrement in Stroop interference time with age. *Perceptual and Motor Skills*, 41, 149–50.

Witkin, H. A., Goodenough, D. R., and Oltman, P. K. (1979). Psychological differentiation: current status. *Journal of Personality and Social Psychology*, 37, 1127–45.

Wittgenstein, L. (1953). *Philosophical Investigations*. New York: Macmillan.

Witvliet, C. V. (1997). Traumatic intrusive imagery as an emotional memory phenomenon: a review of research and explanatory information processing theories. *Clinical Psychology Review*, 17, 509–36.

Wixon, D. R., and Laird, J. D. (1976). Awareness and attitude change in the forced compliance paradigm: the importance of when. *Journal of Personality and Social Psychology*, 34, 376–84.

Wixted, J. T., and Mickes, L. (2010). A continuous dual-process model of remember/know judgments. *Psychological Review*, 117, 1025–54.

Wollen, K. A., Weber, A., and Lowry, D. (1972). Bizarreness versus interaction of mental images as determinants of learning. *Cognitive Psychology*, 3, 518–23.

Wollett, K., and Maguire, E. A. (2012). Exploring anterograde associative memory in London taxi drivers. *NeuroReport*, 23, 885–8.

Wood, N. L., and Cowan, N. (1995). The cocktail party phenomenon revisited: attention and memory in the classic selective listening procedure of Cherry (1953). *Journal of Experimental Psychology: General*, 124, 243–62.

Woodhead, M. M., and Baddeley, A. D. (1981). Individual differences and memory for faces, pictures, and words. *Memory and Cognition*, 9, 368–70.

Woodruff-Pak, D. S., Papka, M., and Ivry, R. B. (1996). Cerebellar involvement in eyeblink classical conditioning in humans. *Neuropsychology*, 10, 443–58.

Woods, A. J., Hamilton, R. H., Kranjec, A., Minhaus, P., Bikson, M., Yu, J., and Chatterjee, A. (2014). Space, time, and causality in the human brain. *NeuroImage*, 92, 285–97.

Woods, B. T., and Teuber, H. L. (1978). Changing patterns of childhood aphasia. *Annals of Neurology*, 3, 273–80.

Woods, D. L., Knight, R. T., and Scabini, D. (1993). Anatomical substrates of auditory selective attention: behavioral and electrophysiological effects of posterior association cortex lesions. *Cognitive Brain Research*, 1, 227–40.

Woodworth, R. S., and Schlosberg, H. (1954). *Experimental Psychology*. New York: Holt, Rinehart & Winston.

Xiong, J., Rao, S., Gao, J., Woldorff, M., and Fox, P. T. (1998). Evaluation of hemispheric dominance for language using functional MRI: a comparison with positron emission tomography. *Human Brain Mapping*, 6, 42–58.

Yamaguchi, S., and Knight, R. T. (1990). Gating of somatosensory inputs by the prefrontal cortex. *Brain Research*, 521, 281–8.

Yang, Y., and Johnson-Laird, P. N. (2000). Illusions in quantified reasoning: how to make the impossible seems possible, and vice versa. *Memory and Cognition*, 28, 452–65.

Yarbus, A. L. (1967). *Eye Movements and Vision*. New York: Plenum Press.

Yates, F. A. (1966). *The Art of Memory*. London: Routledge & Kegan Paul.

Yerkes, R. M., and Dodson, J. D. (1908). The relation of strength of stimulus to rapidity of habit-formation. *Journal of Comparative Neurology and Psychology*, 18, 459–82.

Yin, H. H., and Knowlton, B. J. (2006). The role of the basal ganglia in habit formation. *Nature Reviews Neuroscience*, 7, 464–76.

Yonelinas, A. P. (2002). The nature of recollection and familiarity: a review of 30 years of research. *Journal of Memory and Language*, 46, 441–517.

Yovel, G., and Duchaine, B. (2006). Specialized face perception mechanisms extract both part and spacing information: evidence from developmental prosopagnosia. *Journal of Cognitive Neuroscience*, 18, 580–93.

Yttri, E. A., Wang, C., Liu, Y., and Snyder, L. H. (2014). The parietal reach region is limb specific and not involved in eye–hand coordination. *Journal of Neurophysiology*, 111, 520–32.

Zahn-Waxler, C., Radke-Yarrow, M., Wagner, E., and Chapman, M. (1992). Development of concern for others. *Developmental Psychology*, 28, 126–36.

Zakay, D., and Glicksohn, J. (1985). Stimulus congruity and S–R compatibility as determinants of interference in a Stroop-like task. *Canadian Journal of Psychology*, 39, 414–23.

Zaragoza, M. S., Payment, K. E., Ackil, J. K., Drivdahl, S. B., and Beck, M. (2001). Interviewing witnesses: forced confabulation and confirmatory feedback increase false memories. *Psychological Science*, 12, 473–7.

Zelazo, P. D., Jacques, S., Burack, J. A., and Frye, D. (2002). The relation between theory of mind and rule use: evidence from persons with autism-spectrum disorders. *Infant and Child Development*, 11, 171–95.

Zelniker, T. (1971). Perceptual attenuation of an irrelevant auditory verbal input as measured by an involuntary verbal response in a selective-attention task. *Journal of Experimental Psychology*, 87, 52–6.

Ziessler, M., and Nattkemper, D. (2001). Learning of event sequences is based on response–effect learning: further evidence from a serial reaction task. *Journal of Experimental Psychology: Learning, Memory, and Cognition*, 27, 595–613.

Zigmond, M. J., and Stricker, E. M. (1989). Animal models of Parkinsonism using selective neurotoxins: clinical and basic implications. *International Review of Neurobiology*, 31, 1–78.

Zoellner, L. A., Foa, E. B., Brigidi, B. D., and Przeworski, A. (2000). Are trauma victims susceptible to "false memories"? *Journal of Abnormal Psychology*, 109, 517–24.

Zola-Morgan, S. M., and Oberg, R. G. (1980). Recall of life experiences in an alcoholic Korsakoff patient: a naturalistic approach. *Neuropsychologia*, 18, 549–57.

Zola-Morgan, S. M., Squire, L. R., and Amaral, D. G. (1986). Human amnesia and the medial temporal region: enduring memory impairment following a bilateral lesion limited to field CA1 of the hippocampus. *Journal of Neuroscience*, 6, 2950–67.

Zurif, E. B., Caramazza, A., Meyerson, R., and Galvin, J. (1974). Semantic feature representations for normal and aphasic language. *Brain and Language*, 1, 167–87.

Zurif, E. B., Swinney, D., Prather, P., Solomon, J., and Bushnell, C. (1993). An on-line analysis of syntactic processing in Broca's and Wernicke's aphasia. *Brain and Language*, 45, 448–64.

GLOSSARY

4b Cells – The cells in the primary visual cortex that receive their input from magnocellular neurons and are most sensitive to motion and contrast, so are responsible for the representation of motion.

Action – The movement of a body part in response to some target perceived by an animal.

Agraphia – The inability to write either spontaneously or two dictation despite a normal ability to make fine motor movements.

Alcoholic Korsakoff's Syndrome – When the anterior thalamic nuclei are destroyed as a result of alcohol abuse coupled with thiamine deficiency and the patient survives the Wernicke's phase of the disorder, the principal symptom is a dense learning deficit.

Alexia – When the pathways by which the visual representations of words are recognized are severed so the words are no longer recognized and reading is impossible.

Ambiguous – When a pattern has more than one representation.

Amygdala – The key structure of the avoidance system. The amygdala aggregates and modulates responses of the superior colliculus and inferior colliculus into a comprehensive orienting or startle response that categorizes the stimuli as good or bad and orients the body towards or away from it and prepares the body for action in response to it. The amygdala also initiates the fear response.

Analysis By Synthesis – The process that converges on a single perceptual representation, through the comparison of ambiguous auditory representations with different syntactic and semantic descriptions until a word sequence that is a meaningful phrase is found.

Analytical Intelligence – The use of a person's semantic knowledge and skills to solve problems.

Anchor Value – An initial generated value that is modified to generate an estimate of something.

Anchoring Effect – The effect of the anchor value on the final estimate.

Anomia – Word-finding difficulty caused by damage to in semantic memory within the left temporal cortex.

Anomic Aphasia – When the only language impairments an individual has are anomia and impaired sentence comprehension.

Anosognosia – When the patient denies having a disability.

Anterograde Amnesia – An inability to remember events that occurred after a brain injury.

Aphasia – An impairment of the ability to understand language.

Apperceptive Visual Agnosia – A form of agnosia resulting from a defect in feature analysis or the integration of visual features into perceptual representations in the occipital cortex.

Apraxia – A collective term referring to an inability to perform voluntary actions caused by brain damage.

Arousal – An integrated set of physiological and neural responses that prepare an animal for action and direct it towards a particular goal.

Associative Advantage – When an animal learns what is good and what is bad.

Associative Memory Test – When recognition of a test word pair requires recollection of the study word pair because test pairs are either intact study pairs or members of two different study pairs.

Associative Stage – The second stage of skill learning, in which performance of the skill still requires voluntary control.

Associative Visual Agnosia – A form of agnosia resulting from a disconnection in the temporal cortex that disrupts the comparison of perceptual representations with object representations in memory.

Ataxia – A motor coordination problem in which walking becomes wobbly, reaching attempts lead to overshoots and it becomes difficult to touch your finger to your nose.

Attention – The ability to control perception so that what is important is seen or heard.

Attentional Blink – The failure to detect one target as the result of detecting another target.

Atypical Instance – An instance that is similar to only a few other instances.

Auditory Cortex – The area of the superior temporal cortex which processes auditory information.

Autism – A disorder in which infants are born without normal social attachments or lose them after a year of life.

Autonomous Stage – The third stage of skill learning, in which the skill does not require conscious direction of each of its component actions.

Autostereogram – Two pictures of the same scene taken from slightly different angles that are printed on top of each other so that when the eyes slightly cross, the images fuse, and the scene is perceived in three dimensions.

Availability – A heuristic in which a decision is made on the basis of the ability to retrieve a few examples in a brief period of time.

Ballistic Phase – The time during a motor movement when there is the least amount of control. During this time most of the distance is covered at maximum velocity.

Base Rates or Prior Odds – Knowledge of the frequency of occurrence of something or its prevalence stated as a proportion of a population.

Basolateral Complex – A neural center within the amygdala which influences the probability that a memory of an experience is formed based on its emotional arousal.

Behavior – A sequence of complimentary actions towards a common purpose.

Binaural Processing – Combining the auditory output of both ears.

Binocular Cells – Cells which process the output from corresponding cells in the right and left retinas stimulated by light from the same location in space.

Bipolar Cells – Sensory neurons which are specialized for the transmission of input from areas of the retina.

Blind Sight – A visual phenomenon in which observers can physically indicate the locations of flashes that they have not seen.

Blind Spot – The point in each retina where the optic pathway exits from it.

Blob Cells – A specific kind of neuron that appears as blobs in the primary visual cortex when stained with a dye. Blob cells are most sensitive to color and contrast and so are responsible for the representation of color.

Bottom-Up Processing – The recoding of sensory features into perceptual relations on the basis of the values and relations among the features in the sensory representation.

Broca's Aphasia / Expressive Aphasia / Nonfluent Aphasia – a syndrome consisting of two distinct deficits: Halting, labored speech, filled with pauses and stutters and impaired syntactic knowledge.

Camouflage – When one pattern is contained in but not perceived as a part of another.

Capgras Delusion – A delusion in which a person comes to believe that an exact duplicate has replaced someone close to them.

Category Instances – When the same action may be performed in similar contexts, to many similar targets, with the same result, the various targets are said to be instances of the same category.

Causal Interpretation Of Prior Odds – When prior odds are considered to plausibly cause variations in the outcome.

Change Blindness – The failure to detect a change in successive images.

Chess – A board game which involved strategically moving pieces named after medieval figures to "take" one another, with the goal being to take the opponent's King.

Chunks – A sequence that has been re-coded in memory as a single item.

Classical or Pavlovian Conditioning – When a stimulus that does not elicit a reflexive response is routinely presented just before the stimulus of the reflexive response and as a result comes to elicit the response.

Clauses – syntactic representations that contain subjects and verbs.

Clusters – Groups of one or more words recalled together during list recall. Cluster members are always obviously related in some way.

Cochlear Nuclei – The structures at the top of the brain stem where the auditory pathway divides into the three main contralateral sub-pathways and subordinate ipsilateral pathways.

Complex Span – An elaboration of the running span task which in which a second task is performed in addition to remembering the items in a sequence.

Conclusion – A statement which is deduced from one or more premises, such that if the premises are true then the conclusion must also be true.

Conditioned Response (CR) – A response which has been conditioned to be elicited by a specific stimulus.

Conditioned Stimulus (CS) – A stimulus which has been condition to elicit a specific response.

Conduction Aphasia – When an aphasic individual has lost the ability to repeat verbal sequences.

Cone Neuron – The photoreceptor cells in the retina which respond must strongly to one of three different wavelengths of light.

Confabulation – A false memory.

Confirmatory Bias – The greater availability of positive examples.

Consciousness – Another name for voluntary action; actions which you choose to perform.

Consolidation – The process by which a memory trace becomes stronger over time.

Context-Dependent Recall – When recall of something is better in the context in which it was learned.

Contralateral – The term for opposite when describing hemispheric control, as the left hemisphere controls the right side of the body and the right hemisphere controls the left side of the body.

Corpus Callosum – The structure which transmits information between the left and right cortex.

Correct Rejection – Within the framework of signal detection theory, classifying a distracter as a distracter or noise as noise. More generally, perceiving something novel as novel something absent as absent.

Cortex – The thick outer layer of the forebrain.

Cranial Reflexes – Reflexes in the head.

Creative Intelligence – The ability to perform novel tasks and to create original solutions to problems.

Cryptomnesia – Saying something without being aware that some else has said it earlier.

Crystallized Intelligence – Knowledge and skills that assist cognitive performance.

d′ – The distance between the means of the signal and noise distributions in signal detection theory.

Declarative Memory – Awareness that something has been encountered or done before. Called "knowing what" in philosophy.

Declarative Stage – The first stage of skill learning, in which the individual knows what must be done but does not yet know how to do it.

Deep Dyslexia – When the connection between the phonemic and visual representations of a word is severed.

Delay Conditioning – Conditioning in which the onset of the unconditioned stimulus occurs before the offset of the novel stimulus that is being conditioned.

Delayed Auditory Feedback (DAF) – People speak into microphones while their own speech is played back to them through earphones two-thirds of a second later.

Developmental Prosopagnosia (Face Blindness) – An inability from birth to learn to recognize faces.

Deviation Score – A score which indicates how far an individual's intelligence score deviates (above or below) the mean of the normal population.

Dichotic Presentation – When different speech sounds are presented simultaneously to each ear.

Diffuse System – The subsystem of the auditory pathways which carries information for stress and rhythm.

Disparities – Differences between the right and left retinal images.

Distributed or Spaced Presentation – Intermittent presentation over an extended interval.

Dyslexia – Difficulty in learning to read.

Dysprosody – Inaccurate pitch, rhythm, inflection, intonation, pace, and/or articulation in speech.

Early Infantile Autism – A disorder in which, beginning in infancy, there is an inability to develop normal social relations with people.

Early Selection – Selection of a target based on its perceptual features.

Echolalia – The repetition of words or phrases spoken by others with no apparent intent to communicate.

Electroencephalogram (EEG) – An apparatus which records electrical activity in the brain through electrodes placed on the scalp.

Electronic Convulsive Therapy (ECT) – Therapy technique in which an electric shock is applied to the brain in order to induce a seizure.

Emotional State – The internally generated evaluative response to an experience that is perceived as part of the experience.

Endo-Akinesia – The inability to make a voluntary movement without an external stimulus.

Endowment Effect – People assign more value to things which they own than to things which they could acquire, as we are more prone towards avoiding emotional pain of loss.

Episode – The basic unit of memory, consisting of an action, its target, is consequence, and its context.

Episodic Memory – Memory of a personal experience.

Event-Related Potential (ERP) – An increase in electrical activity in a specific region in the brain in response to a specific event.

Exception Effect – Skilled readers are slower to pronounce low-frequency, irregularly pronounced, exception words than regular words.

External Source Amnesia – Integrating information into a single narrative in memory without preserving when and where each fact was read or heard.

Extinction – When a conditioned stimulus is consistently presented alone so until it no longer elicits the unconditioned response.

False Alarm – Within the framework of signal detection theory classifying a distractor as a target or classifying noise as a signal. More generally, recognizing as old something that one has not seen or heard before.

Familiarity – The perception that something has been experienced or done in the past.

Familiarity Judgment – Making a judgment as to an object's familiarity on the basis of its perceived familiarity.

Familiarity Response – The perception that something has been experienced or done in the past.

Feature Analysis – The second stage of perceptual processing, in which the input is analyzed as maps of features.

Features – Details of the sensory input used to construct its perceptual representation.

Finite-State Network – A formal representation consisting of causal chains.

Fitts' Law – An equation which describes the relationship between movement time and the distance and size of the target.

Flashbulb Memories – Memories of events that evoked strong emotions and are recalled with special vividness.

Fluid Intelligence – The ability of the instrumental system to generate ad hoc responses to novel situations.

Forebrain – The area above the midbrain, by far the largest part of the brain in mammals, which controls cognitive and emotional processing in mammals.

Form Cue – A cue whose perceptual representation is similar to the perceptual representation of the target.

Fovea – The area near the center of the retina most tightly packed with rod neurons and containing virtually of the cone neurons.

Framing – Whether a choice is framed as a gain or loss scenario influences which choice is selected, because emotion guides opposite choices for gains versus losses.

Frontal Eye Fields – A region of the frontal cortex which is responsible for voluntary, non-tracking eye movements.

Fronto-Temporal Dementia – Dementia which afflicts the frontal cortex, the temporal cortex, or both.

Functional Fixedness – A phenomenon in which, if an object has one established use in a situation, subjects have difficulty in imagining using the object in another way.

Ganglion – Cells within the retina which receive signals from bipolar cells.

Garden Path Sentence – An sentence in which the ambiguity occurs early in the sentence and is only resolved late in the sentence such that only one interpretation of the ambiguity results in a meaningful sentence and for which the interpretation that does not result in a meaningful sentence is more likely to be selected before the point of resolution is reached.

Gaze Aversion – When autistic children do not make eye contact when interacting, often actively avoiding it.

Geons – the representations of convex shapes that are assembled in the construction of the representation of a three-dimensional object by the visual system.

Global Features (Spatial Relations) – Features defined by the spatial relations among local features.

Goal – The intended result of an action.

Good Part (Gestalt) – An apparent part of an image that results from the perceptual representation of the part being a distinct component of the perceptual representation of the entire image.

Grid Cells – Cells in the entorhinal cortex which encode the location of an animal as it moves from place to place.

Habit System – The system responsible for encoding sequences of actions repeatedly performed to a target.

Habituation – Repeated presentation of weak stimulus produces successively weaker responses until even a normal stimulus fails to elicit the response.

Hemiballismus – A rare disorder resulting from damage to the subthalamic nucleus that results in precise voluntary action being replaced by violent, flinging motions.

Hemiplegia – Paralysis resulting from damage to any part of the body map in the motor area.

Heterarchy – An organization of a perceptual or motor processing system consisting of parallel sequential pathways over which different features of the same input are first analyzed separately and then combined in a single representation or action.

Heuristic – A decision procedure that usually gives the correct answer, but is not guaranteed to do so.

Hindsight Bias – When the probability of an event is judged as greater after it occurs.

Hippocampus – The small, sea-horse shaped structure within the temporal cortex which makes trace conditioning possible, encodes mental maps, and generates the awareness of temporal order among the immediate experiences that comprise short-term memory.

Hit – Within the framework of signal detection theory, classifying a target as a target or a signal as a signal. More generally, perceiving something that is there or recognizing something one has seen before.

Homophones – Two different letter sequences that are pronounced the same way.

How Pathway – The visual pathway used to direct voluntary action, which extends upwards from the thalamus and occipital cortex into the parietal cortex.

Hue – A perception largely determined by the wavelength of light.

Huntington's Disease – A disease caused by deterioration of nuclei in the striatum, ultimately resulting ultimately in the inability to perform voluntary actions.

Hypermnesia – When the total number of items recalled is higher on a later test than on an earlier test.

Identification – The third stage of attention, in which a match between the target representation and the perceptual of input at some location causes a response indicating that the target has been found.

Illusion of Explanatory Depth – The assumption that you understand the cause of something when you do not.

Illusory Conjunctions – When two perceptual features that occurred at different locations are perceived to have occurred at the same location.

Implicit Learning – Changes in behavior as a result of experience without any accompanying memories of the experience.

Infant Swim Reflex – When a newborn infant is placed in water, the infant swims for a few meters.

Inhibition – Reducing activation.

Insight – When an individual suddenly becomes aware of the solution to a problem.

Instrumental System – The system responsible that constructs a mental map of the environment and uses it to direct ad hoc voluntary responses, hence controlling an animal's response in a novel context.

Intention – When the plan and execution of an action are separated in time, the plan to perform the action at some point in the future is an intention.

Interblob Cells – The cells that fall between blob cells in the primary visual area and are sensitive to location and orientation and so are responsible for the representation of form.

Inter-Modal Pathways – Pathways between representations in different perceptual modalities.

Internal Source Amnesia – The inability to distinguish whether one merely thought of or actually did something.

Intersegmental Reflexes – Spinal reflexes whose junctions between the stimulus and response are in the brain stem.

Inter-Stimulus Interval (ISI) – The interval in between the presentation of successive stimuli.

Intra-Modal Pathways – Pathways between representations within the same perceptual modality.

Joint Attention – When one person is aware of the target of another's attention. Joint attention makes learning the names of objects possible because when the adult utters a new word the infant knows what is being named.

Kinesthetic System – The system which detects body movements and the locations in space of body parts.

Knowledge – A representation of something in the world.

Late Selection – When a target can only be found by successively comparing perceptual representations at different locations with the target representation.

Lateral Geniculate Nucleus (LGN) – The lateral region of the geniculate nucleus, whose principal function is to encode visual information from the retina into different features that are transmitted to the primary visual area in the occipital cortex.

Lateral Lemniscus – The structure at the base of the inferior colliculus that refines binaural representations.

Learning or Operant Conditioning – When a reward follows a voluntary action increases the probability that this action will be performed again.

Lexical Ambiguity – When a word has more than one meaning and/or pronunciation.

Lightning Calculator – A person with the exceptional ability to perform complex numerical calculations in their head.

Lobes – The four different areas of the cortex.

Local Feature – A feature defined by the intersections and orientations among a small number of lines, all close to a single location.

Locomotion System – The motor system which moves the torso and limbs to make it possible for us to crawl, walk, skip, run, jump, climb, swim, etc.

Logogens – The response nodes for words.

Long-Term Depression (LTD) – When learning is associated with a decrease in strength for some neurons associated with the response.

Loss Aversion – The preference to avoid the possibility of a loss rather than risk it to achieve an equal sized, equally probable gain.

Magnocellular Neurons – Large neurons in the lateral geniculate nucleus.

Manipulation System – The motor system which moves the fingers and hands for grasping, catching, writing, pointing, gesturing, etc.

Mask – One of two patterns presented sequentially in the same location that renders the other invisible.

Masked Prime – A masked word which reduces the time to perceive a word that immediately follows it.

Massa Intermedia – The structure which transmits information between the left and right thalamus.

Massed Presentation – Repeated presentation over a brief interval.

Metamemory – An understanding of one's own memory abilities.

Miss – Within the framework of signal detection theory, classifying a target as a distracter or a signal as noise. More generally, a failure to perceive or recognize something.

Modal Action Pattern – A complex sequence of reflexive responses over time in response to a single stimulus for a single purpose.

Modus Ponens – If p, then q. P, therefore q.

Modus Tollens – If p, then q. Not q, therefore not p.

Monocular Neurons – Neurons which process the visual information from cells in a single retina.

Motivated Forgetting or Fugue State – Avoiding a personal crisis by forgetting it, by forgetting one's own identity.

Motor Cortex – The region of the posterior frontal lobe which guides the direction of a body part's movement.

Motor Neglect – The failure to make responses with a particular portion of the body.

Motor Neurons – Response neurons that initiate muscle contraction or relaxation, producing body movement.

Motor Plan – A representation of the final posture of a body part that is moved to achieve a purposeful action.

Negative Priming – When inhibiting an action or representation on one trial slowed its activation on the very next trial.

Neocerebellum – The part of the cerebellum which turns motor plans into motor programs transmitted to the brain stem.

Nervous System – The system of neurons that transmits signals throughout the body and regulates the activities of the various systems in the body.

Neurogenesis – The birth of new neurons in the brain.
Neuropathy – A rare disability in which a patient loses the sensory neurons in a limb so there is no proprioceptive feedback to guide movement.
Neurotransmitter – A chemical signal released by a neuron that floats across the synapse, is taken up by the next neuron and stimulates it.
Non-Accidental Properties – The parts of a figure that have similar representations in different orientations.
Novel Stimulus – A stimulus which has not been recently perceived.
Nucleus Accumbens – The pleasure center of the brain, located at the tip of the caudate.
Object Construction Stage – The stage of perceptual processing in which pattern representations corresponding to surfaces are combined and compared with memory to construct shape representations.
Occlusion – When surfaces overlap so that one covers the other.
Onset – The initial vowel or consonant cluster of a word.
Optic Pathway – The neural pathway from the retina to the superior colliculus, thalamus, parietal cortex, and occipital cortex.
Orbitofrontal Cortex – The lower area of the frontal cortex.
Orientation Features – The simplest local features, which respond to the orientation of lines.
Orientation Reaction or Orienting Response – A collection of reflexes that direct perceptual processing to a novel input.
Parafovea – The area of the retina immediately outside the fovea.
Parkinson's Disease – A disease caused by damage to the substantia nigra, ultimately resulting in an inability to initiate voluntary action in the absence of a strong stimulus.
Parvocellular Neurons – Small neurons in the lateral geniculate nucleus.
Perception – The process of using sensory input to construct a representation of the surroundings.
Performance Advantage – The improvement in performance on a motor or perceptual task as the result of practice.
Perseveration – The inability to alter a previously correct response when a new response is called for.
Phonemes – The smallest part of the speech input that makes a difference in a word's meaning.
Phonemic Restoration Effect – When part of a word in a sentence is occluded by a non-speech sound, the entire word is heard.
Phonological Loop – When saying something generates a phonological representation, which activates the corresponding articulatory representation, which can be executed to say it again.
Photoreceptors – Collective term for rods and cones.
Phrases – A short meaningful sequence of words containing a noun phrase that is related to another phrase.
Pincer Grip – An innate motor program for gripping objects between the thumb and index finger.
Place Cells – Cells in the hippocampus that are activated every time an animal returns to the same location.
Place Learning – When an animal forms a mental map of its surroundings, using this map to reach a goal.
Polymodal Representation – Representations involving more than one sensory modality and more than one representation.
Polysensory System – The subsystem of the auditory pathways which carries information for cross-modal integration.
Pop Out – An area of the visual field that is perceived as distinct because it has a distinctive feature that causes the visual system to organize it as a discrete and distinctive part of the representation of the visual field.

Posterior Parietal Cortex – The posterior area of the parietal cortex, which is involved in sensory-motor integration to direct voluntary movement.

Post-Traumatic Stress Disorder (PTSD) – The resulting disability when a painful memory becomes so intrusive that it disrupts daily life.

Practical Intelligence – The ability to accomplish one's own goals in daily life, often through social intercourse.

Pragmatics – The contribution of the context to language understanding.

Preference Reversal – A change in the selection of identical choices when they are restated in terms of possible losses instead of possible gains.

Premise – A statement which is taken to be true in order to deduce a conclusion.

Primacy Effect – The first and second list items have a higher probability of being recalled than the middle list items.

Primary Visual Cortex (Striate Cortex) – The region of the cerebral cortex which receives visual input from the thalamus.

Proactive Interference (PI) – When the processing of an earlier target interferes with the memory of a later target.

Problem-Solving Set – A strategy for finding a solution that is highly available because it has recently been successfully used to solve similar problems.

Procedural Memory or Procedural Learning – When the change in behavior resulting from implicit learning is an improvement in the performance of some task. Called "knowing how" in philosophy.

Proliferation – The fact that new neurons are born every day in various parts of the brain.

Pronominal Reversal – When someone refers to themselves in the second or third person.

Proprioceptive Feedback – Information transmitted to the brain about the location of body parts.

Prospect Theory – A theory which describes how people make decisions under uncertainty. It states that when people make such decisions, most people, guided by the probability and magnitude of gain versus loss that each option entails.

Pulvinar Nucleus – A nucleus in the thalamus that organizes visual information from the retina into features pathways to the parietal cortex that ultimately direct voluntary actions.

Pupillary Light Reflex – A reflex which varies the size of the pupil so that the right amount of light enters the eye.

Pupils – The small holes in the surface of your eyes.

Rapid Eye Movement (REM) Sleep – A stage of sleep in mammals which is marked by rapid eye movements.

Rapid Reacquisition – When resuming conditioned stimulus – unconditioned stimulus pairings after extinction leads to a rapid return of the response to the conditioned stimulus.

Rapid Serial Visual Presentation (RSVP) – When visual targets are rapidly presented one after the other in the same location.

Recency – The perception that something has just occurred a short time before.

Recency Effect – The high probability of recall for the last four items in a list.

Recency Judgement – Making a judgment as to how recently you last perceived an object.

Recognition – The awareness that something has been perceived or done before.

Recognition By Components – The use of simple, familiar geons to identify the object the object that contains them.

Recollection – The act of remembering a piece of information.

Reduplicative Paramnesia – A delusion in which a person believes that a familiar location is in fact a duplicate of the real location.

Reenactment – When people repeat an action that they have previously performed.

Reflex Arc – A sequence of neurons which perform reflexes, beginning with a sensory neuron and ending with a response neuron.

Reflexive Avoidance Response – The system of coordinated reflexes that prevent or eliminate contact with the stimulus and are associated with the emotion of fear in humans.

Reinstatement – the response to the CS recovers spontaneously recovers even if the unconditioned stimulus is presented by itself again after extinction.

Reminder – Some part of an experience that activates a memory of the entire experience and so strengthens the memory trace as much as if the entire experience had been repeated.

Reminiscence – When list items are recalled on a later test that were not recalled on an earlier test.

Renewal – When the conditioned stimulus is tested in a different environmental context from the extinction context and extinguished responding returns.

Repetition Priming – When something is repeated the time to recognize it decreases.

Representativeness – A heuristic in which the likelihood that an individual will perform an action or a situation will result in an outcome is based on the similarity of other individuals who performed that action or to other situations that resulted in that outcome.

Response Learning – When an animal learns a sequence of actions that result in reaching a goal.

Response Neuron – A neuron which activates a muscle or gland in response to a signal from a sensory neuron.

Response Node – A node in semantic memory activated by a perceptual representation.

Retention Intervals – The period of time between training or study and test.

Retina – The back of the eyeball, which detects light which is focused on it.

Retroactive Interference (RI) – When processing a more recent target interferes with the memory of the earlier one.

Retrograde Amnesia – An inability to remember events that occurred before a brain injury.

Rewards – Positive emotional responses, including joy and pleasure, that increase the probability of an action causing them.

Rod Neuron – The photoreceptor cells which detect light intensity but not wavelength.

Routine – Regularly repeated events that continue into the future.

Running memory Span – A serial recall task in which a sequence of targets is presented one at a time, and the observer has to recall the order in some final part of the sequence were presented.

Saccade – The rapid movement of the eyes from one fixation point to the next. The eyes typically perform about 3 or 4 saccades per second.

Schema – The hierarchical organization of a narrative into a setting, theme, plot, and resolution.

Search – The stage of attention during which perceptual inputs that have a target feature are serially compared with the target representation.

Secondary Recall Cues – Additional recall cues which aid in remembering large data sets.

Secondary Visual Cortex (Prestriate or Extrastriate) – The region where the results of the basic analyses of an image are combined to form patterns that correspond to surfaces in the visual field.

Segmental Reflexes – Spinal reflexes whose junctions between the stimulus and response are in the spinal cord.

Selective Interference – When decline in performance when two tasks each require that a different voluntary action be taken by the same functional system at the same time.

Semantic – Word meaning.

Semantic Cue – A cue whose semantic representation is related to the semantic representation of the target.

Semantic Knowledge – Knowledge of what something is.

Semantic Memory – The representation of semantic knowledge in the brain.

Semantic Priming – The decrease in recognition time for the second of two semantically related items.

Semantic Relationships – Relationships in which there is some obvious connection in the meaning of the items.

Sensation – The effect of a stimulus in the nervous system.

Sensitization – When the response to subsequent stimuli becomes stronger after a very strong stimulus is presented.

Sensory Neglect – The failure to respond to sensory inputs from a particular location

Sensory Neuron – A neuron which detects a change in the environment on in the animal itself.

Sensory Registration – The first stage of perceptual processing, in which a sensory neuron responds to a stimulus.

Sentence – A clause or sequence of clauses that does not contain a function word that connects it in an even longer sequence with yet another clause.

Serial Learning – The decrease in response time to perform a repeated sequence of actions in response to a repeated sequence of targets.

Serial Reaction Time (SRT) Task – A task in which a person repeatedly responds as rapidly as possible to each in a sequence of targets.

Shadowing – When listeners have to repeat what they everything they hear, word for word, as they hear it.

Short-Term Memory – The ability to recall which in sequence of targets has just been perceived and which in a sequence of actions has just been performed.

Simultagnosia – A form of agnosia resulting from a defect in the integration of local features into patterns.

Skill – A routine action which has become faster and more accurate with practice.

Somatosensory cortex – The region of the anterior parietal lobe which receives feedback indicating a body part's location.

Span – The number of items in a sequence that may be repeated accurately.

Specific Language Impairment (SLI) – An impairment in language processing often revealed by the demands of literacy.

Speech Spectrogram – A visual record of the physical wave pattern you produce when you speak.

Spinal Reflexes – Reflexes whose junctions between the sensory, (inter-,) and response neurons are in the spinal cord.

Spinocerebellum – The part of the cerebellum which turns motor plans into motor programs transmitted to the spinal cord.

Spontaneous Confabulation – A false memory that is obviously false to a normal observer but is accepted by the individual constructing it.

Spontaneous Recovery – When a previously conditioned stimulus which had undergone extinction is presented alone and elicits the unconditioned response again.

ß (Beta) – Within the framework of signal detection theory, when the distributions of target and distracter features overlap, creating ambiguous test items that may be either targets or distracters, beta is the criterion value of the ratio of the height of the target distribution to the height of the distracter distribution that is used to classify the ambiguous test item as either a target or a distracter.

Stereopsis – The combination of the separate images from each retina to form a single representation.

Stimulus-Response Compatibility – The spatial relationship between a cue describing the location of a target and the location of the target. The highest level of stimulus-response compatibility is when the locations of the cue and target are the same.

Stop Consonants – /p/ and /t/ are called stop consonants because when you produce them, you momentarily close your vocal tract and stop the flow of air from your lungs.

Striatum – A medial structure of the forebrain involved in the control of voluntary action.

Sub-goal – The goal of a simpler problem that must be solved in order to solve a more complicated problem that contains it.

Substantia Nigra – The part of the basal ganglia extending into the midbrain.

Subthalamic Nucleus – A part of the basal ganglia between the midbrain and thalamus.
Sulci – The deep folds resulting from the crumpling together of the cortex inside the brain. The main sulci partition the cortex into its four lobes.
Superior Olivary Complex – The structure in the brain stem where binaural processing of the auditory input refines the main feature pathways.
Survival in neurogenesis – Learning something new causes a new neuron to survive rather than dying within two weeks.
Symbolic Distance Effect – The further apart the items are on the relevant dimension, the more quickly a comparative judgment can be made.
Synapse – The small gap separating each neuron from the next.
Synaptic Extinction – A decrease in the number of synapses between a pair of neurons.
Synaptic Plasticity – Changes in the strength of the signal from the pre-synaptic to the post-synaptic neuron.
Synaptogenesis – An increase in the number of synapses between a pair of neurons.
Synesthesia – when an input to a single sense modality evokes an image in more than one sense modality.
Syntactic Representations – Word sequence representations that include function words and/or inflections that organize the meanings of the content words into a phrase or clause that describes an episode.
Target – The focus of a voluntary action, hence usually also of the perceptual experience guiding it.
Target Specification – The first stage of attention, all features in the target modality except for those of the target are inhibited.
Task Analysis – Conceptualizing a problem as a hierarchy of the simpler problems that comprise it.
Terminal Nodes – Containers filled with neurotransmitters which lie at the tips of the axons of neurons and spill the neurotransmitters into the synapse when the neuron is activated by a stimulus or a signal from another neuron.
Texture – Similar features organized into a single pattern.
Theory Of Signal Detection – A formal description of the general method for determining the sensitivity of a receiver to a signal.
Tip-of-the-tongue (TOT) or Feeling Of Knowing (FOK) – When you know you know an answer but cannot recall it.
Tonotopic System – The subsystem of the auditory pathways which encodes the tones comprising the input sounds.
Top-Down Processing – A mental representation is decomposed into its global and local features that are ultimately compared with the sensory input or direct the basic motor units of a response.
Tourette's Syndrome – A syndrome caused by a decrease in inhibition from the basal ganglia, leading to involuntary movement in the form of twitches, tics and on rare occasions involuntary vocalizations.
Trace Conditioning – A form of conditioning in which the novel stimulus ends before the unconditioned stimulus begins, so there is a delay between the end of the novel stimulus and the onset of the unconditioned stimulus.
Transient Epileptic Amnesia – Transient amnesia caused by a seizure.
Transient Global Amnesia – A temporary amnesia severe enough to temporarily block memories of recent events and so destroy awareness of the current time and place.
Transitional Probabilities – The probability that the one specific item in a sequence will be followed by another specific item.
Typical Instance – An instance that is similar to many other instances.
Unconditioned Responses (UR) – The response component of a reflex.
Unconditioned Stimulus (US) – The stimulus component of a reflex.

Valid – A deduction is valid when it is the case that, if the premises are true, then the conclusion must be true.

Verbal Agnosia (Pure Word Deafness) – When sounds are still heard but speech sounds are no longer recognized.

Verbal Fluency Task – A task in which participants are asked to generate as many instances of a category in a specified time period.

Verbal Rehearsal – A method of retaining information in which you rehearse the information to yourself through repetition of the same speech sequence.

Verbal Working Memory – Maintaining a representation of a novel target sequence through the voluntary action of verbal rehearsal.

Vestibular System – The neurons in the inner ear that keep track of and signal the orientation of the body.

Vestibulocerebellum – The part of the cerebellum which contains the reflexes for maintaining balance and coordinating eye movements.

Vigilance Task – A task in which an occasional target must be discriminated from many similar distracters over an extended period of time.

Visual Agnosia – A deficit in visual recognition.

Visual Cliff – A clear plate extending over the edge of a table, so it looks as if one is stepping out into empty space.

Visual Dominance – When a light and a tone are presented simultaneously, the light is likely to be detected first.

Visual Field – Everything you can see.

Visual Search System – The system which directs, the eyes and controls the thalamus to efficiently acquire task-relevant visual information.

Visual Working memory – Maintaining a representation of a novel target sequence through the voluntary action of visual imagery.

Visuospatial Disorder / Visuoconstructive Disorder / Visual Ataxia – A deficit in the visual control of actions caused by damage to the visuomotor pathway.

Vocalization/Ingestion System – The motor system which moves the vocal cords, tongue, throat, and mouth for talking, singing, eating, etc.

Voluntary Response – A deliberate action in response to a stimulus.

Wernicke's Aphasia / Receptive Aphasia /Fluent Aphasia / Semantic Dementia – The failure to comprehend or produce meaningful speech that results from damage to semantic memory.

Wernicke-Korsakoff Disorder – A disorder resulting from destruction of the anterior thalamic nuclei through a combination of alcoholism and a thiamine deficient diet involving an initial, acute (Wernicke)phase in which there is confusion and severe motor dysfunction in the eyes and limbs and initial chronic phase in which there is a dense learning deficit.

What Pathway – The visual pathway used for visual recognition, which extends downwards into the temporal cortex.

Word Superiority Effect – When a letter is presented in very small type or for a very short time, it may be identified less often when it is presented by itself than when it is presented as part of a word.

Working Memory – Target specification through the voluntary action of verbal rehearsal or imagery.

Working Memory Tasks – Tasks which test the span of an individual's working memory.

Zero Reference Point – Within the context of prospect theory, the amount you have before you act in a scenario with potential losses and gains.

FIGURE CREDITS

1.1–1.5, 1.7, 1.8, 2.1, 2.5, 2.6, 3.1, 3.3, 3.5–3.7, 3.9, 3.10, 4.3, 4.8, 4.10, 5.8, 6.1–6.3, 6.7–6.10, 6.14, 6.17, 6.18, 6.22, 6.25–6.31, 6.33, 7.1, 7.2, 7.5, 7.8, 7.9, 7.17, 7.18, 8.4, 8.5, 9.3, 9.8, 10.6, 11.7–11.9, 11.14, 12.10, 12.14–12.18, 14.1, 14.4–14.9, 15.2, 15.4–15.9, 15.11 redrawn by Dave Gaskin

1.6, 2.2, 3.2, 4.1, 6.4, 6.5, 7.7, 11.6, 13.1 redrawn by Simon Tegg

1.5 Adapted from House, E.L., Pansky B., A functional approach to neuroanatomy, 1967.

1.6 Redrawn from an original figure by Nicole Owens

2.2 Redrawn from an original figure by Nicole Owens

3.4 Adapted from Collard R., Povel, D. J., Theory of serial pattern production: Tree traversals, Nov 1982, Psychological Review, Vol 89(6), 693–707

3.6 Adapted from Penfield, W., Rasmussen, T., The cerebral cortex of man, 1950, 248 pp

3.7 Adapted from Shokur, S., O'Doherty, J.E., Winans, J.A., Bleuler, H., Lebedev, M.A., & M.A.L. Nicolelis, Expanding the primate body schema in sensorimotor cortex by virtual touches of an avatar (2013), Proceedings of the National Academy of Sciences, 110(37): 15121–15126

3.8 Adapted from Georgopoulos, Current issues in directional motor control 1995, Trends Neurosci 18, 506–510.

3.10 Adapted from Erickson, K.I., Boot, W.R., Basak, C., Neider, M.B., Prakash, R.S., Voss, M.W., Graybiel, A.M., Simons, D.J., Fabiani, M., Gratton, G., & Kramer, A.F., Striatal volume predicts level of video game skill acquisition, 2010, Cerebral Cortex, 2522–30

3.11 Adapted from Crossman, E. R. F. W., A theory of the acquisition of speed-skill, 1959. Ergonomics 2, 153–166

3.12 Adapted from Slachevsky A1, Pillon B, Fourneret P, Renié L, Levy R, Jeannerod M, Dubois B., The prefrontal cortex and conscious monitoring of action: an experimental study. 2003 Neuropsychologia.;41(6), 655–65

4.4 Weichselgartner, E, Sperling G., Dynamics of Automatic and Controlled Visual Attention, 1987, Science, vol 238, 778–780

4.5 Adapted from Rovee-Collier, C., Hankins, E., & Bhatt, R. S., Textons, visual pop-out effects, and object recognition in infancy, (1992), Journal of Experimental Psychology: General, 121, 435–445

4.7 Adapted from Wang, Q., Cavanaugh, P., & Green, M. (1994). Familiarity and pop-out in visual search. Perception & Psychophysics, 56, 495–500

4.8 Adapted from Botella, C., Breton-López, J., Quero, S., BañosR.M., Garcia-Palacios A., Zaragoza I., Alcaniz M., Treating cockroach phobia using a serious game on a mobile phone and augmented reality exposure: A single case study, 2011, Computers in Human Behavior 27, 1, 217–227

4.9 Adapted from Schneider, W., & Shiffrin, R. M., Controlled and automatic human information processing. I. Detection, search, and attention (1977), Psychological Review, 84(1), 1–66.; Shiffrin, R. M., & Schneider, W., Controlled and automatic human information processing. II. Perceptual

5.1 Redrawn from Ziessler, M., Nattkemper D., Learning of event sequences is based on response-effect learning: Further evidence from a serial reaction task, 2001/5, Journal of Experimental Psychology: Learning, Memory, and and Cognition 27/3, 595

5.2 Yarbus, A., Eye Movements and Vision, 1967, Springer, p180

5.3 Adapted from Rayner K., Parafoveal identification during a fixation in reading, Acta Psychologica. 1975 Aug 39/4,271–82

5.4 Adapted from Rayner K., Liversedge S.P., White S.J. and Vergilino-Perez D. (2003). Reading disappearing text:

Cognitive control of eye movements. Psychological Science, 14, 385–388

5.5 Adapted from Just, M. A., & Carpenter, P. A. (1980). A theory of reading: From eye fixations to comprehension. Psychological Review, 87,329 354.

5.6 Adapted from Kolers P. A., Pattern-analyzing memory. Science. 1976 Mar 26, p1280-1

5.8 Adapted from Eriksen, C. W., & Collins, J. F. (1967). Some temporal characteristics of visual pattern perception. Journal of Experimental Psychology, 74, 476–484

5.9 Adapted from Beck, D. Muggleton, N., Walsh, V. & Lavie N. (2006). Right parietal lobe plays a critical role in change blindness. Cerebral Cortex, 16, 712–717

5.11 Nadia Chomyn © Bethlem Museum of the Mind

5.12 Stephen Wiltshire

5.13 Institut Pasteur – Musée Pasteur

6.1 Adapted from Benson, D., Greenberg J.P., Adapted from Visual Form Agnosia A Specific Defect in Visual Discrimination, Arch Neurol. 1969, 20(1), 82–89

6.6 Estes W. K., Allmeyer D. H., Reder S. M., Serial position functions for letter identification at brief and extended exposure durations, 1976, Perception & Psychophysics, Vol, 19 (1), 1–15

6.14 Redrawn from Julesz B., Experiments in the visual perception of texture, Scientific American, 1975 Apr; 232(4): 34–43.

6.17 Yury Kuzmin/Getty

6.22 Adapted from Bregman, A.S. (1981) Asking the "what for" question in auditory perception. In M. Kubovy and J.R. Pomerantz (Eds.), Perceptual Organization

6.26 Adapted from Ramachandran V.S., Perception of shape from shading, Nature. 1988 Jan 14;331(6152): 163–6

6.27 Adapted from Shepard, R and Metzler. J. "Mental rotation of three dimensional objects." Science 1971. 171(972): 701–3

6.28 Adapted from Biederman, I., Bar, M. (1999). One-shot viewpoint invariance in matching novel objects. Vision Research, 39, 2885–2889

6.29 Adapted from Biederman, I., Recognition-by-components: A theory of human image understanding, Psychological Review, Vol 94(2), Apr 1987, 115–147

6.30 Biederman, I., & Cooper, E. E. (1991). Priming contour-deleted images: Evidence for intermediate representations in visual object recognition. Cognitive Psychology, 23, 393–419

6.32 David Cole/Alamy

6.33 Adapted from Biederman, I., Mezzanotte, R. J., & Rabinowitz, J. C. (1982). Scene perception: Detecting and judging objects undergoing relational violations. Cognitive Psychology, l4, l43-l77

7.1 Adapted from Binder, J. R., & Desai, R. H. (2011). The neurobiology of semantic memory. Trends in Cognitive Sciences, 15, 527 – 536

7.5 Adapted from Leeper, R., (1935), A study of a neglected portion of the field of learning: The development of sensory organization. Journal of Genetic Psychology, 46, 41–75

7.6 Adapted from Neely, J. H. (1977). Semantic priming and retrieval from lexical memory: Role of inhibitionless spreading activation and limited capacity attention. Journal of Experimental Psychology: General, 106, 226–254

7.9a Adapted from Hickok, G., & Poeppel, D. (2004).Dorsal and ventral streams: a framework for understanding aspects of the functional anatomy of language. Cognition, 92, 67–99 and Friederici, A. D. (2012). The cortical language circuit: from auditory perception to sentence comprehension. Trends in Cognitive Sciences, 16, 262 – 268.

7.9b Adapted from Friederici, A. D. (2012). The cortical language circuit: from auditory perception to sentence comprehension. Trends in Cognitive Sciences, 16, 262–268

7.11 Adapted from Lindell (2013) Continuities in emotion lateralization in human and non-human primates, Frontiers in Human Neuroscience, 7, 464

7.15 Adapted from Bialystok, E., Craik, F. I. M., & Luk, G. (2012). Bilingualism: Consequences for mind and brain. Trends in Cognitive Sciences, 16, 240–250

8.1 and 8.2 Carolyn Rovee-Collier

8.3 Adapted from Hsu, V.C. (2010). Time windows in retention over the first year-and-a-half of life: Spacing effects. Developmental Psychobiology.10.1002/dev. 20472

8.4 Adapted from Hsu, V. C., & Rovee-Collier, C. (2006). Memory reactivation in the second year of life. Infant Behavior and Development, 29, 91–107

8.6 Adapted from Imada T, Zhang Y, Cheour M, Taulu S, Ahonen A, et al. 2006. Infant speech perception activates Broca's area: a developmental magnetoencephalography study. NeuroReport, 17, 957–962

8.7 Adapted from Casell M.C. et al: Lexical Development in English and Italian from Cognitive Development, 1995. in Tomasello M., Bates, E., Language Development, The essential Readings. John Wiley & Sons 2001

8.8 Adapted from Ganger, J., & Brent, M. R. (2004). Reexamining the vocabulary spurt. Developmental Psychology, 40, 621–632

8.9, 8.10 Adapted from Caselli C1, Casadio P, Bates E., A comparison of the transition from first words to grammar in English and Italian. Journal of Child Language. 1999 Feb; 26(1): 69–111

8.11 Gelman, S. A., & Markman, E. M. (1986). Categories and induction in young children. Cognition, 23, 183–209
9.1 Adapted from Medin, D. L., Schaffer, M. M. (1978). Context theory of classification leaming, Psychological Review, 85, 207–238
9.2 Adapted from Reber, A. S. (1989). Implicit learning and tacit knowledge. Journal of Experimental Psychology: General, 118, 219–235
9.3 Adapted from Labov, W. (1973). The boundaries of words and their meanings. In C. J. N. Bailey & R. W. Shuy (Eds.), New ways of analyzing variation in English. Washington, D.C.: Georgetown University Press
9.4, 9.8 Adapted from Kay, P., & McDaniel, C. K. (1978). The linguistic significance of the meanings of basic color terms. Language, 54, 610-646.
9.5, 9.6 Adapted from Maddox,W. T, Ashby F.G., 1993, Comparing decision bound and exemplar models of categorization, Perception & Psychophysics, January 1993, 53, Issue 1, pp 49–70
9.7 Adapted from Carmichael, L.; Hogan, H. P.; Walter, A. A., An experimental study of the effect of language on the reproduction of visually perceived, Journal of Experimental Psychology, Vol 15(1), Feb 1932, 73–86
10.1 Adapted from Sperling, G. (1960). The information available in brief visual presentations. Psychological Monographs: General and Applied, 74(11), 1–29
10.2 Adapted from Sperling, G. (1960). The information available in brief visual presentations. Psychological Monographs: General and Applied, 74(11), 1–29
10.3 Adapted from Madigan, S. A. (1969). Intraserial repetition and coding processes in free recall. Journal of Verbal Learning and Verbal Behavior, 8, 828–835
10.4 Adapted from Johnston, W. A., & Uhl, C. N. (1976). The contributions of encoding effort and variability to the spacing effect on free recall. Journal of Experimental Psychology: Learning, Memory, and Cognition, 2, 153–160
10.5 Adapted from Bahrick, H.P. et al.,Maintenance of Foreign Language Vocabulary and the Spacing Effect, Psychological Science Vol. 4, No. 5 (Sep., 1993), pp. 316–321, Sage Publications, Inc. on behalf of the Association for Psychological Science Article
10.6 Adapted from Park, DC; Lautenschlager, G; Hedden, T; Davidson, NS; Smith, AD; Smith, PK. (2002). Models of visuospatial and verbal memory across the adult life span. Psychology and aging, 17: 299–320
10.7 Adapted from Rabbitt P., et al. (2008), Sudden declines in intelligence in old age predict death and dropout from longitudinal studies. Journals of Gerontology. Series B (Psychological Sciences and Social Sciences) :P205-11 (41 ref)
10.8 Adapted from Rundus, D. (1971), Analysis of Rehearsal Processes in Free Recall, Journal of Experimental Psychology, 89, 63–77
10.9 Adapted from Detterman, D. K., Ellis, N. R., Determinants of induced amnesia in short-term memory, Journal of Experimental Psychology, Vol 95(2), Oct 1972, 308–316
10.10, 10.12 Adapted from Bower et al., 1969, Hierarchical retrieval schemes in recall of categorized word lists. Journal of Verbal Learning and Verbal Behavior, 8, 323–343
10.13, 10.14 Adapted from Chase, W. G., & Ericsson, K. A. (1982). Skill and working memory. In G. H. Bower (Ed.), The psychology of learning and motivation (Vol. 16, pp. 1–58). New York: Academic Press
10.15 Adapted from Heindel et al. (1988). Impaired learning of a motor skill in patients with Huntington's disease. Behavioral Neuroscience, 102, 141–147
11.1 Brady et al., 2008, Visual long-term memory has a massive storage capacity for object details. Proceedings of the National Academy of Sciences, 105(38), 14325–14329
11.2 Cedric Weber/Shutterstock, Anilah/Shutterstock
11.3 Adapted from Bruce, 1982, Changing faces: Visual and non-visual coding processes in face recognition. British Journal of Psychology, 73, 105–116
11.4, 11.5 Adapted from Rovee-Collier, C. (1993). The capacity for long-term memory in infancy. Current Directions in Psychological Science, 2, 130–135
11.6 Adapted from Suzuki, W. A., & Naya, Y. (2014). The perirhinal cortex. Annual Review of Neuroscience, 37, 39 – 53
11.7–11.9 Adapted from Adapted from Shipstead et al., 2014, The mechanisms of working memory capacity: Primary memory, secondary memory, and attention control, Journal of Memory and Language, 72 (2014) 116–141
11.10 Adapted from Endress, A. D. & Potter, M. C. (2014). Large capacity visual memory. Journal of Experimental Psychology: General, 143, 548–565
11.11 Adapted from Brady et al., 2008, Visual long-term memory has a massive storage capacity for object details. Proceedings of the National Academy of Sciences, 105(38), 14325–14329
11.12 Adapted from Glass, A. L. (1993). The role of generation in recognition. Scandinavian Journal of Psychology, 34, 255–267
11.13 Adapted from Konkle, T., Brady, T. F., Alvarez, G. A., & Oliva, A. (2010). Conceptual Distinctiveness Supports Detailed Visual Long-Term Memory for Real-World Objects. Journal of Experimental Psychology: General, 139, 558–578

11.14 Adapted from Glass, A. L., Holyoak, K. J., & Santa, J. L. (1979). Cognition. Reading MA: Addison-Wesley Publishing Company

11.15 Adapted from Mansour, J. K. et al.(2012). Impact of disguise on identification decision and confidence with simultaneous and sequential lineups. Law and Human Behavior, 36, 513–526

12.1 Adapted from Keppel & Underwood, 1962, Proact ive inhibition in shortterm retention of single items. Journal of Verbal Learning and Verbal Behavior, I, 153–161.

12.2 Adapted from Keppel & Underwood, 1962, Proact ive inhibition in shortterm retention of single items. Journal of Verbal Learning and Verbal Behavior, I, 153–161.

12.3 Wickens et al. 1963 Proactive inhibition and item similarity in short-term memory. Journal of Verbal Learning & Verbal Behavior. 2:440–445.

12.4 Gardiner et al.,(1972). Retrieval cues and release from proactive inhibition. Journal Verbal Learning and Verbal Behavior, 11, 778–783.

12.5–12.7 Gruenewald & Lockhead, 1980, The free recall of category examples. Journal of Experimental Psychology: Human Learning and Memory 6: 225–240

12.8 Erdelyi, M. H. & Kleinbard, J. (1978) Has Ebbinghaus decayed with time? The growth of recall (hypermnesia) over days. Journal of Experimental Psychology: Human Learning and Memory 4:275–89.

12.9 Adapted from Bower, G. H., & Glass, A. (1976). Structural units and the redintegrative power of picture fragments. Journal of Experimental Psychology: Human Learning and Memory, 2, 456–466

12.10 Adapted from Bower, G. H. (1970). Analysis of a mnemonic device. American Scientist, 58, 496 510.

12.11 Adapted from Godden, D. R., & Baddeley, A. D. (1975). Context dependent memory in two natural environments: On land and underwater. British Journal of Psychology, 66, 325 332

12.12 Nickerson, R. A., & Adams, M. J. (1979). Long term memory for a common object. Cognitive Psychology, 11, 287 307.

12.13 Rubin D. C, & Kontis, T. S. (1983). A schematic for common cents. Memory & Cognition, 11, 335 – 341.

12.14 Adapted from Moar, I., & Bower, G. H. (1983). Inconsistency in spatial knowledge. Memory & Cognition, 11, 107–113

12.15 Adapted from Tversky, Barbara (1981). Distortions in memory for maps. Cognitive Psychology Volume 13 Issue 3, 407–433

12.16 Adapted from Tversky, Barbara (1981). Distortions in memory for maps. Cognitive Psychology Volume 13 Issue 3, 407–433

12.17 Adapted from Tversky, Barbara (1981). Distortions in memory for maps. Cognitive Psychology Volume 13 Issue 3, 407–433

12.18 Adapted from Thorndyke, P. W. (1977). Cognitive structures in comprehension and memory of narrative discourse. Cognitive Psychology, 9, 77 110

12.19 Adapted from Fitzgerald, J., Spiegel, D. L., & Webb, T. B. (1985). Development of Children's Knowledge of Story Structure and Content. Journal of Educational Research, 79, 101–108

12.20 Adapted from Stanhope, N. Cohen, G. & Conway, M. (1993). Very Long-Term Retention of a Novel. Applied Cognitive Psychology, 7, 239–256

12.21 Adapted from Stanhope, N. Cohen, G. & Conway, M. (1993). Very Long-Term Retention of a Novel. Applied Cognitive Psychology, 7, 239–256

13.1 Adapted from Cabeza, R., & St Jacques, P. (2007). Functional neuroimaging of autobiographical memory. Trends in Cognitive Sciences, 11(5), 219–227

13.2 Adapted from Shanon, B. (1979). Yesterday, today, and tomorrow. Acta Psychologica, 43, 469 476

13.3 Anderson, R. C., & Pichert, J. W. (1978). Recall of previously unrecallable information following a shift in perspective. Journal of Verbal Learning and Verbal Behavior, 17, 1 12

13.4 Adapted from Spiro, R. J. (1980). Accommodative reconstruction in prose recall. Journal of Verbal Learning and Verbal Behavior, 19, 84 95.

13.5 Bahrick, H. P. (1984). Semantic memory content in permastore: Fifty years of memory for Spanish learned in school. Journal of Experimental Psychology: General, 113, 1 29

13.6 Bahrick, H. P. (1984). Semantic memory content in permastore: Fifty years of memory for Spanish learned in school. Journal of Experimental Psychology: General, 113, 1 29

13.7 Adapted from Rubin, D.C., Wetzler, S.E., & Nebes, R.D. (1986). Autobiographical memory across the life span. In D.C. Rubin (Ed.) Autobiographical memory. Cambridge: Cambridge University Press

13.8 Adapted from Squire, L. R., Slater, P. C., & Chace, P. M. (1975). Retrograde amnesia: Temporal gradient in very long term memory following electroconvulsive therapy. Science,187,77 79

13.9 Adapted from Albert, M. S., Butters, N., & Levin, J. (1979). Temporal gradients in the retrograde amnesia of patients with alcoholic Korsakoff's disease. Archives of Neurology, 36, 211 216

13.10 Adapted from Butters, N. (1984). Alcoholic Korsakoff's syndrome: An update. Seminars in Neurology, 4, 226 244

14.1 Adapted from Daniel Wilmott, James Wilmott, and Karen Ternosky

14.2 Adapted from Glass, A. L., Millen, D. R. Beck, L. G., & Eddy, J. K. (1985). The representation of images in sentence verification. Journal of Memory and Language, 24, 442–465

14.3 Adapted from Holyoak, K. J., & Walker, J. H. (1976). Subjective magnitude information in semantic orderings. Journal of Verbal Learning and Verbal Behavior, 15, 287 299

14.4 Adapted from Bellugi, U., Wang P.P. (1994) Evidence from two genetic syndromes for a dissociation between verbal and visual-spatial short-term memory. Journal of Clinical and Experimental Neuropsychology, 16 (2) 317–322

14.5 Adapted from McCloskey, M., Caramazza, A., & Green, B. (1980). Curvilinear motion in the absence of external forces: Naive beliefs about the motion of objects. Science, 210, 1139–1141

14.6 Adapted from Wason, P. C. (1968). Reasoning about a rule. Quarterly Journal of Experimental Psychology, 20, 273 281

14.7 Adapted from Tversky, A. (1977). Features of similarity. Psychological Review, 84, 327 352

14.8 Adapted from Tversky, A., & Gati, 1. (1978). Studies in similarity. In E. Rosch & B. B. Lloyd (Eds.), Cognition and categorization. Hillsdale, N.J.: Erlbaum

14.9 Adapted from Wason, P. C., & Johnson-Laird, P. N. (1972). Psychology of Reasoning. Cambridge MA: Harvard University Press.

14.10 Bechara, A., Damasio, H., & Damasio, A. R. (2000). Emotion, decision making, and the orbit ofrontal cortex. Cerebral Cortex, 10, 295–307.

15.2 Adapted from Luria, A. R. (1968). The mind of a mnemonist. New York: Basic Books

15.5 Adapted from Knoblich, G., Ohlsson, S., & Raney, G. E. (2001). An eye movement study of insight problem solving. Memory & Cognition, 29, 1000–1009

15.7 Adapted from Chi, M. T. H., Feltovich, P. J., & Glaser, R. (1981). Categorization and representation of physics problems by experts and novices. Cognitive Science, 5, 121 152

15.8 Adapted from Chi, M. T. H., Feltovich, P. J., & Glaser, R. (1981). Categorization and representation of physics problems by experts and novices. Cognitive Science, 5, 121 152

15.9, 15.10 Adapted from Chase, W. G., & Simon, H. A. (1973). The mind's eye in chess. In W. G. Chase (Ed.), Visual Information Processing. New York: Academic Press

15.11 Adapted from Reitman, J. S. (1976). Skilled perception in Go: Deducing memory structures from inter response times. Cognitive Psychology, 8, 336 356

INDEX